ART
THROUGH
THE AGES

SIXTH EDITION

I Ancient and Medieval Art

REVISED BY

Horst de la Croix

SAN JOSE STATE UNIVERSITY

&

Richard G. Tansey

SAN JOSE STATE UNIVERSITY

GARDNER'S
ART
THROUGH
THE AGES

SIXTH EDITION

I Ancient and Medieval Art

HARCOURT BRACE JOVANOVICH, INC.
New York / Chicago / San Francisco / Atlanta

*Chapter-opening illustrations by Veit-Martin Associates and Martin Eichtersheimer
Architectural drawings by Felix Cooper and others*

Hardbound ISBN: 0-15-503753-6
Paperbound ISBN, I: 0-15-503756-0
Paperbound ISBN, II: 0-15-503757-9

Library of Congress Catalog Card Number: 74-22995

PRINTED IN THE UNITED STATES OF AMERICA

A note on the paperbound version

This volume is part of a variant printing, not a new or revised edition, of *Gardner's Art Through the Ages*, Sixth Edition. Many users of the book have requested that it be made available in this alternative format, and, to meet their needs, the publishers have prepared this printing, which consists of two separate volumes that exactly reproduce the text of the one-volume version. The first of these volumes contains Part One, The Ancient World; and Part Two, The Middle Ages. The second contains Part Three, Renaissance and Baroque; Part Four, The Modern World; and Part Five, The Non-European World. The Introduction, all appendixes, and the index appear in both volumes. The variant printing, then, is intended as a convenience to those instructors and students who have occasion to use only half of *Art Through the Ages*. Consequently the pagination and index of the one-volume version, as well as its illustrations, maps, chronologies, and other related material, are retained in the new printing. The difference between the one-volume and the two-volume versions of the book is a difference only in form.

PREFACE

Since publication of the first edition in 1926, Helen Gardner's *Art Through the Ages* has been a favorite with generations of students and general readers, who have found it an exciting and informative survey. Miss Gardner's enthusiasm, knowledge, and humanity have made it possible for the beginner to learn how to see and thereby to penetrate the seeming mysteries of even the most complex artistic achievements. Every effort has been made in this volume to preserve her freshness and simplicity of style and, above all, her sympathetic approach to individual works of art and to the styles of which they are a part.

Miss Gardner completed the third edition shortly before her death in 1946. The fourth was prepared in 1959 by Professor Sumner Crosby and his colleagues at Yale University, and our fifth edition was published in 1970. The popularity of that edition and suggestions for further improvement led us to prepare this sixth edition.

In addition to a revised but undiminished treatment of Western art this edition offers surveys of the arts of Islam, Asia, pre-Columbian America, the North American Indian, Africa, and Oceania. The chapter on the art of the twentieth century has been enlarged to accommodate revisions necessitated by the rapid development and changing interpretations of its subject, and the general introduction to the book now includes a discussion of the formal aspects of art, dealing with fundamental concepts in some detail. There are, of course, corresponding increases in illustrations, in those student aids introduced in the fifth edition, and in the glossary, essay-style bibliography, and index. The book now constitutes a balanced introduction to the art of the world.

Although in some cases, like that of North American Indian art, a sure chronology is impossible, it remains our conviction that a chronological presentation is still the best for introducing the history of art, and this bias is reflected in our use of a linear chronology to open most chapters and in our use of time-lines—short elaborated sections of a chapter chronology that are keyed into the text at the points or periods on which they focus. Most chapters also open with a map that is related to the accompanying chronology; small drawings of key monuments, shown on the chronology, also appear on the map, thus orienting the various works in space as well as time.

Hardest of all aspects of making a book of this nature is selection—in effect, limitation—of the monuments to be discussed and illustrated. Though a corpus of monuments essential to the art-history survey course has long been forming, and though there seems to be considerable agreement as to what constitutes it, there will naturally be differences of choice deriving from differences of emphasis. While this is as it should be, radical departure from the corpus might well obliterate the outlines of the study. To avoid the random, systemless distribution of material that might result we have generally adhered to the corpus, occasionally introducing monuments not well known or not customarily treated in a survey. Our aim throughout has been to present and interpret works as reflections of an intelligible development rather than merely as items of a catalogue or miscellany. We have tried particularly to give coherence to the vast assortment of materials by stressing—in the descriptions of sculpture and painting—the theme of representation as it passes through the many historical variations behind which operate the crucial transformations of humankind's view of itself and the world.

A work as extensive as a history of world art could not be undertaken or completed without the counsel and active participation of experts in fields other than our own. The chapters dealing with Indian, Chinese, and Japanese art were prepared by Professor J. Leroy Davidson of the University of California, Los Angeles; Professor Herbert Cole of the University of California, Santa Barbara, prepared the chapter on the arts of the North American Indian, Africa, and Oceania; and Professor Raphael Reichert of California State University, Fresno, prepared the chapter on pre-Columbian art. They have our sincere thanks, as does Bruce Radde of San José State University, who guided us through the all-important revision of the chapter dealing with the art of the twentieth century. Many valuable comments and suggestions were received from specialists who reviewed portions of the work in progress; among these are: Dr. Richard Ettinghausen, Consultative Chairman, Department of Islamic Art, Metropolitan Museum of Art, and Hagop Kevorkian Professor of Islamic Art, Institute of Fine Arts, New York University; Julie Jones, Curator, Museum of Primitive Art, New York; Dr. Martin Lerner, Metropolitan Museum of Art, New York; Dr. Roy Sieber, Rudy Professor of Fine Arts, Indiana University, Bloomington. Richard McLanathan reviewed all color plates and suggested adjustments necessary to achieve high color fidelity. Patricia Pinkerton and Marguerite Agramonte gave us most valuable bibliographical assistance, and Luraine Tansey of San José City College read proof and offered many useful suggestions.

Philip Ressner, at Harcourt Brace Jovanovich, has now been our editor for two editions of this book; he has done his task with a skill, diligence, and good humor that honor his profession and his house.

We should like, as we thank all those who have helped immeasurably in the production of this book, to affirm that we alone are responsible for whatever may be its deficiencies.

HORST DE LA CROIX
RICHARD G. TANSEY

CONTENTS

Introduction   2

PART ONE   THE ANCIENT WORLD   20

Chapter One   The Birth of Art   24

The Later Old Stone Age (Upper Paleolithic)   26
Cave Art | Engravings and Sculpture

The Middle Stone Age (Mesolithic)   35
Rock-shelter Paintings

The New Stone Age (Neolithic)   36
The Megaliths

Chapter Two   The Ancient Near East   40

The Beginnings   42
Jericho | Çatal Hüyük

Sumer   47
The City-State and the Ziggurat | Sculpture

Akkad   55

Babylonia   57

Assyria 59
Architecture / Relief Sculpture

Neo-Babylonia 65

Persia 67
Architecture / Sculpture / Craft Art / Eclecticism of Persian Art

72 The Art of Egypt *Chapter Three*

The Early Dynastic Period and the Old Kingdom 76
*The "Palette of Narmer" / Architecture / Sculpture /
Painting and Relief*

The Middle Kingdom 87
Rock-cut Tombs / Painting and Sculpture

The Hyksos and the New Kingdom 88
Architecture / Sculpture and Painting

Akhenaton and the Amarna Period 97

102 The Art of the Aegean *Chapter Four*

Minoan and Cycladic Art 104
*The Early Minoan Period / The Middle Minoan Period /
The Late Minoan Period*

Mycenaean Art 115
Architecture / Pottery, Relief, and Craft Art

122 The Art of Greece *Chapter Five*

The Geometric and Archaic Periods 126
*Vase Painting / Sculpture / Kouros and Kore / Architecture /
Architectural Sculpture*

The Fifth Century 147
The Transitional Period / The Early Classical Period

The Fourth Century and the Hellenistic Period 166
The Late Classical Period / The Hellenistic Period

184 Etruscan and Roman Art *Chapter Six*

The Etruscans 186
Architecture / Painting / Sculpture

The Romans 194
The Republican Period / The Early Empire / The Late Empire

Chapter Seven   Early Christian, Byzantine, and Islamic Art   244

Early Christian Art   247
The Catacombs / Architecture / Mosaic and Painting /
The Illuminated Manuscript / Sculpture and Craft Art

Byzantine Art   262
Ravenna / Byzantium

Later Byzantine Art   277
Architecture / Painting

Islamic Art   286
Architecture / Object Art and Textiles / Illumination

PART TWO   THE MIDDLE AGES   300

Chapter Eight   Early Medieval Art   304

The Migration Period   306
Craft Art / Illumination

The Carolingian Period   312
Painting and Illumination / Craft Art / Architecture

The Ottonian Period   320
Architecture / Sculpture / Painting and Illumination

Chapter Nine   Romanesque Art   326

Architecture   329
The Cluniac-Burgundian Style / Germany-Lombardy /
The Norman Style / Tuscany / Aquitania

Sculpture   341

Painting and Illumination   349

Chapter Ten   Gothic Art   352

Early Gothic   356
Architecture / Sculpture

High Gothic   367
Architecture / Sculpture / Stained Glass

Late Gothic   378

Non-French Gothic   381
England / Germany / Italy

907   Glossary

918   Bibliography

931   Plan and Section Conventions

933   Index

ART
THROUGH
THE AGES

SIXTH EDITION

I Ancient and Medieval Art

INTRODUCTION

The goal of art history, the subject of this book, is the discerning appreciation and enjoyment of art, from whatever time and place it may have come, by whatever hands made. Outside the academic world the terms *art* and *history* are not often so juxtaposed. People tend to think of history as the record and interpretation of past (particularly political) human actions, and of art—quite correctly—as something *present* to the eye and touch, which, of course, the vanished human events that make up history are not. The fact is that a work of art, visible and tangible as it is, is a kind of *persisting event*. It was made at a particular time and place by particular persons, even if we do not always know just when, where, and by whom. Though it is the creation of the past, it continues to exist in the present, long surviving its times; Charlemagne has been dead for a thousand years, but his chapel still stands at Aachen.

THE BASES OF ART HISTORY

Style

The time a work of art was made has everything to do with the way it looks—with, in one key term, its *style*. In other words, the style of a work of art is a function of its historical *period*. The historiography of art proceeds by sorting works of architecture, sculpture, and painting into stylistic classes on the bases of their likenesses and the times or periods when they were produced. It is a fundamental working hypothesis of art history that works produced at the same time (and, of course, the same place) will generally have common stylistic traits. Of course all historiography assumes that events derive their character from the time in which they happen (and perhaps from their "great men," also products of their time); thus we can speak of the Periclean Age, the Age of Reason, even—as with the title of a recent historical work—the Age of Roosevelt. We must also know the time of a work if we are to know its meaning, to know it for what it is. Yet if the work of art still stands before us, persisting from the past, is this not sufficient? By virtue of its survival, is not the work in a sense *independent* of time? May not a work of art speak to men of all times as long as it survives? The key to the question is the word "speak." Indeed, it may speak, but what is its language? What does it say to us? Art may be more than a form of communication, yet it is certainly that; and it is the business of art history to learn the "languages" of the art of many different periods as they are embodied in the monuments from their respective times. We can assume that artists in every age expressed in their works a meaning of some sort intelligible to themselves and others. One can get at that meaning only by setting a particular work in relation to others like it that were made about the same time. To works grouped in this way we can infer a community of meaning as well as of form; we will have outlined, then, a style. In a chronological series of works having common stylistic features, one may find that the later and the earlier works show stylistic *differences* as well. The art historian tends to think of this phenomenon as reflecting an evolution, a *development*.

It is obvious that before one can infer stylistic development it is necessary to be sure that the chronological sequence is correct, that each monument is correctly dated; without this certainty art-historical order and intelligibility are impossible. Thus an indispensable tool of the historian is *chronology*, the measuring scale of historical time; without it there could be no history of style, only a confusion of unclassifiable monuments impossible to describe in any sequence of change.

The table of contents of this book reflects what is essentially a series of periods and subperiods arranged in chronological order, the historical sequence that embraces the sequence of art styles. Until the later eighteenth century the history of art was really a disconnected account of the lives and works of individual artists. Now we regard it as a record of the dynamic change of styles in time, the art of individual masters being substyles of the overall period styles. Although one speaks of "change" in the history of art, the objects themselves obviously do not change; as we have said, they persist, although each will of course suffer some material wear and tear with time. But the fact that works of art from one period look different from those of other periods leads us to infer that *something* changes. This something can only be the points of view of the human makers of works of art with respect to the meaning of life and of art. Modern historiography is much influenced by modern philosophies of change and evolution and, from the terms and data of biological science, our modern history of art was bound to borrow a sense of continuous process to help explain art-historical change.

In art history, as in the sciences and in other historical disciplines, we have gone far in knowing a thing once we have classified it. Art historians, having done this, resemble experienced travelers who learn to discriminate the different "styles" peculiar to different places. The latter know that one must not expect the same style of life in the Maine woods as on the Riviera, and when they have seen a great many places and peoples—like art historians who are familiar with a great many monuments—they are not only at ease with them, but can be said to know and appreciate them for what they are. As their experience broadens so does their discrimination, their perception of distinctive differences. As world travelers come to see that the location contributes to the unique quality and charm of a town, so students of art, viewing it in the historical dimension, become convinced that a work's peculiar significance, quality, and charm are a function of the time of its making.

But is not the historical "placing" of a work of art, so visibly and tangibly present, irrelevant to the *appreciation* of it? After all, is not art-historical knowledge *about* a work of art something different from direct experience of it? The answers lie in the fact that uninstructed appreciators, no matter how sincere, will still approach a work with the esthetic presuppositions of their own time rather than those of the time of the work itself. Hence, their presuppositions can be tantamount to prejudices, so that their appreciation, even if genuine, may well be for the wrong reasons; it will, in fact, be undiscerning and indiscriminate, so that dozens of works of art may be viewed in the same way, without any savor of the individual significance and quality of each. Thus, as a work of art is intended for a particular audience at a particular time and place, so may its *purpose* be quite particular, and its purpose necessarily enters into its meaning. For example, the famous *Vladimir Madonna* (FIG. 7-48, p. 285) is a Byzantine-Russian icon, a species of art produced not as a work of "fine art" so much as a sacred object endowed with religio-magical power. It was considered, moreover, the especially holy picture of Russia that miraculously saved the city of Vladimir from the hosts of Tamerlane, the city of Kazan from the later Tartar invasions, and all of Russia from the Poles in the seventeenth century. We may admire it for its innate beauty of line, shape, and color, its expressiveness, and its craftsmanship, but unless we are aware of its special historical function as a wonder-working image we miss the point. We can admire many works of art for their form, content, and quality, but we need a further characterizing experience; otherwise we are admiring very different works without discriminating their decisive differences. We shall be confused and our judgment faulty.

While our most fundamental way of classifying works of art is by the time of their making, classification by *place of origin* is also crucial. In many periods a general style, Gothic for example, will have a great many regional variations: French Gothic architecture is strikingly different from both English and Italian Gothic. Differences of climate helped to make French Gothic an architecture without bearing walls (and with great spaces for stained-glass windows) and Italian Gothic an architecture with large expanses of wall wonderfully suited to mural painting. Art history, then, is also concerned with the spread of a style from its place of origin. Supplementing time of origin with place of origin thus adds another dimension to the picture of art monuments in the process of stylistic development.

The *artist*, of course, provides a third dimension in the history of art. As we have noted, early "histories" of art, written before the advent of modern concepts of style and stylistic development, were simply biographies of artists. Biography as one dimension is still important, for through it we can trace stylistic development within the artists' careers. We can learn much from contemporaneous historical accounts, from documents such as commission contracts, and from the artists' own theoretical writings and literary remains. All of this is of use in "explaining" their works, though of course no complete "explanation" exhausts the meaning of them. Relationships to their predecessors, contemporaries, and followers are describable in terms of the concepts *influence* and *school*: Artists are likely to have been influenced by their masters, and then to have influenced or been influenced by their fellows working somewhat in the same style at the same time and place. We designate a group of such artists as a school, by which we mean not an academy, but a time-place-style classification. Thus we may speak of the Dutch School of the seventeenth century and, within it, of subschools like those of Haarlem, Utrecht, and Leyden.

Iconography

Thus the categories of time and place, the record of the artist, influences, and schools—all are used in composition of the picture of stylistic development. Another kind of classification, another key to works of art, is *iconography*—the study of the subject matter of and symbolism in works of art. By this approach paintings and sculptures are grouped in terms of their themes rather than their styles, and the development of subject matter becomes a major focus. Iconographical studies have an ancillary function in stylistic analysis since they are often valuable in tracing influences and in assigning dates and places of origin.

Historical Context

Another, very broad, source of knowledge of a work of art lies outside the artistic region itself, yet encloses it and is in transaction with it. This is the *general historical context*—the political, social, economic, scientific, technological, and intellectual background that accompanies and influences the specifically art-historical events. The fall of Rome, the coming of Christianity, and the barbarian invasions all had much to do with stylistic changes in architecture, sculpture, and painting in the early centuries of our era. The triumph of science and technology has everything to do with the great transformation of the Renaissance tradition that takes place in what we call modern art, the art of our own time. The work of art, the persisting event, is after all a historical document.

THE WORK OF ART

The work of art is an object as well as an historical event. To describe and analyze it we use categories and vocabularies that have become more or less standard and that are indispensable for understanding this book.

General Concepts

Form, for the purposes of art history, refers to the shape of whatever is the "object" of art; in the made object it is the shape that the expression of content takes. To create forms, to make a work of art, artists must of course shape materials with tools. Of the many materials, tools, and processes available, each has its own potentialities and limitations, and it is part of the artists' creative activity to select the ones most suitable to their purpose. The technical processes they employ as well as the distinctive, personal way they handle them, we call their *technique*. If the material artists use is the substance of art, technique is their individual manner of giving that substance form. Form, technique, and material are interrelated, as can be readily seen in a comparison of the marble statue of Apollo from Olympia (FIG. 5-35, p. 150) with the bronze *Charioteer of Delphi* (FIG. 5-32, p. 148). The *Apollo* is firmly modeled in broad, generalized planes reflecting the ways of shaping stone that are more or less dictated by the character of that material and by the tool used—the chisel. On the other hand, the *Charioteer's* fineness of detail, the crisp, sharp folds of the drapery, reflect the qualities inherent in cast metal. However, a given medium (the material used) can lend itself to more than one kind of manipulation. The technique of Lehmbruck's bronze *Seated Youth* (FIG. 1), for example, contrasts strikingly with Rodin's *The Thinker* (FIG. 2), also bronze. The surfaces of Lehmbruck's figure are smooth, flowing, quiet, while those of Rodin's are rough, broken, and tortuous. Here it is not so much the bronze that determines the form as it is the sculptor's difference of purpose and of personal technique.

Space, in our common-sense experience, is the bounded or boundless "container" of masses or objects. For the analysis of works of art we regard it as bounded and susceptible of esthetic and expressive organization. Architecture provides our commonest experience of the actual manipulation of space, while the art of painting frequently has had the purpose of projecting upon a two-dimensional surface an image (or illusion) of the three-dimensional spatial world we move in.

Area and *plane*, terms that describe limited, two-dimensional space, generally refer to surface. A plane is flat, two-dimensional —like this page and like elements dealt with in plane geometry, such as a circle, square, triangle. An area, also describable in terms of plane geometry, is often a plane or flat surface that is enclosed or bounded. Bernini, when he defined the essentially plane surface in front of St. Peter's by means of his curving colonnades, created an area (FIG. 15-3, p. 582).

Mass and *volume*, in contradistinction to plane and area, describe three-dimensional space. In both architecture and sculpture, mass is the bulk, density, and weight of matter in space. Yet the mass need not be solid; it can be the exterior form of enclosed space. For example, "mass" can apply to a pyramid (FIG. 3-7, p. 80), which is essentially solid, or to the exterior of the Hagia

1 WILHELM LEHMBRUCK, *Seated Youth*, 1918. Bronze. Wilhelm-Lehmbruck-Museum.

2 AUGUSTE RODIN, *The Thinker*, 1880. Bronze. Metropolitan Museum of Art, New York (gift of Thomas F. Ryan, 1910).

Sophia (FIG. 7-32, p. 273), which is essentially a shell enclosing vast spaces. Volume is the space that is organized, divided, or enclosed by mass. It may be the spaces of the interior of a building or the intervals between the masses of a building or between those of a piece of sculpture, ceramics, or furniture. Volume and mass describe the exterior as well as the interior forms of a work of art—the forms of the matter of which it is composed *and* the forms of the spaces that exist immediately around that matter and interact with it. For example, in the Lehmbruck statue (FIG. 1), referred to above, the expressive volumes enclosed by the attenuated masses of the torso and legs play an important part in the open design of the piece. The absence of enclosed volumes in the Rodin figure—equally expressive—closes the design, making it compact, heavy, and locked-in. (Yet both works convey the same mood—one of brooding introversion.) These forms—the closed and the open—manifest through the history of art, demonstrate the intimate connection between mass and the space that surrounds and penetrates it.

In the definition of mass and volume, *line* is one of the most important yet most difficult terms to comprehend fully. In both science and art line can be understood as the path of a point moving in space, the track of a motion. Because the directions of motions can be almost infinite, the quality of line can be incredibly various and subtle. It is well known that psychological responses attach to the direction of a line—a vertical line being positive, a horizontal one passive, a diagonal suggestive of movement, energy, or unbalance, and so on. Hogarth regarded the serpentine or S-curve line as the "line of beauty." Our psychological response to line is also bound up with our esthetic sense of its quality. A line may be very thin, wirelike and delicate, giving a sense of fragility, as in Klee's *Twittering Machine* (FIG. 17-20, p. 742). Or it may alternate quickly from thick to thin, the strokes jagged, the outline broken, as in a 600-year-old Chinese painting (FIG. 19-16, p. 841); the effect is of vigorous action and angry agitation. A gentle, undulating but firm line, like that in Picasso's *Bathers* (FIG. 3), defines a *contour* that is restful and quietly sensuous. A contour continuously and subtly contains and suggests mass and volume. In the Picasso drawing the line is distinct, dark against the white of the paper. But line can be felt as a controlling presence in a hard edge, profile, or boundary created by a contrasting area even when its tone differs only slightly from that of the area it bounds. A good example of this is to be seen in the central figure of the goddess in Botticelli's *Birth of Venus* (FIG. 12-56, p. 468).

When a line serves as an element along which forms are organized, it is known as an *axis*. The axis line itself need not be

3 PABLO PICASSO, detail of *Bathers*, 1918. Pencil drawing. Fogg Art Museum, Harvard University (bequest of Paul J. Sachs).

evident, and there may be several (usually with one dominant), as in the layout of a city. Though we are most familiar with directional axes in urban complexes, they occur in all the arts. A fine example of the use of axis in large-scale architecture is the plan of the Palace of Versailles and its magnificent gardens (FIG. 15-52, p. 624). Axis—vertical, horizontal, or diagonal—is also an important compositional element in painting.

Perspective, no less than axis, is a method of organizing forms in space, yet we use perspective mainly in creating an illusion of depth or space on a two-dimensional surface. Conditioned by exposure to Western single-point perspective, an invention of the Italian Renaissance (see pp. 476–510), we tend to see perspective as a systematic ordering of pictorial space in terms of a single point—a point where those lines converge that mark the diminishing size of forms as they recede into the distance (FIG. 13-16, p. 490). Renaissance and Baroque artists created masterpieces of perspective illusionism. In Leonardo's *Last Supper* (FIG. 4), for example, the lines of perspective (dashed lines) are handled so that they converge on Christ and, in the foreground, project the picture space into the room on whose wall the painting appears, creating the illusion that the space of the picture and of the room are continuous. Yet we must remember that Renaissance perspective is only one of several systems for depicting depth. Others were used in ancient Greece and Rome, and still others,

4 Leonardo da Vinci, *The Last Supper*, c. 1495–98. Fresco. Santa Maria delle Grazie, Milan. Perspective lines are dashed; lines indicating proportions are solid white or black.

5 CLAUDE MONET, Façade of Rouen Cathedral, *c.* 1880. Above, National Gallery of Art, Washington, D.C. (Chester Dale Collection); below, Museum of Fine Arts, Boston (bequest of Hanna Marcy Edwards).

in the East. Some of these other systems, as well as Renaissance perspective, continue to be used. There is no final or absolutely correct projection of what we "in fact" see.

Proportion deals with the relationships (in terms of size) of the parts of a work. The experience of proportion is common to all of us: We seem to recognize at once when the features, say, of the human face or body are "out of proportion," if the nose or ears are too large for the face or the legs too short for the body. An instinctive or conventional sense of proportion leads us at once to regard the disproportionate as ludicrous or ugly. Proportion, formalized, is the mathematical relationship in size of one part of a work of art to the others within the work, as well as to the totality of the parts; it implies the use of a denominator common to the various parts. Recently it has been shown that the major elements of Leonardo's *Last Supper* show proportions found in harmonic ratios in music—12:6:4:3 (FIG. 4). These figures (with the greatest width of a ceiling panel taken as one unit) are the widths, respectively, of the painting, the ceiling (at the front), the rear wall, and the three windows (taken together and including interstices); they apply as well to the vertical organization of the painting. Leonardo found proportion everywhere, "not only in numbers and measures, but also in sounds, weights, intervals of time, and in every active force in existence."[1] The ancient Greeks, who thought beauty to be "correct" proportion, sought a canon (or rule) of proportion, not only in music, but also for the human figure. The famous canon of Polycleitos (p. 164), expressed in his statue of Doryphoros (FIG. 5-53, p. 163), long provided an exemplar of correct proportion. But it should be noted that canons of proportion differ from time to time and culture to culture and that, occasionally, artists have deliberately used disproportion. Part of the task of the students of art history is to perceive and adjust to these differences as they try to understand the wide universe of art forms. Proportional relationships are often based on a *module*, a dimension of which the various parts of a building or other work are fractions or multiples. It might be the diameter of a column, the height of the human body, an abstract unit of measurement. For example, the famous "ideal" plan of the ninth-century monastery of St. Gall (FIG. 8-11, p. 317) has a modular base of $2\frac{1}{2}$ feet, with all parts of the structure multiples or fractions of this dimension.

Scale (like proportion) refers to the dimensional relations of the parts of a work to its totality (or of a work to its setting) but

[1] In Thomas Brachert, "A Musical Canon of Proportion in Leonardo da Vinci's *Last Supper*," *Art Bulletin*, N.Y. December 1971, LIII, 4, pp. 461–66.

usually in terms of appropriateness to use or function. We do not think a private home need be high as an office building, nor an elephant's house at the zoo the size of a hencoop—or vice versa. This sense of scale is necessary for the construction of form in all the arts. Most often, but not necessarily, it is the human figure that gives the scale to form.

Form, with which we began this list of fundamental concepts, is mediated primarily by *light*. The function of light in the world of nature is so pervasive that we often take it for granted, and there are few who realize the extraordinary variations wrought by light alone—whether natural or artificial—on our most familiar surroundings, as daylight, for example, changes with the hour or season. Few realize fully the extent to which light affects and reveals form. One who did was the French artist Monet (pp. 694–96), who painted the reflections in a waterlily pond according to their seasonal variations, and in a series of more than twenty canvases of the façade of the cathedral of Rouen revealed its changing aspect from dawn until twilight in different seasons (PLATE 16-5 and FIG. 5). Light is as important for the perception of form as is the matter of which form is made.

One function of light is *value*. In painting, and in the graphic arts generally, value refers to lightness, or the amount of light that is (or appears to be) reflected from a surface. Value is a subjective experience, as FIGURE 6 shows. In absolute terms—if measured, say, by a photoelectric device—the center bar in this diagram is uniform in value. Yet, where the bar is adjacent to a dark area, it *looks* lighter, and where adjacent to a lighter area, darker. Value is the basis of the quality called *chiaroscuro*— *chiaro* (light), *scuro* (dark)—which refers to gradations between light and dark that produce the effect of *modeling*, or of light reflected from three-dimensional surfaces, as exemplified in Leonardo's superb rendering of *The Virgin and St. Anne* (FIG. 13-2, p. 478).

In the analysis of light an important distinction must be made for the realm of art: natural light, or sunlight, is whole or additive light, whereas the painter's light in art—the light reflected from pigments and objects—is subtractive light. Natural light is the sum of all the wavelengths composing the visible spectrum, which may be disassembled or fragmented into the individual colors of the spectral band. (Recent experiments with lasers—*l*ight *a*mplification by *s*timulated *e*mission of *r*adiation— have produced color of incredible brilliance and intensity, opening possibilities of color composition until now not suspected. The range and strength of color produced in this way approach, though at considerable distance, those of the sun.) Although the

6 Effect of adjacent value on apparent value. Actual value of center bar is constant.

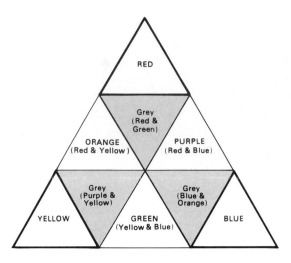

7 Color triangle prepared by Josef Albers and Sewell Sillman, Yale University.

esthetics of color is largely the province of the artist and can usually be genuinely experienced and understood only through intense practice and experimentation, some aspects are susceptible of analysis and systematization. Paint pigments (as well as those of the human body) produce their individual colors by reflecting a segment of the spectrum while absorbing all the rest. A "green" pigment, for example, subtracts or absorbs all the light in the spectrum except that seen by us as green, which it reflects to the eye. (In the case of transmitted rather than reflected light, the coloring matter—as in stained glass—blocks or screens out all wavelengths of the spectrum but those of the color one sees.) Thus, theoretically, a mixture of pigments that embraced all the colors of the spectrum would subtract all light—that is, it would be black; actually, such a mixture of pigments never produces more than a dark gray. (See below, p. 13, the discussion of complementary colors.)

The name of a color is its *hue*—red, blue, yellow. Although the colors of the spectrum merge into each other, artists usually conceive of their hues as distinct from each other, and this gives rise to many different devices for representing color relationships. There are basically two variables in color—the apparent amount of light reflected and the apparent purity, and a change in one must produce a change in the other. Some terms for these variables are (for lightness) *value* (see above) and *tonality*, and (for purity) *chroma*, *saturation*, and *intensity*.

One of the more noteworthy diagrams of the relationships of colors is the triangle (FIG. 7), once attributed to Goethe, in which red, yellow, and blue (the *primary colors*) are the vertexes of the triangle, and orange, green, and purple (the *secondary colors*, which result from mixing pairs of primaries) lie between them. Colors that lie opposite each other (such as red and green) are called *complementary*, since they complement, or complete, one another, each absorbing those colors that the other reflects, leaving a neutral, or gray (theoretically, black), when mixed in the right proportions. The inner triangles are products of such mixing.

Color also has a psychological dimension, red and yellow, quite naturally, having connotations of warmth, and blue and green, coolness. Generally, *warm colors* seem to advance, and *cool colors*, to recede.

The quality of a surface—rough, smooth, hard, soft, shiny, dull—as revealed by light is *texture*. The many painting media and techniques permit creation of a variety of textures. The artist may simulate the texture of materials represented, as in Kalf's *Still Life* (PLATE 15-9), or create arbitrary surface differences, even using materials other than canvas, as in Picasso's *Still Life with Chair-caning* (FIG. 17-8, p. 731).

Specialized Concepts

The terms we have been discussing have connotations for all the visual arts. Certain observations, however, are relevant to only one category of artistic endeavor—to architecture only, or to painting, or to sculpture.

IN ARCHITECTURE

Works of architecture are so much a part of our environment that we accept them as given, scarcely noticing them until our attention is summoned. People have long known how to enclose space for the many purposes of life. Of all the arts it is in architecture that the spatial aspect is most obvious. The architect makes groupings of enclosed spaces and enclosing masses, keeping always in mind the function of the structure, its construction and materials, and of course its design, the correlative of the other two. We experience architecture both visually and by motion through and around it, so that architectural space and mass are given to our perception together. The articulation of space and mass in building is expressed graphically in several ways; the principal ones follow.

A *plan* is essentially a map of a floor, showing the placement

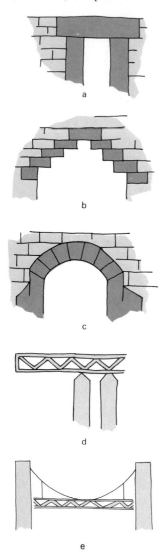

8 Basic structural devices: *a*, post and lintel; *b*, corbeled arch; *c*, arch; *d*, cantilever; *e*, suspension.

a

b

c

d

e

of a structure's masses and, therefore, the spaces they bound and enclose (FIG. 7-35, p. 277). A *section*, like a vertical plan, shows placement of the masses as if the building were cut through along a plane (often one that is a major axis of the building). An *elevation* is a head-on view of an external or internal wall, showing its features and often other elements that would be visible beyond or before the wall. (For details, see p. 930, "Plan and Section Conventions."

Our response to a building can range from simple comfort to astonishment and awe, and such reactions are products of our experience of a building's function, construction, and design. We react differently to a church, a gymnasium, and an office building. For one thing, the very movements required of us in order to experience one building will differ widely and profoundly from those required to experience another. These movements will be controlled by the continuity—or discontinuity—of the plan, or by the placement of its axes. For example, in a central plan—one that radiates from a central point, as in the Pantheon in Rome (FIG. 6-42, p. 223)—we perceive the whole spatial entity at once, while in the long axial plan of a Christian basilica (FIG. 7-24, p. 266) or a Gothic cathedral (FIG. 10-17, p. 367) our attention tends to focus on a given point—the altar at the eastern end of the nave. Mass and space can be so interrelated as to produce effects of great complexity, as, for example, in the Byzantine church of the Katholikon (FIG. 7-39, p. 279) or Le Corbusier's church at Ronchamp (FIG. 17-82, p. 790). Thus, our experience of architecture will be the consequence of a great number of material and formal factors, including training and knowledge and our perceptual and psychological makeup, which function in our experience of any work of art.

The architect must have the sensibilities of a sculptor and of a painter and in establishing the plan of a building must be able, as well, to use the instruments of a mathematician. As architects resolve structural problems they act as—or with—engineers cognizant of the structural principles underlying all architecture (FIG. 8). Their major responsibilities, however, lie in the manner in which they interpret the *program* of the building. We are not talking in architectural terms when we describe a structure simply as a church, a hospital, an airport concourse, a house. Any proposed building presents an architect with problems peculiar to it alone—problems related to the site and its surroundings, the requirements of the client, and the materials available—as well as the function of the building. A program, then, deals with more than function; it addresses itself to all the problems embodied in a specific building.

Like architecture, sculpture exists in the three-dimensional space of our physical world. But sculpture as image is closer to painting than is architecture. Until recently, sculpture has been primarily concerned with the representation of human and of natural forms in tangible materials, which exist in the same space as the forms they represent. Sculpture may also embody visions and ideals and has consistently presented images of deities and of people in their most heroic as well as most human aspects (FIG. 13-18, p. 494, and 5-64, p. 172). Today sculpture often dispenses with the figure as image, and even with the image itself, producing new forms in new materials and with new techniques (FIGS. 17-66 to 17-76, pp. 778–84).

Sculpture may be intimately associated with architecture, often to such a degree that it is impossible to disassociate them (FIG. 10-14, p. 365). Sculpture is called *relief* sculpture (FIG. 3-35, p. 101) when it is attached to a back-slab or back plate; *high relief* if the figures or design project boldly (FIG. 5-66, p. 173); *low relief*, or *bas-relief*, if they project slightly (FIG. 3-35, p. 101).

Sculpture that exists in its own right, independent of any architectural frame or setting (FIG. 13-41, p. 515), is usually referred to as *free-standing* or "sculpture in the round," although there are many occasions in the art of Greece and of the Renaissance when free-standing sculpture is closely allied to architecture. Indeed, sculpture is such a powerful agent in creating a spatial as well as an intellectual environment that its presence in city squares or in parks and gardens is usually the controlling factor in their "atmosphere" or general effect (FIG. 15-57, p. 629).

Some statues are meant to be seen as a whole—to be walked around (FIG. 13-41, p. 515). Others have been created to be viewed only from a restricted angle. How a sculpture is meant to be seen of course has to be taken into account by the sculptor, and by those who exhibit the work. Figure 9 illustrates the effect of ignoring this. The upper photograph is taken directly from the front, as the piece is now seen in the museum, whereas the lower one is taken from below, at approximately the same angle from which the statue was originally meant to be seen in its niche on the façade of the cathedral of Florence.

In sculpture, perhaps more than in any other medium, textures, or tactile values, are important. One's first impulse is almost always to handle a piece of sculpture, to run one's finger over its surfaces. The sculptor plans for this, using a great variety of surfaces from rugged coarseness to polished smoothness (FIGS. 10-43, p. 387, and 12-48, p. 461). Textures, of course, are

9 DONATELLO, *St. John the Evangelist*, 1412–15. Marble. Museo del Duomo, Florence. Above, as seen in museum; below, as intended to be seen on façade of the cathedral of Florence.

often intrinsic to a material, and this influences the type of stone, wood, plastic, clay, or metal that the sculptor selects. There are two basic categories of sculptural technique—*subtractive* and *additive*. Carving, for instance, is a subtractive technique, in that the final form is a reduction of the original mass (FIG. 10). Additive sculpture, however, is built up, usually in clay around an armature. The piece so made is fired and used to make a mold in which the final work is cast in a material such as bronze (FIG. 12-49, p. 462). Casting is a popular technique today, as is direct construction of forms by the welding of shaped metals (FIG. 17-67, p. 778), also an additive technique.

Within the sculptural family must be included ceramics and metalwork, and numerous smaller, related arts, all of which employ very specialized techniques with their own distinct vocabularies. These will be considered as they arise in the text.

10 MICHELANGELO, *Unfinished Bound Slave*, 1519. Marble. Accademia, Florence.

IN THE PICTORIAL ARTS

While the forms of architecture and sculpture exist in the actual, three-dimensional space, the forms of painting (and of its relatives, drawing, engraving, etc.) exist almost wholly on a two-dimensional surface on which the artist creates an illusion—something that replicates what we see around us or something that is unique to the artist's imagination and that has little correspondence to anything seen in the optical world. Human discovery of the power to project illusions of the three-dimensional world upon two-dimensional surfaces goes back thousands of years and marks an enormous step in the control and manipulation of things perceived. To achieve this illusion the artist configures images or representations drawn from the world of common visual experience. Throughout the history of art this has been interpreted in almost infinite variety; yet doubtless there is much that all people *see* in common and can agree on: the moon at night, a flying bird, an obstacle in one's path. They may differ, though, in their interpretation of the seen; for seeing, and then representing what is seen, are very different matters. The difference between seeing and representing determines the variability of artistic styles, both cultural and personal. For what we *actually* see—that is, the optical "fact"—is not necessarily reported in what we represent. In other words, for art there is and need be but little agreement about the likeness of things to the representations of them. This makes a persisting problem in the history of art: How are we to interpret or "read" images or replicas of the seen? Is there a "correct" vision of the "real" world?

THE PROBLEM OF REPRESENTATION

The conundrum of seeing something and making a representation of it is artfully illustrated in FIGURE 11, a cartoon of an ancient Egyptian life-drawing class that Gombrich uses to introduce his invaluable work *Art and Illusion*. The cartoon and the actual representation of an Egyptian queen (FIG. 12) raise many questions: Did Egyptian artists copy models exactly as they saw them? (That is, did Egyptians actually *see* each other in this way?) Or did they translate what they saw according to some formula dictated by conventions of representation peculiar to their cul-

11 ALAIN, drawing.
Copyright 1955
by The New Yorker
Magazine, Inc.

12 *Queen Nofretari*, from her tomb at Thebes, *c.* 1250 B.C. Detail of a painted bas-relief.

ture? Would we have to say—if what was seen and what was recorded were optically the same—that this is the way Egyptians must have looked? Or wished to look? Beginning students usually have questions somewhat like these in mind when they perceive deviation, in historical styles, from the recent Western realism to which they have been conditioned. They will ask whether the Egyptians or others were simply unskilled at matching eye and hand, so to speak, and could not draw from what they saw. But this would be to presuppose that the objective of the artist has always been to match appearances with cameralike exactitude. This is not the case, nor is it the case that artists of one period "see" more "correctly" and render more "skillfully" than those of another. It seems rather to be the case that artists represent what they *conceive* to be real rather than what they *perceive*. They bring to the making of images conceptions that have been instilled in them by their cultures. They understand the visible world in certain unconscious, culturally agreed-upon ways, and thus bring to the artistic process ideas and meanings out of a common stock. They record not so much what they *see* as what they *know* or *mean*. Even in the period of dominant realism in recent Western European art, great deviations from camera realism have set in. Moreover, in our everyday life there are images familiar to all of us, that distort optical

13 Villard de Honnecourt, *Lion Portrayed from Life, c.* 1230–35. Drawing. Cabinet des Manuscripts, Bibliothèque Nationale, Paris.

14 Albrecht Dürer, *Two Lions, c.* 1521. Drawing. Staatliche Museen Preussischer Kulturbesitz, Kupferstichkabinet Berlin.

"reality" quite radically: consider, for one example, those of the ubiquitous comic strip.

Solutions to the problem of representation compose the history of artistic style. It is useful to examine some specimens of sharp divergence in representational approach. Compare, for example, the lion drawn by the medieval artist Villard de Honnecourt (FIG. 13) and lions drawn by the Renaissance artist Albrecht Dürer (FIG. 14). In the de Honnecourt lion, which, it is important to notice, the artist asserts was drawn from life, we have a figure entirely adequate for identification, yet preconceived in the formulas of its time and constructed accordingly. Dürer's lions, drawn some three centuries later, obviously make a much different report of what the artist is seeing or has seen. So do the Assyrian lions of the hunting reliefs (FIG. 2-27, p. 65), the lion of the Ishtar Gate processional way (FIG. 2-28, p. 65), the lion in Rousseau le Douanier's *Sleeping Gypsy* (FIG. 16-61, p. 708), or (in a slight shift of genus) Barye's sculpture of a jaguar in his *Jaguar Devouring a Hare* (FIG. 16-14, p. 663). In each case personal vision joins with the artistic conventions of time and place to decide the manner and effect of the representation. Yet even at the same time and place—for example, nineteenth-century Paris—we can find sharp differences in representation where opposing personal styles, those of Ingres and Delacroix, are recording the same subject (FIGS. 16-35 and 16-36, p. 681).

A final example will underscore the relativity of vision and representation that differences in human cultures produce. We recognize, moreover, that close matching of appearances has mattered only in a few times and places. Although both portraits (FIG. 15) of a Maori chieftain, one by a European, the other by the chieftain himself, reproduce his facial tatooing, the first portrait is a simple commonplace likeness that underplays the tatooing. The latter is a statement by the chieftain of the supreme importance of the design that symbolizes his rank among his people. It is the splendidly composed insignia that is his image of himself, the European likeness being superficial and irrelevant to him.

Students of the history of art, then, learn to distinguish the works before them by scrutinizing them closely in the context of their time and place of origin. But this is only the beginning. The causes of stylistic change in time are mysterious and innumerable; and it is only through the continuing process of art-historical research that we can hope to make the picture even fragmentarily recognizable, never complete. Incomplete though the picture is, the panorama of art, changing in time, lies before the students; and, as their art-historical perspective

15 *The Maori Chief Tupai Kupa, c.* 1800. Left, after a drawing by John Sylvester; right, a self-portrait. From *The Childhood of Man* by Leo Frobenius, 1909. Reproduced by permission of J. B. Lippincott Company.

gains depth and focus, they will come to perceive the continuity of the art of the past with that of the present. It will become clear that one cannot be understood without the other, and that our understanding of the one will constantly change with changes in our understanding of the other. The great American poet and critic T. S. Eliot has cogently expressed this truth for all of art in a passage that suggests the philosophy and method of this book:

> . . . what happens when a new work of art is created is something that happens simultaneously to all the works of art which preceded it. The existing monuments form an ideal order among themselves, which is modified by the introduction of the new (the really new) work of art among them. . . . Whoever has approved this idea of order . . . will not find it preposterous that the past should be altered by the present as much as the present is directed by the past.[2]

[2] "Tradition and the Individual Talent" in *Selected Essays 1917–1932*, by T. S. Eliot (New York: Harcourt Brace Jovanovich, Inc., 1932), p. 5.

PART ONE

THE ANCIENT WORLD

The Christian civilizations of the Western world early distinguished an ancient past from a new age—the times, respectively, before and after Christ. For them the ancient world—the world of the Old Testament—had the character of a preparation; it was related to the new era as promise to fulfillment. This slightly condescending view toward antiquity changed during the Renaissance, when scholars and artists deeply admired especially the Greek and Roman past and often debated the question of which was superior, the "ancient" or the "modern." Interest in Greco-Roman antiquity was broadened later to take in the great civilizations that had preceded it—those of the pre-Greek Mediterranean, Egypt, the Near East, and the very remote, prehistoric cave cultures of western Europe. From the end of the eighteenth century to the present, archeologists and art historians, with ever improving methods of investigation, have recovered great tracts of forgotten history to fill out with increasing accuracy our picture of the distant past. Within the past two decades evidence has been brought forward of the existence of civilizations that flourished as early as 7000 B.C., and the sequence of development that viewed early Egypt and Mesopotamia as concurrent has been shown to be incorrect, Mesopotamia, in fact, preceding Egypt by many centuries.

Cretan fresco of court ladies at a festival, from the palace at Knossos, c. 1600–1400 B.C. Though similar to Egyptian painting in concept, its impressionistic execution stresses lightness of mood and movement.

Historical perspective is likely to produce a distortion of view akin to that of the early Christian depreciation of the pre-Christian world. Until we have become familiar with the ancient world, it seems to us simply *that*—ancient, exceedingly old—and we imagine it in terms and images of faded inscriptions, dusty ruins, fallen idols, and long-outdated institutions. More properly we should see *ourselves* as ancient—that is, as living in the later eras of a great epoch at whose beginning, thousands of years ago, some of our most fundamental beliefs, institutions, folkways, and art and science had their inception.

The precarious, furtive life of the cave-dwelling hunter was, with the development of agriculture and the domestication of animals, succeeded by the more sedentary, predictable, and ordered life of village farmers. Aside from the technological revolutions of our times, this leap from food-gathering to food production brought perhaps the most significant transformation of the human condition and made possible all that has followed. In Mesopotamia, Asia Minor, and Egypt more complex forms of human community were created—cities, city-states, and kingdoms. Formal religion and codes of law were developed to regulate the relationships of gods and men. Writing was invented, as well as numbers and the art of calculation. The courses of the stars were plotted to predict the seasons and the times for planting and harvesting. Architecture, sculpture, and painting flourished in the service of kingly magnificence. The sacred books of Judaism and Christianity were produced in the shadow of mighty and hostile empires, and the legacy of Israel, which has contributed so much to the formation of the Western spirit, was preserved through all the vicissitudes of a remarkable people.

It was with the Greeks that there emerged what might be called the specifically Western intelligence, with its respect for reason, scientific inquiry, the physical concept of nature, and the humanistic view of man. The city-states of Greece were more than seats of commerce and government, and the loyalties of the citizens of each had social, educative, and local religious bases as well. It was in some of these city-states—Athens in particular—that democracy, though in a limited form, first evolved. With the repulse of the Persian invaders in the fifth century B.C., the Greeks inaugurated the first authentic phase of European culture, the content and spirit of which, commingled with Hebraism, is still largely with us in our patterns of life and thought.

Rome, never matching the Greek achievement in intellectual and artistic culture, yet produced the greatest empire of the ancient world. In eight hundred years it passed from its beginnings as a trading center under Etruscan kings to the zenith of its empire, when it extended from what are now the borders of Scotland to Jordan, asserting its hegemony over a multitude of peoples and lands. The dynamic and aggressive Roman spirit was reflected in and supported by an astonishing military machine and technology, although Roman control over diverse peoples was exercised as much by the encouragement of their participation in the empire as in the naked assertion of Roman power. The Romanization of western Europe—through the Roman genius for government and the "Roman Peace"—has still much to do with its character, and the Roman ideal of a single, peaceful community of all mankind is very much in our view today.

Chapter One

The Birth
of Art

PREHISTORIC EUROPE

PALEOLITHIC

Franco-Cantabrian region
● Other cave art
▲ Mobiliary art

MESOLITHIC

East Spanish region

NEOLITHIC
■ Megalithic

Stonehenge

Lascaux

Willendorf

0   100   200   300 miles

W̲ʜᴀᴛ Gᴇɴᴇsɪs is to the biblical account of the fall and redemption of man, early cave art is to the history of his intelligence, imagination, and creative power. In the caves of southern France and northern Spain, discovered only about a century ago and still being explored, we may witness the birth of that characteristically human capability that has made man master of his environment—the making of images and symbols. By this original and tremendous feat of abstraction Aurignacian and Magdalenian men were able to fix the world of their

experience, rendering the continuous processes of life in discrete and unmoving shapes that had identity and meaning as the living animals that were their prey. Like Adam, Paleolithic man gathered and named the animals, and the faculty of imagination came into being along with the concepts of identity and meaning.

In that remote time during the last advance and retreat of the great glaciers man made the critical breakthrough and became wholly human. Our intellectual and imaginative processes function through the recognition and construction of

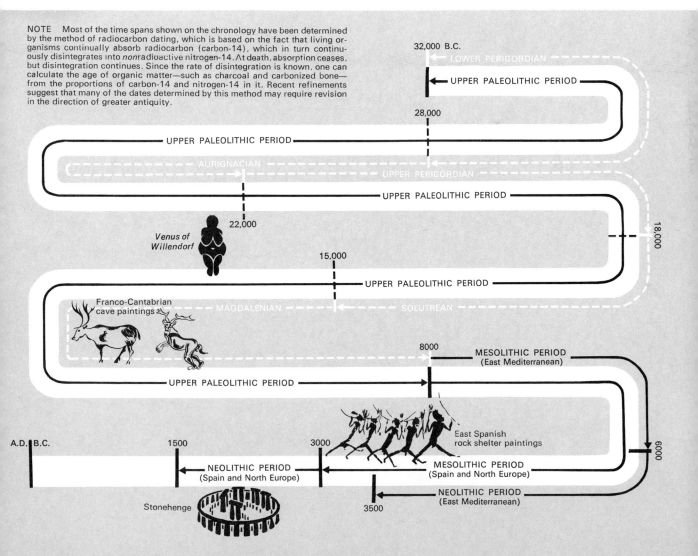

NOTE   Most of the time spans shown on the chronology have been determined by the method of radiocarbon dating, which is based on the fact that living organisms continually absorb radiocarbon (carbon-14), which in turn continuously disintegrates into *non*radioactive nitrogen-14. At death, absorption ceases, but disintegration continues. Since the rate of disintegration is known, one can calculate the age of organic matter—such as charcoal and carbonized bone—from the proportions of carbon-14 and nitrogen-14 in it. Recent refinements suggest that many of the dates determined by this method may require revision in the direction of greater antiquity.

32,000 B.C.
LOWER PERIGORDIAN
UPPER PALEOLITHIC PERIOD
28,000
UPPER PALEOLITHIC PERIOD
AURIGNACIAN
UPPER PERIGORDIAN
UPPER PALEOLITHIC PERIOD
18,000
Venus of Willendorf
22,000
15,000
UPPER PALEOLITHIC PERIOD
Franco-Cantabrian cave paintings
MAGDALENIAN
SOLUTREAN
8000
MESOLITHIC PERIOD (East Mediterranean)
UPPER PALEOLITHIC PERIOD
6000
East Spanish rock shelter paintings
A.D. B.C.
1500
3000
NEOLITHIC PERIOD (Spain and North Europe)
MESOLITHIC PERIOD (Spain and North Europe)
Stonehenge
NEOLITHIC PERIOD (East Mediterranean)
3500

images and symbols; we see and understand the world pretty much as we are taught to by the representations of it familiar to our time and place. The immense achievement of Stone Age man, the invention of representation, cannot be exaggerated.

THE LATER OLD STONE AGE (UPPER PALEOLITHIC)

The physical environment of the cave peoples during the long thousands of years would not, one imagines, be favorable to the creation of an art of quality and sophistication since survival alone would seem to have required most of their energies. Though the Aurignacian period began between the early and main advances of the last glacier and for a while was temperate, it grew cold toward its end. The Solutrean period saw the reign of arctic weather. The great ice sheet advanced south from Scandinavia over the plains of north central Europe, and glaciers spread down from the Alps and other mountain ranges to produce climatic conditions very much like those of Greenland today.With the Magdalenian period began the final recession of the ice and the onset of temperate weather. (Climatically, we are still in the postglacial or, according to some, an interglacial period.) In the cold periods, man, the hunter and food-gatherer, took refuge in caves, and it was here that Cro-Magnon man, who first appeared during the Aurignacian period, replacing Neanderthal man, took the remarkable turn that made him not simply a fabricator of rudimentary stone tools but an artist.

1-1 Diagram of the caves of Lascaux. Dordogne, France. (After Bataille.)

Contour of rock wall at cave floor
Position of paintings and incised figures in relation to passageway floor

FEET
0   10   20   30

FIGURE 1-6

FIGURE 1-4

FIGURE 1-2

PLATE 1-2

PLATE 1-1

Cave Art

This most ancient of all human cultures was the most recently discovered—by amateurs and by accident. In 1879, near Santander in northern Spain, Marcelino de Sautuola, a local resident interested in the antiquity of man, was exploring the Altamira Caves on his estate, in which he had already found specimens of flint and carved bone. With him was his little daughter. Since the ceiling of the debris-filled cavern was only a few inches above the father's head, it was the child who was first able to discern, from her lower vantage point, the shadowy forms of painted beasts on the cave roof. De Sautuola was the first modern man to explore this cave and he was certain that these paintings dated back to prehistoric times. Archeologists, however, were highly dubious of their authenticity, and at the Lisbon Congress on Prehistoric Archeology in 1880 the Altamira paintings were officially dismissed as forgeries. But in 1896, at Pair-non-Pair in the Gironde district of France, paintings were discovered partially covered by calcareous deposits that would have taken thousands of years to accumulate; these paintings were the first to be recognized as authentic by experts. The conviction grew that these remarkable works were of an antiquity far greater than man had ever dreamed. In 1901 Abbé Breuil, dean of archeologists of the prehistoric, discovered and verified the cave art of Font-de-Gaume in Dordogne, France. The skeptics were finally convinced.

The caves at Lascaux, near Montignac, also in the Dordogne region of France, were discovered accidentally in 1941 by two young boys who were playing in a field. Their dog, following a ball, disappeared into a hole, and the boys, hearing barking from below, followed the animal down into the caves. Their lighted matches revealed magnificent drawings of animals, now generally regarded as the most outstanding of all prehistoric art (PLATES 1-1 and 1-2).

While these paintings survived more than ten thousand years in the sealed and dry subterranean chambers, many have deteriorated rapidly since the caves were opened to the public in recent decades. At Lascaux, for example, it was found that moisture (carried into the caves by hordes of visitors) settled on the walls and calcified, creating a film that dims the paintings. To avoid further damage, the cave has been closed to the public.

The Lascaux caverns (FIG. 1-1), like the others, had been subterranean water channels, a few hundred to some four thousand feet long. They are often choked, sometimes almost impassably, by faults or by deposits such as stalactites and stalagmites. Far inside these caverns, well removed from the cave mouths that he chose for habitation, the hunter-artist engraved and painted on the walls pictures of animals—mammoth, bison, reindeer, horse, boar, wolf. For light he must have used tiny stone lamps filled with marrow or fat, with a wick, perhaps of moss. For drawing he used chunks of red and yellow ocher, and for painting he ground these same ochers into powder that he blew onto the walls or mixed with some medium, perhaps animal fat, before applying. A large flat bone may have served him as a palette; he could make brushes from reeds or bristles; he could use a blowpipe of reeds to trace outlines of figures and to put pigments on out-of-reach surfaces; and he had stone scrapers for smoothing the wall and sharp flint points for engraving. Such were the artist's tools. Rudimentary as they were, they were sufficient to produce the art that astonishes us today.

The artist's approach to the figures, as seen at Lascaux and at other sites, is naturalistic; he attempts to represent as convincing a pose and action as possible. Each painting reflects the keen observation and extraordinary memory of the hunter-artist, whose accuracy in capturing fleeting poses is hardly surpassed by today's camera (PLATES 1-1 and 1-2, FIG. 1-10). Yet this observation was selective, the artist seeing and recording only those aspects essential in interpreting the appearance and the character of the animal—its grace or awkwardness, its cunning, dignity, or ferocity. It is almost as if the artist were constructing a pictorial definition of the animal, capturing its very essence.

Any modern interpretation of this cave art must, of course, remain pure speculation. Properties common to all these paintings, how-

1-2 *Three Cows and One Horse*, ceiling of the Axial Gallery, Lascaux, *c.* 15,000–10,000 B.C. Approx. life-size. Dordogne, France.

ever, provide researchers with some fairly definite clues to what they meant to their creators. For instance, the fact that the paintings are never found in those parts of the caves that were inhabited or near daylight rules out any purely decorative purpose. At Font-de-Gaume the first paintings were encountered about seventy yards behind the cave mouth, and in the cave at Niaux the painted animals in the "Salon Noir" are found some 850 tortuous yards from the entrance. The remoteness and difficulty of access of many of these sites and the fact that they appear to have been used for centuries strongly suggest that the prehistoric hunter attributed magical properties to them. And so the paintings themselves most likely had magical meaning to their creators. As Abbé Breuil has suggested, "by confining the animal within the limits of a painting, one subjected it to one's power in the hunting grounds." And, within this context, the artist's aim to be realistic may be explained by his probable conviction that the painting's magical power was directly related to its lifelikeness.

The naturalistic pictures of animals are often accompanied by geometric signs, some of which

seem to represent man-made structures, or *tectiforms* (FIG. 1-2), while others consist of checkers, dots, squares, or other arrangements of lines. Several observers have seen a primitive form of writing in these representations of non-living things, but more likely they, too, had only magical significance. The ones that look like traps or snares, for example, may have been drawn to ensure success in hunting with these devices. In many places there appear representations of human hands, most of them "negative," where the hunter placed his hand against the wall and then painted or blew pigment around it (FIG. 1-3). Occasionally he would dip his hand in paint and then press it against the wall, leaving a "positive" imprint. These, too, may have had magical significance, or may simply have been the "signatures" left by whole generations of visitors to these sacred places, much as the modern tourist leaves some memento of his presence.

Though the figures are in themselves marvelous approximations of optical fact, their arrangement upon the cave walls shows little concern for any consistency of placement in relationship to each other or to the wall space; certainly we find no compositional adjustment to suggest the perspective effect and no notion of separation and enframement. Figures, far from being proportionally related, are often superimposed at random and are of quite different sizes (PLATES 1-1 and 1-2). Generations of artists, working in the same sanctuaries, covered and recovered the crowded walls, though often pains seem to have been taken not to break through the outlines of an earlier figure. It seems that attention to a single figure, the rendering of a single image, in itself fulfilled the purpose of the artist.

The hunter-artist made frequent and skillful use of the naturally irregular surfaces of the walls, of their projections, recessions, fissures, and ridges, to help give the illusion of real presence to his forms. A swelling outward of the wall could be used within the outline of a charging bison to suggest the bulging volume of the beast's body. The spotted horse at Pech-Merle (FIG. 1-3) may have been inspired by a rock formation that resembles a horse's head and neck (on the right of the figure), although the artist's eventual version of the head is much smaller than the formation and highly abstract. Natural forms like those of foliage or clouds, the profile of a mountain, or the shapes of eroded earth and rock can represent for any of us—sometimes quite startlingly—the features of men, animals, or objects. Thus man's first representations may have followed some primal experience of resemblance between a chance configuration of cave wall and the animal he had just been hunting. This might have had for him the effect of an awesome apparition of the very animal, a miraculous and magical reappearance of its vanished life. With the impulse to give the apparition even more presence he could have "finished" the form by cutting an outline around the relief and continuing it until a silhouette more or less complete and familiar had emerged. The addition of color would enhance the reality of the image.

1-3 *Spotted Horses and Negative Hand Imprints*, Pech-Merle, *c.* 15,000–10,000 B.C. 11′ 2″ long. Lot, France.

1-4 *Chinese Horse*, detail of FIG. 1-2. Approx. 56″ long.

1-5 *Bison with Superposed Arrows*, Niaux, *c.* 15,000–10,009 B.C. 4′ 2″ long. Ariège, France.

1-6 *Well Scene*, Lascaux, *c.* 15,000–10,000 B.C. Bison 4′ 7″ high. Dordogne, France.

THE MAGICAL FUNCTION

It is likely that the cave painter did not carefully distinguish between illusion and reality and that for him the bison recreated on the wall was different from the bison he hunted only in its state of being. We have evidence enough that the hunters in the caves, perhaps in a frenzy stimulated by magical rites and dances, treated the painted animals as if they were indeed alive. Not only was the quarry painted as pierced by arrows, as in the *Chinese Horse* at Lascaux (FIG. 1-4), but hunters may have thrown spears at the images— as sharp gouges in the side of the bison at Niaux (FIG. 1-5) suggest—predestinating and magically commanding the death of the animals. This practice would be analogous to that kind of homeopathic magic, still cultivated in parts of the world today, that has as a basis the belief that harm can be done to an enemy by abusing an image of him.

This art produced in dark caverns deep in the earth must have had, as most scholars are now convinced, some profound magical functions. Familiar in religious architecture, which had its beginning thousands of years after the era of the caves, are the cavelike spaces of the sanctuary where the most sacred and hidden mysteries are kept and where the god dwells in silence. The sacred has meant the mysterious, and this means in many cases a place of darkness, lit only by fitful light, where, at the culmination of rituals, absolute silence reigns. These features of the sacred environment were already present in the "architecture" of the caves, and the central theme has never been lost despite its myriad variations.

It is significant that the miracle of abstraction— the creation of image and symbol—should have taken place in just such secret and magical caverns. For abstraction is representation, a human device of fundamental power, by which not only art but ultimately science comes into existence,

1-7 *Sorcerer*, Trois-Frères, *c.* 15,000–10,000 B.C. 2′ high. Ariège, France.

and both art and science are methods for the control of human experience and the mastery of the environment. And that too was the end purpose of the hunter-magician—to control the world of the beasts he hunted. The making of the image was, by itself, a form of magic; by painting an animal, the hunter fixed and controlled its soul within the prison of an outline, and from this initial magic all the rest must follow. Rites before

the paintings may have served to improve the hunter's luck. At the same time, prehistoric man must have been anxious to preserve his food supply, and the many representations of pregnant animals (FIG. 1-4) suggest that these cavalcades of painted beasts may also have served magically to assure the survival of the actual herds.

THE REPRESENTATION OF MAN

The figure of man is almost completely excluded from representation among the vivid troops of painted animals. There are at least two notable exceptions. A very puzzling picture at Lascaux (FIG. 1-6) shows a stick-figure man, falling or fallen, before a huge bison that has been disemboweled, probably by the rhinoceros at the left, which slouches away from the scene. The two animals are rendered with all that skilled attention to animal detail we are accustomed to in cave art; the rhinoceros heavy and lumbering, the buffalo tense and bristling with rage, its bowels hanging from it in a heavy coil. But the bird-faced (masked?) man is rendered with the crude and clumsy touch of the unskilled at any time or place. His position is ambiguous. Is he dead or in an ecstatic trance? The meaning of the bird on the staff and of the spear and throw stick is no more obvious. We shall not add here to the already abundant speculation on the meaning of this picture. More important is the question, Why the difference in treatment of the man and the animal figures? Does man in this dawn of magic distinguish himself so much from the beast that he can find no image suitable to self-depiction? Or is he afraid to cast a spell on himself, as he casts it upon the animals, by rendering his image visible?

At Trois Frères in the Pyrenees there is a very strange humanoid creature, masked and wearing the antlers of a reindeer (FIG. 1-7)—the so-called *Sorcerer*. Is this the memory sketch of a chief shaman or witch-doctor? If so, one can imagine how the fearsome composite apparition—the paws of a bear, tail of a wolf, beard of a man,

1-8 *Reindeer*, Font-de-Gaume, *c.* 15,000–10,000 B.C. Dordogne, France. (After a copy by Abbé Breuil.)

corporal parts of a lion—could have struck terror into the heart of its audience. The chamber in which the figure appears is crowded with beasts, and Breuil has suggested that the figure may be their god, who has descended into the witch-doctor and filled him with his bestial power. It has also been suggested that this is only a hunter camouflaged to stalk deer, but it would again appear that, for Paleolithic man, mankind simply is not to be counted among the animals; at least his figure must be so disguised—perhaps to avoid magical self-involvement—as to be un-recognizable as a man.

QUALITY

In explaining the great accomplishment of Stone Age man—who pictured the world in order to magically control it—we must not forget that his art is *art*. It is not simply that he made images but that he made them skillfully and beautifully. Ancient and modern art have produced, along with masterpieces, images that are dull, prosaic, and of indifferent quality. The art of the caves is of an extraordinary level of quality. The splendid horse in the Axial Gallery at Lascaux (FIG. 1-4) has been called the *Chinese Horse* because its style strangely resembles that of Chinese painting of the best period. Not only do the outlines have the elastic strength and fluency that we find in Chinese calligraphy and brushwork, but the tone is so managed as to suggest both the turning under of the belly of the pregnant animal and the change of the color of the coat. At Font-de-Gaume there is a painted reindeer (FIG. 1-8) executed with deft elegance in the contours and remarkable subtlety in the modeling tones. The grace of the antlers is effortlessly translated into an upward-sweeping line that renders the natural shapes with both strength and delicacy. Breuil, while copying the originals, discerned some highly sophisticated pictorial devices that one expects to find only in the art of far later times; for example, the dark-ening of the forward contour of the left hind leg so as to bring it nearer to the observer than the right leg.

The pictures of cattle at Lascaux and elsewhere (PLATE 1-2, FIG. 1-2) show a convention of represen-tation of the horns that has been called *twisted perspective*, since we see the heads in profile but the horns from a different angle. Thus, the ap-proach of the artist is not strictly or consistently optical—that is, organized from a fixed-view-point perspective. Rather, the approach is de-scriptive of the fact that cattle have two horns. Two horns would be part of the concepts "cow" and "bull." In strict optical-perspective profile only one horn would be visible, but to paint the animal in such a way would, as it were, amount to an incomplete definition of it. And for the cave artist this would have been a defective image, without magic. When we discuss the art of the ancient Near East and Egypt, we shall note again this peculiarity and its significance.

Engravings and Sculpture

The principal bequests of the hunter-artists that can be regarded as fine art are their paintings. However, they have also left us splendid engrav-ings—on stone, ivory, and horn, on both flat and curving surfaces—and sculpture. In the *Bison with Turned Head* (FIG. 1-9) we are impressed by the striking vitality and the simplicity with which the formal beauty is expressed—a sim-plicity and economy of means that distinguishes the great paintings. The head is so turned that it is entirely framed by the massive bulk of the

1-9 *Bison with Turned Head*, La Madeleine, c. 15,000–10,000 B.C. Reindeer horn, 4⅛" high. Dordogne, France. Musée des Antiquités Nationales, St. Germain-en-Laye.

1-10 *Relief Horse*, Cap Blanc, *c.* 15,000–10,000 B.C. 7′ long. Dordogne, France.

1-11 *Venus of Willendorf*, original *c.* 15,000–10,000 B.C. Stone, 4⅜″ high. Naturhistorisches Museum, Vienna. (Cast of original.)

body, and there is a vivid play of curve and countercurve and a surface contrast obtained by the use of decorative hatching to indicate the mane. The artist would have been perfectly familiar with the method of incision of surfaces; incising the outlines of a figure before the tones were introduced was the usual procedure for painting. But the artists of the caves went farther than incision and produced sculpture in deep relief and in the full round. An example of the first is a horse in deep relief (FIG. 1-10) found in the rock shelter of Cap Blanc, not far from Lascaux. The figure is part of a frieze of sculptured horses and bison, some of the figures almost a foot in depth and masterpieces of relief modeling. Though the figures are eroded by weather, we can perceive their characteristics well enough. They are not simply "filled-out" natural rock contours but in parts strongly modeled. The eyes are sharply incised, and, as in the case of the bison incised in reindeer horn (FIG. 1-9), the manes, forelocks, and portions of the head and muzzle have been carefully indicated by hatching.

There are small sculptures in the full round representing the female figure (called Venus figures by archeologists), an exception to the rule of exclusion of the human figure from the cave artist's vocabulary of forms. Perhaps the most famous of these is the *Venus of Willendorf* (FIG. I-11), a figurine of a woman that is composed of a cluster of almost ball-like shapes. The anatomical exaggeration suggests that this and similar statuettes served as fertility fetishes; the needs for game and human offspring were one in the dangerous life of the hunter. But again the artist's approach to the human figure differs from that to animals. He obviously does not aim for that heightened realism so characteristic of his animal representations; facial features, for instance, are seldom indicated in these statuettes, and in some specimens not even the heads are shown. Evidently the artist's aim was not to show the female of his kind but rather the idea of female fecundity; he depicted not woman but fertility.

THE MIDDLE STONE AGE (MESOLITHIC)

Rock-shelter Paintings

As the ice of the Paleolithic period melted in the increasing warmth, the reindeer migrated north, the wooly mammoth and rhinoceros disappeared, and the hunters left their caves. The Ice Age gave way to a transition period known as the Mesolithic, when Europe became climatically, geographically, and biologically much as it is today. During this time there flourished a culture whose art complements that of the caves, from which, indeed, it may partially have originated. Since 1903, diminutive, extraordinarily lively paintings of animals and men in scenes of the hunt, battle, ritual dance, and harvest have been discovered on the stone walls of shallow rock shelters among the barren hills of the eastern coast of Spain (the Spanish Levant). The artists show the same masterful skill in depicting the animal figure as their predecessors of the caves, and it may be that we have here specimens of a

lingering tradition or long-persisting habit of vision and representation of animals. But what is strikingly new is the appearance of the human figure, not only singly, but in large, coherent groups, with wide variety of pose, subject, and setting. We have seen that in cave art the human figure almost never appears; the falling or fallen man of the well scene (FIG. I-6) at Lascaux is quite exceptional. In the rock-shelter paintings the new sentiment for human themes and concerns and the emphasis on action in which man dominates the animal are central. The new vocabulary of forms may have migrated across the Mediterranean from North Africa, where many paintings similar to those in the Spanish Levant have been found. There has been much learned debate about the dating of the whole development, and there is now some agreement that its beginnings were around 8000 B.C. and that the style may have lasted (with many variations) until about 3000 B.C.

Some characteristic features of the rock paintings appear in an energetic group of five warriors (FIG. I-12) found in the Gasulla gorge. The group, only about nine inches in width, shows a customary tense exaggeration of movement, a rhythmic repetition of basic shape, and in general a sacrifice of naturalistic appearance to narrative and to unity of action. Even so, we can distinguish details that are economically descriptive—bows, arrows, and the feathered headdress of the leader. The widely splayed legs read as a leaping stride, perhaps a march to battle or a ritual dance.

Other such paintings show an even greater uniformity of basic shape, and a nervous, sharp angularity, which suggest the pictograph or—as we have proposed—even the phonetic hieroglyph. And over the millennia the rock painting styles do indeed become more abstract and schematic, more symbol than picture, and it is likely that they record a step in the evolution of the symbolic from the pictorial, an evolution that, in the Near East, culminates in the invention of writing. Later on the liveliness and spontaneity of the rock paintings is lost in the rigid uni formities of almost letterlike shapes repeated as if from a limited stock of signs.

The significance of the rock paintings was probably magical-religious, like the paintings of the caves, though some observers believe them

← to *c.* 32,000 B.C.	*c.* **8000**	*c.* **6000**	*c.* 3500 B.C.

UPPER PALEOLITHIC PERIOD	EAST MEDITERRANEAN MESOLITHIC PERIOD	EAST MEDITERRANEAN NEOLITHIC PERIOD
Franco-Cantabrian cave painting	SPAIN AND NORTHERN EUROPE M E S O L I T H I C P E R I O D	
	East Spanish rock-shelter painting	to *c.* **3000** B.C. →

to be no more than pictorial records of memorable events. The paintings are concentrated at particular sites that were used for long periods, while nearby places, better suited for painting, were not used. This suggests that the sites were held sacred, not only by the Mesolithic painters, but by those working well into the historical period. Iberian and Latin inscriptions indicate that supernatural powers were ascribed to some of these holy places as late as the Roman era.

THE NEW STONE AGE (NEOLITHIC)

In Paleolithic art, man, in a supreme feat of intellection, learned to abstract his world by making a picture of it. Thus he sought to control it by capturing and holding its image. In the Neolithic period he made the giant stride toward the actual, concrete control of his environment by

1-12 *Marching Warriors* (ritual dance?), Gasulla gorge, *c.* 8000–3000 B.C. Approx. 9″ wide. Castellón, Spain.

inventing agriculture and domesticating animals. His food supply assured, he changed from hunter to herdsman, to farmer, and, perhaps as early as 7000 B.C., to townsman. The wandering hunter settled down to organized community living in villages surrounded by cultivated fields. Then began the long evolution toward the incredible technological command of the physical environment that exists today. Before the Stone Age had come to a close, as late as 1150 B.C. in parts of Europe, man had invented writing and techniques of measurement, the indispensable intellectual tools with which he could communicate and record his experience and with which he could calculate and predict changes in space and time.

We shall see in the following chapter that it is very likely that these achievements, so enormously important for the making of civilization, were gradually produced in the Near East (western Asia). Slowly, through commerce, colonization, and the quickening migration of ideas, the relatively advanced Near Eastern culture made its influence felt in the comparatively backward region of western Europe, which was still in the Mesolithic and Neolithic stages of its development.

The Megaliths

That influence was exercised not so much through new arts, however, as through new religious and burial customs and a mode of marking sacred and sepulchral places with monumental stone. In the extreme west of Europe—in Brittany, Ireland, and England—there stand monuments of massive, rough-hewn stones that have puzzled and fascinated men for centuries. The very dimensions of the stones, some as high as seventy feet and weighing tons, have prompted the historian to call them *megaliths* (great stones), and the culture that produced them *megalithic*. Megalithic structures appear in western Europe around 3000 B.C. The earliest examples are found in southern Spain and Portugal in association with the first settled and fortified villages in that part of the continent. These villages may have been colonial settlements, perhaps the result of imperial or economic expansion from the Near East, which was the only city-dwelling culture in the western world at that time. Thus the megaliths appear to be manifestations of the arrival of foreign cultural and religious influences, which were adopted by the native populations of Spain and Portugal. From there the culture spread northward along the Atlantic coast, to reach the peoples of the British islands sometime before 2000 B.C.

There are several types of megalithic structures. The *dolmen* consists of several great stones set on end, with a large covering slab. Dolmens may be the remains of passage graves from which a covering earth mound has been washed away. The passage grave, the dominant megalithic tomb type—literally thousands exist in France and England—has a corridor lined with large stone slabs leading to a circular chamber often having a *corbeled* vault, in which each of numerous rings of stones projects inward beyond the underlying course, until the rings close at the top. They were frequently built into a hill slope or covered by mounds of earth, and they may be related to the well-preserved Mycenaean "beehive" tombs (see below and FIG. 4-21). At Carnac in Brittany, great single stones, called *menhirs*, set on end, were arranged in parallel rows, some of which run for several miles and consist of thousands of stones. Their purpose was evidently religious and may have had to do with the cult of the dead or the worship of the sun. Sometimes these huge stones were arranged in a circle known as a *cromlech*; among the most imposing cromlechs are those at Avebury and at Stonehenge, in England (FIGS. 1-13 and 1-14). The structure at Avebury is surrounded by a stone bank about four-fifths of a mile in diameter. The remains at Stonehenge are of a complex of rough-cut sarsen stones and smaller "bluestones." Outermost was a ring of large monoliths of sarsen stones capped by lintels. Next was a ring of bluestones, which, in turn, encircled a horseshoe (open end facing east) of trilithons—five lintel-topped pairs of the largest sarsens, each of which weighs 45 to 50 tons. Standing apart and to the east is the "heel-stone," which, for a person looking outward from the centre of the complex, would have marked the point at which the sun rose at the midsummer solstice.

1-13 Stonehenge, *c.* 1650 B.C. 97′ in diameter. Salisbury Plain, Wiltshire, England.

If this stone was raised to mark exactly the line of sunrise at the summer solstice of the year it was erected, it would naturally follow—owing to astronomical factors—that in the course of time the direction of this line would have slowly changed. The amount of deviation would be commensurate with the time elapsed since erection of the stones, thus supplying the age of the structure. A calculation made early in this century had it that on Midsummer Day, 1680 B.C., the sun rose exactly over the mark-stone and in a direct line with the axis of the temple and avenue of approach. Carbon-14 dating confirmed this, though recent refinements in that method may shift the date back in time considerably.

At the present time, computer-based calculations are raising something of a controversy once again, not so much over the date as over the

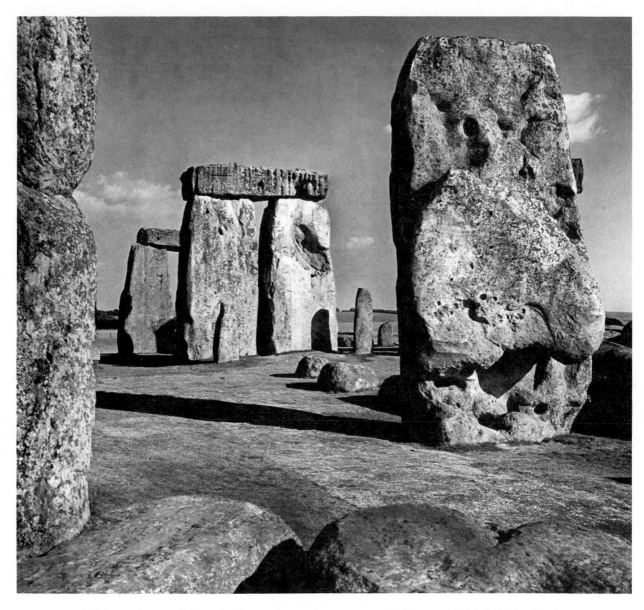

1-14 Stonehenge trilithons (lintel-topped pairs of stones at center). Approx. 24′ high (including lintel).

purpose of Stonehenge. The mysterious structure, believed in the Middle Ages to have been the work of the magician Merlin, who spirited it from Ireland, or the work of a race of giants, comes in our own time to be thought of as a remarkably accurate calendar, a testimony to the rapidly developing intellectual powers of man. Even in their ruined condition the monoliths of Stonehenge possess a solemn majesty, created by heroic human effort, physical and intellectual. At Avebury, as at Stonehenge, there is, in the series of concentric circles with connecting curvilinear pathways or avenues, a feeling for order, symmetry, and rhythm that is evidence not only of well-developed and systematized ceremonial rituals, but perhaps also of a maturing geometrical sense born of observation of the apparent movement of the sun and moon.

Chapter Two

The Ancient
Near East

THE ANCIENT NEAR EAST

JUST HOW AND WHY the state of human society we call civilization began we are not certain; we are more certain where and when it began. Since World War II archeologists have been uncovering the sites in the Near East where the immense transformation began and have pushed back its date as far as 8000 B.C. The onset of civilized life is marked off from all that went before by the development of agriculture. The conventional three-part division of the time preceding recorded history—the Paleolithic, Mesolithic, and Neolithic periods—based on the development of stone implements, is not so basic and decisive as the simpler distinction between an age of food-gathering and an age of food production. In this scheme the Paleolithic period would correspond roughly to the age of food-gathering, with the Mesolithic period, the last phase of that age, marked by intensified food-gathering and the domestication of the dog. The proto-Neolithic would be the period of incipient food production and greater domestication of animals preceding the Neolithic, the period when agriculture and stock-raising become man's major food sources.

According to one view, the area we know today as the Near East—Egypt, Israel, Syria, Iraq, Iran, and Turkey—dried out into desert and semidesert after the last retreat of the glaciers,

to 10,000 B.C.

PALEOLITHIC PERIOD

8000

MESOLITHIC PERIOD
Domestication of animals and incipient agriculture   Incipient agriculture

Jericho resettled

6000

Rise of village farming communities

3500

Çatal Hüyük culture at peak   NEOLITHIC PERIOD   PROTOLITERATE PERIOD

Ziggurat, Ur

Incipient urbanization

3000

Akkadian Head   Head of Abu

2150   2350   2500

NEO-SUMERIAN PERIOD (THIRD DYNASTY OF UR)   AKKADIAN DYNASTY   FIRST DYNASTY OF UR   EARLY DYNASTIC PERIOD

Sargon I c. 2350-2300   Flowering of independent city-states

2000

1900   Stele of Hammurabi   1600   1150

FIRST DYNASTY OF BABYLON   KASSITES AND MITANNI

Hammurabi c. 1790-1750

Winged bull, Khorsabad   Ashurnasirpal II   Rise of Assyrian power

1000

Bull capital, Susa   Ishtar Gate

331   538   612   c. 900

NOTE   Dates prior to 1200 B.C. are approximate and remain controversial.

625

PERSIAN EMPIRE (ACHAEMENID DYNASTY)   NEO-BABYLONIAN KINGDOM (CHALDEAN DYNASTY)   ASSYRIAN EMPIRE

Alexander conquers Persia 323   Darius I 520-486 Xerxes 485-465   Nebuchadnezzar II 605-562   Ashurnasirpal II (Nimrud) 884-859 Sargon II (Khorsabad) 722-705 Ashurbanipal (Nineveh) 669-627 compelling the inhabitants to move to the fertile alluvial valleys of the Nile in Egypt and the Tigris and Euphrates in Mesopotamia (parts of modern Syria and Iraq). But this view is perhaps too simple and may no longer be tenable in light of recent archeological findings. The oldest settled communities are found not in the river valleys but in the grassy uplands bordering them. These regions provided the necessary preconditions for the development of agriculture. Species of native plants like wild wheat and barley were plentiful, as were herds of animals—like goats, sheep, and pigs—that could be domesticated; there was also sufficient rain for the raising of crops. It was only after village-farming life was well developed that settlers, attracted by the greater fertility of the soil, moved into the river valleys and deltas.

There it was that civilized societies originated—in addition to systematic agriculture—government, law, and formal religion, with such instrumentalities and techniques as writing, measurement and calculation, weaving, metalcraft, and pottery.

For a long time it was thought that these developments occurred concurrently in Egypt and Mesopotamia. But again archeology is forcing a revision of our views. It is becoming clear that Mesopotamia and its environs were far ahead of Egypt temporally. Village-farming communities like Jarmo in Iraq and Çatal Hüyük in southern Anatolia (Turkey) date back to the mid-seventh millennium B.C., and the remarkable fortified town of Jericho, before whose walls Joshua appeared thousands of years later, is even older. In Egypt the oldest villages, in the Faiyum district near the Delta, do not seem to have been founded before 4500 B.C., and, furthermore, an urban society like that of Mesopotamia seems never to have developed there. The invention of writing in Mesopotamia preceded that in Egypt by several hundred years, and it may be that the whole development of Egyptian civilization was the result of Mesopotamian influence. Traditionally the history of art in the ancient world begins with Egypt and then passes to Mesopotamia. Archeological studies of Egypt are older, scientific archeology having begun there at the end of the eighteenth century. In addition, the chronology of Egypt is more firmly established, and the general cultural picture is more complete. Nevertheless, in view of the array of new facts presented by the latest archeological investigations, the traditional sequence should be reversed: Mesopotamia should be placed at the beginning of the study of ancient art.

THE BEGINNINGS

Jericho

By 7000 B.C. agriculture was well established in at least three Near Eastern regions: Jordan, Iran, and Anatolia (Turkey). Although no remains of

2-1 Proto-Neolithic fortifications, Jericho, 8000–7000 B.C.

2-2 Human skull, Jericho, 7000–6000 B.C. Features molded in plaster.

this, built with the aid of only the most primitive kinds of stone tools, was certainly a tremendous technical achievement.

Around 7000 B.C. the site was abandoned by its original inhabitants, but new settlers arrived in the early seventh millennium. They built rectangular mudbrick houses on stone foundations and carefully plastered and painted their floors and walls. Several of the excavated buildings seem to have served as shrines, the plan of one of them being remarkably similar to that of the later Greek megaron (see Chapter Five). These settlers fashioned statuettes of a mother goddess and of animals associated with a fertility cult. Most striking is a group of human skulls on which the features have been "reconstructed" in plaster (FIG. 2-2). Subtly modeled, the eyes inlaid sea shells, and the hair painted (a painted mustache has been preserved on one specimen), they present a strikingly lifelike appearance. Since the skulls were detached from the bodies before burial and displayed above ground, they may have been regarded as "spirit traps," implying a well-developed belief in survival after the death of the body.

Çatal Hüyük

Perhaps even more remarkable than the Jericho finds are recent discoveries in Anatolia. Excavations at Hacilar and Çatal Hüyük have shown not only that the central Anatolian plateau was the site of a flourishing Neolithic culture between 7000 and 5000 B.C., but that it may well have been the culturally most advanced region of its time. Twelve successive building levels excavated at Çatal Hüyük between 1961 and 1963 have been dated between 6500 and 5700 B.C. On a single site of thirty-two acres (of which only one acre has been explored) it has become possible to retrace, in an unbroken sequence, the evolution of a Neolithic culture over a period of 800 years, an evolution that led from a predominantly hunting and food-gathering economy to a fully agrarian one.

Along with Jericho, Çatal Hüyük has been called "one of man's first essays in the development of town life." The regularity of the town plan sug-

domestic cereal grains have been found that can be dated before 7000 B.C., the advanced state of agriculture at that time presupposes a long development; indeed, the very existence of a town like Jericho gives strong support to this assumption. The site of Jericho, a plateau in the Jordan river valley with an unfailing spring, was occupied by a small village as early as the ninth millennium B.C. This proto-Neolithic village underwent a spectacular development around 8000 B.C., when a new town was built with houses of mudbrick on round or oval stone foundations. As the town's wealth grew and powerful neighbors established themselves, the need for protection resulted in the first known permanent stone fortifications. By the middle of the eighth millennium B.C. the town, estimated to have had a population of over 2000, had a wide, rock-cut ditch and a five-foot-thick wall surrounding it. Into this wall, which has been preserved to a height of twelve feet, was built a great circular stone tower, thirty feet in height and diameter (FIG. 2-1). Not enough of the site has been excavated to determine whether this tower was solitary, like the keeps in Medieval castles, or one of several similar towers that formed a complete defense system. In either case, a structure like gests that it was built according to some *a priori* plan. A peculiarity of the town is its complete lack of streets, the houses adjoining each other and having access through their roofs (FIG. 2-3). Impractical as such an arrangement may appear today (although it survived in parts of central Anatolia and western Iran), it did offer some advantages: The buildings, braced against each other, had greater stability than free-standing structures, and defense was easier because the town site was surrounded by an unbroken ring of buildings with blank walls facing the country-side. Thus, if an enemy managed to breach the exterior wall, he would find himself not inside the town but inside a single room, with the de-fenders waiting for him on the roof—a dismal prospect at best.

Here and there the dense building mass is interrupted by an open court, which served as a garbage dump. Liberal amounts of ashes mixed in with the refuse acted as sterilizers, although probably not as deodorants. The houses, varying

in size, were of a standard plan and constructed of mudbrick walls strengthened by sturdy tim-ber frames. Walls and floors were plastered and painted, and platforms along walls served for sleep, work, and eating. A great number of shrines have been found intermingled with standard houses. Varying with the different levels, the average ratio is about one shrine for every four houses. This may not hold true for the whole town, only about one thirtieth of which has been excavated.

The shrines (FIG. 2-4) are distinguished from other houses by the greater richness of their interior decoration, which consisted of wall paintings, plaster reliefs, animal heads, bucrania (bovine skulls), and cult statuettes. Bulls' horns, which adorn most shrines, sometimes in con-siderable numbers, were set into stylized, re-modeled heads of bulls or into benches and pillars and may have been thought to protect the inhabitants and ward off evil. Nothing, however, suggests that the bull, or any other animal, was

2-3 Schematic reconstruction of a section of Level VI, Çatal Hüyük, *c.* 6000–5900 B.C. (After J. Mellaart.)

2-4 Reconstruction of a shrine, Level VI, Çatal Hüyük, *c.* 5900 B.C. (After J. Mellaart.)

regarded as a deity. Cult statuettes found at Çatal Hüyük indicate that the people believed their gods to have human form, both male and female. When represented in association with animals—the female deity usually with leopards, the male with a bull—the animals are always shown as subservient.

The statuettes are of stone or baked clay and are quite small, most between two and eight inches high and a few reaching twelve inches. All the female figures, which predominate, seem to represent a mother goddess but in a great variety of aspects: young, old, in ritual marriage, in pregnancy, giving birth, and as ruler of wild animals. These are described explicitly, and, while the bulbous forms of the headless *Seated Goddess* (FIG. 2-5) may remind us of the *Venus of Willendorf* (from which she may indeed have descended), the artist's approach toward his subject is quite realistic. Unlike the Paleolithic artist, who tried to represent the abstract concept of fertility, the Neolithic sculptor converts an abstract being (a goddess) into a human figure. The breasts are sensitively modeled, the small hands carefully rendered, and, judging from other examples, it may be safely assumed that the lost head had fairly well described facial features. The figure is painted with crosslike floral patterns, known also from wall paintings as symbols of agriculture, which here endow the goddess with the specific function of agrarian deity.

Fertility and agricultural symbolism dominate the art of the upper (later) levels of Çatal Hüyük. But hunting also played an important part in the early Neolithic economy, and Paleolithic

hunting rituals survived far into the Neolithic period. Numerous crude animal figurines, intentionally broken and damaged, some pitted with arrow marks, have been found at Çatal Hüyük; they evidently served as animal substitutes during hunting rites and were buried in pits after having served their purpose. The importance of hunting as a food source (until about 5700 B.C.) is reflected also in wall paintings, in which, in the older shrines, hunting scenes predominate. In style and concept, the *Deer Hunt* (FIG. 2-6) recalls the rock-shelter paintings of the Spanish Levant, but these figures are more full-bodied and rendered with greater realism. The

2-5 *Seated Goddess*, Çatal Hüyük, *c.* 5900 B.C. Baked clay.

artist used a full range of pigments, mostly derived from minerals, which he applied with a brush to the white background of dry plaster. A fragment from this hunting scene shows a dancing hunter (PLATE 2-1) dressed in a white loincloth and a leopard skin, holding a bow in one hand, the speed of his movement effectively emphasized by the manner in which the leopard skin whirls around his waist. Once the apparently ritual function of these paintings had been fulfilled, they were covered with a layer of white plaster and later replaced with a new painting of either a similar or a different subject.

In one of the older shrines a painting was uncovered that was to be unique for thousands of years to come. It is a pure landscape and, according to carbon-14 dating, was painted soon after 6200 B.C. (FIG. 2-7). In the foreground is shown a town with rectangular houses neatly laid out side by side, probably representing Çatal Hüyük; behind it, on a smaller scale, as though far away, appears a mountain with two peaks; dots and lines issuing from the higher of the two cones clearly represent a volcanic eruption. The mountain has been identified as the 10,600-foot Hasan Dağ, located within view of Çatal Hüyük, and the only twin-peaked volcano (now extinct) in central Anatolia. Since the painting appears on the walls of a shrine, the recorded volcanic eruption must have had some religious meaning. While the artist may have linked the event with the underworld and witnessed it with fearful awe, his dread may have been mingled with gratitude to a bountiful Mother Earth, for it is believed that Çatal Hüyük derived much of its wealth from trade in obsidian, a vitreous volcanic stone easily chipped into fine cutting edges and highly valued by Neolithic tool- and weapon-makers.

The rich finds at Çatal Hüyük give the impression of a prosperous and well-ordered society that practiced a great variety of arts and crafts. In addition to painting and sculpture, weaving and pottery were well established, and even the art of smelting copper and lead in small quantities was known before 6000 B.C. The society seems conservative in its long retention of Paleolithic traditions and practices, but it was also progressive in effecting, slowly but relentlessly, the revolutionary shift from a food-gathering to a food-producing economy. In the arts this shift is mirrored in a de-emphasis of realism in favor of a more abstract symbolism, in the disappearance of hunting scenes, and in a gradual decline in production of statuettes representing male deities. At the same time representations of the mother goddess increase in number, reflecting perhaps a corresponding change in the importance, if not the social position, of woman. As agriculture took precedence over hunting, female occupations, like the milling of grain, baking, weaving, and the care and feeding of domestic animals, became ever more important. At Çatal Hüyük the change to a fully agrarian economy appears to have been completed by about 5700 B.C. Less than a century later the site was abandoned. A probably related culture at Hacilar, some 200 miles to the west, provides an afterglow. But by about 5000 B.C. the Anatolian Neolithic culture had ceased to exist, and the limelight shifts eastward toward the Mesopotamian valley.

2-6 *Deer Hunt*, detail of a copy of a wall painting from Level III, Çatal Hüyük, *c.* 5750 B.C.

2-7 *Landscape with Volcanic Eruption*, detail of a copy of a wall painting from Level VII, Çatal Hüyük, *c.* 6150 B.C.

SUMER

Some time in the early fourth millennium B.C. in Mesopotamia a critical event took place—the settlement of the great river valleys. It was after this that writing, art, monumental architecture, and new political forms were introduced in Mesopotamia and Egypt, but with striking differences in function. As Henri Frankfort describes it:

The earliest written documents of Mesopotamia . . . facilitated the administration of large economic units, the temple communities. The earliest Egyptian inscriptions were legends on royal monuments or seal engravings identifying the king's officials. The earliest representations in Mesopotamian art are preponderantly religious; in Egyptian art they celebrate royal achievements and consist of historical subjects. Monumental architecture consists, in Mesopotamia, of temples, in Egypt of royal tombs. The earliest civilized society of Mesopotamia crystallized in separate nuclei, a number of distinct, autonomous cities— clear-cut, self-assertive polities—with the surrounding lands to sustain each one. Egyptian society assumed the form of the single, united, but rural, domain of an absolute monarch.

Thus, not one, but *two* civilizations emerged, each having its own special character. From this time forward world history will be the record of the birth, development, and disappearance of civilizations and the rise and decline within them of peoples, states, and nations. It is with these two mighty, contrasting civilizations bordering the eastern Mediterranean region that the drama of Western mankind truly begins.

In the fertile lower valley of the Tigris and Euphrates man may have found the equivalent of the Garden of Eden celebrated in Genesis and long a part of Mesopotamian tradition. Once he had learned the arts of irrigation and, to a degree, the control of floods, the possibility of creating a great oasis was before him, and he realized it. The turbulence of its history strongly suggests that this land, with its promise of a hitherto unknown life of abundance, was enormously attractive to man.

At the dawn of recorded history the lower Mesopotamian valley was occupied by the Sumerians, whose origin is still one of the great puzzles of ancient history. They were an agricultural people who learned to control floods and built strong-walled towns, such as Uruk, the biblical Erech and the modern Warka, and Lagash, the modern Telloh. After several centuries, Semitic nomad shepherds came from the western desert; they adopted agriculture, absorbed much from Sumerian culture, and built their own cities farther north—Kish, Akkad, Mari, and Babylon. Over the centuries, dominion oscillated between the two peoples, but the Semites produced two of the mightiest kings, Sargon and Hammurabi.

2-8 Ziggurat at Ur, *c.* 2100 B.C.

From as early as the Paleolithic caves we have evidence of man's effort to control his environment by picture magic. With the appearance of the Sumerians and the beginning of recorded history the older magic was replaced by a religion of gods, benevolent or malevolent, who personified the forces of nature that often contended destructively with man's hopes and designs. In the fertile valley the fiery heat of summer and the catastrophic floods, droughts, blights, and locusts easily persuaded man that there were powers above and beyond his control, powers that he must somehow placate and win over. Formal religion, a kind of system of transactions between gods and men, may have begun with the Sumerians; and no matter how it has been systematized and diversified since then, religion has retained its original propitiatory devices of prayer, sacrifice, and ritual, as well as a view of man as imperfect by nature and dependent upon and obligated to some higher being. The religion of the Sumerians and of those who followed them centered about nature gods: Anu, god of the sky;

Enlil (Bel), a creator and ruler of earth and "lord of the storm"; Ea (or Enki), lord of the waters (a healing, benevolent god); Nannar (Sin), the moon god; Utu (Shamash), the sun god; and Inanna (associated with the planet Venus), goddess of love and fertility, who, as Ishtar, is later also endowed with the functions of battle goddess.[1]

The City-State and the Ziggurat

Religion, dominating life and investing it with meaning, determined the form of society as well as its expression in architecture and art. The Mesopotamian city-state was under the protection of the god of the city; the king was his representative on earth and the steward of his earthly treasure. The relation of the king to the

[1] Bel and Shamash are Akkadian names; Sin is Babylonian.

gods above and to his subjects below may be read in the prayer of an early Sumerian king to the god Enlil of the city of Nippur:

O En-lil, the king of the lands, may Anu to his beloved father speak my prayer; to my life may he add life, and cause the lands to dwell in security; may he give me warriors as many as the grass; the herds of heaven may he watch over; the land with prosperity endow; the good fortune which the gods have given me, may he not change; and may I ever remain the shepherd, who standeth at the head.

The plan of the city reflected this centrality of the god in its life, his temple being its monumental nucleus. The temple was the focus not only of the religion of the city but of its administrative and economic process. It was indeed the domain of the god, who was regarded as a great and rich holder of lands and herds as well as the protector of the city. The whole function of the city was to serve the god as a master, as the function of all men in general was to serve the gods. The vast temple complex, a kind of city within a city, had a multitude of functions. A temple staff of priests and scribes carried on the business of the city, looking after the possessions of the god and of the king. It must have been in such a setting that writing developed into an instrument of precision; the very earliest examples of it have to do with the keeping of accounts and the description of simple transactions, stores, and supplies.

The most prominent part of a temple compound, and indeed the most characteristic structure of the Mesopotamian valley, was the *ziggurat*. Neither the origin nor the purpose of these huge, multistoried brick structures are known. They have been interpreted as "stairways from heaven" or as artificial mountains and have been linked with the widespread ancient belief that lofty mountain peaks were the homes of the gods (compare Mount Olympus in Greek religion). The shrines atop these ziggurats were called "waiting rooms" or "rooms one passes through," and they may have been thought of as halls in which the faithful might await the manifestation of their deity.

Most of the ruined cities of Sumer—Ur, Warka, Nippur, Larsa, Eridu—are still dominated by their eroded ziggurats. The ziggurat at Ur is a good example, dating from the period called Neo-Sumerian—from the twenty-second to the twenty-first century B.C.—when the builders were pushing for the greatest heights possible (FIGS. 2-8 and 2-9). In one view we see the huge mound of sun-dried brick worn almost into shapelessness by time, weather, and depredation; in the other a conjectural reconstruction. On a massive base, fifty feet high, stand two successively smaller stages, of which presumably the uppermost served as a pedestal for the shrine. Three ramplike stairways of 100 steps each converge toward a tower-flanked gateway from which another flight of steps probably led to the shrine, the focal point of ceremonial pageantry.

2-9 Reconstruction of the ziggurat at Ur. (Adapted from a drawing at the British Museum, London.)

FEET
0   50   100

2-10 *Female Head*, Warka, c. 3500–3000 B.C. Alabaster, approx. 8″ high. The Iraq Museum, Baghdad.

The structure is a solid mass of mudbrick with a thick facing of baked brick laid in bitumen, the latter designed to withstand floods and weathering. Originally the stages may have been of different colors, used symbolically, and trees and gardens may have been planted on the terraces. The very height of the structure and the arduous climb toward its summit shrine may have symbolized, as in other religions, a kind of hard preparation of the spirit for the experience of divine enlightenment. Certainly the loftiness of the great ziggurats, which seemed to reach into the heavens, made a profound impression on the ancient Hebrews, who memorialized the one in Babylon as the Tower of Babel, a monument to the insolent pride of man.

The three great inventions of the Sumerians—a system of gods and god-man relations, the city-state itself, and the art of writing—provided the basis for a new order of human society. In the city-state, consecrated by the presence of the civic deity, men experienced new interrelations with the god and with each other, and these interrelations were formalized and given permanence by being recorded in writing. Life became regularized, and the community assumed functions formerly the individual's, such as defense against man and the caprices of nature. This and the division of labor (specialization), which is encouraged where large numbers of people are concentrated in a coherent community, emancipated the inhabitants from the consuming necessities of daily life so that they could develop and apply skills and talents unthinkable in fluid and unintegrated societies. The relatively fixed character of the city-state also conferred on the community a permanent identity as a city whose king and god were known and present. This sense of identity extended to the individual inhabitant as well, who received his identity from his membership in the community, discovering himself in his interrelations with the city, god, king, and citizens. The new written language may also have contributed to this growing identification, the individual perceiving himself as a name among the names for other things and actions. Thus from the Sumerian creation of stable patterns of life begins that sense of identity, that self-awareness of historical man that will mature and reach its highest development in the civilization of Greece.

Sculpture

We have seen that in the animal paintings of the caves the figure of man almost never appears; he has not come into the field of self-awareness. Though the rock paintings of the Spanish Levant do indeed represent the human figure, they do so only schematically and almost as a kind of picture-writing. Thus we are not prepared for the beautiful female head from Warka (FIG. 2-10). Its ancestry is unknown. Dating from the so-called protoliterate period, when writing first appeared, it is not a complete head but a marble face meant to be attached to a wood backing and wigged, perhaps, in gold. The deep recesses for the eyebrows were filled with colored shell or stone, as were the large eyes. The subject is unknown (goddess, priestess, queen?), but our ignorance of it and of the history of the head does not diminish our appreciation of its exquisite refinement of feature and expression, despite the mutilations of time and accident. The soft modeling of the

2-11 Statuettes from the Abu Temple, Tell Asmar, c. 2700–2500 B.C. Marble, tallest figure approx. 30″ high. The Iraq Museum, Baghdad, and the Oriental Institute, University of Chicago.

cheeks, the sensitivity of the mouth, the hesitancy of the expression between the sweet and the somber not only render for us a person in herself beguiling and mysterious but suggest a sophistication in the artist beyond our expectation of his time.

One notices at once in the Warka head how disproportionately large the eyes are. This is a trait of a whole group of figures from Tell Asmar (FIGS. 2-11 and 2-12). The reason for this convention, which is not only Sumerian but appears throughout ancient art, can only be guessed. Long before Aristotle asserted that man is distinguished from the animals by being rational and that sight is the most "rational" of the organs of sense, men must have perceived and feared the power of the eye to hold, charm, and hypnotize for ends good or ill. The "evil eye" was feared in the ancient world, as it still is feared. It is a popular belief and a part of folklore that one can learn much about another's intentions and character by "looking him straight in the eye";

2-12 *Head of the God Abu*, Tell Asmar, c. 2700–2500 B.C. Marble. The Iraq Museum, Baghdad.

and the modern affectation of dark glasses (curiously Sumerian when oversized!) may be both a defense and a badge of attractive mystery. To the ancient artist, the eyes, the "windows of the soul," could have had several associations: Large eyes fixed in unflagging gaze see all, and frontal, binocular vision, distinguishing human from mere animal seeing, represents the all-seeing vigilance and omniscience of the gods and the guarantee of justice. In the conventionalization of the human image, vision understandably becomes a peculiarly human trait—in its lesser physical sense as well as in its greater intellectual, spiritual, and theistic sense. Godlike vision as the foundation of law and justice is evident in the stories of great law-givers of the ancient world like Hammurabi of Babylon, Moses, Lycurgus of Sparta, and Solon of Athens.

Although it may be that none of our speculations entered the mind of the artist of the Tell Asmar figures, some association of vision with supernatural powers seems to be indicated by the fact that the two largest figures, identified as deities by emblems on their bases, also have the largest eyes in relation to their heads. The other statuettes represent worshipers, the larger ones priests, the smaller laymen; with their hands tightly clasped across their chests in the attitude of prayer, their large eyes seem to express reverent awe in the presence of their gods. The purpose of these votive figures was to offer constant prayers to the gods in behalf of their donors, and thus their open-eyed stares may symbolize the eternal wakefulness necessary if they are to fulfill their duty.

CONVENTIONALIZATION

Just as through formal religion and civic life the Sumerians, at the dawn of recorded history, created a new kind of human experience, so through writing and figurative art they found a new way to represent that experience. Writing had been invented by the simplifying of pictures into signs, wedge-shaped (cuneiform) strokes in numerous combinations pressed by a stylus into wet clay tablets. In figurative art, by an analogous process of simplification, the multitude of appearances of things in the optical world was reduced to a few telling traits sufficient to present the human figure and human action. This process of simplification is variously named schematization, stylization, conventionalization, generalization, and formalization. Conventional simplifications of the human figure are universal and not characteristic of ancient art only. Indeed, all artistic styles are conventional in that, in societies in which they prevail, they are tacitly agreed upon as a comprehensible means of representation. The conventions may be broad or narrow, slow to change or under continual revision, as in our times. In any case, criteria such as fidelity to optical "fact" should not be used in evaluating a style. Although since the 1880's the main trends in modern art have been away from optical "fact," and although today's artists often deliberately disregard photographic "truth," the images they make—such as those seen in comic strips and in commercial art and advertising—are perfectly recognizable to us.

The Sumerians, working out patterns and conventions that regulated the new life that they had in effect devised, also established conventions for the making of the human image. The large eyes of the Warka and Tell Asmar figures are not the only conventionalized details. In the small figures of a shell-inlaid box, the so-called *Standard of Ur* (PLATE 2-2), we find several devices of representation that simplify the narrative, explain the action, and even convey the impression of motion. The panel depicts a Sumerian military victory and its aftermath—the advance of the foot soldiers, the charge of the chariots, lines of prisoners and servants bringing in booty, and finally the king relaxing after the battle, when he drinks with his nobles and listens to harp and song. The figures are carefully arranged in superimposed strips, each strikingly suggestive of a film or comic strip; and doubtless the purpose is the same—to achieve a continuous narrative effect. They are carefully spaced, with no overlapping. (Compare this regularized, formal presentation with the casual and haphazard placements of the figure in Paleolithic and Mesolithic art.) Poses are repeated, as in the line of foot soldiers, to suggest large numbers. The horses of the war chariots, the lines of the legs repeated to suggest the other horses of the team and their alignment in space, change from a walk to a gallop as they attack. The figures are essentially in profile, but it is a convention almost universal in the ancient Near East that the eyes—again, very large—are in front view, as are the torsos. The artist indicates the parts of the human body that enter into our concept of what it looks like, and he avoids positions, attitudes, or views that would conceal or obscure the characterizing parts. For example, were the figures in strict profile, an arm and perhaps a leg would be concealed, the body would appear to have only half its breadth, and the eye would not "read" as an eye at all, since it would not have its distinctive flat oval shape, and the pupil, so important in the Tell Asmar figures, would not appear. We could call this approach "conceptual" rather than "optical," since the artist records not the immediate, fleeting aspect of things but rather his concept of the distinguishing and abiding properties of the human body. It is the fundamental forms of things and his knowledge of them, not their accidental appearance, that direct his hand. But this is simply a reflection of the general *formalism* that was imposed at the beginning of the historical period in an effort to create an enduring order. This formalism continued to rule human conduct through history in thousands of customs, conventions, and ceremonies regarded as sacred and above change. In Greece, many centuries later, Plato conceived the famous philosophy of Forms, claiming that the world of pure form, in which exist the ultimate and unchanging truths of mathematical figures and relationships, is the real world, whereas the world we see, the world of mere appearance, is the realm of the unreal, of illusion, of change, and of death.

THE UNION OF THE FORMAL AND NATURAL

On the inlaid soundbox of a harp from Ur (FIG. 2-13) there are figures representing, in the top register, a Sumerian hero wrestling with two man-headed bulls and, in the lower registers, real and fantastic animals preparing a banquet.

2-13 Soundbox of a harp, Ur, *c.* 2600 B.C. Shell inlay, approx. 9″ high. University Museum, Philadelphia.

The topmost register of the panel presents the figures in heraldic symmetry, and, except that the heads are in front view, they exhibit the conventional formalized pose of the *Standard of Ur*. On the other hand, the figures of the animals in the other registers show the formalism markedly relaxed. The dagger-wearing dog bringing in a laden table, the lion bringing in the wine service, the ass playing the harp, the jackal playing the zither, the bear steadying the harp (or is he dancing?), and the gazelle offering goblets of wine to the scorpion-man—all are seen in more or less true profile. Torsos naturally cut off the view of the far arms, and the near legs obstruct the far legs. Shoulders are properly placed, and features are carefully noted and designated. The heroic human figures have the formality we find in the stylized animals on a coat of arms, but the banquet animals are at ease or seem almost to be burlesquing a stately parade of servants and musicians. Long before the figure of man appears in art we have the naturalistic animal figures of the Paleolithic caves. And for a long time, as if by rule, man is represented with rigid formality, while the animal figure looks and moves much as it would appear to the eye. Our panel shows a delightful Aesop-like scene (the comedy of which may not have been intended) in what is probably a representation of ancient myths. Surely it is a very early specimen of that theme in both literature and art in which animals act as people; thus we pass from the artist of this panel to Aesop's fables, to the Medieval bestiaries, to the zoological creations of Walt Disney.

On the same harp is a splendid bull's head finished in gold leaf and with beard and details in lapis lazuli (FIG. 2-14). (Note where the head is attached to the harp, as it is shown on the third register from the top in FIG. 2-13.) The bull, an

2-14 Bull's head from the soundbox. Gold leaf and lapis lazuli with inlaid eyes, approx. 17″ high. University Museum, Philadelphia.

2-15 Cylinder seal and its impression, Ur, *c.* 2700 B.C. Stone, approx. 1½″ high. The Oriental Institute, University of Chicago.

exemplification of fertility and strength, would naturally become the animal worshiped by early herdsmen, its power invoked against the natural enemies of cattle—drought and predatory beasts. The archaic artist shares with his prehistoric predecessor the genius for rendering with sharp perception the features, almost the personality, of animals. Throughout the ancient Near East and the Mediterranean the bull was revered. In this example, the beard may represent some supernatural amplification of the bull's power. The beard and such humanizing features as the man-heads added to the bulls in the top panel of the soundbox foreshadow the man-headed bulls and lions that appeared much later in Assyria.

The contest of forces natural and supernatural in the Mesopotamians' world is expressed as a struggle between animals and monsters. Such a struggle we find represented in miniature upon a cylinder seal only an inch and a half high (FIG. 2-15), the design cut with exquisite refinement. A seal consisted of a cylindrical piece of stone, usually about an inch or so in height and pierced for the attachment of a cord. Made of various colored stones, both hard and soft, such as rock crystal, agate, carnelian and jasper, lapis lazuli, marble, and alabaster, the seal was decorated with a design in intaglio (incised) so that when it was rolled over soft clay a raised pattern was left. With this device the Sumerian sealed, signed, and identified his letters and documents, which were written on clay tablets. Our illustration shows both the seal and the relief design made from it. A hero fights a bull, and a being—half-man and half-bull—fights a lion. The heraldic attitudes and groupings reflect the formal method of representation, but even in the small area of the seal the skillful artist shows such mastery of animal form that one almost hears the roaring and bellowing of the struggle.

AKKAD

At about 2300 B.C. that loose group of cities we know as Sumer (where the tremendous change from prehistory to civilization had begun) came under the domination of a great ruler, Sargon of Akkad. The Akkadians, though Semitic in origin and speaking a language entirely different from that of Sumer, had assimilated Sumerian culture and under Sargon and his followers introduced a new concept of royal power, its basis unswerving loyalty to the king rather than to the city-state. During the rule of Sargon's grandson, Naram-Sin, governors of cities were called slaves of the king, who, in turn, called himself King of the Four Quarters (of the universe)—in effect, ruler of the earth. A magnificent bronze head of a king from Nineveh (a portrait of Naram-Sin?) embodies this new concept of absolute monarchy (FIG. 2-16). The elaborate coiffure, Sumerian in style, attests the persistence of the tradition of Sumer and serves as crown to the unforgettable face with its expression of majestic serenity. The large eyes, made even larger by the absence of the precious stones once embedded in the sockets, and the emphatic ridgelike brows would seem

2-16 *Head of an Akkadian Ruler*, Nineveh, c. 2300–2200 B.C. Bronze, approx. 12″ high. The Iraq Museum, Baghdad.

2-17 *Victory Stele of Naram-Sin, c.* 2300–2200 B.C. Pink sandstone, approx. 6′ 6″ high. Louvre, Paris.

minded and commanding one, yet in a pensive and composed mood, with perhaps just a trace of irony. The age of metals has come, and the piece demonstrates the craftsman's sophisticated skill in casting and in the engraving of details.

The godlike sovereignty claimed by the kings of Akkad may be seen proclaimed in another masterpiece of Akkadian art, the great *Victory Stele of Naram-Sin* (FIG. 2-17). On the stele the warlike grandson of Sargon is represented leading his victorious armies up the slopes of a wooded mountain and through the routed enemy, who are crushed underfoot, fall, flee, die, or beg for mercy. The king stands alone, far taller than his men, treading upon the bodies of two of the fallen enemy. He wears the horned helmet that signifies his deification, and two auspicious astral bodies, representing Shamash and Ishtar, shine upon his triumph. The artist shows an almost startling originality, not only in his ingenious management of the theme, but in the variety of poses and in the setting. The king's troops, a whole army suggested by eight figures marching in two orderly files, carry spears and flying banners as they encounter the shattered enemy (seven figures), one of whom falls headlong down the mountain side. In comparison with the stele figures, those of the *Standard of Ur* seem rather static and formal. The Naram-Sin artist is a daring inventor, and though he adheres to older conventions, especially in the figures of the king and his soldiers (in simultaneous profile and front view), he nevertheless relies upon his own perception to create the first landscape in Near Eastern art since Çatal Hüyük (FIG. 2-7).

The achievements of Akkad were brought to an end by an incursion of barbarous mountaineers, the Guti, who dominated life in central and lower Mesopotamia for about sixty years, when the cities of Sumer, responding to the alien presence, reasserted themselves and established a Neo-Sumerian polity under the kings of Ur. During this age the most conspicuous contribution came from the city of Lagash under its ruler, Gudea. There are about twenty statues of Gudea, and they show him seated or standing, hands tightly clasped, and sometimes wearing a woolen cap; the statue illustrated is characteristic (FIG. 2-18). Gudea, who attributed his good fortune and that of his city to the favor of the gods,

to go back a long way in tradition, even to the Warka head; the sensitive mouth also recalls that of the earlier work. Here we see to particular advantage that union of the formal with the natural so common in Mesopotamian art. The symmetry of the head and the stylized motifs of the curly locks of hair manage to be consistent with the projection of personality—a strong-zealously looked after the performance of their rites; his statues were numerous so that he could take his (symbolic) place in the temples and there render perpetual service to the benevolent deities. The standing Gudea shown is, like the others, of dolerite, an extremely hard stone that the sculptor works with consummate skill, making an opportunity out of difficulty. The capped figure stands in the formal frontal pose that descends from the age of Tell Asmar; the great eyes and eyebrow ridges are in the Mesopotamian tradition. One shoulder and arm are bare; the drapery pulls about the torso and under the arm and falls almost vertically from the other arm. The overall contour is simple in the extreme, with no irregular or complex relief. There is a singular unity and compactness to the figure that arises from the artist's conceiving of it as a cylindrical or conical form that resides in the mass of the finely textured stone. The smooth sweep of its contours, the elegance of the profile, and the richness of the polished dolerite all complement each other.

BABYLONIA

Lagash, which had retained its independence during the Guti invasion, became a dependency of Ur during that city's brief resurgence in the late third millennium B.C. For a little over a century the Third Dynasty of Ur ruled over a once-more united realm. Its last king fell before the attacks of foreign invaders, and the following two centuries saw the return of the traditional Mesopotamian political pattern in which several independent city-states existed side by side. One of these was Babylon, until its most powerful king, Hammurabi, was able to reestablish a centralized government that ruled the whole country. Perhaps the most renowned king in Mesopotamian history, Hammurabi was famous for his codification of the confused, conflicting, and often unwritten laws of the Mesopotamian towns. Though Hammurabi was not the first to try to bring order out of the chaos, he was the first to succeed; echoes of his code can be found in the Law of Moses.

2-18 *Gudea Worshiping*, Telloh, c. 2100 B.C. Dolerite, approx. 42″ high. Louvre, Paris.

The code, beautifully inscribed on a tall, irregularly surfaced black basalt stele, is capped by a relief sculpture of Hammurabi receiving the inspiration for it from the flame-shouldered sun god, Shamash (FIG. 2-19). The event takes place on a mountain, indicated by toothlike devices beneath the god's feet. Shamash holds the re-

2-19 *Stele of Hammurabi* (upper part), Susa, *c.* 1760 B.C. Basalt, entire stele approx. 7′ 4″ high. Louvre, Paris.

galia of divine power, a baton and a ring, while he dictates the law to Hammurabi, represented in a gesture of reverent attention. We find here again the Mesopotamian artist's instinct for cylindrical volume. Shamash is represented in the familiar convention of combined front and side views, while Hammurabi, his servant, is shown in a position closer to profile. This confrontation between god and man expresses the increasing humanization of natural and supernatural forces, as man, increasingly self-aware, begins (in Babylon) to attribute human form to the gods.

Hammurabi's Babylonian empire was brought down by the Hittites, who, after sacking Babylon around 1595 B.C., retired to Anatolia, the seat of Hittite power, leaving Babylonia in the hands of marauding mountaineers, the Kassites. The Hittites, who spoke an Indo-European tongue, developed an art of great power and originality. Their strongly fortified capital, near the modern Turkish village of Boghazköy, was fronted with massive stone gates set between towers (FIG. 2-20). Projecting from the cyclopean stones—so different from the brick of Mesopotamian architecture!—are rugged figures of lions, blunt and brutal in aspect. Whatever the source for the concept of guardian beasts—Mesopotamia, Syria, or Egypt—the Hittite realization of it is original, the figures being strongly bound to and dominated by the architecture, rather than freestanding and in the round.

ASSYRIA

For centuries the Assyrians, the people of northern Mesopotamia, were frustrated in their impulse to power by the kingdoms of the south—Sumer, Akkad, and Babylon—and, on the northwest, by the Mitanni, to whom for a while they were subject. Their opportunity came when their Mitannian overlords were broken by the Hittites and when the weak Kassite kingdom that had succeeded the Babylonian dynasty proved incapable of effective resistance. By about 900 B.C. the Assyrian destiny was already becoming an actuality and for the next three centuries Assyria was the dominant power in the Near East. Assyrian kings became military commanders, and Assyria itself, with its center successively at Calah (the modern Nimrud), Dur-Sharrukin (the modern Khorsabad), and Nineveh,

2-20 *Lion Gate*, Boghazköy, Anatolia, *c.* 1400 B.C. Lions approx. 7′ high.

became a garrison state with an imperial structure that extended from the Tigris to the Nile and from the Persian Gulf to Asia Minor. Centuries of unremitting warfare against their neighbors and often rebellious subjects hardened the Assyrians into a cruel and merciless people whose atrocities in warfare were bitterly decried throughout the ancient world. Although they held the restless Babylonian south in thrall, the Assyrians respected the religion and the culture of Sumer-Babylon and were, in fact, dependent on its advanced civilization—as the large library of Ashurbanipal attests. (Discovery of this library in the nineteenth century opened an immense field of knowledge about Assyria.)

Architecture

The unfinished royal citadel of Sargon II of Assyria, built at Khorsabad, reveals in its ambitious plan the confidence of the "great kings" in their all-conquering might (FIG. 2-21). The palace covered some twenty-five acres and had over 200 courtyards and rooms. The city, above which the citadel-palace stood on a mound fifty feet high, is itself about a square mile in area. The palace may have been elevated solely to raise it above flood level, but its elevation also served to put the king's residence above those of his subjects and midway between them and the gods. Though the builders probably aimed at symmetry, the plan is rambling, embracing an aggregation of rectangular rooms and halls grouped around square courts (FIG. 2-22). The shape of the long, narrow rooms and the massiveness of the side walls suggest that the rooms were covered by brick barrel vaults (see Chapter Six), the most practical roofing method in a region that lacks both timber and good building stone. Behind the main courtyard, each side of which measures 300 feet, were the residential quarters of the king, who received foreign emissaries in

2-21 Reconstruction drawing of the citadel of Sargon II, Khorsabad, c. 720 B.C.

EDGE OF PLATFORM

ZIGGURAT →

C

N

Probable roofed areas

FEET
0   100   200   300

2-22 Plan of the inner precincts of the citadel of Sargon II.

state in the long, high, brilliantly painted throne room. Such visitors entered from another large courtyard, passing through the central entrance between huge guardian demons, some thirteen feet in height, and into the presence of enthroned power. Waiting in the court for the audience, visitors had time to meditate upon their own insignificance in comparison with the awesome strength of the king, for the walls of the court were lined with giant figures of the king and his courtiers.

Sargon II regarded his city and palace as an expression of his grandeur, which he viewed as founded upon the submission and enslavement of his enemies. He writes in an inscription: "I built a city with [the labors of] the peoples subdued by my hand, whom Assur, Nabu and Marduk had caused to lay themselves at my feet and bear my yoke at the foot of Mount Musri,

above Nineveh." And in another text he proclaims: "Sargon, King of the World, has built a city. Dur Sharrukin he has named it. A peerless palace he has built within it."

In addition to the complex of courtyards, throne room, state chambers, harem, service quarters, and guard rooms making up the palace were the essential temple and ziggurat. The ziggurat at Khorsabad may have had as many as seven stages, of which four have been preserved, each eighteen feet high and each painted a different color. The ascent was made by a continuous ramp spiraling around the building from its base to its summit.

The palace façade consisted of a massive crenelated wall broken by huge rectangular towers flanking an arched doorway. Around the arch and on the towers were friezes of brilliantly colored glazed tiles, the whole effect being sumptuous and grand. Dazzling brilliance seems also to have been part of the royal Assyrian plan to overwhelm the visitor. The doorway was guarded by colossal winged bulls with human heads (FIG. 2-23). These man-headed bulls may be derived from the animal figures at Hittite Boghazköy. Both sets of animals served to ward off enemies, visible and invisible, and to invest the palace façade with an imposing and dramatic aspect. They are partly in the round and partly in high relief, and they combine the front view at rest with the side view in movement, contriving this combination by the addition of fifth legs. The gigantic size; the bold vigorous carving, the fine sweep of wings, and the patterning of the surface by the conventional treatment of details produce together a splendor and a stupendous strength that are awesome even today. But we

2-23 Winged human-headed bull, Khorsabad, c. 720 B.C. Limestone, approx. 13′ 10″ high. Louvre, Paris.

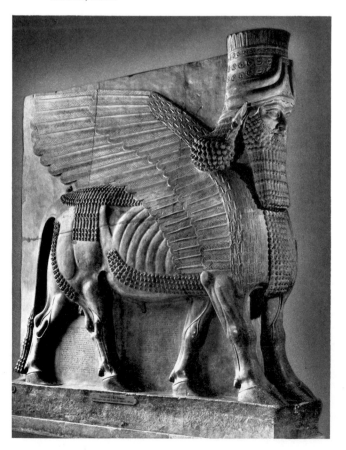

may think of them in all their majesty not so much as guardians of the king as augmentations of his regality. They wear the horned crowns of the god-kings of Akkad and the large-eyed, bearded masks familiar ever since Sumer, and they evidence in their bull and lion bodies the superhuman strength and fierceness of the king and, with their eagles' wings, his swiftness to bring justice or vengeance. The virtues of Assyrian kingship are written large in these hybrid beasts. Ancient art repeatedly testifies to man's persisting fear and admiration of the great beasts that serve as his metaphors for the powers of nature and for the gods themselves.

Relief Sculpture

Although the kings of Assyria had their power depicted in nonhuman forms, they were very much of the world and expected their greatness in their favorite pursuits—war and hunting—to be recorded in unmistakably exact and concrete terms. The chronicle revealed in inscriptions is surprisingly complete, yet we learn of the character of Assyrian royal life quite as much from the numerous relief carvings found in the ruins of Nimrud and Nineveh, those magnificent capitals of Assyria in its prime. The history of Assyrian art is mainly the history of relief carving; very little sculpture in the round survives. Even the great winged beasts are thought of as relief sculpture and are locked into their stone slabs, presenting three relief surfaces. To narrate the royal feasts pictorially required flat, continuous surfaces upon which could be repeated almost without end the campaigns, sieges, conquests and slaughters, and never ending massacres of wild animals that occupied the waking hours of the kings. The artists, working within the limitations of a rectangular surface, devised a vocabulary of forms which, though conventional, was sharply descriptive. The Assyrian reliefs constitute a narrative whose continuity is broken only by the edges of the fitted blocks. What began long before in the *Standard of Ur* here reaches its perfection.

The astonishing multiplicity of a relief of Ashurnasirpal II at war (FIG. 2-24) compels careful study of the composition if one is to discriminate its details. The king stands in his chariot drawing his bow. He is accompanied by officers, and, in

2-24 *Ashurnasirpal II at War*, Nimrud, *c.* 875 B.C. Limestone, approx. 39″ high. British Museum, London.

the sky above him, the winged god of Assyria, Ashur, draws his bow and leads him on. The king's team, the reins tight, is passing an enemy chariot already breaking up, its driver thrown down and one horse fallen. Assyrian foot soldiers cut the throats of the enemy wounded. At upper center an Assyrian soldier slays a foe while his comrade tries to save him. Behind them a soldier is lying dead; and, in the upper right, enemy bowmen desperately defend the towers of their city. What is remarkable is the ease with which we read the incidents, though they are not depicted in perspective or in logical sequence. The artist uses the space of his block for a field to be divided as narrative convenience and his own

sense of both the factual and the dramatic dictate. The liveliness of individual poses and movements is exceptionally fine and convincing, and despite the formality that exists in Mesopotamian art side by side with naturalistic details, sophisticated spatial devices appear throughout. One such is the overlapping of figures to suggest greater or lesser distance from the observer; the king's overlapping of his officers is a good example.

The formality of Assyrian art at its most rigid can be seen in another relief of Ashurnasirpal II (FIG. 2-25), in which the king, seated right of center, solemnly raises a ceremonial cup, while the presence of an august personage—at the far

2-25 *Ashurnasirpal II Drinking*, Nimrud, *c.* 875 B.C. Limestone, approx. 92″ high. British Museum, London.

left a winged genius who sprinkles holy water— makes the king's act part of a sacred ritual. The slow gestures and stately mien are what we expect of some grave liturgy; we recognize them in religious services today. The cuneiform inscriptions on the flat, thin slabs of relief continue across shallow recesses between the slabs, accentuating the neutrality of the planes and suggesting that the carving is meant to be not so much a three-dimensional form (that throws shadows) as a report of an event in pictures as well as writing. An interesting Assyrian convention nevertheless makes itself felt—the representation of the human body as thick-set and weighty and the limbs as bulging with muscle, as witness the advanced left leg of the genius and the arms of the king. The calf and forearm muscles are exaggerated, and the veins are like cables, an example of realistic observation converted to a kind of symbol of brute human strength. Also noteworthy is the way in which the profile view of the arms comprises, with the front-view torso, a kind of three-quarter view. The artist, though subject to the conventions of his time, is experimenting with the problems of representing what his eye sees.

Two centuries later, in a relief from Nineveh showing Ashurbanipal hunting lions (FIG. 2-26),

the conventions of the time of Ashurnasirpal II persist, although more realistic elements are introduced. In this relief, lions released from cages in some large, enclosed arena charge the king, who, in his chariot and with his servants protecting his blind sides, shoots down the enraged animals. The king, menaced by the savage spring of a lion at his back, is saved by the quick action of two of his spearmen. Behind his chariot lies a pathetic trail of dead and dying animals pierced by what would appear to be far more arrows than are needed to kill them. A wounded lioness (FIG. 2-27) drags her hindquarters, paralyzed by arrows that pierce her spine. Blood streams from her wounds—a detail recurring in Assyrian art and revealing the savage character of its patrons. The artist gives a ruthless reading of the straining muscles, the swelling veins, the corrugations of the muzzle, the flattened ears— once more a hard realism under control of the formality of silhouette in low relief. Modern sympathies make of the scene of carnage a kind of heroic tragedy, with the lions as protagonists; but it is unlikely that the artists of the king had any intention other than to aggrandize his image by piling up his kills, by showing the king of men pitting himself against the king of beasts and conquering him.

2-26 *Ashurbanipal Hunting Lions*, Nineveh, *c.* 650 B.C. Alabaster, approx. 5′ high. British Museum, London.

2-27 *Dying Lioness*, Nineveh, c. 650 B.C. Limestone, figure approx. 23″ high. British Museum, London.

NEO-BABYLONIA

The Assyrian empire was never very secure, and most of its kings had to fight revolts in large sections of the Near East. The seventh century B.C. saw a steady rise of opposition to Assyrian rule, and, during the last years of Ashurbanipal's reign, the empire began to disintegrate. Under his son and successor it collapsed before the simultaneous onslaught of the Medes from the east and the resurgent Babylonians from the south. Babylon rose once again, and, in a brief renewal (612–538 B.C.), the old southern Mesopotamian culture flourished, especially under the storied King Nebuchadnezzar, whose exploits we read of in the Book of Daniel. Nebuchadnezzar made Babylon a fabulous city once again and its famous "hanging gardens" one of the seven wonders of the an-

cient world. Of its temple to Bel—the Hebrews' Tower of Babel—only a little of the great ziggurat remains. But Herodotus, the ancient Greek traveler and "father of history," has left us a brief account of his visit to the temple complex during the fifth century B.C.:

In the one [division of the city] stood the palace of the kings, surrounded by a wall of great strength and size: in the other was the sacred precinct of Zeus-Bel, an enclosure a quarter of a mile square, with gates of solid brass, which was also remaining in my time. In the middle of the precinct there was a tower of solid masonry, a furlong in length and breadth, upon which was raised a second tower, and on that a third, and so on up to eight. The ascent to the top is on the outside, by a path which winds round all the towers. When one is about halfway up, one finds a resting-place and

2-28 *Lion from the Processional Way*, Babylon, c. 575 B.C. Glazed brick, approx. 3′ 5″ high. Louvre, Paris.

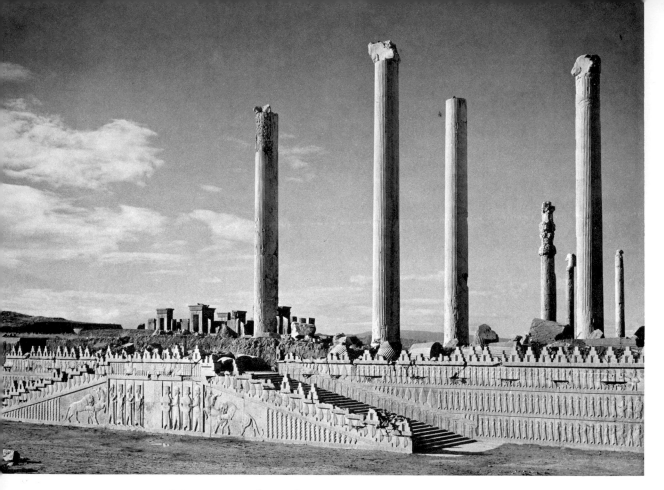

2-29 Stairway to the Royal Audience Hall, Persepolis, *c.* 500 B.C.

seats, where persons are wont to sit some time on their way to the summit. On the top-most tower there is a spacious temple, and inside the temple stands a couch of unusual size, richly adorned, with a golden table by its side . . . . They also declare that the god comes down in person into this chamber, and sleeps upon the couch, but I do not believe it.

A grand approach to the temple complex led down a walled processional way lined with sixty stately figures of lions done in brightly colored glazed bricks (FIG. 2-28). These remarkable beasts, sacred to the goddess Ishtar, are molded in relief and glazed in yellow-brown and red against a ground of turquoise or dark blue. The Babylonian glazes are opaque and hard; possibly each brick was molded and enameled separately. Also, it may be that as a result of this technique these animals, whose vigor is suggested by snarling muzzles, long, nervous tails, and carefully depicted muscles, are more stylized than those of the Assyrian hunting reliefs.

The processional way passed through the monumental, brilliantly glazed Ishtar Gate (PLATE 2-3), the design of which, with its flanking crenelated towers, conforms to the type of gate found in earlier Babylonian and Assyrian architecture. Glazed tiles had been used much earlier, but the surface of the bricks, even of those on which figures appeared, was flat. On the surfaces of the Ishtar Gate, laboriously reassembled, are superposed tiers of figures in profile, the dragon of Marduk and the bull of Adad alternating. Here is the characteristic Mesopotamian formality at its best. The figures make a stately heraldry proclaiming the gods of the temples toward which the Sacred Way leads. The lessons of architectural sculpture from Boghazköy and Khorsabad have been well learned, and the perfect adjustment of figure to wall found in the Ishtar animals has rarely been surpassed; certainly in the history of architecture few more colorful and durable surface ornaments are known.

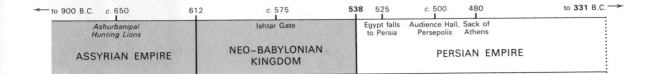

to 900 B.C.	c. 650		612		c. 575		**538**	525		c. 500	480		to **331** B.C.

Ashurbanipal Hunting Lions | Ishtar Gate | Egypt falls to Persia | Audience Hall, Persepolis | Sack of Athens

ASSYRIAN EMPIRE | NEO–BABYLONIAN KINGDOM | PERSIAN EMPIRE

PERSIA

Nebuchadnezzar, Daniel's "King of Kings," boasted: "I caused a mighty wall to circumscribe Babylon . . . so that the enemy who would do evil would not threaten . . . . [and] of the city of Babylon [I] made a fortress." Nevertheless, the handwriting on the wall appeared, the city was taken by Cyrus of Persia, and the line of Nebuchadnezzar came to an end. The impetus of the Persians' expansion carried them far beyond Babylon. Egypt fell to them in 525 B.C. By 480 B.C. the Persian empire extended from the Indus to the Danube, and only the successful resistance of the Greeks in the fifth century prevented it from embracing southeastern Europe as well.

Architecture

The most important source of our knowledge of Persian building is the palace at Persepolis (FIG. 2-29), built between 520 and 460 B.C. by Darius and Xerxes, successors of Cyrus. Situated on the high plateau to the east of the Mesopotamian river valley, the heavily fortified palace stood on a wide platform overlooking the plain toward the sunset. Although destroyed by Alexander the Great in a gesture symbolizing the destruc-

2-30 Plan of the palace at Persepolis.

1. Treasury
2. Harem
3. Palace of Xerxes
4. Palace of Darius I
5. Audience hall of Darius I
6. Throne hall of Xerxes
----- Partially excavated
▨ Originally roofed over (speculative)

FEET
0   100   200

2-31 Bull capital from the Royal Audience Hall of the palace of Artaxerxes II, Susa, *c.* 375 B.C. Gray marble. Louvre, Paris.

descendants. Unknown also remains the genesis of the square, many-columned hall so characteristic of the Persepolis palace. It has been suggested that it may have been derived from Median architecture, which has remained a blank page in archeologists' books. The Medes were the northern allies, later subjects, of the Persians and are believed to have been the intermediaries through whom Persian art received a variety of Iranian stylistic elements.

Stone, easily available at the site, was used liberally at Persepolis for platforms, gateways, stairs, and columns; brick was used for the walls, however, and wood for the smaller columns and the roofs. The ruins of the palace at Persepolis (FIG. 2-32) show that stone was used also for door and window frames. The forms are derived from Egyptian architecture, which had impressed Darius, but here the frames are not composed structurally of posts, lintels, and sills but are cut in an arbitrary manner and used as sculptural ornaments. In fact, the entire complex of buildings, and particularly the apadana, seems to have been designed primarily for visual effect; it is a gigantic stage setting for magnificent ceremonials celebrating not only traditional festivals but the greatness of the Persian empire and the power of its king.

Sculpture

The approach to the apadana leads through a monumental gateway flanked by colossal man-headed bulls and thence at right angles toward the elevated great hall, ascent to which is by broad, ceremonial stairways, designed as though for a stage. The walls of the terrace and staircases are decorated with reliefs representing processions of royal guards, Persian and Median nobles and dignitaries, and representatives from the subjected nations bringing tribute and gifts to the king (FIG. 2-33). These reliefs are thought to represent, in a shorthand version, the actual ceremonies that took place at Persepolis during the great New Year festivals. Traces of color found on similar monuments at other Persian sites suggest that, at least in part, these reliefs were colored. Their original effect must have been

tion of Persian imperial power, its still impressive ruins permit a fairly complete reconstruction of its original appearance.

Unlike the Assyrian palace, which was tightly enfolded around courts (FIG. 2-22), the Persepolis buildings were loosely grouped and separated from each other by streets and irregular open spaces (FIG. 2-30). The dominant structure was a vast columned hall, sixty feet high and over 200 feet square. Standing on its own rock-cut podium, which is about ten feet high, this huge audience hall (*apadana*) has been called "one of the noblest structures of the ancient world." It contained thirty-six forty-foot columns with slender, fluted shafts and capitals composed of the foreparts of bulls or lions arranged to provide a firm cradle for the roof timbers. FIG. 2-31 shows a well-preserved example from the somewhat later palace of Artaxerxes at Susa. These unique capitals are an impressive and decorative Persian invention with no known antecedents or even greater than it is today as the rows of figures sparkled in a blaze of colors rivaling that presented by the court during the festivals. On the other hand, the present denuded state of the reliefs makes it easier for us to appreciate their highly refined sculptural style. The cutting of the stone, both in the subtly modeled surfaces and the crisply chiseled details, is technically superb. Although they may have been inspired by Assyrian reliefs (FIGS. 2-24, 2-25, and 2-26), these Persian reliefs are strikingly different in style. The forms are more rounded and their projection from the background greater; there is less emphasis on such details as straining sinews and bulging muscles; and, most important perhaps, the figures seem organically more unified, as the torsos are now shown in natural side view and are thus more convincingly related to heads and legs. The supposition that most of these modifications of traditional formal elements are the result of Greek (Ionian) influence becomes almost a certainty when we note how the garments worn by the figures have been stylized in accordance with Greek Archaic practice (see Chapter Five). Despite the modifications, the Persepolis reliefs represent a triumph of Near Eastern formality in art. Their purpose and function, to glorify the king in a manner both decorative and monumental, is fulfilled most successfully.

Craft Art

Love for well-ordered forms enabled the designers to create, on a vast scale, a rich and unified setting for official ceremonials. But the Persians could also work successfully on a much smaller scale. They were excellent goldsmiths and silversmiths; the example shown, a jar handle in the form of a winged ibex (FIG. 2-34), typifies their exquisite and enduring art. Made of silver inlaid with gold, the ibex rears up on a palmette growing from the head of a satyr. The leap of the lithe body rises into the higher leap of the horns, and the suave curves of the wings smooth the motion. All that is needed of truth to nature is here, and none of it intrudes upon the effortless play of fancy.

As with most elements of Persian art, it is not difficult to trace the genesis of this winged ibex. Although the animal's body has regained its organic unity, probably through Mesopotamian influence, its original source of inspiration is to be found among the Luristan bronzes. Luristan, a mountainous region to the east of the Mesopotamian valley, inhabited at different times by Kassites, Medes, and other seminomadic tribes, was the home of a flourishing bronze industry that reached its peak during the eighth and seventh centuries B.C. It produced a variety of

2-32 Palace of Darius, Persepolis, *c.* 500 B.C.

portable objects, such as cups, bowls, weapons, bridles, and articles of personal adornment that, collectively, are referred to as nomad's gear. While we do not know by and for whom these objects were made, they form a homogeneous group that is rooted in an old and widespread tradition whose exponents delighted in working with animal forms. This so-called animal style may have originated in the Luristan region; at any rate it spread over much of the ancient world, from the Asiatic steppes to central and western Europe. The Luristan bronzes are characterized by a high degree of abstraction that converts the representations of animals into purely decorative devices. In the handle of the ceremonial cauldron illustrated (FIG. 2-35), the two rearing ibexes make interlocking arcs that echo in linear form

the three-dimensional shape of the vessel to which they are attached. Although wingless, their pose, attitude, and purpose leave little room for doubt that they are the forerunners of the Persian ibex. And, incidentally, the source of inspiration for the Persian animal's wings seems to appear in the embossed decoration of the bowl, where the Luristan artist has boldly copied Assyrian winged bulls and sacred emblems (in Assyrian style and technique).

Eclecticism of Persian Art

Persian art borrowed from so many sources besides Assyria and Luristan that it has been criticized as overly eclectic—that is, as being derivative and lacking originality. A superficial

2-33 *Subjects Bringing Gifts to the King*, detail from the stairway to the Royal Audience Hall, Persepolis, *c.* 500 B.C. Limestone.

2-35 Ritual cauldron, Luristan, eighth century B.C. Bronze, approx. 9″ high.
Cincinnati Art Museum, The Mary Hanna Fund.

2-34 Jar handle in the form of a winged ibex, Persia, fifth to fourth centuries B.C. Silver inlaid with gold, approx. $10\frac{1}{2}$″ high. Louvre, Paris.

survey of Persian art might indeed leave such an impression. The platforms of Persian palaces are of Mesopotamian, the guardian figures of Assyrian origin, the machinelike precision in the carving of details is reminiscent of Assyrian relief sculpture, the columned halls may have been influenced by Egyptian or Median models, and the fluting of columns is derived from Greek (Ionian) practice. And yet, the manner in which these various elements have been combined produces an ensemble that is quite new and different from the art of those nations from which they may derive. A Persian column cannot be mistaken for either an Egyptian or a Greek one, and nothing like the Persian apadana has been found in earlier architecture.

Prior to their conquest of the Near East, the Persians' art had consisted mainly of the small-scale nomad's gear. Their monumental art was created "on the spur of the moment," one might say, when they found themselves masters of the Near East and heirs to its rich culture. To glorify and eternalize their military and political achievements the Persians not only adopted those features of foreign and conquered cultures that seemed to serve this purpose but also brought into the country the artisans who could best realize their ambitious projects. A building inscription at Susa names Ionians, Sardians, Medes, Egyptians, and Babylonians among the workmen who built and decorated the palace. But under the single-minded direction of its Persian masters this mixed crowd with a widely varied cultural and artistic background created a new and coherent style that was perfectly suited to express Persian imperial ambitions. A court style, like that of Louis XIV over two millennia later, it compelled its contributors into a synthesis that was to remain remarkably uniform during the 200-year reign of the Achaemenid dynasty.

Chapter Three

The Art of Egypt

MEDITERRANEAN SEA

SYRIA

Alexandria

Sais

LIBYA

Gizeh • Cairo
Saqqara • Memphis
Faiyum • Medum

SINAI

• Beni Hasan
• Tell el-Amarna

ANCIENT EGYPT

Dendara
Abydos • Karnak
Thebes •
Luxor

Hierakonpolis
Edfu •

▲ GOLD MINES

• Aswan

RED SEA

▲
DIORITE QUARRIES

• Abu Simbel

N U B I A

PUNT

0   100   200   300 miles

OVER 2000 YEARS AGO the admiring Herodotus wrote: "Concerning Egypt itself I shall extend my remarks to a great length, because there is no country that possesses so many wonders, nor any that has such a number of works which defy description." He added a little later: "They [the Egyptians] are religious to excess, far beyond any other race of men." Men of discernment, aware of the profusion of monuments left to the world by the ancient Egyptians, have long been in agreement with these observations. While the Egyptians built their dwellings of impermanent materials, they made their tombs (which they believed would preserve their bodies forever), their temples to the immortal gods, and the statues of their equally immortal god-king of imperishable stone. The cliffs of the Libyan and Arabian deserts and the Nile flowing between them could represent, respectively, the timelessness of the Egyptian world and the endless cycles of natural process. Religion and permanence—these are the elements that characterize their solemn and ageless art and express the unchanging order that for the ancient Egyptians was divinely ordained.

Even more than the Tigris and Euphrates, the Nile defined the cultures that lived by virtue of its presence. Originating deep in Africa, the

NOTE Chronology is well established only from Eleventh Dynasty on.

B.C.

PREHISTORIC (NEOLITHIC) PERIOD

4000

Hierakonpolis painting detail   c. 3500

PREDYNASTIC PERIOD

c. 3000

Union of Upper and Lower Egypt c. 3000

Pyramids, Gizeh

Palette of Narmer

2130   c. 2260   c. 2680

MIDDLE KINGDOM   FIRST INTERMEDIATE PERIOD (civil wars)   OLD KINGDOM (DYNASTIES III–VI)   EARLY DYNASTIC PERIOD (DYNASTIES I–II)

2000

Rock-cut tombs, Beni Hasan

Temple of Amen-Re

Queen Nefertiti

1790   1570   1085

(DYNASTIES XI–XII)   SECOND INTERMEDIATE PERIOD (Hyksos)   NEW KINGDOM (DYNASTIES XVIII–XX)

Amarna Period (Akhenaton) 1377–1358

Abu Simbel

1000

332

LATE PERIOD (DYNASTIES XXI–XXX)

Alexander Conquers Egypt

525 Persia conquers Egypt

3-1 *Men, Boats, and Animals,* wall painting from a shrine at Hierakonpolis, *c.* 3500 B.C. (After Quibel.)

world's longest river descended through many cataracts to sea level in Egypt, where, in annual flood, it deposited rich soil brought thousands of miles from the African hills. Hemmed in by the narrow valley, which even in its widest parts reaches a width of only about twelve miles, the Nile flows through regions that may not have a single drop of rainfall in a decade. Yet, crops grow luxuriantly from the fertilizing silt, as they did in ancient times. Game also abounded then, and the great river that made life possible entered the consciousness of the Egyptians as a god and as a symbol of life.

In predynastic, or prehistoric, and pharaonic times the river held wider sway than it does today. Egypt was a land of marshes dotted with island ridges, and what is now arid desert valley was grassy parkland well suited for grazing cattle and hunting. Amphibious animals swarmed in the marshes and were hunted through tall forests of papyrus and rushes. The fertility of Egypt was proverbial, and, at the end of its history, when Egypt had become a province of the Roman empire, it was the granary of the Mediterranean world.

Before settled communities could be built along the Nile's banks, however, it was necessary to control the annual floods. This was done with dams, and the communal effort needed for construction of them provided the basis for the growth of an Egyptian civilization, just as the irrigation projects in the Mesopotamian valley had furnished the civilizing impetus for that region a few centuries earlier.

In the Middle Ages, when the history of Egypt was thought of as part of the history of Islam, its ancient reputation as a land of wonders and mystery lived on in more or less fabulous report. Until the later eighteenth century, its undeciphered writing and its exotic monuments were regarded as treasures of occult wisdom locked away from any but those initiated in the mystic arts. Scholars knew something of the history of Egypt from references in the Old Testament, from the unreliable reports of travelers ancient and modern, and from a history of Egypt written in Greek by an Egyptian named Manetho in the second century B.C. Manetho described the succession of pharaohs, dividing them into the still useful groups we call dynasties; but his chronology is very inaccurate and his account untrustworthy.

Scientific history, or at least scientific archeology, had its start when, at the end of the eighteenth century, modern Europe rediscovered Egypt; Egypt became the first subject of archeological exploration, and was followed by the uncovering of the ancient civilizations of the Tigris and the Euphrates. In 1799, Napoleon Bonaparte, on a military expedition to Egypt, took with him a small troop of scholars, linguists, antiquarians, and artists. The chance discovery of the famed Rosetta Stone gave the eager scholars what they wanted, a key to the till then undeciphered Egyptian hieroglyphic writing. The stone bears an inscription in three sections, one in Greek, which was easily read, one in *demotic* (people's) Egyptian, and one in priestly hieroglyphic. It was at once suspected that the inscription was the same in all three sections and that with the Greek as a key the other two could be deciphered. More than twenty years later, after many false starts, a young linguist, Jean François Champollion, deduced that the hieroglyphs were not simply pictographs but the signs of a once-spoken language—vestiges of which survived in Coptic—that had relatively recently been written in Greek characters. Champollion's feat made him a kind of Columbus of the new science of archeology, as well as of that special branch within it, Egyptology. Those who followed Champollion, like Auguste Mariette and Gaston Maspero, sought to build classified collections and to protect Egyptian art from the unscrupulous. Men like Flinders Petrie introduced techniques of excavation, preparing the ground for the development of sound methods for validating knowledge of Egyptian civilization.

Ideally the foundation of archeological knowledge is a reliable chronology. Yet, as the body of archeological evidence enlarges and new scientific methods of dating are developed, the chronology must change to accommodate them. Sometimes what was thought close to certain turns problematical; sometimes what was guesswork or speculation suddenly becomes probable. Because this is more often the case the further back one goes in time, the predynastic beginnings of Egyptian civilization are chronologically vague, as are those of Mesopotamia. Some time around 3500 B.C. a people of native African stock may have been exposed to influences from Mesopotamia, or it is possible that, as in Sumer, the sudden cultural development may have been due to an actual incursion of a new people. A wall painting from the late predynastic period, found in a shrine at Hierakonpolis in Upper Egypt (FIG. 3-I), represents men, animals, and boats in a lively, helter-skelter fashion. The boats, symbolic of the journey across the Nile of life and death, are painted white and seem to carry a cargo of tombs mourned over by women. Also shown are a heraldic grouping of two animals (lions?) on either side of a human figure, many figures of gazelles, and, in the lower right corner, men fighting. The heraldic group, a compositional type usually associated with Mesopotamian art, suggests that by this time influences from Mesopotamia not only had reached Egypt but had already made the thousand-mile journey upstream. The stick-figures and their apparently random arrangement remind one of the Mesolithic rock paintings from the Spanish Levant and North Africa, the style of which flourished also in the central Sahara and may have been another impetus to the development of Egyptian art.

The Hierakonpolis mural is the earliest known representative of that millennia-long tradition of painting that reveals to us the funerary customs of Egypt, so much at the center of Egyptian life. Most paintings are found in tombs and provide the principal archeological evidence for the historical reconstruction of Egyptian civilization. Religion pervaded that civilization. In Herodotus' words, the Egyptian was "religious to excess," and his concern for immortality amounted to near-obsession; his overall preoccupation in this life was to ensure his safety and happiness in the next. To this preoccupation we owe the major part of the monuments the Egyptians left behind them.

The sharp distinction between body and soul, long familiar to Christianity and other later religions, was not made in the religion of the Egyptians. Rather they believed that from birth one was accompanied by a kind of other self, the *ka*, which, upon the death of the fleshly body, could inhabit the corpse and live on. For the ka to live securely, however, the dead body must remain as nearly intact as possible; to see that it did, the Egyptians developed to a high art the technique of embalming, their success in which is made evident by numerous well-preserved mummies of kings (like Rameses II), princes, and nobles, as well as of some common persons. The first requirement for immortality, mummification, was followed by others: Food and drink had to be provided, as well as clothing, utensils, and all the apparatus of life, so that nothing would be lacking that had been enjoyed on earth. Images of the deceased, sculptured in the round and placed in shallow recesses, guaranteed the permanence of his identity by providing substitute dwelling places for the ka in case the mummy disintegrated. Wall paintings (for the use and delectation of the ka) recorded with great animation and detail the recurring round of human activities, a cycle of "works and days" that changed with the calendar and the seasons. The Egyptians hoped and expected that the images and inventory of life, set up and collected within the protecting, massive stone walls of the tomb, would ensure immortality; but almost from the beginning of the elaborate interments, the thorough plundering of tombs became a profitable occupation. Only one royal burial place remained intact, that of King Tutankhamen of the Eighteenth Dynasty; its discovery, in 1924, revealed to a fascinated world the full splendor of a pharaoh's funerary assemblage.

THE EARLY DYNASTIC PERIOD AND THE OLD KINGDOM

Egypt has been known as the Kingdom of the Two Lands, a reference to its very early physical and political division into Upper Egypt and Lower Egypt. The upper land was dry and rocky and rustic in culture; the lower land, opulent, urban, and populous. Even in predynastic times there must have been conflict between the two, for the ancient Egyptians began the history of Egypt, as we do, with the forcible unification of the two lands by a certain Menes.

The "Palette of Narmer"

Menes is thought to be King Narmer, whose image we find on a slate slab from Hierakonpolis (FIG. 3-2). The slab, or palette as it is called, was

3-2 *Palette of Narmer,* front and back, Hierakonpolis, *c.* 3000 B.C. Slate, 25" high. Egyptian Museum, Cairo.

originally used as a tablet on which eye makeup (to protect the eyes against sun-glare and irritation) was prepared. The *Palette of Narmer* is an elaborate, formalized version of a utilitarian object common in the predynastic period. Its importance is great, not only as a historical document that records the unification of the two Egypts and the beginning of the dynastic period, but as a kind of early blueprint of the formula of figure representation that was to rule Egyptian art for some 3000 years. On the palette's back, the king, wearing the high, bowling-pin-shaped crown of Upper Egypt, is about to slay an enemy as a sacrifice. Before him a hawk, symbol of the sky god, Horus, protector of the king, takes into captivity a man-headed land from which papyrus grows (a symbol for Lower Egypt). Below the king are two fallen enemies and, above, two heads of Hathor, a goddess favorably disposed to Narmer. The other side of the palette shows Narmer wearing the cobra crown of Lower Egypt and reviewing a pile of the beheaded enemy. In both cases it is significant that the king, towering over his own men and the enemy—by virtue of his superior rank—performs his ritual task alone. Historical narrative as we find it in Mesopotamian reliefs (see the *Victory Stele of Naram-Sin,* FIG. 2-17) is not of primary importance in this work; what is important is the concentration upon the king as a deified figure, isolated from all ordinary men and far above them and alone responsible for his triumph. As early as the Narmer palette (about 3000 B.C.) we see evidence of this Egyptian convention of thought, of art, and of state policy—namely, that the kingship is divine, that its prestige is one with the prestige of the gods.

If what belongs to the gods and to nature is unchanging and if the king is divine then his attributes must be eternal. We have already seen that, in Mesopotamian art, the ever changing natural shapes are formalized into simple poses, attitudes, and actions. The same thing happens in Egypt, even though the instinct for convention leads to a somewhat different style. In the figure of Narmer we find the stereotype of kingly transcendence that, through several slight variations, will be repeated in subsequent representation of all Egyptian dynasts but Akhenaton

(see below) in the fourteenth century. The king is seen in a perspective that combines the profile views of head, legs, and arms with the front views of eyes and torso. While the proportions of the figure will change, the method of its representation will become a standard for all later Egyptian art. Like a set of primordial commandments, the *Palette of Narmer* sets forth the basic laws that will govern art along the Nile for thousands of years. In the Hierakonpolis painting (FIG. 3-1) figures had been scattered across the wall more or less haphazardly; here a surface has been subdivided into a number of bands, and the pictorial elements have been inserted in a neat and orderly way into their organized setting. The horizontal lines that separate the bands also define the ground that supports the figures—a mode that will persist in hundreds of acres of Egyptian wall paintings and reliefs.

Three centuries later we find the basic conventions of Egyptian figure representation that were fixed in the *Palette of Narmer* refined and systematized on a carved wooden panel representing Hesire, a high official from the court of King Zoser (FIG. 3-3). The figure's swelling forms have been modeled with greater subtlety and its proportions have been changed to a broad-shouldered, narrow-hipped, heroic ideal; the artist uses the conceptual approach (see Chapter Two, p. 41) rather than the optical, representing what he knows to be true of the object instead of some random view of it and showing its most characteristic parts at right angles to the line of vision. This conceptual approach expresses a feeling for the constant and changeless aspect of things and lends itself to systematic methods of figure construction (FIG. 3-4). Although perhaps not quite so simple as his description of it, the system has been explained by Erwin Panofsky as follows:

With its more significant lines permanently fixed on specific points of the human body, the Egyptian network [of equal squares] immediately indicates to the painter or sculptor how to organize his figure: he will know from the outset that he must place the ankle on the first horizontal line, the knee on the sixth . . . and so on. . . . It was, for instance, agreed that in a [lunging] figure . . . the length of pace . . . should amount

3-3 *Panel of Hesire*, Saqqara, *c.* 2750 B.C. Wood, 45″ high. Egyptian Museum, Cairo.

3-4 The "Later Canon" of Egyptian Art. (After Panofsky.)

to 10½ units, while this distance in a figure quietly standing was set at 4½ or 5½ units. Without too much exaggeration one could maintain that, when an Egyptian artist familiar with this system of proportion was set the task of representing a standing, sitting, or striding figure, the result was a foregone conclusion once the figure's absolute size was determined.[1]

[1] Erwin Panofsky, *Meaning in the Visual Arts* (Garden City, N.Y.: Doubleday, 1955), pp. 58–61.

In addition to recording an important historical event and to laying down ground rules for the pictorial arts, the *Palette of Narmer* also illustrates several stages in the development of Egyptian writing. The story of Narmer's victories is represented in the different registers with varying degrees of symbolism. Straight pictorial narrative is used to show the king following his standard-bearers in triumphal processsion and inspecting the bodies of his slain enemies. This simple picture-writing becomes symbolic when, in a bottom register, the king is shown as a bull breaking down the walls of an enemy fortress. The symbolism becomes more abstract in the pile of decapitated foes: Here each body, its severed head neatly placed between its legs, probably is a numerical symbol representing a specific number of fallen enemies. Finally, in the signs appearing near the heads of the more important figures, pictographs take on phonetic values, as the names of the respective individuals have been written in true hieroglyphs.

Architecture

Similar principles of permanence and regularity appear in the design of the Egyptian tomb, that symbol of the timeless, the silent house of the dead. We find its standard shape in the *mastaba* (FIG. 3-5). The mastaba (Arabic for "bench") is a rectangular brick or stone structure with battered (sloping) sides erected over a subterranean tomb chamber that was connected with the outside by a shaft. The form was probably developed from mounds of earth or stone that covered earlier tombs. It is significant that in Mesopotamia there was relative indifference to the cult of burial and to the permanence of the tomb, while in Egypt such matters are considered to be of the first importance.

About 2750 B.C. the Stepped Pyramid of King

1. Chapel
2. False door
3. Shaft into burial chamber
4. Serdab (chamber for statue of deceased)
5. Burial chamber

3-5 Mastabas, with plan and (at top) schematic section.

Zoser of the Third Dynasty (FIG. 3-6) was raised at Saqqara, the ancient necropolis (city of the dead) of Memphis. Possibly Egypt's oldest stone building, it was the first monumental royal tomb. In form a kind of compromise between the mastaba and the later "true" pyramids at Gizeh, it is in fact a piling of mastabas of diminishing size one upon another, forming a structure resembling the great ziggurats of Mesopotamia. Unlike them, Zoser's pyramid is a tomb, not a temple, and is elevated above the funerary city arranged around it.

A tomb such as Zoser's had a dual function: to protect the mummified king and his possessions and to symbolize by its gigantic presence his absolute, godlike power. This structure, with its temples (now thought to be a medical shrine), complex of chambered terraces, and great courtyard, was the work of Imhotep, the first artist of recorded history. Grand vizier to King Zoser and a man of legendary powers, he was celebrated in the ancient world not only as an architect but as a wise man, wizard, physician ("the father of medicine"), priest, and scribe—a kind of universal genius who later came to be worshiped as a deity.

At Gizeh, across the Nile from modern Cairo, are three pyramids (FIG. 3-7) of pharaohs of the Fourth Dynasty—Khufu (the Greek Cheops), Khafre (Chephren), and Menkure (Mykerinus). Built after 2700 B.C., they have been associated with mystery and with "hidden" knowledge and have served as symbols for many things—primeval wisdom, Egypt itself, eternal stability, and the arts of magic. The pyramids of Gizeh represent the culmination of an architectural evolution that began with the mastaba. They did not evolve out of necessity; kings could have gone on indefinitely piling mastabas one upon another to make their weighty tombs. Rather, it has been suggested that when the kings of the Third Dynasty moved their permanent residence to Memphis they came under the influence of nearby Heliopolis. This city was the seat of the powerful cult of Re, the sun god, whose fetish was a pyramidal stone, the *ben-ben*. By the Fourth Dynasty the pharaohs considered themselves the sons of Re and, hence, his incarnation on earth. For the pharaohs, then, it would have been only

3-6 Stepped Pyramid of King Zoser, Saqqara, *c.* 2750 B.C.

3-7 Great Pyramids of Gizeh: Menkure, *c.* 2575 B.C.; Khafre, *c.* 2600 B.C.; Khufu, *c.* 2650 B.C.

c. 3000 B.C.		c. **2680**	c. 2600	c. 2500		c. **2260**	2130		1790 B.C.
Palette of Narmer		Great Pyramids of Gizeh	Tomb of Ti						Rock-cut tombs, Beni Hasan
EARLY DYNASTIC PERIOD				OLD KINGDOM		CIVIL WARS		MIDDLE KINGDOM	
DYNASTIES I–II				DYNASTIES III–VI				DYNASTIES XI–XII	

a step from the belief that the spirit and power of Re resided in the pyramidal *ben-ben* to the belief that their divine spirits and bodies would be similarly preserved within pyramidal tombs.

Is the pyramid form, then, an invention inspired by a religious demand rather than the result of a formal evolution? We need not decide here. Our concern is rather with the remarkable features of the Fourth Dynasty pyramid. Of the three at Gizeh, that of Khufu is the oldest and largest. Except for the galleries and burial chamber it is an almost solid mass of limestone masonry, a stone mountain built on the same principle as the Stepped Pyramid of Zoser, the interior spaces in plan and elevation being relatively tiny, as if crushed out of the scheme by the sheer weight of stone (FIG. 3-8). The limestone was quarried in the eastern Nile cliffs and floated across the river during the seasonal floods. After the masons finished cutting the stones, they marked them with red ink to indicate the place of each in the structure. Then great gangs of laborers dragged them (the wheel was not yet known) up temporary ramps and laid them course upon course. Finally the pyramid was surfaced with a casing of pearly white limestone, cut with such nicety that the eye could scarcely detect the joints. A few casing stones can still be seen in the cap that covers the Pyramid of Khafre, all that remain after many centuries during which the pyramids were stripped to supply limestone for the Islamic builders of Cairo. The immensity of the Pyramid of Khufu is indicated by some dimensions in round numbers: At the base the length of one side is 775 feet and its area some 13 acres; its present height is 450 feet (originally 480 feet). According to Petrie, the structure contains about 2,300,000 blocks of stone, each of which averages $2\frac{1}{2}$ tons in weight; it has been calculated that this enormous number of blocks would be enough to build a low wall along the perimeter of modern France. Yet it is not alone huge size and successful engineering that consti-

tute the art of this structure but its formal design —the proportions and immense dignity so consistent with its funerary and religious function and so well adapted to its geographical setting: The four corners are oriented to the four points of the compass, and the grave and simple mass dominates the flat landscape to the horizon. The ironic outcome of the stupendous effort may be read from the cross section (FIG. 3-8). The dotted lines at the base of the structure indicate the path cut into the pyramid by ancient grave robbers. Unable to locate the carefully sealed and hidden entrance, they started some forty feet above the the base and tunneled into the structure until they intercepted the ascending corridor. Many royal tombs were plundered almost as soon as the funeral ceremonies had ended; the very conspicuousness of the pyramid was an invitation to despoilment. The hard lesson was learned by the successors of the Old Kingdom pyramid-builders; they built few pyramids, and those were relatively small and inconspicuous.

3-8 Section of the Pyramid of Khufu. (After Hoelscher.)

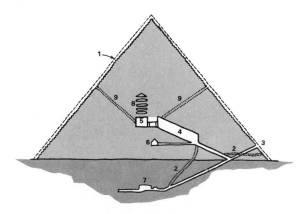

1. Silhouette with original facing stone
2. Thieves' tunnels
3. Entrance
4. Grand gallery
5. King's chamber
6. So-called queen's chamber
7. False tomb chamber
8. Relieving blocks
9. Airshafts

The Early Dynastic Period and the Old Kingdom   81

1. Pyramid of Khafre   3. Covered causeway   5. Great Sphinx   7. Pyramids of the royal family and mastabas of nobles
2. Mortuary temple   4. Valley temple   6. Pyramid of Khufu

3-9 Reconstruction of the Pyramids of Khufu and Khafre. (After Hoelscher.)

From the remains around the middle pyramid at Gizeh, that of Khafre, we can reconstruct an entire pyramid complex (FIG. 3-9). This consisted of the pyramid itself, within or below which was the burial chamber; the chapel, adjoining the pyramid on the east side, where offerings were made and ceremonies performed and where were stored cloth, food, and ceremonial vessels; the covered causeway leading down to the valley; and the valley temple, or vestibule of the causeway. Beside the causeway and dominating the temple of Khafre rose the Great Sphinx, carved from a spur of rock to commemorate the pharaoh. The head is often referred to as a portrait of Khafre, although the features are so generalized that little individuality can be discerned. In size it is unique in ancient sculpture.

The valley temple of the Pyramid of Khafre (FIG. 3-10) was built on the post-and-lintel system—upright supports, or posts, with horizontal beams, or lintels, resting on them. Both posts and lintels were huge, rectangular, red-granite monoliths, finely proportioned, skillfully cut and polished, and devoid of decoration. Alabaster slabs covered the floor, and seated statues, the only embellishment of the temple, were ranged along the wall. The interior was lighted by a few slanting rays filtering in from above. Although the Egyptians knew the arch and the vault and had used them occasionally in predynastic tombs, they rarely used them again after about 3000 B.C., the beginning of the dynastic period. Egyptian architects preferred the static forms of the post-and-lintel system, which, if cast into the heavy, massive shapes of the Khafre temple, express perhaps better than any other architectural style the changeless and eternal.

Sculpture

We have already noted that in the tombs sculpture in the round served the important function of creating an image of the deceased that could serve as an abode for the ka should the mummy be destroyed. For this reason an interest in portrait likenesses developed early in Egypt.

Hence, too, permanence of style and material were essential. Though wood, clay, and bronze were used, mostly for images of those not of the royal or noble classes, stone was the primary material: limestone and sandstone from the Nile cliffs, granite from the cataracts of the Upper Nile, and diorite from the desert.

A seated statue of Khafre (FIG. 3-11) was one of a series of similar statues carved for Khafre's temple of the Sphinx. These statues, the only organic forms in the geometric severity of the temple structure, with its flat-planed posts and lintels, must have created a striking atmosphere of solemn majesty. Khafre is seated on a throne on the base of which is carved the intertwined lotus and papyrus, symbol of united Egypt. Sheltering his head are the protecting wings of the hawk, symbol of the sun, indicating Khafre's divine status as son of Re. He wears the simple kilt of the Old Kingdom and a linen headdress that covers his forehead and falls in pleated folds over his shoulders. The portrait of the king is strongly individualized yet permeated with an imperturbable calm, reflecting the enduring power of the pharaoh and of kingship in general. This effect, common to royal statues of the ka, is achieved by devices of form and technique that we can still admire. The figure has great compactness and solidity, with few projecting, breakable parts; the form manifests the purpose—to last for eternity. The body is attached to a back slab, the arms are held close to the torso and thighs, the legs are close together and attached to the throne by stone webs. Like Mesopotamian statues, the pose is frontal, rigid, and bisymmetrical. This repeatable scheme arranges the parts of the body so that they are presented in a totally frontal projection or entirely in profile. As Panofsky remarked:

> ...we can recognize from many unfinished pieces that even in sculpture the final form is always

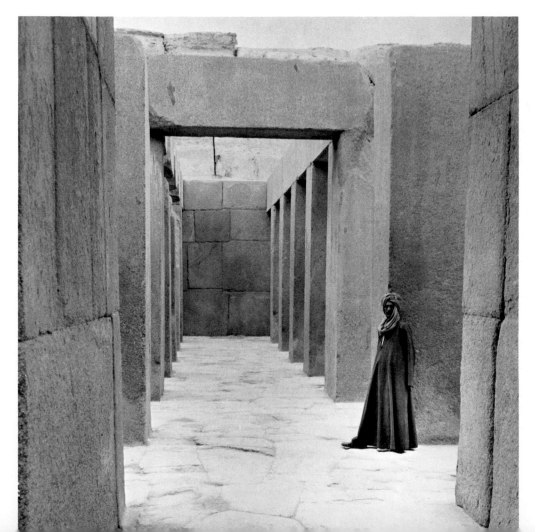

3-10 Middle aisle of the hall of pillars, valley temple of the Pyramid of Khafre, Gizeh, c. 2600 B.C.

3-11 *Khafre,* side and front, Gizeh, c. 2600 B.C. Diorite, 66" high. Egyptian Museum, Cairo.

determined by an underlying geometrical plan originally sketched on the surfaces of the block. It is evident that the artist drew four separate designs on the vertical surfaces of the block . . . that he then evolved the figure by working away the surplus mass of stone so that the form was bounded by a system of planes meeting at right angles and connected by slopes . . . . there is a sculptor's working drawing . . . that illustrates the mason-like method of these sculptors even more clearly: as if he were constructing a house, the sculptor drew up plans for his sphinx in frontal elevation, ground plan and profile elevation . . . so that even today the figure could be executed according to plan.[2]

This subtractive method of "working away the surplus . . . stone" accounts for the blocklike look of the standard Egyptian statue, which strongly differs from the Mesopotamian cylindrical or conical shape seen, for example, in the Gudea statues (FIG. 2-18). The hardest stone was used to ensure the permanence of the image—and Egypt, again unlike Mesopotamia, is rich in

[2] Panofsky, *op. cit.,* pp. 58–59.

stone. Even so, the difficulty of working granite and diorite with bronze tools (much of the finishing had to be done by abrasion) made production too expensive for all but the wealthiest. The hard and costly stones were rarely painted, especially if the stone had a grain that could be brought out by polishing.

As the figure was cut to plan, so were its proportions determined beforehand. A canon of ideal proportions, designated as appropriate for the representation of imposing majesty, was accepted and applied quite independently of optical fact. The generalized anatomy persisted in Egyptian statuary even into the Ptolemaic age, when Greek influence might have been expected to shift it toward realism. The Egyptian sculptor seems to have been indifferent to realistic representation of the body, preferring to strive for fidelity to nature in the art of portraiture, at which Egyptians have not been surpassed.

An example of their skill is a so-called reserve (duplicate, or spare) head of a prince of the family of Khufu (FIG. 3-12). Attention is given only to the execution of the face, which shows the union of the formal with the realistic that gives distinc-

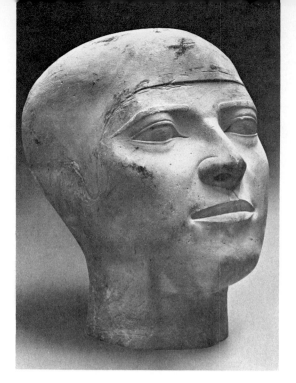

3-12 Reserve head of a prince, Gizeh, *c.* 2600 B.C. Limestone, life-size. Egyptian Museum, Cairo.

covered with painted canvas or plaster, a common procedure when soft or unattractive woods were used. Sensitive to the intrinsic beauty of the material with which he worked, the Egyptian sculptor treated hard woods like hard stones: He polished but did not paint them.

Painting and Relief

The scenes in painted limestone relief that decorate the walls of the tomb of an Old Kingdom official, Ti, typify the subjects favored by the patrons; most often they are of agriculture and hunting (FIG. 3-14), activities that represent the fundamental human concern with nature and that are associated with the provisioning of the ka in the hereafter. Ti, his men, and his boats

tion to so many portrait busts of its type. Reserve heads were not placed in the chamber of the ka, and their purpose is not understood. This head displays the extraordinary sensitivity of Old Kingdom portraiture. The personality—sharply intelligent, vivacious, and alert—is read by the sculptor with a penetration and sympathy seldom achieved in the history of sculpture.

In the history of art, especially portraiture, it is almost a rule that formality is relaxed and realism increased where the subject is a person of lesser importance. The famous wood statue of Ka-Aper (or Sheikh el Beled) is a case in point (FIG. 3-13). The work is a lively representation of a man whose function was to serve the king in the spirit world as he had in life. The face is startlingly alive, an effect that is heightened by eyes of rock crystal. The sheikh stands erect in conventional frontal pose, left leg advanced. His paunchy physique lacks the heroic and idealized proportions one finds in representations of royalty and nobility; he was, after all, only a minor official. The wood medium permitted the artist to omit the backslab and try a freer pose. Actually, what we see is the wood core that was originally

3-13 *Sheikh el Beled*, from his tomb at Saqqara, *c.* 2500 B.C. Wood, approx. 43″ high. Egyptian Museum, Cairo. (Partially restored.)

85

move slowly through the marshes, hunting hippopotamuses, in a dense growth of towering papyrus. The slender, reedy stems of the plants are delineated with repeated fine grooves that fan out gracefully at the top into a commotion of frightened birds and stalking beasts. Beneath the boats, the water, signified by a pattern of wavy lines, is crowded with hippopotamuses and other aquatic fauna. Ti's men seem frantically busy with their spears, while Ti himself, looming twice their size, stands impassive and aloof in the formal stance that we have seen in the figure of Hesire (FIG. 3-3). The outsize and ideal proportions bespeak Ti's rank, as does the conventional pose, which contrasts with the realistically rendered activity of his diminutive servants and particularly with the precisely observed figures of the birds and animals among the papyrus buds.

A rare and fine example of Old Kingdom painting is the frieze called the *Geese of Medum* (FIG. 3-15). In the prehistoric art of the caves, the rock paintings, and the art of Mesopotamia, we admired the peculiar sensitivity of early artists to the animal figure. They seem to have had empathy with the nonhuman creature, what Keats called negative capability—the power almost to share the being of the animal and to feel as it feels.

The *fresco secco* technique used, in which the artist lets the plaster dry before he paints on it, lends itself to slow and meticulous work, encouraging the trained professional to take pains in rendering the image and expressing his exact knowledge of its subject. The delicate, prehensile necks of the geese, the beaks, the suppleness of

3-14 *Hippopotamus Hunt*, tomb of Ti, Saqqara, *c.* 2500 B.C. Painted limestone relief, approx. 48″ high.

3-15 *Geese of Medum*, *c.* 2600 B.C. Dry fresco, approx. 18″ high. Egyptian Museum, Cairo.

The Art of Egypt

the bodies, and the animals' characteristic step and carriage are rendered with an exactitude and discernment that would elicit the admiration of an Audubon. The firm, strong execution of the figures is the work of an expert, with superbly trained eye and hand, probably conscious of his power and proud of it. It is probable, too, that religious motives mingled here with esthetic ones, for, after all, once a tomb was sealed no mortal eyes could ever be expected to see the paintings again. It must have been thought that in the darkness and silence the pictures worked their own spell, creating a force that would serve the ka eternally; something of the magic-working of the cave paintings seems to persist here.

The art of the Old Kingdom is the classic art of Egypt. Its conventions, definitively established, survived three millennia without major change. And the quality of Old Kingdom art at its best, though sometimes equaled, was never surpassed in later periods of Egyptian history.

THE MIDDLE KINGDOM

About 2300 B.C. the power of the pharaohs was challenged by ambitious feudal lords, and for about a century the land was in a state of civil unrest and near-anarchy. Eventually a Theban prince, Mentuhotep I, managed to unite Egypt again under the rule of a single king. In the Eleventh and Twelfth dynasties that followed (called the Middle Kingdom), art was revived, and a rich and varied literature appeared.

Rock-cut Tombs

Among the most characteristic remains of the Middle Kingdom are the rock-cut tombs at Beni Hasan (FIG. 3-16). One of the best preserved is the tomb of Khnumhotep, who boasted in an inscription of its elaborateness, saying that its doors were of cedar, seven cubits (about twenty feet) high. Expressing the characteristic Egyptian attitude toward the last resting place, he added:

> My chief nobility was: I executed a cliff-tomb, for a man should imitate that which his father does. My father made for himself a house of the *ka* in the town of Mernofret, of good stone of Ayan, in order to prepetuate his name forever and establish it eternally.

The rock-cut tombs of the Middle Kingdom largely replaced the Old Kingdom pyramid tombs. The immense cost and the futile effort to protect the king's mummy under a conspicuous and penetrable pyramid led to this new burial custom, in which tombs were hollowed out of the living rock at remote sites. Fronted by a shallow columned portico, the tombs contained the fundamental units of Egyptian architecture— portico or vestibule, columned hall, and sacred chamber (FIG. 3-17). The interior of the rock-cut

3-16 Rock-cut tombs, Beni Hasan, c. 1800 B.C.

FEET
0   30

3-17 Plan and section of a rock-cut tomb.
(After Sir Banister Fletcher.)

tomb of Amenemhet I (FIG. 3-18) shows the hall, the columns of which serve no supporting function, being, like the portico columns, continuous parts of the rock fabric. (Note the broken column in the rear, suspended from the ceiling like a stalactite.) Tomb walls were decorated with paintings and painted reliefs as in former times, and the subjects were much the same.

Painting and Sculpture

A painting from the tomb of Khnumhotep (FIG. 3-19) shows servants feeding oryxes (antelopes), the domesticated pets of the Egyptian gentry. The artist here has made a daring attempt to present the shoulders and backs of both human figures in foreshortening. However, working within the rigid framework of convention, he simply joined their front and side views in an unusual combination. As a result the action reads convincingly enough, but the figures fall short of optical consistency.

In portrait sculpture of the Middle Kingdom a somewhat deepened perception of personality and mood can be noted, as shown in a partially damaged head thought to be of Amenemhet III or Sesostris III (FIG. 3-20). Although the head is small—only five inches high—and can be held in the palm of one's hand, it has the effect of a life-sized representation. It is carved in obsidian, a hard stone that required great skill in cutting, grinding, and polishing. The stylized headdress, the strong modeling, and the accent on clearly defined planes identify it as Egyptian. The strong mouth, the drooping lines about the nose and eyes, and the shadowy brows show a determined ruler, who had also shared in the cares of the world, sunk in brooding meditation. The portrait is strangely different from the typical realistic and "public" Old Kingdom face, being personal, almost intimate, in its revelation of the mark of anxiety a troubled age might leave on the soul of a king.

THE HYKSOS AND THE NEW KINGDOM

This anxiety may have reflected premonitions of disaster. The Middle Kingdom, like that which had preceded it, disintegrated, and power passed to a line of migrant Semitic Asiatics from the Syrian and Mesopotamian uplands, called the Hyksos, or Shepherd Kings, who brought with them a new and influential culture and that practical instrument, the horse. The invasion and domination of the Hyksos, traditionally thought to have been a disaster, was latterly reassessed as a seminal influence that kept Egypt in the mainstream of the Bronze Age culture in the eastern Mediterranean. In any event, the innovations introduced by the Hyksos, especially in weapons and the techniques of war, contributed to their own overthrow by native Egyptian kings of the Seventeenth Dynasty. Ahmose I, final conqueror of the Hyksos and first king of the Eighteenth Dynasty, ushered in the New Kingdom (the Empire), the most brilliant period of Egypt's long history. At this time Egypt extended her borders by conquest from the Euphrates in the east deep into Nubia (the Sudan) to the south. Wider foreign contact was afforded by visiting embassies and by new and profitable trade with Asia and the Aegean islands. The booty taken in wars and the tribute exacted from subjected peoples made possible the development of a new capital, Thebes, which became a great and luxurious metropolis with magnificent palaces,

3-18 Interior of the tomb of Amenemhet I, Beni Hasan, c. 1975 B.C.

3-19 *Feeding of Oryxes*, fresco from the tomb of Khnumhotep, Beni Hasan, c. 1900 B.C.

tombs, and temples along both banks of the Nile. Thutmose III, who died in the fifty-fourth year of his reign, in the first half of the fifteenth century B.C., was the greatest pharaoh of the New Kingdom, if not of all Egyptian history, and his successors continued the grand traditions he established. The optimistic mood of the new era is recorded in an inscription above the heads of revelers in a painting now in the British Museum:

> The Earth-god has implanted his beauty in every body.
> The Creator has done this with his two hands as balm to his heart.
> The channels are filled with waters anew
> And the land is flooded with his love.

3-20 *Head of Amenemhet III (?), c. 1850 B.C. Obsidian, approx. 5″ high. National Gallery of Art, Washington, D.C. (C. S. Gulbenkian Collection).*

Architecture

If the most impressive monuments of the Old Kingdom are its pyramids, those of the New Kingdom are its grandiose temples. Burial still

3-21 Mortuary Temple of Queen Hatshepsut, Deir el-Bahari, *c.* 1500 B.C.

The Art of Egypt

demanded the elaborate care shown earlier, and, following the tradition of the Middle Kingdom, nobles and kings hollowed their burial chambers deep in the cliffs west of the Nile. In the Valley of the Kings, the tombs are rock cut, approached by long corridors extending as deep as 500 feet into the hillside. The entrances to these burial chambers were carefully concealed, and the mortuary temples were built along the banks of the river at some distance from the tombs. The temple, which provided the king with a place for worshiping his patron god and then served as a mortuary chapel after his death, became elaborate and sumptuous, befitting both the king and the god.

The noblest of these royal mortuary temples, at Deir el-Bahari, was that of Queen Hatshepsut (FIG. 3-21), who preceded the conquering pharaoh Thutmose III. A princess who became queen when there were no legitimate male heirs, she boasted of having made the "Two Lands to labour with bowed back for her." Built about 1500 B.C. along the lines of the neighboring Middle Kingdom temple of Mentuhotep I, but without

the original pyramid in the forecourt, the structure rises from the valley floor in three colonnaded terraces connected by ramps. It is remarkable how visually well suited the structure is to its natural setting. The long horizontals and verticals of the colonnades and their rhythm of light and dark repeat, in man-made symmetry, the pattern of the rocky cliffs above. The pillars of the colonnades, which are either simply rectangular or chamfered (beveled, or flattened at the edges) into sixteen sides, are esthetically proportioned and spaced. Statues in the round, perhaps 200, were intimately associated with the temple architecture. So also were the brightly painted low reliefs that covered the walls and whose remnants may still be seen. These reliefs represented Hatshepsut's birth, coronation, and great deeds. In her day the terraces were not the barren places they are now but gardens with frankincense trees and rare plants brought by the queen from an expedition to the faraway "land of Punt" on the Red Sea, an event that figures prominently in the temple's figural decorations.

The immense rock-cut temple of Rameses II,

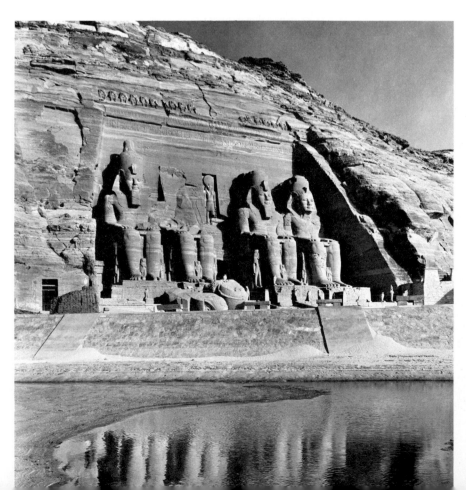

3-22 Temple of Rameses II, Abu Simbel, 1257 B.C. Colossi approx. 60′ high.

3-23 Interior of the Temple of Rameses II.

face each other across the narrow corridor, their exaggerated mass seeming to appropriate the architectural space. The columns are *reserved*— that is, hewn from the living rock—and have no bearing function, in this respect resembling the columns in the tombs at Beni Hasan. The figure-as-column, the *caryatid* form, will appear later in Greek architecture, and its presence at Abu Simbel may be its earliest use.

Distinct from the mortuary temples were the edifices built to honor one or more of the gods and often added to by successive kings until they reached gigantic size as in the temples at Karnak and Luxor (FIGS. 3-27 and 3-28). These temples all had similar plans. A typical pylon temple plan (FIG. 3-24) is bilaterally symmetrical along a single axis that runs from an approaching avenue through a colonnaded court and hall to a dimly lighted sanctuary. The dominating feature of the statuary-lined approach is the façade of the pylon, simple and massive, with sloping walls. The close-up example of a pylon shown in FIG. 3-25 is from the Temple of Horus at Edfu, which was built during the Ptolemaic period and is a striking monument to the persistence of Egyptian artistic traditions. Its broad surface is broken by the doorway with its overshadowing cornice, by deep channels to hold great flag-staffs, and by low reliefs. Moldings finish its top and sides. Within is an open court colonnaded on three sides, followed by a hall between court and sanctuary, its long axis placed at right angles to that of the entire building complex. This "broad" or hypostyle hall (that is, having a roof supported by columns) is crowded with massive columns and roofed by stone slabs carried on lintels that rest in turn on impost blocks supported by the great capitals. In the hypostyle hall of the Temple of Amen-Re at Karnak (FIGS. 3-26 and 3-27) the columns are sixty-six feet high, and the capitals, twenty-two feet in diameter at the top, large enough to hold 100 men. The Egyptians, who did not use cement, depended on the weight of the huge stones to hold the columns in place. In many such hypostyle halls the central rows of columns were higher than those at the sides, raising the roof of the central section and creating a clerestory. Openings in this clerestory permitted light to filter into the interior. This method of construction appears in primitive

Egypt's last great warrior-pharaoh, who lived a little before the exodus from Egypt under Moses, was built far up the Nile at Abu Simbel. Rameses, proud of his many campaigns to restore the empire, aggrandized his greatness by placing four colossal images of himself in the temple façade (FIG. 3-22). The whole monument was moved in 1968 to save it from submersion in the new Aswan Dam reservoir. In later times, the glories of kings and emperors in periods of conquest and imperial grandeur were also celebrated in huge monuments; gigantism seems characteristic of much of the art of empires that have reached their peaks. Here, Rameses' artists use the principle of augmentation both by size and by repetition. The massive statues lack the refinement of earlier periods, since much is sacrificed to overwhelming size. The grand scale is carried out in the interior also (FIG. 3-23). The giant figures of the king, formed as columns,

3-24 Plan of a typical pylon temple.

1. Pylon
2. Court
3. Hypostyle hall
4. Sanctuary
5. Girdle wall
6. Colossal statues of the pharaoh
7. Obelisks
8. Avenue of recumbent animals
   Probable roofed areas

3-25 Pylon Temple of Horus, Edfu, *c.* 237–212 B.C.

The Hyksos and the New Kingdom   93

FEET

0 50 100 200 300		

▦ Thutmose I (c.1530 BC) ▨ Rameses I (c.1314 BC) ▦ Rameses III (c.1198 BC)
▨ Thutmose III (c.1504 BC) ⬛ Seti I (c.1312 BC) ▨ Shishak I (c.950 BC)
▦ Amenophis III (c.1408 BC) Rameses II (c.1301 BC) ▨ Ptolemaic period (323-30 BC)
▨ Probable roofed areas
---- Reconstruction

3-26 Plan of the Temple of Amen-Re, Karnak. Dates in parentheses indicate time of construction. (After Sir Banister Fletcher.)

3-27 Model of hypostyle hall, Temple of Amen-Re, Karnak, c. 1300 B.C. Metropolitan Museum of Art, New York (bequest of Levi Hale Willard).

3-28 Court and pylon of Rameses II, *c.* 1290 B.C., and court and colonnade of Amenhotep III, *c.* 1390 B.C., Temple of Amen-Mut-Khonsu, Luxor.

form as early as the Old Kingdom in the valley temple of the Pyramid of Khafre. Evidently an Egyptian invention, it has remained an important architectural feature down to our times and was particularly important in the design of Medieval cathedrals.

The Egyptian temple plan evolved from ritualistic requirements. Only the pharaoh and the priest could enter the sanctuary; a chosen few were admitted to the hypostyle hall; the mass of the people was allowed only as far as the open court, and a high wall shut off the site from the outside world. The conservative Egyptians did not deviate from this basic plan for hundreds of years. The corridor axis, which dominates the plan, makes the temple not so much a building as, in Oswald Spengler's phrase, "a path enclosed by mighty masonry." Like the Nile that it almost symbolizes, the corridor may have been an expression of the Egyptian concept of life. Spengler suggests that the Egyptian saw himself moving down a narrow, predestined life-path that ended before the judges of the dead. The whole of Egyptian culture can be regarded as illustrating this theme.

The hypostyle hall at Karnak (FIG. 3-27) shows the smooth-shafted (as opposed to fluted) Egyptian columns with the two basic types of capitals: the bud-shaped and the campaniform, or bell-shaped. Though the columns are structural members, unlike the reserve "columns" of the Middle Kingdom tombs at Beni Hasan and the figure-columns at Abu Simbel, their function as carriers of vertical stress is almost hidden by horizontal bands of relief sculpture and painting, suggesting that the intention of the architects was not to emphasize the functional role of the columns so much as to utilize them as surface for decoration. This contrasts sharply with later Greek practice, which keeps the vertical lines of the column emphatic and its function clear by freeing the surfaces of the shaft from all ornament.

The courts and colonnades of the Temple of Amen-Mut-Khonsu at Luxor (FIG. 3-28) exhibit the columnar style especially well. The post-and-lintel structure of the temples appears to have had its origin in an early building technique that used firmly bound sheaves of reeds and swamp plants as roof supports in adobe struc-

| 2130 B.C. | *c.* 1975 | 1790 | 1570 | 1085 | 332 B.C. |

	Tomb of Amenemhet I	HYKSOS DOMINATION	Akhenaton (1377–1358)		
MIDDLE KINGDOM			NEW KINGDOM	LATE PERIOD	
DYNASTIES XI–XII			DYNASTIES XVIII–XX	DYNASTIES XXI–XXV	

tures. Evidence of this origin is seen in the columns themselves, which are carved to resemble sheaves of papyrus or lotus reeds, with the bud-cluster or bell-shaped capitals. Painted decorations, traces of which can still be seen on the surfaces of the shafts and capitals, emphasized these natural details. In fact, the flora of the Nile valley supplied the basic decorative motifs in all Egyptian art. With respect to a possible Mesopotamian influence, it is important to note that, until the time of Persia, Mesopotamian architecture seldom employed the post-and-lintel system; the column was rarely seen. Moreover, the formalization of plant forms into the rigid

profiles of architecture is precisely the same thing as the formalization of human bodies and action that the Egyptians achieved so skillfully in tomb painting and sculpture.

Sculpture and Painting

This radical simplification of form, which preserves in the ka figures the cubic essence of the block, can be seen to advantage in the statue showing Senmut (Queen Hatshepsut's chancellor and the architect of her temple at Deir el-Bahari) with Princess Nefrua (FIG. 3-29). This curious design, evidently popular in the New Kingdom, concentrates attention upon the portrait head, leaving the "bodies" a cubic block, which is given over to inscriptions. With surfaces turning subtly about smoothly rounded corners, it seems another expression of the Egyptian fondness for volume enclosed by flat, unambiguous planes. The polished stone shape has its own simple beauty.

The persistence of the formulas for projection of an image onto a flat surface can be seen in wall paintings in the tomb of Amenemheb at Thebes, which dates from the Eighteenth Dynasty (PLATE 3-1). The deceased nobleman is standing in his boat and driving the birds from a papyrus swamp with his throw-stick. In his right hand he holds three birds he has caught; his hunting cat, on a papyrus stem just in front of him, has caught two more in her claws and is holding the wings of a third in her teeth. His two companions, perhaps his wife and daughter, their figures scaled down in proportion to their rank, are enjoying the lotuses they have gathered. Although the water and the figures are represented by the usual conventions, cat, fish, and birds show a naturalism based upon visual perception like that which we have seen in the *Geese of Medum* (FIG. 3-15).

The tomb chamber, as we see it in the well-

3-29 *Senmut with Princess Nefrua*, Thebes, *c.* 1480 B.C. Black stone, approx. 40″ high. Staatliche Museen, Berlin.

preserved New Kingdom tomb of Nakht, at Thebes (FIG. 3-30), is similar to the tomb chambers of the Old Kingdom; in the mural the system of registers still preserves the rigid separation of the zones of action. But some innovations of detail appear: here and there a new liveliness and a closer inspection of life. A fresco fragment from another New Kingdom tomb (FIG. 3-31) shows four ladies watching and apparently participating in a musicale and dance in which two nimble little nude dancing girls perform. The overlapping of the girls' figures, facing in opposite directions, and the rather complicated gyrations of the dance are carefully and accurately observed and executed. Of the four ladies of the audience, two at the left are represented conventionally, but the other two face us in what is a most unusual and very rarely attempted frontal pose. They seem to beat time to the dance; one of them plays the pipes, and the artist takes careful note of the soles of their feet as they sit cross-legged. This informality may mean a relaxation not only of the stiff rules of representation but of the set themes thought appropriate for tomb painting. We may also have here the reflection of a more luxurious mode of life in the New Kingdom, and it may have been that the ka now required not only necessities and comforts in the hereafter but formal entertainment as well.

AKHENATON AND THE AMARNA PERIOD

These small variations of age-old formulas heralded a short but violent upheaval in Egyptian art, the only major break in the continuity of its long tradition. In the fourteenth century B.C. the emperor Amenophis IV (Amenhotep IV), later known as Akhenaton (or Ikhnaton), proclaimed the religion of Aton, the universal and only god of the sun. He thus contested and abolished the native cult of Amen, sacred to Thebes and professed by the mighty priests of such temples as Karnak and Luxor, as well as by the people of Egypt. He blotted out the name of Amen from all inscriptions, and even from his

own name and that of his father, Amenophis III. He emptied the great temples, embittered the priests and people, and moved his capital downriver from Thebes to a site now called Tell el-Amarna, where he built his own city and shrines to the religion of Aton.

This action by Amenophis IV—now Akhenaton—though it might savor of the psychotic or of the fanaticism of sudden conversion, was portended by events in the formation and expansion of the power of the great Eighteenth Dynasty. Egyptian might had formed the first world empire. Ruling over Syria and Nubia, bordered by the Hittites, and checking the penetration of the Mitanni, the conquering, imperialist pharaohs had gradually enlarged the powers of their old

3-30 Tomb of Nakht, Thebes, c. 1450 B.C. Rear wall 55″ × 60″.

3-31 *Musicians and Dancers*, detail of a wall painting from a tomb in the necropolis at Thebes, *c.*1400 B.C. British Museum, London.

sun god, Amen, to make him not simply god of the Egyptians, but of all men. Even before Egypt had become the main force in the Mediterranean world—before, as James Breasted describes it, "the Egyptian supremacy [was] undisputed from the Greek islands, the coasts of Asia Minor, and the highlands of the Upper Euphrates on the north to the Fourth Cataract of the Nile on the south"—Thutmose I, a founder of the fortunes of the dynasty, could say of the sun god that his kingdom extended as far as "the circuit of the sun." And the military pharaoh, Thutmose III, said of this aggrandized god: "He seeth the whole earth hourly." Thus, Akhenaton was exploiting forces already gathering when he raised the imperialized god of the sun to be the only god of all the earth and proscribed any rival as blasphemous. He appropriated to himself the new and universal god, making himself both the son and prophet, even the sole experient, of Aton. To him alone could the god make revelation. His hymn to Aton survives:

> Thou art in my heart
> There is no other that knoweth thee
> Save thy son Ikhnaton.
> Thou hast made him wise.
> In thy designs and might.
> The world is in thy hand,
> Even as thou hast made them . . .
> Thou didst establish the world,

> And raise them up for thy son,
> Who came forth from thy limbs,
> The king of Upper and Lower Egypt,
> Living in Truth, Lord of Two Lands . . .

Egypt has left us the ingredients, as it were, of the later monotheisms so influential in the world. Akhenaton's brief theocracy seems to have embodied the seeds of later concepts of one god, of an eternal son who is also a king, of a world created by that one god, and of the intimate revelation of that god's spirit to a chosen one.

One of the effects of the new religious philosophy seems to have been a temporary relaxation of the Egyptians' preoccupation with death and the hereafter and a correspondingly greater concern with life on this earth. In art this change is reflected in a different attitude toward the representation of the human figure. Artists aim for a new sense of life and movement, expressed in swelling, curvilinear forms; and their long-fostered naturalistic tendencies, so far confined largely to the representation of animals, are now extended not only to the human figure of the lowly but significantly to royalty also. A colossal statue of Akhenaton (FIG. 3-32), from his capital at Tell el-Amarna, retains the standard frontal pose; but the strange, epicene body with its curving contours and the long, full-lipped face, heavy-lidded eyes, and dreaming expression, show that the artist has studied his subject with care and rendered it with all the physiognomical and physical irregularities that were part of the king's actual appearance. The predilection for curved lines stresses the softness of the slack, big-hipped body that is a far cry indeed from the heroically proportioned figures of Akhenaton's predecessors. In a daring mixture of naturalism and stylization, the artist has given us an informal and uncompromising portrayal of the king that is charged with both vitality and a psychological complexity that has been called expressionistic.

The famous painted limestone bust of Akhenaton's queen, Nefertiti (PLATE 3-2), exhibits a similar expression of entranced musing and an almost mannered sensitivity and delicacy of curving contour. It may be that the sculptor deliberately alludes to a heavy flower on its slender stalk when he exaggerates the weight of the crowned head and the length of the almost serpentine neck. One thinks of those modern descendants of Queen Nefertiti—the models in the fashion magazines, with their gaunt, swaying frames, masklike, pallid faces, and enormous, shadowed eyes. As the modern mannerism shapes the living model to its dictates, so the sculptors of Tell el-Amarna may have had some standard of spiritual beauty to which they adjusted the actual likeness of their subjects. Even so, one is made very much aware of the reality of the queen through her contrived mask of beauty, a masterpiece of cosmetic art. The Nefertiti bust is one more example of that elegant blending of the real and the formal that we have noticed so often in the art of the ancient Near East.

During the last three years of his reign Akhenaton's coregent was his half-brother, Smenkhkare. A relief from Tell el-Amarna shows Smenkhkare and his wife Meritaten (FIG. 3-33) in an informal, even intimate, pose that contrasts strongly with the traditional formality in representation of exalted persons. Once-rigid lines have become undulating curves, and the pose of Smenkhkare has no known precedent. The prince leans casually on his staff, one leg at ease, an attitude that presumes knowledge on the sculptor's part of the flexible shift of body masses, a principle not really grasped until Classical times in Greece. This quite realistic detail accompanies others that are the result of a freer expression of what is observed:

details of costume and the departures from the traditional formality, such as the elongated and bulging head of Meritaten and the prominent bellies that characterize figures of the Amarna school. Proportions of figures no longer depend on rank; the princess is depicted in the same scale as her husband on the basis of their natural proportions.

We have seen that there was some slight loosening of the conventions of sculpture and painting even before Akhenaton. But the Amarna style (and a subsequent return to the earlier tradition) marks breaks too abrupt and emphatic to let us conclude that the style was simply a local, native flowering. It is at least possible that there was some influence from the Mediterranean world. We know that Egypt had commercial relations with Crete beginning in the predynastic

3-32 *Akhenaton*, from a pillar statue in the Temple of Aton, Tell el-Amarna, *c.* 1375 B.C. Sandstone, approx. 13′ high. Egyptian Museum, Cairo.

3-33 *King Smenkhkare and Meritaten* (?), Tell el-Amarna, *c.* 1360 B.C. Painted limestone relief, approx. 9½" high. Staatliche Museen, Berlin.

period, and the livelier, less convention-bound art of the Minoans could have proved suggestive and stimulating to the Amarna artists. Although the Cretan palace culture came to an end around 1400 B.C. (see Chapter Four) and Akhenaton did not ascend the Egyptian throne until 1377 (first as coruler with his father), the time lag does not seem too great to preclude such an influence. It may be that some Cretan artists, finding refuge in Egypt, and a sympathetic artistic climate under Akhenaton's rule, fertilized the Amarna style.

The survival of the Amarna style is seen in a painted panel from a chest of Tutankhamen, the successor to Akhenaton (FIG. 3-34). The panel represents the king hunting droves of fleeing animals in the desert. The theme is traditional, but the fluid, curvilinear forms, the dynamic composition—with its emphasis on movement and action—and the disposition of the hunted animals who, freed of the conventional ground lines, race wildly across the panel, are features reminiscent not only of the Amarna style but of the lively naturalism of Cretan art.

The pharaohs who followed Akhenaton re-established the cult and priesthood of Amen,

3-34 Painted panel from a chest, tomb of Tutankhamen, Thebes, *c.* 1350 B.C. Approx. 20" long. Egyptian Museum, Cairo.

restored the temples and the inscriptions, and returned to the old manner in art. Akhenaton's monuments were wiped out, his heresy anathematized, and his city abandoned. The conservative reaction can be seen in a relief of the pharaoh Seti I (FIG. 3-35). The rigid, flattened shapes repeat the formula of the *Palette of Narmer* (FIG. 3-2) and the static formality of Old Kingdom art. It is as if some fifteen centuries had not passed into history.

Though art by no means died out after the New Kingdom, its lingering life over some thousand years, when Egypt became a backwater of Mediterranean civilization, was feeble indeed—at least in comparison to what it had been. Summing up the New Kingdom and the later decline, Maspero wrote:

Seeing things on a great scale, they sought to create greatness, no longer after the manner of their ancestors, the Pyramid-builders, by the exaggerated bulk of their material, but by the reasoned immensity of their conceptions; thus architects had arrived at the gigantic colonnades of Luxor and Karnak, and sculptors at the colossi of the Theban plain and Abu-Simbel. When they had reached this point, which they could not surpass, they did not long maintain themselves at its level. . . .[3]

The prodigiousness of the effort seemed to have sapped Egypt's creative energies, and her military decline after Rameses III had its parallel in the waning of her artistic vigor.

[3] G. Maspero, *Art in Egypt* (New York : Scribner's, 1922), pp. 207–08.

3-35 *Seti I Offering*, Temple of Seti I, Abydos, *c.* 1300 B.C. Painted limestone, Louvre, Paris.

Chapter Four

The Art of
the Aegean

THE AEGEAN WORLD

Troy

Dimini • • Iolkos

AEGEAN

ASIA MINOR

SEA

Orchomenos • • Arne

• Thebes

• Athens

Mycenae •
Tiryns •

SYROS

C

L

A

D

E

S

NAXOS

• Miletus

PAROS

• Vaphio

C

AMORGOS

Pylos •

MELOS

RHODES

MEDITERRANEAN SEA

THERA

CRETE   Knossos   • Mallia

• Palaikastro

• Zakro

Hagia Triada •   Gournia

Phaistos

0   50   100   150 miles

OMER WROTE of the might and splendor of the Achaean host deployed for war against Troy:

So clan after clan poured out from the ships and huts onto the plain of Scamander, and . . . found their places in the flowery meadows by the river, innumerable as the leaves and blossoms in their season . . . the Locrians . . . the Athenians . . . the citizens of Argos and Tiryns of the Great Walls . . . troops from the great stronghold of Mycenae, from wealthy Corinth . . . from Lacedaemon . . . from Pylos . . . Knossos in Crete, Phaistos . . . and the other troops that had their homes in Crete of the Hundred Towns. . . .

The list goes on and on, outlining the peoples and the geography of the Aegean world in intimate detail. Until about 1870, historians of ancient Greece, though they acknowledged Homer's superb art, discounted him as a historian, attributing the profusion of his names and places to the rich abundance of his imagination. The pre-history of classical Greece remained shadowy and lost—as the historians believed—in an impenetrable world of myth. That they had done

CRETE
c. 3000 B.C.

NEOLITHIC PERIOD → c. 2800 → EARLY MINOAN PERIOD (PRE-PALACE PERIOD)

EARLY HELLADIC PERIOD

c. 3000 B.C.
GREECE

Cycladic idol

EARLY HELLADIC PERIOD

EARLY MINOAN PERIOD (PRE-PALACE PERIOD)

Kamares ware

Snake Goddess, Knossos

Toreador Fresco, Knossos

c. 2000

c. 1700   MIDDLE MINOAN PERIOD (OLD PALACE PERIOD) --- MIDDLE MINOAN PERIOD (NEW PALACE PERIOD) --- c. 1550

MIDDLE HELLADIC PERIODS

c. 1550

Lion Gate, Mycenae

Vaphio Cups

LATE MINOAN PERIOD

c. 950   c. 1100

SUB-MYCENAEAN PERIOD ← → LATE HELLADIC PERIOD

SUB-MINOAN PERIOD ← LATE MINOAN PERIOD

c. 950   c. 1100   c. 1450

NOTE   The period "Late Helladic" is also designated "Mycenaean."

less than justice to the truth of Homer's account or, for that matter, to ancient Greek literary sources in general, was proved by a German amateur archeologist, Heinrich Schliemann, who, between 1870 and his death twenty years later, uncovered some of the very cities of the Trojan and Achaean heroes whom Homer celebrates: Troy, Mycenae, Orchomenos, Tiryns. In 1870, at Hissarlik in the northwest corner of Asia Minor, which his knowledge of the *Iliad* had led him to believe was the site of Homer's Troy, he dug into a vast *tell*, or mound, and found there a number of fortified cities built one upon the remains of another, together with the evidence of their destruction by fire. Schliemann continued his excavations at Mycenae on the Greek mainland, whence he believed Agamemnon and Achilles had sailed to avenge the capture of Helen, and here his finds were even more startling. Massive fortress-palaces, elaborate tombs, quantities of gold jewelry and ornaments, cups, and inlaid weapons revealed a magnificent preclassical civilization.

But further discoveries were to prove that Mycenae had not been its center. An important Greek legend told of Minos, king of Crete, who had exacted from Athens a tribute of youths and maidens to be fed to the Minotaur—half-bull, half-man—which was housed in a vast labyrinth. Might this legend too be based on historical fact? The lesson of Schliemann's success in pursuing hunches based on careful reading of ancient legends was not lost on his successors. An Englishman, Arthur Evans, had long considered Crete a potentially fertile field for investigation, and Schliemann himself, shortly before his death, had wanted to explore the site of Knossos. In 1900, Evans began work on Crete and a short time later uncovered extensive unfortified palaces of the old sea-kings of Crete, which indeed did resemble labyrinths (FIG. 4-6). His findings, primarily at Knossos, were augmented by additional excavations there and at Phaistos, Hagia Triada, and other important sites on the southern coast of Crete. In 1962, excavation of another palace was begun on the eastern tip of Crete at Kato Zakro; more recently, in 1966, a queen's burial chamber judged to be about 3400 years old was discovered near Knossos.

MINOAN AND CYCLADIC ART

The civilization of the coasts and islands of the Aegean emerged about the same time as the river-valley civilizations of Egypt and Mesopotamia. Though there was close contact at various times and active exchange of influences, each civilization manifested a brilliant originality of its own; the Aegean civilization, however, has a special significance as the forerunner of the first truly European civilization—that of Greece. The sea-dominated geography of the Aegean contrasts sharply with that of the Near East, as does its temperate climate. In the ancient world this made for a busy, commercial seafaring culture, with decentralized authority and a way of life vigorous, vivacious, and pleasure-loving. This is especially true of Crete, the ancient center of Aegean civilization from which radiated its creative forces. As a commercial crossroads for the ancient world, Crete was strategically placed in the east Mediterranean, and her remarkable variety of products, both of agriculture and manufacture, was exported widely. The sea provided a natural defense against the frequent and often disruptive invasions that checker the histories of land-bound civilizations like Mesopotamia, and the navies of the sea-kings maintained a prosperous, far-flung maritime empire that served for the transmission of ideas and influences as well as goods. The controlled accessibility to Crete of impulses from abroad, especially from Egypt and Mesopotamia, may account for the initiation of a great culture there. Cretan culture influenced all of the Aegean area, and the particular modifications of it on the Greek mainland and in the islands of the Cyclades north of Crete have been identified. Thus, the art of Crete itself is called Minoan, after King Minos; that of the mainland, Helladic; and that of the islands, Cycladic. The culture associated with Mycenae on the mainland—the Mycenaean—is classed under Late Helladic (about 1550–1100 B.C.).

The archeological problems confronting investigators of Near Eastern civilizations were much less difficult than those of archeologists working in the Aegean area. Here there survived very few documents like the chronicles and inscriptions of Egypt and Mesopotamia with which to correlate the archeological findings, and there were no "absolute" dates expressible numerically. Evans had to construct a "relative" dating in terms of different periods of ceramic and decorative style from various sites on Crete, in the Cyclades, and at Mycenae. Evans' tripartite division of Minoan art into Early, Middle, and Late Minoan and the further division of each large period into three subperiods are a classic example of a relative chronology, used by the archeologist-historian when he lacks absolute dates. A greater firmness was given the Minoan chronology when points of contact with the chronology of Egyptian art were established. Imported objects of a certain style from the one country were uncovered in datable contexts in the other; in this way, for example, the Middle Minoan period was found to be roughly contemporary with the Middle Kingdom in Egypt.

The two earliest of several scripts found on Crete seem to have been inspired by Egyptian hieroglyphs. Of the later scripts, Linear A and Linear B, only the latter has been deciphered (as late as 1953); it is a pre-Homeric form of Greek. But the tablets inscribed with it represent almost exclusively inventories and tallies of objects and are of little aid in delineating the Minoan culture. For Minoan history, pottery remains have been by far the greatest evidence, since figurative art is relatively scarce and often so fragmentary and diminutive as to preclude building a stylistic continuity upon it. Potsherds are one of the mainstays of archeology when documentary and monumental evidence is sparse or missing. Pots (kitchenware, for example) were thrown on the garbage heap when broken. Over the years perishable materials decayed and disappeared leaving only pottery sherds, which settled into firmly stratified mounds. Careful excavation of such mounds can produce relative chronologies. Although the sequence of Cretan pottery styles was well established by Evans, some archeologists now feel that his method of dating has become inadequate in view of increased knowledge of the Minoan civilization. A new chronology has been suggested that is based on the construction of the great Cretan palaces. Its relation to the traditional chronology is shown on p. 103.

Nevertheless, absolute dates are few, and our knowledge of Minoan history remains vague and provisional. Even the origin of the Cretans is problematical. Some believe that they may have come from Anatolia as early as 6000 B.C., bringing with them a well-developed Neolithic culture, complete with pottery, and that the Bronze Age may have been ushered in by a new wave of immigrants (also from Anatolia?) around the year 2800 B.C.

The Early Minoan Period

The Early Minoan (pre-Palace) period is known to us primarily through pottery and a few scattered pieces of minor sculpture. There is the Mochlos stoneware (named after the site where

4-1 Cycladic idol, Syros, *c.* 2500–2000 B.C. Marble, 8½″ high.

it was found and apparently copied from Egyptian pieces of the First to Fourth Dynasties), and there are hand-made clay pots decorated with incised geometric patterns.

The most striking and perhaps the most appealing Aegean products of the Early Bronze Age are the numerous marble statuettes from the Cycladic islands. Most of them are representations of nude females with their arms folded across their abdomens. Varying greatly in size (from a few inches in height to life-size), these flat "plank idols" are highly schematized descendants of the Neolithic mother goddess. Their styles are as varied as their sizes and range from figures of almost normal proportions to shapes that resemble violins rather than human figures. The example shown (FIG. 4-1) occupies a middle ground: The organic forms have been converted into near-geometric shapes (triangles, rectangles, ovals, and cylinders), but the reference to the female figure remains clear, and the manner in which the various stylized parts have been combined has considerable esthetic appeal. Traces of paint found on some specimens show that at least

4-3 Small storage jar, Psyra, c. 2000–1850 B.C. 11″ high.

parts of these figures were colored. The eyes were usually painted, and additional color touches were provided by painted necklaces and bracelets.

Occasionally male figures also occur in the Cycladic repertoire. They usually appear as musicians, like the *Lyre Player* (FIG. 4-2), who, wedged between the echoing shapes of chair and lyre, dutifully performs a task that seems to have been part of funerary rituals. In the rendering of the figure, the disk-shaped head and the long, tubular neck are in the same style as the plank figures, but the body has gained mass and volume, and the composition has a three-dimensional quality lacking in the plank idols. Although it has not been possible to establish a chronological sequence for these Cycladic figurines, most seem to date from the second half of the third millennium B.C.; the *Lyre Player* is believed to belong to the end of the line and may have been contemporary with the Cretan palaces.

The Middle Minoan Period

The Middle Minoan period is marked by the founding of the "old" palaces around the year

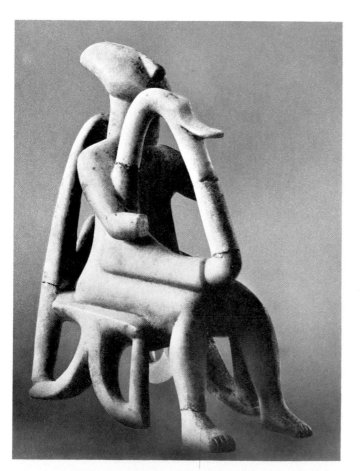

4-2 *Lyre Player*, Keros, c. 2000 B.C. Marble, 9″ high.

2000 B.C. Building in Crete emphasized neither tombs, temples, nor fortresses but, instead, palaces for the king and his retainers, around which grew up royal towns. The absence of fortification on Crete is conspicuous in the Aegean world, since fortified sites appear everywhere in the Helladic and Cycladic areas. It attests either to the power of the Cretan navies, to a long-enduring insular peace (a kind of *Pax Minoica*), or to both. But after only about three centuries, around 1700 B.C., these early palaces were destroyed, probably by one of the frequent earthquakes that ravage this part of the Mediterranean region.

An important technological advance of the beginning of the Old Palace period was the introduction of the potter's wheel, which permitted the throwing of vessels with thinner walls and subtler shapes and led to the development of a thriving industry. In the so-called eggshell ware, the Minoan potter's art reached a degree of excellence that deserves our highest admiration, if for the delicacy of the ceramic technique alone. But the Cretan artist also developed a style of decoration that complemented the delicate fabric and sophisticated shapes of his pottery. Beginning with relatively simple, curvilinear patterns painted dark on light (FIG. 4-3), he moved toward a fully polychrome style of decoration that found its culmination in the splendid pottery (FIG. 4-4) discovered in the cave at Kamares on the slope of Mount Ida. On a surface swelling robustly with the peculiarly Minoan "feel" for the vigor and buoyancy of active life we find a lustrous black ground on which is a quasi-geometric pattern of creamy white interspersed with yellow and red, forming a colorful and harmonious decoration. As in Egypt, the motifs derive from natural forms; here they are simplified into a play of spirals that are beautifully adjusted to and integrated with the shape of the vessel.

The Late Minoan Period

Somewhere between 1600 and 1500 B.C. began the period of the "new" palaces, when the destroyed palaces were rebuilt and the Golden

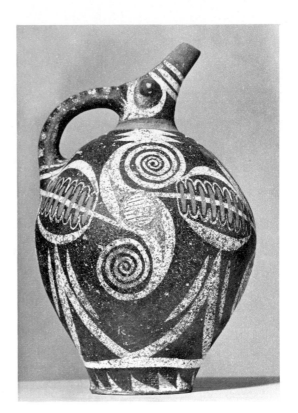

4-4 Kamares pitcher, Phaistos, *c.* 1800–1700 B.C. Approx. 10″ high. Archeological Museum, Herakleion.

Age of Crete produced the first great Western civilization. The bulk of the surviving archeological material—the evidence of an age of unsurpassed creative energy and precocious artistic achievement—dates from this era, which ended about 1400 B.C.

THE PALACES

The palaces rebuilt for the kings and their retainers were large, comfortable, and handsome, with ample staircases and courtyards for pageants, ceremonies, and games. The largest of them, the palace at Knossos (FIGS. 4-5 and 4-6), was a rambling structure built against the upper slopes and across the top of a low hill rising from a fertile plain. The great rectangular court around which the units of the palace are grouped had been leveled in the time of the old palace, and the manner of the grouping of buildings suggests

4-5 Palace at Knossos, *c.* 1600–1400 B.C. (view from the east).

that it was not preplanned but that several building nuclei grew together, with the court as the major organizing element. A secondary organization of the plan is provided by two long corridors. On the west side of the court a north-south corridor separates official and ceremonial rooms from the magazines, where wine, grain, oil, and honey were stored in large jars (*pithoi*). On the east side of the court, an east-west corridor separates the king's and queen's quarters and reception rooms (south) from the workmen's and servant's quarters (north). At the northwest corner of the entire building complex is the "arena," or "theater area," with steps (seats?) on two sides—a possible forerunner of the later Greek theater. Its purpose is unknown, but it is a feature that, like the central court, appears in other Cretan palaces. The complexity of the palace's plan came to be associated for the Greeks with the cult of the double axe (*labrys*), celebrated here; thus, perhaps, the Greek myth of the Cretan *labyrinth*. Certainly it was the product

of wealth and luxurious tastes and of a love for the convenient. Beneath the palace is a re-markably efficient drainage system of terra-cotta pipes that must have made Knossos one of the most sanitary cities existing before the twentieth century.

The practical storage system is exhibited in the magazines of the west wing (FIG. 4-7), where some of the pithoi are still in place. Some of the rooms had flat floors; others, like those shown here, had stone-lined pits. The walls were quite thick, as must have been the roofing over these magazines; the masonry may have been covered with earth to keep the interior cool. In most parts of the palace the masonry composing the walls was rough, consisting of unshaped field stones imbedded in mortar; ashlar masonry, made of shaped blocks of stone, was used at building corners and around door and window openings.

The palace had as many as three stories with interior staircases built around light and air wells

(FIG. 4-8), which provided necessary illumination and ventilation. Distinguishing features of the Minoan columns, which were originally fashioned of wood but were restored in stone (with, it is now thought, mistakenly bulky proportions), are their bulbous, cushionlike capitals and the manner in which the column shafts taper toward the base, being widest at the top. Strong evidence that the column had religious significance for the Cretans is its central position in the Lion Gate at Mycenae (FIG. 4-20) and the fact that the base of a column in one of the lower stories of the palace at Knossos is surrounded by a trough that was used for libations.

PAINTING

A view into the Queen's Megaron, with its pillared hall and light well (FIG. 4-9), shows the typically elaborate wall decoration of the more important rooms at Knossos. Here plastered walls were painted with frescoes, which, together with the red- or blue-shafted columns, must have

4-6 Plan of the palace at Knossos.

Reconstruction

Earlier structures { Existing / Reconstruction

1. West porch
2. Corridor of the Procession
3. South propylon
4. Central court
5. "Theater area"
6. North propylon
7. Pillar hall
8. Magazines
9. Throne room
10. Palace shrine and lower verandas
11. Stepped porch
12. Grand staircase
13. Light area
14. Hall of the Colonnade
15. Hall of the Double Axes (principal reception room)
16. Queen's Megaron

4-7 View of the west magazine, palace at Knossos, with large pithoi *in situ*.

4-8 Reconstruction of a stairwell, palace at Knossos.

provided an extraordinarily rich effect. The frescoes depicted many aspects of Cretan life (bullfights, processions, and ceremonies) and of nature (birds, animals, flowers and—as here—marine life with dolphins frolicking among other fauna of the sea).

One of the most memorable figures from the art of Crete is the *Cupbearer* from the procession fresco of the South Propylon at Knossos (FIG. 4-10). It is the only one preserved from a sequence, shown in two registers, that may have contained over 500 figures—if those from the Corridor of the Procession are included. The ceremonial *rhyton* (vessel for pouring ritual libations) carried by the youth has a typically Minoan shape, found nowhere else except as a Minoan import. And the figure itself is unmistakably Minoan. The youth has long curly hair, wears an elaborately embroidered loincloth with a silver-mounted girdle, and has ornaments on his arms, neck, ankles, and wrist. Although the profile pose with the full-view eye was a familiar convention in Egypt and Mesopotamia, the elegance of the Cretan figure, with its pinched waist, proud, self-confident bearing, and free movement, distinguishes it from all other early figure styles. The angularity of the older styles is typically modified in the curving line that suggests the elasticity of the living and moving being.

Vivacity and spontaneity characterize the *Toreador Fresco* (FIG. 4-11). Although only fragments of it have been recovered, they are extraordinary in their depiction of vigorous movements of the girls and the young man, who is shown in the air, having, perhaps, grasped the bull's horns and somersaulted over its back. We have seen how important the bull is in the Near East, especially in Mesopotamian art. The difference in the Minoan paintings is in the relationship of the bull—it may be that here he is even a god—to human beings. In this fresco, man and beast contest with each other in a dangerous game that takes place in the here and now, the human beings as conspicuous in the action as the bull. In a powerful characterization of the natures of both man and beast, the poise and agility of the toreadors play off against the exploding energy

4-10 *The Cupbearer*, Knossos, *c.* 1500 B.C. Fresco, approx. 5′ high. Archeological Museum, Herakleion.

4-9 Reconstruction of the Queen's Megaron, palace at Knossos.

4-11 *The Toreador Fresco*, Knossos, *c.* 1500 B.C. Approx. 32″ high including border. Archeological Museum, Herakleion.

of the bull. (One thinks back to the charging bisons of the Paleolithic caves.) Everywhere within the frame are curving lines, the directional lines of action, and nowhere more conspicuously and vitally than in the electric energy of the line that sweeps from the head of the bull to the whip of his tail.

Because of her cosmetic prettiness—like that of a sophisticated, modern type of womanhood—a girl represented in a fragment of another fresco has been labeled *La Parisienne* (PLATE 4-1). With her conventionally enlarged and front-view eye, her turned-up nose, full red lips, and elaborate coiffure, she is almost disturbingly of our own times, especially as we conventionalize her type in popular art. Surely there is nothing quite like this sprightly charm, freshness, and *joie de vivre* in the art of the ancient Near East. The painting method used is appropriate to the lively spirit of the Minoans. Unlike the Egyptians, who painted in the dry fresco technique, the Minoans used a true, or wet, fresco method, which required rapid execution and a skill in getting quick, almost "impressionistic" effects. If one is to catch an interesting but fugitive aspect of an object or a scene, one must work quickly, even

spontaneously, allowing for happy accidents. Thus, because the wet-fresco technique compelled the artist to work rapidly, the spirit of *La Parisienne* is also a product of the resultant verve of his hand, and the simple, light delicacy of the technique matches exactly the vivacity of the subject. It is the Minoan sense of immediate life and the Minoan skill in catching it that strike us as novel in the ancient world and prophetic of great changes in man's outlook on nature.

POTTERY

The Minoan feeling for the dynamics of living nature, revealed in their figurative fresco art, is no less visible in their pottery, among the finest in history. In the Kamares ware this interest in animate nature does not at once appear; the taste is for abstract spiral forms, scrolls, whorls, and the like. As time went on, the tendency toward naturalism in decoration increased. Motifs were derived from sea life, such as dolphins, seaweed, and octopuses. The tentacles reaching out over the curving surfaces of the *Octopus Jar* from Gournia (FIG. 4-12) embrace the piece and emphasize its elastic volume. This is a masterful realization of the relation between the decoration of the vessel and its shape, always a problem for the ceramist. From the Kamares silhouetting of light abstract forms upon a dark ground, we go, in the *Octopus Jar*, to a silhouetting of dark naturalistic forms upon a light ground. This manner lasts from about 1600 to 1500 B.C., when the fluid, open, and lively naturalistic style becomes increasingly stiff and abstract. This late style can be seen in a three-handled jar of about 1425 B.C. from Knossos (FIG. 4-13). The stalks of its papyrus decoration grow symmetrically, and the flowers turn into stylized scrolls and fans, symmetrically balanced. Wavy bands, simple concentric circles with crosses, and other rudimentary space-fillers occupy the surface rather than adjust to it and embrace it. Such devolution from naturalism to formalism and abstraction can be observed frequently in the history of world art.

An increasing self-awareness, which we have watched slowly evolving in ancient art, requires that man represent himself ever more as he is, in more conditions and situations, with fewer restrictions imposed by tradition. The *Harvester Vase* (FIGS. 4-14 and 4-15), made of steatite (soapstone), gives a sharp new glimpse of man as he is in his usual physical context. The egg-shaped rhyton, its lower half missing, shows a riotous crowd of olive-harvesters, singing and shouting. Their forward movement and lusty exuberance are most vividly expressed. The pattern of pitchforks fills the upper part of the band, while the figures below, in higher relief, create a variation in surface. The entire design, like the octopus of the Gournia vase, hugs the shape so tightly that it seems to be an integral part of the wall of the vase. But the figures themselves are depicted with a gusto that matches their mood. They are led by a man who carries a *sistrum*, or rattle, and beats time, while his lungs are so inflated with air that his ribs show. The harvesters' facial expressions are rendered with astonishing exactitude; there are degrees of hilarity and degrees of vocal effort, all marked in the tension or relaxation of facial muscles.

4-12 *The Octopus Jar* (amphora), Gournia, *c.* 1600 B.C. Approx. 8″ high. Archeological Museum, Herakleion.

4-13 Right: Three-handled jar with papyrus decoration, Knossos, *c.* 1500 B.C. Approx. 53″ high. Archeological Museum, Herakleion.

This reading of the human face as a vehicle of emotional states is without precedent in ancient art before the Minoans.

SCULPTURE

There is little sculpture in the round in Minoan art, and what there is is diminutive; there is no monumental sculpture of gods, kings, and monsters, such as we find in Mesopotamia and Egypt —at least, none has been found. This absence of large-scale sculpture may reflect an absence of a systematic and formal religion—though this is entirely speculation because of our ignorance of Minoan religion. The small figures of "snake goddesses" like the one shown from Knossos (FIG. 4-16) are hardly more than of talisman or fetish size. They exhibit most of the rigid conventions, including the frontal pose, that we have met in Egypt and Mesopotamia, but their snake-entwined arms have been released from the core of the block and are held forward or aloft. Thus, they are shown to be active and, somehow, seem more alive than their Near-Eastern or Egyptian cousins. The Cretans seem to have worshiped a mother goddess sacred to many places and manifest in many forms. Whether or not these miniature figures brandishing snakes are images of her is not certain, but they are clearly identified as Minoan by their costume—the open bodice and flounced skirt worn by Minoan women as we find them depicted many times over. This touch of the real may be another example of man fashioning his gods in his own image.

The circumstances under which the Minoan civilization came to an end are still hotly disputed. One theory, which seems to be gaining adherents, has it that the Cretan palaces were destroyed around 1450 B.C. as the result of a cataclysmic volcanic eruption on the island of Thera, which lies some eighty miles north of Crete. The seismic catastrophe may have caused such a loss of population that the Mycenaeans could move into the island and establish themselves at Knossos without meeting major resistance. From the repaired palace at Knossos they seem to have ruled the island for at least half a century, perhaps much longer. Parts of the palace continued to be occupied until its final destruction around 1200 B.C., this time by the Dorians, but its importance as a cultural center faded soon after 1400, as the focus of Aegean civilization shifted to the Greek mainland.

4-14 *The Harvester Vase* (rhyton), Hagia Triada, *c.* 1500 B.C. Steatite, approx. 5″ wide. Archeological Museum, Herakleion. (Lower part is lost.)

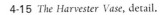

4-15 *The Harvester Vase*, detail.

← to c. 2800 B.C.	c. **2000**	c. 1700	c. **1550**	c. 1500	c. 1450	c. 1300	c. 1100 B.C.

EARLY MINOAN (PRE–PALACE) PERIOD | MIDDLE MINOAN PERIOD — Destruction of Old Palaces | LATE MINOAN PERIOD — Toreador Fresco | Lion Gate

←— OLD PALACES —→ Kamares Style ←— NEW PALACES —→ ←————— MYCENAEAN PERIOD —————→

MYCENAEAN ART

Just as the end of the Minoan, so the origins of Mycenaean culture are still being debated. The primitive Greeks may have moved into the mainland about the time the old palaces were being built in Crete—that is, about the beginning of the second millennium B.C. Doubtless they were influenced by Crete even then, and some believe that for a long time the mainland was a Minoan colony, though the mainlanders developed and held to many cultural features of their own. At any rate, Mycenaean power rose on the mainland in the palmy days of the new palaces on Crete, and by 1500 B.C. a new and splendid culture was flourishing in Greece to which, 700 years later, Homer was to give the epithet "rich in gold." It is possible that the Mycenaeans made close contact in this new era not only with Crete but with Egypt, with which they may have been allied against the Hittites in the early part of the New Kingdom; and the Mycenaeans' taste for gold, as well as their actual treasure, may have been acquired in the mercenary service of Egypt, which was known in the ancient world for its lavish use of the metal. Thus, the awakening of the Mycenaean world may have been the consequence of a kind of three-way route of influence connecting the mainland, Crete, and Egypt. The destruction of the Cretan palaces left the Mycenaean (mainland) culture supreme, but new waves of migrating proto-Greek peoples, the Dorians, finally submerged the Mycenaean civilization. The steady infiltration of these peoples had already made a fortress architecture necessary (unlike the case in Crete) and by about 1200 B.C. the fortified citadels of the mainland were overwhelmed by the invaders. The heroes and battles of these last centuries of Aegean civilization must have provided the tradition that, hundreds of years later, Homer would

immortalize in the first great European epics, the *Iliad* and the *Odyssey*.

Though Mycenae appears to have been the cultural center of the mainland development, the remains of other large palaces have been found at Vaphio, Pylos, Orchomenos, Arne, and (most recently) at Iolkos. The best preserved and most impressive Mycenaean remains are those of the fortified palaces at Tiryns and Mycenae, both built at the beginning of the Late Mycenaean period, about 1400 B.C., and razed (along with the others) between 1250 and 1200 B.C.

4-16 *Snake Goddess*, Knossos, c. 1600 B.C. Faïence, approx. 13½″ high. Archeological Museum, Herakleion.

REFUGE (?)

APPROACH
RAMP

MAIN
GATE

MEGARON

OUTER
PROPYLON

N

Existing
Reconstruction

FEET
0   50   100

4-17 Plan of the Citadel of Tiryns, *c.* 1400–1200 B.C.

4-18 Plan of the megaron, Tiryns.

Architecture

The Citadel of Tiryns (FIG. 4-17), only ten miles from Mycenae, so that at times they may have been under the same lord, was known by Homer as Tiryns of the Great Walls and by the ancient world as the birthplace of Herakles, the mythic hero of great strength. The ancient sightseer and guidebook-writer, Pausanias, thought the walls of Tiryns quite as spectacular as the pyramids of Egypt. The heavy walls are in sharp contrast with the "open" Cretan palaces and clearly reveal their defensive character. The buildings within the twenty-foot-thick walls are aligned axially and seem to have been laid out according to a predetermined plan. Unlike the rambling and often confusing layout of the Cretan palaces, the Mycenaean plan is an example of a clear and simple arrangement of the units. The megaron (FIG. 4-18), the three-chambered structure at the heart of the design and the center of the life of the citadel, embodies the germ of the classical temples of Greece. This fundamental building type does not appear in the palaces of Crete but does appear, surprisingly, at Troy as early as 2000 B.C. A hall of state, the megaron was rectangular, with a central hearth and four columns supporting the roof.

The massive fortification walls at Tiryns and other Mycenaean sites, built of unhewn or

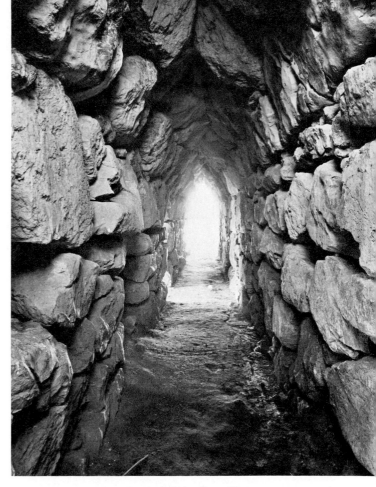

4-19 Corbeled gallery, Tiryns.

roughly dressed stone, were called cyclopean by later Greeks, who imagined them to have been built by that mythical race of giants. Through the walls at intervals run corbeled galleries (FIG. 4-19), which may have been used as part of the defensive structure or as part of a complicated and dramatic ceremonial path leading, through a porch and vestibule, to the chief room of the palace—the megaron. The corbeled gallery pictured makes use, as its name indicates, of the primitive corbeled arch. The rough appearance of these cyclopean structures is most impressive in its crude monumentality; it possesses an earthy dynamism not found in other, more sophisticated ancient architectural styles.

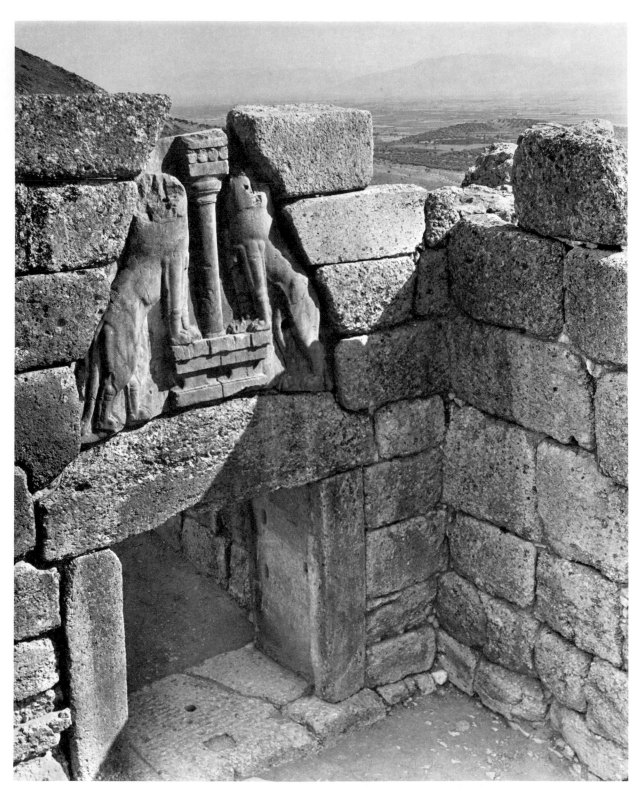

4-20 The Lion Gate, Mycenae, *c.* 1300 B.C. Limestone relief panel, approx. 9½′ high.

The Art of the Aegean

4-21 Plan and sections of the Treasury of Atreus, Mycenae, *c.* 1300 B.C.

THOLOS

DROMOS

FEET
0 10 20 30 40

The sternness of these fortress-palaces was relieved by frescoes, by carvings, and, at Mycenae at least, by monumental architectural sculpture—the Lion Gate (FIG. 4-20). This outer gateway of the stronghold, protected on the left by a wall and on the right by a projecting bastion, is formed of two great monoliths capped with a huge lintel above which the layers of stone form a corbeled arch, leaving a triangular opening that serves to lighten the weight to be carried by the lintel. The arched space is filled with a slab on which two lions carved in high relief confront each other on either side of a column of the probably sacred Minoan type, resting their forepaws on its base. (This column of the Lion Gate supplies evidence of what the vanished wooden Minoan columns looked like.) Holes near the top of the animals indicate that the heads, now lost, were made of separate pieces of stone or metal. The lions are carved with breadth and vigor, and the

whole design admirably fills its triangular space, harmonizing in dignity, strength, and scale with the massive stones that form the walls and gate. We find similar groups in miniature on Cretan seals, and one senses that these lions are not too distant from Mesopotamian heraldic composition.

Within the gate and to the right lies the grave circle, an enclosure containing a number of simple shaft graves, stone-lined pits serving as tombs for kings and their families, covered and marked by a stele. Another similar grave circle was recently discovered outside the walls of Mycenae. Both grave circles date from about 1600–1500 B.C. But at this time shaft graves were gradually being replaced by the so-called beehive tombs, of which the best preserved is the remarkable Treasury of Atreus (FIGS. 4-21 and 4-22), misnamed that by Schliemann, who thought it—the most imposing of a group—to be the storehouse for the treasure of Atreus,

4-22 Interior of the tholos, Treasury of Atreus Vault approx. 45' high.

father of Agamemnon and Menelaus. Built into a hill and approached by a long passage, or *dromos*, the beehive shape of the round tomb chamber, or *tholos*, was achieved by use of corbeled courses of stone laid on a circular base, splendidly fitted to the curve of the wall, and ending in a lofty dome, which in this fine example is about forty feet high. This was the largest vaulted structure without interior supports in all antiquity until the Roman Pantheon was built 1500 years later.

Pottery, Relief, and Craft Art

Most of the beehive tombs had been thoroughly looted long before their modern rediscovery. On the other hand, rich finds were made in shaft graves at Mycenae. Some bronze daggers, inlaid with gold and silver, found in these graves

reveal the influence of the Minoan figure style (PLATE 4-2). On the longest of the three blades illustrated, three hunters with spears, bows, and shields attack a lion that has struck down a fourth hunter, while two other lions flee. The subject is of Mesopotamian derivation, but the costumes are Cretan, and the vigorous, spirited movements of the hunters, the lithe strength and spring of the lions, are of the Minoan taste.

Beaten gold (*repoussé*) masks were found in the shaft graves, attached to the faces of the mummified Mycenaean princes (FIG. 4-23). Powerfully realistic in their record of the features of the deceased, they also testify to the influx of gold from Egypt. This and the elaboration of funeral practices lend strong support to the supposition that the impulse that started this high phase of Mycenaean civilization originated partly in Egypt, partly in Crete.

The golden culture of Mycenae produced such masterpieces as the famous cups from Vaphio (FIG. 4-24). Found in a beehive tomb, these beautiful vessels are still the subject of warm debate among experts who see them as originating in Crete and those who insist that, despite their undoubted resemblance to Minoan figure style, they are Mycenaean. The cups are a pair, each made of two plates of gold, one of which was worked in *repoussé* for the outside, the other left plain to make a smooth surface for the inside.

4-23 Funeral mask from the royal tombs of Mycenae, *c.* 1500 B.C. Beaten gold, approx. 12" high. National Museum, Athens.

4-24 *The Vaphio Cups,* c. 1500 B.C. Gold with *repoussé* decoration, approx. 3½″ high. National Museum, Athens.

The plates were fastened together, the handles riveted on, and some of the details then engraved. The subject seems to be Minoan (the men are costumed in the Minoan manner) and related to the bull-leaping ritual; bulls are being trapped and snared, with a cow used as a lure in one case. One cup shows a bull caught in a net. A second bull, charging furiously, impales with its horns a man whose companion falls to one side. A third bull dashes madly from the fracas. The other cup presents a quieter scene. At the right the bull moves toward the cow; in the center he stands beside her; at the left, captured and hobbled, he is bellowing. The three scenes are integrated by the trees and the man, and the whole design is admirably composed to fit the space. In both cups, areas not filled by the animal and human figures contain landscape motifs of trees, rocks, and clouds similar to those in painting. The shallowness of the relief and the conventional treatment of the trees produce a rich play of light and shade together with a variety of textures.

The *Warrior Vase* (FIG. 4-25) represents a file of Mycenaean soldiers strikingly different in costume, physiognomy, and beards from the Cretan types we have seen in Minoan art. This would seem to strengthen the argument of those who regard the Mycenaeans as being of entirely different racial stock from the Minoans and as the indigenous builders of their own civilization. It may be, too, that we are looking here at the last Mycenaean warriors who marched forth to meet the Dorian invaders, under whose onslaught the Mycenaean civilization collapsed after 1200 B.C. The Dorians carried iron weapons, superior to the softer bronze of the Mycenaeans, and their success illustrates the historical commonplace that a superior technology can overcome an otherwise more highly developed civilization. The centuries-long "dark age" that followed the obliteration of Aegean culture, though little survives from it, cannot be considered merely a historical void. New energies were gathering that would form one of the greatest civilizations the world has known, a civilization new, bold, self-confident, and "modern."

4-25 *The Warrior Vase,* Mycenae, c. 1200 B.C. Approx. 14″ high. National Museum, Athens.

Chapter Five

The Art of Greece

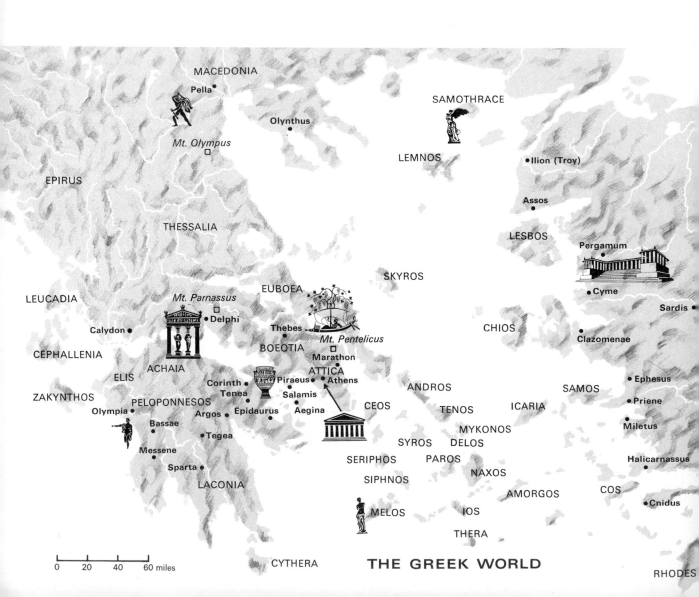

MACEDONIA

Pella•

SAMOTHRACE

Olynthus•

□ *Mt. Olympus*

LEMNOS

•Ilion (Troy)

EPIRUS

•Assos

THESSALIA

LESBOS

Pergamum

SKYROS

•Cyme

Sardis•

LEUCADIA

EUBOEA

Mt. Parnassus □

CHIOS

Calydon•

•Delphi

Thebes•

Clazomenae•

CEPHALLENIA

Mt. Pentelicus

BOEOTIA

•Ephesus

ELIS

ACHAIA

Corinth•

Marathon

ATTICA

ANDROS

SAMOS

ZAKYNTHOS

PELOPONNESOS

Tenea•

Piraeus•

•Athens

•Priene

Olympia•

Salamis•

CEOS

TENOS

ICARIA

Miletus•

Argos•

Epidaurus•

Aegina•

Bassae

MYKONOS

Tegea•

SYROS

DELOS

Messene

PAROS

Halicarnassus•

Sparta•

SERIPHOS

NAXOS

LACONIA

SIPHNOS

AMORGOS

COS

IOS

•Cnidus

MELOS

CYTHERA

THE GREEK WORLD

THERA

RHODES

0   20   40   60 miles

"FOR WE ARE LOVERS of the beautiful, yet with simplicity, and we cultivate the mind without loss of manliness. . . . We are the school of Greece." In the fifth century B.C., the Golden Age of Athens, Thucydides has Pericles make this assertion in praise of the Athenians, comparing their open, democratic society with the closed, barracks state of their rivals, the Spartans. But he might be speaking in general of Greek culture as we have received it and of the ideal of humanistic education and life created by that culture. In the "humanistic" view, man is what matters, and he is, in the words of Protagoras, the "measure of all things."

For the Greeks, what sets man apart is his intelligence, and human intelligence, trained in reasoning, is the highest function nature has created. Moreover, Aristotle assures us that "all men by nature desire to know." And what we know is the order of nature, which is one with the order of human reason.

The order of both nature and reason, said the Greeks, is beautiful and simple, and the beauty of things is one with our knowledge of them;

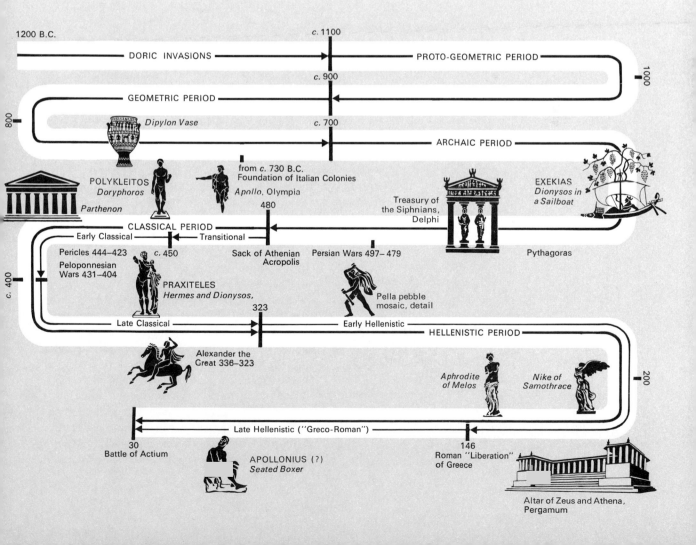

1200 B.C.
c. 1100
DORIC INVASIONS PROTO-GEOMETRIC PERIOD
1000
c. 900
GEOMETRIC PERIOD
800
Dipylon Vase *c.* 700
ARCHAIC PERIOD

POLYKLEITOS *Doryphoros*
from *c.* 730 B.C. Foundation of Italian Colonies
Apollo, Olympia
EXEKIAS *Dionysos in a Sailboat*
Parthenon
Treasury of the Siphnians, Delphi
480
CLASSICAL PERIOD
Early Classical Transitional
Pericles 444–423 *c.* 450 Sack of Athenian Acropolis Persian Wars 497– 479 Pythagoras
Peloponnesian Wars 431–404
c. 400
PRAXITELES *Hermes and Dionysos,*
Pella pebble mosaic, detail
323
Late Classical Early Hellenistic
HELLENISTIC PERIOD
Alexander the Great 336–323
Aphrodite of Melos *Nike of Samothrace*
200
Late Hellenistic ("Greco-Roman")
30 Battle of Actium
APOLLONIUS (?) *Seated Boxer*
146 Roman "Liberation" of Greece
Altar of Zeus and Athena, Pergamum

thus, the good life, the achievement of the "beautiful soul," follows upon compliance with that typically Greek command, "Know thyself!" One achieves the good life, then, through an intellectual process; one lives "according to nature"—that is, according to the natural laws of life discoverable by rational man. The self now becomes of first importance, and as man comes to full self-awareness he necessarily becomes aware of nature as well.

Man is regarded as the highest creation of and value in nature, and it was the Greeks who created democracy as well as the natural image of man in art. The late great scholar of Classical Greece, Werner Jaeger, wrote of their exaltation of man: "As against the Oriental exaltation of one God-king . . . and the . . . suppression of the great mass of the people . . . the beginning of Greek history appears to be the beginning of a new conception of the individual . . . . the history of personality in Europe must start with them [the Greeks]."[1]

This honoring of the individual—and through the individual, the laws of human nature—is so completely part of our habit of mind that we are scarcely aware of it and of its origin in the minds of the Greeks.

From the Paleolithic age we have been surveying man in a world dominated by the great beasts—threatened by them, fighting them, dependent upon them (or their embodiment), worshiping them, conceding their might and his own weakness. Now, in Greece, he asserts that his own peculiar power—the power of intelligence—puts him far above the beasts. But the Greek mind is not dryly or pallidly rationalistic; it knows well the forces of the irrational against which reason must struggle constantly. In fact, Greek art constitutes with Greek culture a compact synthesis of opposites, a harmony between profound passion and rational order. Its clarity and symmetry are not cold but blazing; its forms can be rigorous and mathematical, yet full of life.

In marked contrast to Egypt, with its long horizontals of alluvial plain between desert plateaus and seemingly invariable sunshine, Greece is a country of diversified geography and climate. The bays of its deeply indented, rugged

coastline make the country half land and half sea; mountain ridges divide it into many small units. The climate is vigorous—cold in the winter, dry and hot in the summer. There is almost always a breeze from the sea. The unusually clear, almost crystalline atmosphere is often softened by a haze. Both sky and sea are brilliant in color. It is little wonder that the Greeks, with their joy in nature, should people mountains, woods, streams, sky, and sea with divinities; that they should picture Zeus, the king of this realm of gods, as reigning from their loftiest peak, Olympus; the Muses as dwelling in the deep, cool groves on the long slopes of Parnassus and Cithaeron; and Apollo as speaking from the awe-inspiring rocky clefts of Delphi.

Nature worship evolved into personification. The gods assumed human forms whose grandeur and nobility were not free from human frailty; indeed, unlike the gods of Egypt and Mesopotamia, their only real difference from men was that they were immortal. There is a saying that the Greeks made their gods into men and their men into gods. Man, becoming the measure of all things, must become, if all things in their perfection are beautiful, the unchanging standard of the best; to create the perfect individual became the Greek ideal.

The Greeks, or Hellenes, as they called themselves, appear to have been the product of an intermingling of Aegean peoples and of Indo-European invaders. This intermingling may have been a vitalizing factor that should be considered, together with the climate and the strongly diversified mountain-valley terrain of the Greek peninsula, in hypothesizing the causes of the peculiarly high competitive and creative energy of the Greek peoples.

The first of the invaders began to drift into the area about 2000 B.C., and after 1600 B.C., as we have seen, they formed the Mycenaean civilization on the Greek peninsula. After about 1200 B.C. the Mycenaeans were apparently overwhelmed in turn by new invaders from the north—the Dorians and perhaps the Ionians. The Dorians made the Peloponnesos the center of their power and may have forced the Ionians eastward across the Aegean to the coast of Asia Minor. The origin of the Ionians is still a matter of dispute. Some scholars feel that proto-Ionians

[1] Werner Jaeger, *Paideia: The Ideals of Greek Culture* (New York: Oxford Univ. Press), Vol. I, p. xix.

lived at Athens during Mycenaean times and that they were displaced during the Doric invasions. Others hold that they developed on the coast of Asia Minor between the eleventh and eighth century B.C. out of a mixed stock of settlers. In either case, the Ionians seem to have been more individualistic than the tribally ordered Dorians, whose most characteristic city became conservative Sparta.

In Ionia, on the east coast of Asia Minor, epics of individual greatness had come to be celebrated by the eighth century B.C., and by the seventh century, the rational philosophers of Miletus had begun to interpret the world in terms of reason rather than religion, beginning that immense transformation of the worship of nature into the science of nature, the science that is still expanding today. Between Ionia and the Peloponnesos lay Attica, and there, in Athens, a conservative tribal order and individualistic striving combined to produce the most fruitful of all the *poleis*, or city-states, of Greece, the one that Thucydides could boast was the "school of Greece."

By the eighth century B.C. the separate Greek-speaking states had held their first ceremonial games in common: the Olympiad of 776 B.C., from which time the historical Greeks calculated their chronology. From then on, despite their chronic rivalries and wars, they regarded themselves as Hellenes, distinct from the surrounding "barbarians," who did not speak Greek. The enterprising Hellenes, greatly aided by their indented coasts and island stepping-stones, became a trading and a colonizing people who enlarged the geographic and cultural boundaries of Hellas. Tribal organizations had evolved into city-states, each an individual unit. Political development differed from state to state, but a kind of pattern emerged in which rule was first by kings, then by nobles, then by "tyrants" who seized personal power. At last, in Athens, appeared the dynamic balance that was called democracy.

Athens has in many ways become the symbol of Greek culture; many of the finest products of Greek civilization were created by Athenians or by men who were closely associated with Athens and its traditions. Athens, at the time of its brief flowering after the Persian Wars, was an active business city of about 100,000 people. Above its

olive groves and rooftops towered the Acropolis, or higher city, formerly a Mycenaean fortress but in this age crowned with temples rising in bright colors against an intensely blue sky. Under the covered colonnades (*stoas*) that surrounded the city's central marketplace (*agora*), the citizens congregated to discuss the latest political development or a new philosophical idea. Among the Athenians, philosophical argument was both a public and a private exercise that went on wherever a few disputants could be assembled. This love of intellectual contest, the vigorous forerunner of science itself, was astonishingly popular, and whether in the house of a rich man or in the marketplace, in the gymnasium, or on the street corner, such discussion was the key to the intense political and intellectual life that developed in the Greek city-state. Bodily exercise also played a large part in education and daily life, and the Athenian aim of a balance of intellectual and physical discipline, an ideal of humanistic education, is expressed in the Latin, *mens sana in corpore sano*, "a sound mind in a sound body."

The tragedies of Aeschylus and Sophocles, played before the eager citizens, presented the individual as having an obligation to the gods, and the rise and fall of his fortunes as a reflection of the contest between blind fate and the new-found power of reason.

The constants of Greek culture were man, nature, and reason, and the Greeks understood goodness to be the harmony of all three. Upon this elementary conviction, new to the world, they built their grand achievements in art, poetry, mathematics, philosophy, logic, history, and science—the heritage upon which the modern Western world was in turn constructed. In discovering man the Greeks discovered and confronted the problem of persistence and change; men pass away, but mankind remains. And although they aspired toward the timeless ideal, the Greeks recognized the changes that produce growth and development.

The remains of Greek civilization enable us to reconstruct the development of the Greek style in art. That the Greek style should in fact have "developed," is in itself significant. Development in the art of Egypt, for example, was minimal; the pattern of ritual and of form was not to be broken. Change in Egypt occurred, when it did, *despite* the pattern of the culture as a whole. Of course we must remember that an important factor in the sudden appearance of Greece on the summit of historical eminence was the base on which it rose—the civilizations of Egypt and the Near East, the quality and matter of which the Greeks quite honestly acknowledged borrowing. From these older civilizations they acquired ideas, motifs, conventions, and skills. But from the beginning, the Greeks embraced experiment, even while adopting and holding to the older forms. Development and change were inherent in Greek culture, as conservatism was in Egyptian, and change has recognizable forms, as in the recurring stages of human life from infancy to old age. Greek art displays much more readily discernible stages than the relatively unchanging art of the ancient Near East.

THE GEOMETRIC AND ARCHAIC PERIODS

Pottery serves, as no other artistic medium can, to link the very late Mycenaean (sub-Mycenaean) age with that of historical Greece. For one thing, it has survived. We can trace a continuity from the sub-Mycenaean period into the Classical fifth century B.C. entirely in terms of the figurative decoration of Greek ceramic ware, showing the artist's confrontation with radically new ideas and problems and his equally radical interpretations and solutions. It is appropriate, then, given this continuity and the Greek notion of the development of forms, to begin the study of Greek art with vase paintings that illuminate changes that were profoundly influential in human history and that take place in a curiously logical order. We have already seen numerous examples of how man represents himself, from the strange, falling stick-figure in the well at Lascaux to the agile Minoans of the Vaphio cups. Now we can review changes in the representation of the human body that are the result not of accidental differences of convention but of carefully accumulated increments of knowledge. These were firmed into a tradition of technical

procedure that did not backslide—as was the case in the Egyptian return to old forms after the death of the innovating Akhenaton (see Chapter Three). We can see in the Archaic Greek vases that man for the first time has become the subject of intense analytical study. As the philosopher questions man's nature and purpose, the artist begins to inquire how man looks to others of his kind in the world of optical experience. The old conceptual way of placing him and enumerating his features, which we have seen in the older civilizations, gradually is given up and is replaced by a method of painstaking observation of the pose and motion of the body in life. This did not happen all at once; centuries were involved in the great transformation, and the dated sequence of vases reveals the ordered phases of the change. It is useful to describe these changes at the outset, for, from its earliest appearances on vases, the human figure remains the principal motif of Greek art, as man is central to its thought and interest.

Vase Painting

An *amphora* (FIG. 5-1), a tall, two-handled jar for wine or oil, from about the tenth century B.C. shows us the formative phase of what is called the Geometric style. Though it borrows the decorative devices of the earlier sub-Mycenaean style, its execution is neater and more painstaking. As the Geometric style develops, the Minoan stock of curvilinear forms is gradually replaced by

5-1 Proto-Geometric amphora, Dipylon cemetery, tenth century B.C. Approx. 16½" high. Keramikos Museum, Athens.

126

5-2 *Dipylon Vase* (Geometric amphora), eighth century B.C. Approx. 4′ 11″ high. National Museum, Athens.

possibly of the same date as the Dipylon vase of FIG. 5-2 or somewhat later, shows a certain loss of refinement as the geometric ornament becomes secondary. The figures represent a funeral procession, with horse-drawn chariots occupied by warriors carrying shields; in the conceptual manner both wheels of each chariot are represented, the horses carefully distinguished, and their legs correct in number. The warriors are standing behind their shields, which are shown in front view. The number of represented figures has increased markedly over that of FIG. 5-2, suggesting that the artist was intrigued with the rediscovery of a subject—the human figure—that had been absent from mainland pottery decoration for over 400 years.

The Geometric period was succeeded by the Orientalizing phase of the Archaic period, a time of marked commercial and colonial expansion that brought the Greeks into closer contact with ancient Eastern civilizations. A consequence of these new relationships was the frequent appearance of Oriental animals and composite monsters on Greek vases, motifs familiar to us from Mesopotamian and Egyptian art: lions, sphinxes, griffins, and centaurs. Stylistically, a vase from Eleusis (FIG. 5-4), typical of the Orientalizing

rectilinear shapes arranged in tight bands that cover more and more of the vessel.

The human figure reappears in the decorative scheme in the period of the culminating Geometric style, specifically in the so-called *Dipylon Vase* (FIG. 5-2), from the eighth century B.C. and named after the Dipylon cemetery in Athens, where it was found. The figures are hardly more than symbols, fashioned of diamond and wedge shapes that fit the severe, regular, geometric characteristics of the banded shapes. The extremely abstract figures are arranged on the shoulders of the vessel, toward which the design builds up from below, the decorative bands generally wider the higher their placement on the body of the vase.

Another type of Greek vase, the *krater*, had a larger body and wider mouth than the amphora. A krater from the Dipylon cemetery (FIG. 5-3),

5-3 Geometric Dipylon krater (with prothesis), Dipylon cemetery, eighth century B.C. Approx. 40½″ high. Metropolitan Museum of Art, New York (Rogers Fund).

5-4 *The Blinding of Polyphemos* and *Gorgons* (proto-Attic amphora), Eleusis, *c.* 675–650 B.C. Approx. 56″ high. Museum, Eleusis.

phase, represents a complete and radical break with the orderly Geometric manner. The figurative decor occupies most of the vessel; the arrangement of the motifs is loose, almost casual, and the shapes are mostly curvilinear. It is almost as if the artist were intentionally throwing off the Geometric strait jacket as an awkward restraint upon a new interest—the representation of narrative scenes, some from Homeric legend. On the amphora in FIG. 5-4 where Polyphemos, the one-eyed giant, is being blinded by Odysseus, the human figure—resembling those of the Geometric period, but much more filled out, rounded, and active—now occupies the largest

areas of the vessel, and the ornament retreats to the smaller areas in the neck, shoulder, and base. It was in the Geometric period that the Homeric themes were collected in the great epics; the Orientalizing phase marks their diffusion and their achievement of universal popularity in Greece. The illustration of the epics will occupy the surfaces of vases for centuries to come; it might almost seem that this first great reflection of man and his actions, in Greek epic, launched the enterprise of representing him in art.

During the Geometric and Archaic periods, numerous pottery centers developed throughout the Aegean world. They have been divided into two main groups—those of the mainland and those of eastern Greece (the regions east of the mainland). On the mainland the most important centers were Athens in Attica and Corinth in the Peloponnesos, and after 550 B.C. Athens became the principal ceramic center and the largest exporter of vases in the Mediterranean basin. In this brief survey we shall confine ourselves to Athenian wares.

The number of basic Attic vase shapes was limited to six or seven, each subject to four or five variations. The shapes developed out of specific usages and were entirely functional (FIG. 5-5).

The *François Vase* (FIG. 5-6), which was named after its discoverer and is perhaps the finest existent example of an early Archaic krater, with its volute handles and extraordinarily vigorous shape, was found in an Etruscan necropolis. (We are indebted to the Etruscans for their avid collecting of Greek vases, as many of the best-preserved have been found in Etruscan tombs.) It is especially important, not only for its high quality but for the fact that it is signed by both

5-5 Greek vase shapes: (a) the *hydria* (from the Greek for "water"), a water jar with three handles, two for lifting and one for carrying; (b) the *lekythos*, an oil flask with a long narrow neck adapted for pouring oil slowly, used chiefly in funeral rites; (c) the *krater* (from the Greek "to mix"), a bowl for mixing wine and water, the usual beverage of the Greeks; (d) the *amphora* (meaning "to carry on both sides," referring to the two handles), a vessel for storing provisions (wine, corn, oil, honey), with an opening large enough to admit a ladle and usually fitted with a cover; (e) the *kylix* (from the Greek "to roll," referring to the vases' being turned on the potter's wheel), chief form of the drinking cup; (f) the *oenochoe* (from the Greek "to pour out wine"), a wine jug, the lip pinched into a trefoil shape to facilitate pouring.

the potter ("Ergotimos epoiesen") and the painter ("Kleitias egraphsen"). Signed vases appear for the first time in the early seventh century B.C. and suggest that their makers had pride in their profession and that their art had at least as much prestige, say, as that of the sculptor or wall painter.

The *François Vase* is ornamented with over 200 figures distributed in bands around the vessel. Representing almost the entire Greek pantheon, the figures provide us with one of our first pictorial glimpses of the forms and personages of Greek religion: The subject is the wedding of Peleus, with the gods in attendance. In addition to the scene of the gods and Peleus, father of Achilles, are depictions of the Calydonian boar hunt and the funeral games for Patroklos. On the foot of the vase is an account of an animated battle between cranes and pygmies, above which rays felicitously augment the swelling surface of the krater. The lively scenes are rigidly organized in six bands of varying widths, the widest placed on the vessel's shoulders, a return to the discipline and formality of the Geometric style after the casual and permissive Orientalizing style of the vase from Eleusis (FIG. 5-4).

The François Vase is decorated in an early form of the so-called *black-figure* technique, which is shown fully developed and at its best in a *kylix* (drinking cup) by the potter-painter EXEKIAS (FIG. 5-7). Dark figures are silhouetted against the light background of the natural reddish clay. Details are incised into the silhouettes with a sharp, pointed instrument to expose the red beneath; touches of white and purple, particularly on the earlier wares, add color to the dominantly monochrome decoration. Although the black areas are customarily referred to as glazes, it should be pointed out that the black on these Greek pots is neither a pigment nor a glaze but *engobe*, a slip of finely sifted clay that originally is of the same color as the clay of the pot. In the three-phase firing process used by Greek potters, the first (oxidizing) phase turns both pot and slip red; during the second (reducing) phase the oxygen supply into the kiln is shut off and both pot and slip turn black; in the final (reoxidizing) phase the coarser material of the pot reabsorbs oxygen and becomes red again, while the smooth-

5-6 *The François Vase* (Attic black-figure krater), Chiusi, *c.* 575 B.C. Approx. 26″ high. Museo Archeologico, Florence.

er, silica-laden slip does not and remains black. After long experiment, Greek potters developed a velvety, jet-black "glaze" of this kind. The touches of white and purple were used more sparingly, with the result that the figures stood in even stronger contrast against their reddish

5-7 EXEKIAS, *Dionysos in a Sailboat*, interior of an Attic black-figure kylix, Vulci, *c.* 550–525 B.C. 12″ in diameter. Staatliche Antikensammlungen, Munich.

129

backgrounds. This superb formal control provides the framework for a wealth of naturalistic detail, some of it strikingly novel.

Exekias' kylix, with a representation of Dionysos sailing over the sea carrying his gifts to mankind and accompanied by sporting dolphins, his boat's mast entwined by a joyful grapevine, introduces a still more spectacular innovation, one that heralds the beginning of a revolution in world art. In his drawing of the boat's sail, Exekias does not show a traditional and conventional symbol that "reads" as a "sail" but a sail as a sail would actually look, bellying out and filled with wind. It is an image of the action of wind itself, the wind made palpable as a force, and it must have come from a new awareness of the *physical* presence of nature. This awareness was abroad; it is in the Ionian speculations about the physical constitution of the world, and in the reality-charged poetry of Homer: "But soon an off-shore breeze blew to our liking— a canvas-bellying breeze.... The bows went plunging ... sails cracked and lashed out ...."

Though in Homer the gods are still the manipulators of the elements, it is men who feel their effects, who hear the howl of the great winds, smell the brine, and feel the harsh ropes and drenching rain. Man's experience of the world, as well as the world itself, begins to be understood by him in physical terms. Such a profound change in man's awareness of his relation to nature and, in consequence, of his own nature, is one that is bound to make itself felt in art. From Exekias' sail on, Greek art will manifest an increasing comprehension of physical nature as it is apprehended by vision.

Exekias' skill and subtlety also solve to perfection a difficult compositional problem: how to fix the ship within its circular frame. Part of his solution lies in the down-branching weight of the loaded vines, part in the reverse hooklike dolphins, which seem to stitch the composition to its frame.

Around 530 B.C. a new painting technique was invented that reversed the black-figure style by making the background black and leaving the figures reserved in red. The figures of men and animals no longer are dark and earthy, massive against a light ground, but instead are luminous, like light and air, shining forth from the black background. In this new *red-figure* technique the

major interior markings were rendered with relief lines applied with a syringelike instrument that squeezed out the black "glaze" matter evenly and smoothly. Secondary markings, such as those representing hair, muscles, and sometimes even shading, were painted in "dilute glaze" (engobe diluted with water), which could be applied with a fine brush. The style is freer and more facile than the earlier black-figure style, which it largely replaced within twenty years. The artist felt no need to enlarge his limited color scheme, for the polished coppery red against a velvety black created an effect that was rich and of reserved elegance. The artist usually credited with the invention of the red-figure technique is the ANDOKIDES PAINTER, who is named for the potter Andokides, several of whose signed vases he decorated. Sometimes called a student of Exekias, the Andokides Painter uses pictorial devices that are rooted in the style of the older master. On an amphora that shows Herakles and and Apollo struggling for the tripod (FIG. 5-8) he shows an interest in rich drapery ornaments and textural effects such as are found in the work of his presumed master. His work lacks some of the warmth and sympathy of Exekias' as he is more concerned with exploiting the possi-

5-8 ANDOKIDES PAINTER, *Herakles and Apollo Struggling for the Tripod*, detail from amphora, *c.* 350 B.C. Outline drawing at right indicates relation to whole vessel. Portion shown approx. 11″ high; whole vessel approx. 23″ high.

bilities of his newly discovered technique. And there he breaks new ground, experimenting with novel and varied effects of color (he liked to use both purple and white) and, in a technique that dispenses with the laborious process of incision, creating new decorative schemes of great elegance.

A krater painted by EUPHRONIOS, one of the most forceful red-figure painters working near the end of the sixth century B.C., shows Herakles strangling the giant Antaios (FIG. 5-9). Euphronios was among the first to devote himself seriously to the study of anatomy and was famous for this in his time. Here he shows two male figures in a complicated wrestling pose, one figure from the side, the other from the front. He attempts such radical experiments as the doubled-under leg of Antaios and the rendering of Antaios' face in white to suggest the pallor of impending death. He makes an effort to describe Herakles' and Antaios' straining, powerful bodies with pains-taking attention to the musculature, and though he does not entirely succeed in producing a correct representation, his attempt to apply knowledge gained through observation of bodily action is most significant.

EUTHYMIDES was a contemporary and competi-tor of Euphronios and, like him, an experimenter. As we can see from his picture of revelers done on an amphora (FIG. 5-10), Euthymides is less con-cerned with anatomical description than with the problems of foreshortening in the figures and of showing them from different viewpoints. The fairly tipsy dancers, mightily enjoying them-selves, are a rather popular subject on late Ar-chaic and early Classical vases, and celebrate the Hellenic sense of the comic that served as counter-poise to its genius for tragic art in the drama. In this case it gives Euthymides an opportunity to present the figures in informal motion and in fairly successful three-quarter back and front views. The turning and twisting of the figures indicate that the artist is beginning to think of them as three-dimensional volumes that have free mobility in a space deeper than the flat, two-dimensional surface of the picture plane—a significant departure from pre-Greek tradition. The maturing self-consciousness of the Greeks is shown not only in their concern for the figures of man but also, of course, in their consciousness of themselves as artists. They sign their names to their work and they are aware that they are doing new and revolutionary things as collaborators and rivals in a common professional enterprise. Euthymides, in an inscription on this amphora

5-9 EUPHRONIOS, *Herakles Strangling Antaios*, detail from krater, Cerveteri, *c.* 510–500 B.C. Outline drawing at right indicates relation to whole vessel. Portion shown approx. 12″ high; whole vessel approx. 19″ high.

5-10 EUTHYMIDES, *Revelers*, detail from amphora, Vulci, *c.* 510–500 B.C. Outline drawing at right indicates relation to whole vessel. Portion shown approx. 12″ high; whole vessel approx. 24″ high.

(FIG. 5-10), proclaims with naive pride: "Euphronios never did anything like it."

As revolutionary as Euphronios and Euthymides had been, the BRYGOS PAINTER (an anonymous artist who is named after the potter whose vases he decorated) takes a significant step beyond them, around the year 490 B.C. Again the revelers theme, with its gaily swinging movement, gives the experimenting artist his opportunity (FIG. 5-11). For some 2500 years, since the *Palette of Narmer* (FIG. 3-2), painted figures and figures in relief had advanced the *far* leg to show a stride—which, after all, is the best way if the torso is to be shown in front view with minimum distortion of the figure. Euthymides had broken this rule, advancing the near leg of a figure to show it in a three-quarter rear view (FIG. 5-10). But the Brygos Painter, for the first time, presents a striding figure with the near leg advanced and its shoulder turned diagonally toward the observer. (See the two central figures.) The result is the first true *contrapposto* stance in the history of painting. The figure is now understood as an acting unit, not merely an assemblage of parts; the problem of its engineering has been solved to the extent that it can be represented in convincing movement. This may at first seem to be a small matter, but an apparently superficial detail may be the manifestation of an epoch-making change in the concept of what human beings perceive.

5-11 BRYGOS PAINTER, *Revelers*, detail from kylix, Vulci, *c.* 490 B.C. Outline drawing at right indicates relation to whole vessel. Portion shown approx. 10″ wide; whole vessel approx. 13″ wide. Martin V. Wagner Museen der Universität, Wurzburg.

Sculpture

Trends in the development of sculpture in Greece are just as visible and describable as those we have traced in vase painting, though much less sculpture survives. The earliest pieces go back to the beginning of the ninth century B.C. and consist of small-scale representations of animals (horses, oxen, deer, birds) and of human figures in various materials: copper, bronze, lead, ivory, and terra-cotta. Some of these were ornaments on larger objects like vases and bronze tripods; others were separate votive offerings that have been found near ancient sanctuaries. At Olympia they seem to have been manufactured on the spot for sale to visitors to the shrines.

A bronze warrior from the Acropolis of Athens, from the late eighth century B.C. (FIG. 5-12), shows all the clear simplifications of the Geometric period. The figure, a favorite type in Geometric art, is solid cast. (Given the figure's diminutive size, this would be the reasonable casting method, as hollow casting, which was understood, would not have saved much bronze.) The warrior originally held a spear in one raised arm, and a shield in the other, though both shield and spear are missing in most surviving examples. The rather carefully rendered head and face, with the large eyes and broad grimace, later to become known as the standard "Archaic smile," attest to the fact that this figure is a late specimen of a type whose earlier examples had heads and faces that were little more than shapeless lumps. Moreover, the body forms have become smoother, losing some of their former angularity, as if the artist were trying to rid himself of centuries-old conventions of Geometric figure representation before the new approach—the visual one—could be tried. It is believed that these warrior statuettes were Syrian in inspiration, but a difference important in the evolution of Greek sculpture should be noted: The Greek figures are represented nude, while the Syrian prototypes wear loincloths. As early as this, the Greek instinct for the natural beauty of the human figure, which peculiarly and permanently distinguishes Greek art, is set in contrast with the Near Eastern traditional prejudice against the representation of the nude in sculpture in the round.

5-12 Geometric bronze warrior, front and back views, Acropolis, Athens, late eighth century B.C. Bronze, approx. 8″ high. National Museum, Athens.

Kouros and Kore

A bronze figure of a youth from around 680 B.C. (FIG. 5-13) stands at the beginning of the Archaic period; it is a small forerunner of the later *Kouros* figures (see FIGS. 5-15 and 5-16). The silhouette remains essentially geometric, with a triangular torso, a narrow waist, and bulging thighs; but the forms have gained volume, and the modeling of the pectoral muscles and the description of other anatomical details by means of incised lines show an incipient interest in the structure of the body.

Monumental, freestanding sculpture (life-size or larger) first appeared about 600 B.C., in the earlier stages of the Archaic period. Its rise is contemporary with the Orientalizing phase in vase painting and was probably inspired by foreign sources, most likely Egypt and Mesopotamia, which were in fact the only areas at that time that could show monumental sculpture in abundance. An early example of this monumental, free-standing sculpture is the *Hera of Samos* (FIG. 5-14), which is over six feet tall and has a cylindrical shape that could have been derived only from Mesopotamia (compare FIGS. 2-18 and 2-19). The goddess stands in a frontal pose, feet together, the right arm held tightly to the side, the left bent to the breast and probably originally holding some attribute, or symbol, of authority. She is the goddess as a sheathed column (in origin a tree?), as were the deities of Crete and Mycenae, but here the Greek artist displays his extraordinary sensitivity for surface ornamentation. The stability of the lower portions—where the striations of the *chiton*, or tunic, are placed against the plain surface of the *himation*, a kind of cape—contrasts with the movement in the upper portions, where the himation is drawn in gracefully curving folds around the delicate modeling of the swelling bosom.

We are reminded of Egyptian statues by the early Kouros figures (FIGS. 5-15 and 5-16). Some of these figures are of youths who are dedicated to a god and are apparently advancing into his

5-13 *Mantiklos "Apollo,"* front and back views, Thebes, *c.* 680 B.C. Bronze, approx. 8″ high. Museum of Fine Arts, Boston (Francis Bartlett Fund).

of the figure from the original block of stone. On the broad planes of the figure anatomical details are carefully modeled, as in the chest and knee joints. The head is geometrically simplified into flat planes, the eyes large and protruding, and the nose, mouth, ears, and wig all highly stylized attributes of the almost cubic mass of the head. Though still almost provincial Egyptian, the Tenea Kouros is quite un-Egyptian in its nudity and in its more dynamic, half-striding stance. Moreover, this figure is slender and elegant, with the alert, elastic physique of a sprinter. Description of the anatomy by incised line, typical of the earlier models, has been given up, and the torso, thighs, and calves are modeled in the full round with ever closer approximation of anatomical truth.

With the *Kroisos* from Anavysos (FIG. 5-16), we come to the verge of a breakthrough similar to that which we have seen in vase painting. The statue is, according to an inscription on its base, a funerary monument of a youth, Kroisos, who had died a hero's death in battle. Where the anatomy of the Tenea figure is still somewhat generalized, it here becomes specific and accurate. The artist not only understands the structural parts of the figure and their natural relation and how to represent their surfaces by modeling the stone, but he is able to give us what amounts to a *portrait* of the body, a likeness of a particular physique—in this case, that of a muscular wrestler, strikingly in contrast with the taut, spare Tenea figure. It is noteworthy that the Greeks begin their monumental sculpture with portraits not of the head but of the body. This "bodiliness" of Greek sculpture persisted for centuries until it became lost in a realism that compelled the sculptor to use illusional devices more appropriate to painting.

What we might think of as companion figures to the Kouroi (youths) are the draped *Korai* (maidens), contemporaneous with the former and manifesting in their own style similar features of concept and design. The *Peplos Kore* (PLATE 5-1), contemporary with the *Kroisos*, is one of numerous figures found on the Acropolis of Athens, where they had been thrown down by the Persians after their sack of the city in 480 B.C. Their purpose is obscure, but they may have been

presence; others are memorial statues that stand over graves of noblemen. Thus, they are men, not gods (not, as once thought, "Apollos"), and this is significant, this glorification of men in monumental statues that commemorate their triumph and give them a godlike scale and presence. The Kouroi recall Egyptian statues in the pose (the left foot advanced), in the broad, square shoulders, and in the rigidly frontal and symmetrical design. The Egyptian and Mesopotamian thought of the sculptured human body as a smooth envelope of stone, but the Greek was interested in the structural parts and how they fitted together. The *Kouros from Tenea* (FIG. 5-15) shows us characteristic traits of the type, though the Kouroi differ markedly from each other. Because the figures were freestanding, without the Egyptian stone slab for support, most Kouroi have been found broken at the ankles. Obviously, the Greek sculptor was not aiming for Egyptian permanence so much as for fidelity to appearance, and one of his first steps toward that goal was the liberation votive figures attending the deities in a kind of permanent and perpetual ritual. In contrast with those of earlier types, the face of this Kore has become more expressively modeled; the chin, cheeks, and corners of the mouth subtly planed. The great eyes, originally with painted lids, may have been intended to have a hypnotic power: One thinks back to the ancient head from Warka (FIG. 2-10). The missing left arm was extended, a break from the frontal compression of the arms at the sides in Egyptian statues. The body itself is modeled with a soft smoothness that takes account of the figure beneath the drapery much

like the earlier *Hera of Samos*, yet with a great deal more of the anatomically real. Traces of paint may be seen on parts of the figure, for all Greek stone statues were painted, the powder-white of Classical statues being an error of modern interpretation. But the Greeks did not smear their statues garishly with bright colors, indifferent to their place and effect; only the decisive parts, such as eyes, lips, hair, and the edges of drapery, were painted, to provide accents and contrast to the color of the soft marble itself, the latter being waxed and polished. The whole purpose of coloring was to

5-15 *Kouros from Tenea*, c. 570 B.C. Marble, approx. 5′ high. Staatliche Antikensammlungen, Munich.

5-16 *Kroisos* (Kouros from Anavysos), c. 540–515 B.C. Marble, approx. 6′4″ high. National Museum, Athens.

make the statue more lifelike, more convincing as a kind of person confronting the visitor to the shrines of the Acropolis. The remarkable permanence of the color is partly ascribable to the technique of *encaustic*, in which pigment is mixed with wax and applied to the surface while hot. This method was widely used in ancient wall painting as well as in the embellishment of statues.

The preservation of the color of many of the Kore statues is also a result of the Athenians' use of fragments of broken statues and temples as rubble fill in rebuilding the temples and retaining the walls of the Acropolis after the Persian destruction. Found in this material by modern archeologists have been works such as the *Kore from Chios* (FIG. 5-17). The figures' luxurious gowns may be evidence that they were made in Ionia, where the wealthy Greek states cultivated the Oriental taste for rich ornamentation in both life and art. Ionian influence was strong in Athens during the Archaic period, and Ionian fashions, featuring the intricately folded, chic chiton, interested not only women, but sculptors, who found in the representation of delicate texture and fold a peculiarly difficult challenge. For some time they seemed to take delight in working out the complexities of the pleats and folds made by the thin, soft material and were content to let the matter remain one of decoration rather than structure. Though much must have been learned of the movement of a surface independent of the body beneath it, the Kore figures remain frontal and basically unchanged through a considerable period. Although there are slight changes, the scheme of this example is repeated over and over until the end of the Archaic period. The attractive problem of surface texture appears to have deflected the sculptors of the Kore figures from larger issues.

The larger issues involve not the draped female figure but the nude Kouros type we have been describing; at least, it is there that the break with age-old sculptural traditions takes place. The female nude does not appear in ancient sculpture—with some minor exceptions—until the fourth century B.C. We will see that its appearance in Greek art accompanies changes of a fundamental kind in Greek culture and morals. Why the

5-17 *Kore from Chios* (?), *c.* 510 B.C. Marble, approx. 21½″ high. Acropolis Museum, Athens.

Greek artist should have represented the male figure nude some 300 years before he represented the female so is not known. He may have found, as any student of the living model in art has found, that the male figure is much more revealing of human structure. He may have had available for observation male models in exercises and at the games; we know that in the Dorian world, of which Sparta was the capital, he would also have been able to observe female models, yet the male figure had priority. By the time of Plato, nudity in the context of athletics was commonplace in the Greek world, and the prejudice against it could be regarded as barbarous— that is, merely a prejudice of the non-Hellenic Near East. In Plato's *Republic* Socrates remarks:

Not long ago . . . the Hellenes were of the opinion, which is still generally received among the barbarians, that the sight of a naked man was ridiculous and improper. . . . But experience showed that to let all things be uncovered was far better than to cover them up . . .

Certainly by about 520 B.C. the male nude must have been familiar enough for the artist to construct from the observation of it a convincingly real image. The establishment of a new convention, the propriety of the nude, implied the setting aside of the 3000-year-old convention of the pre-Greek world that inhibited—probably because nudity was the badge of slavery—the study of the structure of the human body as given to the eye.

In the *Kroisos* figure the independent elements of the body have been sufficiently described. The question must now be: How do the elements work together? From the time of King Narmer, there have been more or less successful approximations of the human figure, the parts enumerated, and the attitudes universally stiff and immobile. What can put these parts into motion? The answer appears in a late Kouros—if we can still call it that—found in the Acropolis rubble and dating from just before the Persian destruction. The statue, which must have been the consequence of a mind deliberating upon what had already been done, is called the *Kritios Boy* (FIG. 5-18), from the name of its presumed sculptor. It is not in action but stands at rest; that is to say, it *really* stands at rest and not merely in a stiff-legged pose or a pose bound to a block. The secret of its new and radical naturalness lies in its artist's knowledge of the principle of *weight-shift*, the shifting of position of the main parts of the body around the vertical but flexible axis of the spine. The shifting of the human body in life never takes place in a rigid, stiff-legged manner; indeed we laugh at, or are in terror of, the science-fiction monster that moves in this ponderous, mechanical way. Rather, when we change place and move, the elastic musculoskeletal structure of our bodies dictates a harmonious, smooth motion of all the elements of the body. Greek artists were the first to grasp this fact, and the artist of the *Kritios Boy* was the first to represent it. The youth turns his head

5-18 *Kritios Boy*, front and side views, Acropolis, Athens, *c.* 480 B.C. Marble, approx. 34″ high. Acropolis Museum, Athens.

away from the central axis—only very slightly. There is the slightest dip to the shoulders and to the hips, indicating the shift of weight onto the left leg; the right leg is at ease. (One can easily assume this pose and the contrasting flat-footed poses of the Kouros statues.) Once the principle of weight-shift has been realized, all motion of the human figure is possible in the world of representation; not simply in terms of the signs of motion—simple gesture—but in terms of motion of the whole body as we see and experience it. After the *Kritios Boy* Greek sculpture rapidly passes through the possibilities of the figure understood as having its own physical principle of motion, a principle revealed to the eye in ordinary optical experience and confirmed by the observer's own physical sense of motion.

So far we have been considering sculpture apart from architecture. But the decoration of buildings, especially temples, with sculpture, both in relief and in the round, offered the Greek sculptor a major opportunity. Since sculpture was applied only to very specific and limited areas of temples, it is necessary first to become acquainted with the basic structure of the various buildings that it adorned.

Architecture

Greek architecture is more familiar to us perhaps than any but "modern" architecture. The "revival" of it by European architects in the late eighteenth century brought about a wide diffusion of its style, and especially official public buildings—court houses, banks, city halls, legislative chambers—designed for impressive

5-19 Six representative plans of the Greek temple: (a) Treasury of the Athenians at Delphi, a temple *in antis*, in which the portico is formed by the projecting side walls with two columns set between their ends (*antae*); (b) Temple B at Selinus, Sicily, a *prostyle* temple, in which the columns stand in front of the cella and extend to its width; (c) Temple of Athena Nike on the Acropolis at Athens, an *amphiprostyle* temple, in which the prostyle plan has a porch added at the rear; (d) Temple of Hera at Olympia and (e) Temple of Aphaia at Aegina, *peripteral* temples in which a single colonnade surrounds the cella; and (f) Temple of Apollo at Didyma, near Miletus, a *dipteral* temple, in which two colonnades surround the cella. (Drawings are not to scale.)

a   b   c

d   e   f

← to c. 900 B.C.   c. 750   c. 700 c. 680   c. 575 c. 550 c. 530   490 **480**   to 323 B.C. →

| Dipylon vases | Mantiklos "Apollo" | | François Vase | EXEKIAS Dionysos in a Sailboat | Peplos Kore | Battle of Marathon | Kritios Boy | |
| GEOMETRIC PERIOD | A R C H A I C   P E R I O D | | | | | | | CLASSICAL PERIOD |

formality, imitated the architecture of Classicism, which was fundamentally Greek in inspiration. Although their homes were unpretentious places, they had no monarchs to house royally, and they performed religious rites in the open, the ancient Greeks were industrious builders. Their significant buildings began primarily as simple shrines to protect the statues to their gods. More and more attention was lavished on these until possibly the qualities of the god became embodied in the structures themselves. Figure sculpture played its part in this program, partly to embellish the protective building, partly to tell something of the deity symbolized within, and partly as a votive offering. But the building was itself also conceived as sculpture, abstract in form and possessing the power of sculpture to evoke human qualities. The commanding importance of the sculptured temple, its inspiring function in public life, was emphasized in its elevated site, often on a hill above the city (the *acropolis*). As Aristotle stipulated: "the site should be a spot seen far and wide, which gives due elevation to virtue and towers over the neighborhood." And the reverent awe that must have been attached to the temple and to the genius of its founders echoes in Plato: "Gods and temples are not easily instituted, and to establish them rightly is the work of a mighty intellect."

The earliest temples were of wood, and these wooden forms were in time translated into the more permanent materials of limestone and sometimes marble. Marble was expensive, but mountains of it were available: from Hymettos, just east of Athens, with its bluish-white stone; from Pentelicus, northeast of the city, its glittering white stone particularly adapted for carving; and from the islands of the Aegean, Paros in particular, which supplied marble of varying quantities and qualities.

In its plan the Greek temple discloses a close affinity with the Mycenaean megaron and even in its most elaborate form retains the latter structure's basic simplicity (FIG. 5-19): a single or double room (the *cella*) with no windows and one door (two for a double cella) and with (a) a portico with two columns between the extended walls (columns *in antis*), or (b) a colonnade across the front (*prostyle*), or (c) a colonnade across both front and back (*amphiprostyle*), or any of these plans surrounded by (d and e) a single (*peripteral*) or (f) a double (*dipteral*) colonnade. What strikes the eye first in the Greek scheme, after what has been seen of the architecture of the ancient Near East, is its remarkable order, compactness, and symmetry, in contrast, say, to the rambling groupings of the Egyptian temples. The difference lies in the Greeks' sense of proportion and in their effort to achieve ideal forms in terms of regular numerical relations and the rules of geometry.

We can discern in the plans a kind of development from quite simple units to more complex, without, however, any fundamental change in the nature of the units or of their grouping. For Greek architecture, like classical music, has a simple core theme from which is developed a series of complex, but always quite intelligible, variations. And, to change the analogy, the development of the temple scheme is like that other great invention of the Greeks, geometry, where theorems, propositions, and their corollaries are deduced from a simple original set of axioms. The insistence of the Greeks on mathematical order guided the experiments with the proportions of temple plans. The earlier, Archaic temples tended to be long and narrow (FIG. 5-19d), with a proportion of the ends to the sides roughly expressible as 1:3. Late Classical and Hellenistic (see below) plans approached, but rarely had a proportion of exactly 1:2, with Classical temples tending to be a little longer than twice the width (FIG. 5-19e) and Hellenistic a little shorter (FIG. 5-19f). Proportion in architecture and sculpture, and harmony in music, were much the same to the Greek mind and indeed reflected and embodied the cosmic order just as did the rationally pursued "good life."

The description of the elevation of a Greek

5-20 Doric and Ionic orders. (After Grinnell.)

building is in terms of the column, platform, and superstructure, or *entablature*; this combination and relationship of three units is called an order. The three orders developed by Greek builders are differentiated partly by details but chiefly by the relative proportions of the parts. Each order served different purposes and embodied different meanings. The earliest of the Greek architectural orders to be formulated were the *Doric*, of mainland Greece, and the *Ionic*, of Asia Minor and the Aegean islands (FIG. 5-20). The *Corinthian* order followed much later.

The columns, which rest on a platform (*stylobate*), have two or three parts, depending on the order: the *shaft*, which is marked with vertical channels (*fluting*); the *capital*; and (in the Ionic and Corinthian) the *base*. As the shaft rises, its diameter decreases gradually, giving the profile a subtle curve (*entasis*); the top (in the Doric) is marked with one or several horizontal lines (*necking*) that furnish the transition to the capital. The capital has two elements, the lower of which (the *echinus*) varies with the order: In the Doric it is convex and cushionlike; in the Ionic it is small and supports a bolster ending in scroll-like spirals (the *volute*); and in the Corinthian, a relatively elongated element principally of stylized acanthus leaves that form an inverted-bell shape. The upper element, present in all orders, is

a flat, square block (the *abacus*) that provides the immediate support for the entablature. The entablature has three parts: the *architrave*, the main weight-bearing and weight-distributing element; the *frieze*; and the *cornice*, a molded horizontal projection that, with two sloping (*raking*) cornices, forms a triangle that enframes the *pediment*. The architrave is usually subdivided into three horizontal bands (*fasciae*) in the Ionic and Corinthian orders. The frieze is subdivided into *triglyphs* and *metopes* in the Doric order and left open in the Ionic to provide a continuous field for reliefs.

The Doric order is massive in appearance, its sturdy columns firmly planted on the stylobate. Compared with the weighty and severe Doric, the Ionic seems light, airy, and much more decorative. Its columns are slenderer and rise from molded bases. While the Doric flutings meet in sharp ridges (*arrises*), the Ionic ones are flat. The most obvious differences among the three orders are, of course, in the capitals, the Doric severely plain, the Ionic and Corinthian highly ornamental.

In ancient times the Doric and Ionic orders were contrasted as masculine and feminine. The Corinthian order was not developed until the fifth century B.C., when it appeared inside the temple, like a natural form growing in the darkness of the interior. It was not widely used, however, until Roman times. Since the Renaissance, and until about two generations ago, architecture in the Western world was considered to be in essence the display of the refined beauty of these architectural orders.

The functional placement of the architectural units may have been set by a tradition of building going back to the use of wooden structural members. Thus, many of the parts of the Doric order seem to be translations into stone of an earlier timber architecture. Pausanias, writing in the second century A.D., noted that in the even then ancient Temple of Hera at Olympia (FIG. 5-19d) there was still a wooden column in place; the rest had been replaced by stone columns. It has been inferred, from the varying proportions of these columns, that the wooden columns were replaced at different times, probably as the wood of the original columns rotted. One feature of the Doric order can be explained only as a translation from the wooden original into stone: the organization of the frieze into triglyphs and metopes. The triglyphs most likely derived from the ends of cross beams that rested on the main horizontal support, the architrave. The metopes would then correspond to the voids between the beam-ends in the original wooden structure.

Sculptural ornamentation, which played an important part in the design of the temple, was concentrated on the upper part of the building—in the frieze and pediments. It was basically sculpture that was gaily painted in red and blue, with touches of green, yellow, black, and perhaps a little gold, and was applied only to those parts of the building that had no structural function or that suggested a former structural function. This is true particularly of the Doric style, in which decorative sculpture was applied only to the "voids" of the metopes and of the pediment. Ionic builders were less severe in this respect and were willing to decorate the entire frieze and sometimes even the lower drums of columns. Occasionally they replaced their columns with female figures (*caryatids*), something the Doric builder would probably not have done. Using color, the designer could bring out more clearly the relationships of the structural parts, soften the glitter of the stone at specific points, and provide a background to set off the figures. Although it is

true that color was used for emphasis and to mitigate what might have seemed too bare a simplicity (in Doric buildings as well as in Ionic), the primary dependence in Greek architecture—as in Greek mathematics, science, and philosophy—was on the setting of clear limits. This thesis had to begin with the axiom that the limits themselves must never be encroached upon, must always contain, and must never be vague. The architectural orders described above were embodiments of codified limits, given plainly to the eye as functioning realities. To the Greek it was unthinkable to use surfaces in the way that the Egyptian used his gigantic columns—as fields for complicated ornamentation. The very building itself, the Greek temple as given to the eye, must have the clarity of a Euclidean demonstration. This is borne out not only by its plan, elevation, and function-enhancing ornament but also by its "dry-jointed" construction (that is, construction without mortar), which seems evidence that Greek architects looked upon their temples not as "buildings" but as monumental pieces of sculpture.

The placement of the building strengthened its sculptural aspect. Unlike Egyptian temples, Greek temples faced outward. Rites were performed at altars in front of the temple, and the building itself served to house the cult statue and perhaps trophies and treasure. Private cults were frowned upon and public ritual prevailed. Thus it was on the exterior of the building and its surfaces that the architect generally concentrated his efforts to make the temple a suitable monument to the deity. The studied visual relationships of solids and voids, of light and shade in the colonnades, and the lighter accents of the entablature make a sculptural form out of the rectangular mass of the temple. The history of Greek architecture is the history of the artists' unflagging efforts to express the form of the temple in its most satisfactory—that is to say, perfect—proportions.

The experiment in proportions can be followed rather easily if we begin with the Archaic Doric architecture of the Greek colonies—especially that in Sicily and southern Italy—for it is here that the best-preserved examples of Archaic temples are found. (In examining Greek architecture it is useful to keep in mind the develop-

5-21 "Basilica," *c.* 550 B.C. Paestum, Italy.

5-22 Corner of the "Basilica" colonnade with view of the Temple of Hera beyond.

ment of the human figure in Greek painting and in sculpture, for the architectural events are not only contemporaneous but reflect a similar concern with "true" proportions.) The "Basilica" at Paestum, south of Naples, dates from about 550 B.C., and is a quite typical example of Archaic Doric style (FIG. 5-21). Called "the Basilica" after a Roman building type that early investigators felt it resembled, it is a peripteral temple with heavy columns of pronounced entasis, closely spaced, with large, bulky, pillowlike capitals, supporting a high and massive entablature that makes the columns seem proportionately squat. These parts of the order will be gradually adjusted until a lighter, taller, and more graceful combination is achieved. There is a structural reason, perhaps, for the heaviness of the design and the narrowness of the spans between the columns. The architects at this time may not have been certain of the strength of their materials and may have wisely operated within a broad margin of safety. A corner of the "Basilica" colonnade (FIG. 5-22) shows extreme spread of the cushion capitals and exaggeration of the supporting surface in relation to the spans bridged by the architrave. The columns are built up of separate dry-jointed "drums," fitted with square metal plugs to prevent turning as well as shifting.

The whole temple was of this typically Greek construction, the blocks of stone in a horizontal course being held together by metal cramps, while those of different courses, one above the other, were joined vertically by metal dowels. Through the "Basilica" colonnade one can see the nearby Temple of Hera, which was built eighty to ninety years later and whose columns have proportions strikingly different from those of the "Basilica."

The diagram (FIG. 5-23) showing the evolution in the proportions of the Doric order from Archaic to Classical points up the thesis that Greek art evolves with a certain logic, whether in its figurative forms or its architectural, moving toward a conclusion that is as satisfactory as it is true. Plato, in speaking of the imitative arts, declared that the degree of their truth or rightness is determined by the proportionality of their elements and that if they are to be judged at all they must be judged by the "standard of truth, and by no other whatever." In this diagram we see the architects working toward proportions that could be thought of as "true" and final. Some of the earliest columns (not shown) were extremely slender, under massive capitals. The shafts soon thickened to the shape of the "Basilica" type, as the builders searched for a better relationship between the shaft and the capital. From then on, the forms were constantly refined, the shafts becoming more slender, the entasis subtler, the capitals smaller, and the entablature lighter. The final Classical proportions were considered to be ideal ones beyond which further refinement was impossible.

The Temple of Hera at Paestum (FIG. 5-24) dates from about 460 B.C.; although the forms have been refined, the columns are still massive and closely spaced. This was erected at a time when, on the Greek mainland, the Doric order had already achieved its Classical proportions—as early as 490 B.C.—in the Temple of Aphaia at Aegina. There was a considerable time lag between developments on the mainland and their adoption by the colonies in Italy and Sicily, so that the colonial architecture exhibits the usual provincial conservatism characteristic of styles distant from their source of inspiration in the cultural capital. The plan and section of the

5-23 Changes in Doric-order proportions, Archaic to Classical. Examples are not drawn to same scale.

Temple of Hera (FIG. 5-25) show a noteworthy peculiarity in the support structure of the interior, the columns of which rise higher than the outer, peripteral columns. Each of the two rows of small Doric columns that support the roof is made up of two sets of columns, one resting on a stone course that rests on the set of columns below. This was a standard form where Doric columns were used to support the roof, the reason being, apparently, that a single row of large columns, as in the "Basilica," would produce a distortion of scale and look out of proportion and oppressive inside the relatively small cellas. Later, the support problem was solved by using Ionic or Corinthian columns in the interior, since they were taller in relation to their diameters than were the Doric ones.

One of the earliest Ionic buildings in Greece is the Treasury of the Siphnians at Delphi, constructed about 530 B.C. (FIG. 5-26). Although it has no Ionic columns, the supporting function being assumed by luxuriously carved caryatids, it has the identifying Ionic feature—the con-

5-24 Temple of Hera at Paestum, *c.* 460 B.C.

5-25 Reconstruction of the plan and section of the Temple of Hera at Paestum. (After Sir Banister Fletcher.)

FEET
0   50   100

tinuous frieze—which here appears as part of a heavy Archaic entablature. The caryatids, with their elaborate costume and very irregular silhouettes, could never fit into a context of Doric architecture, with its severity of line and disdain of ornament. Yet as the Athenian Erechtheum (FIG. 5-48) shows, the demands of architecture can quiet the profiles of the caryatids, and architect and sculptor can collaborate in producing a most convincing columnar effect in the motif of the human body as a supporting vertical element.

Architectural Sculpture

We have noted already that decorative sculpture was applied only to those parts of a temple that had no evident structural function—that is, the frieze and the pediment. The caryatids are exceptional, but their use is rare. Ordinarily the weight-carrying columns and the weight-distributing architraves were not decorated, though it may be that war trophies were hung upon the blank Doric architrave. In the Doric order only the metopes bore relief sculpture. It might be argued that the fluting of columns is a form of decoration, but in fact the fluting simply explains and emphasizes the form and function of the column, stressing its verticality—the only vertical in the temple design. It also exhibits the column's rotundity, for when the sunlight strikes sharply upon the shaft (FIG. 5-22) the flutings throw numerous shadows of graduated width and darkness that lead the eye around the shaft in a series of graded steps, making the effect of roundness more evident than in the nonfluted column, in which the sunlight creates a single, indistinct line separating the light and dark sides.

The architectural sculptor had a problem similar to that of the vase painter: how to adjust the image to the surface on which it is placed. This is not apparent in the frieze from the Treasury of the Siphnians (FIG. 5-27), for here the sculptor has merely a continuous blank zone to manage and can arrange his figures in a simple file, their heads on the same level, each filling a unit of space of approximately the same dimension. This is a good example of the formalizing effect of architectural line on figurative composition, just as the surface of the ceramic vessel imposed its necessities on the vase painter, making for simplicity and elegance of style. In fact, in the case of the Siphnian figures there is a resemblance stylistically between them and contemporary painting like that of the Andokides Painter (FIG. 5-8). But an awkward space like that of the triangular pediment of the Archaic Temple of Artemis (early sixth century B.C.) on the island of Corfu (FIG. 5-28) is more troublesome to manage. The figures are heraldically arranged and bring to mind compositions that go back beyond the Lion Gate at Mycenae to the symmetrical man-beast compositions of Mesopotamia. On the thin panel of stone that fills the space between the cornices of the pediment, the sculptor presents a Gorgon flanked by spotted panthers. The Gorgon, a guardian monster, grimaces hideously, exposing her boar's teeth (her look could turn men to stone) and fulfilling her function as a winged demon to repulse all enemies from the sanctuary of the goddess. To the left and the right of the central Gorgon appear, on a smaller scale, the figures of Chrysaor and Pegasus, those mythological creatures that,

according to legend, sprang from the Gorgon's head when she was struck by the sword of Perseus. Still smaller are two groups of figures beyond the panthers: Zeus slaying a giant (on the observer's right) and one of the climactic events of the Trojan War, Neoptolemos killing

5-26 Reconstruction of the façade of the Treasury of the Siphnians in the Sanctuary of Apollo at Delphi, c. 530 B.C. Museum, Delphi.

5-27 *Battle of the Gods and Giants*, from the north frieze of the Treasury of the Siphnians. Marble, approx. 26″ high. Museum, Delphi.

Priam. In the outer ends of the pediment, recumbent figures represent a fallen Trojan and a dead giant. As pieced together from the surviving fragments, the artist's narrative intention is clear enough, but the odd shape of the surface on which he worked compelled him to distribute his figures somewhat haphazardly around the central ones and to show them on different scales. As time progresses, the Greek artist attempts to fill the space more organically, with figures so grouped that they appear to be of the same size and participating in a unified way in a single event.

Toward the end of the Archaic period Greek sculptors were arriving at a solution to the problem of pedimental composition. In the pedimental sculptures of the Temple of Aphaia at Aegina (FIGS. 5-29 to 5-31) we find that the figures in different poses, but of the same scale, have been fitted into the difficult triangular space. The figures, heavily cleaned and over-restored in the nineteenth century, probably represent some episode of the Trojan War. Athena, with aegis and spear, stands in the center, with fighting groups on either side. We notice most the freedom of movement and variety of pose. The figures are modeled with great vigor and an understanding of the human physique that, as we have seen in the contemporary vase paintings, reflect a careful observation of nature. The figure of the fallen warrior from the left angle of the pediment

(FIG. 5-30) exhibits the daring with which the sculptor tackles the challenging problem of a difficult twisted pose. The bold composition of the turning masses of the body manifests his new confidence in his mastery of the science of representation. The dynamics of muscular tension and relaxation are appreciated and are close to life in their rendering. Mistakes are still made, and the transition from chest to pelvis has not been fully solved in this complex pose. (Note the misplaced navel.) These rather technical considerations should not blind us to the marvelously expressive power of this figure. The *Fallen Warrior* brings to mind the spare and monumental nobility of Homer's heroes, and particularly the Homeric simile, "darkness came down upon his eyes, and he crashed in the battle like a falling tower."

The figure of the archer Herakles (FIG. 5-31) from the same pediment is another instance of the Greek sculptor's triumph over age-old taboos and difficulties of representation. It is thought that this nimble archer is executing a maneuver hard to perform without long practice but required in the Greek war games and in actual combat. Running forward, he has dropped suddenly almost to one knee, and from this tense position takes aim and fires a flight of arrows in a matter of seconds. Soon he will spring to his feet to run forward again. The practiced strength

5-28 Reconstruction drawing superimposed on a photograph of the remaining fragments of the pediment of the Temple of Artemis at Corfu, *c.* 600–580 B.C.

5-29 Reconstruction drawing of the east pediment of the Temple of Aphaia at Aegina, *c.* 490 B.C.

5-30 *Fallen Warrior*, from the east pediment of the Temple of Aphaia at Aegina. Marble, 72″ long. Staatliche Antikensammlungen, Munich.

and poise demanded by such a feat is beautifully caught in the elastic, though momentarily rigid, pose. One might read here the expression of a new spirit in Greek life and art, a spirit buoyant and optimistic as it meets the great challenge of the Persians at Marathon and looks to a future that the old Near Eastern world could never envision and never encompass.

THE FIFTH CENTURY

The Transitional Period

The thirty years or so of the Transitional period constitute the heroic age of the Athenians and of all the Hellenes who joined forces against the invasion of Greece by the Persians. Just as we look back to the age of the American Revolution and of the founding fathers of the republic for our models of heroism and of civic wisdom and virtue, so did the Greeks of the later fifth century revere the men of Marathon, Thermopylae, and Salamis, the battles that daunted and finally turned back the mighty hosts of Asia led by Xerxes. The new world of the Greeks—attributed by them to the Homeric feats of their heroes—turned away from Asia, barbarism, tyranny, and ignorance (it was all the same to the Greeks) to build a Hellenic civilization productive of a new species of mankind. Typical of the time were the views of the great dramatist Aeschylus, who celebrated, in his *Oresteia*, the triumph of reason and law over barbarous crime, blood feud, and

mad vengeance. Himself a veteran of Marathon, Aeschylus repudiated in majestic verse all the slavish and inhuman traits of nature that the Greeks at that time of crisis tended to associate with the Persians.

Shortly after Athens was occupied and sacked in 480 B.C., the Greeks won a great naval victory over the Persians at Salamis. This resilient toughness of the Athenians signified a new pride that was to mature into a sense of Hellenic identity so strong that thenceforth the history of European civilization would be distinct from—even though in interaction with—the civilization of Asia. The period of struggle with the Persians, calling repeatedly for courage and endurance, produced in the Hellenes a kind of austere grandeur that is manifested in the art of that period. This quality is rendered in the fine bronze,

5-31 *Herakles*, from the east pediment of the Temple of Aphaia at Aegina. Marble, approx. 31″ high. Staatliche Antikensammlungen, Munich.

5-32 *Charioteer*, from the Sanctuary of Apollo at Delphi, *c.* 470 B.C. Bronze, approx. 71″ high. Museum, Delphi.

and in the conventional way in which the hair is worked. But we notice also the skillful modeling of the hand and the feet, the toes of which cling to the chariot floor, and the slight twist of the torso, giving the feeling of an organic structure beneath the drapery. These subtleties are not seen at first and one might mistake the statue for another example of the Archaic formulas of rigid frontality. But it is only the formality of the pose, not ignorance of the principle of weight distribution, that determines the tight composure of the figure; it is as "alive" as the pose of a soldier at parade rest. The statue is probably a portrait, yet there are few individualized traits. This is typical of most works of the Greek Classical period and distinguishes Greek from Egyptian portrait statues, which had a religious function— the preservation of the deceased's likeness meaning the preservation of the ka. Although with the Greeks, man comes to complete self-consciousness ("Know thyself!") and although the *figure* of man is idealized, he himself, as an individual, is not regarded as being true or perfect nor, consequently, an appropriate subject for representation. In the words of Bruno Snell:

> If we want to describe the statues of the fifth century in the words of their age, we should say that they represent beautiful or perfect men, or, to use a phrase employed in the early lyrics for purposes of eulogy: "god-like" men. Even for Plato the norm of judgment still rests with the gods, and not with men.[2]

Thus, the observations made at the beginning of the chapter must be modified: Though with Protagoras "man is the measure," for art the gods are the measure of man, and to achieve the ideal is to achieve the "godlike."

The rapid process of liberation from Archaic limits continues in the renowned *Discobolos* of the sculptor MYRON (FIG. 5-33), from about 450 B.C. As have most freestanding statues by the "Great Masters" of Greek sculpture, this has survived only in Roman marble copies after the bronze original (see pp. 151–52). Myron's representation of an athlete engaged in the discus throw,

the *Charioteer of Delphi* (FIG. 5-32). The Greek search for ideal beauty is also fully shown here, as well as the culmination of the long-evolving mastery of the structure of the human figure. The statue belonged to a group with chariot and horses, probably erected to commemorate the victory of King Polyzalos of Gela at the races in 478 B.C. It represents a youthful aristocrat who stands firmly on both feet, holding the reins in his outstretched hand. He is dressed in the customary garment of a driver, girdled high and held in at the shoulders and the back to keep it from flapping. The hair is confined by a band tied behind the head. The eyes are made of glass paste and shaded by lashes of hairlike pieces of bronze. We feel the sharp clarity of Archaic work in the figure, especially in the lower part, where the folds of the dress have almost the quality of a fluted column, in the sharp lines of the brow,

---

[2] Bruno Snell, *The Discovery of the Mind: The Greek Origins of European Thought* (New York: Harper & Row, 1960), p. 247.

5-33 MYRON, *Discobolos*, original *c.* 450 B.C. Roman copy, marble, life-size. Museo Nazionale Romano, Rome.

expression of concentrated force. The composition is in terms of two intersecting arcs, creating the impression of a tightly stretched bow a moment before the string's release.

The "severe" early style of the transition finds clearest and most representative expression in the pedimental sculptures of the Temple of Zeus at Olympia (FIG. 5-34). On the west pediment is represented the combat of centaurs and Lapiths at the wedding feast of Peirithous. The centaurs, half beast, had been invited to the celebration but became drunk and attempted to abduct the bride and her maidens. They were prevented from doing so by Peirithous and Theseus, and Apollo, appearing above the combat, approves the heroes' chastisement of this breach of hospitality. The scene symbolizes three things: the Greek victories over the Persians; the sacred truce of Olympia (which outlawed strife within or on the approaches of the consecrated precincts of the temple); and the responsibility of men, who, unlike animals, acknowledge the rule of law.

The grouping of the figures in the Olympia pediments shows considerable improvement over the older Aegina grouping (FIG. 5-29) in the adjustment of the poses to fit the triangular pediment. In the center, Apollo thrusts out his arm amid the tumult (FIG. 5-35). The figure should be compared with the Archaic Kouroi (FIGS. 5-15 and 5-16): From its formality and such lingering archaisms as the tight, decorative treatment of the hair, it seems the last of that great line, although the new understanding of bodily structure shows in the splendid and exact modeling of the athletic physique. The musculature is no longer schematic but swelling with life and power. The

still an athletic event in the Olympic games, was revolutionary because of its vigorous and convincing movement; it has been widely reproduced in both the ancient and modern worlds. However, the motion of the *Discobolos* has clearly been restricted to one plane, which means that only two distinct views are possible. The figure, represented at the point between the backward swing and the forward thrust of the arm, becomes by means of certain formal devices an

5-34 Reconstruction drawing of the west pediment of the Temple of Zeus at Olympia, 468–460 B.C. Approx. 91′ wide.

transitions from one group of muscles to another are smoothly and subtly made, and this soft flow of planes and contours belies the formal rigidity of the pose. The face of the *Apollo,* like those of the *Charioteer of Delphi* and the *Discobolos,* is composed in the expressionless mask of regular beauty deemed appropriate to gods and godlike men, despite their action or potential for action. This ideal mask, expressing the conviction of Greek philosophy that reason must be above and in control of the passions, precludes the distortion of the face by any strain of emotion, even in scenes of the most violent action. In the twisted complication of the group of *Hippodameia and the Centaur* (FIG. 5-36), where the bride of Peirithous tries to wrench from her breast the centaur's clutching hand, the girl's face remains serenely neutral. Her predicament is dire, as the artful sculptor dramatically describes it; yet, and significantly, it is only the centaur's face that is distorted, as befits the low creature that it is, surrendering to drunkenness and lust. This distinction between the calm of noble men and the frenzy of the creature abandoned to impulse prevails for centuries in Greek art. The Greeks were convinced that overwhelming disaster awaited the man who yielded to the spell cast by the dark god of intoxication and madness, Dionysos; this conviction is reflected in their drama and in their persistent appeal to reason and order, both in art and life. Against Dionysos they attempted to raise the shining figure of Apollo, god of light, beauty, and wisdom. Thus, it was with the pediments of Olympia that the visual arts moved into the realm of philosophy and drama, and it was in the presence of these sculptures that the Greek athletes took their oath at the altar of Zeus before the Olympic games.

5-36 *Hippodameia and the Centaur,* from the west pediment of the Temple of Zeus at Olympia. Marble, slightly over life-size. Museum, Olympia.

The Early Classical Period

The prestige that the Athenians won by their leading role in the repulse of the Persians and by virtue of the powerful fleet they had built in the process made them the dominant political force in the Greek world. They acquired a sea empire disguised as a more or less democratic alliance of city and island states throughout the Aegean. Members of the alliance, which was called the Delian League, had cause enough to complain bitterly that they were more the subjects of Athens than her allies and that she siphoned off a large part of the common treasury (raised as a fund for defense against Persia), for her own uses. Despite chronic warfare within the "alliance" (and between it and the rival league led by Sparta), Athens, under the leadership of its adroit statesman, Pericles, became an immensely prosperous and proud community. The brief period of her glory under Pericles saw a concentration of human creative energy and a triumph of drama, philosophy, and art such as has been known in no other place or time in all of the Western world.

Disdaining to reassemble the desecrated stones of the Athenian Acropolis after the sack of the city in 480 B.C., the Athenians, led by Pericles, signalized their new power and independence by completely rebuilding the Acropolis, an undertaking that was one of the greatest building projects of antiquity before Roman times. Their success stands as a rare human achievement against the larger history of human failure. The beauty of the buildings, set upon a towering platform of rock with difficult access (FIGS. 5-37 and 5-38), was recognized and celebrated in ancient times as it is today. Plutarch, writing some 500 years after the rebuilding of the Acropolis, commented:

> Pericles' works are especially admired, as having been made quickly, to last long. For every particular piece of his work was immediately, even at that time when it was new, recognized as ancient, because of its beauty and elegance; and yet in its vigor and freshness it looks to this day as if it had just been done. There is a sort of bloom and newness upon those works of his, preserving them from the touch of time . . . .

The late architect Eric Mendelssohn (1887–1953) made almost the same observation when he first visited Athens. Expecting to be depressed by the view of that original source of the academic classicism from which his generation was fighting to free itself, he found himself exclaiming that the Parthenon is "modern," meaning that good architecture is always good, and so, always "modern."

THE PARTHENON

Of the buildings on the Acropolis, the Parthenon (the temple sacred to Athena Parthenos) was the first and the largest to be constructed (FIG. 5-39). Its architects were ICTINOS and CALLICRATES, and its sculptural ornament was produced under the direction of PHIDIAS, friend of Pericles and one of the great sculptors of all time. In plan (FIG. 5-38) the Parthenon is a peripteral temple, its short side slightly less than half the length of its long. Its cella is subdivided into two parts; the larger contained the cult statue of Athena Parthenos in ivory and gold, some forty feet in height, the work of Phidias; the smaller had been designed to serve as treasury of the Delian League, but most of the revenues contributed by the Aegean members were expended upon Pericles' ambitious building projects. The interiors of the two rooms are organized differently. The cella proper has two double rows of small columns for roof support; although long disputed, the purpose of the rows was, according to some, to provide a second-story gallery from which visitors could view the statue, the foundation of which is still visible. The treasury had four single Ionic columns—one of several Ionic features in the otherwise Doric building, another being the continuous frieze of sculpture that runs around the top of the cella wall on the exterior. Except for these Ionic elements, the Parthenon is the epitome of the classical Doric temple, exhibiting the order at the peak of its refinement.

The building seen today is a restoration. Through the centuries the Parthenon has undergone many transformations, having been at one time a Greek temple, at another a Christian church, and then a Turkish mosque. In 1687

5–37 View (from the west) of the Acropolis today, Athens.

the cella was being used as an ammunition dump by the Turks, who were then at war with the Venetians. A Venetian rocket scored a direct hit, and the resultant explosion blew out the center of the building. During the past century the colonnades have been reassembled, but the core of the structure remains a ruin.

Despite its dilapidated condition, the Parthenon is probably the most carefully surveyed and measured building in the world. The consequence of this searching study is the revelation that the builders aimed for unsurpassable ex-

cellence in every detail; the "refinements" of the structure have become almost a subtopic in the history of Greek architecture. If there is anything we are led to expect from the severe Doric order, it is that its lines must be rigidly and consistently straight and plumb; yet there are few straight structural lines in the Parthenon. The stylobate is convex, so subtly as to be almost imperceptible as a curve; only if one sights along it from one end does the curvature, which is repeated in the entablature, become visible. The columns tilt slightly inward and are not

ERECHTHEUM

SITE OF OLD
TEMPLE OF
ATHENA

STATUE

PARTHENON

CHALKOTHEKE

SITE OF
ATHENA PROMACHUS
STATUE

SANCTUARY OF
ARTEMIS
BRAURONIA

PROPYLAEA

MYCENAEAN
FORTIFICATION

N

FEET

0   50   100

Probable roofed areas
Reconstruction
Perimeter and precinct wall

PINAKO-
THEKE

5-38 Plan of the Acropolis,
restored as of 400 B.C.

TEMPLE OF
ATHENA NIKE

5-39 ICTINOS and CAL-
LICRATES, the Parthenon,
Acropolis, Athens, 448–
432 B.C. (view from the
west).

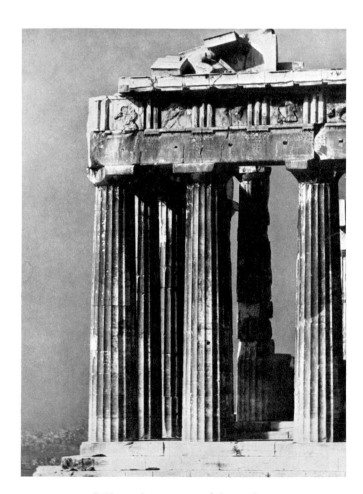

5-40 Southeast corner of the Parthenon.

uniformly spaced, standing closer to each other
at the corners of the buildings. Moreover, not all
the columns are of the same diameter, those at
the corners having somewhat greater girth than
the rest. The entasis, which gives a kind of muscle-
tense elasticity and buoyancy to the profile of the
column, has the same subtlety seen in the curvature of the stylobate and the entablature.

These deviations from the mechanical, plumb-
line, straight-edged norm are plainly intentional;
most have been found in other temples. But interpretations of these refinements do not agree;
some feel that they are purely functional, the
curvature of the stylobate, for example, facilitat-
ing drainage or perhaps anticipating settling of
the central part of the building. Others believe
that the deviations were intended to offset
marginal distortions in the human visual field—
optical illusions that might make columns with
exactly vertical profiles look pinched and weak.
Still other speculation sees the refinements as
required by Greek instinct for completeness in
the look of the building and for integrity with its
surroundings; for example, the downward-
tending curve of the stylobate would find its
limit in the earth, making a visually stable and
strong base for the building's aspect. A reasonable conjecture would be that the Parthenon was
intended to be more than a product of engineering logic, that it was to be viewed and appreciated

as a great work of sculpture, having the elasticity, resilience, and life of the human figure in statuary. Thus, the particulars would be designed to work in smooth relation to each other and to the whole structure in an organic way that, of course, means predominance of the curved line over the straight. The Parthenon columns especially display this in their entasis, appearing to respond to the burden they bear by the seeming swell of their compressed contours, expressing their function not mechanically but organically.

Parts of the building were painted. This painting provided background against which sculpture could be seen clearly and, perhaps more important, delineated the upper parts of the building against the bright sky, so that the temple's basic proportions were crisply shown and could not be misread. Color also ensured that the visible parts of the building would be clearly defined and distinguished one from another.

The insistence upon clarity in argument, which led to the invention of logic by the Greeks, operates just as strongly in the "arguments" of their architectural design. Unfortunately, that early triumph of Greek thought, the syllogism, with its three propositions ending in a logically correct conclusion, cannot quite be matched in the Doric order. As examination of a corner of the Parthenon (FIG. 5-40) will show, Greek architecture was not as "rational" as Greek logic. The Doric frieze was organized according to three inflexible rules: (1) a triglyph must be exactly over the center of each column; (2) a triglyph must be over the center of each intercolumniation; and (3) triglyphs at the corners of the frieze must meet, so that no space is left over. But the architectural "argument" does not work out; the logical syllogism is faulty, for Rule 3, the "conclusion," cannot be harmonized with Rule 1: If the corner triglyphs must meet, they cannot be placed over the center of the corner column. Though irremediable, this might seem to us a minor flaw, even in a building that aimed at perfection in all details. The Greeks wanted to be sure, and they worked out, in logic, a method for making series of statements conform to a rule for validity. But in Doric architecture, there was something left over, something that did not fit. To the Greeks it must have appeared like the in-commensurable, "irrational" numbers (such as the square root of two)—a disturbing thing, since it has no limit or definition. (According to a singular and significant Greek legend, the man who first revealed the mystery of the irrationals perished by shipwreck, "for the unspeakable and the formless must be left hidden forever!") In much the same manner as mathematicians and logicians faced with some disturbing contradiction in their results, the architects and artists who aimed at perfection must have found this problem of the corner triglyph a constant irritation and embarrassment. Indeed, it may have contributed to the eventual decline of the Doric order, which began in the fourth century B.C., and to the rise of the Ionic and Corinthian orders, whose continuous friezes eliminate the problem.

The main purpose of the Parthenon, as already noted, was to house the cult statue of Athena Parthenos. Since the image of Athena—for whom the city of Athens was named—was made of ivory and gold, it did not survive centuries of depredation, although it seems to have been in existence as late as the second century A.D. We know the look of it only from accounts by Pausanias and others and from a few small replicas that differ in detail. Plutarch, in his *Life of Pericles*, tells us that its artist, Phidias, probably the scapegoat in an anti-Pericles plot, was convicted of stealing some of the gold intended for the statue and died in prison (though we know from other sources and recent excavations that he was working on a statue of Zeus at Olympia after he left Athens and that he died in exile). Because work on the colossal cult statue for the cella of the Parthenon must have taken up most of Phidias' time, it is quite likely that he planned and designed the pedimental groups and friezes but left the carving of these architectural sculptures to his students and assistants. Nevertheless, they undoubtedly reflect his style and they are among the most marvelous of all surviving Greek works of sculpture and among the supreme masterworks of all time. The east pedimental group depicted the birth of Athena; the west, her contest with Poseidon for the city of Athens.

Most of these sculptures are now in the British Museum in London, where they are popularly

5-41 *Dionysos* (*Herakles?*), from the east pediment of the Parthenon. Marble, over life-size. British Museum, London.

known as the Elgin marbles. Between 1801 and 1803, while Greece was still under Turkish rule, Lord Elgin, the British ambassador to the Ottoman court at Constantinople, was permitted to dismantle the Parthenon sculptures and to ship the best-preserved ones to England. He eventually sold them to the British government, although at a great financial loss to himself. Although he was severely criticized for having "stolen" the treasures of Athens, Lord Elgin's quite civilized motives in saving the statues from almost certain ruin are no longer doubted. During his time there seemed to be no prospect that the statues, surrounded by rubble and neglected for centuries, might one day be salvaged and protected against further damage and decay.

The figure of Dionysos (recently identified as Herakles) from the Parthenon shows the final relaxing of all the limitations of Archaic figurative art. Phidias and his assistants are in full possession of the knowledge of the organic, coordinated human body and render it effortlessly and with entirely convincing consistency in all its parts. This fidelity to nature was a revelation even in an age (the nineteenth century) that was at the end of a long tradition of respect for nature in art. The artist Benjamin Robert Haydon, writing in that time, described his reaction to the reclining figure of Dionysos (Herakles?) (FIG. 5-41), which he called Theseus:

But when I turned to the Theseus, and saw that every form was altered by action or repose—when I saw that the two sides of his back varied, one side stretched from the shoulder blade being pulled forward, and the other being compressed from the shoulder blade being pushed close to the spine, as he rested on his elbow, with the belly flat because the bowels fell into the pelvis as he sat—when I saw in fact the most heroic style of art, combined with all the essential detail of actual life, the thing was done at once and forever . . . Here were principles which the great Greeks in their finest time established . . .[3]

These principles seem indeed to be the monumental or heroic style "combined," as Haydon wrote, "with all the essential detail of actual life," the calm grandeur and simplicity of the one being in no way weakened by the precise, dynamic anatomical logic of the other.

The three goddesses from the east pediment of the Parthenon (FIG. 5-42), show even more than the *Dionysos* (*Herakles?*) the reinforcing and complementary actions of the principles of monumentality of scale and simplicity of pose with the "essential detail of actual life." The statues are typically Phidian in style, at once majestic and utterly "real" in the reading of the relaxed forms.

[3] In F. H. Taylor, *The Taste of Angels* (Boston: Little, Brown, 1948), p. 502.

5-42 *Three Goddesses*, from the east pediment of the Parthenon. Marble, over life-size. British Museum, London.

In thin and heavy folds, the drapery alternately reveals and conceals the main and the lesser masses of the bodies, at the same time swirling in a compositional tide that subtly unifies the group, the articulation and integration of the bodies producing a wonderful variation of surface and play of light and shade. Not only are the bodies fluidly related to each other, but they are related as well to the draperies, though the latter remain distinct from the bodies materially. The treatment of body and drapery as obviously different stuffs, yet in functional relation to each other, illustrates the thoroughly reasoned laws of appearance that Phidias and his generation had come to know and respect.

The sculptural decorations of the Parthenon are in the pediments (some of the figures of which were just described), on the metopes, and on a continuous Ionic frieze at the top of the external cella wall. Those on the metopes provide an accent of movement, notably by the use of diagonal forms in successive compositions of pairs of struggling interlocking figures done in high relief—centaurs and Lapiths, gods and giants, Greeks and Amazons. The metope illustrated (FIG. 5-43), shows a battle between a Lapith and a centaur, the theme of the Apollo pediment at Olympia (FIG. 5-34). The figures are accommodated with great adroitness to the square spaces offered by the metopes, and the whole series displays the ingenuity of the Phidian school in varying the poses and attitudes of the figures and avoiding the monotony that a regularly repeated space could impose. It is interesting also that the fortunes of the contestants are about equally balanced, the Greeks seeming to win or lose as often as their opponents.

The inner Ionic frieze of figures (FIGS. 5-44 and 5-45) was seen from below in reflected light against a colored ground. It enriched the plain wall and directed attention toward the entrance to the temple. It may represent the Panathenaic

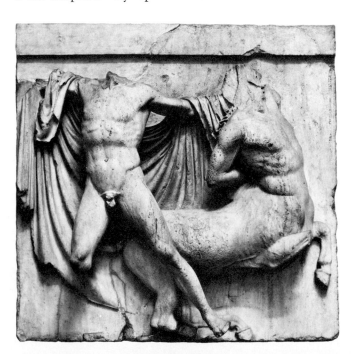

5-43 *Lapith and Centaur*, metope from the Parthenon. Marble, 4′ 8″ high. British Museum, London.

procession, which took place every four years, when the citizens of Athens gathered in the marketplace and carried to the Parthenon the *peplos*, or robe, for the statue of Athena. If so, this is the first known representation of a non-mythological subject in Greek temple reliefs.

The Panathenaic frieze is unique in the ancient world for its careful creation of the impression of the passage of time, albeit a brief fragment of it. The effect is achieved by use of a sequence of figures so posed as to present a gradation of motion—a rudimentary picture of time as an acceleration or deceleration. In order to experience the illusion, the observer must himself be in motion, following the frieze around the colonnade of the temple. In the part of the frieze that decorated the western side of the cella the viewer can see the procession forming: Youths are lacing their sandals and holding or mounting their horses; they are guided by marshals who stand at intervals, and particularly at the corners, to slow movement and guide the horsemen at the turn. In the friezes of the two long sides of the cella the procession moves in parallel lines, a cavalcade of spirited youths, chariots, elders, jar-carriers, and animals for sacrifice. Seen throughout the procession is that balance of the monumental-simple and the actual, of the tactile and the optical, of the "ideal" and the "real," of the permanent and the momentary that, again, is characteristically Greek and the perfect exemplification of the "inner concord of opposites" that Herakleitos, the philosopher, wrote of in the sixth century B.C. The eye follows the movement of light and shade in the drapery, pausing at any point by shifting focus to the broad areas of planes, with their sharply linear outlines. The movement of the procession becomes slower and more solemn as it nears the eastern side of the cella, when, after turning the corner, it approaches the seated divinities, who appear to be guests of Athena at her great festival. Standing

5-46 MNESICLES, the Propylaea, Acropolis, Athens, *c.* 437–432 B.C. (view from the east).

5-47 Temple of Athena Nike, Acropolis, Athens, 427–424 B.C.

5-48 The Erechtheum, Acropolis, Athens, 421–405 B.C. (view from the south).

5-49 Reconstructed elevations of the east and west façades of the Erechtheum.

figures—to note one device of the artists—face against the general movement at ever closer intervals, slowing the forward motion of the procession (FIG. 5-45).

OTHER BUILDINGS OF THE ACROPOLIS

To reach the Parthenon, the Panathenaic procession would have wound its way from the lower level of the city of Athens, up the steep slope of the Acropolis, and through the gate called the Propylaea (FIGS. 5-38 and 5-46), another structure of the Periclean project. Built by MNESICLES between 437 and 432 B.C., it was begun immediately upon the completion of the Parthenon but was never finished, partly because of the financial drain of the Peloponnesian War and partly, it is believed, because one of its wings would have trespassed on the sanctuary of Artemis Brauronia. The design is a monumental and subtle elaboration of a gate unit leading through a city wall, the gate hall itself being flanked by buildings containing a library and perhaps the first picture gallery (*pinakotheke*) in history. Here persons could rest in beautiful surroundings after the steep climb and before they passed on to the sacred buildings on the summit. The Propylaea shows modifications of Doric regularity in the broadening of the space between the central columns to make the passageway more commodious, and, like the Parthenon, it includes Ionic elements such as the columns lining the corridor and giving greater height where it is needed for the support of the central roof structure.

The beautiful little Ionic Temple of Athena Nike (Athena Victorious), built under the direction of Callicrates between 427 and 424 B.C. (FIGS. 5-19C, 5-38, and 5-47), is the earliest completely Ionic building extant on the Acropolis. Before this time the Ionic order had been used for a whole building in a few treasuries at Olympia and Delphi on the Greek mainland (for example, the Treasury of the Siphnians, FIG. 5-26), and these had been constructed by Aegean islanders, not by Greeks of the mainland. It was through Athens' rule of the islands that it became open to eastern Greek and Ionian influences.

←to c. 700 B.C. 480　　　c. 450 448　　　　421　　　c. 400 399　　　　　　　　c. 340　　323 B.C.

| AR-CHAIC PERIOD | Kritios Boy | | Parthenon begun | Erechtheum begun | | Socrates dies | | PRAXITELES Hermes and Dionysos | Alexander dies |
| | ←—— TRANSITIONAL ——→ | | ←———— C L A S S I C A L | E A R L Y ————→ | | | ←—— P E R I O D | L A T E ——→ | |

The little amphiprostyle temple stands on what used to be a Mycenaean bastion near the Propylaea, to the Doric severity of which this slender, exquisitely proportioned building offers a striking contrast, heightening the effect of both.

Another Ionic building situated on the Acropolis is the Erechtheum (FIGS. 5-38 and 5-48), the last of the Periclean program. Constructed between 421 and 405 B.C., the Erechtheum is most unusual in plan and quite unlike any other Greek temple. It was named after the mythic Athenian hero, Erechtheus, to whom it was in part dedicated. Its many unusual features are due partly to the irregularity of its site and partly to the number of shrines included within it. According to the above-mentioned Pausanias, the Greek geographer and historian of the second century A.D., the Erechtheum stood on the traditional site of the contest between Poseidon and Athena for dominion over Athens, the theme of the sculpture group in the west pediment of the Parthenon. Also at the site were a rock supposed to be at the imprint of Poseidon's trident, the spring of salt water that the stroke of the trident produced, and Athena's olive tree. The asymmetrical arrangement of the building, which probably was not intended in the original plan, may also reflect an interruption and a "making-do" caused by the impending and final defeat of Athens in the Peloponnesian War, in 404 B.C. Thus, the Erechtheum was not completed as planned, and it can be assumed that the original plan provided for the west face to extend so that the north and south porches would have had their positions in the centers of the long blank walls. In the reconstructed elevations of the east and the west sides (FIG. 5-49) we can observe that on the east the different levels of the friezes are smoothly adjusted, while the west side appears to have been finished hurriedly with a wall to which are attached half-columns, the spaces between which are closed with bronze grilles. These *engaged* columns are rarely used in Classical Greek architecture, though the device is very popular later in Roman architecture. If one approaches the building with some rigid preconception of Greek architectural order, its overall effect may be disappointing; however, the asymmetry of the Erechtheum is extremely effective as a complement to the symmetrical unity of the Parthenon, just as the Korai of its Porch of the Maidens complement the Parthenon's Doric columns. Moreover, the carved details of the Erechtheum are without rival in their refined beauty.

SCULPTURE

The Porch of the Maidens, the south porch of the Erechtheum, is so called because its caryatids are its dominating feature (FIG. 5-50). It brings

5-50 Porch of the Maidens, the Erechtheum.

5-51 *Grave Stele of Hegeso*, Dipylon cemetery, *c.* 410–400 B.C. Marble, 59″ high. National Museum, Athens.

sumed to be supporting. There are technical as well as esthetic reasons for the Erechtheum adjustment: Although the weight of a full entablature was borne by the Siphnian caryatids, in this case the load could have been too great for the necks of the figures, their weakest point; however, esthetic considerations were probably the more persuasive. Thus, again, we find the Classical architect-sculptor balancing in his wonderfully trained judgment the realities of structure with the necessities of ideal beauty. The figures have enough rigidity to suggest the structural columnar and just the degree of flexibility necessary to suggest the living body. The compromise is quite superbly brought off. The corner figures determine the stance by representing the weight as falling on the outer leg. The inner figures repeat this pose so that the legs not carrying the weight, and bent at the knee, do not determine the architectural verticals, nor disturb their natural plumb-line straightness. These figures have all the monumental majesty of Phidias' on the Parthenon pediments; the pleats and folds of their draperies reveal the quiet power of their bodies, and the very obligation imposed upon them by the architecture serves only to strengthen their noble poise.

The Phidian style dominated Athenian sculpture until the end of the fifth century B.C. Because of the Peloponnesian War fewer large-scale sculptural enterprises were launched, although the style lingered on in smaller works such as the popular grave steles produced in considerable numbers for both local use and export. One of the most harmoniously designed of these is the *Grave Stele of Hegeso* (FIG. 5-51), which was found in the Dipylon cemetery. As was often the case in grave reliefs of the Classical period, the figures are placed in an architectural framework. The deceased is seated on a chair with sweepingly curved back and legs that provides an effective transition from the frozen forms of the architecture to the organic ones of the figures. Hegeso is contemplating a necklace (originally rendered in paint) that she has taken from the box held by her girl servant. The quiet glances of mistress and servant meet at Hegeso's right hand, which, placed exactly in the center of the panel, is the compositional focal point. Although the

to mind that earlier Ionic caryatid design, the Treasury of the Siphnians (FIG. 5-26), and comparison of the two is useful. Unlike the Siphnian caryatids, those of the south porch of the Erechtheum do not carry a full entablature but one that consists of architrave and cornice only, the topmost fascia of the architrave being decorated with medallions to simulate the missing frieze. This seems to be a deliberate proportional adjustment undertaken by the sculptors of the Erechtheum figures to avoid the effect seen in the Siphnian caryatids, which look overloaded by the entablature; the sculptors must have been aware that figures graceful in attitude and dimension could scarcely harmonize with a massive architectural superstructure they would be pre-

5-52 *Nike Fastening her Sandal,* from the parapet of the
Temple of Athena Nike, Acropolis, Athens,
c. 410 B.C. Marble, approx. 42″ high.
Acropolis Museum, Athens.

stele was carved toward the end of the century,
it is devoid of the sentimentality found in many
other works of its day; the solemn pathos of the
scene links the stele with the grandiose conception
of the Parthenon sculptures.

The relief of a Nike fastening her sandal (FIG.
5-52) from a parapet that was constructed around
the Temple of Athena Nike about 410 B.C.
shows how sculptors, having achieved the Classical perfection of the human form, now exhibit
their virtuosity. The function of the concentri-
cally arranged draperies, heavy and clinging to
the form as if drenched with water, is to reveal
the supple beauty of the young body. The interplay of the intricately moving drapery and the
smooth volumes of the body seen in the *Three
Goddesses* of the Parthenon (FIG. 5-42) is here refined to make a deliberately transparent veil for
the female figure, which now fully emerges from
the elaborate costume of the Kore tradition.

In contrast with the Ionian sumptuousness of
the Phidian style is a work of the Argive school of
southern Greece, the *Doryphoros* (FIG. 5-53) of
POLYKLEITOS, a sculptor whose fame rivaled that
of Phidias in the ancient world. The work shown
here, the original of which is dated 450–440 B.C.,
is a Roman copy made much later.

Almost all extant works of the so-called Great
Masters of Greek sculpture are replicas, the
originals having disappeared. Originals of Roman
copies can be identified through descriptions by
ancient authors, especially Pausanias and Pliny
the Elder, and occasionally through representations on ancient coins. There are a number of
reasons for the disappearance of the originals: In
war, statues made of precious materials were
often pillaged and bronze statues melted to make
weapons or utensils; during the barbarian invasions in the time of the fall of the Roman
empire marble statues were used to make lime
for mortar. After the Romans conquered Greece,
in the second century B.C., they took Greek works
of art to Rome to adorn the imperial palaces and
the villas of the rich. Numerous copies were

5-53 POLYKLEITOS, *Doryphoros,* original *c.* 450–440 B.C.
Roman copy, marble, 6′ 6″ high. Museo Nazionale,
Naples.

made of some statues, reflecting their popularity and fame. Many of the copyists took liberties with the originals; changes were made to conform with popular taste, and very few of the copies even approach the quality and refinement that the originals must have had. When the Romans were copying bronze in marble, they used awkward devices to strengthen weak points —such as a tree trunk placed next to a statue's leg and braces and struts to prevent breakage of the arms, as can be seen in the *Doryphoros*. Nevertheless, the copy of the *Doryphoros* does give evidence of the appearance of the original, and we can compare its blocky solidity and strength with the subtle grace of the Phidian style. Although the unity and equilibrium that pervade the works of Phidias are also in the Polykleitan statue, the origins differ, for while the artists at work on the Parthenon seem to have achieved their results with a deft, spontaneous translation of natural appearances, Polykleitos worked according to a canon of proportions in which he formulated the principles that give rise to unity. Although Polykleitos' own treatise enunciating his canon is lost, Galen, the second century A.D. physician, interprets it as follows in his *Placita Hippocratis et Platonis*:

> beauty consists in the proportions, not of the elements, but of the parts, that is to say, of finger to finger, and of all the fingers to the palm and the wrist, and of these to the forearm, and of the forearm to the upper arm, and of all the other parts to each other, as they are set forth in the Canon of Polycleitos.

It was said that in the *Doryphoros* Polykleitos had not simply made a statue but had manifested sculpture itself, and Aristotle uses "sculptor" and "Polykleitos" interchangeably. As the Greeks saw proportion as the central problem in architecture, so did they in sculpture, and they viewed Polykleitos' canon as the embodiment of proportional rationality for sculpture.

In the *Doryphoros*, movement, which began to be expressed successfully in the early fifth century B.C., is disciplined through the use of an imposed system of proportions. The mighty body, with its broad shoulders. thick torso, and muscular limbs, strikes us as the embodiment of the Spartan ideal of the warrior physique, the human equivalent of the Doric order. And, like the Doric order, the figure appeals to the intellect and must be studied long and carefully before it fully reveals itself to the observer. The slow forward walk, the standard Polykleitan pose, stresses the principle of weight-shift—the maneuver that must be made before we can move at all and with which the whole development of the representation of the moving human figure begins. What appears to be a casually natural pose is, in fact, the result of an extremely complex and subtle organization of the various parts of the figure. Note, for instance, how the function of the supporting leg is echoed by the straight-hanging arm to provide the right side of the figure with the columnar stability needed to anchor the dynamically flexed limbs of the left side. If read anatomically, on the other hand, the tensed and relaxed limbs may be seen to oppose each other diagonally (that is, the right arm and the left leg are relaxed, and the tensed supporting leg is opposed by the flexed right arm, which held a spear). Thus, all parts of the figure have been carefully composed to achieve the utmost variety within a compact and stable whole. A most circumspect and subtle artist has combined realism, monumentality, and diversity in a unified design that seems to be beyond the reproach of even the most discriminating critic.

PAINTING

The mural painter POLYGNOTOS enjoyed almost as much fame in antiquity as his contemporaries, Phidias and Polykleitos. Unfortunately, none of his works survive. On the basis of ancient literary sources, it is believed that his style is reflected in the vase decoration of the NIOBID PAINTER, whose *Argonaut Krater* (FIG. 5-54) illustrates a radical break with the traditional decorative style. For over two centuries figures had been arranged isocephalically—that is, with all the heads at one level—in horizontal bands, not only in Greek vase decoration, but also in monumental painting. Evidence for the latter seems to be provided by surviving Etruscan frescoes, which presumably reflect contemporary, or slightly earlier, Greek mural styles (see

Chapter Six). On the *Argonaut Krater* the figures have been placed on different levels, and ground lines on which they stand or recline attempt to introduce into painting the illusion of depth, an effect that is thwarted, however, by the uniform size of the figures. We also read that Polygnotos modeled his figures in dark and light, aiming for three-dimensional and sculptural effects. This last feature was not adopted by the Niobid Painter, whose style remains linear and does not reveal what must have been an impressive statuesque quality of Polygnotan figures. Though important as reflecting—dimly, to be sure—the monumental manner of Polygnotos, the Niobid Painter's works also represent the decline of vase painting as the figurative decoration loses contact with the body of the vessel, the earlier cohesion of figure and surface becoming mere adhesion.

Although the work of the Niobid Painter may give some notion of the general compositional schemes of Polygnotos, it tells nothing of his use of color. A pale reflection of it may be found in the so-called white-ground vases of the fifth century B.C. Experiments with the white-ground technique go back to the Andokides Painter, but the method became popular only toward the middle of the fifth century. It is essentially a variation of the red-figure technique, the pot first being covered with a slip of very fine white clay that, when burnished, provided a glossy or matte white surface for drawing in black glaze or dilute brown wash. The range of colors remained severely limited—purple, brown, and several kinds of red—as few colors known to the Greeks could survive the heat of the kiln. Also, the white slip, although highly effective as background for drawing and coloring, was not durable, tending to flake off. Crucial for wares that saw daily use, such as cups and kraters, this impermanence was less so in vessels that had a more limited use, such as funerary *lekythoi* (oil flasks), which were not handled after they had been deposited in the tomb. After mid-century, the white-ground technique was reserved almost exclusively for funerary vases of this type, some of which were even painted in full polychrome *after* the vase had been fired—naturally at an even greater cost in durability.

5-54 NIOBID PAINTER, *Argonaut Krater*, Orvieto, Italy, *c.* 455–450 B.C. Outline drawing at right indicates relation to whole vessel. Portion shown approx. 15″ high; whole vessel approx. 21″ high. Louvre, Paris.

The example shown in PLATE 5-2 uses the conservative colors that could withstand firing. It shows Hermes handing the infant Dionysos to Papposilenos ("granddad-satyr") and the nymphs in the shady glens of Nysa, where Zeus had sent Dionysos, one of his illegitimate sons, to be raised, safe from the possible wrath of his wife, Hera. The artist has used reds, brown, purple, and a special snowy white, the last for the flesh of the nymphs and for such details as the hair, beard, and shaggy body of Papposilenos. Despite this rather limited color scheme, the painting's effect is warm and rich; in combination with the compositional devices of the Niobid Painter, it may provide a shadowy idea of the appearance of the famed Polygnotan murals, which had so impressed ancient viewers.

The grandeur of the age of Phidias and Polykleitos, when their styles briefly dominated Greek art, passed with them. What followed, though exquisite and virtuoso, constituted a descent from their heights, becoming elegant, slight, more and more naturalistic, less concerned with the lofty themes and majestic forms. The statues of "godlike" men became statues of men of this world.

5-56 PRAXITELES, *Head of Hermes*, detail of FIG. 5-55.

5-55 PRAXITELES, *Hermes and Dionysos*, c. 340 B.C. Marble, approx. 7' high. Museum, Olympia.

THE FOURTH CENTURY AND THE HELLENISTIC PERIOD

The Late Classical Period

The disastrous Peloponnesian War, which ended in 404 B.C. with the complete defeat of Athens, left Greece drained of its strength. Sparta and then Thebes took the leadership of Greece, both unsuccessfully. In the latter half of the fourth century B.C., the Greek states lost their liberty to Philip of Macedon. Athens lost its precedence. The whole structure of life changed; the traditional balance between the city-state and the individual was lost. The serene idealism of the fifth century, born of a simple, robust concept of mind and matter, of man and the state, gave way to chronic civil wars, social and political unrest, skepticism, and cynicism.

The Apollonian command "Know thyself," which Socrates taught as he spoke with the people in their daily gathering places, inevitably changed the Greek point of view to a more individualistic one. Euripides, too, seems to regard the individual as paramount, and his dramas depict a whole spectrum of human passions and crises. Aristophanes, however, ridiculed both Socrates and Euripides for their apparent departures from the good old Classical ways and customs and especially for their emphasis upon the role and value of the individual. During the fourth century B.C. man's intellectual independence was firmly established by Plato—however much he himself regretted the passing of the old ways—whose doctrine of eternal forms such as "virtue," "justice," and "courage" could serve as the rational models upon which the individual could construct his life. Aristotle, perhaps the most versatile of all thinkers, formulated the operations of reason in the science we call logic, converting reason into an instrument applicable to all human experience. Aristotle turned his attention systematically on just about everything that could be of interest to man, and among his fundamental contributions is the outline of the sciences of nature.

Thus, gradually separating himself from the old assurances—the gods, their oracles, and time-honored custom—as prime interpreters of the meaning of life, the Greek carried on his search to know himself and to achieve knowledge of the world and life through observant experience. His dependence upon the city-state lessened, until he boasted with Diogenes: "I am a citizen of the world." Knowing the real, for whatever purpose, becomes the conspicuously Greek faculty and value. In the midst of political disaster, Greece, in the fourth century, enacted a daring drama of human discovery.

SCULPTURE

The humanizing tendency that had been gathering force throughout the fifth century achieved characteristic expression in the sculpture of the fourth century; though themes lose something of the earlier, solemn grandeur and representations of the greater gods give place to those of the lesser, the naturalistic view of the human figure is fully focused. The *Hermes and Dionysos* attributed to Praxiteles (FIGS. 5-55 and 5-56) is a work of such high quality that some authorities insist it must be by Praxiteles himself and not a mere Roman copy. The god is represented standing, with a shift in weight from the left arm (supporting the upper body) to the right leg, so that there is a double distribution of the weight, giving the pose, with its fluid axis, the form of a sinuous, shallow S-curve that becomes a manner with Praxiteles. On his arm Hermes holds the infant Dionysos, who reaches for something (probably a bunch of grapes) Hermes held in his right hand. Hermes is looking off into space with a dreamy expression, half smiling. The whole figure, particularly the head, seems in deep reverie, the god withdrawn in self-admiration. The modeling is deliberately smooth and subtle, producing soft shadows that follow the planes as they flow almost imperceptibly one into another. The delicacy of the features is enhanced by the rough, impressionistic way in which the hair is indicated, and the deep folds of the realistic drapery are sharply contrasted with the flow and gloss of the languidly graceful figure. It needs but a comparative glance at Polykleitos' *Doryphoros* to see how broad a change in artistic attitude and intent took place from the mid-fifth to the mid-fourth century. Majestic strength and rationalizing design are replaced by sensuous languor and an order of beauty appealing more to the eye than the mind. Praxiteles' esthetic of the human nude, with its emphasis on the exquisitely smooth modeling that reproduces the tones of resilient flesh, naturally led him to become the inventor of the nude female statue. His *Aphrodite*

5-57 *Aphrodite of Cyrene*, North Africa, c. 100 B.C. Marble. Museo Nazionale Romano, Rome. (After fourth-century type.)

5-58 *Warrior's Head*, from the Temple of Athena Alea at Tegea, *c.* 350 B.C. Marble. National Museum, Athens.

5-59 *Mausolus*, from the mausoleum at Halicarnassus, *c.* 355 B.C. Marble, approx. 9′ 10″ high. British Museum, London.

of Cnidus was widely regarded in antiquity as the most beautiful of all statues, the pride of Cnidus, the city that owned it. Its charm can best be understood, not from the inferior Roman copy of it, but from a much later, Hellenistic work, the *Aphrodite of Cyrene* (FIG. 5-57), which at two centuries remove conveys a Praxitelean poetry of sensual beauty. For both the male and female nude, Praxiteles set a new, more personal and naturalistic ideal of physical beauty.

Though Praxiteles' style was greatly admired, and though his theme of the bathing Aphrodite was taken up again and again long after his time, he was not the only influential sculptor in the late Classical period. A fellow Athenian, SCOPAS, is known for a robust and vigorous style more suited to the representation of action and perhaps

derived from Polykleitos. A fragmentary head from Tegea in Greece (FIG. 5-58) illustrates Scopas' style and shows a hitherto undepicted tension of facial expression, the features broad and strong, the eyes large, round, and set deeply under knitted brows. As a reflection of inner states through varied facial expressions, this work breaks with the Classical tradition of benign, neutral features and prefigures later Hellenistic art, when the depiction of emotion becomes more important to sculpture.

The monumental Tomb of Mausolus, another of the seven wonders of the ancient world, was built for King Mausolus and his Queen Artemisia. Mausolus was king of Caria, a non-Greek state in southwest Asia Minor, and was in the service of the king of Persia. The colossal portrait-statues of

5-60 LYSIPPOS, *Apoxyomenos*, bronze original *c.* 330 B.C. Roman copy, marble, approx. 6′ 9″ high. Vatican Museums, Rome.

pos was very prolific, his work is extant in copies only, including, notably, the *Apoxyomenos* (FIG. 5-60), which represents a young athlete scraping oil and mud from his body before taking his bath. The figure embodies two important innovations of the time, which may be creditable to Lysippos. One was a new canon of proportions, replacing the Polykleitan canon and reflecting a change in taste noticeable in all the arts. The new canon required a more slender, supple, and tall figure, a conception toward which we have already seen Praxiteles moving. This innovation may indeed have been influenced by the second (also foreshadowed in earlier works)—the full realization of the figure moving in space, not in the two dimensions of the figures hitherto examined (whether Phidian, Polykleitan, or Praxitelean), but in *three* dimensions. Thus, the figure now moves in a kind of free spiral through the space around it; it is made to be seen from a variety of angles, and it is related to things in its environment other than itself. The earliest Greek figures had been in a stiff frontal position, with the planes closely related to the stone block from which they had been carved; they were best seen from only one or two positions. The form was enclosed in space; space was its limit. Even when the figure was treated less rigidly, so that the torso as well as the arms and legs moved in a curve, it was still seen satisfactorily only from one or two points of view. In this respect an Archaic Kouros (FIG. 5-16) and the *Hermes and Dionysos* of Praxiteles (FIG. 5-55) are more nearly alike than are the *Hermes* and the *Apoxyomenos* of Lysippos. In the latter the arms curve forward, the figure enclosing space in its reach and twisting in it; the small head is thrown into stronger perspective by the large hand interposed between it and the viewer. Lysippos said that he wished to make men the way the eye sees them, allowing thus for accidents of perspective.

As Praxiteles prepared the way for developing optical realism in his subtle surface effects, so Scopas and Lysippos foreshadow Hellenistic themes (see below) demanding force, action, and dramatic emotion. Before the new drama could develop in sculpture, space had to be understood

the king (FIG. 5-59) and queen date from about 355 B.C. Presumably they are intended as likenesses; the sculptor, who is unknown, is particular about the hair—curiously reminiscent of the Archaic—and the dynamics of the drapery. He continues that study of the drapery masses begun in the previous century and is at pains to read them so closely and realistically that he differentiates folds and pleats from the minute creases thin drapery would acquire in use. The colossal monument and the large figures reflect Eastern influence, and already we sense that mingling of East and West that is to compose the Hellenistic styles of the last centuries before Christ.

The most renowned sculptor of the second half of the fourth century B.C. was LYSIPPOS, court sculptor to Alexander the Great. Although Lysipin a new way, not as merely the limit of the body, but as an environment in which the body could act freely, as in nature.

ARCHITECTURE

It is noteworthy that, in its full development of the Corinthian order, the architecture of the fourth century also produced a "body" that offered a complete aspect from any angle. The first Corinthian capital—the order differs from the Ionic only in its capital—had appeared on the inside of the cella of the Temple of Apollo at Bassae, around 450 B.C. It crowned a column that, because it stood as a divider between two parts of the cella, could be seen from all sides. Presumably it was designed for that purpose and provided a much more satisfactory solution than the Ionic capital, which is designed to be seen effectively from two sides only. For Ionic colonnades that turn corners, like those of peripteral structures, special "corner capitals" had to be designed that would look the same on the two sides facing outward. The sharply projecting edge formed by the two meeting volutes never quite satisfied Classical architects, who may also have felt that this solution was achieved only at the expense of

the structural logic of the Ionic capital and by a distortion of its functional parts. The problem was solved by the Corinthian capital, which can be seen to equal advantage from all sides. Its original design has been associated with the relief sculptor and metal-worker Callimachos, who may have been at Bassae when the Temple of Apollo was built and of whom the sentimental story was told in antiquity that he was inspired to design the capital when he saw acanthus leaves growing up around a slab-weighted votive basket on the grave of a maiden. Be that as it may, though the Corinthian order appeared in the fifth century B.C., for almost a century it was used on the inside of the temple only. It is uncertain whether this is to be attributed to religious conservatism, which would tend to preserve a feature that had taken on a certain sanctity from its function at the temple's center, or whether experiments with the Ionic were continuing and a Doric tradition persisting. In any event, full emergence of the Corinthian order on a public exterior takes place about the same time as Lysippos' freeing of the sculptured figure from its two-aspect limits.

A capital from the tholos at Epidaurus (FIG. 5-61), where a Corinthian colonnade stood inside the cella of a Doric structure, illustrates a step along the Corinthian order's elaborative route, which culminates in the characteristic Hellenistic and Roman luxuriance. Here the bell is thickly clothed with acanthus leaf and manifests that same increasing attention to the deep and detailed sculpturing of stone surfaces that was noted in sculptured figures.

The monument of Lysicrates (FIG. 5-62), constructed in Athens in 334 B.C., shows the first known use of the Corinthian order on the outside of a building. Significantly, the innovation appears not on a religious but on a commemorative monument. The graceful cylinder to which the Corinthian columns are engaged memorializes the victory of a choric group whose patron was Lysicrates and which had won the prized trophy of the tripod in the wild, dithyrambic contest of song in honor of Dionysos. The little tholos serves as a base for the monumentalized tripod. Henceforth, the Corinthian order will be more and more in use on the exterior of public buildings until it comes to

5-61 Corinthian capital from the tholos at Epidaurus, c. 350 B.C. Museum, Epidaurus.

exclude almost all other orders in the architectural design of the Romans. In addition to having solved the vexing problems of both the Doric and Ionic orders—the corner-triglyph and the corner-volute dilemmas—the Corinthian order, with its ornateness, was bound to suit the developing taste for sumptuous elaboration of form and realistic representation that guided artistic effort in the Hellenistic world.

The Hellenistic Period

Philip of Macedon brought the once free Greek city-states into subjection. His son, Alexander the Great, educated in Hellenism, the culture of Greece, by none other than Aristotle, returned the visit the Persians had made to Greece a century and a half before, overthrew their empire, and conquered all the Near East, including Egypt. Greek conquest of this vast area produced a culture and period called Hellenistic, a curious mingling of Western and Eastern ideas, religions, and arts, and a long period of Greek cultural—and partly political—dominance that made her the cosmopolitan heir of Sumer, Babylon, Egypt, Assyria, and Persia. Greedy for the lands their young leader had conquered, his generals asked Alexander on his death bed, "To which one of us do you leave your empire?" In the skeptical manner of the age, but also with more than a tinge of an older irony, he is supposed to have answered, "To the strongest." Although probably apocryphal, this exchange points up the near inevitability of what followed—the division of Alexander's far-flung empire among his Greek generals and their subsequent naturalization among the Orientals whom they held subject.

The centers of culture in the Hellenistic period were the court cities of these Greek kings—Antioch in Syria, Alexandria in Egypt, Pergamum in Asia Minor, and others. An international culture united the Hellenistic world, and its language was Greek. Hellenistic princes became enormously rich on the spoils of the East, priding themselves on their libraries, art collections, scientific enterprises, and skill as critics and connoisseurs, as well as on the learned men they could assemble at their courts. The world of the small, austere, and heroic city-state passed away

5-62 The monument of Lysicrates, Athens, c. 334 B.C.

as had the power and prestige of its center, Athens, and a "world" civilization, much like today's, took its place.

SCULPTURE

The tendencies traced thus far all the way from the Archaic period are not interrupted by this change but simply go on to anticipated completions. In sculpture, the "environment" that opened up around the *Apoxyomenos* of Lysippos (FIG. 5-60) is opened still more around the *Nike of Samothrace* (FIG. 5-63). The goddess of victory is here represented as alighting upon the prow of a war galley, triumphant in some conflict among the successors of Alexander in the Greek world around 190 B.C. One of the masterpieces of the Hellenistic age, the *Nike*, windswept, her wings still beating, brings strength, weight, and airy grace into an equipoise one would not expect to be achieved in the hard mass of sculptured marble. But it is a fact that the sculptors are here working their stone with a freedom emulative of painters. They achieve shadows and gradations of shadows by variations of surface carving, almost as if they were using broad as against light brush strokes. The gauzelike stretch of material across the stomach and the waves of drapery around the striding thighs and legs amount not only to an exercise in virtuosity of stonecraft but a successful effort to make stone do what poetry and painting do—that is, render at the same time the visual nuances of the moment and the ongoing essence of action. In the end, the sculptor wants us to sense, from the figure itself, an atmosphere of wind and sea. We recall the billowing sail of Exekias' *Dionysos* (FIG. 5-7), where it all seems to have begun.

The extension of the spatial environment of the figure, so as to suggest a stage upon which it may and does act, appears in sculptures associated with the Hellenistic kingdom of Pergamum and the island republic of Rhodes, from the third through the first century B.C. From a group dedicated by Attalus I of Pergamum (241–197 B.C.) there survives a figure, in Roman copy, of a *Dying Gaul* (FIG. 5-64). The figure is on stage, realistic, and also historical, since it is meant to represent a Gallic casualty in the wars Attalus had just fought with barbarian invaders. Comparison of the *Dying Gaul* and the *Fallen Warrior* from Aegina (FIG. 5-30) shows that, in a little more than

5-63 *Nike of Samothrace, c.* 190 B.C. Marble, approx. 8' high. Louvre, Paris.

5-64 *Dying Gaul*, bronze original, Pergamum, *c.* 240 B.C. Roman copy, marble, life-size. Museo Capitolino, Rome.

two centuries, the principle of uniformity of movement has been well learned. The Gaul, dying from a chest wound that bleeds heavily, slowly loses strength, his weight falling rapidly upon his last support, the trembling right arm; its collapse will be his own. This the observer reads at once from the lines and planes of the body, visually, and with no need of interpretation or filling-out of the meaning. The statue is a triumph of realism. It may mark also the surrender of the interests of sculpture to the stage, where, we know, spectacles of human suffering painted with all realism of detail were sapping the great tradition of drama and diminishing human life in bloody scenes that could only present it as worthless. With the *Dying Gaul* the sculpture of action degenerates into brutal stagecraft. Realism can go no further, even while it triumphs.

A later school of Pergamum exhibits a realism not quite so explicit, yet nonetheless belonging to the Hellenistic taste for tableaux of monumental suffering. A section of the great frieze of the *Battle of Gods and Giants* from the Pergamum Altar of Zeus and Athena (FIGS. 5-65 and 5-66) illustrates the highly dramatic kind of figurative sculpture that descended from Scopas and Lysippos. The altar was erected about 180 B.C. by the son and successor of Attalus I to glorify his father's victories. In a representation less factual than the group of dying Gauls, the artists here revert to

the traditional Greek approach of presenting historical events in mythological disguise. The suffering and death, the writhing gesticulation, are somewhat formalized, and we do not feel so much that we are in the presence of pain that ordinary men might feel. In the figure of Alcyoneus, the young giant whom Athena takes by the hair (FIG. 5-66), one finds the anguish of the face to be based upon Scopas and the twisting of the figure upon the athleticism of both Scopas and Lysippos. The tragic content is read through the increasingly dramatic style of stonecraft. The Greek vision of the climactic instant is still seen against a neutral background. Now, however, the background is almost obscured by shadows, from which the figures project like bursts of light. All these devices are "baroque" and closely related to those developed in seventeenth-century Europe. The unity of the design is achieved by a fluid, yet binding organization of parts—not unlike that of the figures of the three goddesses of the Parthenon (FIG. 5-42). Indeed, the two major figures of the frieze, Zeus and Athena, are directly inspired by the figures of Poseidon and Athena from the Parthenon pediments; yet this dynamic integration of the whole composition is unlike the carefully studied relationships of *separate* parts seen in the Early Classical period. In such pictorial unity, produced by the movement of light and the contrast of shade, we again recognize the strong influence of painting.

The theme of suffering is so pervasive in the Hellenistic world and its art that it could almost be understood as *the* interpretation of life by men who felt the hopelessness attendant upon the decline of an older, more reasonable system. A late work of Hellenistic sculpture is the *Laocoön* group, a product of a still quite active school of Rhodes (FIG. 5-67). It shows the Trojan priest, Laocoön, and his sons being strangled by sea serpents—some say because of his defiance of

5-67 Above: *Laocoön* group, early first century B.C. (?) Marble, 8′ high. Vatican Museums, Rome. (Partially restored.)

5-68 Right: AGESANDER, ATHANADOROS, and POLY- DOROS, *Odysseus' Helmsman Falling, c.* 150 B.C. (?) Marble, approx. life-size. Sperlonga Museum.

Apollo, others because he offended Poseidon (who sided with the Greeks) by warning his Trojan compatriots of the strategy of the Trojan Horse. Whatever his offense, Vergil has described his plight with unsparing realism:

> Laocoön . . . they [the sea serpents] seize and bind in mighty folds; and now, twice encircling his waist, twice winding their scaly backs around his throat, they tower above with head and lofty necks. He the while strains his hands to burst the knots, his fillets steeped in blood and black venom; the while he lifts to heaven hideous cries, like the bellowings of a wounded bull that has fled from the altar and shaken from its neck the ill-aimed axe.

The spectacular torment of Laocoön and his sons is presented with all the devices of rhetorical realism available to artists as well as poets—the tortuous poses, straining muscles, and swelling veins—yet curiously there are lapses from consistent visual fact, as in the—perhaps deliberate—disproportion of the size of the sons in relation to the size of the father, indicating them as *sons*, though they appear simply as small men. The exceedingly popular group was reproduced frequently, sometimes on a colossal scale, and in the eighteenth century the analysis of it by Gotthold Lessing led to his designation of art and poetry as opposed in function and to the foundation of the branch of philosophy called esthetics.

Pliny named three Rhodians—ATHANADOROS, AGESANDER, and POLYDOROS—as the sculptors of the *Laocoön* group. The same three names are inscribed on the stern of a marble ship (FIG. 5-68) that formed part of one of several sculptured groups, fragments of which have been found in a large grotto near the sea at Sperlonga, some eighty miles south of Rome. The cave, adjacent to a large imperial Roman villa built early in the first century A.D., had been used as a kind of dining room. Multifigured sculptured groups appear to have been displayed in two niches and in a round central pool within the grotto. At least some of the sculptures must have been brought from Rhodes and were installed in the grotto around A.D. 29, when the cave was refashioned after a partial collapse.

A definitive interpretation of the scenes is most difficult, since the groups were found only in

5-69 AGESANDER, ATHANADOROS, and POLYDOROS, *Head of Odysseus*, c. 150 B.C. (?) Marble, life-size. Sperlonga Museum.

fragments, the figures evidently having been smashed to make lime or out of religious fanaticism. At least two scenes from the *Odyssey* seem to have been represented: the blinding of Polyphemos (among the finds are the legs of a colossus that must have stood nearly twenty feet high) and Scylla attacking Odysseus' ship. FIG. 5-68 shows the terrified helmsman falling from the stern of the ship as his comrades (not shown) battle the monster, which has boarded the vessel. Probably the finest of the fragments is the head of Odysseus (FIG. 5-69). Less convulsed and emotional than Laocoön's head, it nevertheless reflects strikingly the horror of the situation and the fear of impending death. The effect is produced—without the use of grimaces or the exaggerated eyes and anguished mouth of Laocoön—by the wind-tossed, whirling hair and beard that frame the face of the Homeric hero, merely suggesting the blast of terror sparked by the fearful battle aboard the ship. While the dating of the Sperlonga sculptures remains uncertain,

| 323 B.C. | c. 300 | c. 240 | c. 175 | 146 | c. 50 | 30 B.C. |

| Hunter Mosaic, Pella | | Dying Gaul, Pergamum | Altar of Zeus and Athena, Pergamum | Roman "liberation" of Greece | APOLLONIUS (?) Seated Boxer |

H E L L E N I S T I C   P E R I O D

←——————EARLY——————→   ←——————LATE ("GRECO-ROMAN")——————→

it is felt that they must be earlier than the *Laocoön*, as they show the expressive power of the Rhodian sculptors at its height, before it succumbed to the theatrical exhibitionism that marks the latter group.

Side by side with the drama of suffering, Hellenistic sculpture continued the tradition of ideal, Praxitelean beauty, as in the *Aphrodite of Cyrene* (FIG. 5-57) already referred to. Another Hellenistic descendant of this Praxitelean line is the *Aphrodite of Melos* (FIG. 5-70), the famed *Venus de Milo*. Here, as in the former, the ideal is taken out of the hypersensible world of reasoned proportions and made into an apparition of living flesh—like the coming alive of Pygmalion's statue of Galatea. The feeling for stone as stone has quite surrendered to the ambition of

making stone look as though it were the soft, warm substance of the human body. Such effects as these can be obtained only by an artist with brilliant technical facility working in the conviction that the business of the artist is to produce from stone a vision of beauty, faithful to optical reality, yet so modified as to make the keenest appeal to the senses as a flawless manifestation of the human form. Faithfulness to optical fact can also lead the sculptor to represent, with unflattering explicitness, the opposite of beauty, as in the *Old Market Woman* (FIG. 5-71). The bent, hobbling creature is offered to the viewer as an object of contempt, pity, or disgust, depending upon his temperament.

The disparity in subject of these two works reflects the wide scope of theme and the visual curiosity of Hellenistic sculptors. The sculptor aims to move the observer in terms of the theme of his work. He wishes, moreover, for recognition by the observer of those traits in the statue that the observer knows in life, so that a large part of the response to the statue comes from the observer's familiarity with its model or type in the context of his own experience. Thus, while the Classical sculptor generally showed young adults at the height of their physical development, the Hellenistic artist expanded his subject matter to include not only the very old but also the very young. It seems unlikely that a fifth-century B.C. sculptor would have imagined that a boy strangling a goose (FIG. 5-72) could be a subject worthy of representation. The sculpture may strike us as somewhat unpleasant, with its sadistic overtones, but doubtless it was intended to be "cute" and to elicit fond smiles as well as praise of the artist, BOETHOS, for his ingenuity in inventing a curious subject. And it must be admitted that Boethos has succeeded, from the formal point of view, in converting a trivial subject into a remarkably effective work of art. The swirling forms have been contained in a compact, pyra-

5-70 *Aphrodite of Melos*, c. 150–100 B.C. Marble, approx. 6′ 10″ high. Louvre, Paris.

Color Plates 1-1 to 6-4

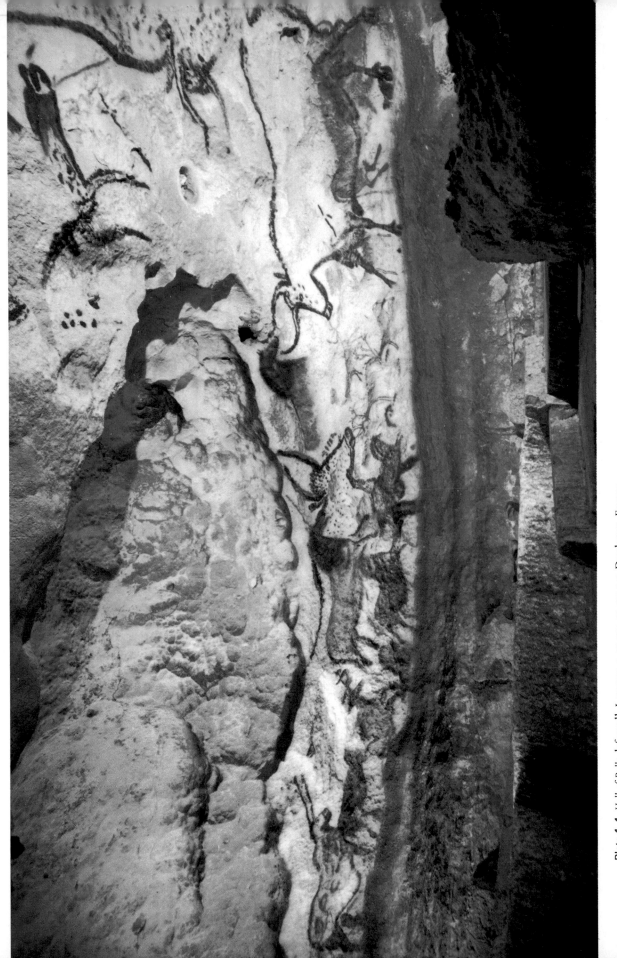

Plate 1-1 *Hall of Bulls*, left wall, Lascaux, *c.* 15,000–10,000 B.C. Dordogne, France.

Plate 1-2 *Second Bull*, detail of Plate I-I. Bull approx. 11′ 6″ long.

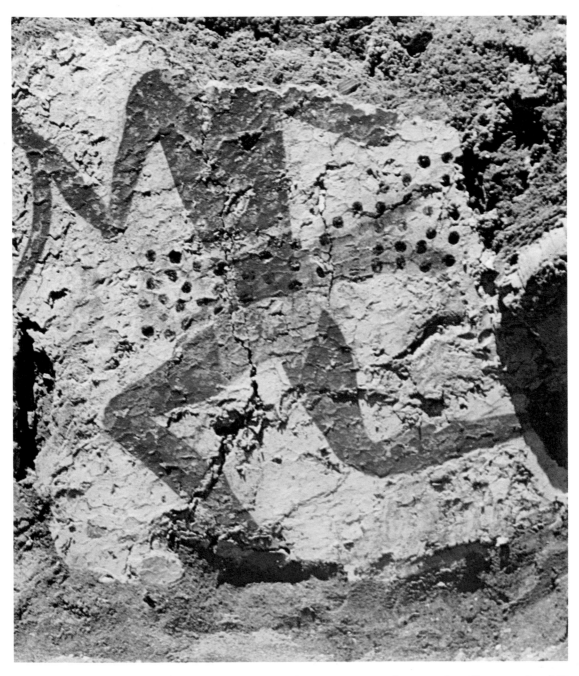

Plate 2-1 *Dancing Hunter*, fragment of a wall painting, Level III,
Çatal Hüyük, *c.* 5750 B.C.

Plate 2-2 *Scenes of War*, panel
from the *Standard of Ur*,
c. 2700 B.C. Panel inlaid with
shell, lapis lazuli, and red
limestone.
Each panel approx. 8″ × 19″.
British Museum, London.

Plate 2-3 The Ishtar Gate (restored), Babylon, *c.* 575 B.C.
Staatliche Museen, Berlin.

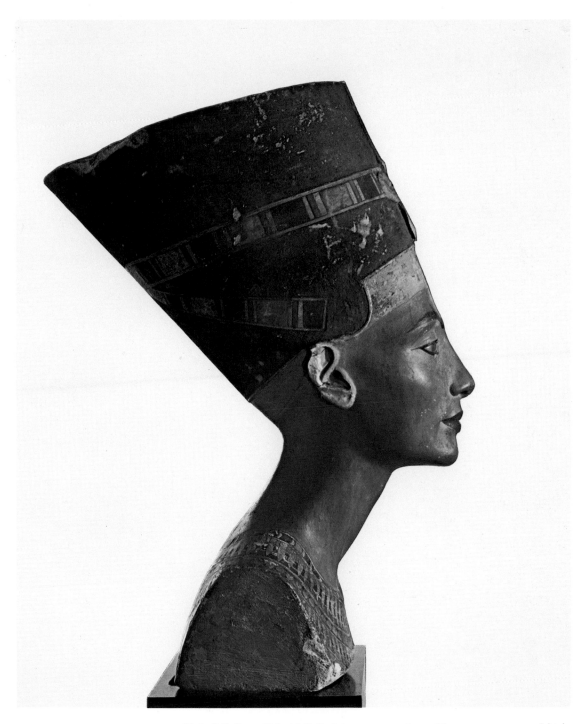

Plate 3-2 *Queen Nefertiti*, Tell el-Amarna, *c.* 1360 B.C. Limestone, approx. 20″ high.
Berlin Ägyptisches Museum.

Plate 4-2 Inlaid dagger blades from the royal tombs at Mycenae, *c.* 1600–1500 B.C. Bronze, longest blade approx. 9″ long. National Museum, Athens.

Plate 5-1 *Peplos Kore*, Acropolis, Athens,
c. 530 B.C. Marble, approx. 48″ high.
Acropolis Museum, Athens.

Plate 5-2 PHIALE PAINTER, *Hermes Bringing the Infant Dionysos to Papposilenos*, krater, Vulci, *c.* 440–435 B.C. Approx. 14″ high. Vatican Museums, Rome.

Plate 5-3 *Hunter*, detail of the *Lion Hunt* mosaic, Pella, *c.* 300 B.C. Pebble mosaic, approx. 5′ 6″ high.

Plate 6-1 *Revelers*, wall painting from the Tomb of the Leopards, Tarquinia, *c.* 470 B.C. Approx. 42″ × 76″.

Plate 6-2 Detail of the *Woman of the Velcha Family*, wall painting from the Tomb of Orcus (Hades), Tarquinia, c. 470 B.C.

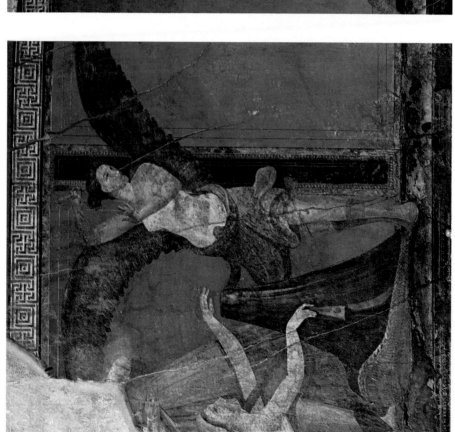

Plate 6-3 Details of a frieze from the Villa of the Mysteries, Pompeii, c. 50 B.C. Second-style ("architectural") wall painting. Figures approx. 4½–5′ high.

Plate 6-4 *Garden Scene*, detail of a wall painting from the House of Livia, Primaporta, late first century B.C. Portion shown approx. 9′ wide. Museo Nazionale Romano, Rome.

midal composition that is at once complex and unified and in which the voids, like the solids, have been carefully studied and used as functioning parts of the whole. Occasional references to the "decline" of Greek art during the Hellenistic period certainly cannot be interpreted as meaning that the artist lost his former skill. What is meant, undoubtedly, is that the artistic sights were lowered from lofty ideals to the trivia of life.

The *Seated Boxer* (FIG. 5-73), a very late Hellenistic work (perhaps more properly referred to as Greco-Roman, since it dates about a century after the absorption of Greece into the Roman empire), shows a heavily battered veteran of the arena resting, perhaps beaten and listening to the berating of his manager. The boxer is a man of huge physique, but his smashed face, broken nose, and deep scars tell the gist of his story. The sculptor appeals not to our intellect but to our emotions as he strives to evoke compassion for

5-73 APOLLONIUS (?), *Seated Boxer*, *c.* 50 B.C. Bronze, approx. 4′ 2″ high. Found in Rome. Museo Nazionale Romano, Rome.

5-71 *Old Market Woman*, second century B.C. Marble, 4′ 1½″ high. Metropolitan Museum of Art, New York (Rogers Fund).

5-72 BOETHOS, *Boy Strangling a Goose*, second century B.C. Marble, approx. 2′ 9″ high. Staatliche Antikensammlungen, Munich.

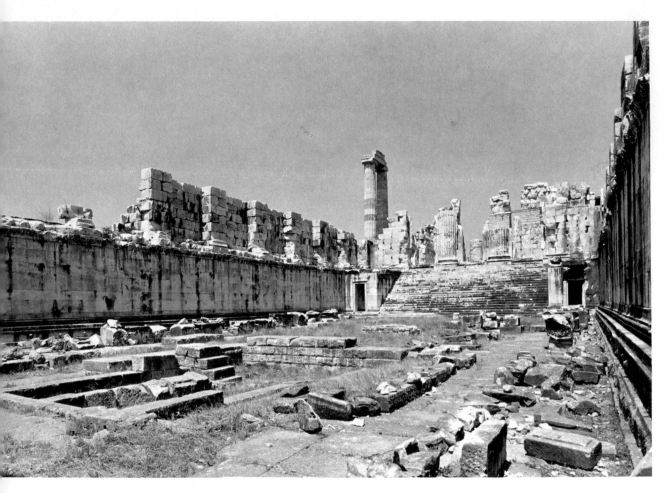

5-74 Interior of the Temple of Apollo at Didyma (the Didymaion), near Miletus, begun 313 B.C.

the battered hulk of a once mighty fighter. Story, realism, and human interest become the Hellenistic artist's interest at the end of the development of Greek sculpture, which thus ran, in a few centuries, a spectrum of possibilities and realizations from the *Apollo* of Olympia to a brutish boxer past his prime.

ARCHITECTURE

The greater variety, complexity, and sophistication of Hellenistic culture called for an architecture on an imperial scale and of wide diversity —far beyond what the Classical city-state could ever require. Building activity shifted from the old centers on the Greek mainland to the opulent cities of the Hellenistic monarchs in Asia Minor,

sites more central to the Hellenistic world. Great scale and ingenious development of interior space, the latter peculiarly a feature of Hellenistic architecture, are shown in the Temple of Apollo at Didyma (the Didymaion) near Miletus, the old Ionian city on the west coast of Asia Minor (FIGS. 5-19f and 5-74). This dipteral Ionic temple is raised upon a seven-stepped base some thirteen feet above the level of the large cella, which was intentionally left open to the sky (*hypethral*). The temple is 167 by 358 feet, the great columns over sixty-four feet high. The deep and column-filled pronaos precedes an antechamber from which a grand flight of steps some fifty feet wide sweeps down to the open courtyard, making a dramatic approach to the diminutive prostyle shrine that protected the cult statue, the foundations of which may be seen in the illustration.

5-75 View of the theater at Epidaurus, *c.* 350 B.C.

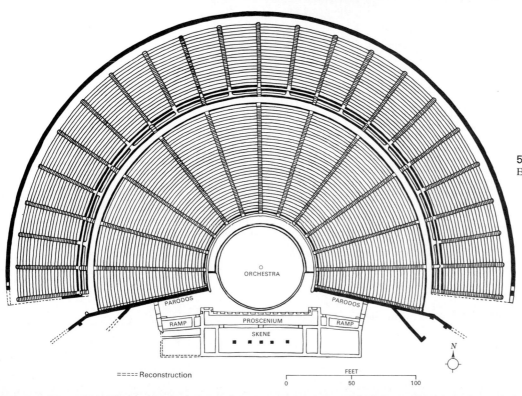

ORCHESTRA

PARODOS

PARODOS

RAMP

PROSCENIUM

RAMP

SKENE

N

5-76 Plan of the theater at Epidaurus.

===== Reconstruction

FEET
0   50   100

5-77 Simplified ground plan of Priene. Darker-toned rectangle indicates area shown in detail below.

1. Temple ruins
2. Wells
3. Fish and meat market
4. Shrine of Asklepios
5. School

▨ Probable roofed areas

═ ═ --- Speculative

This complex spatial planning of large interiors leads directly into later Roman practice and marks a sharp departure from Classical Greek architecture, which stressed the exterior of the building almost as a work of sculpture, and left the interior relatively undeveloped.

Another example of dexterous planning of uncovered space is the theater at Epidaurus, which Pausanias declared to be the best in Greece (FIGS. 5-75 and 5-76). Although the building (about 350 B.C.) is late Classical rather than Hellenistic and belongs to a period when theaters were relatively primitive, it has all the functioning units and formal arrangement of later theaters. The slightly more than semicircular auditorium is built into the side of a hill, and the diameter of its projected circle is 387 feet. Staircase aisles, laid out on radii projected from the center of the circular *orchestra*, where the plays were performed, separate blocks of stone benches, which themselves are separated into two tiers by a broad corridor. The orchestra, the *proscenium*, and the *skene* are arranged for maximum convenience of view of the performance and of preparations of the actors. The *parodos* (passageway between stage and audience) on each side is wide enough to permit rapid exit. This careful thinking-out of the plan for the convenience of an audience marks, as do the New Comedy plays acted at this time, increasing concern for individual views and responses.

The thoughtful adaptation of space to human uses, rather than, as in ancient times, to honor gods and to satisfy the whims of kings, is part of Greek humanism's contribution to history. The Hellenistic Greeks also broadened their conception of architectural design to take in whole cities. The regular street patterns of the gridiron type, which go back to the Archaic period in Greece were systematized during the fifth century B.C. by HIPPODAMOS, a Milesian architect, whose name has been linked with the checkerboard plans of Hellenistic cities like Priene (FIG. 5-77).[4]

[4] Knowledge of ancient urbanism is rather scanty, since archeologists generally prefer to investigate limited sites, and it is rarely economically feasible for them to uncover and trace miles of city streets. The fragmentary evidence shows, however, that cities with regular, usually rectangular street plans existed in both ancient Egypt and Mesopotamia.

The Hippodamian scheme, as illustrated by Priene, consists of a close-meshed network of streets that intersect at right angles, without any particular axial emphasis that might suggest dominant traffic patterns. Here the plan has been superimposed upon an irregular, sloping site without regard to the nature of the terrain. Only the defensive walls on the city's perimeter closely follow the topographical contours, with the result that walls and street plan are unrelated. On the other hand, the system is neat and orderly and, by making few distinctions of either a social or economic nature, essentially democratic.

The major ordering principle of the Hippodamian plan was the agora, which was centrally located and thus easily accessible to all citizens. It was partially surrounded by long, roofed, colonnaded stoas which housed markets and offices and were the architectural expression of

5-78 Plan of House XXXIII, Priene. (Partially restored.)

STREET

COURT

STREET

ENTRANCE

FEET
0   10   20   30

Roofed area

the public life of the city. Here its business and politics, its administration and its gossip went on, and it is from the fact that they taught their rational moral discipline in a stoa that the philosophy of the Stoics takes its name.

It is at this point in the history of architecture that we can speak of domestic building as such and discover (also in Priene) the look of an ordinary human dwelling capable of being called a house (FIG. 5-78). Typically, the lot on which the Hellenistic house stood was enclosed by a wall to shut out the dirt and noise of the narrow street. A single door opened into an office, or service quarters, from which a covered passage led to the main unit through a courtyard into which opened roofed chambers. Wealthier residents had, in addition to the forecourt (similar to the Roman *atrium*) a colonnaded garden, the *peristyle*. On a small scale the Priene house reflects the general Hellenistic interest in designing convenient interior spaces, as well as the growing concern for utility and convenience in the daily life of the ordinary individual.

Priene was a provincial town, and its houses were relatively unpretentious. It was in the capitals of the Hellenistic kingdoms—at Alexandria in Egypt, Pergamum in Asia Minor, and Pella in Macedonia—that life unfolded its richest and most sumptuous aspects. Here the kings and their retainers surrounded themselves with luxury that became proverbial, and their way of life set a standard that was to be surpassed only by the Roman emperors in later antiquity. Among the most lasting symbols of Hellenistic luxury were the floor mosaics with which the wealthy residents of these court cities embellished their houses.

MOSAICS

Mosaic as an art form had a rather prosaic and utilitarian beginning. (The Sumerian custom of covering walls with baked clay cones and the technique of shell inlay, as found in the *Standard of Ur*, PLATE 2-2, were not long-lived.) In the Mediterranean region the mosaic technique seems to have been invented primarily for the purpose of developing a flooring that was both inexpensive and durable. Originally, small pebbles collected from beaches and riverbanks were set into a thick coat of plaster. It was soon discovered, however, that the stones could be arranged in decorative patterns. At first these were quite simple and confined to geometric shapes; examples of this type that date back to the eighth century B.C. have been found at Gordium in Asia Minor. Eventually the stones were arranged to form more complex pictorial designs, and by the fourth century B.C. the technique had been developed to the point where mythological subjects could be represented on a large scale and with rich coloristic effects.

The most famous of these fourth-century pebble mosaics were found at Olynthus, which was destroyed by Philip of Macedon in 348 B.C., and at Pella, the Macedonian capital under King Archelaus around 400 B.C. Although almost forgotten until the late 1950's (excavations there were begun in 1957), it was at Pella that Alexander was born, that Aristotle taught, and that Euripides died. Under Alexander, Pella became virtually the capital of the world, as he ruled his vast empire from there. Although little has been preserved of the buildings' superstructures, furniture, or other works of art, the uncovered floor mosaics give ample evidence of the luxury and beauty of Pella's houses. A detail from one of several well-preserved pebble mosaics shows an almost life-sized figure from a scene representing a lion hunt (PLATE 5-3). The stones that have been arranged to form the picture are neither hewn nor shaped but natural pebbles. A variety of colors has been used to produce a polychrome effect, but the chief pictorial impact is derived from a strong dark and light contrast. Some outlines and interior markings are defined with thin strips of lead, a refinement that increases the clarity of the design but which was to enjoy no lasting favor.

Because they were cheap and durable, pebble mosaics remained popular through Roman times; in fact, they are still used for decorative pavements in Mediterranean countries. However, the desire for ever greater pictorial realism led to the simple but revolutionary practice of cutting stones to desired shapes so they could be fitted together more closely. At first these shaped stones, or *tesserae*, which permitted more precise description of detail, were used together with pebbles in limited areas that were felt to require greater definition. But by the second century B.C., "true" mosaics, composed entirely of cut stones, were designed at Pergamum and Delos, and the technique had been perfected to include colored glass (*smalto*) for strong colors, such as pure blue, red, and green, that are rarely found in natural materials. One of the most durable of the artistic media, mosaic was highly refined and popular in Roman times and became one of the chief vehicles for pictorial expression of early Christian and Byzantine artists.

While Alexander and his successors were Hellenizing the East, a power was rising in the western Mediterranean that in its own way would, like Greece, greatly determine the history of Europe and the Europeanized world. In one fateful year, 146 B.C., that power—Rome— sacked the Greek city of Corinth and destroyed an old enemy, Carthage, absorbing the small Greek states into the Roman province of Achaia and constructing around the ruins of Carthage the province of Africa. Thus, in a double stroke, Rome took under its aegis the culture of Greece and brought to an end in the Mediterranean West the ancient Near Eastern civilization that had continued to flourish in the old Phoenician sea-empire. Although this constituted another step in the Westernizing of the ancient world, it did not mean a blocking of the channels of commercial and intellectual intercourse with the East. For what Rome adopted from Greece it passed on to the Medieval and modern worlds in a form much transformed by the Oriental message of Christianity. If Greece is peculiarly the inventor of the European spirit, Rome is its propagator and amplifier.

Chapter Six

Etruscan and
Roman Art

LIGURIANS

VENETI

Mediolanum

Mantua

Adria

ILLYRIANS

Felsina

Faesulae

Volaterrae

Clusium

Perusia

ETRUSCANS

Volsinii

ADRIATIC SEA

Aleria

Vulci

Tarquinii

Veii

Fidenae

CORSICA

Caere

Roma

ITALIC

Tusculum

Praeneste

PEOPLES

Olbia

Capua

IAPYGIANS

Cumae

Mt.
Vesuvius

Tarentum

Paestum

Metapontum

Hydrus

SARDINIA

TYRRHENIAN SEA

Sybaris

Croton

Panormus

Messana

Drepanum

Rhegium

S I C I L I A

GREEK COLONIES

Selinus

Agrigentum

Syracuse

Carthage

CARTHAGINIANS

AFRICA

MAP OF ROME ABOUT A.D. 350

1 Aurelian Wall   6 Temple of Fortuna Virilis

2 Forum Romanum   7 Arch of Constantine

3 Colosseum   8 Basilica Ulpia

4 Trajan's Column   9 Baths of Caracalla

5 Pantheon   10 Arch of Titus

11 Circus Maximus

ITALY ABOUT 500 B.C.

Area of Etruscan domination

Areas of Greek colonization

Areas of Carthaginian colonization

Area of Italic domination

0   100   200 miles

THE PEOPLE of Italy, while touched at an early date by the radiance of Greece, had deep and tenacious qualities of their own. Etruscan (or Etrurian) and Roman art, like any other, must be recognized as a synthesis of influences from outside sources and of elements indigenous to the country. Roman art, the immediate heir of all earlier Mediterranean cultures, was in many ways a synthesis of the arts of antiquity, in a manner quite distinct from that of Greek art. Rome was also deeply involved in bringing civilization to western Europe. The art of Rome was, therefore, in later times often regarded as the symbol of the art of antiquity.

In terms of political development, the early histories of Greece and Italy are roughly parallel, but the vigorous advance in Greece after the Persian Wars of the fifth century B.C., culminat-

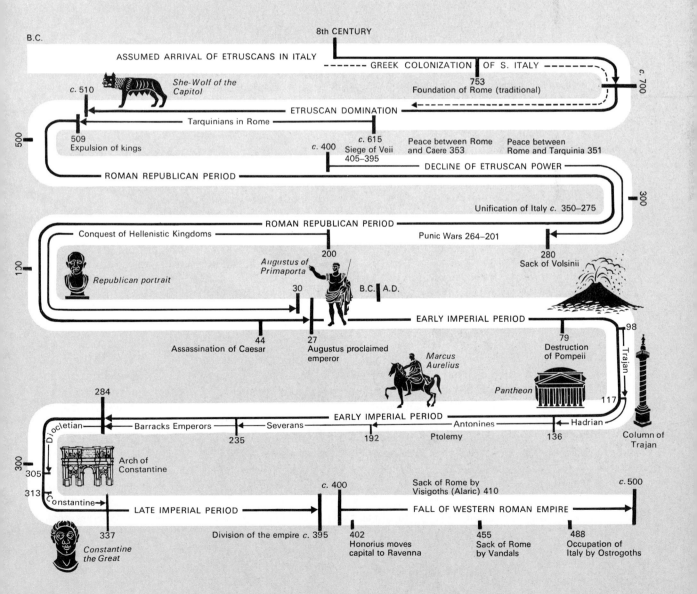

B.C.

8th CENTURY

ASSUMED ARRIVAL OF ETRUSCANS IN ITALY

———— GREEK COLONIZATION OF S. ITALY ————

c. 700

She-Wolf of the Capitol

c. 510

753
Foundation of Rome (traditional)

ETRUSCAN DOMINATION

———— Tarquinians in Rome ————

500

509
Expulsion of kings

c. 400

c. 615
Siege of Veii
405–395

Peace between Rome and Caere 353

Peace between Rome and Tarquinia 351

ROMAN REPUBLICAN PERIOD

DECLINE OF ETRUSCAN POWER

300

Unification of Italy c. 350–275

ROMAN REPUBLICAN PERIOD

Conquest of Hellenistic Kingdoms

Punic Wars 264–201

200

280
Sack of Volsinii

100

Republican portrait

Augustus of Primaporta

30

B.C. A.D.

EARLY IMPERIAL PERIOD

98

44
Assassination of Caesar

27
Augustus proclaimed emperor

79
Destruction of Pompeii

Trajan

Marcus Aurelius

Pantheon

117

284

EARLY IMPERIAL PERIOD

Hadrian

Diocletian

Barracks Emperors

Severans

Antonines

235

192
Ptolemy

136

Column of Trajan

300

Arch of Constantine

305

313

Constantine

LATE IMPERIAL PERIOD

c. 400

Sack of Rome by Visigoths (Alaric) 410

c. 500

FALL OF WESTERN ROMAN EMPIRE

Constantine the Great

337

Division of the empire c. 395

402
Honorius moves capital to Ravenna

455
Sack of Rome by Vandals

488
Occupation of Italy by Ostrogoths

ing in the Age of Pericles, found no counterpart in Italy, where culture was retarded by the bitter struggles among competing Italic peoples and between them and the Etruscans.

THE ETRUSCANS

The origin of the Etruscans, like that of the Mycenaeans, has long been one of the mysteries of the ancient world. Their language, though written in a Greek-derived script and extant in inscriptions that are still obscure, is unrelated to the Indo-European linguistic family. Ancient historians, as fascinated by the puzzle as are modern scholars, generally felt that the Etruscans emigrated from Asia Minor, and Herodotus, the "father of history," specifically declares that they came from Lydia. This tradition has persisted, and since the Etruscan culture emerges as distinct from those of other Italic peoples around 700 B.C., their arrival in Italy has long been put at the eighth century B.C. Such a view seems too simple, however, and does not explain adequately the evident connections between the Etruscan and earlier Italic cultures. Some modern scholars feel that the Etruscans are the direct descendants of very old pre-Indo-European people who had moved into Italy from the north. But this theory, in turn, cannot fully account for certain elements of the Etruscan culture, particularly the elaborate burial cult, which seems to be linked with Oriental customs.

A compromise theory points out that Herodotus gives no dates and that the migration he refers to could well have occurred during the period of the great Mediterranean shake-up and shifting of peoples that occurred around 1200 B.C. and caused the collapse of the Mycenaean civilization. At that time, immigrants from Asia Minor could have settled in Italy, mingled with the native population, and produced the culture of the so-called Villanovans, who, in turn, may have been the direct predecessors of the Etruscans. The changes that produced the Etruscan culture proper would then have to be explained in terms of increasing exposure to foreign influences—first Oriental and then Greek—brought about by expanding commerce and trade. In this connection it is noteworthy that the Etruscans enjoyed high repute as skilled seafarers (or disrepute as pirates) in antiquity and that they emerged into the light of history during the so-called Orientalizing period.

It is now generally conceded that Etruscan art developed largely as a consequence of the Greek colonization of southern Italy during the eighth and seventh centuries B.C. Although responsible for halting further Greek expansion northward along the Tyrrhenian coast, and despite deep-rooted distrust and antagonism toward their southern neighbors, the Etruscans—without relinquishing any of their native characteristics—eagerly absorbed Greek influences. Using the Greek colonial cities as a model, the Etruscans shifted from village life to an urban civilization and established themselves in strongly fortified hilltop cities. By the sixth century B.C. they controlled most of northern and central Italy from such strongholds as Tarquinii (modern Tarquinia), Caere (modern Cerveteri), Veii, Perusia (modern Perugia), and Volsinii (modern Orvieto). But these cities never united to form a state, and so it is improper to speak of an Etruscan nation or kingdom. The cities coexisted, flourishing or fading independently and at different times, and any semblance of unity among them was based primarily upon common linguistic ties and religious beliefs and practices. This lack of political cohesion eventually made the Etruscans relatively easy prey for Roman aggression. During the ten-year siege of Veii, for instance, no Etruscan city came to the aid of its beleaguered cousin.

Architecture

Little is known of Etruscan architecture. Their cities were either razed or rebuilt by the Romans, and those that survived were located on sites so well chosen that they continue to be inhabited to this day, making excavation impossible. Scattered remnants suggest that the Etruscans, at least during their later history, made considerable use of the masonry arch, a structural device not favored by the Greeks but one that was to become of profound importance for later Roman building.

The early Etruscan house is known to us chiefly through clay models that served as cinerary urns, and from tomb chambers in which domestic interiors were re-created. To judge from the interior of the third-century B.C. Tomb of the Reliefs (FIG. 6-3), an originally simple rectangular structure with sloping roof grew progressively more elaborate, reaching its climactic development in the *atrium* houses of Pompeii and Herculaneum. Invention showed itself in the development of the atrium, a high, square or rectangular central hall that was lighted through a large opening in the roof and around which the other rooms were symmetrically arranged. This atrium was the focus of family life and the shrine for the *lares* and *penates*, the household gods. The ancient sacred hearth of Mediterranean family religion found an appropriate architectural expression in the noble atrium, which gave to Italic domestic architecture an importance and dignity beyond that developed by the Greeks.

Our knowledge of the Etruscan temple is based upon a few preserved foundations and a description given by the ancient Roman authority on architecture, Vitruvius (FIG. 6-1). It may very possibly have had its origins in Greece. Its plan, for example, closely resembles the Greek prostyle plan (FIG. 5-19b). Yet the Etruscan adaptation, in typical fashion, developed its own characteristics. Resting on a high base (*podium*) with steps at one end only, it was constructed mostly of wood and sun-dried brick in a post-and-lintel system and had a heavy wooden superstructure richly deco-

rated with brightly painted terra-cotta reliefs. The Etruscan emphasis on a highly ornate façade, with relatively spare treatment of the sides and rear, concentrated attention upon the entrance porch. There was an axial organization quite different from that of the Greek temple. Behind the sunlit pavilion of the porch, the shrine, divided into three cellae of equal size, formed dark cave-like spaces. The temple was not meant to be seen as a sculptural mass from the outside and from all directions, like the Greek temple, but was intended instead to function primarily as an interior space. It was a place of shelter, protected by the wide overhang of its roof.

It is in the remains of their elaborate burial grounds that the Etruscans reveal themselves with the greatest clarity. In a rich array of wall paintings and painted reliefs with which they decorated the interiors of their tombs, they recount their zestful lives, their banquets, and their dances, which, in their suppleness and verve, seem partly Ionian and partly barbarian. They tell us both of their athletic contests and of their wars. Their rise and fall from power is reflected in a gradual change from optimism to pessimism and in the choice of ever more morbid and bloodthirsty subjects as their political fortunes declined. Although the Etruscans' reputation for cruel and unrestrained behavior is based largely upon the testimony of the ancient Greeks and Romans, who were their enemies, elements in their tomb

6-1 Plan and elevations of an Etruscan temple. (After Vitruvius.)

FEET
0   10   20   30

paintings indicate that their society had many aspects that were in fact violent and extravagant. Indeed, these qualities may have played a decisive role in the formation of an energetic and creative culture that was to contribute to the rise to world rulership of their Roman successors.

The Etruscans built their cemeteries at some distance from their cities. Hundreds of tombs arranged in orderly manner along a network of streets produce the effect of veritable cities of the dead (*necropolises*). The tombs varied according to region and local custom. In the northern part of Etruria they were usually constructed above ground, while in the south they were often excavated from the live rock, particularly in areas where tufa soil facilitated digging. Tufa, primarily strongly compressed volcanic ash, is easily excavated and hardens to a concretelike consistency on exposure to the atmosphere. Tufa can also be cut into durable building blocks that require no firing; it was used extensively by the Etruscans and Romans, and a minor tufa brick industry flourishes in Italy today.

The most common Etruscan tomb type is the *tumulus*, a round structure that has been partially excavated and covered with earth (FIG. 6-2). This form was favored in Cerveteri and, in view of its domical shape, seems to carry on an ancient Mediterranean tradition. The majority of Etruscan tomb interiors, however, including those of the tumuli, are rectangular and reproduce the

rooms of domestic architecture. A striking example is the Tomb of the Reliefs (FIG. 6-3), a large underground chamber in Cerveteri, in which massive piers with pseudo-Ionic (Aeolic) capitals support a slanting beamed ceiling. The piers are *reserved*—that is, formed by cutting away the live tufa until the remaining rock has the shape of a column, as in the Egyptian rock-cut tombs at Beni Hasan (FIG. 3-16). This, like most Etruscan tombs, was designed for multiple burials, the final resting place of an entire family and its servants. Sarcophagi, cinerary urns, and other tomb furnishings were placed in niches and on the benchlike projection at the base of the walls. Decoration in the Tomb of the Reliefs consists of painted plaster reliefs representing weapons, tools, and kitchen utensils, and displays a generous inventory of Etruscan objects of daily use.

Painting

Unlike the Caerans, the Tarquinians adorned the walls of their subterranean tomb chambers with colorful and lively murals. Although the subjects of tomb painting in Etruria are sometimes drawn from Greek legend, they are more often concerned with scenes of banquet and revel, as in the Tomb of the Leopards in Tarquinia (PLATE 6-1). This small chamber tomb is decorated in the manner favored in Tarquinia during the fifth century

B.C.: a banquet scene on the wall opposite the entrance and groups of dancers and musicians on the side walls. These wonderfully vital pictures express especially well the peculiarly life-affirming exuberance that fills Etruscan art as it must have filled Etruscan existence. Three young men, one clad only in a light scarf, the other two in the elegant *chlamys* (cloak), seem to be hurrying through a grove of graceful little laurel trees, the leader carrying a cup of wine and beckoning, the others playing the double flute and the seven-stringed lyre. They seem already to be dancing, facing rhythmically in opposite directions as if performing some circling step. The gestures have a kind of choreographic exaggeration, especially those of the enlarged hands and fingers of the flutist, which hold and touch the instrument with such sureness and delicacy. It is rare in the painting of the ancient world that spirited movement is portrayed so convincingly, and it would be difficult to find from that time so fitting a monument to the beauty of youth, springtime, music, and the dance. The picture is a kind of fresco painting on a thin slip applied to the living rock wall or on a stucco paste made from the rock. The colors—blacks, blues, blue-greens, and ocher-reds—still retain much of their original freshness and harmonize easily and naturally with the creamy yellow ground.

But the later Etruscans seem to have surrendered their native, joyous vigor for a quiet, classicizing formalism like that in the *Woman of the Velcha Family*, from a chamber in the Tomb of Orcus (Hades) in Tarquinia (PLATE 6-2). The composed, even reflective, expression of this splendidly painted head suits the somber theme that is its context—the sufferings of the dead in Hades in the midst of the menacing demons of the underworld. The earlier Etruscan euphoria has disappeared, extinguished by the more cosmopolitan religions of the Hellenistic world, which stressed not the last happiness of the funeral revels but the sadness of man's fate.

Sculpture

The Etruscan tombs yield a notable furniture of sculptured objects in both clay and bronze, materials that the Etruscans apparently preferred, though numerous stone sarcophagi survive. The forms are modeled rather than carved, modeling being a technique that would be congenial to the impetuous temperament and fluid style characteristic of the Etruscans. Funerary urns and sarcophagi with recumbent portrait figures present some of the best examples of Etruscan sculpture. A canopic (cinerary) urn (FIG. 6-4) from Clusium

6-3 Tomb of the Reliefs, Caere (Cerveteri), fifth to fourth centuries B.C.

6-4 Canopic urn from Clusium (Chiusi), second half of the seventh century B.C. Hammered bronze with terra-cotta head, approx. 33″ high. Museo Etrusco, Chiusi.

(modern Chiusi) has a terra-cotta head as a lid, the whole set in a bronze model of a chair; the head is obviously intended as a portrait likeness of the deceased whose ashes are here contained. The strongly rounded form of the urn has a crude vitality that is carried into the head, with its blunt, aggressive features and massive neck. The accent upon the individuality of the deceased is specifically Etruscan and is seen to fullest advantage in the reclining effigies of a man and his wife on the lid of a sarcophagus from Cerveteri (FIG. 6-5). The work is a kind of throwing into three dimensions and a formalizing of the animated banquet scenes painted on Etruscan tomb walls to satisfy the demands of some cult ritual of the dead, the details of which are unknown. But there is nothing here of the solemn or the macabre, and the Etruscan instinct for the lifelike is preserved. The figures shown are relaxed and genial—much in contrast with the funerary formality of Egyptian statues—and the Archaic features of style, though present, produce no stiffness or awkwardness.

The *Apollo of Veii* (FIG. 6-6), an acroterion figure from the ridgepole of an Etruscan temple, is evidence that, like the Greeks, the Etruscans made use of architectural sculpture. But the Greek Archaic elements, though immediately evident, are superficial; the awkward, lurching vigor of the powerful figure is a forceful example of Etruscan clay-modeling techniques and the use to which the confident, quick-conceiving, and quick-executing sculptor could put them. In contrast with, say, the serene majesty of the *Apollo at Olympia* (FIG. 5-35), this one moves like a dangerous giant. His overpowering physical presence reflects small concern for the Greek preoccupation with harmonious proportions or idealized humanity. The Ionian elaboration of the drapery lines bespeaks the Eastern component in Etruscan art, but the animal force, the huge, swelling contours, and the plunging motion are anything but Ionian and little enough mainland Greek. The *Apollo of Veii*, given its architectural function, naturally differs from the painted Etruscan forms we have seen; yet it has in common with them the peculiarly Etruscan strength, energy, and excitement.

The absorption of Greek influences by the Etruscans continued during the height of the latter's power—when they were sending their own art commodities throughout the Mediterranean, including Greece—and through the centuries of their decline. The so-called *Mars of Todi* exemplifies Etruscan interpretation of the Greek Classical style (FIG. 6-7) in the beginning of the fourth century B.C. The figure, dressed in more or less contemporary military garb, executes a peculiar movement of the whole body, involving sideways and contrary directions of head, torso, arms, and legs, without seeming to move from his position. The sculptor may have been exaggerating the Polykleitan weight-shift stance, but there is a kind of agility to it, quite unlike the balanced weight-and-poise of the Polykleitan type. We find again, as in the much earlier *Apollo of Veii*, that an Etruscan interpretation of prevailing Greek style brings out the native quality of energy, whether in the blunt drive of the *Apollo* or in the almost sprightly stance of the *Mars*.

One of the most famous animals in the history of world art, the *She-Wolf of the Capitol* (FIG. 6-8) owes her fame not simply to her antiquity and

6-5 Sarcophagus from Caere (Cerveteri), c. 520 B.C. Terra-cotta, approx. 6′ 7″ long. Museo Nazionale di Villa Giulia, Rome.

6-6 *Apollo of Veii*, c. 510 B.C. Terra-cotta, approx. 70″ high. Museo Nazionale di Villa Giulia, Rome.

6-7 *Mars of Todi*, early fourth century B.C. Bronze, approx. 4′ 8″ high. Vatican Museums, Rome.

6-8 *She-Wolf of the Capitol, c.* 500 B.C. Bronze, approx. 33½" high. Musei Capitolini, Rome.

her magnificence as a work of art, but to the fact that for centuries she has been the totem of the city of Rome. Ancient legend tells us that the founding heroes of Rome, Romulus and Remus, being abandoned as infants, were suckled by a she-wolf. The cult of Romulus and Remus was as old as the fourth century B.C., and we know that a statue of a she-wolf was dedicated on the Capitoline Hill in Rome in 296 B.C. We do *not* know whether the present statue of the she-wolf on the Capitoline Hill is the original (the suckling infants were made in the Renaissance); its dating has been hotly debated, but its Etruscan origin is now widely accepted. The vitality we have noted in the human figure of Etruscan art is here concentrated in the tense, watchful animal body, with its spare flanks, gaunt ribs, and taut and powerful legs. The lowering neck and head, the alert ears, glaring eyes, and ferocious muzzle render the psychic vibrations of the fierce and, at the same time, protecting beast; the incised lines along the neck give us its rising hackles as it watches danger approach. Not even the great animal reliefs of Assyria can match, much less surpass, this profound reading of animal temper.

Somewhat later we have the splendid *Chimera* from Arezzo (FIG. 6-9), a bronze monster with a rough-maned lion's head, a serpent's tail (restored in the Renaissance by Benvenuto Cellini), and a second head—that of a goat—whose right horn

is seized by the serpent. Although the *Chimera* bears the wounds inflicted by the hero Bellerophon, who hunted and slew it, it is not merely illustrative of the event; rather, the figure almost certainly has some further demonic significance. The Etruscans, much of whose art is associated with mortuary ritual, had a well-developed demonology, an aggregation of demonic types that plague the dead in the underworld. Unlike the Greeks, who preferred to humanize their demons, the Etruscans, with their roots partly in Asia, employed their customary expressive force to represent them as dreadful animal hybrids. The precedents for the monster types go back to the sphinxes of Egypt and the winged, man-headed bulls of Mesopotamia, as well as to the ornamental animal bronzes of Luristan and the associated animal-heraldic style of much of the metalwork of central Asia. It may be that these traditions lingered in the Etruscan spirit, and the manifestation of them in such powerful form as the *Chimera*—so anti-Greek and so Asiatic—attests most firmly to the Eastern component in Etruscan culture. By the time of the Middle Ages, a whole population of monsters swarmed through the art of the West.

Also assimilated from the East and passed on by the Etruscans to the Romans was the practice of divination, whereby the future, as a product of arcane forces (personified as gods or demons) was

6-9 *Chimera*, Arezzo, fifth to fourth centuries B.C. Bronze, approx. $31\frac{1}{2}''$ high. Museo Archeologico, Florence.

thought to be predictable to some degree. On the assumption that all nature constituted a universe of affinities, prediction—the art of the priesthood —was based on the state of the viscera of sacrificed animals (especially the liver), the flight of flocks of birds, and unseasonable and unusual events. The engraved back of a bronze mirror (FIG. 6-10)—exquisitely wrought, with all the refinement for which the Etruscan craft arts were celebrated—represents a winged figure labeled Calchas, a priest in Homer's *Iliad*, divining from a liver that he holds in his hand and upon which he muses. The figure is a kind of miniature emblem for that world of benign and malign forces that surrounded ancient men and which they tried to approach or fend off by prophecy, sacrifice, oracle, omen, spell, incantation. Greek rationalism made little headway against the ancient world's overwhelming faith in the magical manipulation of nature.

Closely related to the delicately incised, Classical mirrors of the fourth century B.C., like the Calchas one, are the bronze cists of Praeneste (modern Palestrina), which doubtless echo the styles of the great Greek masters of mural painting—Polygnotos, Euphranor, and others. Etruscan bronze vessels and mirrors with incised mythological scenes were famous and highly prized objects in Greece. Perhaps the outstanding member of this type is the so-called *Ficoroni Cist*

of NOVIOS PLAUTIOS (FIG. 6-11). Most significantly, the artist, Novios Plautios, is not Etruscan; he signed his work in Latin and made it in Rome. He has made a skillful adaptation of a frieze of Greek figures, faithfully taking over the idealized naturalism of the Late Classical period. Naturalistic innovations appear: figures seen entirely from behind or in three-quarter rear view, complicated seated poses, figures on several levels rather than rigidly attached to a single groundline, details of landscape, and a kind of approxi-

6-10 Engraved back of a mirror, *c.* 400 B.C. Bronze, approx. 6″ in diameter. Vatican Museums, Rome.

6-11 NOVIOS PLAUTIOS, *The Ficoroni Cist*, Praeneste (Palestrina), late fourth century B.C. Bronze, approx. 21″ high. Museo Nazionale di Villa Giulia, Rome.

mate perspective space. The artist represents in his work the passing of the Etruscan genius and the acceptance of the irresistible influence of Greece. Yet something of the Etruscan sense for the real will persist through the formal Classicism of Greece, which, in turn, will partly direct the course of the art of Rome; and this earlier Etruscan sense will sharpen into the characteristic Roman taste for the factual in art as in human affairs.

THE ROMANS

The Roman power that succeeded and replaced the Etruscan compelled the contesting peoples of Italy into a Roman state and, eventually, the peoples of western Europe, the Mediterranean, and the Near East into a Roman empire. The rise and triumph of Rome, and the awesome spectacles of its decline and fall, make, in the stately words of the great historian of it, Edward Gibbon, "a revolution which will ever be remembered, and is still felt, by the nations of the earth." From the Tigris and Euphrates to the borders of Scotland stretched a single government under whose energetic and efficient—if often ruthless and brutal—rule lived people of innumerable races, creeds, tongues, traditions, and cultures: Britons, Gauls, Spaniards, Germans, Africans, Egyptians, Greeks, Syrians, Arabs, to name only a very few. If the Greek genius, as we review it, shines most brightly in art, science, philosophy, history, and —in general—the things of the intellect and imagination, the Roman genius shines in the realm of worldly action—in law and in government. Roman monuments of art and architecture are distributed throughout the world that the Romans governed and are the most conspicuous and numerous of all the remains of ancient civilizations we have so far studied. But Roman monuments of a kind also survive in our concepts of law and government, in our calendar, in our festivals, rituals, languages, and religions, in the nomenclature of many of the sciences, and, for our special interest here, in the concept of art as worthy of historical study and criticism.

The main energies of Rome were devoted to conquest and administration, conquest opening the way for the spread of Roman civilization. Roman cities sprang up not only all around the Mediterranean basin but also as far north as the Danube, the Rhine, and the Thames. Each city was a center for the propagation of Roman government, language, and customs and was closely connected with the city of Rome itself by a well-planned system of roads and harbors. Rome about A.D. 200 was the capital of the greatest empire the world had known, an empire efficiently organized with 50,000 miles of sea routes and expertly engineered highways safe for travel and commerce. Rome itself was both cosmopolitan and splendid. The size, power, and complexity of the empire called for an impressive capital, and while the practical demands arising from

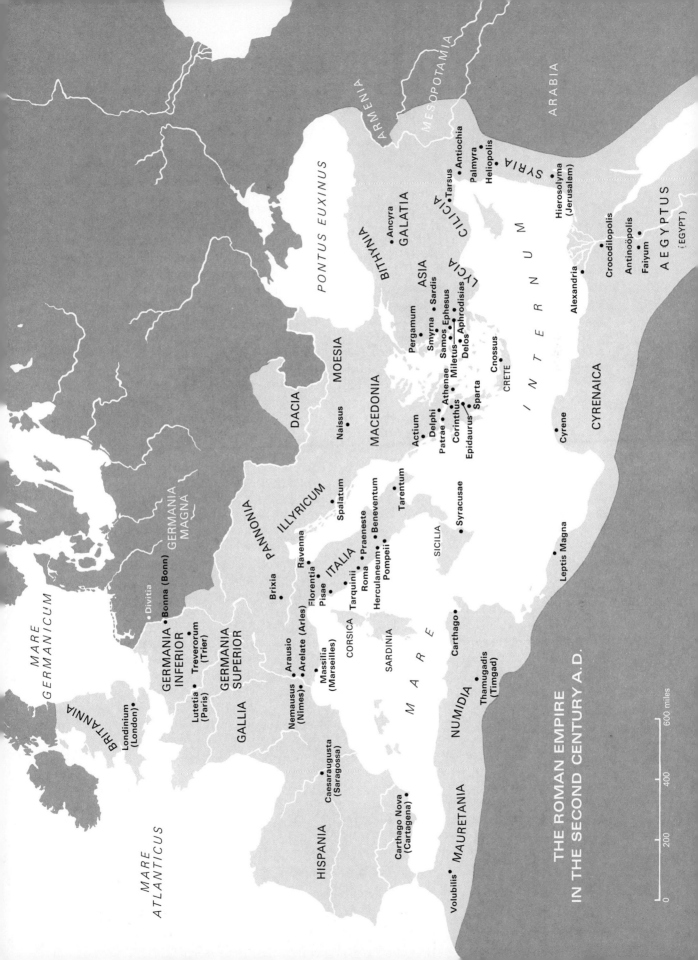

THE ROMAN EMPIRE
IN THE SECOND CENTURY A.D.

MARE ATLANTICUS

MARE GERMANICUM

BRITANNIA

Londinium (London)

GERMANIA MAGNA

Divitia
Bonna (Bonn)
GERMANIA INFERIOR
Treverorum (Trier)
GERMANIA SUPERIOR
Lutetia (Paris)

GALLIA

Arausio
Arelate (Arles)
Nemausus (Nîmes)
Massilia (Marseilles)

HISPANIA

Caesaraugusta (Saragossa)

Carthago Nova (Cartagena)

CORSICA

SARDINIA

Volubilis

MAURETANIA

NUMIDIA

Carthago

Thamugadis (Timgad)

Brixia
Ravenna
Florentia
Pisae
ITALIA
Tarquinii
Roma
Praeneste
Herculaneum
Pompeii
Benevantum
Tarentum

MARE

SICILIA

Syracusae

Leptis Magna

PANNONIA

ILLYRICUM

Spalatum

DACIA

MOESIA

Naissus

MACEDONIA

PONTUS EUXINUS

Actium
Delphi
Patrae
Corinthus
Epidaurus
Athenae
Sparta

Pergamum
Smyrna
Samos
Miletus
Delos

BITHYNIA

Ancyra

GALATIA

ASIA

Sardis
Ephesus
Aphrodisias

ARMENIA

MESOPOTAMIA

CILICIA

Tarsus

LYCIA

Crossus
CRETE

INTERNUM

Cyrene

CYRENAICA

ARABIA

Antiochia
Palmyra
Heliopolis

SYRIA

Hierosolyma (Jerusalem)

Crocodilopolis
Antinoöpolis
Faiyum

Alexandria

AEGYPTUS (EGYPT)

0   200   400   600 miles

← to c. 700 B.C.   c. 510   c. 470   c. 300   146   c. 80   27 B.C.   A.D. 70   118   A.D. 284

Apollo of Veii	Revelers, Tomb of the Leopards	Woman of the Velcha Family, Tomb of Orcus	Conquest of Greece	Sanctuary of Fortuna Primigenia	B.C.|A.D.	Colosseum begun	Pantheon begun	
ETRUSCAN DOMI-NATION	ROMAN	REPUBLICAN	PERIOD		EARLY	IMPERIAL	PERIOD	

the administration of a great empire required high engineering skill for the construction of bridges, roads, sewers, and aqueducts, the imperial ideal called also for public buildings that would adequately express the dignity and diversity of the state. Roman art takes its character in large part from the imperial role the Roman state was required to play.

Although early under both Etruscan and Greek influence, Roman art came to have its own quite distinctive characteristics. The Romans, almost from the beginning of their rise, had been fully aware of Greek art, but it was only in the later Republican and Augustan ages that Hellenism became a conscious fashion. "Conquered Greece," wrote Horace, "led her proud conqueror captive." Shiploads of Greek marbles and bronzes were brought to Rome by generals and provincial governors to adorn their palaces, and, when the supply was exhausted, copies were made or Greek artists were employed to create new works. Fashionable art for a time became to a large extent mere copying of Greek works. Finally a deeper assimilation took place, and the art of Imperial Rome emerged, a product of its richly varied heritage and its unique genius.

This art-historical view of Roman art is comparatively new. Until about 1900 the scholars saw Roman art as merely decadent Greek art, unoriginal and inferior. It is true that, drawing as it necessarily does upon what went before, it does not have the degree of originality that distinguishes the great styles of Egypt, Mesopotamia, Greece, and even Etruria. Yet it is more than a mere "propagator and preserver of the classical heritage"; it is the "first comprehensive stage of western European art." While it makes use of Classical forms, it expresses non-Classical concepts. It combines an interest in individual personality with one in such abstract concepts as "law," "state," and "civilization." The vast body of the material of Roman art—found on three continents, with much of it still not evaluated and with much more still underground—suggests methods almost of mass production, in which the anonymous artist (almost no names survive, in contrast with those of writers and poets) becomes the servant of his patron—private or public, wealthy connoisseur or the Roman state. Nevertheless, in the collective as well as in the individual case, Roman art survives as an imposing style taking its own course from the days of the late republic.

The Republican Period

The Roman republic was founded after the last of the (possibly Etruscan) kings had been driven out. From the fifth century B.C. to the collapse of the republic and the assassination of Julius Caesar in 44 B.C., the external business of Rome was expansion abroad and the consolidation of imperial power in the Western world. In a succession of wars, the most harrowing and dangerous of which were the wars with Carthage, the Romans developed their peculiar qualities of character: disciplined valor, tenacity, practicality, obedience to authority, and a pitiless realism in recognizing the facts of power. Yet the constitutional structure of the republic, adequate to a limited city-state, could not begin to meet the requirements of empire. Internal quarrels between classes—the patricians and the plebeians—were inflamed by dispute over disposition of the enormous wealth won abroad. When successful armies led by popular generals intervened in the politics of the republic, civil war began. Lasting almost a hundred years, during which dictators like Marius, Sulla, Caesar, and Pompey ruled, the war exhausted the state and destroyed its constitution. When the great-nephew of Julius Caesar, Octavian, finally found himself alone at the head of the Roman world (when he called himself Augustus), the republic was no more than a pious, ritualized memory.

It is in this period of the crisis of the republic, even while Greek influence became increasingly strong, that Roman art began to emerge as an entity distinguishable from the late Hellenistic style. In 146 B.C., when Greece was absorbed into the Roman empire as the province of Achaia, a sculptural style came into being that we call Greco-Roman, the term an admission that the two styles cannot be readily separated from each other. Much of the original sculpture of the period was produced by Greek immigrant artists—for instance, the *Seated Boxer* (FIG. 5-73). But the growing Roman fascination with individual traits of personality is apparent in portrait sculpture, a field in which the Romans made one of their most original contributions (the others being architecture and landscape painting) and in which they achieved a quite typical, uncompromising, and often unflattering realism. However, the Hellenizing idealism that is found balancing this hard Roman realism in the last days of the republic bears witness to the peculiar dualism in the Roman attitude toward the defeated Greeks—admiration for their art and grace and contempt for their "unmanly" cleverness and for their lack of skill in managing their own affairs as a people. Cicero described this Roman ambiguity of sentiment and scored the Greeks on their un-Roman insincerity in terms a little like those of nineteenth-century American travelers commenting on the French.

> I grant them literature, I grant them a knowledge of many arts, I do not deny the charm of their speech, the keenness of their intellects, the richness of their diction; finally, if they make other claims, I do not deny them. But truth and honor in giving testimony that nation has never cherished ... Greeks never trouble to prove what they say but only make a display of themselves by talking.

But it was the idealism of Greek art that again and again captivated the Romans. Greek statues in great profusion stood in the Roman forums and in both public and private buildings; villas and baths were museums of Greek sculp-

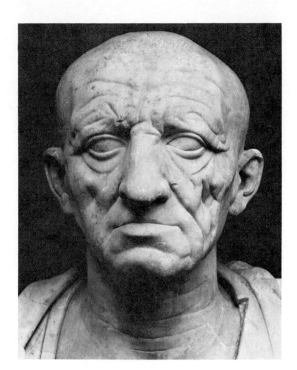

6-12 *Head of a Roman*, c. 80 B.C. Marble, life-size. Palazzo Torlonia, Rome.

ture—whether originals, copies, or adaptations to suit Roman taste. We read of 285 bronze and 30 marble statues brought from Corinth in 146 B.C., after the barbarous sack of that city, and of 500 bronzes brought from Delphi by Nero; when the stockpile of originals ran low, the demand for Greek sculpture was satisfied by copies made after Greek works.

PORTRAIT SCULPTURE

But even while under the spell of Hellenism, Roman portraitists produced works that have no parallel in Greek art. During the Hellenistic period, the quality of generalization that had distinguished earlier portraits had already given way to a style that was more particularizing and descriptive. The Roman's desire for literalness, together with his custom of keeping in his house, always before his eyes, the *imagines* (wax masks) of his ancestors, influenced the sculptor to accentuate individual traits still further. Also operative was the Etruscan influence, which, with its expressionistic realism, persisted in Late Republican portraiture. The *Head of a Roman* (FIG. 6-12), for example, is striking by virtue of its "character," at once alive and masklike. But the character may simply be accidental, the result of the artist's painstaking report of each rise and fall, each bulge and fold, of the facial surface, executed as if he were proceeding like a map-maker, concerned not to miss the slightest detail of surface change. The artist apparently tries neither to idealize the subject—that is, to improve him in conformity with an ideal, as in Greek practice— nor to interpret his personality. The blunt and bald record of his features, the kind given by a life mask or death mask, is quite enough. Thus, this "verism," a kind of superrealism, is the artist's objective, and it is determined not so much by esthetic motives as by religious convention. The habit of mind that demands faithful records of this kind is familiar to us in our curiosity about the fidelity of photographs of our forebears.

A quite different approach to the portrait subject can be seen in a bust of Pompey the Great (FIG. 6-13). A sculptor confronting a powerful and famous man may be conscious of the need for a method different from mere recording; he may want to idealize but also to personalize—that is, interpret the subject's personality. We, coming 2000 years after Pompey, bring to our scanning of him far more knowledge of the man than we could ever bring to the contemplation of a portrait of an unknown Roman. Pompey was first the partner and then the rival of Julius Caesar in the devastating civil war that wrecked the Roman republic in the first century B.C. We know of him as a great general, successful in war and—almost —the proprietor of all the Eastern world held by Rome. We know of him also as a political incompetent and as an ambitious man of the middle class who allowed himself to be made the dupe of the extremists of the Senatorial party. We know of him as hopelessly irresolute, disappointing even his closest friends because he was unable to make up his mind. We know that he lost to Caesar the bloody battle of Pharsalus, after which he was ignominiously assassinated by one of his own men. Yet he was a good man who refused to enrich himself by plunder of the provinces, a practice from which most of his contemporaries

6-13 *Pompey the Great, c.* 55 B.C. Marble, life-size. Frank E. Brown Collection, Rome.

did not scruple to refrain. Cicero wrote of Pompey to a friend: "I knew him as a man honest, grave, and high-minded."

Thus, Pompey is a complex of traits played upon by the accidents of history; yet what kind of man of only slightly more than good talent could have bested Caesar? Knowing what we do about Pompey's strength and weakness, his triumphs and ultimate failure, we naturally approach his portrait bust as we might approach a bust of Washington or Lafayette—with curiosity about the individual man and his history. In the same way, it is likely that the artist of the bust, though different from us in his cultural responses, would still have cared to make a likeness that would be more than a mere facial record. This is evident in the work, which has none of the rigidity of the death mask and possesses a subtly modeled surface over which the light plays softly. The modeling is obviously contrived to suggest rather than to describe. The strong lines of the broad head and the somewhat flat surfaces of the face are softened by a curiously ambiguous expression. Would we be wrong to read in it self-doubt mingled with affectation or bluster under an official mask of power? At any rate, the very fact that we are tempted to such interpretation testifies to the sophisticated artist's power to make us thoughtful before his image of a great and unfortunate man.

ARCHITECTURE

Striking as is the manifestation of Roman originality in its naturalistic portraiture, it is even more so in its architecture. During the Republican period the Roman identity is first and most fully expressed in architecture and city-planning. Unlike the religious architecture of the civilizations (including the Greek) that preceded it, the Roman temple was not a particularly inventive or conspicuous type. Rather it was upon imposing and utilitarian civic structures and plans that the Roman builders concentrated, though of course they also built temples, which were modeled upon schemes in which Greek and Etruscan elements were blended in unique fashion. The Temple of Fortuna Virilis in Rome (FIG. 6-14), dating from the late second century B.C., looks at first glance like an Ionic peripteral temple. It consists of a large cella located behind a deep porch (see FIG. 6-1). But the building stands on a high Etruscan podium, and the cella occupies its entire width. This means that only the porch columns are freestanding, while those along the exterior walls of the cella are engaged, being purely decorative and having no supporting function. Seen from a distance, they give the illusion of being freestanding; hence the designation "pseudoperipteral" for this type of construction. 'A favorite with Roman builders, this temple type has survived in many examples, most of them larger than the one shown and employing the Corinthian order.

The same superficial resemblance to Greek architecture appears in the Temple of the Sibyl at Tivoli (FIG. 6-15). Built in the early first century B.C., it looks at first like a Corinthian tholos. However, like the Fortuna Virilis, it stands upon a podium, ascent to which is by means of a single flight of stairs that leads to the entrance of the cella. This arrangement introduces an axial alignment that is not found in Greek tholoi and

6-14 Temple of Fortuna Virilis, Rome, late second century B.C.

6-15 Temple of the Sibyl, Tivoli, early first century B.C.

6-16 Sanctuary of Fortuna Primigenia, Praeneste (Palestrina), *c.* 80 B.C.

that serves to lessen the isolation of the building from its surroundings, diminishing somewhat the independent sculptural aspect so prized by the Greeks. A closer examination of the Temple of the Sibyl reveals other "un-Greek" features: The columns are monolithic—all of a piece—and not built up in the drum sections that were usual with the Greeks; the Romans preferred to use the monolithic column, often on great scale, wherever possible. The frieze is embellished not with figure sculpture, as would be the case in Greece, but with a favorite Roman decorative motif—garlands held up by *bucrania* (ox skulls), probably symbolic of fertility and of the alternation of death and resurrection; this motif is rhythmically repeated around the whole frieze. Finally, and also in contrast with Greek practice, the cella wall is built not of cut stone but of concrete into which blocks of tufa have been set in an ornamental pattern.

These significant departures from the Greek model are seen even more clearly in the Sanctuary of Fortuna Primigenia at Praeneste (FIG. 6-16), which was dedicated to Fortuna (Fate) and built under the first Roman dictator of the republic, Sulla, around 80 B.C., at a site where oracular lots had long been cast. The great size of the sanctuary reflects the growing taste for colossal Hellenistic designs during the Late Republican period. Seven terraces rising against the hillside are placed with rigid axial symmetry (FIG. 6-17). The top terrace carried a semicircular double colonnade that contained the sanctuary proper, probably in the form of a small round temple. Although something of it had been studied, we have full knowledge of the great temple only by an accident of war: Palestrina, modern successor of the Medieval town that had been built over Praeneste, was bombed during World War II, and clearing of the resultant ruins disclosed the impressive remains of the Roman buildings. It was seen that the Roman builders had converted an entire hillside into a man-made design in a symbolic and ostentatious display of power and dominion. This assertive subjection of nature to man's will and rational order is the first full-blown manifestation of the Roman imperial spirit and contrasts with the more restrained Greek bent, which crowns a chosen hill with sacred buildings rather than transforms the hill itself into architecture.

The substructures for the terraces (FIG. 6-18) were built in concrete (*opus concretum*), and it is here that we can find in grand scale the use of that favorite Roman building material, developed in the second century B.C. and destined for centuries of application throughout the Roman empire. Concrete (of generally inferior quality) had been used in the Near East, chiefly for the building of fortification walls, but its combination with the

6-17 Reconstruction of the Sanctuary of Fortuna Primigenia. Museo Archeologico, Palestrina.

arch and the vault, as here at Praeneste, was revolutionary. As perfected during the Early Imperial period, concrete vaulting permitted Roman builders to cover, without interior supports, spaces of a scale never dreamt of before. Its use enabled the Roman architect to think of architecture in terms radically different from those of earlier builders—as an architecture of space rather than of sheer mass, as was the case in the Egyptian pyramid or the Mesopotamian ziggurat or even the lighter but still space-encumbering post-and-lintel systems of the Greeks. (See discussion of the Roman Pantheon, pp. 222–23.) Roman concrete, a mixture of lime-mortar,

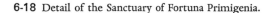

6-18 Detail of the Sanctuary of Fortuna Primigenia.

water, and volcanic dust, was poured over rubble that had been laid in courses between forms. Once solidified, this rubble concrete was cohesive and strong, though rough in appearance; but it was the custom to face the rough surfaces with marble slabs, plaster, or ornamental brick or stone work. In Praeneste, the concrete is faced with small, flat, irregularly shaped stones that produce a figuration called *opus incertum*.

Systematized concrete building methods gave Roman architecture a characteristic uniformity. No matter where its ruins are found today, in France, Spain, Italy, North Africa, or the Near East—usually without their original decorative facing—they can immediately be identified as Roman.

In the eighteenth century the imagination of Europe was excited by the discovery of the buried cities of Pompeii and Herculaneum, which had been overwhelmed by an eruption of Mount Vesuvius in A.D. 79. Their discovery, prior to the first archeological expeditions to Egypt, fascinated Europe and provided the initial impetus for modern archeological curiosity. What made the discoveries—new ones are still being made in the excavations of both cities—of such poignant human interest, as well as so infinitely valuable for scientific history, was that they revealed to modern eyes, in almost perfect preservation and detail, the everyday communal life of these times and places past. Pompeii, a city of about 20,000 and not very important in its time, had been stopped dead in the very motion of everyday life and had been preserved intact in volcanic ashes, invisible and forgotten for some 1600 years. The remains of the city permit us to reconstruct the Roman way of life during the Early Imperial period with a completeness far beyond that achieved at any other archeological site. The fullness of its record, its appeal to our sense of the dramatic and terrible accidents of life, and its usefulness for describing the architectural and artistic environment of quite ordinary men in an ancient city warrant considerable attention.

Though destroyed during the Early Imperial period, the city and most of its architectural monuments date from the Republican period. The plan of Pompeii, as seen in the parts excavated so far (FIG. 6-19), is not that of the ideal *castrum* type, but rather the irregular plan of a *grown* city, one that was subjected at various periods to revisions and regularizing. The Roman castrum type of city plan, based on the layout of a military camp, was used in the outlying, frontier, colonial regions and had its major development during the Early Imperial period (see FIG. 6-35), although early forms of it were used at Ostia in the fourth century B.C. and Cosa in the third century B.C. Pompeii, which started as a small, unplanned settlement in the vicinity of the Greek colony of Neapolis (modern Naples), was founded in the sixth century B.C. by the Oscans, early local rivals of the Romans. It was seized in 425 B.C. by the Samnites—also rivals of the Romans—who fortified and replanned it under the influence of expanding Greek concepts of rational urban planning. But the Greek grid system could not be rigidly applied without tearing down most of the city; as a result, the main organizing features—the north-south and east-west thoroughfares—do not intersect at right angles, and the "islands" between them are irregular. The city was conquered by Sulla in the eighties and refounded as a Roman colony in 80 B.C. In A.D. 62 it was partially destroyed by an earthquake; it had not yet been entirely rebuilt by the time of its final destruction seventeen years later. Pompeii has been especially valuable to the historian of Roman architecture since many building types that later become standard are found there in their early, if not earliest, examples; these include the oldest amphitheater extant and the earliest known public baths.

Next to the Roman Forum, from whose design it differs significantly, the forum of Pompeii (FIGS. 6-20 and 6-21) is the most important example of an early Roman civic center. The Pompeian forum is a rectangular court, in the proportion $3\frac{1}{2}$:1, that is unified by and the boundaries of which are defined by continuous colonnades around three sides. The other type of plan, represented by the Roman Forum, is bordered by more monumental, but individual and disconnected, structures. Like most Roman forums, that of Pompeii is set apart from the major traffic arteries, and vehicles could not enter it. Its long, north-south axis is dominated by the Capitolium, a large temple set on a high podium and dedicated to the three gods who protected Rome and her colonies. Several smaller temples flank the long sides of

6-19 Above: Aerial view of the excavated portion of Pompeii. Boxed area is shown below.

6-20 Left: Plan of the forum of Pompeii.

FEET
0   50   100

1. Arch of Tiberius
2. Macellum (market)
3. Sanctuary of the Lares
4. Building of Eumachia (used by corporation of clothmakers and dyers)
5. Comitium (election hall)
6. Curia (city council)
7. Basilica
8. Temple of Apollo
9. Temple of Jupiter Capitolinus
▨ Probable roofed area

6-21 Forum of Pompeii.

the forum. At the south end stands the triple hall of the Curia (city council), representing civic authority, and the Basilica, the seat of law and business. (This basilica, dating back to about 100 B.C., is an early example of one of the most important and influential classes of Roman buildings, the one from which the basic form of the Christian church building will derive.) Thus, the forum combines the functions of a religious, commercial, and administrative civic center and is the heart of the town. In the same way, it is a kind of imperial center in miniature, and this combination of functions, as architecturally expressed in the Roman Forum, will come to represent the central concerns and focus of the whole Roman empire.

One would not expect the formality of a civic center to be found in the streets that surround it. These would be less monumental and regular, and their spaces less ample—even narrow and cramped. The streets had heavy flagstone pavements with flanking sidewalks. Stepping stones for pedestrians crossing the street were so spaced as to be straddled by the wheels of vehicles. Most intersections had continuously flowing public fountains. The problem of human convenience in an urban society, though not dealt with

on the enormous scale that it is today, was worked out in Pompeii with an efficiency we can believe suited the needs of the people. The town had its commercial sections, like that of the Via dell' Abbondanza, where the streets were flanked by rows of small shops, offices, taverns, bakeries, etc. and where we can still see many painted advertisements on the walls. Here and there the rows of shops were interrupted by a gateway leading into a private residence, which spread out in the back of the shops and was entirely enclosed and isolated from them and from the noise and dust of the street.

The private house is probably the most precious and best-preserved record of urban life to come from Pompeii. The town houses of the well-to-do, like the House of Pansa (FIG. 6-22), an atrium type, protected in Pompeii and Herculaneum by the volcanic ash and lava in which they were buried, are extraordinarily well preserved, with their mural decorations still fresh and sometimes with their equipment and household utensils intact. Such a house stood flush with the sidewalk. Through a narrow door one entered a vestibule that led into the atrium. The latter had an opening in the center of the roof (the *impluvium*) and a depression in the floor below it to collect rainwater. Along the sides were small rooms; at the end, where the atrium extended the full width of the building, were two wings, *alae*. Behind the atrium was the *tablinum*, in which family archives and statues were kept. The tablinum could be shut off or could afford a passage to the peristyle, a large colonnaded court of Hellenistic origin. This court contained fountains and a garden, around which were arranged the family's private apartments. At the back there was sometimes a vegetable garden or orchard. Along the outer sides of the house and opening onto the street were the shops. Thus the house faced inward, depending upon its courts for light and air. As in the Etruscan atrium, units were symmetrically arranged on a long axis that reached back from the street and, when opened through its entire length, afforded a charming vista of open court, gardens, fountains, statues, colored marbles, mosaics, and brightly painted walls. Some of the largest of these atrium houses in Pompeii rivaled, if they did not surpass, the palaces of Hellenistic kings; the House of the Faun, in which the Alexander mosaic (FIG. 6-32) served as a floor ornament, covered almost 30,000 square feet. Of course, these were the houses of patricians and rich merchants; artisans, craftsmen, and shopkeepers lived in much more modest quarters, the latter often in single rooms in back of or above their shops.

In their fullest development, in the late Roman republic, the elaborate, skillfully planned houses of the great combine an older Italic nucleus with features of the Hellenistic house and represent the highest achievements of domestic architecture in antiquity. That domestic architecture had a prominent place in Roman civilization was manifest in every part of the empire. The character of Roman domestic religion, which exhibited a traditional Italic feeling for the home, family, and hearth as sacred, helps explain the careful elaboration of the domestic architecture.

PAINTING AND MOSAIC

The interiorizing design, with its open and independent arrangement of units, guaranteed complete privacy. Because of the small number of doors and windows, it also offered considerable stretches of wall space suitable for decoration, as the atrium of the House of the Silver Wedding in Pompeii (FIG. 6-23) clearly shows. The decoration commonly used varied between types that emphasized the wall as a barrier and others that visually opened the wall and enhanced the space of the room. The colors were sometimes delicate greens and tans, sometimes striking reds and black (to throw the panels or figures into relief), and there was rich creamy white in the borders. The Romans obtained a certain brilliance of surface by a careful preparation of the wall. After the plaster, which was specially compounded with marble dust, was laid on in several layers, it was beaten with a smooth trowel until it became very dense; it was then polished to a marblelike finish.

The progression from flat to spatial wall decoration in Pompeii and Herculaneum has been

6-22 Plan of the House of Pansa, Pompeii, second century B.C. (After Sir Banister Fletcher.)

1. Shops
2. Main entrance
3. Baker's shop
4. Bake house
5. Oven
6. Impluvium
7. Separate house
8. Atrium
9. Peristyle
10. Portico
11. Wagon shed
12. Gardener's shed
13. Winter dining room
14. Dining room (triclinium)
15. Reception room (oecus)
16. Office
17. Kitchen
18. Tablinum
Probable roofed area

FEET
0   25   50

The Romans   205

divided, somewhat arbitrarily, into four successive but overlapping styles. The first style (about 200–60 B.C.), called *incrustation*, divided the wall into bright polychrome panels of solid colors with occasional schematically rendered textural contrasts (FIG. 6-24). This style is a continuation of Hellenistic practice, and examples of it have been found in houses at Priene and on the island of Delos. A wall painting from a villa in Boscoreale, near Pompeii (FIG. 6-25), shows the second, or *architectural*, style (about 60–20 B.C.), in which the decoration is no longer restricted to a single visual plane. The space of the room is made to look as if it extended beyond the room itself by the representation of architectural forms in a visually convincing but not really systematic perspective. Columns, pilasters, and window frames painted on the wall served as enframements of distant views of cities and landscape. In

6-23 Atrium of the House of the Silver Wedding, Pompeii, second century B.C.

the *herringbone perspective* used, the orthogonals, or lines of perspective projection, do not converge on a single vanishing point on the horizon (as in Renaissance perspective), but tend to converge on an axis that runs vertically through the center of the panel. Though this method is not consistently employed, it does give a somewhat convincing illusion of objects receding in space.

A second-style mural in the Villa of the Mysteries, near Pompeii (about 50 B.C.), displays painted figures that are among the finest to have come down to us from the ancient world (PLATE 6-3). While other rooms in the villa are decorated in a style very similar to the pure architectural style of the villa in Boscoreale, the second-style illusionism here is confined to a painted ledge that looks like a shallow extension of the room proper and which affords the figures a kind of narrow supporting stage. The figures, set against a red-paneled background, in the style of a relief, are part of a large composition that once circled the walls of the room, which may have doubled as a banqueting room and as a place for the celebration of the rites of some mystery cult, perhaps that of Dionysos. The meaning of these scenes is in dispute; we may, however, be fairly certain that this group represents the initiation of a young novice into the cult. Whipped by a winged genius or deity, she crouches for solace in the lap of a solicitous older woman while a splendidly painted nude dances in Bacchic frenzy. The mystery cults, which are discussed below in connection with Christianity, made their way into the Roman empire in increasing numbers and variety from the Hellenized East. All included mysteries that were never to be divulged by the initiate, and which, when understood after painful introduction into the secret rites, would afford salvation through mystical union with a deity. The pictured ceremony from the Villa of the Mysteries is not only a work of art of high order, but a most important record of one aspect of the gradual religious transformation of the

Roman world by the westward migration of Oriental spiritualism. As always with Roman paintings of quality, the question arises, Is it original Roman or derivative from a Greek Hellenistic original in some temple now lost? No decisive answer can be given.

The question arises again, and more insistently, when we look at the second-style *Odyssey Landscapes* (FIG. 6-26) from a house on the Esquiline Hill in Rome. In these landscapes, dating from the late first century B.C. and now in the Vatican, the painted columns divide the otherwise continuous stretch of landscape into eight compartments in which are represented scenes from the Homeric epic. The shimmering landscapes extend the space of the room and almost absorb the subordinated, rapidly sketched figures by their luminosity. At the same time the landscapes seem to be brought into the room almost magically. The flickering play of color and light and especially the shaded edges of the solids give a stagelike presence, as of easily shifted props, that suggests distance and isolated action. The second style, though "architectural," here exhibits its versatility, for the sole purpose of the rigid frames is to create the illusion of open and unconstrained landscape. Therefore, if it could be established that the conception of an "all-encompassing" space in works like the *Odyssey Landscapes* is original with Rome, then a solid Roman contribution to the history of art could be acknowledged.

The architectural quality of the second style fades toward the end, and the triumph of the illusionism we see coming forward in the *Odyssey Landscapes* may be seen in the detail of a wall

6-24 First-style ("incrustation") wall painting from a Samnite House, Herculaneum, second century B.C.

6-25 Second-style ("architectural") wall painting from the cubiculum of the Villa Boscoreale, near Pompeii, first century B.C. Metropolitan Museum of Art, New York.

6-26 *Ulysses in the Land of the Lestrygonians*, part of the *Odyssey Landscapes*, second-style ("architectural") wall painting from a house in Rome, late first century B.C. Approx. 5' high. Vatican Library, Rome.

painting from the House of Livia in Primaporta, near Rome, made toward the end of the first century B.C. (PLATE 6-4). The extension of the space of the room—with its complementary effect, the bringing of the landscape into the room—creates the image of a garden just outside the limit of the wall. (This is a curious anticipation of the widely popular "picture window" of recent modern architecture in which one enjoys a "view" by fixing it within a frame, at the same time thinking of the garden as continuous with the room.) Here "deep" perspectives and distant views are not desired, but rather the intimacy and freshness of natural beauty easily within contact. One may think that in the second style, as it develops, the "view" comes ever closer, until it is one's own garden, free of any human intrusion, enclosed and isolated by the painted limits of the fence and by the back-stopping of the foliage itself, which occupies a plane close to the viewer and shuts out distance.

The passing of the wall from the state in which it is a framed view into nature to that in which

it merely supports smaller framed views takes place in the third, or *ornate*, style (about 20 B.C.– A.D. 60), during the time of the early empire. The style retains some degree of illusionism, as may be seen in a wall from Pompeii (FIG. 6-27), but the articulating architectural members lose their functional appearance. Columns and pilasters become attenuated and at times purely fantastic, like the central columns in our illustration; often they are entwined by garlands and tendrils. The painted architectural elements are apparently no longer intended to represent actual architecture but serve primarily as dividers, framing panels on which are small, individual paintings that have no direct relation to the overall design of the wall. These scenes resemble pictures hung on a wall and are placed with exquisite delicacy.

The fourth Pompeian wall style, called the *intricate*, dates from around A.D. 60 to A.D. 79 and may be seen to good advantage in the Ixion Room from the House of the Vetii (FIG. 6-28). Here, the painters, under the influence of contemporary Roman theatrical design, returned to the use of architectural frames and open vistas. An aerial perspective, however, rather than a linear one, is created by areas of color flooded with light and atmosphere. It unites the wall in a complex way, incorporating all the lessons of previous experiments in optical illusion. In fact the fourth style is a kind of résumé of its predecessors: The incrustation manner appears along the lower walls, and architectural panels are set into the ornate third-style wall articulation, which is also reflected in the individual picture panels. Though the aerial perspective produces a certain unifying effect, there is no single point of view from which the designs can be taken in or from which they can be related; obviously it is intended that we pass the pictures as we do in a gallery, stopping at each one, aware that it need have no relation in subject or style to its neighbor.

The small panels show a great variety of subject matter, ranging from still life to genre, from mythology to landscape. A still life with peaches and a carafe, from Herculaneum (PLATE 6-5), about A.D. 50, demonstrates that the Roman painter sought illusionistic effects in depicting small objects quite as much as in depicting archi-

6-27 Third-style ("ornate") wall painting, Pompeii, first century A.D. Museo Nazionale, Naples.

6-28 Fourth-style ("intricate") wall painting from the Ixion Room, House of the Vetii, Pompeii, first century A.D.

6-29 Genre scene (?), detail of a wall painting transferred to panel, from the House of the Dioscuri, Pompeii, first century A.D. Entire painting approx. 15″ × 17″. Museo Nazionale, Naples.

tectural forms and landscape spaces. Here his method involves light and shade with scrupulous attention to contour shadows and to highlights; doubtless he worked directly from an arrangement he made himself, the fruit, the stem and leaves, and the translucent jar being set out on shelves to give the illusion of the casual, almost accidental, relation of objects in a cupboard. But the picture is exact in neither drawing nor perspective, and the light and shade are approximate. Still, the illusion the painter contrives here marks the point of furthest advance made by the ancients in the technique of representation. He seems here to have an inkling that the look of things is a function of light, and he strives to paint *light* as he strives to paint the touchable *object* that reflects and absorbs it. It is interesting that painters like Paul Cézanne—often called the founder of modern art—in discarding the systematic organizing devices of perspective and chiaroscuro (light and dark), produce distortions and irregularities in painted objects that resemble those of this ancient still life.

A painting from the House of the Dioscuri in Pompeii (FIG. 6-29) offers evidence of the high degree of skillful illusionism achieved by the painters of the fourth style. The subject may be a scene from mythology or a genre scene. A woman seated before a stone building and a small hut receives a cup from a bowing man—or does she extend the cup to him? It is difficult to decide. Whatever the interpretation, the brush technique is a deft impressionism, the strokes firm and practiced; and the painter is entirely sure of the poses and the relationship of the figures in space. The problems of figural attitude, anatomy, movement, and proportion, which we have seen confronting the ancient artist for millennia, seem now to have their familiar solutions, so that the artist of this work proceeds easily and confidently, his brush quickly expressive of his knowledge.

That the style of the Dioscuri painting was contemporaneous with other quite different styles is apparent from a painting from Herculaneum representing Herakles finding the infant Telephos in Arcadia (FIG. 6-30). The subject indicates that the picture was copied from some Hellenistic original—or originals, for the artist proceeds as if he were lifting figures from different sources and arranging them with little relation to one another. Thus, the personification of Arcadia, the large seated figure, is not in proportion to Herakles, nor is the treatment the same: The statuesque Arcadia has the pale, hard modeling we associate with sculpture, while the play of light and highlight upon the supple surfaces of the Herakles figure is closely related to the effects we expect in pictorial illusionism, though the technique is by no means the free "painterly" one we see in the Dioscuri work. All the figures are precisely modeled, with firm outlines. The artist is concerned chiefly with the solid volumes of the bodies and not with light or with the space the whole group occupies; each figure is contained, as it were, by its own particular space, the space it "fits." The depiction of space as an enveloping and unifying factor in pictorial design may not be characteristic in Greek art, and this picture, as we have said, copies a Greek model. On the other hand, the special Roman contribution to painting may be precisely the representation of space as *surrounding* the whole group of objects and figures in any given composition and not merely coming between them.

It still seems to be a general tendency to deny any originality to Roman paintings and to insist that they are direct copies of or closely inspired by Hellenistic originals. No doubt, many Roman paintings do appear to be direct copies— for example, the *Herakles and Telephos* just discussed and the Alexander mosaic shown in FIG. 6-32. In fact, many paintings were probably done by transplanted Greek artists, and we might even grant that the Greek-derived style was the dominant one. But the Roman *landscape* seems to represent a radically different approach, particularly in its expression of a concept of space that is simply not evident in Greek art, and all attempts to derive Roman landscape painting from Hellenistic Greece lead us into extremely tenuous speculation based on unknown (or nonexistent) Greek prototypes. All extant Greek works show the Greek artist thinking in terms of solid volumes, like those of human figures—as in the *Herakles* painting—and confining space to a mere separating function rather than an all-containing one. Thus, it might be much simpler to credit the Romans with the development of a new concept in painting—namely, the projection of an enveloping, unifying volume of space on a flat surface. This refinement of abstraction— where space, filled with air and light, is actually represented as just as real as the objects it surrounds and contains—would complete the long development of representation that begins with the silhouettes of early Egypt and Mesopotamia and even earlier. At any rate, many now accept the view that the architectural illusionism of the second style is a Roman development and that this illusionism was a step in the transition to the spaces depicted in the smaller landscape panels (FIG. 6-31, PLATE 6-6). For an artist thinking of the wall surface as a kind of extension of the space of the room (as in architectural illusionism), the next step would be to take a segment of the wall and convert it, windowlike, into a small block of framed space that extends "through" the wall and contains its little universe of depicted objects.

In any case, the artist of the fourth style, chiefly interested in representing space, makes the objects as small as possible and unifies the whole composition, as we have seen, with light and atmosphere. Of course, recession in depth is suggested, not accurately projected. As noted

6-30 *Herakles and Telephos*, wall painting, Herculaneum, *c.* A.D. 70. Approx. 86″ × 74″. Museo Nazionale, Naples.

6-31 Sacral-idyllic landscape, wall painting transferred to panel, from the Villa of Agrippa Postumus, near Pompeii, late first century B.C. Portion shown approx. 26″ high. Museo Nazionale, Naples.

above, the Romans had no system of mathematical perspective but used (effectively, if unsystematically) the diminution of figures and objects and particularly atmospheric perspective, with its hazed and sketchy outlines, the shift from local color toward blue, and the blurring of distant contours (compare FIG. 6-26).

The love of country life and the idealizing of nature—what we may call the Arcadian spirit —prevails in these landscapes. Characteristically, they contain shepherds, goats, fauns, little temples, garlanded columns, copses of trees, and other accessories, which from their mood—part religious, part idyllic—have been called sacral-idyllic scenes. The Arcadian spirit of the time

speaks in the formal, pastoral poetry of Vergil, and in one of his odes Horace, proclaiming the satisfactions afforded the city man by his villa in the countryside, where life is beautiful, simple, and natural in contrast with the urban greed for gold and power, asks, "Why should I change my Sabine dale for splendor full of trouble?"

The attitude that celebrates the virtues of rustic life must be very closely associated with an original Roman development in architecture. Many Arcadian landscapes have been found in *villas*—country houses developed by the Romans when congestion in the cities became severe, as it did in Pompeii during the first century B.C. The villas were never located very far from town (one might call them suburban), and their wealthy owners could enjoy the advantages of city life and the quiet of the countryside. The very spaciousness of the landscape around the villa came to be the subject matter of the wall paintings we have been examining. The modern desire to escape the tensions of the city and to return to nature is ancient in its architectural and pictorial expression, not to mention its appearance in literature. We will encounter this Arcadianism again and again in the history of the West —in the Renaissance and in the nineteenth and twentieth centuries, when urban pressures strain human nerves.

The floors as well as the walls of Roman buildings were ornamented, usually in mosaics. Mosaic had its beginnings in the ancient Near East (see Chapter Five). It was used by the Greeks in place of carpets, often in geometric patterns. The Romans continued the practice and even applied mosaic to walls, though this seems to have been the exceptional case. A striking aspect of Roman mosaics is the attempt frequently made in them to copy not only the subject matter of painting but also the painter's technique in modeling, shading and the like. This was possible only if extremely small tesserae (the bits of glass or stone composing the mosaic) were used, as, for example, in the famous Alexander mosaic from the House of the Faun in Pompeii (FIG. 6-32), which is likely a copy of a Hellenistic original and perhaps should be thought of as more Hellenistic than Roman. The mosaic, which represents the rout of Darius and his army by Alexander the Great, has those qualities of Greek style we have noted: the essentially sculpturesque emphasis upon the solid forms, space defined by the forms themselves, and no attempt to show an enveloping space. Nevertheless, a remarkable taste for fidelity to appearance is shown in the details of action. The horses plunge into and out of the picture at the most daring angles, and the human figures are posed in such variety of descriptive attitude as to convince us the artist was

6-32 *The Battle of Alexander*, from the House of the Faun, Pompeii, third to second centuries B.C. Mosaic, approx. 8′ 10″ × 16′ 9″. Museo Nazionale, Naples.

pursuing an ultimate realism. In keeping with this is the high degree of tonal smoothness that was achieved by the setting-in of tesserae so small that some fifty separate bits were used to describe a single eye perhaps 1½ inches wide. The Romans appear to have developed a taste for this kind of minute workmanship, and the technical quality of mosaics must have been judged by the size of the tesserae used—the smaller the better. Since, after all, the mosaics were seen at a distance of only five or six feet (one walked on them), such a criterion seems natural enough. The standard changes during the Early Christian period, when mosaics were placed high on church walls and apse vaults, making such minute differences scarcely noticeable and such a painstaking technique meaningless.

We may judge the quality of panel painting by a portrait from Faiyum in Egypt, some sixty miles south of modern Cairo (PLATE 6-7). In Greek and Roman times Faiyum was a busy, populous province, and its cemeteries have yielded some 600 portraits painted on wood and attached to the mummy cases of the deceased. The making of such portraits must have been a regional custom, as very few have been found elsewhere; they supply for us our largest gallery of ordinary people of the vast Roman imperial world when it was at the height of its power. While some Pompeian wall frescoes give us hints as to what Greek murals may have looked like, the Faiyum portraits give us the best idea we have of Hellenistic Greek painting techniques. Most of the portraits are done in the encaustic technique (pigments in hot wax—see p. 136), but *tempera* (pigments in egg yolk) was used occasionally. Easel painting, upon small, portable panels, had been highly esteemed in Greece, where the encaustic technique had a long tradition. Polygnotos had worked in it in Classical times and, as mentioned earlier, it had been used for the architectural decoration of buildings like the Parthenon. The example here shows the very highest level of craftsmanship—refined brushwork, soft and delicate modeling, and the subtlest possible reading of a sensitive subject. The Faiyum portraits were probably painted from living persons, and in this instance we have the meeting of an unusually perceptive artist with a subject whose personality would try his whole skill to render. The composure, the emphasized thoughtful eyes, the Hellenizing hairstyle, are familiar in the portraits made during the time of the Stoic emperor Marcus Aurelius (about A.D. 160) and in the portraits of the emperor himself. The calm demeanor of the subject, the gaze that "sees the world steadily and sees it whole," evokes the philosophy of the emperor himself as set forth in his *Meditations*. As earlier we confronted the bust of Pompey, familiar with his history, so it is an aid to us in meeting this image from the age of the Antonines to read the philosophic emperor as we read the painted features of our subject:

> Every moment think steadily as a Roman and a man to do what you have in hand with perfect and simple dignity. . . . do every act of your life as if it were the last, laying aside all carelessness and passionate aversion from the commands of reason, and all hypocrisy, and self-love, and discontent with the destiny which has been given to you.

Our history has taken us beyond the period of the republic into that of the empire in order to show how Rome carried the ancient world's representation of landscape and of human individuality—begun in Mesopotamia and Egypt—to its most complete expression.

The Early Empire

When Octavian Caesar, the great-nephew and heir of Julius Caesar, routed the forces of Antony and Cleopatra at Actium in 31 B.C., he brought to an end some ninety long years of destructive civil war that had shattered the Roman republic. Though Octavian believed and proclaimed himself the restorer of the republic and the protector of its constitution and traditions, he became in fact the first emperor of Rome and to all intents and purposes ruled as emperor, taking the venerable name "Augustus," which was bestowed upon him by a grateful Senate. The peace that began with Augustus has been called the Pax Romana, for, under the auspices of a long line of emperors, peace prevailed within the Roman world for 150 years, a record in world history.

Augustus, determined to establish his authority unshakably, kept command of the military and financial resources of the empire in his own hands and deliberately set out to build a new and magnificent Rome in order to give a splendid image to the imperial reality. As they carried the boundaries of the empire further in all directions, the Julio-Claudian emperors, Augustus' successors in the first century A.D., continued his policy of glorifying by architecture, art, and a vast variety of public works the visible aspect of empire, sometimes to an extravagant degree. In the second century the empire—under Trajan, Hadrian, and the Antonines—reached its greatest geographical extent and the summit of its power (see map, p. 195); the might and influence of Rome was unchallenged in the Western world, though there was always the pressure of the new, Germanic peoples on its northern borders and of the Parthians and resurgent Persians on the east. These pressures increased in the third century, and, combined with the decline of imperial authority within the empire, disintegration of the economic and administrative structure, and military anarchy, almost brought the empire to collapse. In A.D. 285 it was somehow restored—temporarily—by the last pagan emperor, the capable Diocletian, under whom took place the savage persecution of a sect called the Christians. Within a generation the triumph of this sect was to mark a major turning point in the history of the world.

ARCHITECTURE AND PUBLIC WORKS

The grandiose imperial designs of the early empire are of course reflected in its architecture, perhaps most conspicuously there. The relatively stable conditions produced by the Pax Romana made possible the Romanization of the provinces, and urbanism—the planning and building of cities—played in this process a principal role. The rapid growth of population, especially city population, we have mentioned above as a reason for the escape to the suburban villa. The pressure of population in the city itself made the sprawling atrium house—wasteful of space—obsolete. In Rome, a population of close to one million had to be housed in multistory apartment blocks (*insulae*). Some 45,000 of these—built to the maximum legal height of five stories (sixty to seventy feet high)—accommodated almost 90 per cent of Rome's population. Most of the almost 50,000 inhabitants of Ostia, the port city of Rome, were housed in such apartment houses, some of which have been preserved to the level of the third story. Most were built of brick; some of concrete. The ground floors were occupied by shops, above which were the apartments, accessible by individual staircases. Many of the apartments were substantially more spacious than are most of ours today, the suites sometimes containing as many as twelve rooms, arranged on two levels. A reconstruction of an Ostian insula (FIG. 6-33) shows the apartment

6-33 Reconstruction of an insula, Ostia.

6-34 Pont du Gard, near Nîmes, southern France, first century B.C.

blocks built around a central court, which probably was landscaped and sometimes contained a small shrine. Apparently, many apartments had balconies, still a standard feature of modern Italian apartment houses. Only deluxe apartments had private toilets; others were served by community latrines, usually on the ground floor. The insulae had no private baths, but public baths were conveniently located throughout the various quarters of the city and were equipped with highly developed heating systems, which private houses and apartments lacked. (This is still true of parts of modern Italy.) The crowded conditions encouraged rent-gouging and jerry-building. Deficiency in materials was often compounded by bad design, such as a foundation area too small in relation to the height of a building—the latter a means of maximal exploitation of the limited space available. The poet Juvenal wryly complains about the poorly constructed city buildings:

> ... we inhabit a city propped up for the most part by slats: for that is how the landlord patches up the crack in the old wall, bidding the inmates sleep at ease under the ruin that hangs above their heads.

To an extent greater than is commonly known, the convenience of the ancient Roman of ordinary and less than ordinary means depended on facilities provided by the state—by authority imperial, provincial, or municipal. Millions of individuals depended upon the government for food distribution, water supply and sanitation, recreation and entertainment, and roads and bridges, not to mention the protection afforded by police and fire-fighters. The administration of these services in the great days of the empire was efficient even by our standards, given of course the limitations we would expect from a less highly developed technology and communication system. Second only to food distribution, an adequate water supply for the populations of the overcrowded cities was the most imperative need. The Romans were the first to incorporate the methodical development of water-supply systems into urban planning. The city of Rome began to build aqueducts for itself as early as the fourth century B.C., and Roman aqueducts or their ruins still stand in many former Roman cities, both in Italy and in the provinces. Water was carried from the source to the city by gravity flow, requiring the building of channels with a continuous gradual decline over distances often exceeding fifty miles; we can appreciate even in modern terms what an outstanding achievement of surveying and engineering this represents. The Pont du Gard near Nîmes (FIG. 6-34), in southern France, is one of the most impressive specimens of Roman engineering skill. Each large arch spans some eighty-two feet and is constructed of uncemented blocks weighing up to two tons each. The quickening rhythm of the small top arches (which carry the channel), placed in groups of threes over the larger arches, manifest the Roman engineer's sense for the esthetic as well as the practical. The finished aqueduct carried water to Nîmes over a distance of some thirty miles and provided each inhabitant with about 100 gallons a day. Services like this, and the awesome structures through which they were provided, could not help but impress upon the diverse peoples who had come under the rule of Rome the advantages of compliance with such practical power and the benefits that could come from Romanization.

If the construction of aqueducts could show the value of homage to Rome, how much more the erection of a whole city! At Timgad (Thamugadis) in North Africa (FIG. 6-35) the Romans built a city, around A.D. 100, that lasted until its destruction by the Moors in the sixth century A.D. Built along a major military road 100 miles from the sea, it was probably planned to house a military garrison to keep local tribes in check. But this primary function was soon expanded, and no

costs were spared to make this little provincial town into an attractive focal point for the local inhabitants. Here the empire was a physical presence to the Africans, the city representative of the authority of the emperor and the civilization of Rome. Like many other colonial settlements, Timgad served as a key to the process of Romanization. The town was planned with great precision, its design based on the layout of the Roman military encampment (the castrum). The typical provincial Roman city has the form of a square divided into equal quarters by two main arteries crossing at right angles, the *cardo* being the north-south axis, the *decumanus* the east-west; the forum is located near this crossing. The quarters are subdivided into square blocks, and the forum and public buildings like the theater, baths, and library occupy areas that are multiples of these blocks. At Timgad monumental gates led into the city, the streets of which were colonnaded. The city covered some thirty acres, and its original population of 2000

6-35 Plan of Timgad, North Africa, founded *c.* A.D. 100.

1. Forum
2. Theater
3. Library
4. House of Januarius, baptistry
5. East bath
6. North bath
7. Small baths
8. Temple of Ceres

←to 27 A.D. 70	100	118	215	235	**284**	300	315	A.D. 395
B.C.								
Colosseum begun	Timgad founded	Pantheon begun	Baths of Caracalla		Palace of Diocletian begun	Arch of Constantine		Division of the empire

E A R L Y   I M P E R I A L   P E R I O D

←BARRACKS EMPERORS→

L A T E I M P E R I A L
P E R I O D

soon grew to 15,000. The whole plan was essentially a modification of the Hippodamian scheme (see p. 181) but more rigidly ordered and systematized, with the forum set off from the main traffic pattern. The fact that most of these colonial settlements were laid out in the same manner—whether in North Africa, the Near East, or England—expresses more concretely than any building type or other construction project the unity and centralized power of the Roman empire at its height.

The architectural images of Rome set up in the far reaches of the empire had their even more monumental equivalents in the capital itself. When all roads did indeed lead to Rome, they could find their symbolic terminus in such stupendous works as the Colosseum (FIGS. 6-36 and 6-37), which for modern men still represents Rome as does no other building. So closely was it identified in the past with the city and the empire that an aphorism out of the early Middle Ages went: While the Colosseum stands, Rome stands; when the Colosseum falls, Rome falls; and when Rome, the world!

The Colosseum is sometimes called the Flavian Amphitheater, because it was begun by Vespasian, first in the Flavian line of emperors. It was dedicated in A.D. 80 by his successor, Titus, who had employed on the building of it prisoners from the Jewish Wars (see FIG. 6-52). The building type is an invention of the Romans, who expanded the "theater" into an "amphitheater," which is essentially two facing theaters enclosing an oval space, the arena. The Roman Colosseum is the largest of its type, but most major cities in the empire had an amphitheater. Some, like that at Verona, are still being used today for theatrical performances or games. The Colosseum was originally meant for the staging of lavish spectacles, battles between animals and gladiators in various combinations. The mythic beast-men struggles we saw represented in Mesopotamian art here came to bloody reality. The extravagant-

ly inhuman shows cost thousands of lives, among them those of many Christians, and the Colosseum has never quite outlived its infamy. The emperors competed with each other over who could produce the most elaborate spectacles. For the opening performance in A.D. 80 the arena was flooded and a complete naval battle, with over 3000 participants, was duplicated.

The oval arena of the Colosseum (FIG. 6-36) is surrounded by steeply rising rows of seats, which had a capacity of over 50,000 spectators. Its substructure consists of a complex system of radial and concentric corridors covered by concrete vaults that rise to support the upper rows of seats. Originally, tall poles around the top of the structure supported ropes on which awnings could be spread to provide shade for the spectators. The basements below the arena proper contained animal cages, barracks for gladiators, and machinery for raising and lowering stage settings as well as the animal and human combatants. A great deal of technical ingenuity involving lifting tackle was employed to suddenly hurl hungry beasts from their dark dens into the violent light of the arena.

Roman ingenuity in the management of architectural space to fit a complex function may be observed even in the exterior of the Colosseum —namely, the arcuated entrance-exit openings that must have permitted rapid filling and emptying of the vast interior space. The relation of these openings to the tiers of seats within was very carefully thought out and, in essence, may be observed in the modern football stadium. The Colosseum exemplifies the Roman talent for matching public and private convenience within large-scale service structures that require the enclosure and the spanning of great spaces.

The exterior of the building (FIG. 6-37), with its numerous functional openings, consists of ashlar masonry in which dry-jointed blocks were held together by metal cramps and dowels, as in Greek architecture. Its present pock-marked ap-

6-36 Aerial view and interior of the Colosseum, Rome, A.D. 70–82.

pearance (as if it had been blasted by large shrapnel) is due to the fact that the metal fittings were pried from the joints during the Middle Ages, when metal was very hard to come by. With these jointing units gone, vibrations from modern traffic have been shifting the stones, and the entire structure is in danger of collapse. The exterior walls are 161 feet high, and each of the three stories shows the characteristic combination of the Roman arch and vault construction with one of the ornamentally enclosing Greek orders. This setup, in which an arch is enframed by two engaged columns that carry a lintel, is called the Roman arch order; it appears in triumphal arches and other Roman buildings, and, revived in the Italian Renaissance, has a long, illustrious history in Classical architecture. For the moment it is necessary only to note that although this exterior feature serves no structural purpose, it does have an esthetic function, that of integrating the units of the surface by rhythmic horizontal and vertical repetition of the enframed arch. Although the arrangement of the orders finds no correspondence of a functional sort in the interior of the Colosseum, the rule of the arrangement is strict, following the standard Roman vertical sequence for multistoried buildings: Doric-Ionic-Corinthian, from the ground floor up. This sequence is based on the proportions of the orders, the Doric being the heaviest and thus, visually, the one most likely to be able to support the greatest load.

The imperial forums of the emperors rivaled the Colosseum as majestic expressions of the imperial ideal. The forums were erected not so much as fundamental civic units of direct service to the people as ostentatious glorifications of imperial power. They stood witness to the "piety, might, good fortune, magnanimity and happiness"—as their triumphal inscriptions so often proclaimed—of the successive emperors who built them. They were not planned as a unit, but each forum was added to another, their unity being achieved by strict axial alignment (FIG. 6-38). Most consist of large colonnaded courts designed to set off a temple dedicated to the god

6-37 Outer wall of the Colosseum.

who was the special protector of the emperor. The demands of impressive scale and great, sweeping vistas led sometimes to massive transformation of whole neighborhoods. The building of the Forum of Trajan required relocation and rebuilding of a market district and the modification of an entire hillside.

Dominating the Forum of Trajan was the huge Basilica Ulpia of about A.D. 112 (FIG. 6-39). A derivation from the basilica in Pompeii, it was perhaps the single most characteristic building type developed by the Romans. The basilica was a public hall designed to accommodate large numbers of people on various kinds of business. It was the locale of stock exchanges, law courts, business offices, and administrative bureaus and must have provided a center for civic services analogous to those of multiple-building municipal centers today. Later, the Christians adapted the basilica to religious purposes, modifying it into the typical Christian church building. In plan the basilica was rectangular, with two or more semicircular *apses*. In the Basilica Ulpia one of the apses contained the Shrine of Liberty, where

slaves were set free; the other may possibly have served in ceremonies of the emperor's cult. The entrance was on one of the long sides, an orientation that was changed by the Christians. The building was vast—426 by 138 feet; illumination for this great interior space was afforded by clerestory windows provided by elevation of the timber-roofed nave above the colonnaded aisles. In the Basilica Ulpia we once again encounter the Romans' instinctive feeling for broad, uninterrupted architectural spaces enclosed for the convenience of human transaction. The interior space is what counts here, and though it is a colonnaded space, its effect is not like that of the externally perceived Greek temple but rather like a peripteral Greek temple inverted: It is to be experienced from within, not from without.

One of the best preserved of all Roman monuments is the city of Rome itself; and one of the most renowned and influential buildings in the history of architecture is the Pantheon (FIGS. 6-40 to 6-42), built about A.D. 125, in which the effect of interior space is quite overwhelming, especially since its exterior scarcely suggests it. It is a domed

6-38 Plan of the Roman forums. (After Sir Banister Fletcher.)

1. Temple of Trajan
2. Column of Trajan
3. Basilica Ulpia
4. Market of Trajan
5. Temple of Mars Ultor
6. Temple of Peace
7. Basilica Aemilia
8. Temple of Antoninus and Faustina
9. Basilica of Constantine
10. Temple of Venus and Rome
11. The Colosseum
12. Arch of Constantine
13. Arch of Titus
14. House of the Vestal Virgins
15. Basilica Julia
16. Temple of Saturn
17. Rostra
18. Arch of Septimius Severus

rotunda fronted with a rectangular portico that seems not quite fitted to the original round structure and may have been an afterthought. The original effect must have been different, for the building was not freestanding but backed against an older basilica, extensions of which partly covered its sides. Moreover, the portico was preceded and partly embraced by a colonnaded court and originally was the only part of the building that was visible from the front. Built in the time of Hadrian, it may have been designed by that versatile ruler.

The structure is of monumental simplicity and great scale. The circular interior is covered by a hemispherical dome 144 feet in diameter, the summit of the dome being the same distance from the floor. The design is thus based upon the intersection of two circles, one horizontal, the other vertical, imaginable as sections of a globe of "space" inscribed within the building. The

dome is a shell of concrete that gradually thickens toward the base in order to augment structural strength where it is most needed. The center of the dome is dramatically pierced by a round opening (the *oculus*, or "eye") 30 feet in diameter, which, left unglazed and open to the sky, is the only source of light for the interior. Supporting the dome are walls of immense thickness into which have been cut alternating rectangular and semicircular niches, each covered by a vault that channels pressures exerted by the weight of the dome into solid masonry piers. The dome is coffered for the double purpose of making a handsome geometric foil of squares within the vast circle and of reducing the weight and mass of the dome without weakening its structure. The floor of the building is slightly convex, and drains are cut into the shallow depression in the center (directly under the oculus) to carry off any rain that falls through the opening far above.

Giovanni Pannini's painting of the interior of the Pantheon (FIG. 6-42) exhibits better than any photograph the unity and scale of the design, the simplicity of its relationships, and its breathtaking grandeur. It almost records the experience one has on first entering this tremendous, shaped space, a feeling not of the weight of the enclosing masses, but of the palpable presence of space itself, for the architecture here displayed is first of all an architecture of space. In the architectures so far studied, the form of the space enclosed is almost accidentally determined by the placement of the solids, which do not so much shape it as interrupt it. The solids are so prominent in Egyptian and Mesopotamian architecture that it is the solids we *see*; space is only "negative," simply *happening* between the solids. We think of this as an architecture of mass. Greek architecture, also primarily concerned with masses and their relations, and with the shaping of the solid units, is designated as skeletal or sculptural architecture. It is the Roman architects who initially conceive architecture in terms of units of space that can be shaped by enclosures. The interior of

the Pantheon, in keeping with this interest, is a single, unified, self-sufficient whole, uninterrupted by supporting solids; it is a whole that encloses the visitor without imprisoning him, a small cosmos that opens through the oculus to the drifting clouds, the blue sky, the sun, universal nature, and the gods. To escape from the noise and torrid heat of a Roman summer day into the sudden cool and calm immensity of the Pantheon is an experience almost impossible to describe and one that should be promised oneself. Above all, it is an *architectural* experience.

It should not be forgotten that Roman inventiveness in the construction of great interior spaces depended upon engineering knowledge of the properties of solids and of the statics of inert masses. The arch, the vault, and the dome were structural units appropriated and developed by the Romans with skill unsurpassed in the ancient world and not often since. Basically the problem as the Romans met it was this: how to enclose and roof over a vast space and how to give this space proper illumination while still keeping it open and free of the supports necessary

6-40 The Pantheon, Rome, A.D. 118–25.

EYE (UNGLAZED)   4' 0" THICK

FEET
50

25

0

A   A'

6-41 Plan and section of the Pantheon.
(After Sir Banister Fletcher.)

A   A

FEET
0   25   50

under a flat roof. (Compare this approach with
that embodied in the hypostyle halls of Egypt,
as shown in FIG. 3-27.)

The simplest vault used by the Romans was
the *barrel vault* (FIG. 6-43a)—in essence, a deep
arch that forms a half-cylindrical roof over an
oblong space, the edges of the half-cylinder resting directly upon the side walls, which must
be either thick enough to support the weight or
reinforced by buttresses. This vault can be made
of concrete by use of a temporary wooden form
(known as *centering*) that is the size and shape of
the finished vault and that holds the fluid concrete until it hardens. The vaulting of the central
hall of the Thermae (Baths) of Caracalla (FIG. 6-44)
and of the Basilica of Constantine (FIG. 6-67) was

6-42 *Interior of the Pantheon*, painting by Giovanni
Pannini, *c.* 1750. National Gallery of Art, Washington,
D.C. (Samuel H. Kress Collection).

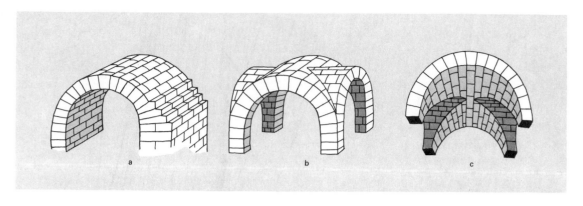

6-43 Roman vaulting systems: (a) barrel vault; (b) cross-barrel vault seen from above; (c) cross-barrel vault seen from below.

made by having the main barrel vault intersected at right angles at regular intervals by other barrel vaults, thus obtaining what is known as the *cross-barrel vault* (FIG. 6-43b and c). If the height of the intersecting and main barrel vaults is the same, the result is a *groin vault*, the line of intersection being called the groin. (Groin lines can be seen readily in FIG. 6-44.) Besides being lighter in appearance than the barrel vault, the cross, or groin, vault requires less buttressing: In the barrel vault the thrust—that is, the downward and outward forces exerted by the vault, like those of the arch—is along the entire length of the wall, requiring a corresponding buttressing; in the groin vault it is exerted only at the points at which the groins converge, and it is only at these points that heavy buttressing is needed. Thus, the interior can be kept free of load-carrying walls, and more light can be admitted through the use of clerestory windows located in the free space where buttressing is not needed (in effect, the ends of the cross vaults). Buttressing can be provided by heavy walls perpendicular to the main wall and pierced by arches, which thus form side aisles to the main hall (FIG. 6-68), and by short wall sections above the aisle roofs that channel part of the vaults' thrust into the outside vaults.

All this was elementary to the builders of the gigantic Baths of Caracalla (FIGS. 6-44 and 6-45), dating from about A.D. 215. The enclosure of great spaces by vaulting was at this time common practice. Although nothing of the covering is left, the baths reveal traces of the vaults that

sprang up from the thick walls to heights of ninety feet; under them, spread out in unending variety, were spaces designed for the intellectual as well as physical recreation of thousands of leisured Romans—all at the expense of the state. Just the central buildings of the huge complex, in which the emperors hoped to keep an unruly and indigent populace preoccupied with pleasure, covered an area roughly 240 by 120 yards; and the baths, which were the center of interest as well as the architectural center of the design, had a capacity of 1600 bathers. The functions of various parts of the complex are still matters of controversy. The design was symmetrical along a central axis occupied by pools that were filled with water of different temperatures: the *frigidarium*, the cold-water pool; the *tepidarium*, the central room containing smaller warm-water pools; and the *calidarium*, a circular hot-water pool in a domed rotunda. The central buildings also contained steam baths, dressing rooms, lounges, lecture halls, and *palaestrae* (exercise rooms). This whole core complex was surrounded by landscaped gardens bordered by secondary buildings that housed shops, restaurants, libraries, gymnasiums, and (perhaps) a stadium. The long side of the entire complex measured almost one-quarter of a mile. Beneath it all was a subterranean world of corridors (some wide enough to accommodate vehicles), storerooms, and heating chambers populated by slaves and stokers, for the halls and the water were heated by a system in which hot air was circulated through tubes and hollow bricks beneath the floors, in the walls, and sometimes in the vaults. The water was plentifully supplied by an individual aqueduct.

This enormous dedication of human ingenuity in the service of human ease! For a negligible admission fee one could lounge for a whole day at the baths in surroundings of the greatest magnificence. In fact, the baths were so lavish, ornate, and luxurious that moralists of the time complained of their wasteful ostentation. Seneca, comparing his degenerate times with those of the heroic Scipio, who bathed in austerely simple surroundings, complained:

> But who in these days could bear to bathe in such a fashion? We think ourselves poor and mean if our walls are not resplendent with large and costly mirrors; if our marbles from Alexandria are not set off by mosaics of Numidian stone, if their borders are not faced over on all sides with difficult patterns, arranged in many colours like paintings; if our vaulted ceilings are not buried in glass; if our swimming pools are not lined with Thasian marble, once a rare and wonderful sight in any temple . . . What a vast number of statues, of columns that support nothing, but are built for decoration, merely in order to spend money! And what masses of water that fall crashing from

level to level! We have become so luxurious that we will have nothing but precious stones to walk upon.

The baths were of course not merely that but social centers in which one could spend the whole day "sweetly doing nothing." And the baths were cultural centers as well, with their libraries, and with their profusion of magnificent statues. A large number of the abovementioned Roman copies after Greek originals were found in public baths, and a few of the most important in the Baths of Caracalla.

SCULPTURE AND MONUMENTAL RELIEF

Sculpture in the empire begins under the influence of Augustan Rome's admiration of Hellenic culture and of the emperor's apparent determination to base a cultural renewal of Rome on it. That the Hellenized glorification of the empire was politically motivated is doubtless true; we have seen in architecture how building was molded to the end of manifesting the imperial authority. But the imperial motivation had the esthetic consequence that work of the highest quality in all

6-44 Tepidarium of the Baths of Caracalla, Rome, c. A.D. 215. (Restoration drawing by G. Abel Blonet.)

6-45 Plan of the Baths of Caracalla. (After Sir Banister Fletcher.)

1. Tepidarium
2. Calidarium
3. Frigidarium, with swimming pool
4. Open peristyles
5. Lecture rooms and libraries
6. Promenade
7. Shops
8. Stadium
9. Aqueduct and reservoirs

FEET
0   500

GARDEN

the arts was produced bearing the seal, as it were, of the Hellenic spirit. The *Augustus of Primaporta* (FIG. 6-46), about 20 B.C., no less than the *Aeneid* of Vergil, is an example of the sedate, idealizing manner we recognize as "Augustan." The statue, which once stood in front of the imperial villa in Primaporta, about ten miles north of Rome, represents Augustus proclaiming a diplomatic victory to the people. The work is of the highest quality and is very likely by a Greek artist. At first glance it might appear to be in the realistic mode of Republican statues, but at the second we find it strongly idealized, made according to Polykleitan proportions and even reminiscent of the *Doryphoros* (FIG. 5-53), especially the walking pose. The reliefs on the emperor's breast plate are Roman in subject and refer to contemporaneous events—at least in the central theme: A Parthian returns a Roman standard to a Roman soldier. But these historical references are enframed by mythological and allegorical figures representing the sky god, the earth goddess, and the pacified provinces of Spain and Gaul. Together the figures symbolize blessings of the new Golden Age expected to come with the Augustan peace. They also place side by side the idealizing and realistic tendencies in Roman art that will alternate and intermingle throughout imperial times.

6-46 *Augustus of Primaporta*, c. 20 B.C. Marble, 6′ 8″ high. Vatican Museums, Rome.

6-47 Ara Pacis Augustae, Rome, 13–9 B.C. Marble, approx. 35′ wide. (Cornice restored.)

The tendencies mingle in the sculptured figures of the Ara Pacis Augustae (Altar of the Augustan Peace) yet remain distinguishable (FIG. 6-47). Completed and dedicated in January, 9 B.C., to commemorate pacification of Spain and Gaul in 13 B.C., the altar can stand as a monument to the pacification of the whole empire in the Augustan years following the establishment of the new government in 27 B.C. The actual altar is raised upon an interior platform that is surrounded by a nearly square enclosure, 39 by 35½ feet. The exterior and interior surfaces of the enclosing walls are decorated with reliefs. On the interior walls are garlands suspended from bucrania (compare the frieze of the Temple of the Sibyl at Tivoli, FIG. 6-15). The exterior walls have a lower zone of a delicately carved, decorative acanthus leaf pattern arranged in spiral designs. The upper zone depicts a procession of men, women, and children and, on separate panels, allegorical subjects. The wall surfaces are framed by florid Corinthian pilasters in a composition reminiscent of the second style of Pompeian wall painting.

The *Tellus Relief* (FIG. 6-48) represents the ancient Roman earth mother, Tellus, flanked by personifications of the elements, their draperies blowing about them, seated in a fertile landscape against clouds simulated in low relief. Although we have come to think of the interest in the illusion of landscape as Roman, the poses, the style of the draperies, and the lateral placement of the figures in a single plane attest the Greek influence. The whole tableau celebrates the Augustan peace as the source of a new bounty of nature and the new richness and fertility of earth as the foundation of Roman wealth and power.

The *Procession* (FIG. 6-49) on the Ara Pacis, led by the emperor himself, may be intended to represent the actual solemnities when the Altar was dedicated. The historical particularity of the frieze is characteristic of the Roman feeling for the factual, especially as we have seen it expressed in the portrait bust, in a pragmatic architecture, and to a degree in landscape painting. This contrasts with the Greek practice of disguising historical events in the mythological, as in the great frieze of Pergamum, where a historical war between Greeks and Gauls becomes a struggle

6-48 *Tellus Relief*, panel from the Ara Pacis Augustae.

6-49 *Procession*, portion of the frieze of the Ara Pacis Augustae. Marble, approx. 63″ high.

between gods and giants. In some respects the Roman feeling for narrative bound to actual events resembles more the Assyrian approach than the Greek. Yet the style of the figures of the procession is Hellenizing, and may be directly inspired by the Panatheniac frieze of the Parthenon (FIGS. 5-44 and 5-45). In the Ara Pacis the procession moves in several files. Differences in distance are signified by differences in degree of relief—the nearer the figure, the higher the relief. There is studied differentiation of individual persons; the heads are moderately idealized portraits; and there are "human interest" touches —for example, the clinging, restless children quieted by the adults. The overall demeanor is solemn, as befits the occasion, and we get the impression of a quiet concourse of participants behaving as they think proper to a quasireligious ceremony. The draperies, the quiet dignity, the ordered deployment within a shallow plane of space echo the older Classical style, and the Ara Pacis, with its blend of real and ideal, signifies the Augustan style and that of the empire in general.

The memorializing of actual events in monumental form finds striking expression in the imperial triumphal arch, one of the most popular types of commemorative monuments. Essentially, the triumphal arch is an ornamental version of a city gate moved to the center of the city to permit entry of triumphal processions into the forum. The Arch of Titus (FIG. 6-50), dated A.D. 81, is located at a point where the Via Sacra enters the Roman Forum. As a building type the triumphal arch exerted considerable influence on the architecture of the Renaissance. Closely related to the Colosseum arch order, it consists of a single arch flanked by massive piers to which the Corinthian order has been attached decoratively. Its typical superstructure, the *attic*, bears the commemorative inscription. Occasionally the flanking piers are also pierced by arches, produc-

6-50 Arch of Titus, Rome, A.D. 81.

6-51 *Spoils from the Temple in Jerusalem*, relief from the Arch of Titus. Marble, approx. 7′ high.

ing a triple arch like that of Constantine (FIG. 6-71). The walls of the passageway of the Arch of Titus are decorated with relief panels representing the triumphal return of Titus from the conquest of Jerusalem at the end of the Jewish Wars (A.D. 66–70). In later arches the sculptural decor is moved to the outside surfaces of the structure as in the Arch of Constantine.

One of the archway reliefs shows soldiers of the Roman army carrying spoils from the temple in Jerusalem, including the seven-branched candelabrum from the Holy of Holies (FIG. 6-51). The panel is much damaged. Beam holes in the upper part date from the Middle Ages, when the family of the Frangipani converted the arch into a private fortress and built a second story into the vault—only one of many examples of later indifference to the esthetic and historic value that recent times have discovered in the ruins of Rome. But enough remains to show that spatial effects aimed at in the Ara Pacis reach full development here. The illusion of movement is complete and convincing. The marching files press forward from the left background into the center foreground and disappear through the obliquely placed arch in the right background. The energy and swing of the column suggest a rapid marching cadence and the chant of triumph. The carving is extremely deep. The heads of the forward figures have been broken off, probably because they stood vulnerably free from the

block, emphasizing their different placement in space from the heads in low relief, which are intact. The deep relief produces dramatically strong shadows, the light and shade quickening the movement and strikingly suggesting the "momentary flash of a passing parade." The work brings to mind the experiments with light and space in Imperial painting and architecture.

Across the archway is represented the *Triumph of Titus* (FIG. 6-52), which has a slower pace, without the thrusting movement of the marching soldiers carrying the spoils from the temple and without the spatial experiments found there. The numerous layers of figures create an illusion of depth, and a bold attempt at representing the overlapping horses turning into the way, drawing the chariot of Titus, persuades us that the sculptor's intentions are alike in both panels. The close correspondence between the event as shown in the panels and a description of it by Josephus (Jewish soldier, statesman, and historian) points up the Roman bent for the factual:

Most of the spoils that were carried were heaped up indiscriminately, but more prominent than all the rest were those captured in the Temple at Jerusalem—a golden table weighing several hundredweight, and a lampstand similarly made of gold. . . . The central shaft was fixed to a base, and from it extended slender branches placed like the prongs of a trident, and with the end of each one forged into a lamp: these numbered seven, signi-

6-52 *Triumph of Titus*, relief from the Arch of Titus. Marble, approx. 7′10″ high.

6-53 Column of Trajan, Rome, A.D. 113.

copied: As late as the nineteenth century, in commemoration of the victories of Napoleon, a Trajanic column was set up in the Place Vendôme in Paris. The original column is 128 feet high. It was once crowned by a statue of Trajan, which was lost in the Middle Ages and replaced by a statue of St. Peter in the sixteenth century. The square base served as Trajan's mausoleum, and his ashes were deposited there in a golden urn in A.D. 117. The column records Trajan's two successful campaigns against the Dacians, as a result of which the Roman dominion was extended across the Danube into what is now Hungary and Rumania. Under Trajan the limits of the empire reached their greatest expansion. The marble reliefs, in a 625-foot band that winds the height of the column, represent a continuous record of the campaigns, told in 150 separate episodes with literally thousands of figures. The band increases in width as it moves toward the top of the column (from thirty-six inches to fifty inches) for better visibility from the ground. But recognition of the upper subjects must have been a problem, although the column originally stood in a small courtyard surrounded by two-story buildings, from the upper story or roofs of which the topmost reliefs may have been recognizable.

The carving is of relatively low relief in order to reduce shadows to a minimum, since they would tend to impair the legibility of the work. This low relief constitutes a significant reduction in illusionistic depth; subsequent reliefs will continue to grow ever flatter. The sculptured narrative puts much emphasis on military architecture, fortifications, bridges, and so on, to show the Roman technical superiority over the barbarian foe. At the bottom appears the famous pontoon bridge built across the Danube by Apollodorus, with the Danube as a river god looking on in amazement at the achievement. On the fourth circuit of the column Trajan is shown speaking to his troops. The emperor's figure is seen many times throughout the narrative, appearing as a kind of major motif. The story of the campaigns is told throughout with objectivity; the enemy is not belittled and the Roman victories are hard won.

The Column of Trajan reliefs embody some features of great importance for the art of the Middle Ages. We have indicated one of them

fying the honour paid to that number by the Jews. After these was carried the Jewish Law, the last of the spoils. Next came a large group carrying images of Victory, all fashioned of ivory and gold. Behind them drove Vespasian first with Titus behind him: Domitian rode alongside, magnificently adorned himself, and with his horse a splendid sight.

The Column of Trajan, another kind of commemorative monument, dating from A.D. 113, stood in his forum before the temple of the Trajanic deities (FIGS. 6-53 and 6-54). The column, the work of Trajan's favorite architect and military engineer, APOLLODORUS of Damascus, was often above, a flattening of relief, and have shown the functional reason for it—better visibility. But the sacrifice of the strong illusionism of the Arch of Titus reliefs, even of those of the Ara Pacis, may have another reason: a desire for completeness of narrative description that requires that a great number of actions be shown in a limited space. Thus *narrative* fact rather than *visual* fact is required, and truth to appearance ("illusionism," "realism"), to greater or less degree, can be sacrificed. A very singular and important sacrifice is made in the Column of Trajan compositions, and that is in the representation of space. In the Ara Pacis and the Arch of Titus the figures are represented as standing and moving on the same groundline, at the eye level of a presumed observer who occupies an imagined place on the same line; thus, all the heads are approximately on the same level. But the figures of the Column of Trajan are placed in rows one above the other, a device altogether different from the approximate perspective of illusionism. From a perspective viewpoint the figures and architecture are entirely haphazard in their arrangement; from the point of view of narrative they occur where the story demands. Often relative proportions are sacrificed: Soldiers are represented as large as the walls they attack, or, though not represented in this illustration, cavalrymen are as large as or larger than their horses. We can say that conventions of Medieval art already appear in the sculptures of the Column of Trajan.

These features were not immediately adopted. They appear in the somewhat later Column of Marcus Aurelius; but in a relief of Marcus Aurelius sacrificing (FIG. 6-55), one of three panels surviving from a triumphal arch dedicated to that emperor and carved about A.D. 180, the older illusionism persists, though not to the degree that we find it in the Arch of Titus. In this relief the procession was cut up into panels (each a part of a larger whole to be imagined by the viewer), since the narrative requirements are not so demanding. There is much of Hellenic Classicism in the poses of the figures and in their draperies. (The drapery of the figure at the left is an echo of the *Nike* of the balustrade of the Temple of Athena Nike on the Acropolis, shown in FIG. 5-52, and the head is an obvious reference to Phidias' Olympian Zeus, FIG. 5-34). Hadrian,

6-54 Detail of the two lowest bands of the Column of Trajan. Marble, bands approx. 36" high.

6-55 *Marcus Aurelius Sacrificing*, from an arch of Marcus Aurelius, late second century A.D. Marble, approx. $10\frac{1}{2}'$ high. Palazzo dei Conservatori, Rome.

6-56 *Head of Augustus*, detail of FIG. 6–46.

6-57 *Livia*, wife of Augustus, *c.* A.D. 20. Marble, head approx. 15″ high. Antiquario, Pompeii.

Antoninus Pius, and Marcus Aurelius were all Hellenophiles, and it is in their reigns that perhaps the last powerful influence of Classical Greece was felt. The figures in the relief are cut to ideal proportions, but a considerable Roman realism appears in the details and in such illusionistic devices as the perspective of the background architecture and the varying depth of relief to show distance. The bland composure of the faces of the Ara Pacis does not appear here; the times have changed, the end of the Golden Age has come. A kind of brooding solemnity prevails as the grave philosopher-emperor—the sculptor gives us a portrait likeness—prepares the sacrifice that may produce omens of a troubled future for the empire.

PORTRAIT SCULPTURE

Two portrait busts from Republican times have already shown us the Roman aptitude for and skill in this art, an expression of the now familiar Roman instinct for the factual. It is scarcely an accident that the historical reliefs just discussed have portrait figures in them. Literally thousands of portrait busts have been found from the times of the republic and of the empire, and it must be conceded that the best are evidence of the important contribution of the Romans to portrait art. Two tendencies of style determine the production of portrait sculpture—the verism of the republic, and the Hellenizing idealism of the empire; in the later period the tendencies alternate and sometimes converge. It is significant that members of the lower social classes generally are portrayed realistically in all periods, while official portraits (of the ruling class, that is) tend to shift between realism and idealism, depending in part upon the general style of the period or perhaps the preference of the sitters or both.

A portrait of the emperor Augustus (FIG. 6-56), a detail of the Primaporta figure (FIG. 6-46), which can be profitably compared with earlier portraits from the republic (FIGS. 6-12 and 6-13), is very subtly idealized without any apparent loss of likeness. The hair, adhering closely to the skull, is reminiscent of fifth-century B.C. Greek style and reflects Augustus' Classical taste prevailing over Hellenistic realism. We have met the Classicism of the Augustan age in the Ara Pacis and have pointed out that Vergil's *Aeneid*, deliberately imitating Homer and commissioned by Augustus himself, reveals in its form the same Classical spirit. Livia, the second wife of Augustus and mother of the emperor Tiberius, is shown in a portrait bust as the comely, tactful, and elegant woman she is believed to have been (FIG. 6-57). There is the same Augustan idealization and the same retention of the likeness. The lifelike quality is enhanced by effective use of color, much of which is preserved in the hair, eyes, and lips.

The emperor Vespasian, succeeding Nero, the last of the Julio-Claudian line, which had begun with Augustus, reigned from A.D. 69 to 79. His portrait bust (FIG. 6-58) forcefully reveals the veteran general who had fought successfully in all parts of the empire. Vespasian was a man of simple origin and simple tastes who desired to return to republican simplicity after Nero's extravagant misrule. He was a good administrator —honest, shrewd, and earthily humorous, all of which qualities speak from his portrait. The artist has attempted no flattery; quite possibly Vespasian himself discouraged him from idealizing overmuch, for he preferred to have the blunt, rugged aspect of the soldier. From the portrait we can understand the active man whose care was restoration of the empire and who is reported to have said on his deathbed: "An emperor should die standing." The portrait, while a little subtler in characterization, is almost republican in its directness.

The bust of a lady from the Flavian period (FIG. 6-59)—embracing the reigns of Vespasian and his sons, Titus and Domitian—is a departure from the usually rather stern portraits of Roman women. It is a rare masterpiece in its inimitable union of sensitive beauty, noble elegance, and lucid intelligence. The elaborate coiffure stands in striking textural contrast to the delicate, softly modeled features, and the technique and effort to reproduce the luminosity and glow of actual flesh recalls the art of Praxiteles. This truly regal work, exemplar of Roman portrait art at its height, can be instructively compared with the head of Queen Nefertiti (PLATE 3-2),

6-58 *Vespasian, c.* A.D. 75. Marble, life-size. Museo Nazionale Romano, Rome.

6-59 *Portrait of a Lady, c.* A.D. 90. Marble, life-size. Musei Capitolini, Rome.

6-60 *Hadrian*, *c*. A.D. 120. Marble, approx. 16″ high. Museo Ostiense, Ostia.

done in the subtle Amarna style of Egypt.

Great persons of ambivalent qualities are particularly interesting to us, and this makes their portraits—such as that of Pompey (FIG. 6-13)—more interesting perhaps than those of persons of more uniform character. This quality of ambivalence was especially true of the emperor Hadrian (FIG. 6-60). We can approach his portrait informed by the account given of his personality by his ancient biographer, Spartianus. Hadrian, beyond all the other emperors a lover of Greek art and culture and himself a skillful artist and architect, poet, scholar, and writer, is thus described:

> He was grave and gay, affable and dignified, cruel and gentle, mean and generous, eager for fame yet not vain, impulsive and cautious, secretive and open. He hated eminent qualities in others, but gathered round him the most distinguished men of the state; at one time affectionate towards his friends, at another he mistrusted and put them to death. In fact he was only consistent in his inconsistency [*semper in omnibus varius*]. Al-

though he endeavored to win the popular favor, he was more feared than loved. A man of unnatural passions and grossly superstitious, he was an ardent lover of nature. But, with all his faults, he devoted himself so indefatigably to the service of the state, that the period of his reign could be characterized as a "golden age."

We might bring also to the contemplation of his portrait the poem, long famous, that he wrote to his soul at the end of his life:

> Charming, fleeting little soul,
> My body's guest and comrade,
> Where now will you go
> Naked, pallid, unmoving
> Never again to play?

In this portrait Hadrian affects the Greek coiffure, in form much like the early Classical ringlets of the *Apollo* from the Temple of Zeus at Olympia (FIG. 5-35). He adopts also the Greek beard, abandoning the age-old tradition of the clean-shaven face. (This may have been inspired by portraits of Pericles.) In any event, from now on most Roman emperors will be represented bearded. The head is idealized, but with restraint, the features a little regularized and retouched, perhaps, but not so as to interfere with the likeness. A certain ambiguity and inscrutability shadows the face. But, when we know a little of him, we are prepared for this.

The last emperor of the great Imperial age that had begun with Augustus was the Stoic Marcus Aurelius. We have touched on his philosophy in looking at the Faiyum portrait of a man from his time, a man whose serenely gentle and reflective face manifests the emperor's philosophy. A great equestrian bronze portrait statue of Marcus Aurelius (FIG. 6-61) has survived from the ancient world, unique in that it *did* survive, for there are no other examples of what must have been a statue type popular with the Roman emperors. (Medieval Christians probably melted the statues down for their bronze and because they were impious images from the pagan, demonic world of the Caesars. It is thought that the Christians mistakenly took the *Marcus Aurelius* statue for that of the first Christian emperor, Constantine, and that that is why it escaped destruction.) The emperor, whom we have seen earlier in his role of head priest, *pontifex maximus*,

6-61 Equestrian statue of Marcus Aurelius, c. A.D. 165. Bronze, over life-size. Capitoline Hill, Rome.

with his toga drawn over his head, is portrayed here exercising his office as commander of the legions, perhaps passing before the people. His gesture here, magisterial, benignly authoritative, much like a later papal blessing, conveys at once the awesome and universal significance of the Roman *imperium*, the almost godlike presiding of the emperor over the whole world. Yet, at closer view, we see the same features as in the sacrifice panel—those of a man calmly aloof, meditative, a little resigned. The magnificent, high-stepping charger, the war horse mettlesome and impatient with the tameness of the parade, breathes hotly through dilated nostrils. This superb bronze was the inspiration and sometimes the despair of the sculptors of the Late Renaissance. It stands today on the Capitoline Hill, the authentic ancient centerpiece of Michelangelo's great architectural design (see Chapter Thirteen), representing as does no other single object the lost authority of empire.

After Marcus Aurelius the downward course of the empire became precipitous, though not at once; Septimus Severus held it level for a while.

6-62 *Caracalla*, c. A.D. 215. Marble, life-size. Vatican Museums, Rome.

His son Caracalla (FIG. 6-62), under whom the great baths named after him went toward completion, was a brutal man, murderer of his own brother. He reigned briefly between A.D. 211 and 217, and his murder grieved no one. Gibbon writes of him: "Caracalla was the common enemy of mankind." To render his violent traits, the sculptor had to return to realism. We find a burly, suspicious, almost snarling man, more a cut-throat than an emperor, a man who could scarcely be more the opposite of Marcus Aurelius. Significantly for what was to follow—the military anarchy of the third century, when the "barrack emperors" were set up (and pulled down) by the army—Caracalla pursued the tyrant's rule that if one has the loyalty of the army, one need not consider the people. His soldiers, however, were not wary enough to protect him from the dagger of an assassin, and his death was the model death of the tyrant, in form repeated again and again throughout the terrible third century. "Such," writes Gibbon, "was the end of a monster who disgraced human nature." Yet Michelangelo was later to base his noble bust of Brutus on this bust of Caracalla.

Internal unrest combined with attacks on frontiers by the new Sassanian line of Persian kings in the east and German tribes in the north brought the empire to the verge of collapse. In the space of fifty years some twenty of the barrack emperors were exalted and then assassinated by factions of the army. This created anguish and foreboding throughout the empire, curiously reflected in numerous portraits like that of one of the barrack emperors himself, Philip the Arab (FIG. 6-63). Philip became emperor after having his predecessor, Gordianus, executed. In considering his portrait it will be useful to know something of the close of his career. An adventurer himself, he knew that he was surrounded by adventurers—especially in the army—who were ready to follow his example. Faced with a revolt, Philip appointed a brave and intelligent aristocrat, Decius, to put it down and to calm the army. The army accepted Decius as its leader on condition that he agree to depose Philip or be put to death himself. Decius then led the best of the army against Philip, who was slain; Decius became emperor. The portrait thus shows the face of a man who knows he is utterly without security. Fear, distrust, suspicion work the face into a mask of guilt and anxiety. The brow is furrowed. The deep-set eyes shift sideways. The eye pupils are carved, an innovation that focuses on the psychic state. The hair is cropped short, the beard stubbly. The short, nervous chisel strokes adapt to the nervous mood. (In the works of later sculptors they will become increasingly abrupt and schematic, leading to the geometric patterning of the fourth century.) But it is the face, with its terrible tensions, that was rarely seen before in the history of art. From the Archaic masks we come at last, in the third century A.D., to a face so "modern" in what it reflects of trouble that we experience a shock of recognition. Both the ideal and the real in Roman sculpture are now replaced by something new—expression—wherein the artist is concerned first of all with expressing an emotional state—either his subject's or his own, and perhaps both.

6-63 *Philip the Arab*, A.D. 244–49. Marble, life-size. Vatican Museums, Rome.

The Late Empire

The anarchy of the third century—when at one time as many as eighteen claimants struggled for the throne and it seemed as if the empire would be divided into a number of small, weak states— was brought to an end by a vigorous leader, Diocletian, in A.D. 285. Diocletian saw the impossibility of ruling the vast empire alone, what with the continual German and Persian attacks in the north and east and countless revolts in the provinces. He restored the political order by dividing authority among four persons, the *tetrarchs*, including himself as prime mover. Diocletian appointed a co-ruler called, like himself, "augustus," and each of the two "augusti" then adopted an assistant of slightly lower rank, the "caesar." One augustus and one caesar ruled in the east, and the other pair in the west. Though political control was restored, a fatal precedent was set: the division of authority within the empire.

Under Constantine, who did away with Diocletian's system and ruled alone, the practice was begun of dividing the empire, like personal property, among the emperor's sons—a crippling, divisive custom that was to last into the Middle Ages. Even more divisive was Constantine's founding of a city named after him (Constantinople, now Istanbul, on the site of the ancient Greek city of Byzantium), which led inevitably to the decline of the city of Rome and the shift of imperial emphasis to the east. Byzantium gives its name to the later civilization of the eastern Roman empire.

After the reign of Theodosius, at the end of the fourth century, the empire was irreparably divided, though the emperors of the east, at Constantinople, continued for centuries to claim the west. These claims were in vain, for in the fifth century the barbarians took power in the West—the Ostrogoths in Italy, the Vandals in Africa, the Visigoths in Spain, the Franks and Burgundians in Gaul, the Angles and Saxons in Britain. These Romano-Germanic petty kingdoms succeeded to the once centralized and almost universal power of Rome and became the predecessors of the nations of modern Europe. The eastern half of the empire lived on as the Byzantine empire for a thousand years, until the conquest of Constantinople by the Turks in 1453.

ARCHITECTURE

Developments in architecture powerfully express the ebbing authority of the Roman empire. In the days of Augustus and Trajan the "walls" of the empire had been the might of the legions on its remotest borders; behind the bulwark of the legions a great empire could rest secure. But late in the third century the emperor Aurelian was forced by circumstances to girdle the city of Rome itself with walls, turning it into a fortress; Rome became what it had been at the start, merely a walled city, now dwindling into the ghost of an empire. Aurelian's insecurity was shared by Diocletian, who, unlike Tiberius in the first century B.C., could not afford to retire to the undefended paradise of Capri but had built for his retirement a well-fortified palace on the Dalmatian coast at Spalato (modern Split, in Yugoslavia), about A.D. 300 (FIG. 6-64). The complex, covering about ten acres, is laid out like a Roman colonial city. The plan is almost identical with that of Timgad (FIG. 6-35), which in turn was planned, as we have seen, like an army camp. The relation can be seen in the peristyle before the palace entrance, which corresponds to the forum at Timgad.

A feature of great importance for the history of Medieval architecture appears in the peristyle of Diocletian's palace (FIG. 6-65). The pediment at the far end is broken through by an arch that carries with it the entablature; or perhaps it should be described as an entablature that suddenly arches itself into the face of the pediment. The feature of the broken pediment had appeared earlier, mostly in the eastern provinces of the empire—for example, in the façade of the great temples at Baalbek, in Syria. It is a quite un-Classical device—hardly imaginable in a building like the Parthenon—and represents a transitional stage between the Classical, column-supported, horizontal entablature and the springing of arches directly from column capitals, as is the case in the flanking colonnades of this same peristyle. We are here in the process of change from the *trabeated* (post-and-lintel) architecture of Greco-Roman antiquity (and earlier) to the *arcuated* (arch-column) architecture of the Middle Ages. There were early anticipations of this novel feature, but the arcade at Spalato is the first appearance of it in a perfected form and on a grand scale. It is interesting to observe its gradual emergence from the Roman arch order (FIG. 6-66) and the Roman architect's reluctance to give up the conventional three-part division of the entablature even when it had become only a blocklike fragment, as in the capital from the Baths of Caracalla. Later, Byzantine architects will retain the entablature-block, but will rid it of the old

6-64 Palace of Diocletian, Spalato (Split), A.D. 300–05. (Reconstruction by E. Hebrard.)

6-65 Peristyle court, palace of Diocletian.

6-66 Development of arcuated architecture from trabeated architecture.
(After Kimball and Edgell.)

1
COLOSSEUM
Roman architectural
order (*c.* AD 70)

2
PANTHEON
Central niche
(*c.* AD 125)

3
BATHS OF
CARACALLA
(*c.* AD 215)

4
SPALATO
Central arch
(*c.* AD 300)

5
SPALATO
Porta Aurea

6
SPALATO
Street arcade

6-67 Basilica of Constantine, Rome, *c.* A.D. 310–20.

6-68 Reconstruction of the Basilica of Constantine.

Classical features, geometrizing it into a flat-sided, trapezoidal "impost" block (FIG. 7-29).

Although the center of empire was moved by Constantine to his new city on the site of ancient Byzantium, he completed some important building projects prior to leaving Rome. One of these was the vast basilica begun between 306 and 310 by Maxentius, rival of Constantine, and finished by Constantine after 313 (FIGS. 6-67 and 6-68). All that remains of the building are three barrel-vaulted bays of the north aisle and brick-faced concrete walls twenty feet thick supporting the coffered vaults. The interior, like that of the Baths of Caracalla, was richly marbled and stuccoed. The ruins are most impressive by virtue of their size and mass yet represent only a small part of the original structure, which measured 300 by 215 feet and had a groin-vaulted central nave

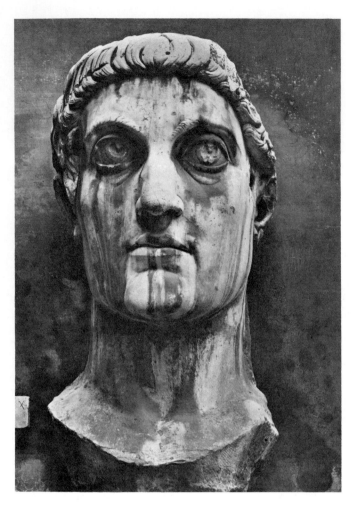

6-69 *Constantine the Great, c.* A.D. *330. Marble, approx. 8′6″ high. Palazzo dei Conservatori, Rome.*

rising 114 feet. The reconstruction (FIG. 6-68) shows a groin vault (over the central nave) that permitted lighting of the interior through the ends of the cross vaults, which were left open in an adaptation of the clerestory manner. Buttresses reinforce the vault (where the groins join vertical supports) and channel part of the pressures exerted by the weight of the vault across the aisles and into the outside walls. Remains of the springing of the central vault and of buttresses can be seen in FIG. 6-67. This structural system prefigures that of the flying buttress, developed by Gothic architects. As the last great building of the ancient world, the Basilica of Constantine is a monument to the ingenuity of Roman architects.

Exemplar of an architecture of space, it is designed on a grand, imperial scale—spacious, fully illuminated, uninterrupted by rows of vertical supports, and constructed of a highly malleable, versatile, fireproof material. In this it fulfills the requirements of architecture in periods of high civilization; not for 800 years will they be so artfully fulfilled again.

SCULPTURE AND MONUMENTAL RELIEF

In the western apse of the Basilica of Constantine was a colossal statue of the emperor, a seated figure some thirty feet high, the head of which has been preserved (FIG. 6-69). The figure was composed of a brick core, a wooden torso covered with bronze, and head and limbs of marble. The head alone is 8½ feet high and weighs over eight tons. The characteristics of the earlier busts we have described, in which the real and the ideal alternate or blend, are here no longer dominant. Rather we have the onset of traits familiar in the earlier, Archaic period: simplification of detail, with a regularizing of the features and a flattening that make of the face a rigid mask uncompromisingly frontal in aspect. The eyes become enormously large in proportion to the rest of the features, though in the Constantine head they still turn slightly to the side and upward as in certain third-century portraits like that of Philip the Arab (FIG. 6-63). Those unchanging qualities of the permanent form, which we have seen in Egypt and Mesopotamia—particularly in the representation of kings—once more make their appearance. The personality of the emperor is lost in the immense image of eternal authority. It is his authority, not his personality or his psychic state, that the sculptor exhibits. The colossal size, the Archaic rigidities, the eyes directed at no thing or person of this world—all combine to make a formula of overwhelming power appropriate to the exalted position of Constantine as absolute despot, which, by the early fourth century, he had certainly become. It is not surprising that the first of the Christian emperors, in authority the European equivalent of a Rameses II, should be embodied in colossal form like the giant statues of the Egyptian king at Luxor and (formerly) Abu Simbel.

The profound changes in style that occur at an accelerated pace in the fourth century, introducing the epoch of Medieval art, can be seen in the group called the *Tetrarchs*, dating from about A.D. 305 (FIG. 6-70). Although it is an earlier work than the portrait of Constantine, it reflects much more strongly the trend toward Archaism. Carved from porphyry in one of the eastern provinces (perhaps Egypt), the group represents the four co-rulers of the empire: Diocletian and Maximian (the augusti) and Galerius and Constantius "Chlorus," father of Constantine (the caesars). They embrace each other to symbolize their hoped-for but not realized unity. They seem, even as they embrace, to be huddled in fear and foreboding, facing some impending disaster, in an expression of the already noted prevalent anxiety of the age. Classical features have disappeared; the figures are ill proportioned, with large heads on squat bodies, giving them a gnomelike appearance. The drapery is schematic, the bodies shapeless. Seven hundred years of Greek and Roman idealism and naturalism here terminate. No portrait likenesses are tried; the masklike faces are the same face in quadruplicate. Individuality and personality already belong to the past.

The waning creative power and technical skill of Rome in the west can be seen in the Arch of Constantine (A.D. 312–15) in the city of Rome (FIG. 6-71). It is the last great triumphal arch preserved in the declining city. Dedicated to Constantine by the now figurehead Senate, it commemorates the victory over his rival Maxentius, a victory which made him the absolute monarch of the Roman empire. But the occasion produced no corresponding stimulus for the imagination of his builders. The design of the arch is copied from that of the earlier Arch of Septimius Severus, of the early third century, and most of its decorative sculpture is taken from the monuments of rulers like Trajan, Hadrian, and Marcus Aurelius.

Beneath two Hadrianic medallions are reliefs belonging to Constantine's own period (FIGS. 6-72 and 6-73), which give us an opportunity to estimate the degree of change from the style of the Early Imperial age to a new style that it is not

6-70 *The Tetrarchs*, c. A.D. 305. Porphyry, approx. 4′ 3″ high. Piazza San Marco, Venice.

inappropriate to call Medieval. Constantine, surrounded by his entourage, stands at the center of a rostrum, addressing the people. His central position corresponds here to the frontality of his colossal statue and expresses a new, rigid formality of composition that will more and more depend upon fixed positions of figures rather than representation of action. The figures are nonclassical in their lack of proportionality; in this respect they are like the *Tetrarchs*. Moreover, they do not move on any principle of classical-naturalistic movement but rather with the mechanical and repeated stances and gestures of puppets. The relief is flattened back into the block, the forms no longer fully modeled, the details

6-71 Arch of Constantine, Rome, A.D. 312–15.

incised. The lines of figures are superposed (a device seen in the Column of Trajan); the spatial arrangement is, as noted, not casual, but a careful head-counting lineup. The gestures are few and, like the uniform heads, reproduced again and again. We have not so much a historical narrative of action as the labeling of an event frozen into a tableau; thus, the ordered groups could quickly be read and labeled as "crowd," "emperor," "servants of the emperor," the artist desiring to include all the essential participants without the ambiguity that can accompany description of particulars. The latter have been reduced to the absolute minimum, their place having been taken by formal placement and repetition of attitude and gesture.

The Archaizing of Greek and Roman figurative art in the Constantinian reliefs reflects a trans-formation in the way the peoples of the late Roman world interpret the structure of appearance. Underlying this change in interpretation is a mighty spiritual change—the assimilation of Christianity into Greco-Roman civilization, a phenomenon so far-reaching in its influence as to separate the psychologies of two millennia, that of Greece-Rome and that of Medieval Christianity. Now, in the words of the medievalist Ferdinand Lot:

The gods are dead, killed by the one God whose commandments impose a rule of life so new that henceforth this world will assume a secondary role; the sage imbued with "the new Philosophy" will place the object of his desires in the sphere of the world beyond. Between the men of the new and those of the ancient times there will no longer be a thought in common.

6-72 Above: Reliefs from the Arch of Constantine: medallions, A.D. 117–38; frieze, early fourth century A.D. Marble, frieze approx. 40″ high.

6-73 Left: Detail of the frieze shown in FIG. 6–72.

Chapter Seven

Early Christian,
Byzantine,
and Islamic Art

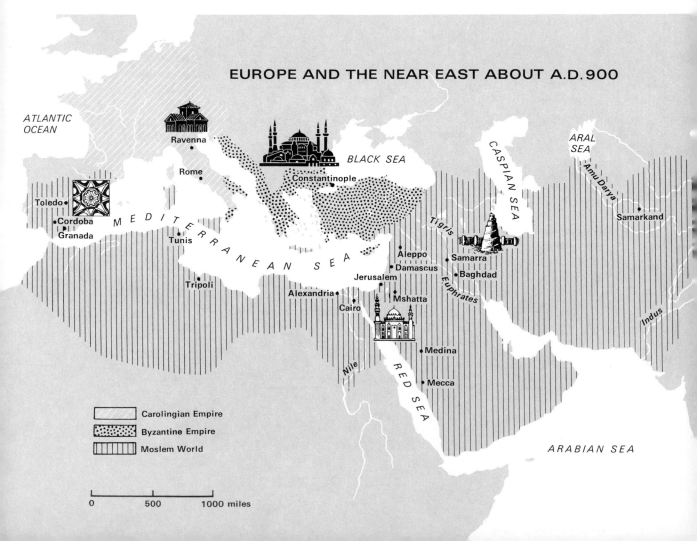

EUROPE AND THE NEAR EAST ABOUT A.D. 900

ATLANTIC
OCEAN

Ravenna

Rome

BLACK SEA

Constantinople

ARAL
SEA

CASPIAN SEA

Amu Darya

Toledo

Cordoba

Granada

M E D I T E R R A N E A N   S E A

Tunis

Samarkand

Tigris

Samarra

Aleppo

Baghdad

Damascus

Euphrates

Jerusalem

Tripoli

Alexandria

Mshatta

Cairo

Indus

Nile

Medina

Mecca

RED SEA

ARABIAN SEA

Carolingian Empire
Byzantine Empire
Moslem World

0   500   1000 miles

CHRISTIANITY, like many Eastern cults, was a peculiarly persuasive religion of salvation. Its immense success in making converts among the teeming populations of the great imperial cities brought it to the attention of the Roman authorities. Because Christians refused to acknowledge the state religion, which was the cult of the emperor, and because they refused to participate in its rather perfunctory rites, they were regarded as politically subversive and were bitterly persecuted. Tacitus, reflecting the attitudes of his time, regarded the Christians as believers in a degenerate doctrine and practitioners of obscene and perverse rites that, he felt, were typical of Eastern cults.

The deep misunderstanding between pagan Roman and Christian Roman can symbolize the even more profound contrast in their world views; indeed, to repeat Ferdinand Lot: "Between the men of the new and those of the ancient times there will no longer be a thought in common." The fundamental opposition between the Eastern and Western spirit proclaimed in Zechariah—"when I have raised up thy sons, O Zion, against thy sons, O Greece ..." (LX.13)—rings angrily once again in the words of the early

A.D.100

PERIOD OF PERSECUTION

200

325 Constantine recognizes Christianity

PERIOD OF RECOGNITION

400

Division of Roman Empire; beginning of Byzantine Era 395

Mausoleum of Galla Placidia

Theodoric at Ravenna 493-526

c.526

Sant' Apollinare in Classe, detail

c.565

Honorius at Ravenna 402–23

Galla Placidia at Ravenna 425–50

JUSTINIAN (FIRST FLOWERING)

Fall of Rome to Visigoths under Alaric 410

Fall of Ravenna to Odoaker; end of western Roman empire 476

539 Investment of Ravenna

Justinian Mosaic detail, S. Vitale

600

Hagia Sophia

726

ICONOCLASTIC CONTROVERSY

TERRITORIAL LOSSES

c. 800

732 Battle of Poitiers

711 Conquest of Spain

Paris Psalter

637 Conquest of Jerusalem

622 Moslem era begins

Great Mosque, Samarra

Mosque, Cordoba

MOSLEM ERA

SECOND FLOWERING

843

c. 900

1000

Mausoleum of Sultan Hasan

Crusaders' capture Constantinople 1261

St. Mark's begun 1063

Vladimir Madonna

Katholikon c. 1020

1390

1297

THIRD FLOWERING

DECLINE

1453 Ottoman conquest of Constantinople

The Harrowing of Hell

Baghdad captured by Mongols 1258

c. 1100

Abelard (1079-1142)

1031 End of Caliphate of Cordoba

Christian Tertullian: *Quid Athenae Hierosolymis!* —"What is there in common between Athens and Jerusalem? What between the Academy [of Plato] and the Church?" While the unmitigated hostility of Tertullian was by no means shared by all Christians, an antagonism between the ancient Semitic East and the Hellenic world that had for a while conquered it was inevitable and could not be suppressed. Greek naturalism and rationalism had become integral to the western Roman world and at the same time had become changed through contact with the old civilizations of the Middle East. The mystery cults, with their suspiciously secret rites, their savior gods, their redemptive messages and occult sciences, their solar and fertility myths, drew heavily upon Egypt, Babylon, Persia, and even India; and, although they borrowed a good deal of the intellectual apparatus of Hellenic philosophy, they mysticized it and made of it a kind of magical formulary and a *gnosis*, the privileged knowledge of only an initiated few.

Although Christianity, based as it was on Jewish teaching and tradition, differed radically from many of the crude cults with which Romans like Tacitus confused it, it joined with those cults in the long, vast historical reaction against the Hellenized West—both its world view and that material manifestation of it, the increasingly oppressive Roman empire. To Christians, the empire, with its exactions, cruelties, materialism, wars, and false gods, became *regnum Caesaris regnum Diaboli*—"the kingdom of Caesar, the kingdom of the Devil." But the empire would be inherited by the Christians in A.D. 325 when Constantine recognized Christianity and made it the official religion of the state.

In the eighteenth century, Gibbon, in his monumental history, *The Decline and Fall of the Roman Empire*, accused Christianity of being the principal cause of that—to his times—calamity. We do not now believe that Christianity had that role, but as early as the fifth century A.D., Augustine wrote his *City of God* to defend the Church against the pagan accusation that the sack of the city of Rome (in A.D. 410 by the Goths) was a punishment sent by the ancient gods upon the city because it had become Christian. The disintegration of the empire, beginning with its nominal separation into the western and eastern

empires toward the end of the third century, was a phenomenon of considerable complexity and cannot be laid at the door of the Christians, nor entirely at that of the "barbarians"—those Celtic, Germanic, Slavic, and other peoples who had been pressing slowly into the Mediterranean world for thousands of years. (We have met their predecessors in the great migrations that disturbed Egypt, Mesopotamia, Asia Minor, Crete, and Greece.)

At any rate, from the end of the third century on, there was a slow, sometimes hardly perceptible takeover of the empire, not indeed the unified empire, but its already fragmented remains. The spiritual and ideological conquest made by the Christians in the politically consequential form of mass conversion paralleled the gradual infiltration and settlement by the "barbarians," who, for that matter, had long been present in the administrative and military structure as well as in recognized possession of imperial territories. The subsequent actions of these "barbarians," Christianized and in control of the western empire by the end of the fifth century, make up the history of the Middle Ages in the west. The eastern empire, actually but not officially severed from the western by the beginning of the fifth century, goes its own continuous way as the Byzantine empire, reverting to its Greek language and traditions, which, to be sure, had become much "Orientalized." The Byzantine world was a kind of protraction of the life of the late empire and the Early Christian culture that filled it. With a quite Oriental conservatism, which reminds us somewhat of the ancient Near Eastern civilizations, the Byzantine empire remains Greek, orthodox, unchanging for a thousand years, preserving the forms of its origin, oblivious to and isolated from the new.

In the seventh century, Islam, a new spiritual force, erupted from Arabia and swept across the Near East and the southern Mediterranean world with amazing speed. Islam created a new civilization that rivaled Christianity and would have far-ranging influence in medieval Europe. Arabic translations of Aristotle and other Greek writers of antiquity were eagerly studied by Christian scholars of the twelfth and thirteenth centuries; Arabic love lyrics and poetic descriptions of nature inspired the early French troubadours; Arab scholars laid the foundations of arithmetic and algebra as they are still taught in our schools, and their contributions to astronomy, medicine, and the natural sciences have made a lasting impression in the Western world. While Islamic art may not properly fall within the scope of Western art in the more limited sense, it nevertheless deserves our attention at this point in our survey, particularly since its early monuments share with those of Early Christian and Byzantine art derivation from earlier Near Eastern and Mediterranean artistic traditions. Most early monuments of Islamic art thus belong to the succession of late Roman, early Byzantine, and Iranian art, although different social and religious needs soon transformed similar prototypes into forms quite different from those they were to take in the Christian world.

EARLY CHRISTIAN ART

The style we call Early Christian we could as accurately call Late Roman, or, as art-historical usage has it, Late Antique. Christian works are distinguished from pagan only by subject, not by style. After all, the Christians of the time were as much "Roman" as the pagans; they were trained in the same crafts, were brought up in the same environment, and spoke the same language. The Christian church itself, both in its organization and its philosophy, owed much to the Greco-Roman structure of life; and Early Christian art shows simple transformation of pagan themes into Christian and the freest kind of borrowing of pagan motifs and manners. Hybrid forms are produced throughout the Christianized late empire in the greatest profusion and with the greatest intermingling of regional styles, making it almost impossible to recognize any one style—or even half a dozen—that could definitely be called Early Christian or that could serve as an exclusive exemplar of what we mean by Early Christian.

What happens in the plastic arts is a kind of "denaturing" of Greco-Roman naturalism, something we have seen beginning as early as the Column of Trajan and well advanced in the

reliefs from the Arch of Constantine. Archaizing modes supervene upon the old naturalism, and things come to look less and less like the Greco-Roman prototypes from which ultimately they derive. This denaturing process, variously influenced by barbarian styles, continues well into the western Medieval period. It should by no means be thought merely the negation of the Greco-Roman style, or a clumsy botching of it by men who had lost the sense of it and the necessary manual skill. Rather it is the product of an entirely new world view—one that inevitably brings about the transformation of the naturalistic tradition. Early Christian art shows that transformation in process.

The Early Christian era divides conveniently into the Period of Persecution—from the establishment of the earliest communities, in the first century A.D.—and the Period of Recognition—from A.D. 325, when Constantine established Christianity as the official religion of the Roman empire, until about A.D. 500, when the western provinces of the empire had come under the sway of barbarian princes. In the earlier period, as we have seen, the Christians were, in the Roman view, a troublesome, even dangerous, sect that needed to be curbed. During this time it is likely that the Christians, shrinking from the kind of attention public shrines might attract, worshiped in the private houses of their wealthier communicants, perhaps the elaborate atrium houses of the type we have seen in Pompeii (see p. 204). It is quite possible that the atrium forecourt of the later public churches, the basilicas, derived from their liturgical relation to the earlier atrium of the private house.

The Catacombs

The most significant monuments of the Period of Persecution are the least conspicuous of all the monuments of Rome; they are entirely underground. The catacombs, so called, are vast networks of galleries and chambers beneath Rome and other cities, designed as cemeteries for the burial of the Christian dead, many of them sainted martyrs. From the second through the fourth century the catacombs were in constant use, and it is estimated that as many as four

7-1 Plan of the catacomb of Callixtus, Rome, second century A.D., and section through main gallery of oldest region.

1 and 2. Main galleries
3. Collapsed lower floor
4. Cubicula

FEET
0   10   20   30

NOTE: Open rectangles indicate loculi.

million bodies were accommodated in the Roman catacombs alone. In times of persecution they could have served as places of concealment for fugitives; evidence of this function survives in blocked and cut-off staircases, secret embrasures and passages, and concealed entrances and exits. Doubtless the Christian mysteries must have been enacted here, although the principal function of the catacombs was mortuary.

In Rome the catacombs were tunneled out of the granular tufa stratum, the convenient properties of which had been exploited earlier by the Etruscan necropolis-builders (see p. 188). After a plot of ground had been selected for the cemetery (Christians were not prevented by Roman law from owning property), a gallery three to four feet wide was dug around its perimeter at a convenient level below the surface (FIG. 7-1). In the walls of these galleries, embrasures were opened parallel to the gallery axis to receive the bodies of the dead; these openings, called *loculi*, were one above the other, like shelves (FIG. 7-2). Often, small rooms, called *cubicula*, were constructed in the walls to serve as mortuary chapels,

7-2 Gallery and loculi of the catacomb of Pamphilius, Rome, third century A.D.

and these were variously vaulted. When the original perimeter galleries were full of *loculi* and *cubicula*, other galleries would be cut at right angles to them, the process continuing as long as lateral space permitted. Then lower levels would be dug and connected by staircases, some systems going as deep as five levels. When adjacent burial areas belonged to members of the same Christian confraternity, or by gift or purchase fell into the same hands, communications were opened between the respective cemeteries, which thus spread laterally and gradually acquired a vast extent. After Christianity received official sanction, the catacombs fell into disuse except as holy places, monuments to the great martyrs, which were visited by the pious.

Many cubicula were decorated with frescoes that were Late Antique (pagan) in manner and even in subject, the latter interpreted by the Christians to conform with their own beliefs. The geometric patterning of a ceiling in the catacomb of Saints Pietro and Marcellino in Rome (FIG. 7-3) becomes the Dome of Heaven (the large circle), which has been inscribed with the basic symbol of the Christian faith, the cross. The cross-arms terminate in lunettes in which are represented the key episodes from the Old Testament story of Jonah, who is thrown from his ship on the left, emerges from the whale on the right, and, safe on land on the bottom, contemplates the miracle

of his salvation and the mercy of God. The compartments between these lunettes are occupied by *orans* figures, members of the Christian community with arms raised in the attitude of prayer, a priestly gesture still made in the ritual of the Roman Catholic mass and likely of great antiquity. The central medallion shows the figure of Christ as the Good Shepherd whose powers of salvation are underscored by his juxtaposition with the story of Jonah. As a theme, the Good Shepherd can be traced back through Greek Archaic to Egyptian art, but here it becomes the symbol for the loyal protector of the Christian flock who said to his disciples, "Feed my lambs, feed my sheep." It is noteworthy that in the catacombs, during the Period of Persecution, Christ was almost invariably represented either as the Good Shepherd or as a teacher. Only later, when Christianity became the official state religion of the Roman empire, did Christ take on imperial attributes such as the halo, the purple robe, the throne, and others denoting rulership.

The style of the catacomb painters is most often the quick, sketchy impressionism we have seen in earlier Roman painting of the last Pompeian period, and the execution ranges from good to inferior, most often the latter. We must take into account that the catacombs were very unpromising places for the art of the mural decorator. The air was spoiled by decomposing corpses, the

7-3 Painted ceiling from the catacomb of Saints Pietro and Marcellino, Rome, fourth century A.D.

humidity was excessive, and the lighting, provided largely by oil lamps, was entirely unfit for elaborate compositions and painstaking execution. For ceiling designs and those on arches and lunettes the painter was required to assume awkward and tiring poses, and it is no wonder that he proceeded hastily and that his results were poor.

Architecture

Although some ceremonies were held in the catacombs, it is likely that regular services were held in private houses that were rearranged to make "community" houses or in simple columned halls. The latter have not survived intact, having been destroyed in the last great persecutions under Diocletian; the remains of one, a kind of rudimentary basilica, dating from A.D. 311, have been found beneath the cathedral of Aquileia. When Christianity achieved imperial sanction under Constantine, there was suddenly the urgent need to set up buildings that would meet the requirements of the Christian liturgy and

would help aggrandize the Christian cult. All the architectural ingredients were present: the atrium house, the catacomb chapel, the Roman basilica. How these combined into the masterful composition that was one of the first Christian church buildings of the new age, old St. Peter's in Rome (FIGS. 7-4 to 7-6), we do not know; discussion about the origins of the Christian basilica has not ended. Dedicated about 330, St. Peter's is probably the most important design in the history of church architecture. Its wide influence was augmented by the belief that it stood where Peter, first of the Apostles, had been buried. Its extraordinary dimensions are difficult to realize from the old drawings; the nave was as long, as high, and twice as wide as the nave of a great Gothic cathedral. Its interior was "one of the most spacious, most imposing, and most harmonious . . . ever built, imperially rich in its marbles and mosaics, grandiose yet forthright and large in the best Roman sense of the word."[1]

[1] Kenneth Conant, *Early Medieval Church Architecture* (Baltimore: Johns Hopkins Press, 1942), p. 6.

7-4 Reconstruction of the plan and section of old St. Peter's, Rome, *c.* A.D. 333. Approx. 215' wide.

1. Nave
2. Aisles
3. Transept
4. Apse
5. Narthex
6. Atrium

	c.A.D. 250		306	**325**	c. 333	c. 350		c. 395	410	c. 425		493	c. 526
	"Ludovisi Battle Sarcophagus"		Constantine becomes emperor		Old St. Peter's	Santa Costanza, Rome		Division of the empire	Fall of Rome	Mausoleum of Galla Placidia begun		Theodoric at Ravenna	
PERIOD OF PERSECUTION					PERIOD	OF		RECOGNITION					

The plan of St. Peter's (FIG. 7-4) shows a rectangular building entered through an open colonnaded court, the atrium, which leads to the *narthex*, or vestibule; the body of the church consists of the nave, low side aisles, apse, and transverse aisle, or *transept*, which is placed between the nave and the apse and projects slightly beyond the walls of the nave and aisles. This fundamental arrangement was used in subsequent Christian architecture, though it would be wrong to think that there is some rigid, standardized basilican design; for instance, the transept, an occasional feature of churches in the city of Rome, is often lacking in other churches, especially in the smaller ones.

The cross section shows a great columned hall that obviously relates to such Roman secular basilicas as the Basilica Ulpia in the Forum of Trajan (FIG. 6-39). Unlike the slightly earlier Basilica of Constantine, St. Peter's was not vaulted, but timber roofed; concrete and vaulted buildings were expensive, and one supposes that the light materials used in the Christian buildings were adopted out of expediency and because they were adequate for the purpose of the ritual. The pagan basilica's lateral entrance is moved to the short side of the Christian church. Only one of the multiple apses is retained, and that is placed opposite and at a dramatic distance from the entrance. Evenly spaced columns no longer surround but flank the central nave, and at St. Peter's they carried a horizontal entablature in the classical tradition (FIG. 7-5). In subsequent church buildings, more and more often the columns support arches in the manner of the peristyle of the Palace of Diocletian at Spalato (FIG. 6-64). All these modifications of the pagan basilica make for a sweeping perspective that converges on the shrine as the focus of the whole design and the place of the central mystery of the Christian faith. The "spiritualizing" of the secular Roman design is expressed not only in the realignment of the building's axis (so as to focus one's whole experience on the center) but in its extreme simplicity of structure and the lightness of its bearing walls and columns. Roman mass—huge walls and ponderous weight, sculptured surfaces in relief and recess, and whole populations of statuary—has been lightened, rarefied, smoothed; we could say it has been "dematerialized" to suit the new orientation toward a spiritual rather than a physical world.

The bird's-eye view of St. Peter's in reconstruction (FIG. 7-6), though partly conjectural, shows the very Roman stepped podium, which we have seen before in the Temple of Fortuna Virilis (FIG. 6-14) and which has Etruscan predecessors; a propylaea and forum-become-atrium are other elements with not only Roman but ancient antecedents. We believe that the exterior was, like that of Christian basilicas in general, unadorned, the whole decorative enterprise being reserved for the interior. It is as if the building imitated the ideal Christian, with grave and plain exterior and a soul glowing and beautiful within.

7-5 Interior of Old St. Peter's in a miniature by Fouquet showing the coronation of Charlemagne.

7-6 Conjectural reconstruction of old St. Peter's. (After K. J. Conant.)

The rectangular basilican church design was long the favorite of the western Christian world. But the Early Christians also adopted another classical building type—the central-plan, a round or polygonal domed structure; this was later favored in the east, where Byzantine architects developed it to monumental proportions and amplified its theme in numerous ingenious variations. In the west the central-plan building type was used generally for smaller structures adjacent and subsidiary to the main basilicas, like mausoleums, baptistries, and private chapels. A highly refined example of this central-plan design is Santa Costanza in Rome (FIGS. 7-7 to 7-9), built in the mid-fourth century. Perhaps a baptistry at first (attached to a now destroyed basilica), it was soon converted to serve as the mausoleum of Constantia, daughter of the emperor Constantine. Its antecedents can be traced to the beehive tombs of the Mycenaeans, although its direct inspiration may have been the Pantheon, or the pool-enclosing rotunda of some public baths, like those of Caracalla. The Pantheon's mass, however, has been metamorphosed, as with the mutation

7-7 Interior of Santa Costanza, Rome, c. A.D. 350.

7-8 Plan and section of Santa Costanza.

of the pagan into the Early Christian basilica. In Santa Costanza the circle of paired columns that carries the domed cylinder is well free of the external walls, free enough to leave space for a barrel-vaulted corridor, or *ambulatory*. In fact, it is as if the basilican wall-arcade has been bent around a circle, the ambulatory corresponding to the basilican aisles and, like them, equipped with a high, ample clerestory. The exuberant naturalism of the luxurious mosaics in the vault of the ambulatory (FIG. 7-9) suggests a lingering influence of the pagan spirit.

All the important buildings of the fourth century, including Santa Costanza and the great longitudinal basilicas, are closely associated with Constantine and his immediate relatives, for it was through their patronage and supervision

7-9 Detail of mosaics in the vault of the ambulatory, Santa Costanza.

and as an expression of the new ideal of the Christian *imperium* that these buildings came to be. This close relationship of the Constantinians with Constantinian architecture may help to explain a certain consistency of design in the apparently diverse basilicas of the fourth and early fifth centuries. It might also partly explain how such apparently contradictory and opposed designs as the long church and the central church could be imagined as working together in meeting the requirements of Christian belief and ritual. Given centuries of tradition, it would have been perfectly natural for Constantine to memorialize the place of Jesus' death and burial by a traditional type of monument, the domed rotunda. At the same time the existing basilica scheme might have been seen as offering the space needed for the congregations of pilgrims coming to the holiest place in Christendom. For several centuries then, the architectural problem—though never explicitly stated—was how to integrate the long plan and the central plan.

The mausoleum and basilica types, the central and the long designs, one memorializing a person, the other designed for a congregation, are seen in rather loose relation for the first time in a conjectural reconstruction of the Church of the Holy Sepulcher in Jerusalem (FIGS. 7-10 and 7-11). The emperor, in a letter to the bishop of Jerusalem, asserted that he wanted this basilica to be "more beautiful than any of the others anywhere." There is little if anything to be seen of the original structure. Begun before 333, it was destroyed by the Persians in 613, then built and rebuilt in subsequent centuries. What we can reconstruct shows a relatively small basilica preceded by a shallow atrium leading to the portico on the Roman street. In a courtyard behind the basilica are the two most venerated spots, the rock of Calvary, to one side, and the

7-10 Reconstruction plan of the Church of the Holy Sepulcher, Jerusalem, *c.* A.D. 345. (After K. J. Conant.)

7-11 Conjectural reconstruction of the Church of the Holy Sepulcher. (After K. J. Conant.)

Holy Sepulcher, covered by a rotunda, in the rear. The buildings are related to each other by ritual function and, architecturally, by a precinct wall. Although superficially resembling that of Santa Costanza, the rotunda of the Holy Sepulcher, the perhaps conical dome of which was timber, may go back to circular buildings, like the tholos at Epidaurus, which were also timber roofed. In any event, the Holy Sepulcher shows us the central- and long-plan building types in architectural relation, even if a rather loose and rambling one. The perfect union of the domed central unit and the basilica will come two centuries later in the great church, Hagia Sophia, in Constantinople. After that synthesis the two structural types will go their separate ways, the long church (often with domed crossing) in the west, the central type in the east.

Mosaic and Painting

As the church-building enterprise under Constantine and his successors was designed to meet the urgent ceremonial needs of Christianity, now suddenly become official and public, so wholesale programs of decoration for the churches were also called for. To advertise the new faith in all its diverse aspects—its dogma, scriptural narrative, and symbolism—and to instruct and edify the believer, acres of wall in dozens of new churches had to be filled in a style and medium that would most effectively carry the message. Brilliantly ornamental mosaics—with sparkling tesserae of reflective glass, rather than the opaque marble tesserae that had been preferred by the Romans—became the standard vehicle of expression almost at once. Mosaics were particularly suited to the flat, shell-like surfaces of the new basilicas, becoming a durable, tangible part of the wall, a kind of architectural tapestry. The light flooding through the clerestories was caught in vibrant reflection by the mosaics, which produced abrupt effects and contrasts and sharp concentrations of color that could focus attention on the central, most relevant features of a composition. Mosaic, worked in the Early Christian manner, is not intended for the subtle changes of tone that a naturalistic painter's approach would require; although, as we have seen in the Roman mosaics, tonality is well within the mosaicist's

reach. But in mosaic, color is placed, not blended; and bright, hard, glittering texture, set within a rigorously simplified pattern, becomes the rule. As noted earlier, for mosaics placed high on the wall, far above the observer's head, the painstaking use of tiny tesserae, seen in Roman floor mosaics, becomes meaningless. Early Christian mosaics, designed to be seen from a distance, employ larger stones; the surfaces are left uneven so that the tesserae's projecting edges can catch and reflect the light, and the designs are simple, for optimum legibility. Through several centuries, in the service of Christian theology, mosaic was the medium of some of the supreme masterpieces of world art.

Content and style find their medium; the content of Christian doctrine took centuries to fashion, and for a long time even the proper manner of representing the founder of Christianity was in question. When Christianity became official, Jesus' status changed. In early works he is shown as teacher and philosopher, in later, his image becomes imperialized as the ruler of heaven and earth. In the fourth and fifth centuries there was hesitation about how he should be represented, and variant types of images were produced. After some crucial theological questions on Jesus' nature were resolved, a more or less standard formula for his depiction emerged.

In the minds of simple Christians only recently converted, Jesus could be easily identified with the familiar deities of the Mediterranean world, especially Helios (Apollo), the sun god, or his romanized eastern aspect, Sol Invictus (the Unconquered Sun). The late third-century vault mosaic of a small Christian mausoleum in a pagan cemetery, excavated underneath St. Peter's in Rome in the 1940's (FIG. 7-12), shows Jesus as Apollo, driving the horses of the sun-chariot through the heavens—a conception far more grandiose than that of the Good Shepherd.

The style, or styles, of Christian art came of the transmutation of Greco-Roman art; for the mosaicists, the point of departure was Roman illusionism. In the great mosaic cycles, like those in the Santa Maria Maggiore of early fifth-century Rome, we can witness the union of the old naturalism and the new symbolism. The panel representing the parting of Lot and Abraham (FIG. 7-13) tells its story (Gen. XIII.5–13) succinctly:

7-12 Detail of a vault mosaic from the mausoleum of the Julii, Rome, A.D. 250–75.

flexibility of naturalism toward the significant gesture and that primary method of Medieval representation, *pantomime*, which simplifies all significance into body attitude and gesture. The wide eyes turned in their sockets, the broad gestures of enlarged hands, the opposed movements of the groups, remind us of some silent, expressive chorus that comments only by gesture upon the action of the drama. Thus, the complex action of Roman art stiffens into the art of simplified motion or dumb show, which has great power to communicate without ambiguity and which, in the whole course of Medieval art, will produce the richest kind of variety. Also foreshadowing the character of Christian art is the fact that the figures of the panel have been moved to the foreground and that the artist takes no great pains to describe either space or landscape setting; background town and building are symbolic rather than descriptive. But within this relatively abstract setting, the figures themselves loom with massive solidity. They cast shadows and are modeled in dark and light to give them that three-dimensional appearance that testifies to the artist's heritage of Roman pictorial illusionism. It will require another century and much modification under Eastern influence before he will be able to think of his figures entirely as symbols rather than plastic bodies.

The Illuminated Manuscript

Santa Maria Maggiore is an early and outstanding example of the complementarity of the new basilican architecture and the new, detailed mosaics and paintings designed for them. But the earlier art of the catacombs could not have provided the resources for narratives as elaborate as those of Santa Maria Maggiore; catacomb painting was much too narrow in scope of subject and much too rudimentary in style and technique. Rather, the church decorators must have drawn upon a long tradition of pictures in manuscripts going back to pharaonic Egypt and highly developed by the Hellenistic Greeks of Alexandria; thousands of texts must have been available to the Constantinian artists, richly illustrated with themes—Hebrew, Greek, and Christian,

Agreeing to disagree, Lot leads his family and flocks to the right, toward the city of Sodom, while Abraham moves toward a building on the left (the church?). Lot's is the evil choice, and the instrumentalities of the evil, his two daughters, are represented in front of him, while the figure of the yet unborn Isaac, the instrument of good, stands before his father, Abraham. The cleavage of the two groups is emphatic, and each is represented by a shorthand device one could call a "head-cluster," which will have a long history in Christian art. The figures turn from each other in a kind of sharp dialogue of glance and gesture and we recognize here a moving away from the

7-13 *The Parting of Lot and Abraham*, mosaic from Santa Maria Maggiore, Rome, c. A.D. 430.

and combinations of all three. We know that Constantine summoned numerous savants and literati of Alexandria and that he established a library where they gave instruction; we know also that he was a generous donor of manuscripts to the Church. Hence, it is no wonder that Constantinople became a center of traditional and Christian learning that was transmitted by the copying and recopying of manuscripts through the centuries. The dissemination of manuscripts, as well as their preservation, was greatly aided by an important invention in the early Imperial period. The long manuscript scroll used by Egyptians, Greeks, and Romans and made of the fragile papyrus was superseded by the *codex*, which was made much like the modern book, of separate pages bound together at one side and having a cover. Papyrus was replaced by much more durable *vellum* (veal skin) and *parchment* (lamb skin), which provided better surfaces for painting than did papyrus. These changes in the durability, reproduction, and format of texts greatly improved the possibility that the records of ancient civilization could survive long centuries of neglect, even if not in great number.

The sacred texts were copied as faithfully as possible, and so were the pictures in them. After the great fathers of the Eastern Church recommended the didactic use of pictures in churches and books, the picture came to have a significance only slightly less than that of the text from which it drew its authority. The passage from the scroll to the codex—that is, from continuous narrative to a series of individual pictures—can be seen in two manuscripts of different date, the later still reflecting the scroll procedure. The *Vatican Vergil* (FIG. 7-14), from the early fifth century and the oldest painted manuscript known, is pagan in content, representing a scene from Vergil's *Georgics*, in which a seated farmer, at the left, instructs two of his slaves in the art of husbandry, while Vergil, at the right, listens and records the

7-14 Miniature from the *Vatican Vergil*, early fifth century A.D. Approx. 12″ × 12½″. Vatican Library, Rome.

instructions. (One remembers the Roman idealization of country life and nature.) The style is Late Antique and reminiscent of Pompeian landscapes. The quick, impressionistic touches that suggest space and atmosphere, the foreshortened villa in the background, the small, active figures in their wide, spacious setting—all these are familiar features of Roman illusionistic painting. We saw the heavy black frame isolating a single episode in the late Pompeian styles; it contrasts with the form of the *Vienna Genesis* (FIG. 7-15), which uses the continuity of a frieze, or in this case a scroll. The episode from Genesis represents Joseph receiving his brothers (who do not recognize him) in Egypt, where he has become the Pharaoh's chief administrator. They have come from Israel destitute and starving and, forgetting their cruelty to him, Joseph permits them to gather food. Overcome with emotion, he has withdrawn behind a screen to weep. Three distinct episodes are represented, with Joseph in two of them. The picture might almost have been cut out of a continuous scroll, for it seems as if it should continue to the left and right. (Although this is not the case here, pictures often *were* cut out of scrolls and fixed to the pages of a codex.) The figures are the reduced Hellenistic types, acting in a neutral space entirely without land-scape and performing in the silhouetted, pantomimic way that presents the story with all possible economy. While the figures retain only a narrative importance, the page itself becomes sumptuous, a rich purple ground lettered in silver. The luxuriousness of ornament that will be more and more typical of sacred books absorbs the human figure or relegates it to a secondary function. What will come to count above all are the spiritual beauty of the text and the material beauty of the vehicle that serves and intensifies it. The luster of holy objects—"sages standing in God's holy fire"—becomes the intent and being of Byzantine art.

Sculpture and Craft Art

The transformations that take place in architecture in the period of early Christianity—whereby the multipurpose pagan basilica is adapted to the single purpose of Christian ritual, and the heavy materiality of Roman buildings is "dematerialized" in the screenlike thinness and lightness of Christian structure—is paralleled in the sculpture of the time. We have seen anticipations of the change as early as the second century in the

7-15 *Joseph Recognizes His Brothers*, from the *Vienna Genesis*, early sixth century A.D. Approx. $4'' \times 7\frac{1}{2}''$. Österreichische Nationalbibliothek, Vienna.

7-16 *Battle Between Romans and Barbarians*, front panel of the so-called *Ludovisi Battle Sarcophagus*, third century A.D. Marble, approx. 4′ 8″ high. Museo Nazionale, Rome.

Column of Trajan (FIG. 6-53), and we have seen the change almost complete in early fourth-century reliefs of the Arch of Constantine (FIGS. 6-72 and 6-73). A third-century relief on the so-called *Ludovisi Battle Sarcophagus* (FIG. 7-16) should be interpolated between them. This representation of a struggle between Romans and barbarians is most instructive as an illustration of the "flattened relief" and the "piled-up" perspective so characteristic of the denaturing of Greco-Roman naturalism and the emerging Medieval style. While a strong descriptive realism persists in details of physiognomy, dress, action, gesture, and accessories, pattern has taken over from figure composition. The writhing figures are all within the same plane; at the same time the "foreground" figures (those at the base of the pattern) are relatively small, while the "background" figures at the top of the pattern are the largest. This *reverse perspective* strengthens the surface into a dense mass with no illusion of space beyond (behind) it. Carving has less and less a role, and quick effects of light and dark are had by gouging, punching, and drilling the surface. As yet the formal placing

of the figures that we find in the Arch of Constantine has not appeared; but of course the subject does not call for that, and the sarcophagus composition represents more the dissolution of the style of the Trajanic reliefs than the advent of Constantinian formalism. But the patterning and constriction of surface, the sacrifice of realism of space and proportion, are all present and recognizably Early Medieval.

Toward the end of the fourth century we find the flattening and patterning process well advanced. The *Good Shepherd Sarcophagus* (FIG. 7-17) has a thick, spaceless surface that is perforated rather than carved, producing a kind of hard lacing of flat darks and lights. This sarcophagus is interesting, too, for what it reveals of Christian adaptation of pagan material. We have seen that the Good Shepherd theme appears in pre-Christian times and that the Christians take it to signify Christ. Here the motif appears three times, possibly in an allusion to the Trinity. Around the Good Shepherd twines a grapevine heavy with grapes and through which climb busy cupids bringing in the harvest. Three cupids crush the

7-17 *The Good Shepherd Sarcophagus*, from the catacomb of Praetextus, Rome, late fourth century A.D. Musei del Laterano, Rome.

grapes in a wine press, and their wine, once sacred to Bacchus, has now become symbolic of the blood of Christ; the cupids themselves, once associated with love and erotic passion (Cupid is the son of Venus), are forerunners of Christian cherubs. Thus, a purely pagan theme with orgiastic overtones is transmuted by Christian intention into a symbol of redemption through the blood of Christ. The figure style, with its stumpy proportions, frontalizing pose, and stereotyping of action, had its predecessor in the reliefs on the Arch of Constantine and is common (with many variations) to a great number of sarcophagi from the fourth, fifth, and sixth centuries.

Monumental sculpture begins its decline in the fourth century and does not recover its place in the history of art until the twelfth. The Christian tended to be suspicious of the freestanding statue, linking it with the false gods of the pagans. In his *Apologia*, Justin Martyr, a second-century ecclesiast mindful of the First Commandment admonition to shun graven images, accuses the pagans of worshiping statues as gods. But the Greco-Roman experience was still a living part of the Mediterranean mentality and, at least in the west, the Semitic ban on images in sacred places was not likely to be adopted. The reasoning of the fathers of the early Church—that the use of pictures and statues could be justified on the grounds that they instructed the illiterate in the mysteries and stories of the faith—was

later supplemented by the theological argument that since Jesus was "made flesh and dwelt among us," he had a human nature and human likeness that could be represented in art.

In any event, and perhaps for many reasons, sculpture dwindled to craft art and small work —sarcophagus reliefs, commemorative ivory panels, church furniture and accessories, book covers, and the like. A very fine example of the quality that could be achieved by the ivory carvers of the eastern empire is a leaf from a diptych dating from the early sixth century and representing St. Michael the Archangel (FIG 7-18). It is evidence that the classical spirit and form had by no means died out or been entirely denatured. The prototype of the *St. Michael* must have been a pagan Victory; the flowing classical and still naturalistic drapery. the delicately incised wings, and the facial type and coiffure are of the pre-Christian tradition. But there are significant divergences from it, even so—misinterpretations or misreadings of the rules of naturalistic representation. Subtle ambiguities in the relation of the figure to its architectural setting appear in such details as the placing of the wings (one in front of the column at the left, one behind the column at the right), the placing of the scepter, and the hovering of the feet above the stair without real relation to it. These matters have, of course, little to do with the striking beauty of the form; they simply indicate the course that stylistic change is taking, as the Greco-Roman world fades into history and the Medieval era begins.

We find that change almost completed in the *Diptych of Anastasius* (FIG. 7-19), which represents the emperor Anastasius I, as consul, about to throw down the *mappa* (handkerchief), the signal for the games to start. Though the diptych, dated A.D. 517, is about contemporary with the *St. Michael* ivory, the mutation of classical naturalism is much further advanced (a reminder that the process does not proceed evenly along the same historical front or at the same tempo). The figure of the emperor in both panels is elevated above the lively scenes taking place in the arena. He is enthroned in rigid frontality, making a static, suspended gesture, entirely symbolic, the abstraction of his consular authority. His features are

masklike, and his quasidivine status is announced by a halo. The halo, a shell form, would originally have been an architectural feature, part of the pediment of the niche; here—in an excellent example of a misreading of a prototype—it has migrated to its place behind the emperor's head. The details of the architecture are confused and have lost their original architectural significance, and the flattening and patterning of the surface is as we have seen it developing earlier. The work is entirely ornamental and symbolic; the living man is lost in the concept—in this case, the concept of supreme and suprahuman authority. One hundred years after the *Diptych of Anastasius*, the *Sarcophagus of Archbishop Theodore* (FIG. 7-20) is not only ornamented with entirely symbolic forms, but the human figure is dismissed alto-

7-18 *St. Michael the Archangel*, leaf of a diptych, early sixth century A.D. Ivory, approx. 17″ × 15½″. British Museum, London.

7-19 *Diptych of Anastasius*, A.D. 517. Ivory, each leaf 14″ × 5″. Bibliothèque Nationale, Paris.

7-20 *Sarcophagus of Archbishop Theodore,* seventh century A.D. Marble. Sant' Apollinare in Classe, Ravenna.

gether. Peacocks, symbolic of eternity, flank a *chi-rho* monogram (XP are the first two letters of "Christ" in Greek). The XP is supplemented in the monogram with the alpha (A) and the omega (Ω), the first and last letters of the Greek alphabet, representing the words of Christ: "I am the Beginning and the End." The fruiting vines behind the peacocks represent, as we have seen, the source of the redeeming blood of Christ. Set within wreaths on the lid of the tomb, the *chi-rho* monogram appears three times, serving as the *labarum* carried upon the standards of the Imperial Christian army. Thus, the hope of the deceased archbishop and the guarantee of his salvation are expressed entirely in symbol: eternity; redemption through the blood of Christ, who stands at the beginning and the end of time; and the triumph of Christianity. The accidents and irregularities of figural representation, the busyness of narrative, are replaced by timeless signs of salvation and immortality.

BYZANTINE ART

The transition from Early Christian to Byzantine art is neither abrupt nor definite and, in fact, defies accurate definition. The almost contemporary diptychs of St. Michael (FIG. 7-18) and of

Anastasius (FIG. 7-19) are both products of eastern carvers and might well be classified as Byzantine works. Yet the *St. Michael* is still firmly rooted in the Greco-Roman tradition, while the *Anastasius* panels show the Medieval stress on the event rather than its appearance. In this latter approach, essentially Near Eastern or Semitic, forms evolved into decorative symbols placed before a shallow, often neutral background that makes little if any allusion to optical space.

One point of departure for the abstract, symbolic Eastern Christian art may be a mural painting from Dura-Europos, a small garrison town on the west bank of the Euphrates in the heart of ancient Mesopotamia and on the very edge of the Roman empire (FIG. 7-21). It dates from the second to third century A.D., the time of the Roman occupation. The detail shown here may depict an attendant and priests of a forgotten pagan cult of Parthia or Palmyra (modern Tadmor). The figures stand with formal frontality in front of (within?) an architectural background. Their drapery is rendered by line, not tone, and their gestures are slow, ceremonial, and grave. Each figure is in itself a single vertical design entity, isolated from its neighbor. The bodies are hovering, weightless, their feet in ambiguous relation to the ground and to the architectural setting, reminding us of the *St. Michael* ivory carved centuries later. Although the meaning of the enacted ceremony is lost to us, it must have been represented with utmost clarity to initiates, who could read the depicted symbols and gestures like a pictorial script, a script that moved laterally across the surface of the printed wall unobstructed by perspective and other illusionistic devices.

As Christian dogma developed, this form of symbolic interpretation of reality was more and more favored, and a flat, decorative, abstract "Byzantine" style, rooted in such Near-Eastern works as the Dura-Europos murals, began to dominate Christian art. And, although Western illusionism was tenacious and enjoyed repeated revivals, the transition was more or less complete by the middle of the sixth century. It can be conveniently observed in the monuments of a single city, Ravenna.

Ravenna

Early in the fifth century, when the Visigoths, under their king, Alaric, threatened to overrun Italy, Emperor Honorius moved the capital of his crumbling empire to Ravenna, an ancient Roman harbor on Italy's Adriatic coast, some eighty miles south of Venice. There, in a city surrounded by swamps and, thus, easily defended, his imperial authority survived the fall of Rome to Alaric in 410. Honorius died in 423, and the reins of government were taken over by his half-sister, Galla Placidia, whose biography reads like an outrageously exaggerated adventure story. Galla Placidia died in 450, some twenty-five years before the last of her weak successors was deposed. In 476 Ravenna fell to Odoacer and eventually, in 493, it was chosen by Theodoric, the Goths' greatest king, to be the capital of his Ostrogothic kingdom, which encompassed much of the Balkans and all of Italy. During the short history of his unfortunate successors the importance of the city declined. But in 539 the Byzantine general Belisarius conquered Ravenna for his emperor, Justinian, and led the city into the third and most important stage of its history. Reunited with the (eastern) "empire," Ravenna remained the "sacred fortress" of Byzantium, its foothold in Italy for 200 years, until its conquest successively by the Lombards and the Franks. It enjoyed its greatest cultural and economic prosperity during the reign of Justinian, at a time when the "eternal city" of Rome was threatened with complete extinction by repeated sieges, conquests, and sackings.

The seat of Byzantine dominion in Italy, ruled by Byzantine governors, or *exarchs*, Ravenna and its culture became an extension of Constantinople, and its art, more than that of the Byzantine capital (where relatively little has survived outside of architecture), clearly reveals the transition from Early Christian to Byzantine style.

The climactic points of Ravenna's history are closely linked with the personages of Galla Placidia, Theodoric, and Justinian. Each left his stamp on the city with monuments that have survived to our day (one might say miraculously, since the city was heavily bombed in World War II) and that make Ravenna one of the most complete repositories of fifth- and sixth-century mosaics in Italy. The monuments of Ravenna,

7-21 *Priests with Attendant*, detail of a mural from the Temple of the Palmyrene Gods, Dura-Europos, second to third centuries A.D.

7-22 Above: Mausoleum of Galla Placidia, Ravenna, A.D. 425–50.

7-23 Left: Interior of the mausoleum of Galla Placidia.

particularly the Justinianic ones, represent ideas that ultimately will determine the forms of culture, and certainly art, of the Middle Ages.

Galla Placidia's own mausoleum (the identity of which has recently been questioned) is a rather small cruciform structure with a dome-covered crossing (FIGS. 7-22 and 7-23). Built shortly after 425, it was originally attached to the narthex of the now greatly altered basilican palace church of Santa Croce. Although its plan is that of a Latin cross, the cross-arms are very short and appear to be little more than apsidal extensions of a square. Thus, all emphasis is placed on the tall, dome-covered crossing, and the building becomes, in effect, a central-plan structure. On the other hand, this small, unassuming building also represents one of the earliest successful fusions of the two basic early church plans, the longitudinal and the central, and introduces us, on a small scale, to a building type that will have a long history in Christian architecture—the basilican plan with a domed crossing.

The mausoleum's plain, unadorned brick shell encloses one of the richest mosaic ensembles in Early Christian art. Every square inch of the interior surfaces above the marble-faced walls is covered with mosaic decor: the barrel vaults of nave and cross-arms with garlands and decorative medallions reminiscent of snowflakes on a dark blue ground; the dome with a large golden cross against a star-studded sky; other surfaces with representations of saints and apostles; and the lunette above the entrance with a representation of Christ as the Good Shepherd (PLATE 7-1). We have seen earlier versions of the Good Shepherd, but none so regal as this. Jesus no longer carries a lamb on his shoulders but is seated among his flock in splendid isolation, haloed and robed in gold and purple. To his left and right the sheep are evenly distributed in groups of three. But their arrangement is rather loose and informal (compare PLATE 7-3), and they have been placed in a carefully described landscape that extends from foreground to background and is covered by a blue sky. All forms are tonally rendered; they have three-dimensional bulk, cast shadows, and are disposed in depth. In short, the panel is replete with devices of Roman illusionism and its creator still has roots deep in the Hellenic tradition. Some fifty years later his successors will work in a much more abstract and formal manner.

Around 504, shortly after he settled in Ravenna, Theodoric ordered the construction of his own palace church, a three-aisled basilica dedicated to the Savior. In the ninth century, the relics of Apollinaris were transferred to this church, which was rededicated and has been known since as Sant' Apollinare Nuovo. The rich mosaic decorations of the interior nave walls (FIG. 7-24) are arranged in three zones, of which the upper two date from the time of Theodoric. Between the clerestory windows are represented Old Testament patriarchs and prophets, and above them scenes from the life of Christ alternate with decorative panels. The lowest zone originally bore subjects of either Arian or political character. Although Christians, Theodoric and his Goths were Arians—followers of the teachings of Bishop Arius—a sect declared heretical by the Orthodox Church. After the Byzantine conquest of Ravenna, Bishop Agnellus ordered all mosaics that bore reference to Theodoric or to Arianism removed and replaced with the present procession of orthodox saints, male on one side, female on the other. Since Agnellus had no quarrel with the subjects on the upper two levels, they were left intact, and our example, which shows the miracle of the loaves and the fishes (PLATE 7-2), must date from about 500. It well illustrates the stylistic change that has occurred since the decoration of Galla Placidia's mausoleum. Jesus, beardless and in the imperial dress of gold and purple, faces directly toward us as he directs his disciples to distribute the miraculously augmented supply of bread and fish to the great crowd to which he has preached. The artist makes no attempt to supply details to the event. Rather he emphasizes the sacramental character of it, the spiritual fact that Jesus, outstanding in the group, is performing a miracle by the power of God. The fact of the miracle takes it out of the world of time and of incident, for what is important in this scene is the presence of almighty power, which requires nothing but an unchanging presentation in terms of formal, unchanging aspect. The story is told with the bare minimum of figures necessary to make its meaning explicit, and these figures have been aligned laterally, moved close to the foreground, and placed in a shallow picture box that

7-24 The nave of Sant' Apollinare Nuovo, Ravenna, c. A.D. 504.

is cut off by a golden screen close behind the back of the figures. The landscape setting, which was so explicitly described by the artist who worked for Galla Placidia, is here merely suggested by a few rocks and bushes that enclose the figure group like parentheses. That former reference to the physical world, the blue sky, is now replaced by a neutral gold, which is to be the standard background color from now on. Remnants of the former illusionism are to be found only in the handling of the individual figures, which still cast shadows and retain some of their former volume. But the shadows of the drapery folds have already narrowed into bars and will soon disappear.

The Ravenna epoch closes with the church of Sant' Apollinare in Classe where, in the great apse mosaic, the Byzantine style reaches full maturity. Here, until the ninth century (when it was transferred to Ravenna, as described above), rested the body of St. Apollinaris, who suffered his martyrdom in Classe, Ravenna's port city. The building itself (FIG. 7-25) is of the Early Christian type, a three-aisled basilica with a plan quite similar to that of Theodoric's palace church in Ravenna. The peculiar design of the apse,

which combines a semicircular interior with a polygonal exterior, is typical for Ravenna churches and is probably of Byzantine origin. As usual for the period, the outside of the building is plain and unadorned. (The cylindrical bell tower, or *campanile*, is of later date.) The interior decoration in this case is confined to the triumphal arch and the apse behind it. Of these mosaics the one decorating the semivault above the apse (PLATE 7-3) was probably completed by 549, when the church was dedicated. It shows, against a gold ground, a large blue medallion with a jeweled cross, symbol of the transfigured Jesus. Just above, the hand of God and the dove issue from the clouds on an axis with the cross, the three together symbolizing the Trinity. On either side in the clouds appear the figures of Moses and Elijah, who had appeared before Christ during his transfiguration; below these two figures are three sheep, the three disciples who accompanied Christ to the foot of the Mount of the Transfiguration. Beneath, in the midst of green fields with trees, flowers, and birds, stands with uplifted arms the patron saint of the church, Apollinaris, accompanied by twelve sheep representing the twelve apostles and forming, as they march in regular file across the apse, a wonderfully decorative base.

Comparison with the Galla Placidia mosaic (PLATE 7-1) shows how the style and the artist's approach to his subject have changed during the course of a century. In each case we are looking at a human figure and some sheep in a landscape. But now, in the mid-sixth century, the artist no longer tries to re-create a segment of the physical world but tells his story in terms of flat symbols, lined up side by side. All overlapping is carefully avoided in what must have been an intentional effort to omit all reference to the three-dimensional space of the material world and physical reality. Shapes have lost their volume to become flat silhouettes into which details have been inscribed with lines. The effect is that of an extremely rich flat tapestry design that tells its story directly and explicitly without illusionistic devices. The Byzantine style becomes the ideal vehicle for the conveyance of the extremely complex symbolism of the fully developed Christian dogma. Our apse mosaic, for example, has much more meaning than first meets the eye. The transfiguration of Christ—here into the image of the cross—symbolizes his own death, with its redeeming consequences, but also the death of his martyrs—in this case, St. Apollinaris. The lamb is also a symbol of martyrdom and is appropriately used to represent the martyred apostles. The whole scene expands above the altar, where the sacrament of the Eucharist is celebrated, the miraculous recurrence of the supreme redemptive and transfigurative act. The very altars of Christian churches, where the mystery of the Eucharist takes place, were from early times sanctified by the bones and relics of martyrs; thus the mystery and the martyrdom were joined in one concept—namely, that the death of the martyr, in imitation of Christ, is a triumph over death that leads to eternal life. The images above the altar present a kind of inspiring vision to the eyes of the believers, for the way of the martyr is open to them, and the reward of eternal life is within their reach. The organization of the symbolism and of the images is hieratic, and the graphic message must have come to the faithful with overwhelming force. Looming above

7-25 Sant' Apollinare in Classe, Ravenna, c. A.D. 533–49.

their eyes is the apparition of a great mystery ordered in such a way as to make perfectly simple and clear the "whole duty of man" seeking salvation. That the anonymous artists working under the direction of the priests expended every device of their craft to render the idea explicit is plain enough; believing men could read it as easily as an inscription. The martyr's glorification beneath the cross inscribed in the starry heavens presented in one great tableau the eternal meaning of Christian life in terms of its deepest mystery.

The Byzantine style, born of the Orientalizing of Hellenistic naturalism, appears in monumental grandeur and ornamental splendor in the mosaics of San Vitale (PLATE 7-4), which, in the high quality they share with the beautiful building itself, symbolize the achievements of the age of the emperor Justinian and are worthy representatives of the First Byzantine Golden Age. Begun shortly after Theodoric's death and dedicated by Bishop Maximianus in 547, San Vitale (FIG. 7-26) shares with the other Ravenna churches its plain exterior (slightly marred by a Renaissance portal) and the polygonal apse. But beyond that it is an

7-26 San Vitale, Ravenna,
A.D. 526–47.

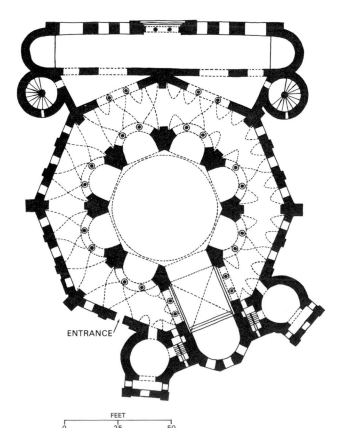

ENTRANCE

FEET
0   25   50

7-27 Plan of San Vitale.

entirely different building (FIG. 7-27). The structure is centrally planned and consists of two concentric octagons of which the dome-covered inner one rises above the surrounding one to provide the interior with clerestory lighting. The central space is defined by eight large piers that alternate with curved, columned niches, pushing outward into the surrounding ambulatory and creating, on the plan, an intricate, multifoliate design. These niches effect a close integration between inner and outer spaces that otherwise would simply have existed side by side as independent units. A cross-vaulted sanctuary preceding the apse interrupts the ambulatory and provides the plan with some axial stability. This effect is weakened, however, by the unsymmetrical placement of the narthex, the odd angle of which has never been fully explained. (The no longer extant atrium may have paralleled a street that ran in that direction.) As shown in FIG. 7-28, the ambulatory has been provided with a second story, the so-called gallery, which was reserved for women and is a typical feature of Byzantine churches. Probably also of Byzantine origin are the so-called impost blocks, which have been inserted between the simply profiled but richly patterned column capitals and the springing of the arches (FIG. 7-29). Resembling an inverted, truncated pyramid, these impost blocks appear in most Ravenna churches (compare FIG. 7-24) and may be highly abstracted reflections of entablature segments that had been inserted between column and arch by Late Roman architects.

The sum of San Vitale's intricate plan and elevation produces an effect of great complexity. Walking through the building, one is struck by the rich diversity of ever changing perspectives. Arches looping over arches, curving and flattened spaces, and shapes of wall and vault seem to change constantly with the viewer's position. Light filtered through alabaster-paned windows plays over the glittering mosaics and glowing marbles that cover the building's complex surfaces, producing an effect of sumptuousness that is not Western but Oriental. And, indeed, the inspiration for this design is to be found in Byzantium rather than Rome. In Constantinople, some ten years before the completion of San Vitale at Ravenna, a church had been dedicated to the Saints Sergius and Bacchus that looks like a rough preparatory sketch for the later church in which the suggestions of the earlier plan may be seen developed to their full potential.

Slightly earlier than those of Sant' Apollinare in Classe, but of higher quality, the mosaics that decorate the sanctuary of San Vitale, like the building itself, must be regarded as one of the climactic achievements of Byzantine art. Completed less than a decade after the surrender of Ravenna by the Goths, the decorations of apse and forechoir proclaim the triumph of Justinian and of the orthodox faith. The multiple panels of the sanctuary form a unified composition, a theme of which is the holy ratification of the emperor's right to Ravenna and to the whole of the western empire of which it was now the principal city. The apse mosaics are portrait groups representing Justinian on one wall and his empress, Theodora, on the other (FIGS. 7-30 and 7-31). The monarchs are accompanied by their retinues in a

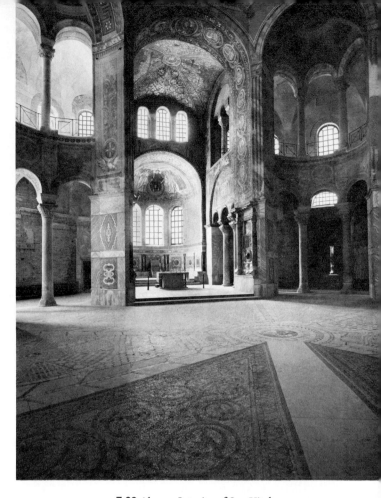

7-28 Above: Interior of San Vitale.

7-29 Capital from San Vitale.

7-30 *Justinian and Attendants*, apse mosaic from San Vitale.

depiction of the offertory procession, that part of the liturgy when the bread and wine of the Eucharist are brought forward and presented. Justinian, represented as a priest-king, carries a vessel containing the bread, and Theodora the golden cup with the wine. Images and symbols covering the entire sanctuary express the single idea of man's redemption by Christ and the reenactment of it in the Eucharist. Moses, Melchizedek, Abraham, and Abel are represented as prefigurations of Christ and also as priestly leaders of the faithful whose offerings to God were declared acceptable to Heaven. In the representation of the Second Coming (PLATE 7-5), Christ, seated on the orb of the world, with the four rivers of Paradise beneath him and rainbow-hued clouds above, extends a golden wreath of victory to Vitalis, the patron saint of the church, who is here introduced by an angel. At Christ's left another angel introduces Bishop Ecclesius, in whose

time the foundations of the church were laid, and who carries a model of it. The arrangement recalls Christ's prophecy of the last days of the world: "And then shall they see the Son of man coming in the clouds with great power and glory. And then shall he send his angels, and shall gather together his elect from the four winds, from the uttermost part of the earth to the uttermost part of heaven" (Mark XIII.26-27). It appears that Justinian's offering is also acceptable, for the crown extended to St. Vitalis is also extended to him where he stands in a dependent mosaic (FIG. 7-30 and PLATE 7-6). Thus, his rule is confirmed and sanctified by these rites in which, as is so typical of such expressions of the Byzantine imperial ideal, the political and the religious are one:

In the atmosphere of Byzantium, the Christian emperor appeared as a Christ-like high priest and . . . the principles of his administration seemed to be symbolized in the liturgical rite. In the offer-

7-31 *Theodora and Attendants*, apse mosaic from San Vitale.

tory procession he appeared like the priest-king Melchizedek, "bringing forth bread and wine" on behalf of his people, to propitiate God.[2]

The laws of the Church and the laws of the state, united in the laws of God, are manifest in the person of the emperor and in his God-given right. The pagan emperors had been deified; it could not have been difficult, given that tradition, to accept the deification of the Christian emperor. Justinian is distinguished from his dignitaries not only by his wearing of the imperial purple, but by the halo, a device emanating from ancient Persia and originally signifying the descent of the honored one from the sun—and hence his godlike origin and status.

The etiquette and protocol of the imperial court fuse here with the ritual of the liturgy of the church. The positions of the figures are all-important, since they express the formula of precedence and the orders of rank. Justinian is exactly at center. At his left is Bishop Maximianus, the architect of his ecclesiastical-political policy and the one responsible for the completion of San Vitale and its consecration in 547. The bishop's importance is stressed by the label giving his name, the only identifying inscription in the composition. The figures are in three groups—the emperor and his staff (standing for the imperial administration), the clergy, and the army, who bear a shield with the *chi-rho* monogram seen on the *Sarcophagus of Archbishop Theodore* (FIG. 7-20). Each group has a leader, one of whose feet precedes (by overlapping) the feet of those who follow. There is a curious ambiguity in the positions of Justinian and Maximianus; though the emperor appears to be slightly behind the bishop, the sacred vessel he carries overlaps the

[2] Otto von Simson, *Sacred Fortress: Byzantine Art and Statecraft in Ravenna* (Chicago: Univ. of Chicago Press, 1948), p. 35.

bishop's arm. Thus, symbolized by place and gesture, the imperial and churchly powers are in balance. The paten carried by Justinian, the cross carried by Maximianus, and the book and censer carried by his attendant clerics produce a movement that modifies strikingly the rigid formality. There is no indication of a background; the observer is expected to understand the procession as taking place in this very sanctuary, where the emperor will appear forever as participant in the sacred rites and proprietor of this royal church, the very symbol of his rule of the western empire. The portraits of the empress Theodora and her entourage, on the other hand, are represented within a definite architecture, perhaps the narthex of San Vitale. The empress stands in state beneath an imperial canopy, waiting to follow the emperor's procession and to pass through the curtained doorway to which she is beckoned by an attendant. The fact that she is outside the sanctuary and only about to proceed attests that in the ceremonial protocol her rank is not quite that of her consort—even though the representation of the Three Magi on the border of her robe recalls their offerings to the infant Christ and makes an allusive connection between Theodora and the Virgin Mary.

The figure style shows the maturing of conventions of representation that go back to Dura-Europos and earlier. Tall, spare, angular, and elegant, the figures have lost the rather squat proportions characteristic of much Early Christian work. The gorgeous draperies fall straight, stiff, and thin from the narrow shoulders; the organic body has dematerialized, and, except for the heads, we have a procession of solemn spirits gliding noiselessly in the presence of the sacrament. Byzantine style will preserve this hieratic mood for centuries, no matter how individual variations will occur within its conventions.

One can hardly talk of Byzantine art without using the term "hieratic." Christianity, originating as a mystery cult, kept mystery at its center;

one might say that the priest becomes a specialist in mystery. The priestly supernaturalism that disparages matter and material values prevails throughout the Christian Middle Ages, especially in orthodox Byzantium, and it is that hieratic supernaturalism that determines the look of Byzantine figurative art—an art without solid bodies or cast shadows, with blank, golden spaces, with the perspective of paradise, which is nowhere and everywhere.

The portraits in San Vitale are individualized despite the prevailing formality (PLATE 7-6); however, this is true only of the principals, those of the lesser personages on the outskirts of the groups being more uniform. There can be little doubt that in these portrait groups, which memorialize the dedicatory ceremony, it was intended that close likenesses be made of those centrally involved—the emperor and empress and the high officials of church and state. Since pagan times, the image of the deified emperor in public and sacred places had been tantamount to his actual presence, for the image and the reality were taken to be essentially one. The setting up of the image of the emperor was "an act which furnished the occasion for the declaration of submission on the part of the people";[3] and those who gazed on the images must have known that they owed them absolute reverence: "In these awe-inspiring images the sovereigns, though far away in Byzantium, had actually set foot on the soil of Italy."[4]

Thus the symbol, the image, and what they represent are most often one and the same. Just as the image of Justinian or Theodora or a saint is venerated as if it were the person, so are a cross, relics, and mementoes. Even vessels associated with holy rites come to be venerated as real presences of sacred powers that can cure not only spiritually but physically. To the believer, this

[3] *Ibid.*, p. 28.
[4] *Ibid.*, p. 39.

7-32 Hagia Sophia, Constantinople, A.D. 532–37.

communion of reality between objects and what they represent is logical enough; if the body of Christ is reproducible through the ritual of the Eucharist, then representations of all holy things ought to be just as real as what they represent. Symbols, images, narratives, sacramental objects —the furniture and accessories of ritual—can all be venerable and spiritually potent in themselves; this is like the magic of the Paleolithic caves, where the hunter-artists believed they summoned and controlled their animal quarry by the miracle of representation.

In Ravenna a powerful statecraft under the management of Justinian and Maximianus had been able to combine in a group of monuments the full force of Christian belief and political authority. In the process there was made a model of religious art, sacramental-magical in its power, that could work in the service both of the Church and the sanctified imperial state; this model, image, or ideal unity of the spiritual and temporal would strongly influence the Middle Ages in

both east and west. The hieratic style of Byzantium, matured and exemplified in Ravenna, will remain as both the standard and the point of departure for the content and form of the art of the Middle Ages.

Byzantium

Ravenna, the city that had become the successor to Rome as imperial capital in Italy, and then, as the so-called Exarchate, the beachhead of Byzantium in the Germanized west, finally passed from Byzantine control. The images of Justinian and Theodora in San Vitale, proclaiming that the empire was still whole, were powerless to make it so. But the east remained firmly in the hands of successions of emperors for a thousand years, and Constantinople became the magnificent citadel of Byzantine civilization whence streamed its influence to all points of the compass. At the time the imperial presence in Ravenna was being symbolized in architecture and art, the vast church of Santa Sophia, or more properly Hagia Sophia, Church of the Holy Wisdom, was being built for Justinian in Constantinople by the architects ANTHEMIUS of Tralles and ISIDORUS of Miletus between 532 and 537. The church remains today one of the supreme achievements in the history of world architecture (FIGS. 7-32 to 7-35). Its dimensions alone, formidable for any structure not made of steel, would attract attention. In plan it is about 240 by 270 feet; the dome is 108 feet in diameter, its crown some 180 feet above the pavement. It rivals in scale the great buildings seen so far in pagan and Christian Rome—the Pantheon, the Baths of Caracalla, the Basilica of Constantine. In exterior view the great dome dominates the structure; but the external aspects of the building are much changed from their original appearance—by huge buttresses added to the original design and by four towering Turkish minarets added after the Ottoman conquest of 1453, when Hagia Sophia became an Islamic mosque. The building was secularized in the twentieth century and is now a museum.

7-33 *Interior of Hagia Sophia*, lithograph by Gaspare Fossati, *c.* 1850.

The characteristic Byzantine plainness and unpretentiousness of exterior, which in this case also disguises the great scale, scarcely prepares us for the interior of the building (FIG. 7-33). One encounters first the huge narthex with its many entrances, and then the open, tremendous space above, where the soaring dome, canopylike, rides on a halo of light provided by windows in the dome's base. The impression made on the people of the time, an impression not lost on us, is given in the words of the poet Paulus, an usher at the court of Justinian:

About the center of the church, by the eastern and western half-circles, stand four mighty piers of stone, and from them spring great arches like the bow of Iris, four in all; and, as they rise slowly in the air, each separates from the other . . . and the spaces between them are filled with wondrous skill, for curved walls touch the arches on either side and spread over until they all unite above them . . . The base of the dome is strongly fixed upon the great arches . . . while above, the dome covers the church like the radiant heavens . . . Who shall describe the fields of marble gathered on the pavement and lofty walls of the church? Fresh green from Carystus, and many-colored Phrygian stone of rose and white, or deep red and silver; porphyry powdered with bright spots; emerald-green from Sparta, and Iassian marble with waving veins of blood-red and white; streaked red stone from Lydia, and crocus-colored marble from the hills of the Moors, and Celtic stone, like milk poured out on glittering black; the precious onyx like as if gold were shining through it, and the fresh green from the land of Atrax, in mingled contrast of shining surfaces . . . . [5]

The dome rests upon four *pendentives*. In pendentive construction (FIG. 7-36)—developed, apparently after many years of experiment, by builders in the Near East and *the* contribution of Byzantium to architectural engineering—a dome rests upon what is in effect a second and larger dome from which have been omitted the top portion and four segments around the rim—the latter forming four arches whose planes bound a square. By transferring the weight to piers rather than to the wall itself, pendentive construction

[5] In W. R. Lethaby, "Santa Sophia, Constantinople," *Architectural Review*, April 1905, p. 12.

makes possible a lofty, unobstructed interior space such as is particularly evident in Hagia Sophia. In our view of the interior the arches that bound two of the great pendentives supporting the central dome can be seen converging on their massive piers. The domes of earlier central-type buildings, like the Pantheon, Santa Costanza, or even San Vitale, had sprung from the circular or polygonal bases of a continuous wall or arcade. The pendentive system is a dynamic solution to the problem of setting a round dome over a square or rectangle. It made possible the union of the central structure and the long basilican type seen in awkward relationship in the Church of the Holy Sepulcher (FIGS. 7-10 and 7-11). Hagia Sophia, in its successful fusion of the types, becomes a domed basilica, a uniquely successful conclusion to several centuries of experiment in Christian church architecture. However, the thrusts of its pendentive construction make other elements necessary: huge wall piers to north and south, and, east and west, half-domes whose thrusts descend in turn into still smaller domes (FIG. 7-34) covering columned niches that give a curving flow to the design, reminiscent of San Vitale. And, as in San Vitale, the wandering space, the diverse vistas, the screenlike, ornamented surfaces, mask the lines of structure. The arcades of the nave and galleries have no real structural function; like the walls they pierce they are only part of a fragile "fill" between the great piers. Structurally, though Hagia Sophia may seem Roman in its great scale and majesty, it does not have Roman organization of its masses. The very fact that what appears to be wall in Hagia Sophia is actually a concealed (and barely adequate) pier indicates that Roman monumentality was sought after as an *effect* and not derived directly from Roman building principles.

What struck early visitors to Hagia Sophia, and many generations of them since, was the quality of light within it and the effect it had upon one's spirit. The forty windows at the base of the dome gave the peculiar illusion that the dome rested upon the light that flooded through them, so that an observer of the time thought that it looked as if the dome were suspended by a "gold chain from Heaven." Procopius, the historian of the age of Justinian, wrote: "One would declare that the place were not illuminated from the outside

7-34 Vaults of Hagia Sophia.

by the sun, but that the radiance originated from within, such is the abundance of light which is shed about this shrine." Paulus, whom we have already quoted, observed: "the vaulting is covered over with many little squares of gold, from which the rays stream down and strike the eyes so that men can scarcely bear to look." We thus have a vastness of space shot through with light and a central dome that *appears* to be supported by the light it admits. Light is the mystic element, light that glitters in the mosaics, that shines forth from the marbles, that pervades and defines spaces that in themselves seem to escape definition; light becomes the agent that seems to dissolve material substance and transform it into an abstract, spiritual vision. At Hagia Sophia, the intricate logic of Greek theology, the ambitious scale of Rome, the vaulting tradition of the Near East, and the mysticism of Eastern Christianity

MINARET

STAIRWELL

SACRISTY

BUTTRESS

BUTTRESS

A

MINARET

BUTTRESS

BUTTRESS

BAPTISTRY

STAIRWELL

STAIRWELL

NARTHEX

MINARET

OUTER NARTHEX

CLOCK
TOWER

MINARET

BUTTRESSES

A'

THEODOSIAN FORECOURT

ATRIUM

	Theodosian
	Justinian intact
	" speculative
	" foundation remains
	" standing remains
	Later additions
	Turkish additions
	Reconstruction

BYZANTINE

FEET

0   25   50

FEET
0   10   20

---------- Not extant

7-35 Plan (left) and section (above) of Hagia Sophia. (After drawings by Van Nice and Antoniades.)

are combined to create a monument that is at once a summation of antiquity and a positive assertion of the triumph of Christian faith.

Hagia Sophia was a unique hybrid, uniting the western basilican with the eastern central plan in a design (FIG. 7-35) without successors, for after it the east forsook the long church for a thousand years or more, developing the central plan, while in the west the basilican plan was consciously revived in Carolingian times.

LATER BYZANTINE ART

Between the later tenth and the twelfth century there occurred, under the auspices of the Macedonian dynasty, what has been called the Second Flowering or Second Byzantine Golden Age, when Byzantine culture reencountered its Hellenistic sources and accommodated them to the styles inherited from the Age of Justinian, the time of the *First* Flowering.

Architecture

In architecture a brilliant series of variations on the domed central theme appeared. From the exterior the typical later Byzantine church building is a domed cube (less often some rectangular form having other than a square as its basis), the dome rising above the square on a kind of cylinder or drum. The churches are small, vertical, high-shouldered, and, unlike earlier Byzantine buildings, have exterior wall surfaces with ornament in relief. In the Church of the Theotokos (FIGS. 7-36 and 7-37), about 1040, at Hosios Loukas in Greece, one can see the form of a domed cross with four equal-length, vaulted cross-arms (the "Greek Cross"). Around this unit, and by the duplicating of it, Byzantine architectural design developed bewilderingly involved spaces. The adjacent, larger Church of the Katholikon (FIGS. 7-36 and 7-37) uses a dome over an octagon inscribed within a square, the octagon formed by *squinches*—arches, corbeling, or lintels that bridge the corners of the square (FIG. 7-38). This arrangement represents a subtle extension of the older

7-36 Monastery churches at Hosios Loukas, Phocis, Greece: Church of the Katholikon, *c.* 1020 (left), and Church of the Theotokos, *c.* 1040 (right).

7-37 Plans of the Church of the Katholikon (bottom) and the Church of the Theotokos (top).

FORMER COURT

FEET

0   5   10   15   20   25

Upper level
Closed with masonry

schemes such as Santa Costanza's circular plan, San Vitale's octagonal, and Hagia Sophia's dome on pendentives rising from a square. The complex core of the Katholikon lies within two rectangles, the outermost being the exterior walls. Thus, in plan, from the center out there is a circle-octagon-square-oblong series whose parts exhibit a remarkably intricate interrelationship.

The interior elevation of the Katholikon reflects its involved plan (FIG. 7-39). Like earlier Byzantine

buildings it creates a mystery out of space, surface, and light and dark. High and narrow, it forces our gaze to rise and revolve: "The overall spatial effect is overwhelmingly beautiful in its complex interplay of higher and lower elements, of core and ancillary spaces, of clear, dim, and dark zones of lighting."[6] Middle and Late Byz-

[6] Richard Krautheimer, *Early Christian and Byzantine Architecture* (Baltimore: Penguin, 1965), p. 244.

7-38 Domes on pendentives (left) and squinches (right).

Pendentives Squinches

antine architecture thus seems to aim for complex interior spaces that issue into multiple domes in the upper levels; these, in exterior view, produce spectacular combinations of round forms that shifting perspectives develop dramatically. The splendid Church of Holy Apostles, built in the time of Justinian and now no longer in existence, is reflected in plan in St. Mark's in Venice, which reproduces it (FIGS. 7-40 to 7-42). The original structure of St. Mark's, dating from the eleventh century, is disguised on its lower levels by Romanesque and Gothic additions. But in plan, or from an air view, the domes, grouped along a cross of equal arms (the Greek Cross again) make the Byzantine origins at once evident. The inner masonry shells are covered with swelling, wooden, helmetlike forms sheathed in gilded copper; these not only protect the inner domes but make an exuberant composition appropriate to this great community church of the proud Venetian republic. Venice was, like Ravenna some eighty miles to the south, under strong Byzantine influence, despite the independence it had won early in the Middle Ages and preserved for centuries. The interior of St. Mark's is, like its plan, Byzantine in effect, though its great Justinianic scale and intricate syncopation of domed bays are modified slightly by western Romanesque elements. Certainly its light effects and its rich cycles of mosaics are entirely Byzantine.

Byzantine influence was wide-ranging, not only in Italy but in the Slavic lands and in the regions of the east where Islam had expanded. Byzantium brought its script, its religion, and much of its culture to Russia. The "holy" Russia before the revolution of 1917 was largely Byzantine in its traditions—one might even say, in its mood. Russian architecture, magnificently developed in the Middle Ages, is a brilliant provincial variation on Byzantine themes. In Moscow, within the walls of the Kremlin, stands the Cathedral of the Annunciation, dating from the later fifteenth century (FIG. 7-43). The domed-cross system of Byzantium here receives a most spirited expansion. The domes rise in a kind of crescendo to the triumphant climax of the central unit, with its characteristically Russian onion-shaped form con-

7-39 Interior of the Church of the Katholikon (view facing east).

7-41 Plan of St. Mark's. (After Sir Banister Fletcher.)

Additions to original structure

Tetrarchs of San Marco (see fig. 6-70)

ENTRANCE

ENTRANCE

FEET
0   25   50

7-40 St. Mark's, Venice, begun 1063.

Painting

While architecture enjoyed a fairly continuous development throughout the Byzantine period, that of the representation arts (painting and sculpture) suffered a severe setback during the eighth and ninth centuries, when they became the subject of a violent controversy. The Iconoclastic Controversy over the propriety of religious imagery, which raged for more than 100 years (730–843), began with the temporary victory of the image-destroyers (iconoclasts), who interpreted

trasting with the helmetlike shapes of its auxiliaries. The bright metal caps, peaked with crosses like miniature masts, reflect the moody Russian skies and proclaim, as if in architectural polyphony, the glory of the orthodox faith.

the biblical ban against graven images literally. In 730 an imperial edict banned religious imagery throughout the Byzantine empire, and artists were either forced to migrate to the west, where the edict was unenforceable, or, if they chose to remain in Byzantium, to turn their talents to secular subject matter, which was not affected by the ban. Although little has survived of their work, it may be assumed that those who worked in the secular vein discovered in the classical style a vehicle better suited to the depiction of nonspiritual subjects than the austere, abstract Byzantine manner; for when the ban was lifted in 843 and religious painting was again encouraged, a style emerged that represents a subtle blending of the pictorial Hellenic and the abstract Byzantine.

An eleventh-century crucifixion scene on the wall of the monastery church at Daphne in Greece (FIG. 7-44) shows the simplicity, dignity, and grace

7-42 Interior of St. Mark's (view facing east).

of classicism fully assimilated by the Byzantine artist in a perfect synthesis with Byzantine piety and pathos. Christ is represented on the cross, flanked by the Virgin and St. John. A skull at the foot of the cross indicates Golgotha, the "place of skulls." Nothing is needed to complete the tableau. In quiet sorrow and resignation, the Virgin and St. John point to Christ as if to indicate the meaning of the cross. Symmetry and closed space produce an effect of the motionless and unchanging aspect of the deepest mystery of the Christian religion; and the timeless presence is, as it were, beheld in unbroken silence. The picture is not a narrative of the historical event of the Crucifixion but a devotional object, a thing sacramental in itself, to be viewed by the monks in silent contemplation of the mystery of the Sacrifice. Although elongated, these figures from the Second Golden Age of Byzantine art have regained their organic structure to a surprising

7-43 Cathedral of the Annunciation, Moscow, 1482–90.

A.D. 726	752		843	878	c.900		975	c.1020	1063	c. 1100
	Ravenna lost to Lombards			Sicily lost to Arabs	Paris psalter		Damascus retaken	Katholikon, Hosios Loukas	St. Mark's begun, Venice	

to c.
A.D. 565

ICONOCLASTIC CONTROVERSY · TERRITORIAL DECLINE

SECOND FLOWERING

degree, particularly as compared with those of the Justinian period (compare FIGS. 7-30 and 7-31). The style is a masterful adaptation of Greek statuesque qualities to the linear Byzantine style.

The elongation of saintly figures to stress their noncorporeal, spiritual essence, found in the Ravenna mosaics, becomes a typical "mannerism" of Late Byzantine art. A striking example is the solemn, majestic *Virgin* in the apse mosaic of the cathedral of Torcello, an outlying island of Venice (FIG. 7-45). Tall, slender, small-headed, she stands utterly and triumphantly alone in a golden Heaven, pointing to the Christ child she carries, elevated above the twelve apostles and above all mankind. The mystery of the *Theotokos* ("Mother of God") is made visible in her commanding image. One remembers the great god-

desses of the ancient world, their awesome stature and superhuman powers; the Virgin here represented is their spiritual descendant, purged of all dross of matter, a near-hypnotic apparition. The hieratic style we have seen forming in the Age of Justinian and earlier has here reached a peak of expression.

But Byzantine art of the later periods can also represent vigorous action. A recently uncovered fresco in the vault of a side chapel of the Mosque of the Ka'riye in Istanbul (built in 1320 and originally the Church of the Blessed Savior of the Chora) represents, although inscribed *Anastasis* ("Resurrection"), the harrowing of hell (FIG.7-46). Christ, after his death upon the cross, descends into hell, tramples Satan, and rescues Adam and Eve, while other worthies of the Old Testament stand by awaiting their liberation. The movement of the central figures is highly dramatic. The white-robed, aureole-surrounded figure of Christ is laden with energy as he literally tears the parents of mankind from their tombs. The dynamic postures of the figures are reinforced by swirling draperies, agitated by the winds of a supramaterial force. But we also notice that, here and there, the carefully and precisely drawn drapery folds tend to take on a life of their own, as the Late Byzantine artist often shows delight in creating linear patterns for their own sake. These abstract, decorative, linear patterns tend to obscure the fact that, in its late stages, Byzantine art becomes increasingly realistic.

While the characteristics of Byzantine painting were developed in large-scale mural decorations, it was through miniatures in manuscripts and through small panel paintings, more popularly known as *icons*, that the elements of the style were spread abroad. A fine example of the former is a page from a book of the Psalms of David, the so-called *Paris Psalter* (FIG. 7-47), which reasserts the artistic values of the classical past with astonishing authority. It is believed to date from the

7-44 *The Crucifixion*, mosaic from the monastery church at Daphne, Greece, eleventh century.

7-45 *The Virgin with Apostles*, apse mosaic from the cathedral of Torcello, eleventh century.

early tenth century, a time of enthusiastic and careful study of the language of ancient Greece as well as its literature, a time when the classics were regarded with humanistic reverence. It was only natural that, in art, inspiration should be drawn once again from the Hellenistic naturalism of the pre-Christian Mediterranean world, especially Alexandria. David, the psalmist, is represented seated with his harp in a flowering, Arcadian landscape recalling those of Pompeian murals. He is accompanied by an allegorical figure of Melody and surrounded by sheep, goats,

Later Byzantine Art   283

HANATACIC

ĪC XC

7-46 Above: *The Harrowing of Hell*, fresco from the Mosque of the Ka'riye, Istanbul, *c.* 1310–20.

7-47 Right: *David Composing the Psalms*, page from the so-called *Paris Psalter*, *c.* 900. Approx. 15″ × 11″. Bibliothèque Nationale, Paris.

7-48 *The Vladimir Madonna*, eleventh century. Original dimensions of panel approx. 21″ × 30½″. State Historical Museum, Moscow.

and his faithful dog. Echo peers from behind a trophied column, and a reclining male figure, doubtless the river god, Jordan, points to an inscription that identifies him as also representing the mountains of Bethlehem. None of these allegorical figures appears in the Bible; they are the stock population of Alexandrian and Pompeian landscape. Apparently the artist had before him a work from Late Antiquity or perhaps earlier, which he partly translated into Later Byzantine pictorial idiom. In the figure of Melody we find some incongruity between the earlier and later style. Her pose as well as her head and torso are quite Hellenistic; Hellenistic too is the light, impressionistic touch of the brush, but the dra-

pery enwrapping the legs is a pattern of hard line. Byzantine illuminations like this will again and again exert their influence on Western painting in the Romanesque and Early Gothic periods.

An example of the devotional panel is the famous *Vladimir Madonna* (FIG. 7-48), which was probably painted by an artist in Byzantium in the eleventh century, exported to Vladimir, and then taken to Moscow in 1395 to protect that city from the Mongols. As these icons were quickly blackened by incense and the smoke from devotional candles burned before them, they were frequently repainted, often by inferior artists. In our panel, only the faces show the original surface, but the painting retains its Byzantine characteristics in the typical configuration of the Madonna's face, with its long, straight nose and tiny mouth, and in the decorative sweep of the unbroken contour that encloses the two figures and creates a flat silhouette against a golden background. Easily transportable and widely copied, icons spread the Byzantine style throughout the Balkans and Russia, where icon painting flourished for centuries and extended the life of the style well beyond the collapse of the Byzantine empire in 1453.

ISLAMIC ART

In 622 Mohammed fled from Mecca to Medinet-en-Nabi ("City of the Prophet," now Medina). From this flight, known as the Hegira, Islam[7] dates its era.

During the century that followed, the new faith spread with unprecedented speed from Arabia, where it was first espoused, through the Middle East to the Indus Valley and westward across North Africa to the Atlantic Ocean. By 640 Syria, Palestine, and Iraq had been conquered by Arab warriors in the name of Islam. In 642 the Byzantine army abandoned Alexandria, marking the Moslem conquest of Lower Egypt. By 710 all of North Africa had been overrun, and a Moslem army crossed the straits of Gibraltar into Spain. A victory at Jerez de la Frontera in 711 seemed to open all western Europe to the Mohammedans. By 732 they had advanced north to Poitiers in France, where an army of Franks under Charles Martel, the grandfather of Charlemagne, opposed them successfully. Although they continued to conduct raids in France, they were unable to extend their control beyond the Pyrenees. But in Spain the great Caliphate of Cordoba flourished until 1031 and, indeed, it was not until 1492, when Granada fell to Ferdinand and Isabella, that Mohammedan

influence and power in the West came to a close. In the East the Indus River had been reached by 751, and only in Anatolia was stubborn Byzantine resistance able to slow the Mohammedan advance. But relentless Moslem pressure against the shrinking Byzantine Empire eventually caused its collapse in 1453, when the Ottoman Turks conquered Constantinople.

The early lightning successes of Islam were due largely to the zeal and military prowess of Arab warriors who set out to conquer the earth for Allah and who burst upon the Near Eastern and Mediterranean worlds when Persian and Byzantine military power was at a low ebb. But the fact that these initial conquests had effects that endured for centuries can be explained only by the nature of the Islamic faith and its appeal to millions of converts.

Many of the features of the Islamic faith are derived from the Judeo-Christian tradition. Its sacred scripture is the Koran, the collection of Mohammed's revelations ordered to be gathered by the caliph Othman (644–56) and unchanged to the present day. Its basic teachings and ethics are similar to those of the Bible, and the Old Testament prophets as well as Jesus are counted among the predecessors of Mohammed. On the other hand, every Moslem believes he has direct and equal access to Allah without need for complex ritual or an intervening priesthood. Furthermore, a new social order, quite different from the Christian one, was established by Mohammed in that he took charge of the temporal as well as the spiritual affairs of his community. This practice of uniting religious and political leadership in the hands of a single ruler was continued after Mohammed's death by his deputies, the caliphs, who based their claims to authority on their descent from the families of the Prophet or those of his early followers.

Architecture

During the early centuries of Islamic history, the political and cultural center of the Moslem world was the Fertile Crescent (Palestine, Syria, Iraq), that melting pot of East and West strewn with

---

[7] Islam, "exclusive worship of the one God (Allah)" was Mohammed's name for his new religion. Mohammedan, Muhammadan, Muslim, Moslem—all refer to the same faith.

impressive ruins of earlier cultures that became one of the fountainheads of the development of Islamic art. The vast territories conquered by the Arabs were governed by deputies, originally sent out from Damascus or Baghdad, who eventually gained relative independence by setting up dynasties in various territories and provinces —the Umayyads in Syria (661–749) and in Spain (756–1031), the Abbasids in Iraq (749–945), the Fatimids in Egypt and Tunisia (909–1171), and so on. Despite the Koran's strictures against sumptuousness and license, the caliphs were not averse to surrounding themselves with luxuries commensurate with their enormous wealth and power. This duality is expressed by the two major architectural forms developed during the early Islamic period: the mosque and the palace.

Moslem religious architecture is closely related to Moslem prayer, the performance of which is an obligation laid down in the Koran for all Moslems. Prayer as a private act requires neither liturgical ceremony nor a special locale; only the *qiblah*—the direction (toward Mecca) in which the prayer is addressed—is important. But prayer also became a communal act for which a simple ritual was established by the first Moslem community. Once a week the community convened—probably in the Prophet's house, the main feature of which was a large, square court with two *zullahs*, or shaded areas, along the north and south sides. These zullahs consisted of thatched roofs carried by rows of palm trunks; the southern one, wider and supported by a double row of trunks, indicated the qiblah. During these communal gatherings, the *imam*, or leader of collective worship, standing on a pulpit known as *minbar*, near the qiblah wall, pronounces the *khutbah*, which is both a sermon and an act of allegiance of the community to its leader. The minbar thus represents secular authority even as it serves its function in worship. The requirements of this ritual were satisfied by the hypostyle mosque, the origin of which is still in dispute, but one of whose prototypes may well have been the Prophet's house in Medina. Once the Moslems had firmly established themselves in their conquered territories, they began to build on a large scale, impelled perhaps by a desire to create visible symbols of their power

that would surpass those of their non-Islamic predecessors in size and splendor; the great size of some of the early mosques, however, may also be explained by the fact that they were intended to contain the entire Moslem population of a given city.

The Great Mosque of Samarra on the Tigris River (FIGS. 7-49 and 50), built between 848 and 852 but now ruined, is the largest mosque of the Islamic world, measuring 800 by 520 feet. Over half its ten-acre area was covered by a wooden roof carried by 464 supports arranged in aisles around the open central court and leading toward the qiblah wall, the importance of which was emphasized by the greater number of aisles on its side. In the center of the qiblah wall is a niche, the *mihrab*, which became a standard feature in all later mosques. Its origin, purpose, and meaning are still matters of debate; Oleg Grabar feels that it may originally have honored the place where the Prophet stood in his house at Medina when he led the communal prayers. If the mihrab has this symbolic function, it is unusual, since one of the characteristics of early Islamic art is its concerted avoidance of symbols. In this respect, early Islamic art offers a striking contrast to medieval Christian art; the avoidance of religious symbolism, in fact, may reflect conscious rejection of Christian customs and practices.

On the north side of the Great Mosque of Samarra stands a single, large minaret from which a *muezzin* called the faithful to prayer. Although its shape is reminiscent of the ancient ziggurats of Mesopotamia, it was probably inspired not by them but by a certain kind of spiral tower of unknown purpose found in Sassanian Iran. More numerous were minarets that were square in plan and derived from the towers of Early Christian churches in the Near East. Cylindrical minarets, from which evolved the slender needles that are so characteristic of later mosques became popular only in the eleventh century.

The early Moslem hypostyle system, as illustrated by the Samarra mosque, was diffused and, except for the orientation of the building and the position of the qiblah wall, lacked architectural focus and direction. On the other

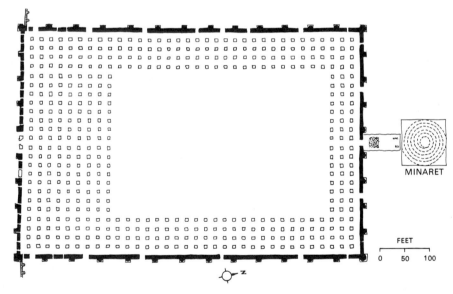

7-49 Above: Great Mosque, Samarra, Iraq, A.D. 848–52.

7-50 Right: Plan of the Great Mosque, Samarra.

MINARET

FEET
0   50   100

hand, it was a flexible system that permitted enlargement and addition with minimum effort. Its main element was the single support, either a column or a pier, which could be multiplied at will and in any desired direction. A striking illustration of the flexibility of this system is the mosque of Cordoba (FIGS. 7-51–52), which was begun in 784 and enlarged several times during the ninth and tenth centuries. The additions followed the original style and arrangement of columns and arches, and the builders were able to maintain a striking stylistic unity for the entire building. The 36 piers and 514 columns are topped by a unique system of double-tiered arches that carried a wooden roof, now replaced by vaults. The lower arches are horseshoe-shaped,

7-51 Plan of the mosque at Cordoba, Spain, eighth to tenth centuries.

MIHRAB

N

Years of Construction
◼ 784   ◻ 965-66
▨ 833-48   ▨ 987-88

MINARET

FEET
0 50 100 150

a form probably adapted from earlier Near Eastern architecture and now closely associated with Moslem architecture. Visually these arches seem to billow out like sails blown by the wind, and they contribute greatly to the light and airy effect of the mosque's interior.

In areas the builders wished to emphasize, like that near the mihrab (FIG. 7-53), the arches become highly decorative, multilobed shapes. Other early Islamic experiments with arch forms had led to the pointed arch, which, however, was not used to cover variable spaces, as in Gothic buildings. Early Islamic buildings had wooden roofs, and the experiments with arch forms were motivated not by structural necessity, but by a desire to create rich and varied visual

7-52 Interior, mosque at Cordoba.

7-53 Mihrab, mosque at Cordoba.

effects. The same desire for decorative effect seems to have inspired the design of the dome that covers the area in front of the mihrab (FIG. 7-54), one of four domes built during the tenth century to stress the axis leading to the mihrab. Here the large ribs that subdivide the hemispherical surface of the dome into a number of smaller sections are primarily ornamental. Only in the hands of Gothic builders, centuries later, were ribs in combination with the pointed arch to become fundamental structural ingredients of a new and revolutionary architectural vocabulary.

Of the early palaces there are only scattered remains, and they are of limited historical importance, serving primarily to illustrate the way of life of Moslem aristocrats and to provide us with some notion of the decorative styles of early Islamic art. Even the purpose of these early palaces is not quite certain. They were built both

7-54 Dome before mihrab, mosque at Cordoba.

7-55 Plan of the palace at Ukhaydir, Iraq, late eighth century.

Well○

GREAT HALL

M O S Q U E

N

FEET

0   50   100

in cities and in the open country. The rural palaces, which are the better investigated, seem to have had a function similar to that of Roman villas. That they reflect an Islamic taste for life in the desert seems too simple an explanation, although a desire to avoid plague-infested cities may well have been at least a partial motivation of their builders. But these rural palaces probably also served as nuclei for the agricultural development of conquered territories; and they may also have been symbols of authority over conquered and inherited lands, as well as expressions of the newly acquired wealth of their owners.

One of the better preserved of these early Moslem palaces is that of Ukhaydir in Iraq (FIGS. 7-55 and 56), built in the second half of the eighth century. Rather larger than most, the palace here is a separate entity within a fortified enclosure. From the outside the high, tower-studded walls look much like those of the Great Mosque of Samarra (FIG. 7-49). This similarity illustrates a flexibility that is characteristic of early Islamic monuments, as relatively minor

changes could convert them from one purpose to another. Differences between a mosque, a palace, or a caravanserai were rarely evident from the exterior; the structures tended to share a rather grim, fortified look that belied their military inefficiency. The high walls may have offered safety from marauding nomadic tribes but, more important to the builders, they may also have fulfilled abstract considerations, like the promise of seclusion for a mosque or, for a palace, privacy for the prince and the symbolic assertion of his power over newly conquered territories.

The plan of the palace at Ukhaydir (FIGS. 7-55 and 56) expresses its dual residential and official function. An elaborate entrance complex, consisting of a monumentalized gate and a Great Hall between two small domed rooms, leads onto the large central court beyond which is a reception hall surrounded by satellite rooms. Flanking this ceremonial axis are four smaller courts, all with three rooms on each of two sides. These grouped rooms appear to be self-contained and

7-56 Palace at Ukhaydir.

probably served as family living units or guest houses. To the right of the entrance hall is a standard feature of these early palaces—a mosque, here incorporated into the main building complex, though sometimes standing by itself. Most palaces also were provided with fairly elaborate bathing facilities, whose technical features, such as heating systems, were taken over from the Roman tradition of baths. (The baths at Ukhaydir, only recently discovered near the mosque, are not shown on the plan.) Just as in classical antiquity, these baths probably served more than merely hygienic purposes. Large halls frequently attached to them seem to have been used as places of entertainment. Thus a characteristic amenity of classical urban culture that died out in the Christian world survived in medieval Islamic culture.

The decoration of the Ukhaydir palace seems to have been rather sparse and confined to simply molded stucco and occasional decorative brickwork. In this respect, finds made in the western palaces in Syria and Palestine (modern Israel and Jordan) have been much richer. At Mshatta, an unfinished palace in the Jordanian desert, for instance, gate and façade were decorated by a wide, richly carved stone frieze (FIGS. 7-57 and 58). Its design, arrangement, and rela-

7-57 Portion of stone frieze, palace at Mshatta, Jordan, c. A.D. 743.

tion to its carrier serve well to illustrate the major characteristics of early Islamic decoration.

A long band, almost fifteen feet high, is decorated with a series of triangles of the same size framed by an elaborately carved molding. Each triangle contains a large rosette that projects from a field densely covered with curvilinear vegetal designs; no two of the triangles are treated the same way, and into some of them, as in the example shown, figures of animals are introduced. The sources of the various design elements are easily identified as late Classical, early Byzantine, and Sassanian Persian, but their combination and arrangement are typically Islamic.

Most of the design elements of Islamic ornament are based on plant motifs, which are sometimes intermingled with human and animal shapes. But the natural forms often become so stylized that they are lost in the purely decorative tracery of the tendrils, leaves, and stalks. These arabesques form a pattern that will cover an entire surface, be it that of a small utensil, a manuscript page, or the wall of a building. (This *horror vacui* is similar to tendencies in barbarian art, although other aspects of Islamic design distinguish it from the abstract barbarian patterns.) The relationship of one form to another in the Islamic is more important than the totality of the design: the patterns have no function but to decorate. This system offers a potential for unlimited growth, as it permits extension of the designs in any desired direction. Most characteristic, perhaps, is the design's independence of its carrier, since neither its size (within limits) nor its forms are dictated by anything but the design itself. This arbitrariness

imparts a certain quality of impermanence to Islamic design, a quality that, it has been said, may reflect the Moslem taste for readily movable furnishings, such as rugs and hangings.

Stone carving was only one of several techniques used for architectural decoration. Floor mosaics and wall paintings continued a long Mediterranean tradition. Particularly popular were stucco reliefs, a method of decoration that was known, but not common, in pre-Islamic Iran and Iraq. Cheap, flexible, and effective, the basic material—wet plaster—was particularly adaptable to the execution of the freely flowing line that distinguishes Islamic ornament, and it became a favorite technique.

Some of the very richest examples of stucco decoration are found in the Alhambra palace in Granada, Spain, the last Moslem stronghold in western Europe in the late Middle Ages. In the Court of the Lions and the rooms around it (FIGS. 7-59 and 60) stucco decoration runs the gamut of the medium's possibilities and creates an exuberant atmosphere of elegant fantasy that seems to be the visible counterpart of the visions of the more ornate Moslem poets.

The court itself (FIG. 7-59), proportioned according to the Golden Mean, is framed by rhythmically spaced single, double, and triple columns with slender, reedlike shafts that carry richly decorated block-capitals and stilted arches of complex shape. All surfaces above the columns are covered by colored stucco moldings that seem aimed at denying the solidity of the stone structure that supports them. The resulting buoyant, airy, almost floating appearance of the building is enhanced by the "stalactite" decorations that break up the structural appearance of

7-58 Reconstruction (after Schulz) of façade of the palace at Mshatta reflects the mistaken belief that the structure was essentially Roman.

7-59 Court of the Lions, The Alhambra, Granada, Spain, 1354–91.

the arches, transforming them into near-organic forms.

This same tendency to disguise architectural forms is shown even more vividly in the Hall of the Two Sisters (FIG. 7-60), which adjoins the Court of the Lions. Here, all surfaces are covered by a polychromed lacework of stucco and tile in which an almost limitless variety of designs is held together by symmetry and rhythmic order. The overall effect of the incredibly rich decoration is that of tapestries suspended from walls and dome, the "stalactites" resembling pendant tassels. In this hall, the Moorish (North African and Spanish) style, heralded in the Mosque of Cordoba (FIG. 7-52), has reached its ultimate refinement. Its influence on Spanish art remained strong throughout the Middle Ages and well into the Renaissance, and traces of it may be observed in the art of the Hispanic colonies of America.

A very different architectural concept is expressed in the Madrasah and Mausoleum of Sultan Hasan in Cairo (FIGS. 7-61 and 7-62). The madrasah, a combined school and mosque, was a building type developed in Iran and brought westward by the advancing Seljuk Turks during the eleventh century. It shares with the hypostyle mosque the open central court but replaces the Arabic forests of columns with austere masses of brick and stone. The court is now surrounded by four vaulted halls, the one on the qiblah side larger than the other three. Crowded into the angles formed by these halls are the various apartments, offices, and schoolrooms of the Moslem educational institution. Decoration of the main building is confined to moldings around the wall openings and a frieze below the crenellated roofline. These serve to accentuate, rather than disguise, the geometric clarity of the massive structure, which presents a striking contrast to the filigreed elegance of the contemporary Alhambra.

Attached to the qiblah side of the madrasah is the mausoleum, which is a simple cubical structure covered by a dome of Byzantine derivation. Mausoleums—central-plan domed structures—were adopted from the West, as they had not been a part of the original inventory of Islamic architecture. First built as memorials to Holy Men, they were eventually converted to the secular function of commemorating Islamic rulers. By the tenth century the building type was well established in Iran, whence it spread both east and west; it became especially popular in Egypt, which, of course, had its own age-old tradition of large-scale funerary monuments.

The most famous of all Islamic mausoleums is the fabled Taj Mahal at Agra (FIG. 7-63), which was built by one of the Moslem rulers in India, Shah Jahan, as a memorial to his wife, Mumtaz

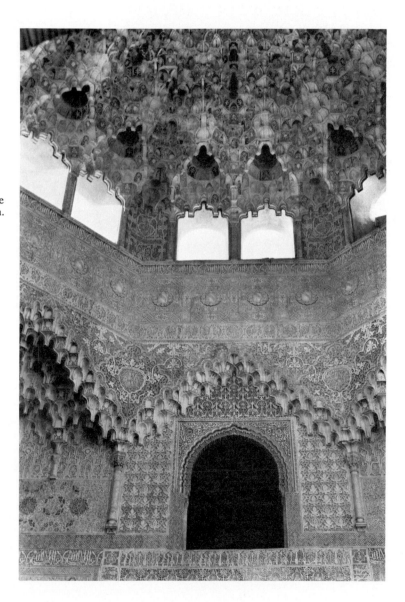

7-60 Hall of the Two Sisters, The Alhambra.

7-61 Madrasah and attached mausoleum of Sultan Hasan, Cairo, Egypt, 1356–63.

7-62 Plan of the Madrasah and mausoleum of Sultan Hasan, Cairo, Egypt.

MAUSOLEUM

FEET

0 50 100 150

Mahal. The basic shape of the monument is that of the Cairo mausoleum, but modifications and refinements have converted the massive, cubical structure into an almost weightless vision of cream-colored marble that seems to float magically above the tree-lined reflecting pools. The interplay of shadowy voids with gleaming marble walls that seem paper-thin creates an impression of translucency, and elimination of the Cairo structure's heavy, projecting cornice (which separated the blocky base of the earlier building from its dome) ties all the elements together. The result is a sweeping upward movement toward the climactic, balloon-shaped

dome. Carefully related minarets and corner pavilions introduce, and at the same time stabilize, this soaring central theme. While the entire monument recalls the fragile elegance of the Alhambra, it far surpasses the latter in subtle sophistication and represents the high-water mark of Moslem architecture.

Object Art and Textiles

The furnishings of the palaces as well as the mosques reflected a love of rich and sumptuous effects. Metal, wood, glass, and ivory were art-

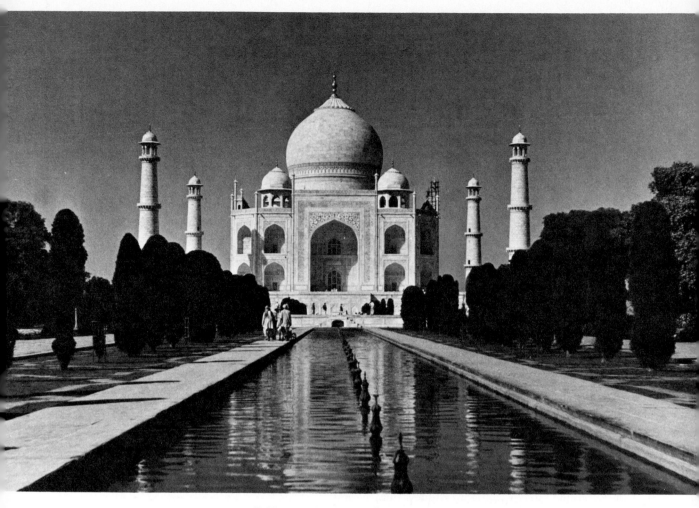

7-63 Taj Mahal, Agra, India, 1632–54.

fully worked into a great variety of objects for use in mosque or home. Basins (often huge), ewers, jewel cases, writing boxes were made of wrought copper or brass, chased and inlaid with silver; enameled glass was used with striking effect in mosque lamps; richly decorated ceramics of high quality were produced in large numbers. Islamic potters, experimenting with different methods of polychrome painting of their wares, developed luster painting, a new and original technique that gives a metallic shine to a surface. Their designs used the motifs found in architectural decoration. This ready adaptability of motifs to various scales as well as to various techniques again illustrates both the flexibility of Islamic design and its relative independence from its carrier.

The most prestigious and highly valued objects of all were textiles, which, in the Islamic world, served more than purely utilitarian or decorative purposes. Produced by Imperial factories, they were used not only in homes, palaces, and mosques, but served also as gifts, rewards, and signs of political favor.

The art of the Moslem weavers was probably acquired from the Sassanians in Iran and the Copts in Egypt, where weaving was well developed at the time that the countries were conquered by the Arabs in the seventh century. From there the art spread across the Islamic world and, by the tenth century, Moslem textiles were famous and widely exported. The art of carpet-making was developed to a particularly high degree in Iran, where the need for protection against the winter cold made carpets indispensable both in the shepherd's tent and in the prince's palace. In houses and palaces built of stone, brick, plaster, and glazed tile, carpets also provided a contrasting texture as floor and divan coverings and wall hangings.

The carpet woven for the tomb-mosque of Shah Tahmasp at Ardebil (PLATE 7-7) is a large example of the medallion type and bears a design of effectively massed large elements surrounded and enhanced by a wealth of subordinated details. The field of rich blue is covered with leaves and flowers (chiefly peonies, a Chinese influence) attached to a framework of delicate stems that weave a spiral design over the whole field. Great royal carpets like the Ardebil are products of the joint effort of a group of weavers who probably were attached to the court. Pile weaving is a slow process at best, and, since a carpet like the Ardebil often has more than 300 knots to the square inch, a skilled weaver working alone would probably have needed about twenty-four years to complete it.

Since the Ardebil carpet was made for a mosque, its decoration excludes human and animal figures, although other carpets from Ardebil show that the Koran's strictures against the representation of man and animal were not taken as seriously in secular art. The ban against the worship of idols, however, had practically eliminated the image of man from Islamic religious art, and even in early secular art it appeared only occasionally in secluded parts of palaces as part of royal imagery. For this reason also, large sculpture in the round and mural or panel painting, as developed in Europe and in the Far East, was rather rare in early Islamic art. Contributing to this lack of interest in monumental plastic art may have been the predilections of the people that made up the Moslem world; many of them—Arabs, Turks, Persians, and Mongols—were nomads, who traditionally preferred small, movable objects (the so-called

"nomad's gear") to large-scale works of art. And so, perhaps, it should not be surprising that, when painting did develop in later times, it was mainly on the small scale of book illumination.

Illumination

The Arabs had no pictorial tradition of their own, and it seems possible that their interest in book illumination developed almost accidentally, as a by-product of their practice of translating and copying illustrated Greek scientific texts. In some of the earliest Islamic illuminated manuscripts, none dating earlier than about A.D. 1200, the illustrations seem to have been drawn by the scribes who copied the texts. From such rather modest beginnings one of the world's great schools of book illumination developed in Persia.

The Persian shahs were lovers of fine books and maintained at their courts not only skilled calligraphers, but also some of the most famous artists of their day. The secular books of the Timurids and the Safawids were illustrated by a whole galaxy of painters. Famous among them were Bihzad (c. 1440–1536), Mirak, and Sultan Muhammad, court painters of Shah Tahmasp (1524–1576), a great art patron. Although the shahs were Moslems, orthodox Islamic restrictions regarding the human figure were rather liberally interpreted by them and did not affect their secular arts, so that the gay scenes of their life of pleasure—the hunt, the feast, music, and romance—and battle scenes fill the pages of their books. In them we feel the luxury, the splendor, and the fleeting happiness of Omar.

In *Laila and Majnun* (PLATE 7-8) the painter Mirak illustrates one of Nizami's romantic poems. The scene represents a school, apparently in a mosque. Seated on a rug is a turbaned *molla*, or teacher, lash in hand, listening to a youth reading; around him are other youths studying, all seated on their knees and heels or with one knee raised, the customary sitting postures of the East. Here and there are cross-legged bookrests. In the foreground one boy is pulling his companion's ear, and at the left, near the large water jar, two are playing ball. In the middle distance are the lovers Laila and Majnun, each obviously aware of the other's presence. Although the figures are drawn expressively with delicate, flowing lines, they are flat, with no shading and with but a hint of perspective; the tiles in the court and the rugs on the floor appear to be hanging vertically. The painting is conceived from a point of view concerned not with natural appearance but with pattern and vivid color. To this end the tones are kept bright and clear. The decorative quality of the miniature is emphasized by the broad margins of the page, which is tinted pale blue and flecked with gold.

In its general appearance the miniature is much more closely related to the Ardebil carpet than to any European painting or, for that matter, to Chinese painting, by which it was certainly influenced. It falls within the general framework of the Islamic decorative style, which, despite early religious restrictions and the constraints of a limited formal vocabulary, became one of the richest and most harmonious decorative styles in the world.

PART TWO

THE MIDDLE AGES

The poets of the Augustan age were singing the glories of "eternal Rome" while Jesus of Nazareth, obscure founder of the religion that was to transform the city of man into the city of God, was born and died. Within three centuries Christianity had become the official cult of the dying empire and the faith of the new peoples, the barbarians, who were to inherit its remains. While Byzantium, eastern remnant of the Christianized Roman empire, maintained a continuous sovereignty, the empire in the west disintegrated. What had been the imperial provinces broke up into contesting barbarian kingdoms—those of the Franks, Burgundians, Visigoths, Anglo-Saxons, Lombards, and others. Historians have called the ensuing epoch, the thousand years from about 400 to 1400, the Middle Ages or the Dark Ages. For centuries it was thought that this interval between the passing of the Roman empire and the rebirth of its civilization in the Renaissance was rough and uncivilized—in a word, "barbarous." Between the ancient and the modern world life was empty, cruel, and dark, simply a blank between (in the "middle" of) two great civilizations. Even today the word "medieval" is often used disparagingly. But since the late eighteenth century, historians have been thoroughly revising the view, long held, that Medieval art was crude and primitive. The same romantic enthusiasm for past

View of the cloister of St. Pierre, Moissac, twelfth century. The capitals are of both the historiated and decorative types, which appear regularly in Romanesque sculptured capitals in southern France.

civilizations that motivated the archeological revolution and the recovery of the ancient past sent scholars in quest of the meaning of Medieval culture, the meaning of monuments that existed in great number, aboveground and visible. Although we now see these centuries with very different eyes, perceiving their innovation and their greatness, the names "Middle Ages" and "Medieval" remain, simply because it is convenient to use them.

Medieval civilization represents an interrelation of Christianity, Roman tradition, and the new, energetic spirit of the Celtic-Germanic peoples, the barbarians, as the Romans had called them. Christianity, firmly established, provided a unifying force even in the midst of anarchy and chronic warfare. It mitigated the harsh passions of rough warriors. It kept alive learning and knowledge of the useful arts. Though itself often corrupted, it was just as often reformed. By the thirteenth century, when the Church was at the height of its power, western Europe had evolved as a great and original civilization, constantly stimulated by influences from the Greco-Roman past and from Byzantium and the world of Islam but ever reworking those influences in novel ways. The Christian Church, with its monopoly on education, also preserved and handed on Roman materials not directly related to religion: the Latin language, Roman law, Roman administrative organization and practice, the idea and ideal of the Roman empire—all elements used by the Church but, as the Renaissance would show, susceptible of entirely secular application.

Though the spirit of Christianity was oriented toward the world of the supernatural and though its learning was centered in theology, which regarded questions about the nature of the physical world both irrelevant to salvation and irreverent in intention, by the thirteenth century there was stirring, even within the Church, a new curiosity about man's natural environment that could not be entirely stifled by the prevailing religious disposition. In a thirteenth-century summation of Medieval knowledge—the influential encyclopedia called the *Speculum Majus* (*Great Mirror*)—Vincent of Beauvais included the "Mirror of Nature," a compendium of lore about natural things. By no means an objective or scientific analysis of nature in the modern sense, it was rather a descriptive record of the appearances of things as the reflection of God's glory and beneficence. Within the Medieval setting, notwithstanding its thoroughly religious view of nature, a different impulse was being felt, a secular and intellectual curiosity about the world that was to mature into modern science.

In addition, there were technological achievements that pointed to consequences far beyond anything the ancient world had known. The invention of tools and mechanisms that extended man's powers over his environment and facilitated manufacture were encouraged not least by the new dignity conferred on manual labor and skills by the Church's condemnation of slavery. The free craftsman, not, as in the ancient world, the slave, was the Medieval agent of production; organized in guilds, he constituted the firm foundation of Medieval urban economy. Thriving towns, populated by free men, provided a stimulus for commerce and industry, and most of the prosperous European cities of today were established or underwent renovation at about the twelfth century. Indeed Florence, mother city of the modern world, had early laid the foundations of its wealth and, by the fifteenth century, had the spirit and the means to lead Europe into the bold, creative age of discovery we call the Renaissance.

Chapter Eight

Early Medieval
Art

MEDIEVAL EUROPE A.D. 800–1000
With Routes of Early Migrations

0   200   400 miles

Kingdom of Ostrogoths

Kingdom of Visigoths

Kingdom of Franks

Kingdom of Burgundians

Carolingian Empire

Territory of Byzantine Empire

Arab Caliphate

ATLANTIC OCEAN

Lindisfarne

DANES

SAXONS

Sutton Hoo

FRANKS

Hildesheim

c.420

BURGUNDIANS

LOMBARDS

VANDALS 401

GOTHS 150–200

VANDALS c. 170

HUNS

375

OSTROGOTHS 455

VISIGOTHS 375

Tours

443   St. Gall

568

Roncesvalles

VANDALS 409

VISIGOTHS 480

Ravenna
488

VISIGOTHS 397

Rome

410

455

Constantinople

VANDALS 439

FOR THOUSANDS of years waves of migrating people had moved slowly across the great Eurasian steppes down into the Mediterranean world; we have met them as the Achaeans and Dorians of Mycenaean times, and again as the Gauls, who invaded Asia Minor and were defeated by Attalus I of Pergamum in the third century B.C.

In the second century A.D. the Goths moved southward from the Baltic region and settled on the north shore of the Black Sea, subjugating the Scythians and Sarmatians who had inhabited the area for some eight centuries. On their march, the Goths had met and defeated the Vandals, pushing them toward central Europe and setting in motion one of the longest and most infamous migratory treks in history, one that was to end only in the fifth century with the establishment of a Vandal kingdom in North Africa. The Goths themselves split into two groups in the early

Frankish ornaments

Death of Attila 453

Huns reach Gaul 451

375

376 Invasion of Huns

Anglo-Saxons in Britain 5th Century

400

482–750 Franks in Gaul (Merovingian)

Visigoths in Spain 412–672

500

Ostrogoths in Italy 489–540

—— MIGRATION PERIOD ——   —— GERMANIC KINGDOMS ——

600

Lombards in Italy 568–774

Sutton Hoo purse cover

Book of Lindisfarne

c. 700

CELTIC CULTURE IN IRELAND 600–850

End of Merovingian Period

750 Pippin "the Short" 741–68

754 Donation of Ravenna to Pope

St. Matthew from Gospel Book of Charlemagne

Coronation of Charlemagne

800

Codex Aureus

Charlemagne 768–814

—— CAROLINGIAN PERIOD ——

900

850

Otto I ("the Great") 936–73

Otto III Enthroned from Gospel Book of Otto III

—— OTTONIAN PERIOD ——

1002   1015

Adam and Eve, St. Michael's, Hildesheim

fourth century—the Ostrogoths (eastern Goths), who remained in Sarmatia, and the Visigoths (western Goths), who moved on into the Danube river basin.

For centuries these migratory movements had been checked by Roman military might along the Rhine and Danube rivers. Despite constant friction with them since the first century B.C., the Romans had been able to contain the barbarians along their northern frontiers. In the fourth century, however, the eruption of the Huns from the east pressed those tribes and nations against the Roman boundaries, which Rome found more and more difficult to defend. In A.D. 376 the Roman emperor Valens allowed the Visigoths, hard-pressed by the Huns, who had already conquered their Ostrogothic cousins, to settle west of the Danube. Maltreated by Roman officials, the Visigoths revolted two years later and, in a battle near Adrianople, killed the emperor and nearly two-thirds of his army. After this, Rome offered little resistance to the different barbarian nations, who crossed into western Europe almost at will. It is the following four centuries of ethnic upheavals in Europe that we refer to as the Migration period.

THE MIGRATION PERIOD

As the name implies, the invasions of Roman territory by barbarian tribes were in reality migrations of ethnic groups seeking not to overthrow the Roman empire, for which they often had great admiration, but a place where they could settle peacefully. However, they were seldom allowed to do so, as other tribes and nations would press in behind them and force them to move on. The Visigoths, for example, who moved in and out of Italy and formed a kingdom in southern France, were forced southward into Spain under pressure from the Franks, who had crossed the lower Rhine and established themselves in nothern France. The Huns themselves, the force that triggered this chain reaction of ethnic dislocations, reached France and Italy in mid-fifth century, and only the death of their great leader, Attila, in 453 prevented them from consolidating their vast conquests. As Hunnish power waned, the Ostrogoths shook off their yoke, moved first to Pannonia (junction of modern Hungary, Austria, and Yugoslavia) and then to Italy, where, under Theodoric, they established their kingdom only to have it fall less than a century later to the Lombards.

During this time of upheaval, strife, fear, and uncertainty, the Church, benefiting from the prestige of such early leaders as Augustine and Gregory the Great, constituted the only central authority, political as well as spiritual; the popes had in effect succeeded the Roman emperors. It was at this time that the foundations for the later authority of the Church were firmly established. In this connection, we should bear in mind that most of the barbarian tribes entering the Roman empire were already Christian, although of the Arian creed, which had been condemned as heretical by the Orthodox Church. In its contest with the eastern Orthodox Church for leadership in Christendom, papal Rome was strengthened when the Frankish king, Clovis, was converted to Catholicism. During his reign (481–511) the Franks gained control over the Burgundians (who had moved from the Baltic area into the region around Lake Geneva in the early fifth century), the Visigoths, and other groups in the area now France. With the recognition of the pope in Rome by this Frankish kingdom and with the success (in the sixth century) of Augustine's mission to England, where he became the first archbishop of Canterbury, Catholicism and the authority of Rome became firmly established in western Europe.

Accounts of the barbarian character vary. Tacitus, pointing up a moral for his Roman contemporaries, praises their courage, good looks, moral purity, fidelity, and good treatment of women but finds them guilty of drunkenness and wanting in perspicacity in matters of money. We can get a better picture of the Germanic character from their epics, songs, and sagas, which show a somber pessimism built upon a fundamental belief in fate, in the inevitable. Their heroes, like Siegfried and Beowulf, struggle against a pagan world of dreadful monsters.

Fierce joy in battle alternates with bragging and carousing; and narratives of stoic valor, with expressions of despair. Interpersonal loyalty, which became the basis of feudal ties and feudal law, is glorified in their poetry, as in this fragment of an Anglo-Saxon epic describing the last stand of a band of Saxons against the Danes:

Remember the times when we spoke over our mead, when we raised up our boasts along the benches, heroes in the hall in anticipation of a hard fight! Now let us see who is brave. . . . Byrhtvold spoke up, an old retainer . . . he taught his warriors their duty: "Mind shall be the harder, heart the keener, courage the greater as our strength grows less."

The imagination of these wandering people teemed with fantastic creatures of all sorts. Their belief that the deep, dark forests of the north virtually swarmed with zoomorphic and demonic populations was widely shared by the nomadic hunters of all tribes. Dragons, like Siegfried's Fafnir and Beowulf's Grendel, symbolize the mysterious and threatening universe of fierce forces that the later Medieval world will picture as the devils and demons of hell. Medieval man, long after he ceased his wandering and despite Christianization, remained more than half pagan; his terrors were bound up with his tribal experience and the memory of fiend-filled forests and pagan rites. (Charlemagne, in suppressing the Saxons, decreed against human sacrifice.) Against this background, it is not surprising to find that the Germanic tribes readily adopted an art form that, although foreign, was ideally suited to their imagination—the Eastern "animal style" already encountered in Mesopotamian art.

Craft Art

The original art of the Germanic peoples was abstract, decorative, and geometric and ignored the world of organic nature. It was confined to the decoration of small, portable objects—weapons or items of personal adornment such as bracelets, pendants, and belt buckles. Most characteristic, perhaps, and produced in considerable numbers by almost all tribes, was the *fibula,* a decorative pin usually used to fasten

8-1 Frankish ornaments, fifth to sixth centuries. Bronze and silver gilt fibula (approx. 3¾" long) with glass and paste inlays (left) and rosette disk fibula (1¼" in diam.) inlaid with beaded silver wire in the cloisonné technique (right). Metropolitan Museum of Art, New York (gift of J. Pierpont Morgan, 1917).

garments (FIG. 8-1). The fibulae were made of bronze, silver, or gold and were profusely decorated, often with inlaid precious or semiprecious stones. The entire surface of objects is covered with decorative patterns, reflecting the *horror vacui* so common in the art of primitive cultures. But we also note that the decorative patterns are carefully adjusted to the basic shape of the object they adorn and that they describe and amplify its form and structure, becoming an organic part of the object itself.

This highly disciplined, abstract, and functional type of decorative design was wedded to the animal style during the early centuries of the Medieval era. Probably of prehistoric origin, the animal style had reasserted itself in the Luristan bronzes of the ninth and eighth centuries B.C. and was a dominant element of the artistic repertoire of the Scythians, who passed it on to their Gothic overlords in the third century A.D. From that time on, the Goths became the main transmitters of this style, which was readily adopted by many of the other Germanic tribes. But its application was severely controlled by the native Germanic sense of order and design. Abstracted to the point of absolute integration with dominantly geometric patterns, the zoomorphic elements frequently become almost unrecognizable, and one must often examine a fibula (FIG. 8-1) carefully to discover that it terminates in an animal head.

The art of the Germanic people was expressed primarily in metalcraft. One of their preferred methods of decoration was *cloisonné*, a technique that may be of Byzantine and, ultimately, of Near Eastern origin. In this technique, used in the circular ornament shown in FIG. 8-1, small metal strips (the *cloisons*), usually of gold, are soldered edge-up to a metal background. An enamel paste (to be subsequently fired) or semiprecious stones, such as garnets, or pieces of colored glass, are placed in the compartments thus formed. The edges of the cloisons remain visible on the surface and are an important part of the design. This cloisonné personal gear was highly prized and handed down from generation to generation. Dispersion of some of the princely hoards at an early date would account for discovery of identical techniques and designs in widely divergent areas. Certainly cloisonné ware must have been given to vassals as gifts and tokens of gratitude; everywhere in barbarian poetry the name for the prince and lord is "treasure-giver." Other collections or "treasures" must have been accumulated over time, which could explain the different forms present in the magnificent discovery made

at Sutton Hoo in Suffolk, England, one piece from which is shown in PLATE 8-1.

Excavated in 1939, the Sutton Hoo site is now associated with the ship burial of the East Anglian king Anna, who died in 654. The purse lid shown is by no means the best of the pieces found, fine as it is. There are four symmetrically arranged groups of figures: The end groups consist of a man standing between two beasts, he frontal, they in profile, a heraldic type of grouping that goes back to ancient Mesopotamia (FIG. 2-13), though of course with variation. The two center groups represent eagles attacking ducks, again a familiar predatory motif that both Mesopotamian and Egyptian art yield us. The animal figures are adjusted to each other with the cunning design we associate with the whole animal style through centuries; for example, the convex beaks of the eagles fit against the concave beaks of the ducks. The two figures fit together so snugly that they seem at first to be a single dense, abstract design; this is true also of the man-animals motif. Above these figures are three geometric designs, the outer ones clear and linear in style, the central one showing an interlace pattern, the interlacements turning into writhing animal figures. Although interlacement had been known outside the barbarian world, it was seldom used in combination with animal figures. It has been suggested that the barbarian fondness for the interlace pattern came from the quite familiar experience of interlacing leather thongs. In any event, the interlacement, with its possibilities for great complexity, had natural attraction for the adroit jeweler.

Metalcraft and its vocabulary of interlace patterns and other motifs, beautifully integrated with the animal form, is without doubt *the* art of the Early Middle Ages in the West. Interest in it was so great that the colorful effects of jewelery designs were imitated in the painted decorations of manuscripts, in stone sculpture, in the masonry of the early churches, and in sculpture in wood. A striking example of the last is an animal head from another ship burial, one found near Oseberg in Norway (FIG. 8-2) that dates from the early ninth century. The Oseberg animal head expresses, as do few monuments of its age, the animal fierceness, the untamed, pagan energy of

8-2 "Academic" animal head from the Oseberg ship burial, *c.* 825. Wood, approx. 5" high. University Museum of National Antiquities, Oslo, Norway.

	Mohammed dies	Sutton Hoo ship burial		Book of Lindisfarne	Codex Amiatinus			
	M E R O V I N G I A N				P E R I O D			CAROLINGIAN PERIOD

the merciless northern sea-rovers who harassed the Christian-German settlements of western Europe from the late ninth until the eleventh century. It brings together in one composition a strikingly real description of the muzzle of a snarling animal, its eyes protruding in predatory excitement, with a vigorously carved passage of interlacements in areas that would bear a lesser burden of expression—the neck and the space between the flaring nostrils and the grimacing mouth. It is thus a powerfully expressive example of the union of the two fundamental motifs of barbarian art, the animal form and the interlace.

Illumination

When we remember that barbarian art was essentially one of small portable objects, part of the collection of accessories and instruments that made up the nomad's gear, it is not surprising that monumental art—whether architecture, painting, or sculpture—is not to be found in what the migrating peoples have left. The masterpieces of barbarian art, which show the meeting of its decorative tradition with those of the art of the Mediterranean world, are illuminations in liturgical books, for with Christianization of the barbarians, the book became an important vehicle of their art. These books were easily transportable, and we can follow the movements of some of them from place to place, since their styles, copied in or copying other books, are traceable in sequences of influence.

The complicated interchanges of influences recorded in manuscript illumination from the sixth to the eleventh century are the consequence not only of the restless migration of the new people, but also of the missionary activities of the Church as it sought to stabilize the wandering groups and to establish its authority. Foremost

in this activity from the sixth century to the time of Charlemagne was the monastically organized Church of Ireland. Monasticism, a system by which communities of persons lived away from the world and dedicated themselves to the spiritual life, was instituted in the eastern Christian world by Basil in the fourth century and in the west by Benedict in the sixth century. The Celts of Ireland, converted to Christianity in the fifth century, adopted eastern rather than western monasticism and were not firmly connected to the Roman rule or to the papacy. Their independence was strengthened by their historical good luck: They were not invaded by the Germanic migrants. While western Europe from about 400 to 750 sank gradually into conflict, confusion, and ignorance, Ireland experienced a golden age. Irish monks, filled with missionary zeal, founded monastic establishments in the British islands— at Iona, off the coast of Scotland, and at Lindisfarne, on the Northumbrian (northeastern) coast of Anglo-Saxon England. From these foundations, which became great centers of learning for both Scotland and England, Irish monks, filled with a "wonderful spirit of missionary enterprise," journeyed through Europe, founding great monasteries in Italy, Switzerland, Germany, and France and making the names of "Scot" (the old term for "Irish") and "Ireland" familiar in all western Christendom. The spread of Irish-Christian influence was countered by the Church of Rome, which felt that the Irish, long isolated from Roman Christianity, were tainted by heresy and separatism. The right hand of the papacy in this action was the Anglo-Saxon Winfred, or, as he is known to history, St. Boniface, Apostle to the Germans.

This encounter between Irish and Germanic Christianity is curiously reflected in the mingling of design elements in the illuminated pages of gospel books produced in Ireland and England between the seventh and ninth centuries. These

"Hiberno-Saxon" manuscripts combine Irish and Anglo-Saxon motifs, sharing essentially, but by no means in all details, the same style. An ornamental page—only one of several from a gospel book, the *Book of Lindisfarne*—is an exquisite example of Hiberno-Saxon art at its best (PLATE 8-2). Here the craft of intricate ornamental patterning, developed through centuries, is manifested in a tightly compacted design. Serpentine interlacements of fantastic animals devour each other, curling over and returning upon their writhing, elastic shapes. The rhythm of expanding and contracting forms gives a most vivid effect of motion and change, a palpable rippling as in the surface of a rapids. The inscribed cross, a variation upon the stone Celtic crosses familiar in Ireland, regularizes the rhythms of the serpentines and, perhaps by contrast with its heavy immobility, seems to heighten the effect of motion. The motifs are placed in detailed symmetries, with inversions, reversals, and repetitions that must be closely studied with the mag-nifying glass if one would appreciate not so much their variety as their mazelike complexity. The zoomorphic forms are intermingled with clusters and knots of line, and the whole design pulses and vibrates like an electromagnetic energy field. The color is rich yet cool, the entire spectrum being embraced but in hues of low intensity. Shape and color are so adroitly adjusted that a smooth and perfectly even surface is achieved, a balance between an overall, steady harmony of key (color) with maximum motion of figure and line. The discipline of touch is that of a master familiar with long-established conventions; yet neither the discipline nor the convention stiffens the supple lines that tirelessly and endlessly thread and convolute their way through the design. This joy at working in the small on infinitely complex and painstaking projects—this goldsmith's, jeweler's, and weaver's craft—will live in Northern art throughout the Middle Ages in architectural detail, ivory carving, illumination, stained-glass work, and, ultimately, in panel painting. The instinct and taste for intricacy and precision, propagated in the art of the wandering Celt-Germans, will broaden beyond art into technology and the making of machines. Modern historians make much of Medieval technological invention, declaring that it innovated well beyond Greek and Roman achievement and pointed the way to the technological revolutions of modern times.

The barbarian craft remained, but the Hiberno-Saxon ornamental style, with its gorgeous essays in interlacements, was fated to be replaced by the Mediterranean styles descended from Early Christian and Late Antique art. Political realities hastened its demise. Irish Christianity lost its influence in Anglo-Saxon England and on the continent; the adherents to the rule of Benedict, the Benedictine order of monks, who wholeheartedly followed the papacy and the Roman version of Christianity, gained the upper hand in power and influence, and though the Irish Church held out for some time, eventually it accepted the Roman form. Even while Hiberno-Saxon art prevailed in Ireland, Scotland, and Northumbria, other monastic foundations in England were copying Mediterranean prototypes. Naturally, the ascendancy of the Roman Church would be

8-3 *The Scribe Ezra Rewriting the Sacred Records*, from the Codex Amiatinus, Jarrow, early eighth century. Approx. 14″ × 10″. Biblioteca Medicea-Laurenziana, Florence.

expressed in manuscripts from the Mediterranean area, and wherever the Roman orthodoxy was accepted an orthodox style of manuscript illumination had to follow. The contrast between the two very different styles is particularly striking in juxtaposition. The *Ezra* of the Codex Amiatinus (FIG. 8-3) was copied from an Italian manuscript, the Codex Grandior of Cassiodorus, early in the eighth century by an illuminator with Italian training in some Anglo-Saxon monastery, probably Jarrow. The same original must have been seen and "translated" a few years earlier by an artist trained in the abstract Hiberno-Saxon manner; his version appears as the St. Matthew figure in the *Book of Lindisfarne* (FIG. 8-4). The *Ezra* of the Codex Amiatinus, as well as the architectural environment, is closely linked with the pictorial illusionism of Late Antiquity. The style is essentially that of the brush, the color, though here and there in flat planes, blended smoothly to model the figure and give gradual transitions from light to dark. This procedure must have been continued in the Mediterranean world throughout the Early Middle Ages, despite the formalizing into line that we have seen taking place in mosaics. But the Hiberno-Saxon artist of the *Lindisfarne Matthew*, trained in the use of hard, evenly stressed line, apparently knows nothing of the illusionistic, pictorial technique, nor, for that matter, of the representation of the human figure. Though he carefully takes over the pose, he interprets the form in terms of line exclusively, "abstracting" the unfamiliar tonal scheme of his model into a patterned figure not unlike what we see in the King, Queen, and Jack of a deck of cards. The soft folds of drapery in the *Ezra* become in the *St. Matthew* a series of sharp, curving lines regularly spaced. There is no modeling, no light and shade. The long training in the peculiar linear style of barbarian art made it necessary for the *Lindisfarne* artist to convert the strange Mediterranean forms into the linear idiom familiar to him; he finds before him a tonal *picture* and makes of it a linear *pattern*.

The Medieval artist did not go to nature for his model but to a prototype—another image, a statue or a picture in a book. His copy might be one in a long line of copies, and in some cases we can trace these copies back to a lost original, in-

8-4 *St. Matthew*, from the *Book of Lindisfarne*, Lindisfarne, late seventh century. Approx. 11″ × 9″. British Library, London.

ferring its former existence. The Medieval practice of copying pictures is of course closely related to the copying of books, especially sacred books like the Scriptures and the books used in the liturgy. The Medieval scribe or illuminator (before the thirteenth century, most often a monk) could have reasoned that just as the text of a holy book must be copied faithfully if the copy is also to be holy, so must the pictures be rendered faithfully. Of course, in the process of copying, mistakes are made; and, while scholars seek to purge the book of these textual "corruptions," "mistakes" in the copying of pictures yield new pictorial styles, or represent the confluence of different styles, as in the relationship of the Codex Amiatinus and the *Book of Lindisfarne*. In any event, one should realize that the style of Medieval images, whether in sculpture or painting, was the result of copying from sources thought

8-5 Above: *St. Matthew*, from the *Gospel Book of Charlemagne*, c. 800–10. Approx. 6¾″ × 9″. Kunsthistorisches Museum, Vienna.

to have sacred authority, and not from the imitation of natural models. Thus, one learned what was true from authorities who declared the truth—the Scriptures and the fathers of the Church—and one painted "true" pictures or sculpted "true" statues from authoritative images. To question authority on one's own, to investigate "nature" on one's own, would be to question God's truth as revealed and interpreted. This would be blasphemy and heresy. It would be wrong, however, to leave the impression that dependence upon authority in art is characteristic solely of the Middle Ages. In the Renaissance and since—and certainly today—new styles gain sudden authority and win widespread reverence and imitation, even if for reasons different from those operative in the Middle Ages.

THE CAROLINGIAN PERIOD

The late eighth and the early ninth century saw the remarkable historical phenomenon now called Charlemagne's renovation, an energetic, brilliant emulation of the art and culture, not to say the political ideals, of Christian Rome. Out of the confusions attendant upon the migrations and settlement of the barbarians, Charlemagne's immediate forerunners built by force and political acumen a Frankish empire that contained or controlled a large part of western Europe. Charlemagne, wishing, like Constantine, whom he consciously imitated, to create a unified Christendom as a visible empire, was crowned by the pope in Rome in A.D. 800 as head of the restored empire; the new entity became the Holy Roman Empire, which, waxing and waning over a thousand years and with many hiatuses, existed as a force in central Europe until its extinction by Napoleon in 1806.

Charlemagne was a sincere admirer of learning and the arts, and in order that his empire should be as splendid as that of Rome (he thought of him-

8-6 *St. Matthew*, from the *Gospel Book of Archbishop Ebbo of Reims*, Hautvilliers near Reims, c. 816–35. Approx. 10″ × 8″. Bibliothèque Nationale, Paris.

self as successor to the Caesars) he invited to his court at Aachen the best minds and the finest craftsmen of western Europe and of the Byzantine East. Though himself unlettered and scarcely able to write, he could speak Latin fluently and loved the discourses he frequently held with the learned men he gathered around him. He must also have admired the splendid works created in the scriptorium of the school he had established in his palace. One of his dearest projects had been the recovery of the true text of the Bible, which, through centuries of miscopying by ignorant scribes, had become almost hopelessly corrupt. Part of the great project, undertaken by the renowned scholar Alcuin of York at the new monastery at Tours, was the correction of the actual script used, which, in the hands of the scribes, had become almost unreadable. The Carolingian rehabilitation of the inherited Latin script produced a clear, precise system of letters; the letters on this page are descended from the alphabet renovated by the scribes of Tours.

Painting and Illumination

Charlemagne, his successors, and the scholars under their patronage imported whole libraries from Italy and Byzantium. The painted illustrations in these books must have astonished northern painters, some of whom had been trained in the Hiberno-Saxon pattern-making manner, others in the weak and inept Frankish styles of the seventh and eighth centuries. Here suddenly they were confronted with a sophisticated realism that somehow had survived from the Late Antique amidst all the denaturing tendencies that followed. The famous *Coronation Gospels* (the *Gospel Book of Charlemagne*), formerly in the Imperial Treasury in Vienna, may have been a favorite of Charlemagne himself: An old tradition records that it was found on the knees of the dead emperor when, in the year 1000, Otto III had the imperial tomb at Aachen opened. The picture of St. Matthew composing his gospel (FIG. 8-5) descends from ancient depictions in sculpture and painting of an inspired philosopher or poet seated and writing; its technique is of the same antiquity—deft, illusionistic brushwork that easily and accurately defines the masses of the dra-

pery as they wrap and enfold the body beneath. The acanthus of the frame of the "picture window" recalls the fourth Pompeian style, and the whole composition seems utterly out of place in the north in the ninth century. How were the native artists to receive this new influence, so alien to what they had known and so strong as to make their own practice suddenly obsolete?

The style evident in the *Coronation Gospels* was by no means the only one that appeared suddenly in the Carolingian world; a wide variety of styles in all stages of change from antique prototypes were distributed through the court schools and the monasteries—a bewildering array, one can believe, for the natives, who now attempted their appropriation by copying them as accurately as possible. Thus, Carolingian painting is extremely diverse and uneven, and classification becomes a difficult matter of ascertaining prototypes and the descendants of prototypes. If the *Coronation Gospels* painting is by a Frank, rather than an Italian or a Byzantine, it is an amazing feat of approximation, since, except for the Jarrow copyist, there is nothing to prepare the way for it in the Hiberno-Saxon or Frankish West. Another *St. Matthew*, in a gospel book made for Archbishop Ebbo of Reims (FIG. 8-6), may be an interpretation of a prototype very similar to that used by the *Coronation Gospels* master, for it resembles it in pose and in brushwork technique. But there the resemblance stops: The classical calm and solidity have been replaced by an energy that amounts to frenzy, and the frail saint almost leaps under its impulse. His hair stands on end, the folds of his drapery writhe and vibrate, the landscape behind him rears up alive. He appears in frantic haste to take down what his inspiration, the tiny angel in the upper right hand corner, dictates. All fidelity to bodily proportions or structure is forsaken in the artist's effort to concentrate on the act of writing; the head, hands, inkhorn, pen, and book are the focus of the composition. This contrasts strongly with the settled pose of the *Matthew* of the *Coronation Gospels* with its even stress so that no part of the composition starts out at us to seize our attention. The native power of expression is unmistakable and will become one of the important distinguishing traits of Late Medieval art. Just as the painter of the *Lindisfarne Matthew* transformed the *Ezra* por-

LAUDINTNOMENEIUSIN   EXSULTATIONESDIINGUT   UTFACIANTINEISIUDICIU
CHORO·INTYMPANO   TURFEORUM·ETGLADII   CONSCRIPTUM·GLORIA
ETPSALTERIOPSALLANTEI   ANCIPITESINMANIBEOR   HAECESTOMNIBUSSCIS
QUIABENEPLACITUMEST   ADFACIENDAMUINDICTA   EIUS

8-7 *Psalm 150*, from the *Utrecht Psalter*, Hautvilliers near Reims, *c.* 830, 4¾″ × 9½″. Utrecht University Library Ms. 32, fol. 83r.

trait in the Codex Amiatinus (FIGS. 8-3 and 8-4) into something original and strong, translating its classicizing manner into his own Hiberno-Saxon idiom, so the Ebbo artist translated his classical prototype into a Carolingian vernacular that left little classical substance. The four pictures should be carefully studied and compared.

Narrative illustration, so richly developed in Early Christian and Byzantine art, was revived by the Carolingians, and many fully illuminated books—some, large Bibles—were produced. One of the most extraordinary and enjoyable of all Medieval manuscripts is the famous *Utrecht Psalter*, written at Hautvilliers near Reims, France, about 830. The text, in three columns, reproduces the Psalms of David and is profusely illustrated by pen-and-ink drawings in the margins. The example shown in FIG. 8-7 depicts figures acting out Psalm 150, in which the psalmist exhorts us to praise the name of God in song and with timbrel, trumpet, and organ. The style shows a vivid animation of much the same kind as the *St. Matthew* of the *Ebbo Gospels* and may have been produced in the same school. The bodies are tense, shoulders hunched, heads thrust forward. The spontaneity of their actions and the rapid, sketchy technique with which they are rendered have the same nervous vitality as the figure in the *Ebbo Gospels*. From details of the figures, their dress and accessories, scholars feel certain that the artist was following one or more

manuscripts done some 400 years earlier; but his interest in simple human emotions and actions, the pantomimic skill in the variety and descriptiveness of gesture, are essentially Medieval characteristics, though they begin in Early Christian art. Note, for example, how the two musicians playing the pipe organ shout at their helpers to pump air more strenuously. It is this candid observation of man, often in his unguarded moments, that is to lend both truth and charm to the art of the Late Middle Ages.

Craft Art

To our knowledge there was little or no monumental sculpture in the Carolingian age. The traditional taste for sumptuously wrought and portable metal objects, which produced the barbarian works we have seen, persisted under Charlemagne and his successors and produced numerous precious and beautiful works like the book cover of the Codex Aureus of St. Emmeram (PLATE 8-3). Dating from the second half of the ninth century, it probably originated at either the St. Denis or Reims court of Charles the Bald, a grandson of Charlemagne. Its golden surface is set with pearls and precious jewels. Within the inscribed, squared cross, Christ appears in an attitude not far removed from that in the apse mosaic of San Vitale (PLATE 7-5). Round him are seated the Four Evangelists, and there are four scenes from the life of Christ. The style of the figures echoes that of the *Ebbo Gospels* and the *Utrecht Psalter*, though it is modified by influences from other Carolingian schools. There is no trace of the intricate patterns of Hiberno-Saxon art. At the centers of the Carolingian renovation the translated, classicizing style of Italy prevails, in keeping with the tastes and aspiration of the great Frankish emperor who fixed his admiring gaze upon the culture of the south.

Architecture

In his eagerness to reestablish the imperial past, Charlemagne also encouraged the revival of Roman building techniques, and in architecture, as in sculpture and painting, innovations made in the reinterpretation of earlier Roman-Christian sources became fundamental for Medieval designs. Perhaps "importation" is more appropriate here than "revival," since the Mediterranean tradition of stonemasonry could never have been more than an admirable curiosity to northern builders. Although northern Europe was dotted with Roman colonial towns that contained many large and impressive stone structures, the Germanic tribes had always relied upon their vast forests to supply them with building materials; northern architecture was a timber architecture and continued to be so well into the Middle Ages. The typical north European dwelling was a timber-frame structure (FIG. 8-8) that, in its essentials, has survived into our time. Its basic structural unit is the *bay*, which is constructed of four posts placed at the corners of a rectangle and interconnected and braced against each other with horizontal or oblique members. Such a unit is self-supporting; it can be roofed, and, depending upon the desired size of the building, it can be multiplied at will. Thus, the interior of such a structure is characterized by a repetition of identical units that move in orderly progression down the length of the building. The plan of such a building is related to the size and proportions of one of its bays in that the bay is the module, or basic unit of measurement, and the structure a multiple of that unit.

Charlemagne's adoption of southern building principles for the construction of his palaces and churches was epoch-making for the subsequent development of the architecture of northern Europe. For his models he went to Rome and Ravenna, one the former heart of the Roman empire that he wanted to revive, the other the long-term western outpost of Byzantine might and splendor that he wanted to emulate in his own capital at Aachen. Ravenna fell to the Lombards in 751 but was wrested from them only a few years later by the Frankish king, Pippin the Short, founder of the Carolingian Dynasty and father of Charlemagne. Pippin donated the former Byzantine exarchate to the pope and thus founded the papacy's temporal power, which was to last until the late nineteenth century. In 789 Charlemagne visited Ravenna, and historians have long thought that he chose one of its churches as the model for the chapel of his own palace at Aachen. But although its plan (FIG. 8-9) shows a resemblance to San Vitale's (FIG. 7-27), recent study disproves a direct relation between the two buildings. The Aachen plan is simpler, for the apselike extensions reaching from the central octagon into the ambulatory have been omitted, so that the two main units stand in greater independence of one another. This solution may lack the subtle sophistication of the Byzantine building but gains in geometric clarity. A view of the interior of the Palatine Chapel (FIG. 8-10) shows that the "floating" quality of San Vitale has been

8-8 Conjectural reconstruction of an Iron Age house upon foundations excavated at Ezinge, Holland. (After W. Horn.)

8-9 Restored plan of the Palatine Chapel of Charlemagne at Aachen, 792–805.

8-10 Interior of the Palatine Chapel of Charlemagne.

converted into blunt massiveness and stiffened into solid geometrical form. The conversion of a complex and subtle Byzantine prototype into a building that expresses robust strength and clear structural articulation foreshadows the architecture of the eleventh and twelfth centuries and the style we call Romanesque.

It was, however, the basilican, not the central plan, that was to provide the basis for and determine the development of Romanesque architecture. Although several churches of the basilican type were built in northern Europe during the reign of Charlemagne, none has survived; nevertheless it is possible to reconstruct the appearance of some of them with fair accuracy. Some appear to have followed their Early Christian examples quite closely, as the abbey church of Fulda (begun in 802), which derives directly from Old St. Peter's and other Roman basilicas with transepts. But in other instances, Carolingian builders subjected the basilica plan to some very significant modifications, converting it into a much more complex organism.

The study of a most fascinating Carolingian document, the ideal plan for a monastery at St. Gall, Switzerland (FIG. 8-11), may give some insight into the motivations of the Carolingian planner. The monasteries, as we have seen, were of central importance in the revival of learning. Monasticism held that the most perfect Christian life should be led in seclusion, removed from the temptations of ordinary life. In 526, Benedict had adapted the earlier regulations to the needs of western Europe. This "Benedictine Rule," which won out over Irish monasticism and which demanded among other things vows of poverty, chastity, and obedience, provided the basic organization for most western monasteries. Daily life was rigidly controlled and each monastic community was self-sufficient. About 819 a schematic plan for such a community was copied from a lost original—probably designed by the abbot

8-11 Schematic plan for a monastery at St. Gall, Switzerland, *c.* 819. (Redrawn after a ninth-century manuscript.)

ECCLESIAE AB ANGILBERTO APVD CENTVLAM AN DCC XCIX
CONSTRVCTARVM E SCRIPTO CODICE   EKMATEION

S·RICHARIVS

S·BENEDICTVS

S·MARIA

CVRA·P·PE·C·R·   ·1612·

8-12 Left: Monastery church of St. Riquier at Centula, France, c. 800. Engraving made in 1612 after a destroyed eleventh-century miniature:

8-13 Above: Plan of St. Riquier (reconstructed).

of Reichenau—and sent to the abbot of St. Gall as a guide in his planned rebuilding of that monastery. Near the center, dominating everything, was the abbey church, with the cloister (not unlike the early colonnaded atrium) at one side. Around the cloister were grouped the most essential buildings: chapter house (meeting room), dormitory, refectory, kitchen, and storage rooms. Other buildings—including an infirmary, school, guest house, bakery, brewery, and workshops—were grouped around this central core of church and cloister. That the scheme may have

been meant to be more than an ideal and actually to have been built is indicated by Walter Horn's recent discovery that the original plan must have been laid out on a modular base of $2\frac{1}{2}$ feet and that parts or multiples of this module have been used consistently throughout the plan. Therefore, the width of the nave, indicated on the plan as forty feet, would equal sixteen $2\frac{1}{2}$-foot modules; the length of the monks' beds, $2\frac{1}{2}$ modules (6 feet, 3 inches); and the width of the paths in the the vegetable garden, $1\frac{1}{4}$ modules.

Although the church is essentially a three-aisled

basilica, it has features not found in any Early Christian churches. Most immediately noticeable, perhaps, is the addition of a second apse on the west end of the building. The origin and purpose of this feature have never been satisfactorily explained, but it remains a characteristic regional element of German churches to the eleventh century. Not quite as evident, but much more important for the subsequent development of church architecture in the north, is the fact that the transept has the same width as the nave. Early Christian builders had not been concerned with the proportional relationships among the various portions of their buildings, which they assembled only in accordance with the dictates of liturgical needs. On the St. Gall plan, however, the various parts of the building have been related to each other in a geometric scheme that ties them together into a tight and cohesive unit. Equalizing the widths of nave and transept automatically makes the area in which they cross (the *crossing*) a square. This feature is shared by most Carolingian churches. But the St. Gall planner has also taken the subsequent steps that become fundamental for the development of Romanesque architecture: He has used the crossing square as the unit of measurement for the remainder of the church plan. The arms of the transept are equal to one crossing square; there is one square between transept and apse; and the nave is $4\frac{1}{2}$ crossing squares long. The fact that the aisles are half as wide as the nave integrates all parts of the church in a plan that is clear, rational, lucid, and extremely orderly.

The St. Gall plan reflects a Medieval way of thinking and is important for Romanesque art and architecture. As a guide for the builder of an abbey, it expresses the authority of the Benedictine Rule and serves as a kind of prototype. In the interest of clarity and orderliness the "rule" is worked out with systematic care. There is balancing of units and a kind of division and subdivision of the site. (This parallels the Medieval invention of that most convenient device, the division of books into chapters and subchapters.) The neat "squaring" that characterizes the scheme will especially dominate Romanesque architectural design together with the principle of the balance of clearly defined, simple units. The eagerness of the Medieval mind to explain the Christian faith in terms of an orderly, rationalistic philosophy built upon carefully distinguished propositions and well-planned arguments finds visual expression in the plan of St. Gall.

Although the rebuilding project for St. Gall was not consummated, the church of St. Riquier at Centula in northeast France gives some idea of what the St. Gall church would have looked like (FIG. 8-12). A monastery church like that of St. Gall, the now-destroyed St. Riquier was built toward the very end of the eighth century and therefore predates the St. Gall plan by approximately twenty years. The illustration, taken from a seventeenth-century copy of a much older drawing, shows a feature not indicated on the plan of St. Gall but most likely common to all Carolingian churches—multiple, integrated towers. The St. Gall plan shows only two towers on the west side of the church, but they stand apart from it in the manner of the Italian campaniles. If we assume a tower above the crossing, the silhouette of St. Gall would have shown three towers rising above the nave. St. Riquier had six towers (not all are shown in the illustration) built directly onto or rising from the building proper. As large, vertical, cubic and cylindrical masses, these towers rose above the horizontal roofline, balancing each other in two groups of three at each end of the basilican nave. Round stair towers on the west end provided access to the upper stories of the so-called *westwork* (entrance structure) and to the big, spired tower that balanced the similar one above the eastern crossing. Such grouping of three towers at the west, quite characteristic of churches built in the regions dominated by the Carolingians and their successors in German lands, probably foreshadows, in rudimentary form, the two-tower façades that were to become an almost universal standard in Late Romanesque and Gothic architecture. The towered westwork contained on the second floor a complete chapel flanked by aisles—a small upper church that could be used for parish services, the main floor of the building being reserved for the use of the clergy. (One must remember that this was a monastery church.) A gallery opened upon the main nave, and from it, on occasion, the emperor and his entourage could watch and participate in the service below. The plan of St. Riquier, as reconstructed (FIG. 8-13), shows an emphatic handling of the crossing square, which has been set apart from the rest of the building by massive arches. The dimensions of the square have been used once for the fore-choir, and again for the westwork chapel. But beyond that, the plan is not as fully developed as that of St. Gall. The aisles are only one third the width of the nave, the transept arms are about two thirds the crossing square, and the length of the nave has not been related to either the crossing square or any other components of the building's plan. However, the St. Riquier design, particularly the silhouette with its multiple integrated towers, was highly influential, especially in Germany.

THE OTTONIAN PERIOD

Charlemagne's empire survived him by less than thirty years. Intensified incursions of the Vikings in the west helped bring about the collapse of the Carolingians and the suspension of their great cultural effort. The breakup of the empire into numerous weak kingdoms, ineffectual against the invasions, brought a time of darkness and confusion perhaps even deeper than the seventh and eighth centuries. The scourge of the Vikings in the west was complemented by invasions of the Magyars in the east and by the plundering and piracy of the Saracen corsairs in the Mediterranean. Only in the mid-tenth century did the eastern part of the former empire consolidate under the rule of a new line of German emperors called, after the names of the three most illustrious members of the family, the Ottonians. The three Ottos made headway against the invaders from the east, remained free from Viking depredations, and were able to found an empire that, nominally at least, became the successor to Charlemagne's Holy Roman Empire. The culture and tradition of the Carolingian period were not only preserved but advanced and enriched. The Church, which had become corrupt and disorganized, recovered in the tenth century under the influence of a great monastic reform encouraged and sanctioned by the Ottonians, who also cemented ties with Italy and the papacy. When the last of the Ottonian line, Henry II, died in the

8-14 Abbey church of St. Michael at Hildesheim, Germany, *c.* 1001–31. (Restored.)

8-15 Plan and section of St. Michael's.

early eleventh century, the pagan marauders had become Christianized and settled, the monastic reforms had been highly successful, and there were signs of a cultural renewal that was destined soon to produce greater monuments than had been known since ancient Rome.

Architecture

Ottonian architects followed the direction of their Carolingian predecessors. St. Michael's, the abbey church at Hildesheim (FIG. 8-14) built between 1001 and 1031, retains the tower groupings and the westwork of St. Riquier, as well as its massive, blank walls. But the addition of a second transept and apse result in a better balancing of east and west units. The plan and section of St. Michael's (FIG. 8-15) clearly show the east and west centers of gravity, the nave being merely a hall that connects them. Lateral entrances leading into the aisles from north and south are additional factors making for an almost complete loss of the traditional basilican orientation toward the east. More refined and precise than St. Riquier, the marked-off crossing squares have now been used as a module for the dimensions of the nave, which is three crossing squares long and one square wide. This fact is emphasized visually by the placement of heavy piers at the corners of each square. These piers alternate with pairs of columns as wall supports and the result-ant "alternate-support system" will become a standard feature of many of the Romanesque churches in northern Europe. Contrary to one view, the alternate-support system is not related to the development of Romanesque systems of vaulting. It made its first appearance in timber-roofed structures of the tenth century (such as St. Cyriakus at Gernrode, begun in 961) and ap-pears to be the logical outcome of the Carolingian suggestion that the length of a building could be a multiple of the crossing square. Thus, the suitability of the alternate-support system to some Romanesque vaulting systems is only in-cidental; it seems to have been adopted not as a structural but as an esthetic device that furnishes

8-16 The nave of St. Michael's. (Restored.)

visual proof of the geometrical organization of the building's plan. It has been suggested that the alternate-support system is an importation from the Eastern Empire, perhaps from Thessalonica (modern Saloniki). If so, it seems to have been adopted enthusiastically by northern architects who, it has been lately proposed, may have seen it as an ideal means of converting un-broken basilican interiors into the modular units to which they were accustomed in their native timber architecture (see p. 315).

A view of the interior of St. Michael's (FIG. 8-16) shows the a-b-b-a rhythm of the alternating light and heavy wall supports. It shows as well that this rhythm is not yet reflected in the upper nave walls, that in fact it has not yet been carried further than the actual supports themselves. Although its proportions have changed—it has become much taller in relation to its width than a Roman basilica—the nave retains the continu-ous and unbroken appearance of its Early Chris-tian predecessors. Only when the geometric or-ganization of the church plan is fully reflected in the elevation of the nave walls and the interior space takes on the appearance of being composed of a number of vertical segments do we see a fully developed Romanesque interior.

Sculpture

St. Michael's is an important and highly refined transitional monument that fills a gap between the Carolingian and Romanesque styles. Its builder, Bishop Bernward, who made Hildesheim a center of learning, was not only skilled in affairs of state, but an eager scholar, a lover of the arts, and, according to his biographer, an expert crafts-man and bronze-caster. His stay in Rome in 1001 as guest of the emperor, Otto III, whom he had tutored and whose friend he was, must have acquainted him with monuments like the Col-umn of Trajan, which may have influenced the great columnlike paschal candlestick he set up in St. Michael's; and the Early Christian wooden doors of Santa Sabina may have inspired the remarkable bronze doors he had cast for his splendid church. The doors were cast in a single piece, the first of their kind since ancient Rome.

Carolingian sculpture, like most sculpture since antiquity, had been small art in ivory and metal; the St. Michael's doors anticipate the coming reinstatement of large-scale sculpture in the Romanesque period. The style of the figures on the doors derives from Carolingian manuscript illumination but has an expressive strength of its own—once again a case of the form derived from a prototype becoming something new and firmly itself (FIG. 8-17). God is accusing Adam and Eve after their fall from grace. As he lays upon them the curse of mortality, the primal condemnation, he jabs his finger with the force of his whole body, the force concentrating in the gesture, the psychic focus of the whole composition. The frightened pair crouch not only to hide their shame but to escape the lightning bolt of the divine wrath. Each passes the blame, Adam pointing backward to Eve, Eve pointing downward to the deceitful serpent. The setting, the starkly flat ground, throws into relief the gestures and attitudes of rage, accusation, guilt, and fear; once again the story is given with all the simplicity and impact of skilled pantomime.

We have seen how the instinct for pantomimic pose and gesture guides the representations and narratives of Medieval art from the very beginning. Such pantomime, emphasized by telling exaggeration, appears in an ivory carving that surely is among the masterpieces of the art of

the Middle Ages (FIG. 8-18). Only nine by four inches, the panel carries a composition of two intertwined figures beautifully adjusted to the space. The theme is that of the persuasion of Doubting Thomas when, after the Resurrection, Christ appears to his sorrowing disciples. All believe that he is truly Christ and truly risen except the skeptical Thomas, who demands to feel the bodily wounds of the master he has seen crucified. In the panel he explores the wound in Christ's side in a kind of climbing, aggressive curiosity. Christ, his right arm raised to reveal his side, bends over Thomas in an attitude that wonderfully combines gentleness, benign affection, protectiveness, and sorrow. The figures are represented entirely in the context of emotion; the concentration on the single act of Christ's revelation to the doubter, the emotional vibrations that accompany the doubt, and the ensuing conversion of Thomas determine every line of the rendering. We are not aware of the presence here of the influence of a prototype; we seem to have before us an original work of great power.

Painting and Illumination

It must be assumed that by Ottonian times artists had become familiar enough with the Carolingian figurative modes to work with considerable independence, developing a functional, vernacular style of their own. A supreme example of this is an illumination in the *Gospel Book of Otto III* (FIG. 8-19), in which an angel announces to the shepherds the birth of Christ. The angel has just alighted upon a hill, his wings still beating, and the wind of his landing agitates his draperies. He looms immense above the startled and terrified shepherds, filling the sky, and bends upon them a fierce and menacing glance as he

extends his hand in the gesture of authority and instruction. Emphasized more than the message itself is the power and majesty of God's authority. The electric force of God's violent pointing in the Hildesheim doors is seen again here with the same pantomimic impact. Although the figure style may ultimately stem from the Carolingian school at Tours, the painters of the scriptorium of Reichenau (an island in Lake Constance in Switzerland) who produced the *Gospel Book* have made of their received ideas something fresh and powerful; there is a new sureness in the touch that is epitomized by the way the draperies are rendered in a hard, firm line, the planes partitioned in sharp, often heavily modeled shapes. We saw this in Middle and Late Byzantine art, and indeed there was close connection between the Ottonian and Byzantine spheres. Yet, for the most part, the Ottonian artists went their own way, for Ottonian painting was produced for the court and for the great monasteries, for learned princes, abbots, and bishops, and thus had an aristocratic audience that could appreciate independent and sophisticated variations on inherited themes. While an illumination like the *Annunciation to the Shepherds* could by no means be called classical, there is a sculpturesque clarity about it, a strong, relieflike projection and silhouette, that suggests not a hesitating approximation of misunderstood prototypes from antiquity but a confident, if unconscious, catching of the antique spirit. At the same time, the powerful means of expression of the *Annunciation* miniature imply an intensification of Christian spirituality, perhaps related to the broad monastic reforms of the tenth and eleventh centuries. With that force of expression goes a significantly new manner of fashioning the human figure in art, one that is not slavishly dependent upon prototypes, even while prototypes are exchanged and studied. Ottonian figurative art reveals a translation of prototypal material into a kind of ready idiom of forms and a native way of drawing. Although there are exceptions, for the most part Ottonian figures will have lost the old realism of the *Coronation Gospels* (FIG. 8-5), inherited from the antique, and will move with an abrupt, hinged, jerky movement not "according to nature" but nevertheless with sharp and descriptive expressiveness.

8-18 ECHTERNACH MASTER, *Doubting Thomas*, from the *Magdeburg Antependium*, c. 970–90. Ivory, approx. 9″ × 4″. Staatliche Museen, Berlin.

This new manner will be passed on to the figurative artists of the Romanesque period. As the western European spoken and written languages emerge from the polyglot Latin-Germanic of the early centuries into the vernacular tongues we recognize today, so figurative art gradually develops out of the same kind of mixture of Latin, Germanic, and Celtic elements into a new, strong, and self-sufficient vernacular of representation.

Another picture from the *Gospel Book of Otto III*, representing the emperor himself (FIG. 8-20), sums up much of what went before and points to what is coming. The emperor is represented enthroned under a canopy (the *baldachin*), holding the scepter and cross-inscribed orb that represent his universal authority. He is flanked by the clergy and the barons—the Church and the State—both aligned in his support. Stylistically remote, the picture still has a clear political resemblance to the Justinianic mosaic in San Vitale. It was the vestigial imperial ideal, awakened in the Frankish Charlemagne and preserved for a while by his Ottonian successors in Germany, that had given some partial unity to western Europe while the barbarians were settling down. This imperial ideal, salvaged from ancient Rome and bolstered by the experience of Byzantium, would survive long enough to give an example of order and of law to the barbarians; to this extent, ancient Rome lived on to the millennium. But native princes in England, France, Spain, Italy, and eastern Europe would aspire to a sovereignty outside the imperial Carolingian and Ottonian hegemony; staking their claims, they make the history of the Medieval power contests that lead to the formation of the states of Europe as we know them. In the illumination, Otto, sitting between the rival Church and State, represents the very model of the Medieval predicament that will divide Europe for centuries. The controversy of the Holy Roman Emperors with the popes will bring the German successors of the Ottonians to bitter defeat in the thirteenth century; and with that defeat, the authority of ancient Rome will come to an end. The Romanesque period that is to follow will in fact deny the imperial spirit that had prevailed for centuries. A new age is about to begin, and Rome, an august memory, will cease to be the deciding influence.

8-19 Above: *The Annunciation to the Shepherds*, from the *Gospel Book of Otto III*, Reichenau or Court School of Otto III, 997–1000. 13″ × 9⅜″. Bayerische Staatsbibliothek, Munich.

8-20 *Otto III Enthroned Receiving the Homage of Four Parts of the Empire* (flanked by nobility and clergy), from the *Gospel Book of Otto III*. 13″ × 9⅜″. Bayerische Staatsbibliothek, Munich.

Chapter Nine

Romanesque Art

EUROPE ABOUT 1100

NORMAN KINGDOM

KINGDOM OF FRANCE

HOLY ROMAN EMPIRE

LEON-CASTILE

ARAGON

MOSLEM DOMINIONS

NORMAN KINGDOM

0 200 400 miles

❶ Durham	⓯ Arles
❷ Caen	⓰ Roncesvalles
❸ Jumièges	⓱ Tahull
❹ Cologne	⓲ Burgos
❺ Mainz	⓳ Santiago de Compostela
❻ Worms	⓴ Cordova
❼ Speyer	㉑ Milan
❽ Paris	㉒ Venice
❾ Vézelay	㉓ Pisa
❿ Autun	㉔ Florence
⓫ Cluny	㉕ Rome
⓬ Angoulême	㉖ Naples
⓭ Moissac	㉗ Palermo
⓮ Toulouse	

—— Principal pilgrimage routes

THE MID-ELEVENTH century marks a turning point in European history; Europe *as* Europe begins to emerge. In the past there was a boiling confusion of barbarian movements coalescing into settlements that aggregated into "empires" like the Carolingian and Ottonian, which had their spiritual and political roots in the memory of the Roman *imperium*. Now, although a Latin culture and tradition persist and are still accepted with reverence, the Medieval people are not so retrospective; they have new experiences and take new directions.

After the disintegration of the Carolingian state, when the successors to the imperializing Ottonians had begun to limit their concerns to Italy and the German duchies, numerous feudal political entities—petty and great, within and without the outlines of the old Frankish and Saxon "empires"—pursued their own interests and developed in their own ways. Two institutions gave them a certain coherence—the Christian Church and feudalism. If the descendants of the barbarians had anything in common, it was their Christianity above all else. Feudalism, which had

c. 1000

Pisa Cathedral (1053-1272)

Speyer Cathedral (1030)

1030

——— ROMANESQUE PERIOD ———

1060

——— NORMAN CONQUEST OF SOUTH ITALY AND SICILY ———

1066 Norman conquest of England (battle of Hastings)

1071 Turkish conquest of Jerusalem

St. George and the Dragon from the *Moralia in Job*

Durham Cathedral (1093)

1090

1101

1095 First Crusade

The Scribe Eadwine from the *Eadwine Psalter*

1120

The Mission of the Apostles, Vézelay (1120-1132)

1147 Second Crusade

c. 1150

its origins both in barbarian custom (see Chapter Eight) and in late Roman institutions, preserved a stability, but it was a stability of a local kind, being naturally antagonistic to broad, centralized government.

Essentially, feudalism was an economic system involving a complicated series of interpersonal relations, obligations, and services based on land tenure: One held a piece of land, a *fief*, and paid for it not in money but in service, often military. Feudal obligation led downward from a lord to his vassal to the lower orders of society and ultimately to the serf, who was bound to the land and to the unquestioning service of the lord. The lords or nobles held fiefs in various ways from each other or from an overlord, such as a king. Inevitably many of them became large landowners and so powerful that they ignored their obligations and defied their king. Their time was spent in petty wars to protect or to increase the extent of their holdings. The *château fort*, or castle, surrounded by walls and moats, was the symbol and seat of feudal authority; today the moldering ruins of these castles in the countrysides of Europe recall the modern visitor to an age when government was always visible, singular, personal, and absolute.

The Romanesque baron or knight, still in the heroic tradition of the Germanic hero, was loyal, defiant, and proud. However, being a Christian, he was without the deep barbarian fatalism of the earlier Saxons and Norse and hoped not only for immortal honor in battle (won as much by the power of religious faith as by his own strength and courage), but for life eternal in heaven. This was the mood—the psychological "set"—of the aristocratic, warring magnates who led the crusades and maintained the feudal system.

Monasticism, which reached its peak at the same time as feudalism, provided seclusion from the world, an assurance of salvation, and almost the only means of receiving an education. The history of monasticism, which, as we have seen, began in the Early Middle Ages, is essentially a series of reform movements. Since gifts and bequests to them were potent means of assuring salvation, monasteries grew wealthy. With wealth came luxury and laxness and recurrent reforms to combat them. The reforms led to the formation of new monastic orders. The two great Romanesque orders were the Cluniac and the Cistercian. The former, which especially fostered the arts, was founded early in the tenth century and had its main abbey at Cluny near Mâcon in France. Encouraged by the Ottonian emperors, it owed allegiance only to the pope in Rome and formed, with the vast number of its priories scattered all over Europe, a centrally organized administration in sharp contrast to the decentralizing tendencies of feudalism. The Cluniac reform, based on a liberal interpretation of St. Benedict's original rule, stressed intellectual pursuits, the study of music, and the cultivation of the other arts. The wealth and the vastness of the resources of the Cluniac order soon provoked still another reform, one that emphasized self-denial and the virtues of manual labor and gave rise to the Cistercian order, which also grew rapidly.

Thus, with feudalism and monasticism triumphant and replacing the emperors, the barons and the monastery clergy—the latter often themselves feudal lords—played a peculiarly cooperative role, and the feudal stratification of society into strictly separated classes was given religious sanction. Notwithstanding this cooperation, however, the chief conflict of the time was between the popes and the feudal principals not over the justice or injustice of the feudal system but over the question, Who is the supreme feudal lord; who is king?

There was great movement of population in the endless pilgrimages to innumerable shrines and in the Crusades (the first two of which belong to this period), which saw treks of thousands of people from western Europe to the Holy Land. Most important of the immediate results of the Crusades were the establishment of the Church as a leader of the people and the reopening of commerce with the great trading centers in the Near East.

Pisan ships carried the crusading barons to the Holy Land and brought back their bones. The Pisans prospered, as did the burghers of the towns that the barons left behind them and to whom they had given charters of liberty in return for financing their campaigns. Thus, the Crusades created subcurrents of independence: The towns got their charters, and a middle class of merchants and craftsmen grew up to countervail the power of feudal barons and the great monasteries. A growing city culture was quick to receive new impulses from abroad. The lines of commerce, often the arteries of ideas, conveyed new learning to Europe. The Crusades, destructive as they were, effected a new insight into Greek science and philosophy through contact with Islam, which had assimilated the Greek culture much earlier. Within a century, the relatively limited knowledge possessed by the Carolingians and Ottonians was expanded to an enormous store. It was from this store that men would draw the materials and inspirations for renaissance after renaissance until, in the sixteenth century, a distinction would come to be made between pagan and Christian antiquity. Within this context of an emerging world, unique though shadowed with a tremendous past, the art called Romanesque appeared. It is a confident art, one that does not hesitate among alternatives and is sure even in the midst of its own changes.

ARCHITECTURE

"Romanesque" is a term first used in the nineteenth century to designate buildings that were supposed to be developing toward a perfected thirteenth-century type called "Gothic." Their round arches and blunt, heavy walls were supposed to bear some resemblance to ancient Roman architecture, just as the developing "Romance" languages were related to Latin. Although the Romanesque style varies widely and embraces numerous provincial differences within its two-century span, architectural historians now regard it as complete within itself and not as the imperfect antecedent of Gothic. Thus, despite its variety, Romanesque architecture is readily recognizable as such and is the first architecture truly of the Middle Ages. An air view of the church of St. Sernin at Toulouse in the south of France (FIG. 9-1) shows certain features that appear in Romanesque buildings no matter how their arrangement differs. There is an overall blocky appearance, a grouping of large, simple, easily definable geometrical masses—rectangles, cubes, cylinders, and half-cylinders. The main masses are sub-divided by enframing buttresses or colonnettes. Exterior wall surfaces, which had been plain and unadorned through the Ottonian period, now reflect the interior organization of the structure. This enlivening of formerly blank wall surfaces foreshadows the structural translucency that was to typify Gothic architecture.

The new demands of a people with religious as well as commercial reasons to travel shaped the new architecture. The building impulse, which became almost a Medieval obsession, was noted by an eleventh-century monk, Raoul Glaber, who wrote:

> ... there occurred, throughout the world, especially in Italy and Gaul, a rebuilding of church basilicas. Notwithstanding the greater number were already well established and not in the least in need, nevertheless each Christian people strove against the others to erect nobler ones. It was as if the whole earth, having cast off the old ... were clothing itself everywhere in the white robe of the church.[1]

Great building efforts were provoked not only by the pilgrimages and the Crusades and the needs of growing cities, but by the fact (notably in Italy and France) that hundreds of churches had been destroyed during the depredations of the Northmen and the Magyars. Architects of the time seemed to see their fundamental problem in terms of providing a building that would have space for the circulation of its congregations and visitors and would be solid, fireproof, and well lighted. These, of course, are the necessities of any great civic or religious architecture, as we saw in ancient Rome, but in this case fireproofing must have been foremost in the builders' minds, for the wooden roofs of the pre-Romanesque churches of Italy, France, and elsewhere had burned fiercely and totally when set aflame by the marauders from north, east, and south in the ninth and tenth centuries. The memory was fresh in the victims' minds; the new churches would have to be covered with cut stone, and the structural problems arising from this need for a solid masonry were to help determine the "look" of Romanesque architecture.

[1] In E. G. Holt, ed., *Literary Sources of Art History* (Princeton: Princeton Univ. Press, 1947), p. 3.

9-1 Aerial view of St. Sernin, Toulouse, *c.* 1080–1120.

9-2 Plan of St. Sernin.

FEET
0   25   50

The Cluniac-Burgundian Style

St. Sernin was one of the churches constructed in the Cluniac-Burgundian style, that met the requirement for a stone ceiling by the use of a semicircular barrel vault above which was a timber-roofed loft. These churches dominated much of southern France and were closely related to those built along the pilgrimage road to Santiago de Compostela in northwest Spain. The plan of St. Sernin (FIG. 9-2) is of extreme regularity and geometric precision. The crossing square, flanked by massive piers and marked off by heavy arches, has been used as the module for the entire body of the church. In this *square schematism* each nave bay measures exactly one half and each square in the aisles one quarter of a crossing square, and so on throughout the building. The first suggestion of such a planning scheme is seen almost three centuries earlier in the St. Gall plan. Although St. Sernin is neither the earliest nor the only (perhaps not even the ideal) solution, it does represent a crisply rational and highly refined realization of the germ of an idea first seen in Carolingian designs. A view of the interior (FIG. 9-3) shows that this geometric floor plan is fully reflected in the nave walls, which are articulated by half-columns that rise from the corners of each bay to the springing of the vault and are continued across the nave as transverse arches. Ever since Early Christian times, basilican interiors had been framed by long, flat walls between arcades and clerestories that enclosed a single, horizontal, unbroken volume of space. Now the aspect of the nave is radically changed so that it seems to be composed of numerous, identical, vertical volumes of space that have been placed one behind the other, marching down the length of the building in orderly procession. This segmentation of St. Sernin's interior space corresponds with and renders visual the geometric organization of the building's plan, and as noted above, is also reflected in the articulation of the building's exterior walls. The result is a structure in which all parts have been integrated to a degree unknown in earlier Christian architecture, a structure that is a full-blown representative of the first genuinely Medieval architectural style—the Romanesque.

The grand scale of St. Sernin at Toulouse is frequent in Romanesque churches. The popularity of pilgrimages and of the cult of relics brought great crowds even to relatively isolated places, and large congregations were common at the shrines along the great pilgrimage routes and in the reawakening cities. Additional space was provided by increasing the length of the nave, by doubling the side aisles, and by building, over the inner aisle, upper galleries, or *tribunes*, the latter for overflow crowds on special occasions. Circulation was complicated, though, since the monks' choir often occupied a good portion of the nave. The extension of the aisles around the eastern end to make an ambulatory facilitated circulation, and the opening of the ambulatory (and often the transepts) into separate chapels (as at St. Sernin) provided more space for worshipers and for liturgical processions. Not all Romanesque churches were as large as St. Sernin, however, nor did every one have an ambulatory with radiating chapels, but such chapels are typical Romanesque features, especially when treated as separate units projecting from the mass of the building.

The continuous, cut-stone barrel (or tunnel)

9-3 The nave of St. Sernin.

vaults at St. Sernin (FIG. 9-3) put constant pressure along the entire length of the supporting masonry. If, as in most instances, including St. Sernin (FIG. 9-2), the nave was flanked by side aisles, the main vaults rested on arcades, the thrust being carried to the thick outer walls by the vaults that were over the aisles. In larger churches the tribune galleries and their vaults (in cross section, often a quadrant, embracing a 90-degree arc), were an integral part of the structure, buttressing the high vaults over the nave. The wall-vault system at St. Sernin is successful in its supporting function; its great scale provides ample space, and its squaring-off into cleanly marked bays, as well as the relief of wall and pier, are thoroughly Romanesque. But the system fails in one critical requirement—that of lighting: Because of the great thrust exerted by the barrel vault a clerestory was impossible, and windows cut into the haunch of the vault would make it unstable.

9-4 Speyer Cathedral, Germany, begun 1030. Pen-and-ink drawing by Wenzel Hollar, *c.* 1620. Graphische Sammlung Albertina, Vienna.

9-5 Plan of Speyer Cathedral.

A more complex and efficient type of vaulting was needed; one might say that, structurally, the central problem of Romanesque architecture was the development of a masonry vault system that admitted light.

Romanesque architectural ingenuity in working toward this end had numerous experimental consequences that appear as a rich variety of substyles. We have already mentioned that one of the apparently confusing features of Romanesque architecture is the great variety of regional and local building styles, a variety that makes classification, coordination, and interpretation still very difficult for scholars. Ten or more types may be identified in France alone, each with its distinctive system of vaulting and its varying solutions to the lighting of the interior. To the informed student of Romanesque architecture, savoring the distinctive beauties of its local styles is somewhat like sampling the endless varieties of local wines.

Among the numerous experimental solutions, the groin vault turned out to be the most efficient and flexible. The groin vault had been widely used by Roman builders, who saw that its concentration of thrusts at four supporting points would allow clerestory fenestration. The great Roman vaults were made possible by an intricate system of brick-and-tile relieving arches as well as by the use of concrete, which could be poured into forms and which solidified into a homogeneous mass. The technique of mixing concrete did not survive into the Middle Ages, however, and the technical problems of building groin vaults of cut stone and heavy rubble, which had very little cohesive quality, limited their use to the

9-6 Interior of Speyer Cathedral.

covering of small areas. But during the eleventh century, Romanesque masons, using cut stone joined by mortar, developed a groin vault of monumental dimensions, which, while still using heavy buttressing walls, eventually evolved into a self-sufficient skeletal support system.

Germany-Lombardy

The progress of vaulting craft can best be seen in two regions, Germany-Lombardy and Normandy-Britain. The cathedral of Speyer in the German Rhineland (FIG. 9-4) was begun in 1030 as a timber-roofed structure. When it was rebuilt by the emperor Henry IV between 1082 and 1106, it was covered with groin vaults. It thus may be one of the earliest fully vaulted Romanesque churches in Europe. Its exterior preserves the Ottonian tradition of balanced groups of towers east and west but adds to it a rich articulation of wall surfaces. A great many of the decorative features, such as the arcades under the eaves, the stepped arcade gallery under the gable, and the moldings marking the stages of the towers, may be of Lombard origin. So may be the inspiration for the groin vaults covering the aisles, since groin-vaulting on a small scale had been used by Lombard builders throughout the Early Middle Ages. The large groin vaults covering the nave (FIG. 9-6), however, probably the achievement of German masons, represent one of the most daring and successful vaulting enterprises of the time. (The nave is 45 feet wide, and the crowns of the vaults 107 feet high.) The plan (FIG. 9-5) shows that the west apse and the Ottonian lateral entrances have been given up, that the entrance has been moved back to the west end, and that the processional axis leading to the sanctuary has been reestablished. The marked-off crossing, covered by an octagonal dome, has obviously been used as the module for the arrangement of the building's east end. Since the nave bays are not square, use of the crossing as a unit is not so obvious. In fact, however, the length of the nave

9-7 Reconstruction of the original nave of Speyer Cathedral, c. 1030–60.

9-8 Right: Sant' Ambrogio, Milan, late eleventh to early twelfth centuries.

9-9 Below: Plan of Sant' Ambrogio.

is almost exactly four times the crossing square, and every third wall-support marks off an area in the nave the size of the crossing; the aisles are half the width of the nave. Although the plan has some irregularities and has not been worked out as neatly and precisely as that of St. Sernin, the builders' intention to apply the square schematism is quite clear. Curiously, the alternate-support system, which is now carried all the way up into the vaults (FIG. 9-6), seems to be unrelated to the geometric facts of the plan. This discrepancy may be explained by the fact that the original building of 1030 was a timber-roofed structure and that the walls were articulated by a series of identical shafts that rose to enframe the

clerestory windows (FIG. 9-7). The alternate-support system was introduced in the 1080's (when the building was vaulted) perhaps partially to strengthen the piers at the corners of the large vaults and to provide bases for the springing of the transverse arches across the nave. That every other support was chosen to anchor a nave vault may simply have been because the walls were not as stable as the massive piers that carry the crossing dome, so that it would be safer to reduce each area to be vaulted by one third. The resultant bay arrangement, in which a large unit in the nave is flanked by two small units in each aisle, becomes almost standard in northern Romanesque architecture. Speyer's interior (FIG. 9-6) shows the same striving for height and has the same compartmentalized effect as that of St. Sernin. By virtue of the use of the alternate-support system, the rhythm of the Speyer nave is a little more complex, a little richer perhaps, and since each compartment is individually vaulted, the effect of a sequence of vertical blocks of space is even more convincing.

From Carolingian times, Rhineland Germany and Lombardy had been in close political and

9-10 Interior of Sant' Ambrogio.

cultural contact, and it is generally agreed that the two areas cross-fertilized each other artistically. But no such agreement exists as to which source of artistic influence was dominant—the northern or the southern. The question, no doubt, will remain the subject of controversy until the date of the central monument of Lombard architecture—the church of Sant' Ambrogio in Milan—can be established unequivocally. Dates ranging from the tenth to the early twelfth century have been advanced for the present building (preceded by an earlier church that dated back to the fourth century), with the late eleventh and early twelfth centuries apparently most popular with architectural historians today. Whether or not a prototype, Sant' Ambrogio remains a remarkable building. As shown in FIG. 9-8, it has an atrium (one of the last to be built); a two-story narthex pierced by arches on both levels; two towers joined to the building; and, over the east end of the nave, an octagonal tower that recalls the crossing towers of German churches. Of the façade towers, the shorter one dates back to the tenth century, while the taller north tower was built during the

twelfth. The latter is a sophisticated and typical example of Lombard tower design; it is articulated by pilasters and shafting and divided, by means of corbel tables (horizontal projections resting on corbels), into a number of levels, of which only the topmost (the bell chamber) has been opened by arches. In plan (FIG. 9-9) Sant' Ambrogio is three-aisled and without a transept. The square schematism has been applied with consistency and greater precision than at Speyer, each bay consisting of a full square in the nave, which is flanked by two small squares in each aisle, all covered with groin vaults. The main vaults are slightly domical, rising higher than the transverse arches, and the last bay is covered by an octagonal dome that provides the major light source (there is no clerestory) for the otherwise rather dark interior (FIG. 9-10). The geometric regularity of the plan is perfectly reflected in the emphatic alternate-support system, in which the light supports are interrupted at the gallery level while the heavy ones rise to support the main vaults. These ponderous vaults have supporting arches along their groins and are sometimes claimed to be the first examples of rib-vaulting (see p. 359); in fact, however, these vaults are solidly constructed groin vaults that have been strengthened by diagonal ribs.

The dating of the Sant' Ambrogio vaults remains controversial. Most scholars seem to feel that they were not built until after 1117, when a severe earthquake caused great damage to the existing building. If so, the Speyer vaults would be earlier than those of Sant' Ambrogio, and the inspiration and technical knowledge for the construction of groin vaults of this size would seem, then, to have come from the north. But such possible influence did not affect the proportioning of the Milanese building, which does not aspire to the soaring height of the northern churches. Sant' Ambrogio's proportions are low and squat and remain close to those of Early Christian basilicas. As we will see, Italian architects never—not even during the height of the Gothic period—accepted the verticality found in northern architecture.

The fame of German architecture rests on its achievements in the eleventh and early twelfth centuries. After the mid-twelfth century it made no major contribution to architectural design. The architectural statements at Speyer were repeated at Worms and Mainz and other, later churches. German builders were content with refining their successful formula; beyond that, they tended to follow the lead of the more adventurous and progressive Franks and Normans.

The Norman Style

The predatory pagan Vikings settled in northwest France after their conversion to Christianity in the tenth century and almost at once proved themselves skilled administrators and builders. With astounding rapidity they absorbed the lessons to be learned from Ottonian architecture and went on to develop the most progressive of the many Romanesque styles and the one that was to become the major source in the evolution of Gothic architecture. The church of St. Étienne at Caen in Normandy is generally considered to be the master model of Norman Romanesque architecture. It was begun by William the Conqueror in 1067 and must have been completed when he was buried there in 1087. The west façade (FIG. 9-11) is a striking design that looks forward to the two-tower façades of later Gothic churches. Four large buttresses divide it into three bays that correspond to the nave and aisles in the interior. There is also a triple division of the towers above their buttresses and a progressively greater piercing of their walls from lower to upper stages. The spires are a later (Gothic) feature. The tripartite division is employed throughout the façade, both vertically and horizontally, organizing it into a close-knit, well-integrated design that reflects the careful and methodical planning of the entire structure. Like the cathedral of Speyer, St. Étienne was originally planned to have a wooden roof, but from the beginning the walls were articulated in an alternating rhythm

9-11 West façade of St. Étienne, Caen, begun c. 1067.

(simple half-columns alternating with shafts attached to pilasters) that mirrors the precise square schematism of the building's plan (FIGS. 9-12 and 9-13). This alternate-support system was effectively utilized some time after 1110—significantly later than Speyer or Milan—when it was decided to cover the nave with vaults. Its original installation, however, must have been motivated by esthetic rather than structural concerns. In any event, the alternating compound piers soar all the way to the springing of the vaults, and their branching ribs divide the large, square vault compartments into six sections, making a so-called sexpartite vault (FIG. 9-12). These vaults, their crowns slightly depressed to avoid the "domed-up" effect of those at Sant' Ambrogio, rise high enough to make an efficient clerestory; they are also viewed as some of the earliest true *rib vaults*, in which the diagonal and transverse ribs compose a structural skeleton that partially supports the as yet fairly massive paneling between them. Rib-vaulting was to become universal practice during the Gothic period, and its development by Norman builders must be rated as one of the major structural innovations of the Middle Ages. There are other elements in St. Étienne that point to the future: the complex piers, their nuclei almost concealed by attached pilasters and engaged columns, forecast the Gothic "cluster-pier"; and the reduction in interior wall surfaces that resulted from use of very large arched openings anticipate the bright curtain walls of Gothic architecture. In short, St. Étienne at Caen is not only a very carefully designed structure but a highly progressive one in which the Romanesque style begins to merge into the Early Gothic.

The conquest of Anglo-Saxon England in 1066 by William of Normandy began a new epoch in English history; in English architecture it signaled the importation of Norman building and design methods. The cathedral of Durham in northern England, begun in 1093, was apparently designed for vaulting at the outset. As with most Romanesque churches in England, it was subjected to many later alterations that, in this case, fortunately were largely confined to the exterior; the interior (FIG. 9-14) has its original, masculine, Romanesque appearance. Ambitious in scale—

9-12 Interior of St. Étienne, vaulted c. 1115–20.

9-13 Plan of St. Étienne.

wider and longer than either St. Sernin at Toulouse or St. Étienne at Caen—its 400-foot length compares favorably with that of the great imperial cathedral of Speyer. With the latter it also shares its reliance upon mass for stability. But unlike Speyer, this building was conceived from the very beginning as a completely integrated skeleton in which the vaults stood in intimate and continuous relation to the vertical elements of

9-14 The nave of Durham Cathedral, England, begun
c. 1093 (view facing east).

9-15 Plan of Durham Cathedral.

FEET
0 25 50

Addition

the compound piers that support them. At
Durham the alternate-support system is interpreted with blunt power and more emphasis,
perhaps, than in any other Romanesque church.
Large, simple pillars ornamented with abstract
designs—diamond, chevron, and cable patterns
descended from the metalcraft ornamentation of
the migrations—alternate with compound piers
that carry the transverse arches of the vaults. The
pier-vault relationship could scarcely be more
visible or the structural rationale of the building
better expressed. The plan (FIG. 9-15), typically
English in its long, slender proportions and the
strongly projecting transept, does not develop
the square schematism with the same care and
logic as that of Caen. But the rib vaults of the
choir (1104) are the earliest in Europe, and, when
they were combined with slightly pointed arches
in the western parts of the nave (before 1130), the
two key elements that were to determine the
structural evolution of Gothic architecture were
brought together for the first time. Only the
rather massive construction and the irregular
division into seven panels prevent these vaults
from qualifying as Early Gothic structures.

Among the numerous regional Romanesque
styles of architecture it is the northern—more
specifically, the Norman—style that will influence the development of the Gothic; no other
style had as great a potential for evolution.

Tuscany

Italy south of the Lombard region retained its
ancient traditions and for the most part produced
a conservative Romanesque architecture. The
buildings of Tuscany seem to adhere more closely
than those of any other region to the traditions of
the Early Christian basilica. The cathedral group
of Pisa (FIG. 9-16) manifests, in addition to these
conservative qualities, those of the great classical
"renaissance" of the late eleventh and twelfth centuries, when architects, craftsmen, poets, and
philosophers again confronted classical-Christian
prototypes and interpreted them in an original
yet familiar way. The cathedral is large, five-aisled
and one of the most impressive and majestic of all
Romanesque churches. At first glance, it resem-

bles an Early Christian basilica, but the broadly projecting transept, the dome over the crossing, the rich marble incrustation, and the multiple arcade galleries of the façade soon distinguish it as Romanesque. The interior (FIG. 9-17) also at first suggests the basilica, with its timber roof rather than vault (originally the rafters were exposed as in Early Christian basilicas), nave arcades, and classical (imported) columns flanking the nave in unbroken procession. Above these columns is a continuous, horizontal molding on which rest the gallery arcades. The gallery, of course, is not a basilican feature but is of Byzantine origin. There are other divergences from the basilica, such as the relatively great verticality and, at the crossing, the markedly unclassical pointed arch, which was probably inspired by Islamic architecture. The striped incrustation, produced by alternating dark green and cream-colored marble, provides a luxurious polychromy, which becomes a hallmark of Tuscan Romanesque and Gothic buildings. The leaning campanile, the result of a settling foundation, tilted from the vertical even while it was being built and now inclines some sixteen perilous feet out of plumb at the top. Round, like the Ravenna campaniles, it is much more elaborate, and its stages are marked by graceful, arcaded galleries that repeat the motif of the cathedral's façade and effectively relate the tower to its mother building. Although the baptistry, with its partly remodeled Gothic exterior, may strike a slightly discordant note, the whole composition of the three buildings, with the adjacent Campo Santo (cemetery), makes one of the handsomest ensembles in the history of architecture and expresses dramatically the new building age that was made possible by the prosperity enjoyed by the busy maritime cities of the Mediterranean.

Another Tuscan church, San Miniato al Monte (FIG. 9-18) in Florence, conservatively recalls Early Christian architecture, although the wall arcading and its elaborate, geometrical incrustation in colored marbles make for a rich ornamental effect foreign to the austere exteriors of the earlier buildings. Conservative as San Miniato may appear externally, the interior (FIG. 9-19) is another matter. Though the church is timber-roofed, as are most Tuscan Romanesque churches, the nave is divided into three equal

9-16 Aerial view of the cathedral group of Pisa (baptistry, cathedral, and campanile), 1053–1272.

9-17 The nave of the cathedral of Pisa.

9-18 San Miniato al Monte, Florence, completed *c.* 1062.

compartments by *diaphragm arches* that rise from compound piers. The piers alternate with simple columns in a–b–b–a rhythm that recalls St. Michael's in Hildesheim. The diaphragm arches, which appear here for the first time (before 1060), had multiple functional and esthetic purposes: They braced the rather high, thin walls; they provided fire-breaks within the wooden roof structure; and they compartmentalized the basilican interior in the manner so popular with most Romanesque builders. Antique, or neo-Antique, motifs appear in the capitals as well as in the incrustation, expressing again the persistence of the classical tradition in Tuscany.

Aquitania

Influences criss-crossed in Romanesque architecture, helping to diversify it and creating exotic hybrids. In the region of Aquitania in southwest France, for instance, it became customary to roof the churches with domes, reflecting the

9-19 Interior of San Miniato al Monte.

c. 1000	1030	1053	**1060** 1066	c.1080	1095–99 **1101**	c.1120	1147 c.1150
	Speyer Cathedral begun	Pisa Cathedral group begun	Norman conquest of England	St. Sernin begun	First Crusade	*Mission of the Apostles*, Vézelay	Second Crusade

R O M A N E S Q U E   P E R I O D

NORMAN CONQUEST OF
SOUTHERN ITALY AND SICILY

influence of Byzantium or Armenia. Curiously, most of these Aquitanian churches mate the dome with a longitudinal plan to which, at first glance, it seems ill suited. In the typical Aquitanian church, a longitudinal, aisle-less nave is covered by a sequence of domes, which, in turn, are usually covered by a pitched wooden roof. The result turns out to be highly practical, as the pendentive-supported domes require much less buttressing than, for instance, continuous barrel vaults. Also, the system automatically produces the cherished compartmentalized effect mentioned above. Although they never aimed at the soaring height of northern Romanesque structures, these Aquitanian domed churches not only represent an almost perfect fusion of geometric plan with elevation, but also are visually most effective, clearly exhibiting the functions of all their structural parts (FIG. 9-20).

From about 1050 on, the old dependence of the pre-Romanesque—Carolingian and Ottonian—upon Late Antique and Early Christian design concepts fades gradually, though never completely. Romanesque architecture develops a number of clear characteristics: the square schematism, the alternating-support system, and the increased relief and depth of walls and piers as they connect with the vaults above. The Romanesque architect conceives a building in terms of the geometric relation of its parts, a view basically different from that of the Early Christian architect, who never thought of large units as related geometrically and who thought of the wall not as essentially a structural element, but as a surface to receive applied decoration.

SCULPTURE

The first definite relation of architecture and sculpture appears in the Romanesque style. Figurative sculpture, confined for centuries to small art, flowers again in the new Romanesque churches of the mid-eleventh century. The rich profusion of sculpture and something of its nature may be guessed from Bernard of Clairveaux's famous tirade against it, written in 1127:

I say naught of the vast height of your churches, their immoderate length, their superfluous breadth, the costly polishings, the curious carvings and paintings.... [Men's] eyes are feasted with relics cased in gold, and their purse-strings are loosed. They are shown a most comely image of some saint, whom they think all the more saintly that he is the more gaudily painted. Men run to kiss him, and are invited to give; there is more admiration for his comeliness than veneration for his sanctity. Hence the church is adorned with gemmed crowns of light....candelabra standing like trees of massive bronze, fashioned with marvellous subtlety of art, and glistening no less bright-

9-20 Interior of St. Pierre, Angoulême, twelfth century.

ly with gems than with the lights they carry. . . .
O vanity of vanities, yet no more vain than insane!
The church is resplendent in her walls, beggarly
in her poor; she clothes her stones in gold and
leaves her sons naked . . . . in the cloister, under
the eyes of the Brethren who read there, what
profit is there in those ridiculous monsters, in that
marvellous and deformed comeliness, that comely
deformity? To what purpose are those unclean
apes, those fierce lions, those monstrous centaurs,
those half-men, those striped tigers, those fighting
knights, those hunters winding their horns?
Many bodies are there seen under one head, or
again, many heads to a single body. . . . For God's
sake, if men are not ashamed of these follies,
why at least do they not shrink from the expense?[2]

As we have noted, stone sculpture had almost
disappeared from the art of western Europe
during the eighth and ninth centuries. The revival of the technique is one of the most important Romanesque achievements. As stone buildings began to rise again, so did the impulse to
decorate parts of the structure with relief carving
in stone. It was to be expected that the artists
should turn for inspiration to surviving Roman
sculpture and to sculptural forms such as ivory
carving or metalwork; it is obvious that they
also relied upon painted figures in manuscripts.
But these Romanesque artists developed their
own attitude toward ornamental design and its
relation to architecture. At first this relation was
somewhat random and haphazard; one placed
the sculpture wherever there seemed to be a
convenient place. A little later, the portals of the
church seemed the appropriate setting, both for
religious reasons and for the practical matter of
display. As Romanesque sculpture turns into
Gothic the statuary of the portals becomes integrated with the design of the whole façade,
following the lines of the architecture. An example of the earlier, random placement is a
figure of Christ in majesty, set into the wall of
the ambulatory of St. Sernin at Toulouse (FIG.
9-21). It clearly shows that its source is some prototype made of metal, perhaps a book cover like
that of the Codex Aureus of St. Emmeram
(PLATE 8-3). The figure has the bulge of metal
hammered out from behind, as in the *repoussé*
method, and even here in stone one senses the
gloss of smooth metal. The signs of the Evangelists at the four corners square off the book-cover-
like design and remind one of the corner screws
that fix the plate to the book. As yet there is no
relation between the relief and its architectural
setting: it is "portable," like a work of craft art,
and could find its place on any wall. In the later
mode the architectural limits of the parts of a
portal or the shape of a capital were respected
as frames to which the sculptors accommodated

[2] *Ibid.*, pp. 17–18.

9-21 *Christ in Majesty*, late eleventh century, from the ambulatory of St. Sernin, Toulouse.

9-22 Tympanum of the south portal of St. Pierre, Moissac, *c.* 1115–35.

their work. A typical Romanesque portal can be seen in the façade of St. Trophime at Arles in the south of France (FIG. 9-27). Architectural elements of such a portal are: jambs, lintel, semicircular tympanum (beneath the arches or archivolts) and in some instances a pier, or *trumeau*, in the middle of the doorway.

The stirring of the peoples in Romanesque Europe, the Crusades, the pilgrimages, and the commercial journeyings brought a slow realization that Europeans were of the same religion, even if of different ethnic stock. The reception of hitherto unknown documents of Greek thought and learning strongly influenced theology, bringing to it, along with new and deep challenges, a kind of order and concentration. There can be little doubt that theologians dictated the subjects of the Romanesque portals; it was just as important to have the right subjects carved

in the right places as to have the right arguments rightly arranged in a theological treatise. The apocalyptic vision of the Last Judgment, appalling to the imagination of twelfth-century man, was represented conspicuously at the western entrance portal as an inescapable reminder to all who entered.

The semicircular tympanum of the portal of Moissac shows the Second Coming of Christ as King and Judge of the World (FIG. 9-22). As befits his majesty, Christ is centrally enthroned, reflecting a rule of composition we have seen followed since Early Christian times. The signs of the Evangelists flank him: on his right side the Angel of Matthew and the Lion of Mark; on his left, the Eagle of John and the Ox of Luke. To one side of each pair of signs is an attendant angel holding scrolls upon which to record the deeds of mankind for judgment. The figures of crowned

9-23 Left, *The Prophet Jeremiah*, from the trumeau of the south portal of St. Pierre, Moissac. Above, the head in detail.

musicians are the twenty-four music-making elders who accompany Christ as the kings of all this world and make music in his praise; each turns to face him, much as would the courtiers of a Romanesque monarch in attendance on their lord. The central group, reminiscent of the heraldic groupings of ancient Mesopotamian art, is set among the elders, who are separated into three tiers by two courses of wavy lines that symbolize the clouds of heaven.

There are as many variations within the general style of Romanesque sculpture as in Romanesque architecture, and the figures of the Moissac tympanum constitute no exception. The architecture of the portal is Islamic and very Spanish in its scalloped jambs, in the intricate rosette motifs

of the lintel, and in the refined arabesquelike treatment of the ornament of the archivolts. Islamic influence may be present in the figures themselves, especially those of the elders; but there are elements here familiar in painting and sculpture throughout western Europe in the eleventh and twelfth centuries. The extremely elongated figures of the recording angels; the curious, cross-legged, dancing pose of the Angel of Matthew; and the jerky, hinged movement are characteristic in general of the emerging vernacular style of representing the human figure. Earlier Carolingian, Ottonian, and Anglo-Saxon manners diffused and interfused to produce the now sure, unhesitating style languages of the Romanesque. The zigzag and dovetail lines of the draperies (the linear modes of manuscript painting are everywhere apparent), the bandlike folds of the torsos, the bending back of the hands against the body, and the wide cheekbones (reminiscent of the ancient Archaic mask) are also common features of this new, cosmopolitan style.

A triumph of the style is the splendid figure of the prophet Jeremiah carved in the trumeau of the Moissac portal (FIG. 9-23). His position below the apparition of Christ as the apocalyptic Judge is explained by his prophecy—recalled by his

9-24 Capitals from the cloister of St. Pierre.

scroll—of the end of the world, when "ruin spreads from nation to nation." He is compressed in the mass of the trumeau behind roaring, interlaced lions of the kind familiar not only in barbarian art but in the art of ancient Mesopotamia and Persia and Islamic Spain. (The totemistic animal is never far from the instinct and imagination of the Medieval artist and certainly not far from Medieval man in general; kings and barons are often named by association with animals thought the most fiercely courageous—for example, Richard the Lion-heart, Henry the Lion, and Richard III of England, whose heraldic animal was the wild boar. It is not unthinkable that the Medieval artist, with millennia of animal lore and ornament in his background, would associate animal strength with architecture, the animal body being thought of as providing support and symbolizing the very forces locked in the architectural fabric. The sphinxes and winged monsters at the palace gates in the ancient world—at Boghazköy, Khorsabad, Persepolis, and Mycenae—are the ancestors of the interlaced lions at Moissac.) The figure of Jeremiah is very tall and thin, in the manner of the angels of the tympanum, and, like the Angel of St. Matthew, he executes a cross-legged step that repeats the criss-crossing of the lions. There is as yet no representation of movement in terms of the actual structure of the body or its natural proportions. At this beginning of a new epoch in the history of sculpture, movement is a kind of grotesque, mechanical dance. The placing of the parts of the body is dependent upon the architectural setting, the sculptor's interpretation of his carved or painted model, or the vocabulary of the prevailing vernacular styles; the artist's originality could also play a large part, as in this case. The folds of the drapery are incised in flowing, calligraphic line that ultimately derives from manuscript illumination and here plays gracefully around the elegant figure.

A detail of the head and shoulders (FIG. 9-23) reveals the artist's striking characterization of his subject. The long, sepentine locks of hair and beard (familiar in the vocabulary of French Romanesque details) frame an arresting image of the dreaming mystic. The prophet seems entranced by his vision of what is to come, his eyes wide but unseeing the light of ordinary day; there is an expression slightly melancholy, at once pensive and wistful. For the man of the Middle Ages there were two alternative callings, one to the active life (*vita activa*), the other to the religious life of contemplation (*vita contemplativa*), the pursuit of the beatific vision of God. The

9-25 West tympanum of St. Lazare, Autun, *c.* 1130.

sculptor of the Moissac *Jeremiah* has given us the very image of the *vita contemplativa*. It has been said that in Greek sculpture the body becomes "alive" before the head (as in the *Fallen Warrior* from Aegina, FIG. 5-30); in the epoch that begins in the eleventh century, the head becomes humanly expressive well before the body is rendered as truly corporeal. The *Jeremiah* is a remarkable instance of this.

Romanesque sculpture is not confined to the portals but appears in delightful variety in the carved capitals within the church and in the cloister walk; it was such sculpture that Bernard complained distracted the monks from their devotions; we are distracted, too, by its ingenuity and decorative beauty. Fifty of the capitals of the Moissac cloister (opening illustration, Part Two and FIG. 9-24) are historiated and some thirty purely decorative. The foremost capital in the general view has an intricate leaf-and-vine pattern with volutes, an echo of the Corinthian capital. The abacus carries rosettes, and its upper edge the fish-scale motif. The capital just beyond has figures seated at a table, probably a representation of the Marriage Feast at Cana. The other capitals (FIG. 9-24) reveal the richness and color of the Romanesque sculptors' imagination; monsters of all sorts—basilisks, griffins, lizards, gargoyles— cluster and interlace and pass grinning before us. We have the Medieval bestiary in stone.

The relatives of the monsters of the Moissac capitals appear as the demons of hell in the awesome tympanum of the church of St. Lazare at Autun in Burgundy (FIG. 9-25). At Moissac we saw the apparition of the Divine Judge before he has summoned man; at Autun the Judgment is in progress. The detail shows the weighing of souls, while below in the lintel, the dead are rising, one plucked from the earth by giant hands. Mankind's pitiful weakness and littleness are distilled in these terror-stricken, weeping dolls, whom an angel with a trumpet summons to judgment. Angels and devils contest at the scales where souls are being weighed, each trying to manipulate the beam for or against a soul. Hideous demons guffaw and roar; their gaunt, lined bodies, with legs ending in claws, writhe and bend like long, loathesome insects. A devil leaning from the dragon-mouth of hell drags souls in, while above him a howling demon crams souls head first into a furnace. The resources of the Romanesque imagination, heated by a fearful faith, provide an appalling scene; one can appreciate the terror the Autun tympanum must have inspired in the believer who passed beneath it as he entered the cathedral.

Another great tympanum, this one at the church of La Madeleine at Vézelay, not far from Autun, varies the theme of the apocalyptic Last Judgment, representing the Ascension of Christ and the Mission of the Apostles (FIG. 9-26). As related in scripture (Acts i.4–9), Christ foretold that the apostles would receive the power of the Holy Ghost and become the witnesses of the truth of the gospels throughout the world. The rays of light emanating from his hands represent the promise of the coming of the Holy Ghost. The apostles, holding the gospel books, receive their spiritual assignment. Christ had assigned three specific tasks to the apostles and given them the power to perform them: to save or to condemn; to preach the gospel to all nations; to heal the sick and drive out devils. The task of saving or condemning is indicated in the central scene and in the lower four of the compartments surrounding it. The task of preaching the gospel to all nations (some at the very edge of the world) is represented on the lintel. The task of healing the sick and driving out devils is indicated in the upper four compartments. The outer archivolt has a repeated ornamental device, and the inner, medallions with the signs of the zodiac, the seasons, and the works of the months.

The Vézelay tympanum reflects, like a vast mirror, religious and secular writings and the influence of antiquity and the Byzantine East. It is a complete, encyclopedic Mission of the Apostles, in which the mission and the power to perform it are merged in a single subject. The theme has its sources in the Acts and in the gospels, in the prophecies of Isaiah, and in writings of antiquity and of the Middle Ages. The crowding, agitated figures reveal wild deformities. We find people with the heads of dogs, enormous ears, fiery hair, snoutlike noses; there are hunchbacks, mutes, blind men, lame men—a whole lexicon of human defects and ailments. Mankind, still suffering, awaits the salvation to come. The whole world is electrified by the promise of the ascended Christ, whose great figure, seeming to whirl in a vortex of spiritual energy, looms above human misery and deformity. Again, as in the Autun tympanum, we are made emphatically aware of the greatness of God and the littleness of man.

Vézelay is more closely associated with the Crusades than any other church in Europe. Pope Urban II had intended to preach to the First Crusade at Vézelay in 1095, about thirty years before the tympanum was carved. In 1146, some fifteen years after the tympanum was in place, Bernard preached to the Second Crusade, and King Louis VII of France took up the cross. In

9-26 *The Mission of the Apostles*, tympanum of the center portal of the narthex of La Madeleine, Vézelay, 1120–32.

9-27 Portal on the façade of St. Trophime, Arles, late twelfth century.

1190 it was from Vézelay that King Richard the Lion-heart of England and King Philip Augustus of France set out upon the Third Crusade. Doubtless the spirit of the Crusades determined the iconography of the Vézelay tympanum, for it was believed that the Crusades were a kind of second mission of the apostles to convert the infidel: "When the tympanum was created the crusaders had already fulfilled the most important part of their mission. They had recaptured Jerusalem on the 15 July, 1099. Contemporary writers stress the fact that this is the day on which the apostles had dispersed throughout the world to fulfill their mission."[3]

Stylistically, the figures of the Vézelay tympanum display characteristics similar to those of Moissac and Autun: abrupt, jerky movement

[3] Adolf Katzenellenbogen, "The Central Tympanum at Vézelay: Its Encyclopedic Meaning and Its Relation to the First Crusade," *Art Bulletin*, Vol. 26, No. 3 (Sept. 1944), pp. 141–51.

(strongly exaggerated at Vézelay), rapid play of line, wind-blown drapery hems, elongation, angularity, and agitated poses, gestures, and silhouettes. The figure of the Vézelay Christ is a splendid essay in calligraphic theme and variation, and is almost a summary of the Romanesque skill with decorative line. The lines of the drapery shoot out in rays; break into quick, zigzag rhythms; and spin into whorls, wonderfully conveying a spiritual light and energy flowing from Christ over and into the animated apostles. The technical experience of centuries of working with small art—with manuscripts, ivories, and metalcraft—is easily read from this monumental translation of such work into stone.

In Provence, in the extreme southeast of France, the vivid linear style of Languedoc (Moissac) and Burgundy (Autun and Vézelay) is considerably modified later in the twelfth century by the influence of the art of antiquity, the Rhône basin (the Provence region) being very rich in the remains of Roman art and architecture. The quieting influence of this art is seen at once in the figures of the façade of St. Trophime at Arles and in the design of the portal, which reflects the artist's experience of a Roman triumphal arch (FIG. 9-27). The tympanum shows Christ surrounded by the signs of the Evangelists. On the lintel, directly below him, appear the twelve apostles at the center of a continuous frieze that depicts the Last Judgment; the outermost parts of the frieze depict the saved (on Christ's right) and the damned (on his left) in the flames of hell. Below this, in the jambs and the front bays of the portals, stand grave figures of saints draped in Classical garb, their quiet stance contrasting with the spinning, twisting, dancing figures seen at Autun and Vézelay. The stiff regularity of the figures in the frieze also contrast with the animation of the great Burgundian tympana and remind us of the "lining up" seen in Early Christian sarcophagus sculpture. Their draperies, like those of the large statues below, are also less agitated and show nothing of the dexterous linear play familiar at Moissac, Autun, and Vézelay. The rigid lines of the architecture of the façade as a whole (rather than just an enframing element such as a tympanum) are now determining the placement and look of the sculpture, and the freedom of execution appropriate to small art is sacrificed to a simpler and more monumental adjustment to the architecture. In the north of France, in the area around Paris, a new system of portal sculpture was developing some thirty years earlier than that at St. Trophime. In the Royal Portal of the cathedral of Chartres we shall see the expansion of the whole portal design into a magnificent frontispiece in which the architectural and sculptural elements are in balanced relation, the sculptural style firmly determined by the lines of the building (FIG. 10-13).

PAINTING AND ILLUMINATION

Monumental mural painting, like monumental sculpture, comes into its own once again in the eleventh century. Although we have examples of it from Carolingian and Ottonian times, and al-though there is an unbroken tradition of it in Italy, it blossoms in the Romanesque period. As with architecture and sculpture there are many regional styles and many degrees of sophistication. Sometimes a provincial style—that is, a style that appears at some distance from its origin, in an artistic "province" rather than at an artistic "capitol"—can reveal more clearly than its sophisticated source the elements common to both. Such is the case in the mural painting in the apse of the little church of Santa Maria, at Tahull in Catalonia in the extreme northeast corner of Spain. This painting (PLATE 9-1) could be called provincial Byzantine, as, for that matter, could much Romanesque painting. If we compare it with a Byzantine mosaic like that at Daphne (FIG. 7-44) or the apse mosaic at Torcello (FIG. 7-45), we find that its distance from the Byzantine source —much greater than the distance from Venice or Torcello to Byzantium—results in a loss of subtlety and refinement and some misunderstanding of motifs in the original style. On the other hand, the Tahull painting has a simple and strong directness, even bluntness, that gives it a peculiarly expressive force. One emphatic feature is the partitioning of the draped figures into separate decoratively modeled segments that almost break the figure itself into independent parts. (Note the similarity to the modulation and articulation of Romanesque architecture.) This is especially well seen in the pattern made by the pipelike legs and the ladderlike folds between them. This decorative banding of the surface serves to keep the figures flat and contributes to the effect of stiff formality. The drapery, also with decorative partitioning, is scarcely distinguished from the body. Even the hands of the Madonna are subdivided, as are the heads and necks of other figures. This technique, which had begun to appear in Ottonian painting (FIG. 8-19), is almost universal in Romanesque; it may be seen beneath the whirling linear draperies of Autun and Vézelay and in the angels of the Moissac tympanum. Here the sharp patterning of the figures is assisted by bold coloring, and the whole effect is one of rude strength, not a little of which derives from the architectural planes to which the patterned figures are masterfully adjusted.

The vernacular Romanesque style can be seen almost in exaggeration in a manuscript illumination from northern France illustrating the life of St. Omer (FIG. 9-28). Here the figures are cut into patterns by hard lines, and the action is remote from even an approximation of organic motion. St. Omer (bound and pulled by the beard) and his captors seem to be performing some bouncing ritual ballet. Although the group is enframed, the frame creates no sense of containment as it did in Anglo-Saxon and Carolingian manuscripts, and bodies and feet move arbitrarily in and out of and across it. Locally different from the Tahull mural, the St. Omer illumination shares its fundamental vocabulary.

The vocabulary, richly applied and gracefully modulated, appears in what surely must be one of the masterpieces of Medieval art, a manuscript illuminated in Bernard's great abbey of Citeaux, the motherhouse of the Cistercian order. Citeaux, and its sister abbey, Clairvaux, where Bernard was abbot, produced magnificent illuminated manuscripts throughout the twelfth century, among which was Gregory's *Moralia in Job*, painted before 1111. A splendid example of Cistercian illumination, the historiated initial from this manuscript (FIG. 9-29) represents St. George, his servant, and the roaring dragon intricately composed to make the letter "R." St. George, a slender, regal figure, raises his shield and sword

against the dragon, a distinguished representation of the age-old animal style so often encountered, while the servant, crouching beneath St. George, runs a lance through the monster. The ornamented initial goes back to the Hiberno-Saxon eighth century; the inclusion of a narrative within the initial is a practice that will have an important future in Gothic illumination. The banding of the torso, the fold partitions (especially evident in the skirts of the servant), and the dovetail folds—all part of the Romanesque manner—are done here with the skill of a master who deftly avoids the stiffness and angularity that result from less skillful management of the vocabulary. Instead, he makes a virtue of stylistic necessity; the partitioning accentuates the verticality and elegance of the figure of St. George, as it does the thrusting action of his servant. The flowing sleeves add a spirited flourish to St. George's gesture. The knight, handsomely garbed, cavalierly wears no armor and aims a single stroke with proud disdain. This miniature may be a reliable picture of the costume of a Medieval baron and of the air of nonchalant gallantry he cultivated.

An illumination of exceeding refinement of execution, exemplifying the sumptuous illustration common to the large Bibles produced in the wealthy Romanesque abbeys, is the frontispiece to the Book of Deuteronomy from the Bury Bible (PLATE 9-2). Produced at the abbey of Bury St. Edmunds in England around the middle of the twelfth century, the work shows two scenes from Deuteronomy enframed by symmetrical leaf motifs in softly glowing, harmonized colors. The upper register shows Moses and Aaron proclaiming the Law to the Israelites; the lower, Moses pointing out the clean and unclean beasts. The gestures are slow and gentle and have quiet dignity; the figures of Moses and Aaron seem to glide. This is quite different from the abrupt emphasis and spastic movement of the earlier Romanesque; here, as the patterning softens, the movements of the figure become more integrated and smooth. Yet the patterning does remain in the multiple divisions of the draped limbs, the lightly shaded volumes being connected with sinuous lines and ladder-folds; the drapery and body are still thought of as somehow the same. The frame now has a quite definite limiting function, and the figures are carefully fitted within it.

9-28 *The Life and Miracles of St. Audomarus (Omer),* illuminated manuscript, eleventh century. Bibliothèque Municipale, Saint-Omer, France.

to fall softly, to wrap about the frame, to overlap parts of it, and to follow the movements beneath. The arbitrariness of the Romanesque vernacular style is yielding, slightly but clearly, to the requirements of a more naturalistic representation. The artist's instinct for decorative elaboration of his surface remains, as is apparent in the whorls and spirals of the gown, but it is significant that these are painted in very lightly and do not conflict with the functional lines that contain them.

With the distinction of body and drapery finally achieved in the Gothic art of the thirteenth century, an epoch of increasing naturalism will begin. As did the billowing sail of Exekias' ship of Dionysos (FIG. 5-7), the Eadwine figure marks a turning point—in this case, in the history of Medieval representation. The Late Romanesque and Early Gothic "feel" of body and drapery as surfaces that interact forcefully implies not only a sense of their materiality but also a sense of depth. That sense will sharpen and deepen into the representational art of the Renaissance.

9-29 Above: *St. George and the Dragon,* from the *Moralia in Job* illuminated manuscript, early twelfth century. 13¾″ × 9¼″. Bibliothèque Municipale, Dijon.

The transition from the Romanesque vernacular style to something new seems to reach a midpoint in a work of great expressive power, the portrait of the scribe Eadwine in the *Eadwine Psalter* (FIG. 9-30), made in Canterbury about the same time as the Bury Bible. Particularly noteworthy is the fact that the portrait represents a living man, a priestly scribe, not some sacred person or King David, who usually dominates the Psalter. While it is true that Carolingian and Ottonian manuscripts included portraits of living men, they were of reigning emperors, whose right to appear in sacred books was God-given, like the right of Justinian and Theodora and their court to be depicted in the sanctuary of San Vitale. Here, the inclusion of his own portrait sanctified the scribe's work, marking a change in attitude that points to the future emergence of the artist as a person and a name.

The style is related to that of the Bury Bible, but, though the patterning is still firm—notably in the cowl and the thigh—the drapery has begun

9-30 Right: *The Scribe Eadwine,* from the *Eadwine Psalter,* c. 1150, 19″ × 13″. Trinity College, Cambridge, England.

Chapter Ten

Gothic Art

GOTHIC EUROPE ABOUT 1200

ENGLAND

Gloucester
London
Wells
Salisbury
Amiens
Rouen
Noyon
Beauvais
Laon
St. Denis
Reims
Paris
Chartres
Étampes
Sens
Le Mans

Cologne
Marburg
Naumburg
Prague
Bamberg
Nuremberg
Ulm
Basel

HOLY ROMAN EMPIRE

Lyons
Milan
Verona
Venice
Bologna
Lucca
Florence
Avignon
Pisa
Toulouse
Siena
Orvieto

PAPAL STATES

Rome

LEON
NAVARRE
ARAGON
CASTILE
Zaragoza
Barcelona

DOMINION OF THE ALMOHADES

0   100   200   300 miles

GOTHIC WAS FIRST used as a term of derision by Renaissance critics who scorned the lack of conformity of Gothic art to the standards of classical Greece and Rome: "May he who invented it be cursed," wrote one of them. Mistakenly, they thought the style had originated with the Goths, who thus were responsible for the destruction of the good and true classical style. The men of the thirteenth and fourteenth centuries, however, referred to the Gothic cathedrals as *opus modernum* (modern work) or *opus francigenum* (Frankish work). They recognized in these structures that towered over their towns a style of building and of decoration that was original. It was with confidence in their own faith that they regarded their cathedrals as the

Laon Cathedral (c. 1180-1205)

Chartres Cathedral

1140

1194

EARLY GOTHIC PERIOD c.1140–94

Louis VII of France 1137–80
St. Francis of Assisi (1182–1226)
Third Crusade 1189–92

Abbot Suger (1081–1151)
Frederick Barbarossa 1152–90
Henry VI (Hohenstaufen) 1190–97
Norman Kingdom joined to Holy Roman Empire under Henry VI

1200

Louis IX (St. Louis) 1226–70
Fourth Crusade (Constantinople) 1204

HIGH GOTHIC PERIOD c.1194–1300

Sixth Crusade 1228–29
St. Thomas Aquinas (c. 1225–74)
Frederick II (Hohenstaufen) 1215–50
Franciscan Order founded 1210

Cologne Cathedral

Amiens Cathedral (1220-36)

1250

Charles of Anjou conquers Sicily (end of Hohenstaufen rule in Italy) 1266
Bamberg Rider
Marco Polo in China 1271–92

Palazzo Pubblico (1288-1309)

Doge's Palace (1345-1438)

Machaut (c. 1300-77)

1300

Babylonian Captivity of papacy at Avignon
The Black Death 1346–48

Virgin of Paris

1309

1350

Milan Cathedral

1377

The Great Schism 1378–1417

LATE GOTHIC PERIOD c.1300–16th Century

1400

1500

1417

Façade of St. Maclou, Rouen (c. 1500-14)

real image of the City of God, the Heavenly Jerusalem, which they were privileged to build on earth.

There are strong contrasts between the Gothic and the Romanesque environment and point of view. Romanesque society was dominated by the uncertainties inherent in the anarchical tendencies of feudalism. The great barons of the countryside and the great abbeys enjoyed an almost total independence, and the conflict of their claims to privilege led to constant warfare. Gothic society was also feudal, but it was a comparatively ordered feudalism. Here and there powerful barons had been able to make themselves kings, and monarchy, especially in England and France, asserted itself strongly to limit the independence of lesser lords and the Church. Centralized government was established, and law and order instilled confidence in people of all walks of life. The cities, entirely new or built on the foundations of old Roman ones, began to thrive and become strong; allied for common defense, they were very often powerful enough to defy kings and emperors. Within their walls men who had escaped from the land could find freedom: "The air of the city is the breath of freedom," one slogan had it. City life took on a complex but ordered form; craft guilds, resembling strong unions, were formed to give protection and profit to artisans of the same specialties. A middle class, made up of the craftsmen, merchants, and professionals (lawyers, doctors, teachers, and many others) came to constitute a new and puissant force to check and balance the feudal aristocracy. The fear and insecurity that pervaded the Romanesque world was mitigated by the new alignment of economic and social forces, and the Gothic world emerged.

Romanesque society had been dominated by men. In Gothic society women took on a new importance. Wandering minstrels sang less of the great deeds of heroes in war and more of love, beauty, and springtime. Eleanor of Aquitaine, wife to Louis VII of France and Henry II Plantagenet of England and mother of Richard the Lion-heart and John, was one of the first to rule over a "court of love," where respect for the lady was prerequisite and from which was to emanate the code of chivalry that so decided social relations in the later Middle Ages. The monastic prejudice against women no longer determined the representation of them in art. In the twelfth century *luxuria*, sensual pleasure, is represented at Moissac as a woman with serpents at her breasts; in the thirteenth century it is represented as a pretty girl looking into a mirror. It is almost with relief that the Gothic upper classes turn from the *chansons de geste* to the new amorous songs and romances, in which the lover adores his lady and in which such immortal lovers as Tristan and Isolde are celebrated. Marie de France, herself a noblewoman, introduced this tale, along with many others of the new Arthurian legends, to northern French feudal society. The poetry of the times nicely illustrates the contrast between Romanesque and Gothic taste and mood: While in the Romanesque *Song of Roland* the dying hero waxes rhapsodic over his sword, the German minnesinger of the Gothic period, dreaming in a swooning ecstasy of his lady, is "woven round with delight."

The love of woman, celebrated in art and formalized in life, received spiritual sanction in the cult of the Virgin Mary, who, as the Mother of Heaven and of Christ and in the form of Mother Church, loved all her children. It was Mary who stood compassionately between the judgment seat and the horrors of hell, interceding for all her faithful. The later twelfth and thirteenth centuries sang hymns to her, put her image everywhere, and dedicated great cathedrals to her. Her image was carried on banners into battle, and her name sounded in the battle cry of the king of France: "Sainte Marie . . . Saint Denis . . . Montjoie!" Thus, Mary became the spiritual lady of chivalry, and the Christian knight dedicated his life to her. The severity of Romanesque themes stressing the Last Judgment yields to the gentleness of the Gothic, in which Mary is represented crowned by Christ in Heaven.

It was not alone the new position of women, the lyrical and spiritual exaltation of love, or the cult of the Virgin that softened barbarous manners. In concert with the new mood was the influence of one remarkable man, St. Francis of Assisi, who saw Christ not as the remote and terrible Judge but as the loving Savior who had walked among and had himself been one of the "rejected of men." The series of reform movements that make up the history of Medieval monasticism culminates in St. Francis' founding of the religious order that bears his name, the Franciscans. St. Francis felt that the members of his order must shun the cloistered life and freely walk the streets of the busy cities as mendicants, preaching the original message of Christ—the love of oneself and one's neighbor. Shortly after Francis' death and against his wish that his followers never settle in monasteries, they commenced the great basilica in his name at Assisi. The historical importance of the Franciscan movement lies in its strengthening of religious faith, its stimulating of the religious emotion among people in cities, and its weakening of the power and influence of the old, Romanesque, countryside abbeys. St. Francis could be said to have brought a kind of democracy to religion in Europe at the expense of its feudal establishment.

Courtly love, the development of chivalry, the cult of the Virgin Mary, and the teaching and example of St. Francis could not, of course, nullify, though they could mitigate, the cruel realities of Medieval life. While St. Francis was still living, the Fourth Crusade sacked Christian Constantinople, visiting atrocities upon it that would outdo those of the later conquest by the Ottoman Turks. The papacy and king of France collaborated in the annihilation of the peoples of Languedoc and Provence in the south of France, the so-called Albigensians, who were accused of heresy but who also stood in the way of the territorial ambitions of royal France. It was this region that had fostered the new poetry of the troubadours and produced the Romanesque sculpture examined earlier. The Albigensian "crusade" produced also that grim and fateful instrument of heretic-hunting, the Inquisition, or "Holy Office," instituted by St. Dominic. The Dominicans, called in fearful derision Domini Canes ("dogs of the Lord"), were in many ways rivals of the Franciscans and saw themselves as rooting out unbelievers and heretics and guarding the purity of orthodox dogma. The Dominicans' concern for theology led them to be teachers, and they produced one of the great Christian theologians and philosophers, St. Thomas Aquinas, who at mid-century was the leading light of the University of Paris.

The institution of the university begins to appear in the early Gothic period, its natural setting the city. The monastic and cathedral schools of the earlier Middle Ages had sought to keep the learning of the fathers of the Church alive and to reassess these teachings in the light of developing Christian thought. From these schools the universities, communities of scholars and their pupils, evolved in the twelfth and thirteenth centuries at Bologna and Padua, Oxford, and Paris. The most important study at the university was theology, but several other subjects were taught, among them mathematics, astronomy, music, grammar, logic, law, and medicine. Ancient Greek philosophy, principally that of Aristotle, was recovered from Arabic translations and had an enormously stimulating effect upon theology. Here appeared a reasoned, systematic method of argument and a treasury of lore and observation of natural things. The philosophers set to work to find some way to adjust this new authoritative knowledge to Christian belief; they sought, in short, to rationalize religion. Their method was to arrive at proofs for the central dogmas of the faith by argument, or disputation. This method, taught in the schools and universities, came to be called scholasticism, and its proponents schoolmen. Scholastic philosophy is still the official philosophy of the Roman Catholic Church. The greatest exponent of this systematic procedure was St. Thomas Aquinas. Typical of the method is his treatise, the *Summa Theologica*, which was laid out into Books, the Books into Questions, the Questions into Articles, each Article into objections with contradictions and responses, and, finally, answers to the objections.

Within this framework the shrewdest and subtlest arguments of the Middle Ages were advanced. The habit of mind it created lasted for centuries, an obstacle to the rise of what we call empirical thought and science; yet much of value is still found in it today. It is quite possible that the scholastic habit of disputation is reflected in the thought processes of Gothic architects, as Erwin Panofsky suggested.

St. Thomas wrote his summary of Christian theology at a time when the great cathedrals were manifesting a kind of architectural "summation" of the Christian universe. At the time, the papacy ruled supreme in Europe, not only spiritually but temporally. At the beginning of the thirteenth century, Pope Innocent III, who took England away from King John, could claim: "Single rulers have single provinces, and single kings single kingdoms; but Peter . . . is pre-eminent over all, since he is the Vicar of Him whose is the earth and the fulness thereof, the whole wide world and all that dwell therein."

The thirteenth century represents the summit of achievement for unified Christendom. It represents the triumph of the papacy; a successful and inspiring synthesis of religion, philosophy, and art; and the first firm formation of the states that will make modern history. The scene of this great but brief equilibrium of forces favoring religion is the Gothic city; within the city, the soaring cathedral, "flinging its passion against the sky," asserts the nature of the Gothic spirit.

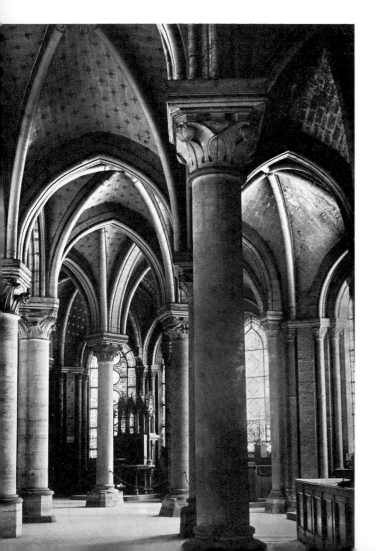

EARLY GOTHIC

Architecture

On June 11, 1144, Louis of France, Eleanor of Aquitaine (his queen), members of the royal court, and a host of distinguished prelates, including five archbishops, as well as a vast crowd, converged on the royal abbey of St. Denis, just a few miles north of Paris, for the dedication of the new choir. This choir, with its crown of chapels radiant with stained-glass windows, set a precedent that the builders in the region surrounding Paris, the Ile-de-France, were to follow for the next half century.

Two eminent persons were particularly influential in the formation of the Gothic style: Bernard of Clairvaux and Suger, abbot of St. Denis. Bernard held the belief that faith was mystical and intuitive rather than rational. In his battles with Abelard, a contemporary scholastic philosopher whose views were a basis for the dialectical method of Aquinas, he upheld this position with all the persuasiveness of his powerful personality and eloquence and by the example of his own holiness. The Cistercian architecture that was being built under Bernard's influence reflected his theology, stressing purity of outline, simplicity, and a form and light peculiarly conducive to meditation.

Although Bernard denounced lavish decoration and elaborate architecture, the Gothic style was initiated by a fellow-abbot who, accepting Bernard's admonitions to reform his monastery, built his new church in a style that surpassed the Romanesque in splendor. The fellow-churchman was the Abbot Suger, who had risen from humble parentage to become the right-hand man of both Louis VI and Louis VII, and, during the latter's absence in the Second Crusade, the regent of France. From his youth, Suger wrote, he had dreamed of the possibility of embellishing the church that had nurtured him, the royal Church of France, within whose precincts its kings had been buried since the ninth century. It was in fact his intention to confer authority on the claims of the kings of royal France to the territory we recognize as France today, for in Suger's time the power of the French king, ex-

10-1 Ambulatory of the abbey church of St. Denis, near Paris, 1140–44.

10-2 Plans of the crypt (left) and choir (right) of St. Denis. (After Sumner Crosby.)

cept for scattered holdings, was confined to an area not much larger than Ile-de-France. Thus, Suger's political role and his building role were one: to construct a kingdom and an architectural expression of it. In 1122 he was elected abbot of St. Denis and within fifteen years was at work rebuilding the old monastery, which had been in use for almost 300 years. As he made his plans for the new building, he must have recalled many of the churches seen during his travels, and the workmen and artists who labored to raise the church were summoned from many regions. St. Denis, one of the last great abbey churches to be built, became the monastic inspiration for the city cathedrals and is known as the cradle of Gothic art.

Suger described his new choir at St. Denis (FIG. 10-1) as follows:

Moreover, it was cunningly provided that—through the upper columns and central arches which were to be placed upon the lower ones built in the crypt—the central nave of the new addition should be made the same width, by means of geometrical and arithmetical instruments, as the central nave of the old [Carolingian] church; and, likewise, that the dimensions of the new side-aisles should be the same as the dimensions of the

old side-aisles, except for that elegant and praise-worthy extension . . . a circular string of chapels, by virtue of which the whole [church] would shine with the wonderful and uninterrupted light of most luminous windows, pervading the interior beauty.[1]

The abbot's description is a key to the understanding of Early Gothic architecture. As he says, the major dimensions of the structure were dictated by an older church, but it was the "elegant and praiseworthy extension," the "string of chapels" with "luminous windows," that proclaimed the new style.

Although the crypt at St. Denis served as a foundation for the choir above it, a comparison of their plans and structure of each reveals the major differences between Romanesque and Gothic building (FIG. 10-2). The thick walls of the crypt create a series of separate volumes—careful Romanesque "partitioning" into units—whereas the absence of walls in the choir above produces a unified space. The crypt is essentially a wall construction, and it is covered with groin vaults; the choir, on the other hand, is a skeletal

[1] Erwin Panofsky, trans., *Abbot Suger on the Abbey Church of St. Denis and its Art Treasures* (Princeton, N.J.: Princeton Univ. Press, 1951), p. 101.

construction, and its vaults are Gothic rib vaults (FIG. 10-3).

The ancestors of the Gothic rib vault (at Caen and Durham) were discussed above. A rib vault is easily identified by the presence of crossed, or diagonal, arches under the groins of a vault. These arches form the armature, which serves as the framework for Gothic skeletal construction. The Gothic vault may be distinguished from other rib or arched vaults by its use of the pointed, or broken, arch as an integral part of the skeletal armature; by the presence of thinly vaulted webs, or severies, between the arches; and by the fact that, regardless of the space to be vaulted, all the arches have their crowns at approximately the same level—something the Romanesque architects could not achieve with their semicircular arches (FIG. 10-4). Thus, flexi-

bility is a major advantage of the Gothic vault, permitting the vaulting of compartments of varying shapes, as may be readily seen in the plan of the choir of St. Denis and in many other Gothic choir plans. Moreover, although it does not entirely support the webs, the Gothic armature allows predetermining of the alignment and concentration of thrusts to be buttressed.

Although the Medieval mason unquestionably derived great satisfaction from his mastery of these technical problems and at times must have been preoccupied with them, he did not permit them to be an end in themselves. The ambulatories and chapels at St. Denis are proof that the rib vault was exploited, as Suger wrote, so that the whole church "would shine with wonderful and uninterrupted light." This was, in Medieval terms, the *scientia*—the theory—that motivated the creation of the Gothic style; and it was *ars*—technical knowledge and practical skill—that made it possible. The difference between the two was akin to that between modern physics and engineering; when a Medieval architect spoke of the "art of geometry," he meant not the abstract nature of geometrical forms, but the practical uses to which mathematical formulations might be put in designing a piece of sculpture or in erecting a building. An understanding of Gothic architecture will not be reached, however, by trying to decide whether it was predominantly concerned with *ars* or with *scientia* but rather by realizing that the cathedrals were the result of both. And it is in the stones themselves, in the extraordinary sensitivity of the Gothic mason for stone as a building material that the spirit of Gothic architecture is to be discovered. The fact is that procedure was often hit or miss and rule of thumb; buildings often collapsed and were rebuilt with very large margins of safety. There was no one sure way and certainly no fundamental agreement about method. The certainties of modern engineering—themselves sometimes not so certain—were centuries beyond the Gothic reach. Even so, what still stands of Gothic architecture is a monument to the supreme skill, persistence, and vision of the Gothic architects.

It was the *scientia* of light that led Suger to the invention of the Gothic building, the slender skeletal structure that permitted the flooding

10-3 Vaults of the ambulatory and radiating chapels of the choir of St. Denis.

of the interior with light. This "theory" came from the writings of a fifth-century mystic called the pseudo-Dionysius the Areopagite because of his claim to be the true Dionysius, a first-century Athenian follower of St. Paul. This "'pseudo-Dionysius" had become confused with the patron saint of royal France, St. Denis, making it natural for Suger to take the former's mystical identification of light with the divine as a kind of prescription for any building dedicated to St. Denis. When Suger, steeped in the theology of the Areopagite, envisioned the new St. Denis, he saw it as a mystic radiance. This is another example of the significance of religious authority in the Middle Ages. Not only scripture, but the works of the fathers of the Church were the key to reality, and things had to be interpreted in terms of their authority.

The evolution of Gothic architecture is a continuing adjustment of scale, proportion, buttressing, vault arrangement, and wall and façade design that, in Panofsky's image, is like the steps of a complex scholastic argument. Only the choir of St. Denis was completed in the twelfth century; for a fairly complete view of the Early Gothic style of the second half of the century, one must turn to the cathedral of Laon (FIGS. 10-5 to 10-8). Begun about 1160 and completed shortly after 1200, the building retains many Romanesque features but combines them with the new Gothic structural devices—the rib vault and the pointed arch. Shortly after the building's completion the choir was enlarged and the present plan, relatively long and narrow with a square east end, has a decidedly English flavor. Among the plan's easily discernible Romanesque features are the strongly marked-off crossing square and the bay system composed of a large unit in the nave flanked by two small squares in each aisle (FIG. 10-5). The nave bays are defined by sexpartite rib vaults and an alternate-support system that, in combination, continue the Romanesque tradition of subdividing the interior into a number of separate compartments. Both features, as well as the gallery above the aisles, have been derived from Norman Romanesque architecture, which enjoyed great prestige in northern France throughout the twelfth century (FIGS. 9-12 and 9-13). A new feature of the interior, however, is the *triforium*, the band of arcades below the clerestory that occupies the space corresponding to the exterior strip of wall covered by the sloping timber roof above the galleries. The triforium expresses a growing desire to break up and eliminate all continuous wall surfaces. Its insertion produces the characteristic Early Gothic nave-wall elevation of four parts: nave arcade, gallery, triforium, and clerestory (FIGS. 10-6 and 10-7).

At Laon the alternate-support system is treated less emphatically than in other Early Gothic

10-4 The Gothic rib vault and the domical vault differ in ways that derive from the fact that they are based on the pointed arch and the semicircular arch, respectively. The diagram (1) illustrates this: *ABCD* is an oblong bay to be vaulted; *AC* and *BD* are the diagonal ribs; *AB* and *DC*, the transverse arches; and *AD* and *BC*, the wall arches. If semicircular arches (the dotted arcs) are used, their radii, and therefore their heights (*EF*, *GH*, and *IJ*), will be different. The result will be a domical vault (2), irregular in shape and difficult to light. If pointed arches are used, the points (and hence the ribs) can have the same heights (*IK* and *GL*). The result will be a Gothic rib vault (3), a lighter, more flexible system than the domical, affording ample space for large clerestory windows.

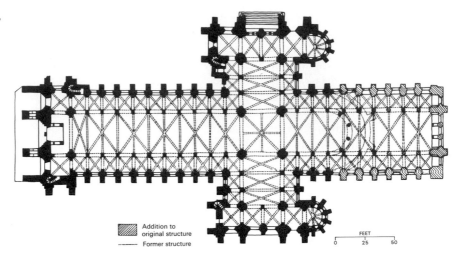

10-5 Plan of Laon Cathedral, *c.* 1160–1205. Choir extended after 1210. (After E. Gall.)

Addition to original structure
------ Former structure

FEET
0   25   50

10-6 Section through the aisle, gallery, triforium, and clerestory of Laon Cathedral. (After E. Gall.)

10-7 Nave of Laon Cathedral.

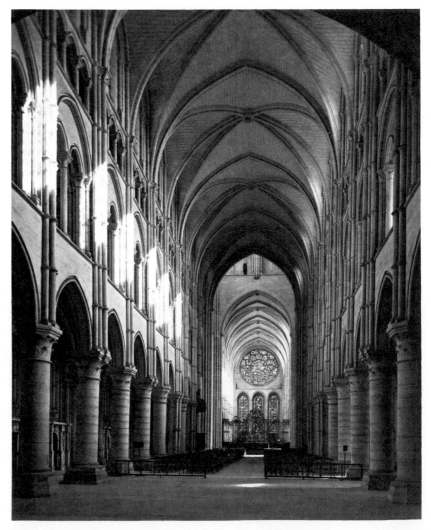

churches (for example, Sens, Noyon). It is not reflected in the nave arcade (although colonnettes were added to a few of the columns as an after-thought), as alternating bundles of three and five shafts have their origin above the level of the main wall supports (FIG. 10-7). It appears that the Laon architect was no longer completely happy with the compartmentalized effect of Roman-esque interiors, which tend to make the visitor pause as he advances from unit to unit. Gothic builders aim, as yet rather timidly at Laon, to create an integrated, unified interior space that sweeps uninterruptedly from west to east. The alternate-support system, hugging the ground in Ottonian times and rising to dominate nave walls in northern Romanesque, has lost its foot-ing at Laon and, like the solid masonry of Ro-manesque walls, is about to evaporate.

Important changes in the design of the church exterior were also part of the Early Gothic ex-perience. At Laon the doorways, under protec-tive porches, and the towers have been treated as integral parts of the mass of the building (FIG. 10-8). The interior stories are reflected in the levels into which the façade is divided. (A notice-able discontinuity between the central and flank-ing portions of the façade was to be regulated in later designs.) Typically Gothic are the deep em-brasures of the doorways and windows and the open structure of the towers. A comparison of the façades of Laon and St. Étienne at Caen (FIG. 9-11) reveals how deep the penetration of the mass of the wall has become. Here, as in Gothic generally, there is operating a kind of principle of reduction of sheer mass by its replacement with intricately framed voids.

Laon has a pair of towers flanking each arm of the transept (only two completed) and a lantern tower over the crossing, which, with the two western towers, gives a total of seven, the perfect mystic number. (Composed of three and four, it represents the Trinity and the Evangelists or the gospels.) This complement of towers was the Early Gothic ideal and continues the German Romanesque tradition of multiple integrated towers. Rarely, however, did building funds suffice for the completion of all towers. Even the façade towers of French cathedrals were seldom finished, most, including those of Laon, lacking the crowning spires planned for them. Eventu-ally the massed towers of the east end were omitted from building plans and the Norman two-tower façade became the French High Gothic standard.

Transept towers were not part of the plan for the cathedral of Paris, the renowned Notre Dame (FIG. 10-9). Thus, this essentially Early Gothic building has a High Gothic silhouette in which only the slender crossing spire interrupts the long horizontal roof line that extends east-ward behind the massive façade towers (FIG. 10-10). Notre Dame of Paris was begun in 1163, only a few years after Laon, and embodies a fascinating mixture of conservative and progressive ideas. Choir and transept were completed by 1182, the nave by 1225, and the façade by 1250. The plan (FIG. 10-11) shows an ambitiously scaled, five-aisled structure in which a Romanesque bay

10-8 Façade of Laon Cathedral, begun c. 1190.

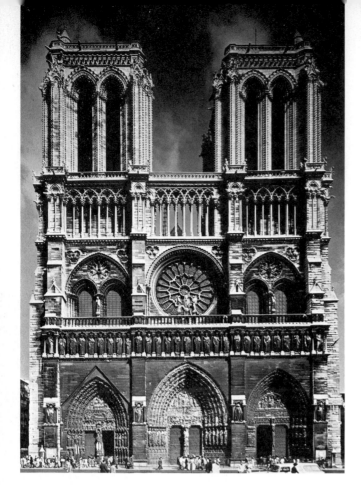

gallery by suppressing the rosettes of the triforium. This, in turn, required that the gallery roof be lowered and redesigned. The solution, a pitched roof with one of its slopes inclined toward the nave wall, created a difficult drainage problem that was solved only in the nineteenth century, when Viollet-le-Duc designed a single-slope roof that throws the water outward.

Like the interior, the façade seems to waver between the old and the new (FIG. 10-9). Begun after the Laon façade had been completed, it appears much more conservative and, in the preservation of its "mural presence," more closely related to Romanesque than to High Gothic façades. From the modern observer's point of view, this may be one of its great assets. Less perforated and more orderly than Laon's, Notre Dame's façade exudes a sense of strength and permanence that is lacking in many contemporary and later designs. Careful balancing of vertical against horizontal elements has achieved a quality of restful stability that makes this façade one of the most satisfying and memorable in Gothic architecture.

system is combined with Early Gothic six-part nave vaulting. The original transept was short and did not project beyond the outer aisles. The original nave wall was four-part, in the Early Gothic manner, with a triforium in the form of a series of rosettes.

Barely completed, the building was extensively modified. Between 1225 and 1250, chapels were built into the spaces between buttresses, and in 1250 the transept arms were lengthened. At the same time, perhaps as the result of a fire (according to Viollet-le-Duc, the cathedral's nineteenth-century restorer), but probably to admit more light into the nave, changes were made in the nave wall, although the bays adjacent to the crossing were left in their original form (FIG. 10-12). By this time the nave of the cathedral of Chartres had been completed (see below) and had rendered Early Gothic galleries and four-level wall elevations obsolete. Since the galleries had already been built at Paris, the "modernization" of the nave had to be a compromise. The clerestory windows were lowered to the top of the

Sculpture

Gothic sculpture first makes its appearance in the Ile-de-France and its environs with the same dramatic suddenness as Gothic architecture, and, it is likely, in the very same place, the abbey church of St. Denis. Almost nothing of the sculpture of the west façade of St. Denis remains to be studied, but it was there that sculpture emerged completely from the interior of the church and dominated the western entrances, which were regarded as the "gateways to Heavenly Jerusalem" and as the "royal portals." These royal portals, so called because of the statues of kings and queens on the embrasures flanking the doorways, are typified by the west portals of the cathedral of Chartres (FIG. 10-13), carved between 1145 and 1170. This west façade and its portals are the only surviving parts of an Early Gothic cathedral that was destroyed in a disastrous fire in 1194 before it had been completed. The cathedral was reconstructed immediately, but in the High

10-10 Above: South flank of Notre Dame.

10-11 Below: Plan of Notre Dame. (After Frankl.)

FEET
0   50   100

10-12 Right: East end and part of the nave of Notre Dame, begun *c.* 1180, modified 1225–50.

10-13 West ("royal") portals of Chartres Cathedral, *c.* 1145–70.

Gothic style (see below). The portals, however, constitute the most complete and impressive corpus of Early Gothic sculpture.

The three west portals of Chartres, treated as a unit, proclaim the majesty and omnipotence of Christ. His birth, the Presentation at the Temple, and Christ in Majesty with his Virgin Mother are shown on the right portal, and his Ascension into heaven on the left. Scenes from his life and from the passion are vividly carved on the capitals, which continue as a frieze from one portal to the next. On the central portal is depicted the Second Coming, surrounded by the symbols of the four Evangelists, with the apostles below, seated as representing the corporate body of the Christian Church. The Second Coming, in essence the Last Judgment theme, remains, as in the Romanesque works we have seen (and which are only some twenty years older than the west portals of Chartres), centrally important. Here, however, it has become a symbol of salvation rather than damnation. It is, moreover, combined with other scenes and symbolic figures as part of a larger theme rather than as symbol of the dogma itself. In the archivolts of the right portal are shown

the seven liberal arts, the core of Medieval learning, and therefore symbolic of man's knowledge, which will lead him to the true faith. The signs of the zodiac and scenes representing the various labors of the months of the year are carved into the left-portal archivolts as symbols of the cosmic and of the terrestrial worlds; and around the central tympanum are the twenty-four elders of the Apocalypse, accompanying the Second Coming. Decorating the multiple jambs flanking each doorway are the most striking figures, the great statues of the kings and queens of the Old Testament, the royal ancestors of Christ (FIG. 10-14). It is almost certain that the Medieval observer also regarded them as the figures of the kings and queens of France, symbols of secular as well as of biblical authority. The unity of the triple portal in its message and composition complements the unity of the cathedral itself, which in its fluent, uninterrupted, vast and soaring space compounds earth and heaven in a symbol of the spiritually perfected universe to come.

The jamb statues are among the few original forms of architectural sculpture to have appeared in any age. At first glance they seem—in their

Color Plates 6-5 to 13-5

Plate 6-5 *Still Life with Peaches*, wall painting transferred to panel, Herculaneum, *c.* A.D. 50. Approx. 14″ × 13½″. Museo Nazionale, Naples.

Plate 6-6 *Pastoral Scene*, detail of a wall painting transferred to panel, Pompeii, first century A.D. Approx. 20″ high. Museo Nazionale, Naples.

Plate 6-7 *Mummy Portrait of a Man*, Faiyum, second century A.D. Encaustic painting on wood panel, approx. 13¾″ × 8″. Albright-Knox Art Gallery, Buffalo (Charles Clifton Fund).

Plate 7-1 *Christ as the Good Shepherd*, mosaic from the entrance wall of the mausoleum of Galla Placidia, Ravenna, A.D. 425–50.

Plate 7-2 *The Miracle of the Loaves and the Fishes*, mosaic from the nave wall of Sant' Apollinare Nuovo, Ravenna, c. A.D. 504.

Plate 7-3 Apse mosaic from Sant' Apollinare in Classe, c. A.D. 549.

Plate 7-4 Sanctuary of San Vitale, Ravenna, A.D. 526–47.

Plate 7-6 *Justinian and Maximianus,* detail of an apse mosaic (FIG. 7-30)
from San Vitale.

Plate 7-7 Carpet from the tomb-mosque of Shah Tahmasp at Ardebil, Iran, 1540. Approx. $34\frac{1}{2}' \times 17\frac{1}{2}'$. Victoria and Albert Museum, London.

Plate 7-8 *Laila and Majnun in Love at School*, miniature from a manuscript of the Khamsa of Nizami, 1524–25. Colors and gilt on paper. Metropolitan Museum of Art, New York.

Plate 8-3 *Christ in Majesty, Four Evangelists, and Scenes from the Life of Christ*, cover of the Codex Aureus of St. Emmeram, c. 870. Gold set with pearls and precious stones, 17″ × 13″. Bayerische Staatsbibliothek, Munich.

Plate 9-1 *Adoration of the Magi*, apse fresco from Santa Maria, Tahull, Catalonia, eleventh century.

Plate 9-2 MASTER HUGO, *Moses Expounding the Law*, frontispiece of the Book of Deuteronomy of the Bury Bible, the abbey of Bury St. Edmunds, early twelfth century. Illuminated manuscript, approx. 20″ × 14″. Reproduced by permission of the Master and Fellows of Corpus Christi College, Cambridge, England.

Plate 10-1 *Crucifixion*, window from St. Remi, Reims, c. 1190. Stained glass, approx. 12′ high.

Plate 10-2 Detail of the *Good Samaritan* window, Chartres Cathedral, early thirteenth century. Stained glass.

Plate 11-1 GIOTTO, *Lamentation*, fresco, c. 1305. Arena Chapel, Padua.

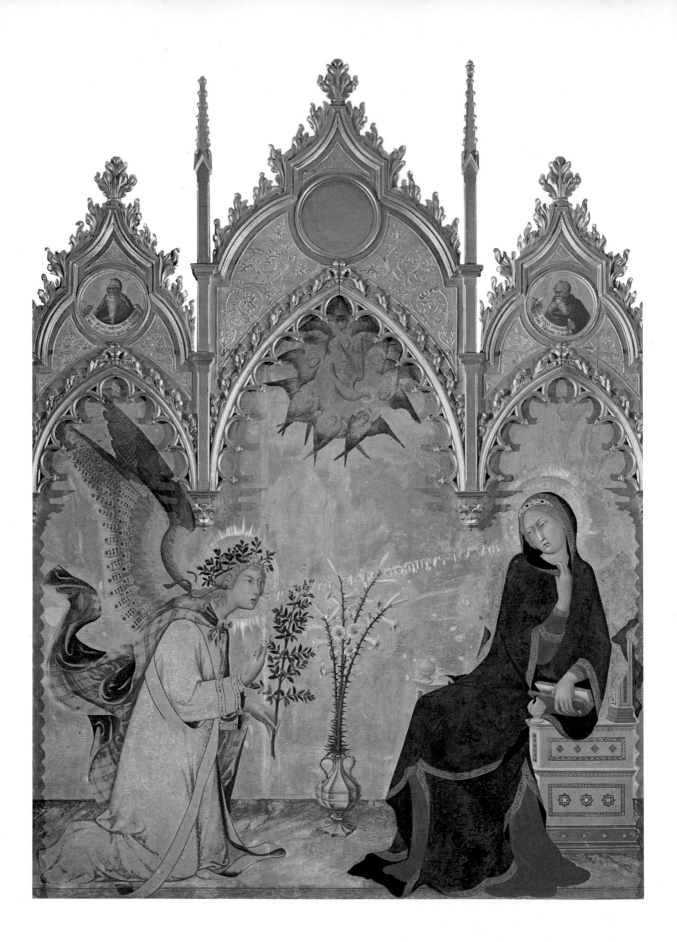

Plate 11-2 SIMONE MARTINI, *The Annunciation*, 1333. Tempera on wood panel, approx. 10′ 1″ × 8′ 8¾″. Galleria degli Uffizi, Florence.

Plate 12-1 GENTILE DA FABRIANO, *The Adoration of the Magi*, 1423. Tempera on wood panel, approx. 9′ 11″ × 9′ 3″. Galleria degli Uffizi, Florence.

Plate 12-2 DOMENICO VENEZIANO, *The St. Lucy Altarpiece, c.* 1445. Tempera on wood panel, approx. 6′7½″ × 7′. Galleria degli Uffizi, Florence.

Plate 12-3 LUCA DELLA ROBBIA, *Madonna and Child, c.* 1455–60. Terra-cotta with polychrome glaze, approx. 6′ in diameter. Or San Michele, Florence.

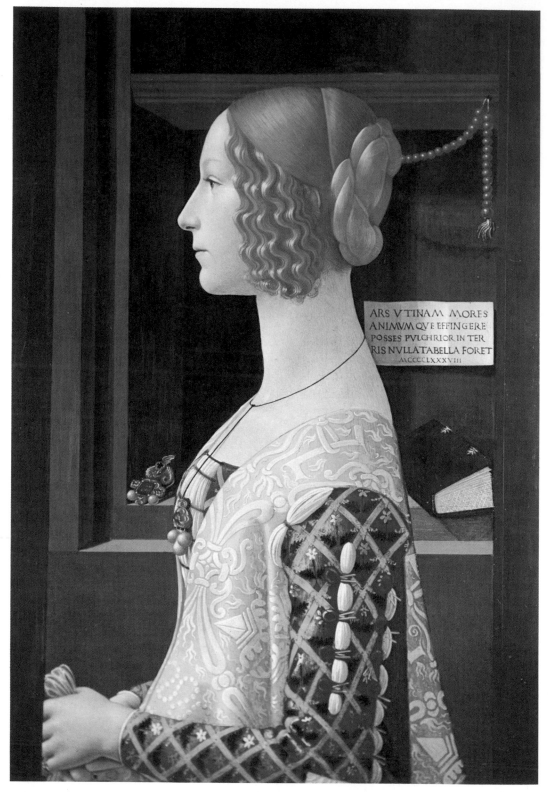

Plate 12-4 Domenico Ghirlandaio, *Giovanna Tornabuoni* (?), 1488. Approx. 30″ × 20″. Sammlung Thyssen-Bornemisza, Lugano.

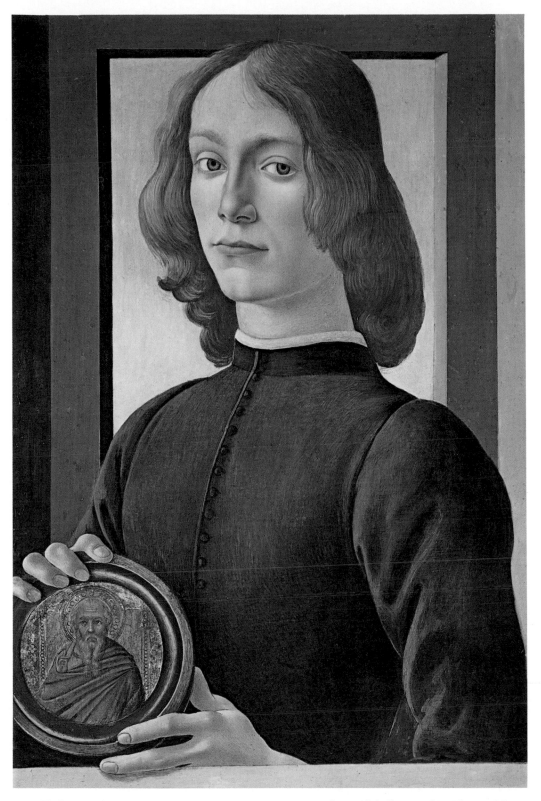

Plate 12-5 SANDRO BOTTICELLI, *Portrait of a Young Man*, 1444–45, 23″ × 15½″. Collection of Sir Thomas Merton, Berkshire, England.

Plate 12-6 ANDREA MANTEGNA, ceiling of the *Camera degli sposi*, fresco, 1474. Ducal Palace, Mantua.

Plate 12-7 ANTONELLO DA MESSINA, *The Martyrdom of St. Sebastian*, c. 1475–77. Approx. 5′ 8″ × 2′ 10″. Gemäldegalerie Abt. Alte Meister, Staatliche Kunstsammlungen Dresden.

Plate 13-1 Raphael Sanzio, *Baldassare Castiglione, c.* 1514. Approx. 30¼″ × 26½″. Louvre, Paris.

Plate 13-2 Michelangelo, *The Creation of Adam*, detail of the ceiling of the Sistine Chapel (fig. 13-23), the Vatican, Rome, 1508–12.

Plate 13-3 ANDREA DEL SARTO, *Madonna of the Harpies*, 1517. Approx. 82″ × 70″. Galleria degli Uffizi, Florence.

Plate 13-4 Jacopo Pontormo, *The Descent from the Cross*, 1525–28. Approx. 11′ × 6′6″. Capponi Chapel, Santa Felicitá, Florence.

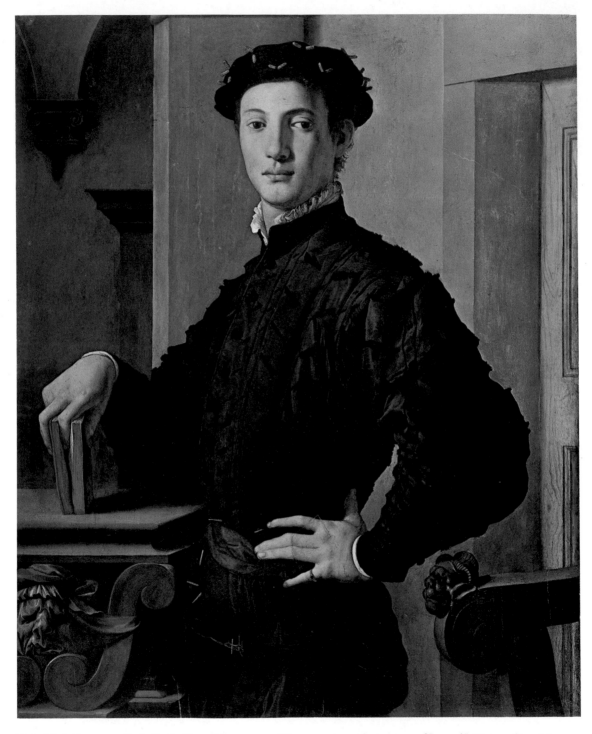

Plate 13-5 BRONZINO, *Portrait of a Young Man, c.* 1550. Oil on wood panel, approx. $37\frac{5}{8}'' \times 29\frac{1}{2}''$. Metropolitan Museum of Art, New York (H. O. Havemeyer Collection, bequest of Mrs. H. O. Havemeyer, 1929).

disregard of normal proportions and their rigid adherence to an architectural frame—to follow many of the precepts of Romanesque architectural sculpture. Yet the differences are striking and important. The statues stand out from the plane of the wall; they are not cut back into it. They are conceived and treated as three-dimensional volumes. They move into the space of the observer and participate in it with him. Most significant of all is the first trace of a new naturalism: drapery folds are no longer calligraphic exercises translated into stone; they now either fall vertically or radiate naturally from their points of suspension. Although carefully arranged in regular patterns, these folds suggest that the artist is no longer copying painted images, but that actual models have become his guides. This is true particularly of the figures flanking the central doorway (left foreground in FIG. 10-13), which are the work of the anonymous HEADMASTER, the artist in charge of the overall design and decoration of the portals. The advanced nature of his style becomes particularly noticeable when his figures are compared with those on the outside jamb of the lateral portal (right background in FIG. 10-13), which evidently were carved by a different, perhaps older, certainly more conservative artist. The latter's approach is still deeply rooted in the Romanesque tradition. His figures seem more agitated, their silhouettes curvilinear and broken. The drapery folds are treated decoratively and, here and there, continue to rotate in abstract swirls. Only the wind-blown lower garment edges, characteristic of much Romanesque sculpture, have come to rest —reluctantly it seems and, perhaps, at the Headmaster's insistence. Even so, the figures fail to adjust themselves as neatly and consequently to their architectural setting as do the Headmaster's. The latter's statues, although they have stepped out of the wall and have become corporeal, are severely disciplined and have been rigorously subordinated to their architectural background. Seen from a distance, they appear to be little more than vertical decorative accents within the larger designs of portals and façade. And yet, within and despite its architectural strait jacket, the incipient naturalism has softened the appearance of the figures. This is particularly

10-14 Detail of the jamb statues, Royal Portal, Chartres Cathedral.

noticeable in their faces, in which the masklike features of the Romanesque are being converted into human likenesses. Here is the faint beginning of a personalizing naturalism that will become transformed first into idealized portraits of the perfect Christian and finally into the portraiture of specific individuals.

At this time, the early twelfth century, great changes were taking place in Western man's view of himself, especially with respect to the relation of body and soul. Previously, the old Augustinian view had prevailed: that the essence of the soul is completely unlike that of the body, the soul being spiritual and immortal, the body material and subject to corruption. With the rediscovery of the main works of Aristotle, it came to be gradually believed that the soul and the body were closely interrelated, that the soul had the *form* of the body, and that, therefore, the body was no longer to be despised as merely the corruptible prison of the soul from which the latter is released when the body dies. One scholastic philosopher saw the soul and the body as meeting, and the combination as responsible for the personality of the individual. Another saw

10-15 Aerial view of Chartres Cathedral, begun 1194.

10-16 Plan of Chartres Cathedral. (After Frankl.)

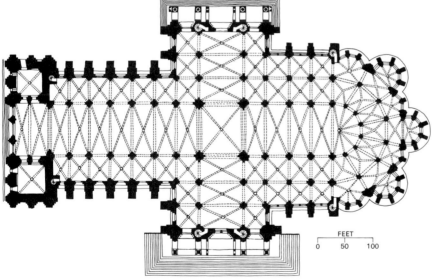

FEET
0   50   100

the soul as ruling the body but also cherishing its prison. These views, in which the body is seen as coming into its own, reflect a universally changing outlook. John of Salisbury, the great English humanist, took the perhaps radical view that the soul is stimulated and acted upon by sensations from the world, rather than directly inspired and moved by entirely spiritual principles. He even declared that some of the principal problems of scholastic philosophy could be solved by psychological examination of the way we think. The West was now speaking with a new voice: Souls must be manifested through bodies, the individual bodies of men and women. Thus, the new

10-17 Nave of Chartres Cathedral.

individualized heads of Chartres herald an era of artistic concern with the realization of personality and individuality that may only now, in our times, be terminating. The figures of the Royal Portal hold a place analogous to the works of Greek artists in the late sixth century B.C.; they turn the corner into a historical avenue of tremendous possibility.

HIGH GOTHIC

Architecture

On June 10, 1194, a great fire consumed the town of Chartres. Its cathedral, which had only recently been completed, was again destroyed, except for the crypt, the western towers, and the Royal Portal between them. A new cathedral was begun almost immediately, to be completed for the most part by 1220. This new cathedral of Chartres is usually considered the first of the High Gothic buildings, the first to have been planned from the beginning for the use of flying buttresses.

The flying buttress, that exceedingly useful and characteristic Gothic structural device, seems to have been employed by about 1180 for the bracing of the nave of Notre Dame in Paris, and shortly thereafter at Laon. A section through the latter church (FIG. 10-6) shows how the flying buttress reaches across the lower vaults of aisle and gallery and abuts the nave walls directly at those points where the vaults exert their major thrusts. Similar methods to strengthen the walls of vaulted naves had already been used in Romanesque architecture, but there the buttresses had been concealed under the aisle roofing. Now, however, they are left exposed in a manner that has been either condemned as "architectural crudity" or praised as "structural honesty." An air view of the cathedral of Chartres (FIG. 10-15) shows that a series of these highly dramatic devices have been placed around the *chevet* (the east end of the church), supporting the vaults with permanent arms, like scaffolding left in place. With the mastery of this structural form, the technical

vocabulary of Gothic architecture is complete. The buttress eliminates the need for Romanesque walls and permits the construction of a skeletal structure that is self-consistent and self-supporting. The Chartres architect was the first to arrive at this conclusion and to design his building accordingly.

At Chartres, after the great fire, the overall dimensions of the new structure were determined by the towers left standing at the west and by the masonry of the crypt to the east, which, for reasons of economy, was used as a foundation. The earlier forms did not limit the plan (FIG. 10-16), however, and it shows an unusual equilibrium between chevet, transept, and nave, which are almost equal in dimension; more important, perhaps, the plan shows a new kind of organization. The last remnants of square schematism, still present in Early Gothic churches, have been replaced by a "rectangular bay system" that will become the High Gothic norm. Now a rectangular unit in the nave, defined by its own vault, is flanked by a single square in each aisle. This new bay arrangement is accompanied by a change in vault design. The new High Gothic vault, covering a relatively smaller area and more

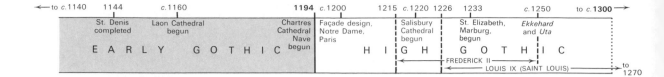
easily braced than its Early Gothic predecessor, has only four panels. The visual effect of these changes is of an interior that has been decompartmentalized (FIG. 10-17), identical units having been so aligned that they are seen in too rapid a sequence to be discriminated as individual volumes of space. The alternate-support system, of course, is gone, and the nave, though richly articulated, has become a vast, continuous hall.

The organic, "flowing" quality of the High Gothic interior was enhanced by a new nave wall elevation, which admitted more light to the nave through greatly enlarged clerestory windows. The use of flying buttresses made it possible to eliminate the tribune gallery above the aisle, which had partially braced Romanesque

and Early Gothic naves. The new High Gothic tripartite nave elevation, consisting of arcade, triforium, and clerestory, emphasizes the large clerestory windows; those at Chartres are almost as high as the main arcade. A comparison of the elevations of Laon and Chartres (FIG. 10-18) illustrates what radical changes could be achieved by the logical application of the new structural device—the flying buttress—that had been used only tentatively at Laon.

Despite the vastly increased size of the clerestory windows, some High Gothic interiors remain relatively dark, largely because of the light-muffling effects of their colored glass. Chartres has retained almost the full complement of its original stained glass (see below), and though it

10-18 Elevations of the nave walls of the cathedrals of Laon (left) and Chartres (right). The latter is drawn to a smaller scale than the Laon elevation. Umschau-Verlag, Frankfurt/Main.

10-19 Façade of Amiens Cathedral, c. 1220–36.

10-20 Plan of Amiens Cathedral. (After Frankl.)

FEET
0   50   100

dims the interior, it sheds a color-shot light of great beauty that has helped to make the cathedral of Chartres the favorite church of lovers of Gothic architecture.

The cathedral of Amiens (FIGS. 10-19 to 10-22) continues the Chartrian manner, gracefully refining it. Amiens was begun in 1220 according to designs of ROBERT DE LUZARCHES. The nave was finished in 1236 and the radiating chapels in 1247, but work on the choir continued until almost 1270. The façade (FIG. 10-19), slightly marred by uneven towers (the shorter dates from the fourteenth, the other from the fifteenth century), was begun at the same time as the nave (1220). Its

lower parts seem to reflect the influence of the Laon façade in the spacing of its funnel-like and gable-covered portals. Unlike Laon's, the Amiens portals do not project from the façade, but are recessed behind the building's buttress-defined frontal plane. The upper parts of the façade, on the other hand, seem to be related to Notre Dame in Paris, the rose window (with fifteenth-century tracery) being placed above the "king's gallery" and between double-arched openings in the towers. But the Amiens façade goes well beyond its apparent models in the richness and intricacy of its surface decoration. The deep piercing of walls and towers seems to have left few continuous

10-21 Nave of Amiens Cathedral.

10-22 Choir vault of Amiens Cathedral.

surfaces to be decorated, to be sure, but the remaining ones have been covered with a network of articulating colonnettes, arches, pinnacles, rosettes, and other decorative stone work that screens and nearly dissolves visually the structure's solid core. Despite its decorative intricacy, the façade retains its monumental grandeur and is one of the first to achieve full integration with the building behind it. The cavernous portals correspond in width and placement to the nave and aisles and, although in slightly different proportions, the façade's three-part elevation reflects that of the nave, the rose window corresponding to the clerestory.

The plan of Amiens (FIG. 10-20), like the façade, is exemplary of the grand High Gothic style. Derived from Chartres and perhaps even more elegant in its proportions, it reflects the builder's unhesitating and confident use of the complete Gothic structural vocabulary: the rectangular bay system, the four-paneled rib vault, and a buttressing system that permits almost complete

dissolution of the heavy masses and thick bearing walls of the Romanesque. The concept of a self-sustaining skeletal architecture has reached full maturity; what remains of the walls has been stretched like a skin between the piers and seems to serve no purpose other than to provide a weather screen for the interior (FIG. 10-21). From a height of 144 feet the tense, strong lines of the vault ribs converge to the colonnettes and speed down the shell-like walls to the compound piers, almost each part of the superstructure having its corresponding element below—the only exception being the wall rib (the rib at the junction of the vault and the wall). There is an appearance of an effortless strength (that counters the fact of great weight), of a buoyant lightness one would never associate with the obdurate materiality of stone. Viewed directly from below, the vaults of the choir seem like a canopy, tentlike and suspended from bundled masts (FIG. 10-22). The light flooding in from the clerestory imparts even more "lift" and at the same time blurs structural outlines. The effect is visionary, and we are reminded of another great building, utterly different from Amiens, in which light plays an analogous role—Hagia Sophia in Constantinople. Not only is the physical mass of the building reduced by structural ingenuity and daring, but what remains is further dematerialized visually by light. As with scholastic philosophy, the logic of the structure is here in the service of mystery. While philosophy might prove the existence of God with reason, the experience of the beatific vision gave the believer a mystical proof, like Dante's experience in Paradise as he gazed, rapt, into the "heart of Light, the heart of Silence."

In examining the interior of Amiens it may be useful to reconsider Panofsky's abovementioned suggestion of a connection between Gothic architecture and scholastic philosophy and the description of the method as typified in Aquinas' *Summa Theologica*. Most striking in the propositions of Aquinas and in the structure of Amiens is an insistence upon an order and unity made up of clearly distinguished and clearly related parts, the philosopher aiming at logical consistency, and the architect at structural coherence. In neither is the order intended to be less than total. Aquinas' *Summa* was designed to treat *all* possible questions where faith and reason touch; in Amiens all individual elements are subordinated to the whole, unlike the case of the sharply subdivided—often opposed—units of Romanesque design. This principle of *manifestatio* ("manifestation," "transparency") determines the look of the philosophic system as it does the look of the cathedral. As Panofsky wrote:

A man imbued with the Scholastic habit [of thought] . . . would look upon the mode of architectural presentation, just as he looked upon the mode of literary presentation, from the point of view of *manifestatio*. He would have taken it for granted that the primary purpose of the many elements that compose a cathedral was to ensure stability, just as he took it for granted that the primary purpose of the many elements that constitute a *Summa* was to ensure validity.

But he would not have been satisfied had not the membrification of the edifice permitted him to re-experience the very processes of architectural composition just as the membrification of the *Summa* permitted him to re-experience the very

processes of cogitation. To him, the panoply of shafts, ribs, buttresses, tracery, pinnacles and crockets was a self-analysis and self-explication of . . . architecture much as the customary apparatus of parts, distinctions, questions and articles was, to him, a self-analysis and self-explication of reason . . . the Scholastic mind demanded a maximum of explicitness. It accepted and insisted upon a gratuitous clarification of function through form, just as it accepted and insisted upon a gratuitous clarification of thought through language.[2]

The other principle Panofsky saw at work in philosophy and architecture is that of *concordantia* ("harmony"), whereby contradictory possibilities are accepted and ultimately reconciled. This is achieved by careful debate, the *disputatio*, in which a possibility is stated, one authoritative view is cited, another authoritative view is cited in objection, the solution (a reconciliation of positions) is given, and finally a reply is given to each of the original arguments now rejected. Panofsky saw this process in the resolution of three "questions" in Gothic architecture: the placement and design of the rose window in the west façade, the design of the interior wall beneath the clerestory, and the conformation of the pier. (Very likely the development of the Gothic plan could also be seen as an evolved "solution" to a "question.") Evidence that the habit of mind reflected in the *disputatio* was not exclusive with the scholastics in the universities, but was more broadly shared, is found in a page from the "album" of drawings by the thirteenth-century architect VILLARD DE HONNECOURT. According to the inscription, an ideal plan for a chevet was drawn by Villard and another architect, PIERRE DE CORBIE, the design being arrived at after a discussion—that is, a *disputatio*.

THE RAYONNANT STYLE

From the grand style of the first half of the thirteenth century came a period of great refinement, the so-called *rayonnant* ("radiant") style, which dominated the second half of the century and was associated with the royal Paris court of Louis IX (St. Louis), famed throughout Europe for his justice, chivalry, and piety, and the Medi-

[2] Erwin Panofsky, *Gothic Architecture and Scholasticism* (Latrobe, Pa.: Archabbey Press, 1951), pp. 58–60.

eval ideal of the "saint-king." Royal France, growing increasingly wealthy, powerful, and prestigious, radiated its art and culture through Europe. The king was lavish in embellishing the realm, especially with religious architecture.

A handsome and characteristic example of the new rayonnant style is the Sainte-Chapelle in Paris (FIGS. 10-23 and 10-24). The building, joined to the royal palace, was intended to be a repository for relics of the Passion of Christ brought back by Louis IX after the ill-fated Sixth Crusade. Here the dissolution of the wall and the reduction of the bulk of the supports has been carried to the point where more than three-quarters of the structure is composed of stained glass. The supporting elements have been so reduced that they

are hardly more than large mullions that separate the enormous windows, which measure approximately 49 by 15 feet and are the largest designed up to their time. Although the chapel was heavily restored during the nineteenth century (after being damaged in the French Revolution), it has retained most of its original thirteenth-century glass, which filters the light and fills the interior with an unearthly rose-violet atmosphere. Amid richly colored stone surfaces and shimmering strips of decorative mosaic stand statues of the Apostles. Multicolored also, they stand on soffits almost independent of the architecture, and their related poses, with multiple axes, foreshadow the graceful rhythms of later thirteenth- and fourteenth-century sculpture. Here are technical

10-23 Sainte-Chapelle, Paris, 1243–48. The rose window was installed after 1485.

10-24 Interior of Sainte-Chapelle.

and esthetic refinements that would have upset the solemn harmonies and monumentality of the art of the earlier part of the century. The emphasis upon extreme slenderness of the architectural forms and upon linearity in general, with exquisite color and precise carving of details, recalls the richly ornamented reliquaries of the time; and it has been suggested that the whole building intentionally has been designed to call one to mind.

The rayonnant manner can be appreciated also in the transepts of Notre Dame in Paris (FIG. 10-10), especially if they are compared with those parts of the building that are some sixty years older. The whole wall seems to open into glass; in the south transept the spectacular rose window, echoed by a smaller window in the gable, contrasts strikingly with the earlier rose in the west façade, which still is framed by massive wall. The south transept rose is the wall become transparent, a filigree of bar tracery seeming as fragile and insubstantial as lace.

The choir of the unfinished cathedral of Beauvais (FIG. 10-25) is an example of the Gothic "rush" into the skies. That skyward impulse, seen first in the height of the nave at Paris (at the turn of the century), became an obsession with Gothic builders. With their new skeletal frames of stone, they attempted goals beyond limit, pushing with ever slenderer supports to new heights, aiming always at effects of insubstantial visions floating far beyond the reach of man. The nave vaults at Laon had risen to a height of about 80 feet; at Paris, to 107 feet; at Chartres, to 118 feet; and at Amiens, to 144 feet. In 1272 the builders of the choir of Beauvais tormented stone to what was to be its limit—157 feet. In 1284 the Beauvais vaults collapsed. The piers had been too widely spaced, and the major buttresses too slim; the choir, rebuilt with a broad margin of safety, has intermediate piers and old-fashioned, six-part vaults. Wide-spaced piers and slender buttresses were exactly the features the rayonnant architects had advocated in their effort to make an architecture out of virtually nothing but line and light. This could be done on the scale of Sainte-Chapelle but not on that of Beauvais. Henceforth, the great structural innovations of the High Gothic, and the vast scale in which they were worked out, would be things of the past. Late

10-25 Choir of Beauvais Cathedral, 1272; vaults rebuilt after 1284.

Gothic architecture, born of the linear rayonnant, would be confined to buildings of quite modest size, conservative in structure and ornamented with restless designs of intricately meshed pointed motifs.

Sculpture

Sculpture was subservient to architecture during the High Gothic period, as it had been since the Romanesque. But rapid changes were taking place. The unity of idea that controls the design of the Royal Portal of Chartres expanded to

10-26 *St. Martin and St. Jerome, c.* 1220–30, from the Porch of the Confessors, Chartres Cathedral.

accounts of natural phenomena, scriptural themes, and moral philosophy serve a didactic religious purpose.

Nature begins to come forward as important, and man comes forward with it. Two figures from the Porch of the Confessors in the south transept of the cathedral of Chartres illustrate how much the incipient realism of the Royal Portal has advanced (FIG. 10-26). The figures represent St. Martin and St. Jerome, and date from the period 1220–30. Although attached to the architectural matrix, their poses are not determined by it as much as formerly. The setting now allows the figures to communicate quietly with one another, like dignitaries waiting for some solemn procession to begin; they turn slightly toward each other, breaking the rigid vertical lines that, on the Royal Portal, fix the figures immovably. Their draperies are no longer described by the stiff and reedy lines of the figures of the Royal Portal; they fall and lap over the bodies in soft, if still regular, folds.

The faces are most remarkable; they show for the first time since the ancient world the features of specifically Western men, with no admixture whatever of the denatured mask that had come down through a thousand years. Moreover, they seem to have been taken from particular persons as models, and we have no difficulty characterizing them. St. Martin is tall, ascetic, the intense priest with the gaunt features of the Gothic visionary (compare the spiritually moved but not particularized face of the Moissac *Jeremiah* of FIG. 9-23); he may have been a saintly canon of Chartres, reluctantly become a bishop; in any event—another realistic touch—his vestments are the liturgical costume of the time. His companion, St. Jerome, appears the humorous, kindly, practical administrator-scholar, who holds his Vulgate translation of the Scriptures. Thus, the two men are not simply contrasted by their poses, gestures, and attributes but most particularly and emphatically as *persons*, so that personality, revealed in human faces, makes the real difference—something that had been rare even in classical art. In another century or so the identifiable portrait will emerge.

The fully ripened Gothic style appears in the west portals of the cathedral of Reims (FIG. 10-27), built in the mid-thirteenth century. At first

embrace the whole cathedral (see the façade of Amiens, FIG. 10-19). The sculptural program came to include not only the huge portals but the upper levels of the building as well. This was at the height of Gothic art, the cathedral-building and cathedral-adorning age, covering the years 1210 to 1260. The range of the iconography of the sculpture is as vast and complex as the building. Most of the carved figures are symbolic, but many, particularly the grotesque gargoyles, used as rain-spouts, and other details of the upper portions, are purely decorative and show the vivacity and charm of the Medieval spirit of this moment, when it was confident in its faith. The iconographic program, no longer (as in Romanesque art) confined almost entirely to the letter of the dogma, is extensive enough to embrace all the categories of Medieval thought. Indeed Émile Mâle showed that many iconographic schemes are based upon the *Speculum majus* ("Great Mirror") of Vincent of Beauvais, a comprehensive summary of Medieval knowledge in which glance, the jamb statues appear completely detached from their architectural background. The columns to which they are attached have shrunk into insignificance and in no way impede the free and easy movement of the full-bodied figures. (On the Royal Portal of Chartres the background columns occupy a volume equal to that of the figures; see FIG. 10-14.) However, two architectural devices limit the statues' spheres of activity and tie them to the larger design of the portal—the pedestals upon which they stand and the canopies above their heads. Less submissive than their predecessors from the Royal Portal of Chartres, these Reims figures create an electric tension within the portal design; they were designed for this portal, however, and would look incongruous in any other setting. Gothic portal statues placed in museums to protect them from weathering look, without exception, forlorn and out of place.

On the right jamb of the central portal, four figures (FIG. 10-28) represent the Annunciation (left) and the Visitation (right). In their different styles they show the hands of several anonymous

10-27 Central portal of the west façade of Reims Cathedral, c. 1225–90.

10-28 *The Annunciation* and *The Visitation*, detail of FIG. 10–27.

masters. The master of the *Visitation* group, quite original in his manner, manifests a classicizing bent startlingly unlike anything seen since Roman times. The group illustrates the impact on its master carver of either actual classical statuary he had seen or of manuscripts or ivories from Late Antiquity or Byzantium. Whatever the artist's source, the facial types, costumes, and drapery treatment are an astonishing approximation of the naturalistic style traits of ancient figure sculpture. He has even tried to represent the classical contrapposto stance, although the only partially successful result betrays the sculptor's ignorance of human anatomy. The two figures of the *Annunciation* group evidently were carved by different masters. The *Virgin* is by a sculptor who may have worked at Amiens before he came to Reims and whose style is characterized by a weighty, massive quality. Drapery resembling a thick, flannel-like material heavily falls from the figure's shoulders to her feet and, by stressing mass and verticality, imparts an aspect of grave solemnity.

The *Angel* of the *Annunciation* group differs strikingly from the *Virgin*. It is tall and slender, animated by a kind of swaying curve, the head quite small, the face bright with a winsome smile. This almost dainty figure, contrasting with the still and somber *Virgin*, represents the new, courtly style—corresponding to the rayonnant in architecture—that comes in with the reign of Louis IX and the cultural dominance of the Ile-de-France after mid-century. The influence of these great cathedral statues must have been widely felt by those who contemplated them. John of Garland, writing in the thirteenth century on how university students should conduct themselves, advises: "... regard as models of deportment the graven images of the churches, which you should carry in your mind as living and indelible pictures."

Stained Glass

The Gothic accomplishment in architecture and sculpture is matched by the magnificent stained glass of the time. This medium is almost synonymous with the Gothic style; no other age has

managed it with such craft and beauty. The mysticism of light that induced Suger to design an architecture that would allow for great windows is widespread in Gothic theology. "Stained glass windows," writes Hugh of St. Victor, "are the Holy Scriptures . . . and since their brilliance lets the splendor of the True Light pass into the church, they enlighten those inside." St. Bernard compares the manner in which light is tinted by a stained-glass window to the process of the Incarnation and virgin birth of Jesus. The Gothic mood seems almost to take its inspiration from the Gospel of John: "In him was life; and the life was the light of men. And the light shineth in darkness."

The difference between these words and the sonorous verses of Revelation, which provide the program of the Romanesque "Last Judgments," reflects the difference between the shining walls of colored light, which change with every passing hour or cloud, and the painted walls of Romanesque churches or the shimmering mosaics of the Byzantine.

Colored glass was used as early as the fourth century to decorate the windows of churches. Perfection of the technique must have been gradual, with the greatest advances during the tenth and eleventh centuries. The first accurately dated windows, those of the choir of St. Denis in 1144, show a high degree of skill; Suger states that they were "painted by the exquisite hands of many masters from different regions," proving that the art was widely known at that time. Yet the stained-glass window may be said to be the hallmark of the Gothic style, particularly in northern Europe, where the almost total dissolution of walls left few surfaces suitable for decoration with frescoes.

Imperfections or unexpected results in making colored glass were frequent; yet this was not an art left entirely to chance. The different properties of colors were well understood and carefully controlled. The glass was blown and either "spun" into a "crown" plate of varying thickness or shaped into a cylindrical "muff," which was cut and rolled out into square pieces. These pieces were then broken or cut into smaller fragments and assembled on a flat table, on which a design had been marked with chalk dust. Many of the pieces were actually "painted" with a dark pigment so that details, as of a face or clothing, could be rendered. The fragments were then "leaded," or joined by strips of lead that were used to separate colors or to heighten the effect of the design as a whole (PLATES 10-1 and 10-2). The completed window was strengthened with an armature of iron bands, which in the twelfth century had the form of a grid over the whole design (PLATE 10-1), but in the thirteenth century was shaped to follow the outlines of the medallions and surrounding areas (PLATE 10-2).

The technical difficulties of assembling a large stained-glass window and fixing it firmly within its frame were matched by compositional problems. Illuminated manuscripts, which had been the painter's chief vehicle during the earlier Middle Ages, had little instructional value for artists who had not only to work on an unprecedented scale, but who had to adjust their designs to the larger whole of the church building and its architecture. Sculptors, of course, had already solved these problems and it may not be too surprising to find that painters turned to them for instruction. Certainly the saints flanking the cross in the Reims window (PLATE 10-1) seem vaguely familiar. Their erect poses, the straight, almost unbroken silhouettes, and the rather precarious manner in which they perch upon their hilltop pedestals stamp them as not too distant relatives of the jamb statues from the Royal Portal at Chartres. Here the Romanesque process has been reversed, and the sculptors, the former students who had found their inspiration in paintings, have now become the teachers.

Like the architects and sculptors with whom they worked in close collaboration, the stained-glass artists relied heavily on the *ars de geometria* for their designs, layouts, and assemblies. The sketchbook of Villard de Honnecourt, the mid-thirteenth-century architect referred to earlier, was intended as a text for Villard's students. But he does not confine his instruction to architecture alone. In addition to details of buildings, plans of choirs with radiating chapels, and church towers, he also presents information on lifting devices, a saw mill, and stained-glass windows. Sprinkled liberally through the pages are drawings of figures, religious and worldly, and animals—some surprisingly realistic, others purely fantastic. In the page shown (FIG. 10-29) Villard is evi-

dently informing his students of the usefulness of the *ars de geometria* in designing human heads and animals. In some instances Villard claims to have drawn his animals from nature, but even these appear to have been composed around a skeleton not of bones but of abstract geometrical figures. It seems likely that the designers of stained-glass windows proceeded in a similar manner. No matter how arrived at, the effect of these glowing, translucent paintings, which often seem to be suspended in space, is as spellbinding today as it must have been to the Medieval churchgoer. For the first time in centuries the art of painting had been made accessible to the common man—painting in a form so compelling that the desire to have more and more of it, from pavement to vault, may well have influenced the development of Gothic architecture. By the middle of the thirteenth century, architectural

10-29 VILLARD DE HONNECOURT, page from a notebook, c. 1240. Bibliothèque Nationale, Paris.

techniques were so advanced that the space of cathedrals seems to be defined by the burning intensity of the stained-glass windows rather than the stone structure.

LATE GOTHIC

The collapse of the vaults of Beauvais would seem to have brought the great thirteenth-century architectural debate to an unarguable conclusion. Analogously, the followers of Aquinas came to believe that his accommodation of faith and reason was impossible and that both must go their separate ways. It was the beginning of the dissolu-

10-30 *The Virgin of Paris*, Notre Dame, early fourteenth century.

tion of the Medieval synthesis, which would lead to the eventual destruction of the unity of Christendom. The resolution of opposites could not be achieved; the conflict must now begin that would reshape western Europe.

Villard de Honnecourt has left us a record of these years when so much was expected of art since so much had been achieved. The search for an ideal solution for a building and the codification of artistic—as well as philosophic—procedures were essentially academic in spirit, conscious evaluations of a style that had already reached and passed its complete definition. Artistic practice and scholastic method would now spend a long time going over ground already covered but would no longer attempt grandiose enterprises. Both were to be concerned with elaborations of surface forms rather than innovations in structure.

By the early fourteenth century the monumental and solemn sculpture of the High Gothic portals was replaced by the courtly style developed from the *Angel* of Reims (FIG. 10-28), a quite rarefied example of which may be seen in the statue of the Virgin and Child within Notre Dame in Paris (FIG. 10-30). The curving sway of the figure, emphasized by the bladelike sweeps of drapery that converge to the child, has a mannered elegance that will mark Late Gothic sculpture in general. This is the famed Late Gothic S-curve that one encounters again and again during the fourteenth and fifteenth centuries. Superficially it may resemble another S-curve seen much earlier—that of Praxiteles in the fourth century B.C. But, unlike its classical predecessor, the Late Gothic S is not organic, coming from within the figure, nor is it the result of a rational, if pleasing, organization of the figure's anatomical parts; it is an artificial form imposed upon the figure, a decorative device that may produce the desired effect of elegance but which has nothing to do with the figure's structure. In fact, in our example, the body is quite lost behind the heavy drapery, which, deeply cut and hollowed, would almost deny the figure solid existence. The ornamental line created by the flexible fabric is analogous to the complex, restless tracery of the flamboyant style in architecture, which dominated northern Europe in

10-31 Above: St. Maclou, Rouen, *c.* 1500–14;
right: Detail of façade.

the fourteenth and fifteenth centuries; and the emphasis upon ornament for its own sake is in harmony with the artificial prettiness the artist contrives in the Virgin's doll-like face, large-eyed and tiny-mouthed under her heavy, gem-encrusted crown.

The change from rayonnant architecture to the Late Gothic or flamboyant (so called because of the flamelike look of its pointed tracery) took place in the fourteenth century; the style reached its florid maturity toward the end of the fifteenth. This period was a difficult one for royal France; long wars against England and Burgundy sapped its economic and cultural strength, and building projects in the royal domain were either halted or not begun. And so the new style found its most fertile soil in regions outside the Ile-de-France. Normandy is particularly rich in flamboyant architecture, and its close ties with England suggest that the Anglo-Norman school of "decorat-ed" architecture may have had much to do with the development of the flamboyant style. The

church of St. Maclou (FIG. 10-31), in Rouen, the capital of Normandy, presents a façade widely different from those of the thirteenth century. St. Maclou, some 180 feet long and 75 feet high, is almost diminutive compared with the great cathedrals. The five portals, two blind, bend outward in an arc and are crowned by five gables pierced through and filled with sinuous, wiry, flamboyant tracery. Pierced galleries of spidery arcades climb steeply to the center bay, marching along behind the transparent gables. The overlapping of all features, pierced as they are, confuses the structural lines and produces a bewildering complexity of views. It is almost as if the Celtic-Germanic instinct for intricate line, expressed in works like the *Book of Lindisfarne*, was manifesting itself once again against the form and logic newly abstracted from the traditions of the Mediterranean. Yet the Renaissance is not far off, and, within a generation or two of St. Maclou, France will have adopted a new classical style from Italy.

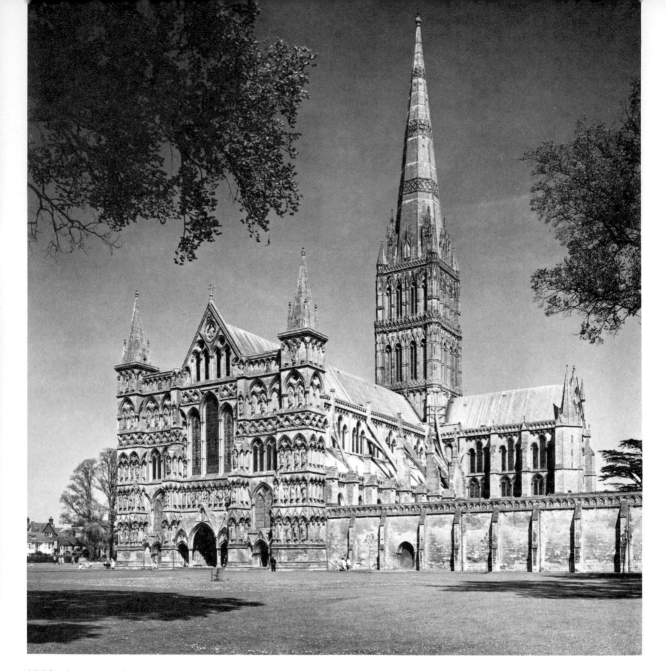

10-32 Above: West façade of Salisbury Cathedral, begun *c.* 1220.

10-33 Right: Plan of Salisbury Cathedral.

Feet
0   50   100

NON-FRENCH GOTHIC

Around 1269 the prior of a German monastery "hired a skilled architect who had just come from the city of Paris" to rebuild his monastery church. The architect reconstructed the church *opere francigeno,* "in the Frankish manner"—that is, in the Gothic style of the Ile-de-France. In 1268, Pope Clement IV, stipulating the conditions for the building of a new cathedral at Narbonne, wrote that the building was "to imitate the noble and magnificently worked churches... which are built in the kingdom of France." The diffusion of the French Gothic style had begun even earlier, but it was in the second half of the thirteenth century that the new style became dominant and that European architecture, in many different ways, turned Gothic. Because the old Romanesque traditions lingered on in many places, each area, marrying its local Romanesque to the new style, developed its own brand of Gothic architecture.

England

The characteristics of English Gothic architecture are admirably embodied in the cathedral of Salisbury (FIGS. 10-32 to 10-35), built between 1220 and 1260. Its location in a park (or close), surrounded by lawns and stately trees, contrasts markedly with that of continental churches, around which the city dwellings nestle closely. The screenlike façade (FIG. 10-32) reaches beyond and does not correspond to the interior; with its dwarf towers, horizontal tiers of niches, and small entrance portals, it is emphatically different from the façades or either Paris or Amiens. Also different is the emphasis on the great crossing tower, which dominates the silhouette. The height of Salisbury is modest compared with that of the almost contemporary cathedral of Amiens; and since height in the English building is not a decisive factor, the flying buttress is used sparingly—as a rigid prop rather than as an integral part of the armature of arches. The exterior of the building, were it not for its pointed features, would look more like an "additive" Romanesque than a Gothic building—if we accept "Gothic" as essentially French.

10-34 Nave of Salisbury Cathedral.

Equally distinctive is the long rectilinear plan (FIG. 10-33), with its double transept and flat eastern end, the latter a characteristic of Cistercian churches and favored in England since Romanesque times. The interior (FIG. 10-34), though Gothic in its three-story elevation, in its pointed arches and rib vaults, and in its compound piers, shows conspicuous differences from French Gothic. The pier colonnettes do not ride up the wall to connect with the vault ribs; instead, the vault ribs rise from corbels in the triforium, producing a strong horizontal emphasis. There is rich detail in the moldings of the arches and the tracery of the triforium, which, enhanced by the contrasts of colored stone, gives a peculiarly crisp and vivid sparkle to the interior. The structural craft of the English stonemason is at its best in the Lady Chapel (dedicated to the Virgin Mary) of Salisbury Cathedral (FIG. 10-35). Incredibly slender piers composed of unattached shafts of Purbeck marble seem to tether the billowing vaults to the ground, rather than support them. Not only is this daring construction, but its linear-

10-35 Lady Chapel of Salisbury Cathedral, *c.* 1225.

ity and slender forms may well be forerunners of the rayonnant style on the continent.

English architecture early finds its native language in the elaboration of architectural pattern for its own sake; structural logic, expressed in the building fabric, is secondary. The pier, wall, and vault elements become increasingly complex and decorative in the fourteenth century, and English Gothic of that period is described as "decorated." The choir of the cathedral of Gloucester (FIG. 10-36), built about a century after Salisbury, illustrates the passage from the "decorated" to the last English Gothic style, the "perpendicular."

The characteristically flat east end at Gloucester is opened in a single, enormous window divided into horizontal tiers of "transom" windows of like shape and proportion, reminiscent of the screen façade of Salisbury. In the nave wall, however, the strong horizontal accents of Salisbury have been erased, as the vertical wall elements, the *responds*, lift directly from the floor to the vaulting, pulling the whole elevation into

a fluent unity. The vault ribs, which had begun to multiply soon after Salisbury, have now become a dense thicket of entirely ornamental strands having no structural function. This vault, in fact, is no longer a rib vault, but a continuous barrel vault with applied decorations.

The culmination of the English perpendicular style can be seen in the vault of the Chapel of Henry VII, which adjoins Westminster Abbey (FIG. 10-37) and was built in the first two decades of the sixteenth century. The linear play of ribs has become a kind of architectural embroidery pulled into "fan vault" shapes with pendent keystones resembling stalactites. The vault looks like something organic that has been petrified in the process of melting. The chapel represents the dissolution of structural Gothic into decorative fancy, its original lines being released from function and multiplying, variegating, and flowering into uninhibited architectural virtuosity and theatrics. The "perpendicular" style in this Tudor structure (named after the reigning dynasty founded by Henry VII) expresses peculiarly well the precious, affected, even dainty style of life codified in the dying etiquette of chivalry at the end of the Middle Ages. Life was, of course, as violent as ever, but the description and expression of it in art comes in forms that are delicate rather than robust.

Germany

The architecture of Germany remained conservatively Romanesque well into the thirteenth century. The plan and massing of German churches include the familiar Rhenish double-apse system, with towers flanking both apses, and in many of these the only Gothic feature is the rib vault, which is buttressed, however, by the heavy masonry of the walls. By mid-century, though, the French influence became strongly felt, and the great 150-foot-high choir of the cathedral of Cologne (FIG. 10-44), discussed on p. 360, is a skillful and energetic interpretation of Amiens. A design, probably of French origin, that met with great favor and was broadly developed in Germany is that of the *Hallenkirche*, or hall church. The term applies to those buildings in which the aisles rise to the same height as the

10-36 Right: Choir of Gloucester Cathedral, 1332–57.

10-37 Below: Detail of the vault of the Chapel of Henry VII, 1503–19, Westminster Abbey, London.

10-38 St. Elizabeth, Marburg, 1233–83.

nave (FIG. 10-39). An early and successful example of this type is the church of St. Elizabeth at Marburg (FIGS. 10-38 to 10-40), built between 1233 and 1283. Since the aisles provide much of the bracing for the central vault, St. Elizabeth's exterior is without the dramatic parade of flying buttresses that circle French Gothic chevets and appears rather prosaic. But the interior (FIG. 10-40), lighted by double rows of tall windows, is more unified and free-flowing, less narrow and divided, than those of other Gothic churches. The hall church, widely used by later Gothic architects, heralds the age of the Protestant Reformation in Germany, when the old ritual that focused on the altar will be modified by the new emphasis on preaching, which will center attention on the pulpit.

French sculpture, like architecture, had its effect abroad. Two stately statues from the choir of the German cathedral at Naumburg (FIG. 10-41) show the quiet, regal deportment of the French statuary of the High Gothic portals, but with a stronger tincture of realism. *Ekkehard* and *Uta* represent persons of the nobility who, in

10-39 Plan and section (through nave) of St. Elizabeth.

former times, had been patrons of the church; the particularity of costume and visage almost make these figures portrait statues, though the subjects lived well before the sculptor's time. *Ekkehard*, blunt and teutonic, contrasts with the charming *Uta*, who with a gesture wonderfully graceful draws the collar of her gown partly across her face while she gathers up a soft fold of drapery with a jeweled, delicate hand. The drapery and the body it enfolds are now understood as distinct entities. The shape of the arm that draws the collar is subtly and accurately revealed beneath the drapery, as is the full curve of the bosom. The drapery folds are rendered with an accuracy that indicates the artist's use of a model. We have before us an arresting image of Medieval people—a feudal baron and his handsome wife —as they may well have appeared in life. By mid-thirteenth century images not only of sacred but of secular personages had found their way into the cathedral.

The equestrian figure of a Gothic nobleman mounted against a pier in the cathedral of Bamberg (FIG. 10-42) is familiarly known as the *Bamberg Rider*. Like *Ekkehard* and *Uta*, it has the quality of portraiture; some believe it represents the German emperor Conrad III. The artist carefully describes the costume of the rider, the high saddle, the caparison of the horse. The proportions of horse and rider are real, though the anatomy of the animal is not quite comprehended, and thus its shape is rather stiffly schematic. An ever present pedestal and canopy firmly establish the group's dependence upon its architectural setting and manage to hold the horse in strict profile. The rider, however, is turning easily toward the observer, as if presiding at a review of troops, and is beginning to break away from the pull of the wall. The stirring and turning of this figure seem to reflect the same impatience with subordination to architecture as did the portal statues at Reims.

Along with the gradual growth of naturalism during the thirteenth century was its modification during the fourteenth by an impulse toward charmingly ornamental effects and courtly convention, as seen in the *Virgin of Paris* (FIG. 10-30). Also rising was a new intensity of expression, which concentrated on such themes as the Cruci-

10-40 Interior of St. Elizabeth.

fixion, the Man of Sorrows, and the Sorrows of the Virgin Mary. The head of a crucifix in St. Maria im Kapitol in Cologne (FIG. 10-43), the features wrenched with pain and sorrow, shows the new preference for interpretations of sacred story in terms of human feeling rather than of dogma and mystery. The humanizing that began in the twelfth century is here accelerated. The anguish of the suffering Christ is represented with such force that it could not fail to stir the emotions powerfully, to arouse deep empathy in the observer. As motion is introduced into portal sculpture, so motion, which reads as emotion, activates the human face. Increasingly, images reach out to the observer, not only into his physical space, but into his emotions. The artist wants to do more than simply present the theological tenet in terms of some impersonal symbol; the mystery is brought back to earth once more, incarnate in the image of physical and psychic suffering.

Italy

Few Italian architects accepted the northern Gothic style, and the question has been raised whether it is proper to speak of buildings like the cathedral of Florence (FIGS. 10-45 to 10-47) as Gothic structures. Begun in 1296 by ARNOLFO DI CAMBIO and so large that it seemed to Alberti to cover "all of Tuscany with its shade," the cathedral looks scarcely Gothic at all. Most of the familiar Gothic features are missing: There are no flying buttresses, no stately clerestory windows, and the walls are pierced only here and there by relatively small openings. Like San Miniato's (FIG. 9-18), the building's surfaces are ornamented, in the old Tuscan fashion, with marble-incrusted geometric designs to match it to the eleventh-century Romanesque baptistry nearby. Beyond an occasional ogival window and the fact that the

nave is covered by rib vaults, there is very little that identifies this building as Gothic. The vast gulf that separates this Italian church from its northern European cousins is strikingly evident when the former is compared with a full-blown German representative of the High Gothic, the cathedral of Cologne (FIG. 10-44).

Cologne Cathedral has one of the longest building histories on record. Begun in 1248, it stood without a nave and with only its chevet, transept, and lower parts of the façade towers completed for some five centuries. Only in the early nineteenth century, when the original designs for the building were discovered, was it decided to finish the structure. Its emphatic stress on the vertical produces an awe-inspiring upward rush of almost unmatched vigor and intensity. The building has the character of an organic growth shooting heavenward, its toothed upper portions engaging the sky, the pierced, translucent stone tracery of the spires merging with the atmosphere.

The cathedral of Florence clings to the ground and has no aspirations to flight. All emphasis is on the horizontal elements of the design, and the building rests firmly and massively on this earth. Simple geometric volumes are clearly defined and show no tendency to merge either into each other or into the sky. The dome, although it may seem to be rising because of its ogival section, has a crisp, closed silhouette that sets it off emphatically against the sky behind it. But, since this dome is the monument with which architectural historians usually introduce the Renaissance (it was built by Brunelleschi between 1420 and 1436), a comparison of the campanile with the Cologne towers may be somewhat more appropriate. Designed by the painter Giotto in 1334 (and completed with some minor modifications after his death), the Florence campanile stands apart from the cathedral in the Italian tradition. In fact, it could stand anywhere else in Florence without looking out of place; it is essentially self-sufficient. This can hardly be said of the northern towers; they are essential elements of the building behind them and it would be unthinkable to detach one of them and place it somewhere else. Heinrich Wölfflin has compared buildings of this kind to a flame, from which no single tongue can be separated. This holds true for every part of the structure, down to its smallest details; no single element seems to be capable of an independent existence; one form merges into the next, in an unending series of rising movements that pull the eye upward and never permit it to rest until it reaches the sky. This structure's beauty is of an amorphous rather than a formal kind; it is a beauty that speaks to the heart rather than to the intellect.

How different the Italian tower! Neatly subdivided into cubic stages, Giotto's tower is the sum of its clearly distinguished parts. Not only could this tower be removed from the building without adverse effects, but each of the component parts, cleanly separated from each other by continuous, unbroken moldings, seems capable of continued, independent existence as an object of considerable esthetic appeal. This compartmentalization is reminiscent of the Romanesque, but it also forecasts the ideal of Renaissance architecture, which was to express itself in clear, logical relationships of a structure's component parts and which aimed for works that were self-sufficient and could exist in complete independence. Compared to the northern towers, Giotto's campanile has a cool and rational quality that appeals more to the intellect than the emotions.

From the plan of the Florence Cathedral (FIG. 10-46) it would seem that the nave was added to the crossing complex as an afterthought; in fact, the nave was built first, pretty much according to Arnolfo's original plans, and the crossing was redesigned in mid-fourteenth century to increase the cathedral's interior space. In its present form the area beneath the dome is the focal point of the design, and the nave leads to it, as Paul Frankl says, "like an introduction of slow chords, to a goal of self-contained finality." To

10-43 Head of a crucifix, 1301. Wood. St. Maria im Kapitol, Cologne.

10-44 Right: Cologne Cathedral, 1248–nineteenth century.

10-45 Below: South flank of Florence Cathedral, 1296–1436.

the visitor from the north, the nave seems as strange as the plan; neither has a northern European counterpart. The cathedral dimensions are about the same as those of Amiens, but there the similarity ends. The Florence nave bays (FIG. 10-47) are three times as deep as those of Amiens; the wide arcades permit the shallow aisles to become part of the central nave; the result is an interior that has an unmatched spaciousness. The accent here, as in the exterior, is on the horizontal elements. The substantial capitals of the piers prevent them from soaring into the vaults and emphasize their function as supports. While this interior may lack the mystery of northern naves, its serene calm and clarity tell the visitor that the Tuscan architects had never entirely rejected nor forgotten their classical heritage, and that it is indeed only here, in central Italy, that the Renaissance could have been born.

The façade of the cathedral of Florence was not completed until the nineteenth century, and then in a form much altered from its beginnings. In

10-46 Plan of Florence Cathedral. (After Sir Banister Fletcher.)

FEET
0   50   100

10-47 Nave of Florence Cathedral.

389

10-48 Façade of Orvieto Cathedral, begun *c.* 1310.

fact, Italian builders seemed little concerned with the façades of their churches, dozens being left unfinished to this day. One of the reasons for this may be that the façades were not conceived as integral parts of the structures but rather as screens that could be added to the fabric at any time. The façade of the cathedral of Orvieto (FIG. 10-48) is a typical and handsome example. Begun in the early fourteenth century, it pays a graceful compliment of imitation to some parts of the French Gothic repertory of ornament, especially in the four large pinnacles that divide the façade into three bays; but these pinnacles—the outer ones serving as miniature substitutes for the big northern west-front towers—grow up, as it were,

from an old Tuscan façade and ultimately from the Early Christian. The rectilinearity and triangularity of the old Tuscan marble incrustation, here enframing and pointing to the precisely wrought rose window, is clearly seen behind the transparent Gothic overlay. The whole effect of the Orvieto façade is that of a great altar screen, its single plane covered with carefully placed carved and painted ornament. In principle, Orvieto belongs with San Miniato al Monte or the cathedral of Pisa, rather than Amiens or St. Elizabeth.

Since Romanesque times, northern European influences had been felt more strongly in Lombardy than in central Italy. When the

to c.1194	1296	c.1300	1309	c.1322	c.1345	1377 1378 1386	1417 to 16th C.

Florence Cathedral begun | Palazzo Pubblico completed, Siena | Façade of Cologne Cathedral begun | Doge's Palace begun, Venice | Milan Cathedral begun |

HIGH GOTHIC | L A T E G O T H I C

←———— BABYLONIAN CAPTIVITY ————→ ←——— GREAT SCHISM ———→

citizens of Milan, in 1386, decided to build their own cathedral (FIG. 10-49), they invited and consulted experts not only from Italy, but also from France, Germany, and England. These experts must have carried on a rough *disputatio* about the strength of the foundations and the composition and adequacy of the piers and the vaults—the application of the true geometric *scientia* in working out plan and elevation. The result was a compromise; the proportions of the building, particularly those of the nave, became Italian (that is, wide in relation to height), and the surface decorations and details, Gothic. But even before the cathedral was half finished, the new classical style of the Renaissance had been well launched and the Milan design had become anachronistic. The elaborate façade represents a confused mixture of late Gothic with classical elements, and stands as a symbol of the waning of the Gothic style.

The city churches of the Gothic world were monuments of civic pride quite as much as they were temples or symbols of the spiritual and natural world. To undertake the construction of a great cathedral a city had to be rich, its commerce thriving; and the very profusion of large churches during the Gothic period attests to the affluence of those who built and maintained them, as well as to the general revival of the economy of Europe in the thirteenth century.

The secular center of the community, the town hall, was almost as much the object of civic pride as the cathedral. A building like the Palazzo Pubblico of Siena (FIG. 10-50), the proud

10-49 Milan Cathedral, begun 1386.

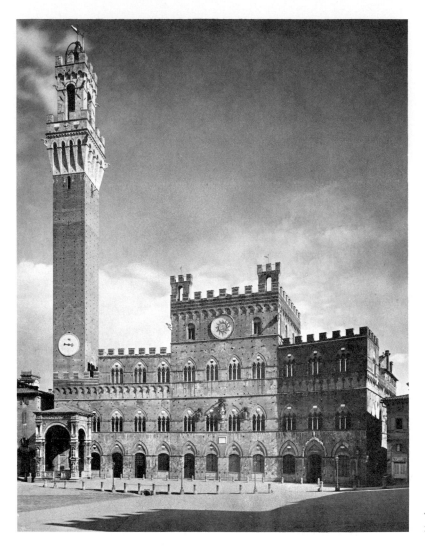

10-50 Palazzo Pubblico, Siena, 1288–1309.

commercial and political rival of Florence, must have drawn the admiration of Siena's citizens as well as of visiting strangers, inspiring in them respect for the city's power and success. More symmetrical in its design than most buildings of its type and period, it is flanked by a lofty tower, which, along with Giotto's campanile in Florence, is one of the finest in Italy. It served as lookout over the city and the countryside around it and as a bell tower from which signals of all sorts could be rung to the populace. The Medieval city, a political unit in itself, had to defend itself against its neighbor cities and often against kings and emperors; but in addition it had to be secure against internal upheavals, in which the history of the Italian city-republics abounds. Feuds between rich and powerful families, class struggle, as well as uprisings of the whole populace against the city fathers were constant threats to a city's internal security. The heavy walls and battlements of the Italian town hall eloquently express the frequent need of city governors to defend themselves against their own citizens. The high tower, out of reach of most missiles, is further protected by machicolated galleries, built out on corbels around the top of the structure to provide openings downward for a vertical defense of the tower's base.

The secular architecture of the Italian mainland tends to have this fortified look. But Venice, some miles out in the Venetian lagoon, was secure from land attack and could rely on her powerful navy to protect her against attacks coming from the sea. Internally, she was a tight corporation of ruling families that for centuries provided an unshakable and efficient establishment, free from disruptive tumults within. This stable internal structure made possible the development of an unfortified, "open" architecture like that of the Doge's Palace (FIG. 10-51), the seat of government of the Venetian republic. This, the most splendid public building of Medieval Italy, seems to invite the passerby to enter rather than to ward him off. In a stately march, the short and heavy columns of the first level support low-pointed arches and look strong enough to carry the weight of the upper structure. Their rhythm is doubled in the upper arcades, where taller and more slender columns carry ogival arches, which terminate in flamelike tips between medallions pierced with quatrefoils. Each story is taller than the one beneath it, the topmost being as high as the two lower arcades combined. And yet the building does not look top-heavy, a fact that is due in part to the complete absence of articulation in the top story and in part to the delicate patterning, in cream and rose-colored marbles, of its walls, which somehow makes them appear paper-thin. The Doge's Palace is the monumental representative of a delightful and charming variant of the Late Gothic. Its slightly exotic style reminds us of Venice's strategic position at the crossroads of the West and the Orient, where it could synthesize artistic stimuli received from either direction. Colorful, decorative, light and airy in appearance, and never overloaded, Venetian Gothic is ideally suited to the lagoon city, which floats between water and air.

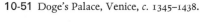

10-51 Doge's Palace, Venice, c. 1345–1438.

GLOSSARY

Italicized terms are themselves defined in the glossary.

abacus (ab′a·kus) The uppermost portion of the *capital* of a *column*, usually a thin slab.

abstract In painting and sculpture, emphasizing a derived essential character having little visual reference to objects in nature.

academy A place of study, derived from the name of the grove where Plato held his philosophical seminars. Giorgio Vasari founded the first academy of fine arts, properly speaking, with his Accademia di Disegno in Florence in 1563.

Achaean (a·kee′an) Of or pertaining to *Achaia*.

Achaia (a·ka′ya) An ancient section of the northern Peloponnesos; loosely, Greece in general.

addorsed Set back-to-back, especially as in heraldic design.

adobe (a·do′bee) The clay used to make a kind of sun-dried brick of the same name, or a building made of such brick.

aerial perspective See *perspective*.

agora (ag′e·ra) An open square or space used for public meetings or business in ancient Greek cities.

alabaster A variety of gypsum or calcite of dense, fine texture, usually white, but also red, yellow, gray, and sometimes banded.

alla prima (a′la pree′ma) A painting technique in which pigments are laid on in one application, with little or no drawing or underpainting.

altarpiece A panel, painted or sculptured, above and behind an altar.

ambulatory A covered walkway, outdoors (as in a *cloister*) or indoors, especially the passageway around the *apse* and *choir* of a church.

amphora (am′fe·ra) A two-handled, egg-shaped jar used for general storage purposes.

apadana (ap·a·dan′a) The great hall in ancient Persian palaces.

apse (aps) A recess, usually singular and semicircular, in the wall at the east end of a Roman *basilica* or Christian church.

arabesque Literally, Arabian-like. A flowing, intricate pattern derived from stylized organic motifs, usually floral, often arranged in symmetrical *palmette* designs; generally an Islamic decorative motif.

arcade A series of *arches* supported by *piers* or *columns*.

arch A curved structural member that spans an opening and is generally composed of wedge-shaped blocks (*voussoirs*) that transmit the downward pressure laterally. See also *thrust*.

architectonic Having structural or architectural qualities (usually as elements of a nonarchitectural object).

architrave (ark'i·trayv) The *lintel* or lowest division of the *entablature*, sometimes called the epistyle.

archivolt (ark'i·volt) One of a series of concentric *moldings* on a Romanesque or Gothic arch.

armature In sculpture, a skeletonlike framework to support material being modeled.

aspara In India, a nymph of the sky or air; in Chinese Buddhism, a heavenly maiden.

atlantes (at·lan'teez) (pl. of atlas) Male figures that function as supporting columns. See *caryatid*.

atmospheric perspective See *perspective*.

atrium (ay'tree·um) The court of a Roman house, near the entrance and partly open to the sky. Also, the open colonnaded court in front of and attached to a Christian *basilica*.

Aurignacian (o'rig·nay'shun) Of or pertaining to the first epoch of Upper *Paleolithic* culture, remains of which were found at Aurignac (Haute-Garonne), France.

avant-garde (a·vahn·gard') Artists whose work is in (or work that reflects) the latest stylistic direction.

avatar (ah'vuh·tar) In Hinduism, an incarnation of a god.

axial plan See *plan*.

axis An imaginary line, or lines, about which a work, a group of works, or part of a work is visually or structurally organized, often symmetrically.

baldacchino (bal·da·kee'no) A canopy on columns, frequently built over an altar.

barrel vault See *vault*.

bas (bah) relief See *relief*.

basilica (ba·sil'i·ka) In Roman architecture, a public building for assemblies (especially tribunals), rectangular in plan and having an entrance on a long side. In Christian architecture, an early church somewhat resembling the Roman basilica, usually entered from one end and with an *apse* at the other, creating an *axial plan*.

batter To slope inward, often almost imperceptibly, or such an inward slope of a wall.

bay A subdivision of the interior space of a building. In Romanesque and Gothic churches the transverse *arches* and *piers* of the *arcade* divide the building into bays.

beehive tomb A beehive-shaped type of subterranean tomb constructed as a *corbeled vault* and found on prehistoric Greek sites.

ben-ben A pyramidal stone; a *fetish* of the Egyptian god Re.

blind arcade (wall arcade) An *arcade* having no actual openings, applied as decoration to a wall surface.

bodhisattva (bo·dee·sot'vuh) In Buddhism, a person who is a potential *buddha*.

bottega (but·tay'ga) A shop; the studio-shop of an Italian artist.

broken color A painting technique using short, thick strokes laid over a ground color to create rich textures and vibrant effects of light.

broken pediment A *pediment* in which the *cornice* is discontinuous at the apex or the base.

buddha One who is an embodiment of divine wisdom and virtue.

burin (byoor'in) A pointed steel tool for *engraving* or *incising*.

buttress An exterior masonry structure that opposes the lateral thrust of an arch or vault. A pier buttress is a solid mass of masonry; a flying buttress consists typically of an inclined member carried on an arch or series of arches and a solid buttress to which it transmits lateral *thrust*.

calligraphy Handwriting or penmanship, especially elegant or "beautiful" writing as a decorative art.

campanile (kam·pa·neel'eh) A bell tower, usually free-standing.

capital The upper member of a *column*; it serves as a transition from the *shaft* to the *lintel*.

cardo The north-south road in Etruscan and Roman towns, intersecting the *decumanus* at right angles.

cartoon In painting, a full-size drawing from which a painting is made. Cartoons were usually worked out in complete detail and the design then transferred to the working surface by coating the back with chalk and going over the lines with a stylus, or by pricking the lines and "pouncing" charcoal dust through the resulting holes.

cartouche (kar·toosh') A scroll-like design or medallion, purely decorative or containing an inscription or heraldic device; also, in ancient Egypt, an oval device containing such elements as *hieroglyphic* names of Egyptian kings.

caryatid (kar'ee·at'id) A female figure that functions as a supporting *column*. See also *atlantes*.

casting In sculpture, duplication of a clay original in plaster or metal by use of a mold.

cella (sel'a) An enclosed chamber, the essential feature of a Classical temple, in which the cult statue usually stood.

centering A wooden framework to support an *arch* or *vault* during its construction.

central plan See *plan*.

ceramics The art of making objects such as pottery of clay; also, the objects themselves.

chaitya (chight'yuh) A Buddhist assembly hall having a votive *stupa* at one end.

chalice A cup or goblet, especially that used in the sacraments of the Christian Church.

chamfer The surface formed by cutting off a corner of a board or post; a bevel.

champlevé (shahn·le·vay') A process of enameling in which a design is cut into a metal plate in such a way as to leave thin raised lines that create compartments to hold the enamel.

chandi A Javanese temple.

chevet (sheh·vay') The eastern end of a Romanesque church, including *choir*, *ambulatory*, and radiating chapels.

chevron A zigzag or V-shaped motif of decoration.

chiaroscuro (kee·ar'eh·skoor'o) In painting or drawing, the treatment and use of light and dark, especially the gradations of light that produce the effect of modeling.

chinoiserie (shee·nwaz·eh·ree') Chinese motifs used as decorations for furniture, in wallpaper, etc., applied largely to eighteenth-century Rococo style.

chiton (kite'en) A Greek tunic, the essential (and often only) garment of both men and women, the other being the mantle (*himation*).

choir The space reserved for the clergy in the church, usually east of the *transept*, but in some instances extending into the *nave*.

ciborium (sih·bor'ee·um) A canopy, usually freestanding and supported by four columns, erected over an altar; also, a covered cup used in the sacraments of the Christian Church. See *baldacchino*.

cinquecento (cheenk·way·chain'toh) The sixteenth century in Italian art.

cire-perdue (seer·pair·dew') The "lost-wax" process. A bronze-casting method in which a figure is modeled in wax and covered with clay. When the clay dries, the wax is melted away and the resulting mold is filled with molten metal.

clerestory (kleer'sto·ry) The part of a building that rises above the roofs of the other parts and whose walls contain openings for light.

cloison (klwa·zohn') Literally, a partition. A cell made of metal wire or a narrow metal strip, usually gold, soldered end-down to a metal base to hold enamel or other decorative materials.

cloisonné (klwa·zoh·nay') A process of enameling employing *cloisons*.

cloister A court, usually with covered walks or *ambulatories* along its sides.

closed form A form, especially in painting, whose contour is not broken or blurred.

clustered pier See *compound pier*.

codex (*pl.* codices) A manuscript in the form of a volume with pages bound together between hard covers.

coffer A sunken ornamental panel in a *soffit*, *vault*, or ceiling.

coin type The pattern or design used to decorate a coin.

collage (kul·lahzh') A composition made by pasting together on a flat surface various materials such as newspaper, wallpaper, printed text and illustrations, photographs, and cloth. See *montage*.

colonnade A series or row of *columns*, usually spanned by *lintels*.

colonnette A small *column*.

color See *hue*, *saturation*, and *value*.

color solid A conceptual device in which the principal variables of *color* are visualized as having a three-dimensional relationship in the form of two cones base-to-base. The vertical *axis* is *value*, the *hues* are arranged around the axis, and *saturation* is the distance from the surface of the solid to the axis.

column A vertical, weight-carrying architectural member, circular in cross section, and consisting of a base (sometimes omitted), a *shaft*, and a *capital*.

complementary after-image The image, in a *complementary color*, that is retained briefly by the eye after the stimulus is removed.

complementary colors Those pairs of colors, such as red and green, that together embrace the entire spectrum. Thus the complement of one of the three *primary colors* is a mixture of the other two. In pigments they produce a neutral, or gray, when mixed in the right proportions.

compound or clustered pier A pier composed of a group or cluster of members, especially characteristic of Gothic architecture.

connoisseur (kon·nuh·ser') An expert on works of art and the individual styles of artists.

contour A visible border of a *mass* in space; a *line* that creates the illusion of *mass* and *volume* in space.

contrapposto (kon·tra·poh'stoh) The disposition of the human figure in which one part is turned in a direction opposite that of the other (usually hips and legs one way, shoulders and chest another)—thus, a counter-positioning of the body about its central *axis*. Sometimes called "weight-shift," since the weight of the body tends to be thrown to one foot, creating tension on one side and relaxation on the other.

cool color Blue, green, or violet. Psychologically, cool colors are calming, unemphatic, depressive; optically they generally appear to recede. See *warm color*.

corbel (kor'bel) A projecting wall member used as a support for some element in the superstructure. Also, courses of stone or brick in which each course projects beyond the one beneath it. Two such structures, meeting at the topmost course, create an archlike form.

cornice The projecting, crowning member of the *entablature*; also, any crowning projection.

cosmati (koz·ma'tee) Cut-stone *mosaic* inlay decoration in geometric patterns.

cramp A device, usually metal, to hold together blocks of stone of the same course. See *dowel*.

crenelated Notched or indented, usually with respect to tops of walls, as in battlements.

crocket A projecting foliate ornament of a *capital*, *pinnacle*, *gable*, *buttress*, or *spire*.

Cro-Magnon (kro-mag'non) Of or pertaining to the *homo sapiens* whose remains, dating from the *Aurignacian* period, were found in the Cro-Magnon cave of Dordogne, France.

cromlech (krom'lek) A circle of monoliths.

crossing The space in a cruciform church formed by the intersection of the *nave* and *transept*.

crown The topmost part of an *arch*, including the *keystone;* also, an open *finial* of a tower.

crypt A *vaulted* space under part of a building, wholly or partly underground; in Medieval churches, normally the portion under an *apse* or *chevet.*

cuneiform (kyoo·nee'ih·form) Literally, wedge-shaped; thus a system of writing used in Babylonia-Assyria, the characters of which were wedge-shaped.

cyclopean (sike·lo·pee'an) Gigantic; vast and rough; massive. Cyclopean architecture is a style of stone construction using large irregular blocks without mortar.

dado (day'doh) A horizontal band, often decorated, at the base or lower part of a wall or pedestal.

decumanus (dek·yoo·man'us) The east-west road in an Etruscan or Roman town, intersecting the *cardo* at right angles.

diptych (dip'tik) A two-paneled *altarpiece;* also, an ancient Roman and Early Christian two-hinged writing tablet, or ivory memorial panels.

dolmen (dohl'men) Several large stones capped with a covering slab, erected in prehistoric times.

dome A hemispherical *vault;* theoretically, an *arch* rotated on its vertical *axis*.

donjon (don'jun) A massive tower forming the stronghold of a Medieval castle.

dowel In ancient architecture, wooden or metal pins placed between stones of different courses to prevent shifting. See *cramp*.

dromos The passage to a *beehive tomb*.

drum The circular wall that supports a dome; also, one of the cylindrical stones of which a non-monolithic *shaft* is made.

dry point An *engraving* in a soft metal such as copper in which the burr raised by the *burin* is retained to produce a soft, richly black effect in the print. See *etching, intaglio*.

duecento (doo·ay·chain'toh) The thirteenth century in Italian art.

earth colors Pigments, such as yellow ochre and umber, that are obtained by mining; they are usually compounds of metals.

echinus (eh·kee'nus) In architecture, the convex element of a *capital* directly below the *abacus*.

eclecticism (eh·klek'ti·sism) The practice of selecting from various sources, usually in order to form a new system or style.

écorché (ay·kor·shay') A flayed figure painted or sculptured to show the muscles of the body.

elevation In drawing and architecture, a geometric projection of a building on a plane perpendicular to the horizon; a vertical projection.

embrasure A flared frame around a doorway or window.

enamel A vitreous, colored paste that solidifies when fired. See *champlevé, cloisonné*.

encaustic An ancient method of painting with colored molten wax in which the wax is fused with the surface by application of hot irons.

engaged column A columnlike, nonfunctional form projecting from a wall and articulating it visually.

engobe (en·gohb') A slip of finely sifted clay used by Greek potters; applied to a pot it would form a black *glaze* in firing.

engraving The process of *incising* a design in hard material, often a metal plate, usually copper; also, the print or impression made from such a plate. See *burin, dry point, etching, intaglio*.

entablature The part of a building, usually the *façade*, between the *capitals* of *columns* and the roof or upper story.

entasis (en·tay'sis) An almost imperceptible convex tapering (an apparent swelling) in the *shaft* of a *column*.

epistyle See *architrave*.

esthetic The distinctive vocabulary of a given style.

etching A kind of *engraving* in which the design is *incised* in a layer of wax or varnish on a copper plate. The parts of the plate left exposed are then etched, or slightly eaten away, by acid in which the plate is immersed after incising. Because wax and varnish are relatively soft materials, the etcher is freed from the restrictions imposed upon the woodcutter and engraver by their media. Etching is thus one of the most facile of the graphic arts and the one most capable of subtleties of line and tone. See *dry point, engraving,* and *intaglio*.

extrados (eks·trah'dohs) The upper or outer surface of an *arch*.

façade Usually, the front of a building; also, the other sides when they are emphasized architecturally.

faïence (feye·ahnce') Pottery (except porcelain) glazed with compounds of tin; also, any glazed earthenware.

fan vault See *vault*.

fenestration The arrangement of the windows of a building; by extension, the arrangement of all openings (windows, doors, *arcades*).

ferroconcrete See *reinforced concrete*.

fête galante (fet ga·lahnt') An elegant and graceful celebration; applied to the works of Antoine Watteau and other Rococo painters.

fetish An object believed to possess magical powers, especially one capable of bringing to fruition its owner's plans; sometimes regarded as the abode of a supernatural power or spirit.

figure-ground The visual unity, yet separability, of

a form and its background; usually with "relationship."

finial A knoblike ornament, usually with a foliate design, in which a vertical member such as a *pinnacle* terminates.

flamboyant Flamelike, flaming; applied to aspects of a late Gothic style, especially architectural tracery.

flute or **fluting** Vertical channeling, roughly semicircular in cross section and used principally on *columns* and *pilasters*.

flying buttress See *buttress*.

foreshortening Seeming visual contraction of an object viewed as extended in a plane not perpendicular to the line of sight; also, the representation of this phenomenon.

form In its widest sense, total organic structure; a synthesis of all the elements of that structure and of the manner in which they are united to create its distinctive character. The form of a work is what enables us to apprehend it. See *closed form* and *open form*.

formalism Strict adherence to, or dependence on, prescribed forms of execution and traditional rules of composition.

fresco Painting on plaster, either dry (dry fresco) or wet (wet or true fresco). In the latter method the pigments are mixed with water and become chemically bound to the plaster. Also, a painting executed in either method.

fret or **meander** An ornament, usually in bands but also covering broad surfaces, consisting of interlocking geometric motifs.

frieze (freez) The part of the *entablature* between the *architrave* and *cornice*; also, any sculptured or ornamented band in a building, on furniture, etc.

gargoyle In architecture, a waterspout, usually carved, often in the form of a *grotesque*.

genre (zhahn'reh) A style or category of art; also, a kind of painting realistically depicting scenes from everyday life.

gesso (jess'oh) Plaster mixed with a binding material and used for *reliefs* and as a *ground* for painting.

glaze A vitreous coating applied to pottery to seal the surface and as decoration; it may be colored, transparent or opaque, and glossy or *matte*. In oil painting, a thin, transparent or semitransparent layer put over a color to alter it slightly.

golden mean or **golden section** A proportional relationship obtained by dividing a line so that the shorter part is to the longer as the longer is to the whole. These proportions have an esthetic appeal that has led artists of varying periods and cultures to employ them in determining basic dimensions.

gopuram (go'pur·om) The massive, ornamented entrance structure of East Indian temples.

gouache (goo·ahsh') *Watercolor* rendered opaque by the addition of a filler such as zinc white. It has more body and dries more slowly than the trans-parent watercolor and lends itself to bright color effects and meticulous detail. Also, a picture painted in this medium.

granulation In jewelry, a method of ornamenting in which small grains of metal, usually gold, are soldered to a flat surface.

graphic arts Those visual arts that are linear in character (such as drawing and *engraving*); also, generally, those that involve impression (printing and printmaking).

graver A cutting tool used by engravers and sculptors.

Greek cross A cross in which all the arms are the same length.

grisaille (greez·eye') A monochrome painting done mainly in neutral grays to simulate sculpture.

groin The edge formed by the intersection of two *vaults*.

groin vault See *vault*.

grotesque In art, a kind of ornament—sometimes called (imprecisely) *arabesque*—used in antiquity and consisting of representations of medallions, sphinxes, foliage, and imaginary creatures.

ground A coating applied to a canvas or other surface to prepare that suface for painting; also, background.

guilloche (gi·lush') An ornament consisting of interlaced curving bands.

hallenkirche (holl'en·keer·kheh) A hall church. In this variety of Gothic church, especially popular in Germany, the aisles are almost as high as the *nave*.

hammer-beam ceiling An English Gothic open-timber ceiling whose support elements resemble the claws of a hammer.

hatching A technique used in drawing, engraving, etc., in which fine lines are cut or drawn close together to achieve an effect of shading.

haunch The part of an *arch* (roughly midway between the *springing* and the *crown*) where the lateral *thrust* is strongest.

herringbone perspective See *perspective*.

hieroglyphic A system of writing using symbols or pictures; also, one of the symbols.

himation (him·mat'ee·on) A Greek mantle worn by men and women over the tunic and draped in various ways.

historiated Ornamented with representations—such as plants, animals, or human figures—that have a narrative, as distinct from a purely decorative, function. Historiated initial letters were a popular form of manuscript decoration in the Middle Ages.

hue The name of a color. The *primary colors* (blue, red, and yellow) together with the *secondary colors* (green, orange, and violet) form the chief colors of the spectrum. See also *complementary colors*, *cool color*, *saturation*, *value*, *warm color*.

hydria An ancient Greek three-handled water jar.

hypostyle hall A hall whose roof is supported by columns; applied to the colonnaded hall of the Egyptian *pylon* temple.

icon (eye′con) A portrait or image, especially, in the Greek church, a panel with a painting of sacred personages that are objects of veneration. In the visual arts, a painting, a piece of sculpture, or even a building regarded as an object of veneration.

iconography (eye·con·og′ra·fee) The study dealing with the symbolic, often religious, meaning of objects, persons, or events depicted in works of art.

iconostasis (eye·con·os′ta·sis) In eastern Christian churches, a screen or partition, with doors and many tiers of *icons*, that separates the sanctuary from the main body of the church.

idealization The representation of things according to a preconception of ideal *form* or type; a kind of esthetic distortion to produce idealized forms. See *Realism*.

illumination Decoration with drawings, usually in gold, silver, and bright colors, especially the initial letters of a manuscript.

imam One who leads worshipers in prayer in Moslem services.

impasto (im·pah′stoh) A style of painting in which the pigment is applied thickly or in heavy lumps, as in many of Rembrandt's paintings.

impost block A stone with the shape of a truncated, inverted pyramid, placed between a *capital* and the *arch* that springs from it.

Impressionism A type of *Realism* whose aim is to render the immediate sense impression of the artist. It had its origins in nineteenth-century France with the work of Édouard Manet and was developed and altered by Claude Monet and others. A main concern of the Impressionists was the study and representation of light.

incising Cutting into a surface with a sharp instrument; also, a method of decoration, especially on metal and pottery.

intaglio (in·tal′yoh) A category of graphic technique in which the design is *incised*, so that the impression made is in *relief*. Used especially on gems, seals, and dies for coins, but also in the kinds of printing or printmaking in which the ink-bearing surface is depressed. Also, an object so decorated. See *dry point, engraving, etching*.

intarsia (in·tahr′sya) Inlay work, primarily in wood and sometimes in mother-of-pearl, marble, etc.

intercolumniation The space or the system of spacing between *columns* in a *colonnade*.

intrados (in·trah′dohs) The underside of an *arch* or *vault*.

isocephaly Arrangement of figures so that the heads are at the same height.

jātaka (jah′tuh·kuh) Tales of the lives of the Buddha.

jube (joo′bee) A *choir* screen treated as an architectural ornament.

ka (kah) In ancient Egypt, immortal human substance, the concept approximating the Western idea of soul.

kakemono A Japanese hanging or scroll.

karma (kar′muh) In Buddhist and Hindu belief, the ethical consequences of a person's life, determinant of his or her fate.

keystone The central, uppermost *voussoir* in an *arch*.

khutbah (koot′buh) In Moslem worship, a sermon and a declaration of allegiance to a community's leader.

kiln A large stove or oven in which pottery is fired.

krater (or crater) (kray′ter) An ancient Greek wide-mouthed bowl for mixing wine and water.

kuang A Chinese covered libation vessel.

kylix (or cylix) (kye′liks) An ancient Greek drinking cup, shallow and having two handles and a stem.

lacquer A resinous spirit varnish such as shellac, often colored.

lantern In architecture, a small, often decorative structure with openings for lighting that crowns a *dome*, turret, or roof.

lapis lazuli (la′pis la′zyoo·lye) A rich ultramarine semiprecious stone used for carving and as a source of *pigment*.

Latin cross A cross in which the vertical member is longer than the horizontal member, through whose midpoint it passes.

lierné (lyair·nay′) A short *rib* that runs from one main rib of a *vault* to another.

line The mark made by a moving point and having psychological impact according to its direction and weight. In art it defines space and may create a silhouette or define a *contour*, creating the illusion of *mass* and *volume*.

linear perspective See *perspective*.

lintel A beam of any material used to span an opening.

lithography In graphic arts, a printmaking process in which the printing surface is a polished stone (or metal plate) on which the design is drawn with a greasy material. Greasy ink, applied to the moistened stone, is repelled by all surfaces but the lines of the drawing. The process permits linear and tonal values of great range and subtlety.

local color In painting, the actual color of an object.

loggia (luh′jee·uh) A gallery that has an open *arcade* or *colonnade* on a side or sides.

lunette A semicircular opening, with the flat side down, in a wall over a door, niche, or window.

luster A thin *glaze*, usually metallic, sometimes used on pottery to produce a rich, often iridescent color. Used particularly in Persian pottery and in *majolica*.

madrasah (muh·dros′uh) A combined Moslem school and *mosque*.

Magdalenian (mag·de·lee′nee·an) Of or pertaining to the climactic cultural stage of the Upper *Paleolithic* and named after archeological findings at La Madeleine (Dordogne), France.

majolica (ma·jah′lik·uh) A kind of Italian Renaissance pottery coated with a whitish tin-compound enamel, brilliantly painted and often *lustered*.

makimono A Japanese horizontal scroll.

malanggan Intricately carved Melanesian ceremonial masks.

mandala (man′duh·luh) In Hinduism and Buddhism, a magical geometric symbol of the cosmos.

mandapa (man·dop′uh) A Hindu assembly hall, part of a temple.

mandorla An almond-shaped nimbus, or glory, surrounding the figure of Christ.

mass The effect and degree of bulk, density, and weight of matter in space. As opposed to plane and area it describes *form* in three-dimensional space. See also *volume*.

mastaba (mah′sta·buh) A bench-shaped ancient Egyptian tomb.

matte (mat) In painting, pottery, and photography, a dull finish.

mbari Ceremonial houses filled with clay sculptures, honoring community deities of the Ibo tribe in Africa.

meander See *fret*.

medium The substance or agency in which an artist works; also, in painting, the vehicle, usually liquid, that carries the pigment.

megaron (meh′ga·ron) A large rectangular living hall, fronted by an open two-columned porch, traditional in Greece since Mycenaean times.

menhir (men′heer) A prehistoric monolith, uncuts or roughly cut, standing singly or with other in rows or circles.

Mesolithic (Middle Stone Age) Of or pertaining to the period between the *Paleolithic* and *Neolithic*, characterized by food-gathering and incipient agriculture.

metope (met′a·pee) The space between *triglyphs* in a Doric *frieze*.

mihrab (mee′rob) In the wall of a *mosque*, the niche that indicates the direction of Mecca.

minbar (meen′bar) The pulpit in a *mosque*.

miniature A small picture illustrating a manuscript; also, any small portrait, often on ivory or porcelain.

modeling The shaping of three-dimensional forms in a soft material such as clay; also, the gradations of light and shade reflected from the surfaces of matter in space, or the illusion of such gradations produced by alterations of *value* in a drawing or painting.

module (mod′yool) A basic unit of which the dimensions of the major parts of a work are multiples. The principle is used in sculpture and other art forms, but it is most often employed in architecture, where the module may be the dimensions of an important part of a building, such as a column, or simply some commonly accepted unit of measurement such as the centimeter or the inch, or, as with Le Corbusier, the average dimensions of the human figure.

molding In architecture, a continuous narrow surface, either projecting or recessed, plain or ornamented, whose purpose is to break up a surface, to accent, or to decorate by means of the light and shade it produces.

monochrome A painting in one color; also, the technique of making such a painting.

montage (mohn′tahzh) A composition made by fitting together pictures or parts of pictures; also, motion-picture effects produced by superimposing images or showing them in rapid sequence. See *collage*.

monumental In art criticism, any work of art of unpretentious grandeur and simplicity, regardless of its size.

mosaic Patterns or pictures made by embedding small pieces of stone or glass (*tesserae*) in cement on surfaces such as walls and floors; also, the technique of making such works.

mosque A Moslem place of worship.

mudra (muh·drah′) A stylized gesture of mystical significance, usually in representations of Hindu deities.

mullion A vertical member that divides a window or separates one window from another.

mural A painting on a wall; a *fresco* is a type of mural.

narthex A porch or vestibule of a church, generally colonnaded or arcaded and preceding the *nave*.

Naturalism The doctrine that art should adhere as closely as possible to the appearance of the natural world. Naturalism, with varying degrees of fidelity to appearance, recurs in the history of Western art.

nave The part of a church between the chief entrance and the *choir*, demarcated from aisles by *piers* or *columns*.

Neanderthal (nee·an′der·tal) A species of *Paleolithic* man.

necking A groove at the bottom of the Greek Doric capital between the *echinus* and the *flutes* that masks the junction of *capital* and *shaft*.

necropolis (neh·krop′o·liss) A large burial area; literally, a city of the dead.

Neolithic (New Stone Age) Of or pertaining to the period that saw the first elements of a farming economy and fixed settlements.

niello (nee·el′o) Inlay in a metal of an alloy of sulfur and such metals as gold or silver. Also, a work made by this process, or the alloy itself.

nirvana (neer·vah′nuh) In Buddhism and Hinduism,

a blissful state brought about by absorption of the individual soul or consciousness into the supreme spirit.

obverse On coins or medals, the side that bears the principal type or inscription. See *reverse*.

odalisque (oh'de·lisk) An Oriental slave girl or concubine, a favorite subject of artists such as Ingres and Matisse.

oenochoe (eh·nuk'oh·ee) An ancient Greek wine pitcher.

oeuvre (uh'vreh) The whole of an artist's output; literally, his "work."

ogee (oh'jee) A *molding* having in profile a double, or S-shaped, curve. Also, an *arch* of this form.

oil color *Pigment* ground with oil.

open form A *mass* penetrated or treated in such a way that space acts as its environment rather than as its limit. See *closed form*.

order In Classical architecture, a style represented by a characteristic design of the *column* and its *entablature*. See also *superimposed order*.

Paleolithic (Old Stone Age) Of or pertaining to the period preceding the *Mesolithic* and characterized by stone implements and cave painting. Lower Paleolithic man (to 32,000 B.C.) was a nomadic hunter, while Upper Paleolithic man (32,000–8000 B.C.) was a specialized hunter.

palette (pal'it) A thin board with a thumb hole at one end upon which an artist lays and mixes his colors; any surface so used. Also, the colors or kinds of colors characteristically used by an artist.

palmette A conventional decorative ornament of ancient origin composed of radiating petals springing from a calyxlike base.

Panathenaea (pan'a·then·ee'a) The most ancient and important festival of Athens, held in honor of the goddess Athena.

Pantheon All the gods of a people, or a temple dedicated to all such gods; especially, the Pantheon in Rome (though it is not certain that this was its function).

papyrus A plant native to Egypt and adjacent lands used to make a paperlike writing material; also, any writing on papyrus.

passage grave A burial chamber entered through a long tunnel-like passage.

pastel Finely ground *pigments* compressed into chalklike sticks. Also, work done in this *medium*, or its characteristic paleness.

patina (pa·teen'a) The green oxidized layer that forms on bronze and copper.

pediment In Classical architecture, the triangular space (gable) at the end of a building, formed by the ends of the sloping roof and the *cornice*; also, an ornamental feature having this shape.

pendentive (pen·den'tiv) A concave, triangular piece of masonry (a triangular section of a hemisphere), four of which support a *dome* erected over a square.

peripteral (per·ip'ter·al) A style of building in which the main structure is surrounded by a *colonnade*.

peristyle A *colonnade* surrounding a building or a court.

perspective A scheme or formula for projecting an illusion of the three-dimensional world on a two-dimensional surface. In linear perspective, the most common type, all parallel lines or lines of projection seem to converge on a single point on the horizon, known as the *vanishing point*, and associated objects are rendered smaller the further from the viewer they are intended to seem. Atmospheric or aerial perspective creates the illusion of distance by the greater diminution of color intensity, shift in color toward an almost neutral blue, and blurring of contours as the intended distance between eye and object increases. In herringbone perspective the lines of projection converge not on a vanishing point, but on a vertical *axis* at the center of the picture.

pi (pee) The Chinese symbol of heaven, a jade disk.

piano nobile (peea'no no'bee·lay) The principal story, usually the second, in Renaissance buildings.

pictograph A picture, usually stylized, that represents an idea; also, writing using such means. See *hieroglyphic*.

picture plane The surface of a picture.

pier A vertical, unattached masonry support.

Pietà (peeay·ta') A work of art depicting the Virgin mourning over the body of Christ.

pigment Finely powdered coloring matter mixed or ground with various vehicles to form paint, crayon, etc.

pilaster (pi·las'ter) A flat, rectangular, vertical member projecting from a wall of which it forms a part. It usually has a base and a *capital* and is often *fluted*.

pillar Usually a weight-carrying member such as a *pier* or a *column*; sometimes an isolated free-standing structure used for commemorative purposes.

pinnacle A tower, primarily ornamental, but functioning in Gothic architecture to give additional weight to a *buttress* or *pier*. See *finial*.

pithos (pith'oss) (*pl.* pithoi) A large clay storage vessel frequently set into the earth, and, therefore possessing no flat base.

plan The horizontal arrangement of the parts of a building, or a drawing or diagram showing such arrangement as a horizontal *section*. An axial plan is one in which the parts of a building are organized longitudinally, or along a given *axis*; a central plan is one in which the parts radiate from a central point.

plasticity In art, the three-dimensionality of an object.

plinth The lowest member of a base; also, a block serving as a base for a statue.

polychrome Done in several colors.

polyptych (pol'ip·tik) An *altarpiece* made up of more than three sections.

porcelain Translucent, impervious, and resonant *pottery* made in a base of kaolin, a fine white clay; sometimes any pottery that is translucent, whether or not made of kaolin.

portico A porch with a roof supported by *columns* and usually having an *entablature* and a *pediment*.

pottery Objects, usually vessels, made of clay and hardened by firing.

predella The narrow ledge on which an *altarpiece* rests at the back of an altar.

primary colors The *hues* red, yellow, and blue. From these three, with the addition of white, it is theoretically possible to mix the full color spectrum. The primary colors cannot be produced by mixing others.

program The architect's formulation of a design problem with respect to considerations of site, function, materials, and aims (of the client); also, in painting and sculpture, the conceptual basis of a work.

pronaos (pro·nay'os) The enclosed space in front of the *cella* of a Greek temple.

provenance Origin, source.

psalter A book containing the Psalms of the Bible.

putto (*pl.* putti) A young child, a favorite subject in Italian painting and sculpture.

pylon (pie'lon) The *monumental* entrance of an Egyptian temple.

qiblah (keeb'lah) The direction (toward Mecca) in which Moslems face in prayer. (Often *kibla*.)

quatrefoil (kat're·foyl) An architectural ornament having four lobes or foils. See *trefoil*.

quattrocento (kwat'tro·chain'toh) The fifteenth century in Italian art.

quoin (koin) Large, sometimes *rusticated*, usually slightly projecting stone or stones that often form the corners of the exterior walls of masonry buildings.

raking cornice The *cornice* on the sloping sides of a *pediment*.

Rāmāyana A Sanskrit epic telling of Rama, an incarnation of the Hindu god Vishnu.

Realism The doctrine that art should represent nature without *idealization*.

reinforced concrete (ferroconcrete) Concrete whose tensile strength is increased by iron or steel mesh or bars embedded in it.

relief In sculpture, figures projecting from a background of which they are part. The degree of relief is designated high, low (or bas), or sunken (or hollow). In the last, the backgrounds are not cut back and the points in highest relief are level with the original surface of the material being carved. A kind of low relief that is hardly more than a scratching of the surface was originated by Donatello and is termed **stiacciata** or **sciacciata**. See *repoussé*.

reliquary A small receptacle for a sacred relic, usually of a richly decorated precious material.

repoussé (ruh·poo·say') Formed in relief by beating a metal plate from the back, leaving the impression on the face. The metal is hammered into a hollow mold of wood or some other pliable material and finished with a *graver*. See *relief*.

respond An engaged *column*, *pilaster*, or similar structure, either projecting from a *compound pier* or other supporting device, or bonded to a wall and carrying one end of an *arch*, often at the end of an *arcade*. A nave arcade, for example, may have nine pillars and two responds.

retable (ruh·tay'bl) An architectural screen or wall above and behind an altar, usually containing painting, sculpture, carving, or other decorations.

reverse On coins or medals, the side opposite the *obverse*.

rhyton (right'on) An ancient Greek ceremonial drinking vessel whose base is usually in the form of the head of an animal, woman, or mythological creature.

rib A relatively slender molded masonry *arch* that projects from the surface. In Gothic architecture the ribs form the framework of the *vaulting*.

ribbed vault See *vault*.

rinceau (ran·so') An ornamental design composed of undulating foliate vine motifs.

rose or **wheel window** The large circular window with *tracery* and stained glass frequently used in the *façades* of Gothic churches.

rusticate To bevel or rabbet the edges of stone blocks in order to emphasize the joints between them. The technique was popular during the Renaissance, especially for stone courses at the ground-floor level.

samsāra (som·sah'ruh) In Hindu belief, rebirth of the soul into a succession of lives.

sarcophagus A stone coffin.

saturation The purity of a *hue*; the higher the saturation, the purer the hue. *Value* and saturation are not constantly related: For example, high-saturation yellow tends to have a high value, while high-saturation violet tends to have a low value.

satyr (sat'er) In Greek mythology, a kind of demigod or deity, a follower of Dionysos, wanton and lascivious and often represented with goatlike ears and legs and a short tail.

scale The dimensions of the parts or totality of a building or object in relation to its use or function. In architectural *plans*, the relation of the actual size of a structure to the size of its representation.

sculpture in the round Free-standing figures, carved or modeled in three dimensions.

secondary colors The colors (green, orange, purple) that result from mixture of pairs of the *primary colors*.

section In architecture, a diagram or representation of a part of a structure or building along an imaginary plane passing through it vertically.

seicento (say·chain'toh) The seventeenth century in Italian art.

serdab A small concealed chamber in a pyramid for the statue of the deceased.

sfumato (sfoo·ma'toh) A smokelike haziness that subtly softens outlines in painting, particularly applied to the painting of Leonardo.

sgraffito (zgra·fee'toh) Decoration produced by scratching through a surface layer of plaster, glazing, etc., to reveal a different-colored ground; also, pottery or other ware so decorated.

shaft The part of a *column* between the *capital* and base.

shaft grave A grave in the form of a deep pit, the actual burial spot being at the base of the shaft or in a niche at the base.

sikara (shih'kuh·ruh) In Hindu temples of Vishnu, the tower above the shrine.

silver point A drawing technique involving use of a silver-tipped "pencil" on a paper with a white *matte* coating; also, the delicate drawings so made.

sinopia Reddish-brown earth color; also, the *cartoon* or underpainting for a *fresco;* often spelled sinopie.

sistrum An instrument of metal rods loosely held in a metal frame, which jingle when shaken. Peculiarly Egyptian, it was used especially in the worship of Isis and is still used in Nubia.

slip Potter's clay dispersed in a liquid and used for *casting,* decoration, and to attach parts of clay vessels such as handles.

socle (soh'kel) A molded projection at the bottom of a wall or *pier,* or beneath a pedestal or *column* base.

soffit The underside of an architectural member such as an *arch, lintel, cornice,* or stairway. See *intrados.*

Solutrean Of or pertaining to a period of the Upper *Paleolithic.* Named after the site of Solutré, France, the culture appears to have been intrusive between the *Aurignacian* and *Magdalenian.*

spandrel The roughly triangular space enclosed by the curves of adjacent arches and a horizontal member connecting their vertexes; also, the space enclosed by the curve of an arch and an enclosing right angle.

splay A large bevel or *chamfer.*

splayed opening An opening (as in a wall) that is cut away diagonally so that the outer edges are farther apart than the inner. See also *embrasure.*

springing The lowest stone of an *arch,* resting on the *impost block.*

square schematism A church plan in which the crossing square is used as the *module* for all parts of the design.

squinch An architectural device used to make a

transition from a square to a polygonal base for a *dome.* It may be composed of *lintels, corbels,* or *arches.*

stele (stee'lee) A carved stone slab or pillar used especially by the ancient Greeks for grave or site markers and similar purposes.

still life A painting representing inanimate objects such as flowers and household articles.

stoa In ancient Greek architecture, an open building whose roof is supported by a row of columns parallel to the back wall.

stringcourse A horizontal *molding* or band in masonry, ornamental but usually reflecting interior structure.

stucco Fine plaster or cement used as a coating for walls or for decoration.

stupa (stoo'puh) A large mound-shaped Buddhist shrine.

style A manner of treatment or execution of works of art that is characteristic of a civilization, a people, or an individual; also, a special and superior quality in a work of art.

stylobate The upper step of the base of a Greek temple, which forms a platform for the *columns.*

superimposed orders *Orders* of architecture placed one above another in an *arcaded* or *colonnaded* building, usually in the following sequence: Doric (the first story), Ionic, and Corinthian. Superimposed orders are found in Greek *stoas* and were used widely by Roman and Renaissance builders.

sūtra (soo'truh) In Buddhism, an account of a sermon by or dialogue involving the Buddha.

swag A kind of decoration for walls, furniture, etc., done in *relief* and resembling garlands and gathered drapery. It was particularly popular in the eighteenth century.

symmetry Esthetic balance, usually achieved by disposing forms about a real or imaginary *axis* so that those on one side correspond more or less with those on the other. The correspondence may be in terms of shape, color, texture, etc.

tectiforms Rooflike shapes found painted on the walls of *Paleolithic* caves.

tell In Near Eastern archeology, a hill or mound, usually ancient sites of habitation.

tempera A technique of painting using as a *medium pigment* mixed with egg yolk, glue, or casein; also, the medium itself.

Tenebrists A group of seventeenth-century European painters who used violent contrasts of light and dark.

terra-cotta Hard-baked clay used for sculpture and as a building material. It may be *glazed* or painted.

tesserae (tess'er·ee) Small pieces of glass or stone used in making *mosaics.*

tholos (thoh'los) A circular structure, generally in

Classical Greek style; also, an ancient circular tomb.

thrust The outward force exerted by an *arch* or *vault*. It must be counterbalanced by *buttresses*.

tondo A circular painting or piece of *relief* sculpture.

torana (tor'uh·nuh) Gateways in the stone fence around a *stupa*, located at the cardinal points of the compass.

torus A convex *molding* or part of a molding, usually the lowest in the base of a *column*.

totem An animal or object and its representation or image considered a symbol of a given family or clan.

trabeated Having horizontal beams or *lintels*.

tracery Branching ornamental stonework, generally in a window, where it supports the glass. It is particularly characteristic of Gothic architecture.

transept The part of a cruciform church whose *axis* crosses at right angles the axis running from the chief entrance through the *nave* to the *apse*.

trecento (tray·chain'toh) The fourteenth century in Italian art.

trefoil An architectural ornament having three lobes or foils. See *quatrefoil*.

triforium In a Gothic cathedral, the gallery between the principal *nave* arcades and the *clerestory*, and opening on the nave through an *arcade*.

triglyph A projecting grooved member of a Doric *frieze* that alternates with *metopes*.

triptych A three-paneled *altarpiece*.

trompe l'oeil (trohmp loy') A form of illusionistic painting that attempts to represent an object as though it existed in three dimensions at the surface of the painting; literally, "eye-fooling."

trumeau (troo·moh') A *pillar* in the center of a Romanesque or Gothic portal.

tympanum The space enclosed by a *lintel* and an *arch* over a doorway; also, the recessed face of a *pediment*.

ushnisha Stylized protuberance of the Buddha's forehead, emblematic of his superhuman consciousness.

value The amount of light reflected by a *hue;* the greater the amount of light, the higher the value. See also *saturation*.

vanishing point In *linear perspective*, that point on the horizon toward which parallel lines appear to converge and at which they seem to vanish.

vault A masonry roof or ceiling constructed on the *arch* principle. A barrel **vault,** semicylindrical in cross section, is in effect a deep arch or an uninter-rupted series of arches, one behind the other. A **fan vault** is a development of *lierné* vaulting characteristic of English Perpendicular Gothic, in which radiating *ribs* form a fanlike pattern. A **groin vault** is formed at the point where two barrel vaults intersect at right angles. A **ribbed vault** is one in which there is a framework of ribs or arches under the intersections of the vaulting sections.

veduta (veh·doo'ta) A painting of a view.

vignette Originally, a decorative element of vine leaves and tendrils. Hence, any rather small decorative design in a book or manuscript that has no definite boundaries or frame.

vimana (vih·mah'nuh) In Hindu and Buddhist temples, the pyramidal tower above the shrine.

volute A spiral scroll-like form characteristic of the Greek Ionic *capital*.

voussoir (voo·swahr') A wedge-shaped block used in the construction of a true *arch*. The central voussoir, which sets the arch, is the *keystone*.

wainscot A wooden facing for an interior wall, usually paneled.

wall arcade See *blind arcade*.

warm color Red, orange, or yellow. Psychologically, warm colors tend to be exciting, emphatic, and affirmative; optically they generally seem to advance or project. See *cool color*.

wash In *watercolor* painting especially, a thin, transparent film of color.

watercolor A painting technique using as a *medium*, *pigment* (usually prepared with gum) mixed with water and applied to an absorbent surface. The painting is transparent, with the white of the paper furnishing the lights. See *gouache*.

westwork A multistoried mass, including the *façade* and usually surmounted by towers, at the western end of a Medieval church.

woodcut A wood block from whose surface those parts not intended to print are cut away to a slight depth, leaving the design raised; also, the printed impression made with such a block.

yaksha (*f.* yakshi) A divinity in the Hindu and Buddhist pantheon.

yu A covered Chinese libation vessel.

ziggurat (zig'oor·at) Roughly pyramidal structures built in ancient Babylonia and Assyria and consisting of stages, each succeeding stage stepped back from the one beneath.

zoomorphism The representation of gods in the form or with the attributes of animals; the use of animal forms in art or symbolism.

BIBLIOGRAPHY

Chapter One: The Birth of Art

The standard works on prehistoric art are Paolo Graziosi, *Paleolithic Art* (1960); A. Leroi-Gourhan, *Treasures of Prehistoric Art* (1967); and Henri Breuil, *400 Centuries of Cave Art* (1952). The last-named volume contains over 500 pictures of specimens from ninety Franco-Cantabrian and two Italian sites. Less profusely illustrated, but of wider geographical range, is H. G. Bandi and Johannes Maringer, *Art of the Ice Age* (1953), which includes examples of the rock-shelter paintings of the Spanish Levant. H. G. Bandi, Henri Breuil *et al.*, *The Art of the Stone Age* (1961) contains a series of short essays by various experts on specific periods and areas, including non-European ones. A handy summary of prehistoric art down to the Roman period, including the art of the Spanish Levant and of the Megalithic culture, is Herbert Kuhn, *The Rock Pictures of Europe* (1956). Dealing only with the most famous of the French caves is Fernand Windels, *The Lascaux Cave* (1949), which, in black-and-white photographs, presents what seems to be an almost complete inventory of that cave's paintings. Somewhat less comprehensive, but visually more appealing, is Georges Bataille, *Lascaux: Prehistoric Painting* (1955), in which the author, using sixty color plates, takes the reader on a tour of the cave.

Chapter Two: The Ancient Near East

The prehistoric archeology of the Near East is lucidly interpreted by R. J. Braidwood, *The Near East and the Foundations for Civilization* (1952), and by James Mellaart, *The Earliest Civilizations of the Near East* (1966). Mellaart also gives a fascinating and readable account of the important recent Anatolian finds in *Çatal Hüyük, a Neolithic Town in Anatolia* (1967), while Kathleen Kenyon breezily reports on the Jericho excavations in *Digging up Jericho* (1957).

For the art of the historical period, the standard work is still Henri Frankfort, *Art and Architecture of the Ancient Orient* (1959). A more recent, unillustrated general introduction to the region's complex history is given by A. L. Oppenheim, *Ancient Mesopotamia* (1964). Sir Charles L. Woolley, an archeologist and one of the outstanding specialists on the region, has written popular introductions to ancient Mesopotamian art and life in *Ur of the Chaldees* (1954) and *The Middle East* (1961). Well-illustrated surveys are

Seton Lloyd, *The Art of the Ancient Near East* (1961); Giovanni Garbini, *The Ancient World* (1966); and Eva Strommenger, *Five Thousand Years of the Art of Mesopotamia* (1964); the last-named work is illustrated by Max Hirmer, probably the best of art-historical photographers. Siegfried Giedion, *The Eternal Present: The Beginnings of Architecture* (1963) deals handily with the subject.

Beautifully illustrated also are two works by André Parrot: *Sumer* (1961) and *The Arts of Assyria* (1962). In the same series as Parrot's books is Roman Ghirshman, *Persia from the Origins to Alexander the Great* (1964), which offers abundant pictures, maps, and chronologies. Also recommended are S. N. Kramer, *History Begins at Sumer* (1959) and *The Sumerians* (1963). Finally, the sources and ramifications of Persian art have been the subject of two recent studies: William Culican's *The Medes and the Persians* (1965), and Edith Porada and R. H. Dyson's *The Art of Ancient Iran* (1965).

Chapter Three: The Art of Egypt

The best general works on the civilization of ancient Egypt are J. A. Wilson, *The Burden of Egypt* (1951), and J. H. Breasted's classic *History of Egypt* (1909). Well-rounded surveys of Egyptian art are presented by two eminent Egyptologists: W. Stevenson Smith, *The Art and Architecture of Ancient Egypt* (1958), and Cyril Aldred, *The Development of Ancient Egyptian Art*, 3 vols. (1949–62). Some of the most impressive photographic coverage of Egyptian art is offered in three fairly recent publications: Kurt Lange (with Max Hirmer), *Egypt: Architecture, Sculpture and Painting in 3000 Years* (1961, 1968), and Irmgard Woldering, *The Art of Egypt* (1962) and *Gods, Men and Pharaohs* (1967).

Dealing with more specific aspects of Egyptian art, either by period or medium, are W. B. Emery, *Archaic Egypt* (1961), and E. Baldwin Smith, *Egyptian Architecture as Cultural Expression* (1938) and *Egyptian Sculpture and Painting in the Old Kingdom* (1946). Alexander Badawy, *A History of Egyptian Architecture*, 3 vols. (I, 1954; II, 1966; III, 1968) is the most comprehensive publication on the subject; the numerous plans, elevations, sections, and reconstructions with which the three volumes are illustrated will appeal particularly to the architectural student. Finally, Arpag Mekhitarian, *Egyptian Painting* (1954) is still popular for its fine color plates.

Chapter Four: The Art of the Aegean

The literature of Aegean archeology begins with the three volumes in which Heinrich Schliemann reported his findings: *Ilios* (1880), *Mycenae* (1880), and *Tiryns* (1885). After a hiatus of several decades, Sir Arthur Evans revived interest with the detailed account of his Cretan excavations, *The Palace of Minos*, 4 vols. (1921–35). The polarization of scholarly opinion into "islander" and "mainlander" theories is expressed in two works now considered classics in the field of Aegean archeology: J. D. S. Pendlebury, *Archeology of Crete* (1939, 1963), and A. J. B. Wace, *Mycenae, an Archeological History and Guide* (1949). The problems involved in the interrelationship of the two cultures are discussed (among other things) in J. W. Graham, *The Palaces of Crete* (1962), and E. T. Vermeule, *Greece in the Bronze Age* (1964). A. W. Persson examines the enigmatic subject of the *Religion of Greece in Prehistoric Times* (1942). More recent works, which stress pictorial coverage, are Pierre Demargne, *Aegean Art* (1964), and Spyridon Marinatos (with Max Hirmer), *Crete and Mycenae* (1960). Informative and nicely illustrated is Friedrich Matz, *The Art of Crete and Early Greece* (1962). Some very important recent excavations have been reported in Blegen and Marion Rawson, *The Palace of Nestor at Pylos in Western Messenia*, 2 vols. (1966).

Chapter Five: The Art of Greece

Beyond the exemplary survey by J. D. Beazley and Bernard Ashmole, *Greek Sculpture and Painting to the End of the Hellenistic Period* (1932, 1966), selections from the voluminous literature on Greek art are perhaps best grouped according to art forms. The standard works on architecture are A. W. Lawrence, *Greek Architecture* (1957); W. B. Dinsmoor, *The Architecture of Ancient Greece* (1950); and D. S. Robertson, *A Handbook of Greek and Roman Architecture* (1954). More recent publications are Robert Scranton, *Greek Architecture* (1962), and V. J. Scully's evocative and controversial *Earth, the Temple, and the Gods* (1962). An excellent pictorial survey is Helmut Berve and Gottfried Gruben (with Max Hirmer), *Greek Temples, Theatres, and Shrines* (1963).

The literature on Greek sculpture is largely dominated by Gisela Richter, whose *Sculpture and Sculptors of the Greeks* has been an invaluable aid to students since its first publication in 1929. Also recommended are her *Kouroi* (1960), *Three Critical Periods in Greek Sculpture* (1951), and the informative *Handbook of Greek Art*, 4th ed. (1965). Primarily concerned with techniques is Charles Blümel, *Greek Sculptors at Work* (1955), while Rhys Carpenter, *Greek Sculpture* (1960), studies techniques in their relationship to style. The best illustrations of Greek sculpture are provided by Max Hirmer in Reinhard Lulliès, *Greek Sculpture* (1957).

General works on Greek painting are Mary Hamilton Swindler, *Ancient Painting* (1929); Ernst Buschor, trans. by G. C. Richards, *Greek Vase Painting* (1922); and J. D. Beazley's translation of Ernst Pfuhl, *Masterpieces of Greek Drawing and Painting* (1955). Archaic vase painting receives careful attention in two works by J. D. Beazley: *The Development of Attic Black-Figure* (1951) and *Attic Black-Figure Vase Painting* (1956). Gisela Richter deals as efficiently with vase painting as she does with sculpture in *Attic Red-Figure Vases: A Survey* (1946). Good pictorial surveys of the field are Martin Robertson, *Greek Painting* (1959), and the Hirmer-illustrated volume by Paolo Arias, *A History of 1000 Years of Greek Vase Painting* (1963). Techniques are investigated by J. D. Beazley, *Potter and Painter in Ancient Athens* (1946), and more recently by J. V. Noble, who reports the fascinating results of his years-long efforts to reproduce the forgotten methods of Greek painters in *The Technique of Painted Attic Pottery* (1965).

Chapter Six: Etruscan and Roman Art

The literature on Roman art begins with Franz Wickhoff, *Roman Art* (1900), which challenged art history's long-standing bias in favor of Greek art. Wickhoff's translator, Eugenie Strong, published her own two-volume work, *Art in Ancient Rome*, in 1928. Since then research in the field of Roman art has accelerated greatly, to produce such richly illustrated works as G. A. Mansuelli, *The Art of Etruria and Early Rome* (1965), and its thematic sequel, Heinz Kahler, *The Art of Rome and Her Empire* (1963), both liberally supplemented with maps, plans, chronological charts, and other study aids. Handsomely illustrated also is George Hanfmann, *Roman Art* (1964), a book whose rather unorthodox organization may shock, but which is filled with valuable information.

Works on Roman architecture include G. T. Rivoira, *Roman Architecture* (1925); D. S. Robertson, *A Handbook of Greek and Roman Architecture* (1954); and F. E. Brown's brief survey, *Roman Architecture* (1961). The most recent and perhaps most interesting study in the field is W. L. MacDonald, *The Architecture of the Roman Empire* (1965). Amedeo Maiuri, *Pompeii* (1957) takes the reader on a tour through that excavated site; the same author deals with a rather neglected subject in *Roman Painting* (1953), a book that is valuable primarily for its plates. Roman portrait sculpture has been the subject of several studies, among which Ludwig Goldscheider, *Roman Portraits* (1940) remains the most profusely illustrated.

Chapter Seven: Early Christian, Byzantine, and Islamic Art

Earlier general works that have been brought more or less up to date are O. M. Dalton, *Byzantine Art and Archaeology* (1961), and G. K. Hamilton, *Byzantine Architecture and Decoration* (1956). C. R. Morey's *Early Christian Art*, 2nd ed. (1953) is a very good survey, as is Ernst Kitzinger, *Early Medieval Art* (1955), which continues the account of Christian art to the twelfth century. A comprehensive anthology of articles on Byzantine history, culture, and art, written by a number of authorities and edited by N. H. Baynes and H. St. L. B. Moss, is *Byzantium* (1948). Recent general works of fundamental value are W. F. Volbach and Max Hirmer, *Early Christian Art* (1962), important for its fine plates and concise text and notes; André Grabar, *The Beginnings of Christian Art 200–395* (1967) and *The Golden Age of Justinian: From the Death of Theodosius to the Rise of Islam* (1967), large, beautifully illustrated picture books with rather brief text; and Richard Krautheimer's *Early Christian and Byzantine Architecture* (1965), a distinguished representative of the scholarly Pelican History of Art series. William MacDonald's *Early Christian and Byzantine Architecture* (1962) is a briefer yet quite dependable survey. A handsomely illustrated book is David Talbot Rice, *The Art of Byzantium* (1959), and a work of broad scope, profusely illustrated, is René Huyghe, ed., *Larousse Encyclopedia of Byzantine and Medieval Art* (1963). In the Skira series of art books, which specializes in color illustrations, the relevant work for this period is André Grabar, *Byzantine Painting* (1953).

The characteristic Early Christian and Byzantine medium, mosaic, is studied in some well-illustrated books: E. W. Anthony, *A History of Mosaics* (1935); Otto Demus, *Byzantine Mosaic Decoration* (1948); W. F. Volbach, *Early Christian Mosaics* (1948); Peter Meyer, *Byzantine Mosaics* (1952); and André Grabar and Manolis Chatzidakis, *Greece: Byzantine Mosaics* (1948). Early manuscript illumination is dealt with by Kurt Weitzmann in *Illustrations in Roll and Codex* (1947) and in *Ancient Book Illumination* (1959). Small sculpture is studied in the above-mentioned works of Morey and of Kitzinger, and in Joseph Natanson, *Early Christian Ivories* (1935).

Emerson Swift, *Hagia Sophia* (1940) is a thoroughgoing study of this most important of Byzantine buildings. E. Baldwin Smith's *The Dome* (1950) and his *Architectural Symbolism of Imperial Rome and the Middle Ages* (1956) are important and suggestive contributions to what might be called the iconography of architecture. For the iconography of Early Christian art W. S. Lowrie, *Art in the Early Church* (1947) is valuable, and Henry Bettenson, *Documents of the Christian Church* (1943) supplies in its early chapters something of the doctrinal background of Christian art. Otto von Simson's *Sacred Fortress* (1948) is an interesting investigation of Ravenna in the sixth century in terms of the iconography of its art and architecture within the context of the city's history under Theodoric and Justinian. John Beckwith makes a detailed study of *The Art of Constantinople* (1968) in the context of the history and culture of the capital of the Byzantine empire.

Many of the key works on Islamic art are written in either French or German and have not yet been translated. Still, a fair number of introductory books on Islamic art, some well illustrated, are available to the English-speaking reader. Among the more recent ones are: Ralph P. Wilson, *Islamic Art* (1957); Ernst Kuehnel, *Islamic Art and Architecture* (1966); and Katerina Otto-Dorn, *Islamische Kunst* (1964), an English edition of which was published in 1971. Oleg Grabar, *The Formation of Islamic Art* (1973) deals authoritatively with the early phases of Moslem art and the art-historical problems raised by its formation. The notion of a "classical" moment in Islamic culture is presented by Gustav von Grunebaum, *Classical Islam* (1970).

More specific aspects of Islamic art are treated by T. W. Arnold, *Painting in Islam* (1928), which contains a convenient general statement on the Islamic attitude toward the arts. More recent is Richard Ettinghausen, *Arab Painting* (1962), which probably is the best introduction to that subject. K. Archibald, C. Creswell, and Marguerite van Berchem, *Early Muslim Architecture* (1969) presents most of the significant early architectural monuments and contains an extensive bibliography. Studies on Islamic urbanism tend to stress its social and institutional aspects; an exception is Jacob Lassner, *The Topography of Baghdad in the Early Middle Ages* (1970). The fundamental introductory work on ceramics is Arthur Lane, *Early Islamic Pottery* (1947). Information on textiles may be found in Walter A. Hawley, *Oriental Rugs, Antique and Modern* (1937). Finally, among various works that deal with the art of specific regions of the Islamic world, the most ambitious and comprehensive is Arthur U. Pope and Phyllis Ackerman, *A Survey of Persian Art from Prehistoric Times to the Present*, 7 vols. (1939).

Chapter Eight: Early Medieval Art

The historical background of the period is presented, with good illustrations and maps, in Gerald Simons, *Barbarian Europe* (1968). A good general survey is John Beckwith, *Early Medieval Art* (1964), though it begins with Carolingian art, omitting the art of the Migrations and Hiberno-Saxon art. The latter area is described in Françoise Henry, *Irish Art in the Early Christian Period* (1940, 1965) and *Irish Art During the Viking Invasions* (1967). Also noteworthy are A. Kingsley Porter's seminal, stimulating study, *The Crosses and Culture of Ireland* (1931); E. T. Leeds, *Early Anglo-Saxon Art and Archaeology* (1936); and the early chapters of Bruce Arnold, *A Concise History of Irish Art* (1968). The art of the Migrations is taken up in David M. Wilson and Ole Klindt-Jensen, *Viking Art* (1966). The architecture of the period is described and interpreted in K. J. Conant,

Carolingian and Romanesque Architecture 800–1200 (1959), and a very comprehensive study of a particular architectural region is H. M. and Joan Taylor, *Anglo-Saxon Architecture*, 2 vols. (1965). For manuscript illumination a fundamental work, in two volumes of concise text and fine illustrations, is Adolf Goldschmidt, *German Illumination* (1928). Roger Hink's *Carolingian Art* (1962), a reissue, is an interpretive survey of the manuscript illumination and small sculpture of the period, and André Grabar and Carl Nordenfalk, *Early Medieval Painting* (1957) is a thorough survey illustrated in color.

Chapter Nine: Romanesque Art

General studies of the Romanesque can be found in C. R. Morey, *Medieval Art* (1942); in Joan Evans, *Art in Medieval France 987–1498* (1948); and especially in the first volume of Henri Focillon, *The Art of the West in the Middle Ages* (1962), where the renowned scholar applies his theory of the evolution of art forms to the monuments of the period. For the most part, however, the Romanesque bibliography is specialized in media and regions: Hans Decker, *Romanesque Art in Italy* (1959), and Joseph Gantner, Marcel Pobé, and Jean Roubier, *Romanesque Art in France* (1959) are handsomely illustrated examples of the almost necessarily regional approach to the study of the Romanesque. General accounts of the media have been given, however, like the monumental work of A. Kingsley Porter, *Medieval Architecture*, 2 vols. (1912), available in reprint since 1966. A much less ambitious but still useful study for the general reader is A. W. Clapham, *Romanesque Architecture in Western Europe* (1936), which has been succeeded by the already mentioned K. J. Conant, *Carolingian and Romanesque Architecture*. A more recent and briefer survey is Howard Saalman, *Medieval Architecture: European Architecture 600–1200* (1962). The regional study of Romanesque architecture first concentrated in the area of Lombardy, long thought to be the source of rib-vault construction. A. Kingsley Porter's *Lombard Architecture* (1915–17) competes in interpretation and emphasis with G. T. Rivoira, *Lombardic Architecture*, rev. ed. (1933). Other regional histories of Romanesque architecture are Bernard Bevan, *History of Spanish Architecture* (1939); A. W. Clapham, *English Romanesque Architecture after the Conquest* (1934); Corrado Ricci, *Romanesque Architecture in Italy* (1925); Geoffrey Webb, *Architecture in Britain: The Middle Ages* (1956); and Julius Baum, *Romanesque Architecture in France* (1928). A recent comprehensive treatment of Medieval art and architecture in France is Whitney Stoddard, *Monastery and Cathedral in France* (1966). A general survey of sculpture, especially bronzes, is Hanns Swarzenski, *Monuments of Romanesque Art* (1954). Sculpture is studied regionally also in Paul Deschamps, *French*

Sculpture of the Romanesque Period—Eleventh and Twelfth Century (1930); A. Kingsley Porter's monumental study of southern French sculpture, Romanesque Sculpture of the Pilgrimage Roads (1923), available in reprint since 1966; G. M. Crichton, Romanesque Sculpture in Italy (1954); and Lawrence Stone, Sculpture in Britain in the Middle Ages (1955). The bronze church portals of this period are splendidly illustrated in Hermann Leisinger, Romanesque Bronzes (1957). Carl Nordenfalk, Romanesque Painting (1958) covers the material with emphasis on manuscript illumination, and wall painting is the focus in P. H. Michel, Romanesque Wall Paintings in France (1949). Edgar Anthony gives a general treatment of the mural medium in Romanesque Frescoes (1951).

Chapter Ten: Gothic Art

The best introduction to the period is the second volume of the classic work by Henri Focillon, The Art of the West in the Middle Ages (1963). Joan Evans, Art in Medieval France (1948) is supplemented by The Flowering of the Middle Ages (1966) by the same author. Good general picture surveys appear in Marcel Aubert, The Art of the High Gothic Era (1964), and André Martindale, Gothic Art (1967). John Harvey, The Gothic World (1950) is a study primarily of the English scene. Paul Frankl, The Gothic Literary Sources and Interpretations (1960) thoroughly documents the style and its history and is especially valuable for its exposition of Medieval spiritualism, the force behind Gothic creativity. By the same author, Gothic Architecture (1962) describes Gothic analytically, and carefully follows the steps of its development. Robert Branner, Gothic Architecture (1961) covers concisely the whole European development of Gothic and provides a short general bibliography that is most valuable. George Duby, The Europe of the Cathedrals (1966) is beautifully illustrated in color. In a fascinating analogical comparison of scholastic thinking in architecture and philosophy, Erwin Panofsky, in Gothic Architecture and Scholasticism (1958), demonstrates the underlying intellectual unity of the Gothic world. Otto von Simson, The Gothic Cathedral (1956) describes the history, iconography, and philosophy of Gothic architecture. Marcel Aubert, Gothic Cathedrals of France and Their Treasures (1959), though its picture captions are in French, is a useful collection of fine plates. Whitney Stoddard, Monastery and Cathedral in France (1966) is an excellent narrative that embraces developments in France from Romanesque through late Gothic, taking in architecture, sculpture, stained glass, manuscript illumination, and the art of the church treasures. An early but still quite adequate account of Gothic architectural structure is Clarence Ward, Medieval Church Vaulting (1915); a later study is John Fitchen, The Con-

struction of Gothic Cathedrals (1961). Chartres, perhaps the most appreciated of Medieval cathedrals, has been widely studied. Henry Adams, in Mont Saint Michel and Chartres (1904), identified it—at least to his English-speaking audience—with the Gothic spirit itself. Most recently Robert Branner, ed., Chartres Cathedral (1969) gives a brief history of the building, with documentation from Medieval texts and a selection of essays on Chartres by critics and scholars through the centuries. Chartres is included among the three great "classical" buildings of the Gothic era in Hans Jantzen, The High Gothic: The Classic Cathedrals of Chartres, Reims, and Amiens (1962). The arts that adorn the cathedral are described in Adolf Katzenellenbogen, The Sculptural Programs of Chartres Cathedral (1959), a thorough stylistic and iconographical study, and in Peter Kidson and Ursula Pariser, Sculpture at Chartres (1959); the cathedral's well-preserved stained glass is reproduced and described in J. R. Johnson, The Radiance of Chartres (1965). There are many elaborate picture books and guidebooks, of which Louis Grodecki, Chartres (1963) is a fine example. The figurative art of Chartres provides many of the illustrations in Emile Mâle's definitive study of Medieval iconography in The Gothic Image: Religious Art in France of the Thirteenth Century (1958).

Erwin Panofsky, in Abbot Suger on the Abbey Church of St. Denis and its Art Treasures (1951), has translated the document perhaps most important to the development of Gothic architecture. A description of that characteristic Gothic art, stained glass, is given in Hugh Arnold, Stained Glass of the Middle Ages in England and France (1940), and Gothic painting is discussed in Daniel Thompson, The Materials and Techniques of Medieval Painting (1956), and, with color illustrations, in Jacques Dupont and Cesare Gnudi, Gothic Painting (1954).

Chapter Eleven: The "Proto-Renaissance" in Italy

A good, complete survey of the period is John White, Art and Architecture in Italy 1250–1400 (1966), and, for sculpture alone, the same function is performed by John Pope-Hennessy, Introduction to Italian Sculpture (1955–62). The first eight chapters of E. T. De Wald, Italian Painting: 1200–1600 (1961) are a detailed survey of the painting of the Proto-Renaissance; less complete, but with fine color plates, are the first five chapters of Lionello Venturi and Rosabianca Skira-Venturi, Italian Painting: The Creators of the Renaissance, 3 vols. (1950–52). A comprehensive study of the period is found in Millard Meiss, Painting in Florence and Siena after the Black Death (1951). An encyclopedic description of Italian painting is Raimond van Marle, The Development of the Italian Schools of Painting, 19 vols. (1923–38). An interesting recent specialized study is James Stubblebine, ed., *Giotto: The Arena Chapel Frescoes* (1969), in which a number of leading scholars examine the masterwork of the leading master of the Proto-Renaissance. A documentary supplement of backgrounds and sources is supplied. The social-economic background of the period is given in Frederick Antal, *Florentine Painting and Its Social Background* (1948). A most important document surviving from the period is Cennino Cennini's handbook for the craftsman-artist, translated by Daniel Thompson, *Cennino Cennini, Il libro, dell' arte* (1933).

Chapter Twelve: Fifteenth-Century Italian Art

Though necessarily requiring revision and updating, there are two nineteenth-century classics that still serve as effective introductions to the Renaissance: the broad study by Jacob Burckhardt, *The Civilization of the Renaissance in Italy* (1860 and numerous later editions), and the much more detailed John Addington Symonds, *The Renaissance in Italy* (1875–86 and later editions). More recently there have been collections of essays on the Renaissance that are valuable for obtaining a good general view of it: Wallace Ferguson *et al.*, *The Renaissance* (1962); Wallace Ferguson *et al.*, *Facets of the Renaissance* (1963); and Tinsley Helton, ed., *The Renaissance: A Reconsideration of the Theories and Interpretations of the Age* (1964). The last contains an especially important essay by Earl Rosenthal, "Changing Interpretations of the Renaissance in the History of Art." All three books are in essence revisions of earlier views of the period. Ferdinand Schevill, *The Medici* (1960), is a good concise study of the family that endowed the Renaissance. There have been a number of general treatments of the art of the period; especially useful is René Huyghe, ed., *The Larousse Encyclopedia of Renaissance and Baroque Art* (1960). Heinrich Wölfflin, whose stylistic polarity of Renaissance-Baroque was enormously influential, gives an introductory survey in *Classic Art* (1953). The concept of the phenomenon "renaissance" is analyzed historically in Erwin Panofsky, *Renaissance and Renascences in Western Art* (1960). André Chastel, *The Age of Humanism* (1963) considers Humanism as a Europe-wide phenomenon. Peter and Linda Murray, *The Art of the Renaissance* (1963) is a concise survey and, considering its ambitious scope, so is Heinrich Decker, *The Renaissance in Italy: Architecture, Sculpture, Frescoes* (1969). Bates Lowry, *Renaissance Architecture* (1965) is a sound survey, as is Peter Murray, *Architecture of the Italian Renaissance* (1963). Rudolf Wittkower, *Architectural Principles in the Age of Humanism* (1952) is a learned and fascinating explication of Renaissance theories of architectural proportion and their relation to

harmonic ratios in music. An invaluable document of the time, Alberti's *De re aedificatoria* is edited by Joseph Rykwert as *Ten Books on Architecture* (1955).

For sculpture there is John Pope-Hennessy's survey cited in the chapter above, and the comprehensive study by Charles Seymour, *Sculpture in Italy, 1400–1500* (1966); and for painting, De Wald and Van Marle, also mentioned in the previous chapter. Bernard Berenson, *Italian Pictures of the Renaissance* (1957) and *The Drawings of the Florentine Painters* (1938) are surveys by the renowned connoisseur. Eve Borsook, *The Mural Painters of Tuscany* (1960) presents the foremost masters of the leading schools of paintings in the fifteenth century; and F. M. Godfrey, *Early Italian Painting: 1250–1500* is another broad survey of Proto-Renaissance and Early Renaissance painting. A fundamental document of the Renaissance, still a valuable reference, is Giorgio Vasari, *The Lives of the Most Eminent Painters, Sculptors and Architects* (1550, 1568 ... 1959). There is much valuable documentary material from the fifteenth century in E. G. Holt, ed., *A Documentary History of Art*, Vol. I (1957).

Chapter Thirteen: Sixteenth-Century Italian Art

Since there is overlapping of the periods of the Renaissance and their divisions are somewhat arbitrarily defined, titles listed for Chapters Eleven and Twelve will in many cases have application to this one. The early years of the sixteenth century are surveyed in Linda Murray, *The High Renaissance* (1967), in John Pope-Hennessy, *Italian High Renaissance and Baroque Sculpture* (1963), and in Sydney J. Freedberg, *Painting of the High Renaissance in Rome and Florence* (1961). Lionello Venturi, *The Sixteenth Century: From Leonardo da Vinci to El Greco* (1956) is the second volume of a work cited earlier. James S. Ackerman, *The Architecture of Michelangelo* (1961) and *Palladio: The Architect and Society* (1967) taken together give a kind of overview of the main trends in the middle and late years of the century. An invaluable guide to artistic theory in Italy from Alberti to the Mannerists is Sir Anthony Blunt, *Artistic Theory in Italy 1450–1600* (1956). Linda Murray, *The Late Renaissance and Mannerism* (1967) is a recent example of the growing bibliography on Mannerism represented also by John Shearman, *Mannerism* (1967), a particularly fine, scholarly yet concise work; Giuliano Briganti, *Italian Mannerism* (1962); Franzsepp Würtenberger, *Mannerism* (1963), an elaborately illustrated work that considers the European phenomenon; and *Renaissance and Mannerism, Studies in Western Art*, the published Acts of the Twentieth International Congress of the History of Art, Vol. II (1963), a collection of scholarly essays in pursuit of agreement on the meaning of

"Mannerism." A seminal work, written years ago but now in a fairly recent edition, is Walter Friedlaender, *Mannerism and Anti-Mannerism in Italian Painting* (1957). There are many documents surviving from the age itself, principally Benvenuto Cellini's autobiography, the letters and poems of Michelangelo, and *The Courtier* of Baldassare Castiglione, all of which are available in popular editions. E. G. Holt, *A Documentary History of Art*, Vol. II (1957) has much appropriate material, as does the recent Robert Klein and Henry Zerner, *Sources and Documents in Italian Art: 1500–1600* (1964).

Chapter Fourteen: The Renaissance in Northern Europe

The classic work that gives the mood of the fifteenth century in the North is still Johan Huizinga, *The Waning of the Middle Ages* (1956). The first twelve chapters of F. J. Mather, *Western European Painting of the Renaissance* (1939), reissued in 1967, are still a readable and entertaining introduction to the period. Otto Benesch, *Art of the Renaissance in Northern Europe* (1945, 1967) is an excellent survey and at the same time a study of the intellectual-historical background of Northern art. Most recently there has been the comprehensive and lavishly illustrated survey by C. P. Cuttler, *Northern Painting from Pucelle to Brueghel* (1968). Of the regions of Northern Europe, Flanders has been favored in English publications. Surveys of Flemish art include W. M. Conway, *The Van Eycks and Their Followers* (1921); M. J. Friedlaender, *From Van Eyck to Bruegel* (1956) and *Early Netherlandish Painting* (1966); Leo van Puyvelde, *The Flemish Primitives* (1958); Erwin Panofsky, *Early Netherlandish Painting* (1953); and Jacques Lassaigne and Robert Delevoy, *Flemish Painting* (1956). R. H. Wilenski, *Flemish Painters* (1960) in one part places the artists within their historical setting and in a second makes a dictionary of them. For French art there is the comprehensive survey by Sir Anthony Blunt, *Art and Architecture in France 1500–1700* (1953). Earlier French art is studied by Louis Réau, *French Painting in the XIV, XV, and XVI Centuries* (1939), and Millard Meiss, *French Painting in the Time of the Duc de Berry* (1967) and *The Boucicaut Master* (1968). German art is considered in Wilhelm Waetzold, *Dürer and His Time* (1950); Erwin Panofsky, *The Life and Art of Albrecht Dürer* (1955); Otto Benesch, *German Painting, Dürer to Holbein* (1967); Francis Russell, *The World of Dürer 1471–1528* (1967); and T. Mueller, *Sculpture in the Netherlands, Germany, France and Spain* (1966). The history of the graphic arts, the popular Northern medium, is given in two works by A. M. Hind, *A History of Engraving and Etching* (1923, 1963) and *An Introduction to a History of Woodcut* (1963). Wolfgang Stechow, ed., *Northern Renaissance Art 1400–1600* (1966)

is a very valuable collection of sources and documents for the period.

Chapter Fifteen: Baroque Art

The picturesque and colorful Baroque style lends itself to elaborate illustration, and there have been a number of general books on it that make full use of the advances in reproduction techniques of the last decade: Germain Bazin, *Baroque and Rococo Art* (1964); Michael Kitson, *The Age of Baroque* (1966); James Lees-Milne, *Baroque Europe* (1962); Victor L. Tapié, *The Age of Grandeur: Baroque Art and Architecture* (1966); Harold Busch, *Baroque Europe* (1962); and Nicolas Powell, *From Baroque to Rococo* (1959). Though prior to what might be called the classical age of the colored print, Fiske Kimball, *The Creation of the Rococo* (1943), revised in paperback in 1964, is still a fine fundamental study of French design in the early eighteenth century. Henry A. Millon, *Baroque and Rococo Architecture* (1961) is a good brief introduction to the subject; and a scholarly and comprehensive treatment of a region is Rudolf Wittkower, *Art and Architecture in Italy 1600–1750* (1958). In the same series of regional studies are Horst Gerson and E. H. ter Kuile, trans. by Olive Renier, *Art and Architecture in Belgium 1600–1800* (1960); Jakob Rosenberg, Seymour Slive, and E. H. ter Kuile, *Dutch Art and Architecture 1600–1800* (1966); George Kubler and Martin Soria, *Baroque Art and Architecture in Spain and Latin America* (1959); Eberhard Hempel, *Baroque Art and Architecture in Central Europe* (1965); and Margaret Whinney and Oliver Millar, *English Art 1625–1714* (1957). For architecture by region there is T. H. Fokker, *Roman Baroque Art: The History of a Style* (1938), a thorough study that stresses architecture while dealing also with sculpture and painting. The work of that most Baroque of architects, Borromini, is brilliantly studied in the context of the city of Rome in the seventeenth century in Paolo Portoghesi, *The Rome of Borromini* (1968). The consummate matter of Baroque sculpture in Italy is studied in Rudolf Wittkower, *Gian Lorenzo Bernini, the Sculptor of the Roman Baroque* (1955), and Howard Hibbard, *Bernini* (1966). E. K. Waterhouse surveys the subject in *Italian Baroque Painting* (1962), expanding and updating A. K. McComb, *The Baroque Painters of Italy* (1934). Special accounts of the influential art of Caravaggio are presented in R. P. Hinks, *Michelangelo Merisi da Caravaggio* (1953), and in Walter Friedlaender, *Caravaggio Studies* (1955). Sir Anthony Blunt, *Art and Architecture in France—1500–1700* (1953) stops short of Rococo, but thoroughly describes the Renaissance-Baroque continuum. A continuous narrative of French painting is given in two books by Albert Châtelet and Jacques Thuillier: *French Painting from Fouquet to Poussin* (1962) and *French Painting from Le Nain to Fragonard* (1964). Sculpture and painting in Great Britain are surveyed in Margaret Whinney, *Sculpture in Britain 1530–1830* (1967), and in E. K. Waterhouse, *Painting in Britain 1530–1790* (1966). John Summerson, *Architecture in Britain 1530–1830* (1963) completes the survey of British art and architecture in the Pelican History of Art. The bibliographies of these more or less general studies of the regions of Baroque art and architecture can furnish the titles of numerous special studies and monographs. A recent title reviewing in detail the rich production of the Dutch School of landscape painting is Wolfgang Stechow. *Dutch Landscape of the Seventeenth Century* (1968), Valuable accounts of the artistic theory of the age can be found in Denis Mahon, *Studies in Seicento Art and Theory* (1947), and in E. G. Holt, *A Documentary History of Art*, Vol. II (1957). Heinrich Wölfflin, *Principles of Art History* (1932), now reprinted in a Dover edition, offers the classic comparison of the Renaissance and Baroque styles.

Chapter Sixteen: The Nineteenth Century

A fundamental detailed narrative of modern architecture is Henry-Russell Hitchcock, *Architecture—Nineteenth and Twentieth Centuries* (1958), and, by the same author, *The Architecture of H. H. Richardson and His Times* (1936) is a study of the American architectural environment at the time that the modern style was being generated. Kenneth Clarke, *The Gothic Revival* (1950) gives a full account of this branch of Romantic eclecticism in architecture. Carl W. Condit, *The Rise of the Skyscraper* (1952); Hugh Morrison, *Louis Sullivan* (1958); and Louis Sullivan, *Kindergarten Chats and Other Writings* (1947) present a portrait of the times and the career of the influential architect and his contemporaries. Nikolaus Pevsner, *Pioneers of Modern Design* (1964) relates the story of the revolution in taste and design in architecture, arts and crafts, and painting from William Morris to Walter Gropius. Modern sculpture is presented in a series of well-selected monuments, handsomely illustrated, in Fred Licht, *Sculpture—Nineteenth and Twentieth Centuries* (1967); and Fritz Novotny, in a detailed encyclopedic study that includes the central European and Russian schools, describes nineteenth-century art in *Painting and Sculpture in Europe 1780–1880* (1960). Alan Cowans surveys an even broader span in *The Restless Art: A History of Painters and Paintings 1760–1960* (1966). John Canaday, *Mainstreams of Modern Art* (1959) is a reliable text for nineteenth-century art, giving much valuable information on the often-neglected phenomena of the academy and the salon. E. G. Holt, *From the Classicists to the Impressionists* (1966) is a most valuable documentary anthology of nineteenth-century art theory and criticism, as are Linda Nochlin, *Impressionism and Post-Impressionism 1874–1904* (1966), and, by the same author, *Realism and Tradition in Art 1848–1900* (1966). Werner Hofmann, *The Earthly Paradise: Art in the Nineteenth Century* (1961) is an interesting survey that stresses little-known and often bizarre works, and Jean Leymarie, *French Painting in the Nineteenth Century* (1962) describes that school with the help of a series of fine plates. Geraldine Pelles, in an interesting study of painting in England and France from 1750 to 1850 called *Art, Artists and Society: Origins of a Modern Dilemma* (1963), examines the ambiguous relation between early modern artists and their publics.

The Romantic period has been presented in a number of well-illustrated volumes, among which are Marcel Brion, *Art of the Romantic Era: Romanticism, Classicism, Realism* (1966); Pierre Courthion, *Romanticism* (1961); Henry Hawley, *Neo-Classicism, Style and Motif* (1964); and Eric Newton, *The Romantic Rebellion* (1963), which attempts to characterize the nature of the general phenomenon of Romanticism. Walter Friedlaender, *From David to Delacroix* (1952) is a fundamental text for the period. J. S. Sloane, *French Painting Between the Past and the Present* (1951) gives a very interesting account of the role of the critics, who were so often hostile to artistic innovation. Indispensable to the "feel" of the period is the brilliant criticism of Baudelaire in *The Mirror of Art* (1955), and *The Journals of Eugène Delacroix* (1948), wherein the great master reveals himself, his ideals, and his methods. John Rewald, *The History of Impressionism* (1962) is the indispensable historical guide through that rich period, as is his *Post-Impressionism from Van Gogh to Gauguin* (1956) for the *fin de siècle*. An important book that analyzes the esthetics of nineteenth-century French art as it is documented by the painters themselves and in relation to contemporary philosophy and science is Charles Gauss, *Aesthetic Theories of French Artists* (1949). Wylie Syphers' interesting synthesis of the arts unifies a large period in *Rococo to Cubism in Art and Literature* (1960).

Chapter Seventeen: The Twentieth Century

The art of our own times has been, and contineus to be, much written about. In the last fifteen years lavishly produced studies, both general and specialized, have recorded the artistic events of the period almost as soon as they have happened. One of the most recent and impressive treatments of the period as a whole is H. H. Arnason, *History of Modern Art: Architecture, Sculpture and Painting* (1968), with more than 1100 black-and-white reproductions, more than 200 in color, and with a very extensive bibliography. A very general background is provided by Norbert Lynton, *The Modern*

World (1965), and an introduction by J. A. Morris, *On the Enjoyment of Modern Art* (1968). Other useful general works are M. Oto Bihalji, *Adventures in Modern Art* (1966), which compares modern with primitive images; William Gaunt, *The Observer's Book of Modern Art* (1964); Gaston Diehl, *The Moderns* (1961), a treasury of worldwide modern painting; E. B. Hanning, *Fifty Years of Modern Art* (1966); Gyorgy Kepes, *The Visual Arts Today* (1966); Gregory Battock, ed., *The New Art: A Critical Anthology* (1968); Jean Cassou, Emile Langui, and Nikolaus Pevsner, *Gateway to the Twentieth Century* (1962); and Charles McCurdy, *Modern Art: A Pictorial Anthology* (1958), which has numerous small illustrations, short historical essays, and an excellent annotated bibliography. Norman Schlenoff, *Art in the Modern World* (1965) is a short, handy history. John Canaday, *Mainstreams of Modern Art* was noted in the bibliography for Chapter Sixteen, as was Henry-Russell Hitchcock, *Architecture—Nineteenth and Twentieth Centuries.*

An excellent and brief introduction to architecture is Vincent Scully, *Modern Architecture* (1962), and some other recent introductions and surveys are Reyner Banham, *Guide to Modern Architecture* (1963); Georges and Rosamond Bernier, *The Best in Twentieth-Century Architecture* (1963); John Jacobus, *Twentieth-Century Architecture: The Middle Years 1940–1964* (1966); and Peter Blake, *The Master Builder* (1960), which studies particularly Le Corbusier, Mies van der Rohe, and Frank Lloyd Wright. Peter Collins, *Changing Ideals in Modern Architecture 1750–1950* (1965) is a study of both the history and the meaning of the great changes taking place in two centuries. Reyner Banham, *Theory and Design in the First Machine Age* (1967) is an analysis of what might be called the philosophy of modern architecture. One of the most influential of all books on modern architecture is Siegfried Giedion, *Space, Time and Architecture* (1954), which traces the development of the new architectural tradition. Talbot Hamlin, ed., *The Forms and Functions of Twentieth-Century Architecture*, 4 vols. (1952) is a monumental reference work on the elements, principles, and building types of modern structures. Arnold Whittick, *European Architecture in the Twentieth Century* (1950) is a detailed survey, and can be supplemented by G. E. K. Smith, *The New Architecture of Europe* (1961). Paul Heyer, *Architects on Architecture* (1966) presents the views of the builders themselves; and John Fleming, Hugh Honour, and Nikolaus Pevsner, *Penguin Dictionary of Architecture* (1966) is an indispensable reference work. G. H. Hamilton, *Painting and Sculpture in Europe 1880–1940* (1967) surveys the "classic" phase of modern art up to World War II. A good short survey of American developments is Sam Hunter, *Modern American Painting and Sculpture* (1959), as is Barbara Rose, *Readings in American Art Since 1900* (1968). A. C. Ritchie, *Abstract Painting and Sculpture in America* (1951), and Sidney Janis, *Abstract and Surrealist Art in America* (1944), cover the reception of abstract art and its naturalization and independent development here. For sculpture, a very good introductory survey is Herbert Read, *A Concise History of Modern Sculpture* (1964), and treating the most recent developments are Udo Kultermann, *The New Sculpture* (1968); John Baldwin, *Contemporary Sculpture Techniques* (1967); and Jack Burnham, *Beyond Modern Sculpture* (1968), an interesting account of the effect of science and technology on modern sculpture. Fred Licht, *Sculpture of the Nineteenth and Twentieth Centuries* was noted in the previous chapter. For painting there are the large, three-volume works edited by Maurice Raynal, *History of Modern Painting* (1949–50), and Werner Haftmann, *Painting in the Twentieth Century: A Pictorial Survey* (1965), a comprehensive survey with more than a thousand illustrations. A shorter survey is Herbert Read, *A Concise History of Modern Painting* (1956). Sam Hunter, *Modern French Painting* (1967) is a brief survey from Manet to Picasso. The first school of abstract art is studied in Robert Rosenblum, *Cubism and Twentieth-Century Art* (1961), and in John Golding, *Cubism* (1967). Christopher Gray, *Cubist Aesthetic Theories* (1953) reviews the intellectual and literary world in which the art movement developed. Peter Selz, *German Expressionist Painting* (1957) thoroughly surveys the art and artists of Expressionism. Marianne W. Martin, *Futurist Art and Theory* (1968) gives an enlightening account of the development of Futurism between 1909 and 1915. Robert Motherwell, *The Dada Painters and Poets* (1951) is an anthology documented with essays and poetry as well as illustrations, and W. S. Rubin, *Dada, Surrealism and Their Heritage* (1968) reviews their development and the strong influence they exert today. Recent developments are surveyed in Mario Amaya, *Pop Art and After* (1966); L. Lippard, *Pop Art* (1966); Allan Kaprow, *Assemblage, Environments and Happenings* (1966); Michael Kirby, ed., *Happenings: An Illustrated Anthology* (1965); and Maurice Tuchman, *American Sculpture of the Sixties* (1967). Valuable references are Wolfgang Pehnt, *Encyclopedia of Modern Art* (1964); Carlton Lake and Roger Maillard, eds., *Dictionary of Modern Painting* (1964); and Paul Cummings, *Dictionary of Contemporary American Artists* (1966). R. L. Herbert, *Modern Artists on Art* (1964) presents theoretical essays written by the artist-pioneers of the modern movement. A treasury of documentation is the Wittenborn series, *Documents of Modern Art* (1970), edited by Jurg Spiller. Some of the important works of the modern movement are by its leaders: Guillaume Apollinaire, *The Cubist Painters* (1949); Piet Mondrian, *Plastic Art and Pure Plastic Art* (1947); László Moholy-Nagy, *The New Vision* (1949); Vasily Kandinsky, *Concerning the Spiritual in Art* (1947); Hans Arp, *On My Way* (1948); Max

Ernst, *Beyond Painting* (1948); D. H. Kahnweiler, *The Rise of Cubism* (1949); Marcel Raymond, *From Baudelaire to Surrealism* (1950); Georges Duthuit, *The Fauvist Painters* (1950); Carola Giedion-Welcker, *Contemporary Sculpture* (1955). Another very important source, descriptive and documentary, is the list of publications of the Museum of Modern Art in New York, beginning in 1930 and current today.

Chapter Eighteen: The Art of India

The continuous reassessment of the chronology of Indian monuments requires that many dates be regarded as tentative. This is no less the case in Ananda K. Coomaraswamy, *History of Indian and Indonesian Art* (1927, 1965) and Benjamin Rowland, *Art and Architecture of India* (1953, 1959), which are recommended as excellent surveys of art in India and its extension in Southeast Asia. Stella Kramrisch, *The Art of India* (1955) provides a sensitive appreciation and fine illustrations. The best book for illustrations is Heinrich Zimmer, *The Art of Indian Asia*, 2 vols. (1955). Bachhofer, *Early Indian Sculpture* (1972) has many fine illustrations; it should be used with care in reference to dates. Two concise surveys of architecture are Krishna Deva, *Temples of North India* (1969) and K. R. Srinivasan, *Temples of South India* (1972). More specialized are Vidya Dehijia, *Early Buddhist Rock Temples* (1972) and John Rosenfield, *Dynastic Arts of the Kushans* (1967). South Indian architecture is carefully discussed in S. R. Balasubrahmanyan, *Early Chola Art*, Part I (1966) and *Early Chola Temples* (1971). Related bronzes are analyzed in Douglas Barrett, *Early Cola Bronzes* (1965) and C. Sivaramamurti, *South Indian Bronzes* (1963). Indian painting traditions can be traced in Douglas Barrett and Basil Gray, *Painting in India* and A. Ghosh, ed., *Ajanta Murals* (1967), which has good illustrations of early Indian painting. Sivaramurti's *South Indian Paintings* (1968) illustrates some lesser-known examples from that area. Miniature painting is discussed generally in W. C. Archer, *Indian Miniatures* (1960) and specifically in his *Indian Paintings from the Punjab Hills*, 2 vols. (1973).

The major iconographical studies are the pioneering T. A. Gopinatha Rao, *Elements of Hindu Iconography*, 4 vols. (1968) and J. N. Banerjea, *The Development of Hindu Iconography* (1956). Ananda K. Coomaraswamy, *Yaksas* (1971) is a brilliant, stimulating study that goes well beyond simple identification of a limited theme. Historical and cultural background are given succinctly in A. L. Basham, *The Wonder that Was India* (1954), while the complicated aspects of Hinduism are clarified in P. Banerjee, *Early Indian Religion* (1973) and in S. Bhattacharji, *The Indian Theogony* (1970). Another aspect of the relationship between architecture and religion is explored in Stella Kramrisch, *The Hindu Temple*, 2 vols. (1946), a monumental work.

A handy survey is Philip Rawson, *The Art of Southeast Asia* (1967). The classic A. J. Bernet Kempers, *Ancient Indonesian Art* (1959) is a more detailed study of the more limited area. Paul Mus, *Barabudur*, 2 vols. (1935) is a masterly work with implications beyond the monument discussed. Outstanding of the many books on Cambodia is Pierre Dupont, *La Statuaire Préankorienne* (1955). Other good studies are G. Groslier, *La Sculpture Khmère Ancienne* (1925); H. Parmentier, *L'Art Khmer Classique* (1939); and Sherman E. Lee, *Ancient Cambodian Sculpture* (1968). There are few introductory studies of Sri Lanka (Ceylon) and Thailand; T. Bowie, ed., *The Art of Thailand* (1960) is useful.

Periodicals include *Artibus Asiae*, *Arts Asiatiques*, *Oriental Art*, *Marg*, and *Lalit Kala*, as well as others essential for current information. The Archaeological Survey of India has issued various series that are indispensable, including *Memoirs*, *Annual Reports*, *Ancient India*, and *Indian Archaeology*.

Chapter Nineteen: The Art of China

Lawrence Sickman and Alexander Soper, *The Art and Architecture of China* (1956) is recommended as a sound, comprehensive view of the subject. Michael Sullivan, *A Short History of Chinese Art* (1970) is a useful summary, and H. G. Creel, *The Birth of China* (1936, 1954) remains a worthwhile classic. Three solid works by Cheng Te-k'un are *Prehistoric China* (1958), *Shang China* (1960), and *Chou China* (1966). Max Loehr, *Ritual Vessels of Bronze Age China* (1968) is a systematic chronology, while Charles D. Weber, *Chinese Pictorial Bronze Vessels of the Late Chou Period* (1968) provides a thorough study of the last great ritual bronzes. S. Mizuno, *Bronzes and Jades of Ancient China* (1959) is a beautiful, well-illustrated Japanese text with a good English summary. Osvald Sirèn, *Chinese Sculpture from the Fifth to the Fourteenth Centuries*, 4 vols. (1925) is an indispensable resource. For specific sites and areas the following are recommended: Richard Rudolph, *Han Tomb Art of West China* (1951); Michael Sullivan and Dominique Darbois, *The Cave Temples of Maichishan* (1969); and S. Mizuno and T. Nagahiro, *Unko Sekkutsu: Yunkang, The Buddhist Cave Temples of the Fifth Century A.D. in North China*, 16 vols. (1951–56) and *A Study of the Buddhist Cave Temples at Lung-men, Honan* (1940). The latter two are in Japanese with English summaries.

Osvald Sirèn, *Chinese Painting, Leading Masters and Principles* (1956–58) is a monumental survey, thoroughly illustrated. More recent research is incorporated in James Cahill, *Chinese Painting* (1960), Sherman E. Lee, *Chinese Landscape Painting* (1971), and Michael Sullivan, *The Birth of Landscape Painting in China* (1961). New information about one of China's greatest sites is furnished in Basil Gray and John B. Vincent, *Buddhist Cave Paintings at Tun-huang*

(1959). A rich source of references useful in research is Alexander Soper, *Literary Evidence for Early Buddhist Art in China* (1959). J. LeRoy Davidson, *The Lotus Sutra in Chinese Art* (1954) is a study of the pragmatic relationships between the arts and cultural attitudes, as expressed in illustrations from religious texts. An adequate starting point in the voluminous literature on ceramics is W. B. Honey, *The Ceramic Art of China and other Countries of the Far East* (1945). A work incorporating more recent research is John Ayers, *The Seligman Collection of Oriental Art: Vol. II, Chinese and Korean Pottery and Porcelain* (1964). Exciting new archeological finds in China are well illustrated in *Historical Relics Unearthed in New China* (1972), published in Peking. Periodicals recommended are *Artibus Asiae; Arts Asiatiques; Oriental Art; Archives of Asian Art; New China.*

Chapter Twenty: The Art of Japan

Recommended as introductory texts are Robert T. Paine and Alexander Soper, *The Art and Architecture of Japan* (1955) and the Japanese sections of Sherman E. Lee, *A History of Far Eastern Art* (1973). Although prepared as an exhibition catalog, John M. Rosenfield and Shojiro Shimada, *Traditions of Japanese Art* (1970) has not only superb illustrations but a commentary that serves as an excellent history of Japanese culture. J. Edward Kidder, *Early Japanese Art* (1964) and *The Birth of Japanese Art* (1965) are comprehensive studies of archeological material but must be supplemented by reports of later discovies, which appear chiefly in Japanese periodicals. The pictorial traditions are concisely and brilliantly treated in T. Akiyama, *Japanese Painting* (1961). J. Edward Kidder, *Japanese Temples: Sculpture, Painting and Architecture* (1965) is particularly useful in its sculpture sections. Specialized studies include John M. Rosenfield, *Japanese Art of the Heian Period, 749–1185* (1967) and Sherman E. Lee, *Japanese Decorative Style* (1961). J. Fontein and M. C. Hickman, *Zen Painting and Calligraphy* (1970) and James F. Cahill, *Scholar Painters of Japan: the Nanga School* (1972) are excellent introductions to their subjects. Arthur Drexler, *The Architecture of Japan* (1955) is a perceptive analysis by a specialist in Western architecture. One of many good books on ukiyo-e, C. Hirano's monograph *Kiyonaga* (1939) also contains an excellent discussion of the Japanese woodblock print in general. Comprehensive and well illustrated are Harold P. Stern, *Master Prints of Japan, Ukiyo-E Hanga* (1969) and *Ceramic Art of Japan* (1972), issued by The Seattle Art Museum, with a text by Henry Trubner; both have extensive, up-to-date bibliographies. Among other periodicals on Asian Art, *Bijutsu Kenkyu* is recommended specifically for its coverage of Japanese art.

Chapter Twenty-one: Pre-Columbian Art

The most comprehensive general work on pre-Columbian art is still George Kubler, *The Art and Architecture of Ancient America* (1962). Excellent general texts providing cultural background material for Meso-America and the Andes are Frederick Peterson, *Ancient Mexico* (1962) and J. Alden Mason, *The Ancient Civilizations of Peru* (1969). Intensive coverage of individual periods, areas, and mediums may be found in the following: Michael D. Coe, *The Jaguar's Children: Pre-Classic Central Mexico* (1965); Merle Greene, Robert Rands, and John Graham, *Maya Sculpture* (1972); Tatiana Proskouriakoff, *A Study of Classic Maya Sculpture*, Carnegie Institute of Washington, D. C. publication no. 593 (1950); William Coe, *Tikal, a Handbook of the Ancient Maya Ruins* (1967); John Paddock, ed., *Ancient Oaxaca* (1966); Donald Robertson, *Pre-Columbian Architecture* (1963); John H. Rowe, *Chavin Art: An Inquiry into its Form and Meaning* (1962); Wendell C. Bennett, *Ancient Arts of the Andes* (1954); André Emmerich, *Sweat of the Sun and Tears of the Moon, Gold and Silver in Pre-Columbian Art* (1965); and Junius B. Bird and Louisa Bellinger, *Paracas Fabrics and Nazca Needlework* (1954). Key handbooks are J. Eric Thompson, *Maya History and Religion* (1970); George C. Vaillant, *Artists and Craftsmen in Ancient Central America* (1973); Sylvanus G. Morley, *The Ancient Maya* (1956); Julian H. Steward, ed., *Handbook of the South American Indians*, 7 vols. (1956); and Robert Wauchope, ed., *Handbook of Middle American Indians*, 16 vols. (1969).

Recent exhibition catalogs have reached new levels of excellence. Of particular value are the Guggenheim Museum's *Mastercraftsmen of Ancient Peru* (1968); the Metropolitan Museum of Art's *Before Cortez, Sculpture of Middle America* (1970); the Los Angeles County Museum of Art's *Sculpture of Ancient West Mexico, The Proctor Stafford Collection* (1970); and the Los Angeles County Museum of Natural History's *Ancient Art of Veracruz* (1971).

Chapter Twenty-two: North American Indian, African, and Oceanic Art

A few general books survey the arts of North America, Africa, and Oceania, each from a different perspective. Paul Wingert, *Primitive Art: Its Traditions and Styles* (1962) employs the "style area" method, whereas Douglas Fraser, *Primitive Art* (1962) employs a theoretical, diffusionist, historical approach. A third, more recent work, still more broadly inclusive, is L. Pericot-Garcia, J. Galloway, and A. Lömmel, *Prehistoric and Primitive Art* (1967). Earlier approaches, now less popular, are found in F. Boas, *Primitive Art* (1927) and L. Adam, *Primitive*

Art (1945). Various methods are surveyed in D. Fraser, ed., *The Many Faces of Primitive Art* (1966).

It is best, perhaps, to consult works on the individual areas. General introductions to Indian arts, all very well illustrated, include: Norman Feder, *Art of the American Indian* (1971); Frederick Dockstader, *Indian Art in America* (1961) and, a new version that treats the entire continent, *Indian Art of the Americas* (1973); A. H. Whiteford, *North American Indian Arts* (1970) and two exhibition catalogues—Norman Feder, *Two Hundred Years of North American Art*, Whitney Museum of American Art (1971), and *American Indian Art: Form and Tradition*, Walker Art Center and Minneapolis Institute of Arts (1972), which contains thirteen essays by specialists on subareas. Another fine, scholarly catalog, this one devoted to Northwest Coast and Eskimo traditions, is H. B. Collins *et al.*, *The Far North*. A wealth of data on arts is contained in E. S. Curtis, *The North American Indian*, 30 vols. (1903–1930), and for bibliography one can consult A. Harding and P. Boling, *Bibliography of Articles and Papers on North American Indian Arts* (1938), as well as the later but more general G. P. Murdock, *Ethnographic Bibliography of North America* (1960). More specific studies include C. Grant, *Rock Art of the American Indian* (1967); V. Scully, *Pueblo Architecture of the Southwest: A Photographic Essay* (1971); J. C. Ewers, *Plains Indian Painting* (1939, out of print); E. Gunther, *Art in the Life of the Northwest Coast Indians* (1966); and, on the Eskimo, D. J. Ray, *Artists of the Tundra and the Sea* (1961).

General surveys of African arts, primarily sculpture, are Frank Willett, *African Art, An Introduction* (1971) and W. R. Bascom, *African Art in Cultural Perspective* (1973), both in paperback; M. Lieris and J. Delange, *African Art* (1968); R. S. Wassing, *African Art, Its Background and Traditions* (1968); J. Laude, *The Arts of Black Africa* (1966); E. Elisofon and W. B. Fagg, *The Sculpture of Africa* (1958, out of print); and M. Trowell, *Classical African Sculpture* (1964). More specific studies include F. Willett, *Ife in the History of West African Sculpture* (1967); W. Forman and P. Dark, *Benin Art* (1960); J. Cornet, *Art of Africa; Treasures from the Congo* (1971); Walker Art Center, *Art of the Congo*; R. Goldwater, *Bambara Sculpture from the Western Sudan* (1960) and *Senufo Sculpture from West Africa* (1964); W. B. Fagg, *Nigerian Images* (1963); B. Brentjes, *African Rock Art* (1969); and R. F. Thompson, *Black Gods and Kings, Yoruba Art at U.C.L.A.* (1971). Specific themes are developed in two anthologies of essays by specialists, W. d'Azevedo, ed., *The Traditional Artist in African Societies* (1973) and D. Fraser and H. M. Cole, eds., *African Art and Leadership* (1972). Useful for bibliography is L. J. P. Gaskin, *A Bibliography of African Art*; and, for articles on traditional as well as modern African Arts, the quarterly periodical *African Arts*, published by the University of California, Los Angeles is good.

An early but still valuable overview of Oceania is R. Linton and Paul Wingert, *Arts of the South Seas* (1946). Finer illustrations, many in color, are found in J. Guiart, *Arts of the South Pacific* (1963) and C. A. Schmitz, *Oceanic Art* (1954). General works on Polynesia are T. Barrow, *Art and Life in Polynesia* (1973) and E. Dodd, *Polynesian Art* (1967). Specific Polynesian studies include P. H. Buck, *Arts and Crafts of Hawaii* (1957) and T. Barrow, *Maori Wood Sculpture of New Zealand* (1969). General New Guinea studies are R. Firth, *Art and Life in New Guinea* (1936) and D. Newton, *New Guinea Art in the Collection of the Museum of Primitive Art* (1967). A few good studies on single areas are D. Newton, *Art Styles of the Papuan Gulf* (1961) and *Crocodile and Cassowary* (1971), which deals with the Upper Sepik River area; M. C. Rockefeller, *The Asmat of New Guinea* (1967); S. Kooijman, *The Art of Lake Sentani* (1959); and R. M. Berndt *et al.*, *Australian Aboriginal Art* (1964). For bibliography: C. J. R. Taylor, *A Pacific Bibliography* (1951).

PLAN AND SECTION CONVENTIONS

The plans and sections (see Introduction, pp. 13–14) in this book use the following conventions: *In plans* masses are generally solid black. (Reconstructions are shown shaded.) Elements such as steps and sills or other structures that do not extend from floor (plan) level to roof or ceiling are shown in line. Structures above or below floor level and not integral with it are shown in dashed line. Section lines, indicating the plane along which a section is drawn, are shown by a dash-dot line. *In sections* structures are generally shown as in a simple line drawing, with masses that are cut by the plane of the drawing shown in gray. The section plane is the foremost; the first surface beyond is untinted, and surfaces beyond that are shown in light grays. Labeled specimen plans and a section are shown below.

PLAN

WALL (Reconstruction)
NICHE
WALL
GROINED VAULT (Reflected)
STAIRS
COLUMN
WINDOW
WALL
STEPS
ALTAR PLATFORM
ARCH } Reflected
DOME }
WINDOW
GROINED VAULT
Reflected { ARCH
STEP
WALL
NICHE
SPIRAL STAIRS
STEPS

PLAN

PLAN

Ⓐ
Ⓑ
SECTION LINE,
indicating location of section plane at right.

SECTION PLANE
SURFACES BEYOND SECTION

SECTION PLANE

SECTION

931

INDEX

(*Page numbers in italic indicate illustrations.*)

A

Abrams, Isaac: *Untitled*, 786, *Plate 17-16*

Abstract Expressionism, 769, 770, 772–74

Abstract Formalism, 770, 775–82; in painting, 775–77; in sculpture, 777–82

Abu Temple, Tell Asmar: statuettes from, *51*, 51–52

Accordionist (Picasso), 730, *730*

Acropolis, Athens, 139, 151, *152*, 153; Erechtheum, 144, *160*, 161, 161–62; Parthenon, *123*, 151–58, *153*, *154*, 185, 214; Propylaea, *159*, 160; Temple of Athena Nike, *138*, *159*, 160–61, *163*, 163

Action painting, 770, 772–74

Actor (Kiyotada), *864*, 865

Adam, Robert, 651, 655–56; Etruscan Room, Osterley Park House, 655–56, *Plate 16-1*

Adam and Eve (Dürer), 562, *563*

Adam and Eve Reproached by the Lord, detail of bronze doors, St. Michael's, Hildesheim, (Bishop Bernward), 305, 322–23, *323*

Adena art, 885, 886

Adena Pipe, 885, *885*

Admonitions of the Instructress to the Young Ladies of the Palace (Ku K'ai-chih), 836; *Lady Feng and the Bear*, from, *836*

Adoration of the Magi (fresco), Santa Maria, Tahull, 349, *Plate 9-1*

Adoration of the Magi (Gentile da Fabriano), 442–43, *Plate 12-1*

Adoration of the Mystic Lamb, from *The Ghent Altarpiece* (H. and J. van Eyck), *540*, 540–43, *541*, *542*

Adoration of the Shepherds, The (van der Goes), 549, *Plate 14-5*

Aegean art, 102–21

Aerial (atmospheric) perspective, 212, 568

African art, 882–84, 892–98

After-image, complementary, 616n

Agesander, Athanadoros, and Polydoros, 175–76; *Head of Odysseus*, *175*, 175–76; *Odysseus' Helmsman Falling*, *174*, 175

Agora: of Athens, 125; in Hellenistic cities, 181–82

Agrippa Postumus, Villa of, Pompeii, wall painting from, 211, *212*

Ajanta, cave painting at, 817

Akhenaton, 73, 97–101; statue of, 98–99, *99*

Akkadian art, 40, 41, 55–57

Alain, drawing, *17*

Alberti, Leon Battista, 399–400, 425, 435, 448–49, 454–59; Palazzo Rucellai, Florence, 455, *455*; San Francesco, Rimini, 456, *456*; Sant' Andrea, Mantua, 456–58, *457*; Santa Maria Novella, Florence, façade of, 425, *455*, 455–56

Alcuin of York, 313

Alessandro dei Filipepi. *See* Botticelli, Sandro

Alhambra palace, 293–94, *294*, *295*

Allegri, Antonio. *See* Correggio

Alloway, Lawrence, 782

Altamira caves, 27

Altar of the Hand, Benin, 893, *893*

Altar of Zeus and Athena, Pergamum, 123, *173*, 173–74

Altarpiece of the Holy Sacrament: The Last Supper from (Bouts), *547*, 548

Altdorfer, Albrecht, 557–58; *The Battle of Issus*, 557–58, *558*

Alternate-support system in Romanesque churches, 322

Amarāvatī, stupa relief from, 814, *814*

Amarna period, Egypt, 73, 97–101

Amenemheb, tomb of, *Fowling Scene* from, 96, *Plate 3-1*

Amenemhet I, tomb of, 88, *89*

Amenhotep III, court and colonnade of, Luxor, *95*, 95–96

Amen-Mut-Khonsu, Temple of, Luxor, *95*, 95–96

Amen-Re, Temple of, Karnak, 92, *94*, 95

American art. *See* North American Indian art; Neoclassicism; Op Art; Pop Art; Pre-Columbian art

American Indian art. *See* North American Indian art

Amida Triad, from *Shrine of Lady Tachibana*, Horyu-ji, 851–52, *852*

Amiens Cathedral (Luzarches), 353, *369*, 369–71, *370*

Amphiprostyle temple, *138*, 139

Amphoras, *126*, 126–27; *The Blinding of Polyphemos* and *Gorgons*, 127–28, *128*; *Dipylon Vase*, 123, 127, *127*; *Herakles and Apollo Struggling for the Tripod* (Andokides Painter), 130, *130*; *Revelers* (Euthymides), *131*, 131–32

Analytic Cubism, 731

Anatolian art, 42, 43–47

Ancestral figure, Papuan Gulf, 902, *902*

Ancestral figures, Kongo, 895–96, *896*

Ancestral poles, Asmat, 902, 902–03

Andean art, 874–79

Andokides Painter, 130–31, 165; *Herakles and Apollo Struggling for the Tripod*, 130, *130*

Andrea del Castagno, 446–47

Andrea del Sarto, 508–09; *Madonna of the Harpies*, 508, *Plate 13-3*

Angelico, Fra, 450, 452; *Annunciation*, 425, 450, *452*

Angkor Thom, *822*, 823, *823*

Angkor Wat, 821, *822*

Angkorean style, 821

Animal caricatures, detail of scroll (Abbot Toba), 856, *857*

Animal style: in Germanic craft art, 307–09; in Luristan bronzes, 69–70; in Romanesque sculpture, 345

Annunciation (Fra Angelico), 425, 450, *452*

Annunciation (Piero della Francesca), 449, *449*

Annunciation, The (jamb statues), Reims Cathedral, *375*, 375–76

Annunciation, The (Simone Martini), 419–20, *Plate 11-2*

Annunciation and the Nativity, The (N. Pisano), 403, 406, 408

Annunciation of the Death of Mary, from *Maestà Altarpiece* (Duccio), 411, 411–12

Annunciation to the Shepherds, The, from *Gospel Book of Otto III*, 324, *325*

Antheil, George, 733

Anthemius of Tralles: Hagia Sophia (with Isidorus of Miletus), 245, *273*, 274, 274–77, *275*, *276*, *277*

Antonello da Messina, 472–73; *Martyrdom of St. Sebastian*, 473, *Plate 12-7*

Antonio da Sangallo: Farnese Palace, Rome, 475, 485, 486, 487

Aphaia, Temple of, Aegina, *138*, *143*, 146, 146–47, *147*

Aphrodite of Cnidus (Praxiteles), 167–68

Aphrodite of Cyrene, 167, *168*

Aphrodite of Melos, 123, *176*, *176*

Apollo, from Temple of Zeus, Olympia, 7, 149–50, *150*

Apollo, Temple of, Bassae, 170

Apollo, Temple of, Didyma, *138*, *178*, *178*

Apollo and Daphne (Pollaiuolo), 465–66, *466*

Apollo Attended by the Nymphs (Girardon), 628–29, *629*

Apollo of Veii (acroterion), 190, *191*

Apollodorus of Damascus: Column of Trajan, 185, 230, 230–31, *231*

Apollonius(?): *Seated Boxer*, 123, *177*, 177–78

Apotheosis of the Pisani Family, The (Tiepolo), 636, *636*

Apoxyomenos (Lysippos), 169, *169*, 171

Aqueducts, Roman, *216*, 216–17

Aquitania, Romanesque architecture in, 340–41

Ara Pacis Augustae, 226, 226–28, *227*

Arapaho art, 890; shield, 890, *891*

Arcadianism: in Roman painting, 212–13; in Venetian painting, 523–24; in work of Watteau, 637

Arch: corbeled, 14; diaphragm, 340; Etruscan, 186; Gothic, 358; Islamic, 289; Roman, 219, 223–25, 228–29, 237, 238; Romanesque, 340

Arch of Constantine, 185, 241–42, *242*, *243*

Arch of Titus, 228, *228*

Archaic period, Greece, 123, 126–47

Archers of St. Adrian (Hals), 609–10, *610*

Archipenko, Alexander: *Woman Combing Her Hair*, 749, *749*

Architectural wall painting, 206–08, *207*, *208*

Architecture: arcuated, 237, *238*; Art Nouveau, 758–59; Assyrian, 60–62; Baroque, 581–92, 623–28, 629–35, 640–41; basic structural devices, 14; Byzantine, 277–80; Chinese, 847; Early Christian, 250–55; Early Medieval, 315–20, 321–22; Egyptian, 79–82, 90–96; English, 337–38, 380–82, 629–31, 640–41, 652–56, 658–59; Etruscan, 186–88; French, 329, 330–33, 336–37, 340–41, 356–62, 367–73, 378–79, 572–75, 623–28, 631–34, 656–58, 660; German, 333–35, 336, 382, 384, 634–35; Gothic, 356–62, 367–73, 378–84, 386–93; Greek, 123, 138–47, 151–61, 170–71, 178–82; in India, 804–07, 810–23; International style, 762–68; Islamic, 286–96; Italian, 335–36, 338–40, 386–93, 437–42, 454–59, 481, 483–87, 498–506, 515–21, 581–92; Japanese, 849, 850, 853–54, 859–60, 867; Javanese, 818–20; Mannerism in, 515–18; Mycenaean, 117–20; Neoclassic, 654–57; nineteenth-century, 652–60, 711–15; North American Indian, 887; Persian, 67–69; pre-Columbian, 871–72, 873–74, 876, 877, 879; program of a building, 14; Realism in, 711–15; Renaissance, 437–42, 481, 483–87, 498–506, 515–21, 572–75; Rococo, 632–35; Roman, 199–205, 215–25, 236–40; Romanesque, 329–41; Romantic, 652–60; twentieth-century, 757–68, 788–95

Arcuated architecture, 237, *238*

Areogun: door from palace at Ikerre (Yoruba), 894, 894–95

Argonaut Krater (Niobid Painter), 164–65, *165*

Aristophanes, 166

Aristotle, 51, 123, 139, 166–67

Arnolfo di Cambio: Florence Cathedral, 386–87, *388*, 389, *389*

Art Nouveau, 721–22; in architecture, 758–59

Artaxerxes II, palace of, Susa: bull capital, 231, *231*

Artemis, Temple of, Corfu, 145–46, *146*

Aryans, influence on art of India, 803

Ashanti art, 893–94

Ashikaga period, Japan, 858–59

Ashurbanipal Hunting Lions (Assyrian relief), 18, 63, *64*

Ashurnasirpal II at War (Assyrian relief), 62–63, *63*

Ashurnasirpal II Drinking (Assyrian relief), *63*, 63–64

Asmat art, 902–03

Aśoka: palace of, Pāṭaliputra, 804–05; lion capital from, 804, *804*

Assumption of the Virgin, The (Correggio), *509*, 509–10

Assumption of the Virgin, The, from

Creglingen Altarpiece (Riemenschneider), 554–55, *556*
Assyrian art, 40, 41, 59–65
At the Moulin Rouge (Toulouse-Lautrec), 706, *Plate 16-11*
Athanadoros. *See* Agesander, Athanadoros, and Polydoros
Athena Nike, Temple of, Acropolis, Athens, *138*, *159*, 160–61; parapet relief, 163, *163*
Athena Parthenos, 151, *155*
Athena Taking Young Alcyoneus by the Hair (frieze, Altar of Zeus and Athena), *173*, 173–74
Atmospheric (aerial) perspective, 212, 568
Atrium: Etruscan, 187; Roman, 204–05, *205*, 206, *206*
Augustus of Primaporta, 226, *226*
Aurier, Albert, 720
Aurora (Guercino), 594, *595*
Aurora (Reni), 594, *594*
Australian art, 904–05
Avignon Pietà, The (Anonymous Master), 554, *Plate 14-7*
Axis, 8, *9*
Aztec art, 874

B

Babylonian art, 40, 41, 57–64; neo-, 65–66
Back I (Matisse), 748, *748*
Back IV (Matisse), 748, *748*
Bacon, Francis, 769; *Number VII from Eight Studies for a Portrait*, 769, *771*
Baldacchino, St. Peter's (Bernini), 585, *586*
Baldassare Castiglione (Raphael), 492, *Plate 13-1*
Ballet Rehearsal (Adagio) (Degas), 697, *697*
Balthasar Coymans (Hals), 579, 608–09, *Plate 15-6*
Balzac (Rodin), 710, *711*
Bamberg Rider, 385, *387*
Bamboo (Wu Chen), 843, *844*
Banner, Lake Sentani, 901, *901*
Banqueting Hall, Whitehall, London (Jones), 630, *630*
Bar at the Folies-Bergère (Manet), 693–94, *694*
Barabudur, Java, stupa at, 818, *819*, 820
Barbizon school, 686–87
Bare Willows and Distant Mountains (Ma Yüan), 840, 840–41
Bark of Dante, The (Delacroix), 677, *Plate 16-3*
Barlach, Ernst, 747; *War Monument*, Güstrow Cathedral, 716, 747, *747*
Baroque art, 578–649; architecture, 581–92, 623–28, 629–35, 640–41; Dutch, 606–17; eighteenth-century, 631–45; English, 629–31, 640–45; Flemish, 603–06; French, 617–29, 631–34, 636–40; German, 634–35; Italian, 581–97, 635–36; painting, 592–623, 635–40, 641–45; Rococo style, 632–40; sculpture, 586–88, 628–29, 639; seventeenth-century, 581–631; Spanish, 598–603
Barrel vault: Roman, 223, *224*; Romanesque, 331
Barry, Charles: Houses of Parliament, London (with A. W. N. Pugin), 651, 658, *659*
Bartolomeo, Michelozzo di. *See* Michelozzo di Bartolomeo
Bartolomeo Colleoni (Verrocchio), 463, 463–64
Barye, Antoine-Louis: *Jaguar Devouring a Hare*, 18, 662, *663*
Basilica, Paestum, *142*, 142–43
Basilica of Constantine, Rome, 223–24, *239*, 239–40
Basilica Ulpia, Rome, 220, *221*
Basilicas, 220; Christian, 250–55
Bathers (Picasso), 8, *8*
Baths of Caracalla, Rome, 223–25, *225*
Battle Between Romans and Barbarians, from *Ludovisi Battle Sarcophagus*, 259, *259*
Battle of Alexander, The (mosaic), House of the Faun, Pompeii, *213*, 213–14
Battle of Gods and Giants (frieze), Altar of Zeus and Athena, *173*, 173–74
Battle of Issus, The (Altdorfer), 557–58, *558*
Battle of Naked Men (Pollaiuolo), 464–65, *465*
Battle of San Romano, The (Uccello), 446, *447*
Battle of the Gods and Giants (frieze), Treasury of the Siphnians, 145, *145*
Baudelaire, Charles, 552, 672, 673, 690
Bauhaus School, 765–66
Bauhaus, Shop Block, Dessau (Gropius), 716, *766*
Bayon, Angkor Thom, 822, 823, *823*
Beautiful Bodhisattva Padmapani ("Great Bodhisattva"), 817, *Plate 18-1*
Beauvais Cathedral, 373, *373*
Beckmann, Max, 716, 724–25; *Departure*, 724–25, *725*
Behrens, Peter, 762–63
Belgian art. *See* Flemish art
Belleville Breviary (Pucelle), 533, 537, *Plate 14-1*
Bellini, Giovanni, 473, 521–24; *Feast of the Gods*, 523, *Plate 13-6*; *San Giobbe Altarpiece*, *522*, 522–23; *San Zaccaria Altarpiece*, *522*, 522–23
Benin art, 893
Bergson, Henri, 760
Berlinghieri, Bonaventura, 410; *St. Francis Altarpiece*, 409, *409*; *St. Francis Preaching to the Birds*, 409, 409–10
Bernard, Émile, 727
Bernard of Clairvaux, 341–42, 346, 350, 356
Bernini, Gianlorenzo, 584–88; *Baldacchino* for St. Peter's, 585, *586*; *Cathedra Petri*, 585–86, *Plate 15-1*; Cornaro Chapel, Rome, 586–87, *587*; *David*, 586, *587*; *The Ecstasy of St. Theresa*, 586–87, *588*; St. Peter's, piazza adjoining, *582*, 584, *584*; Scala Regia, Vatican, 579, 584–85, *585*; Triton Fountain, Rome, *395*, 588
Bernward, Bishop: *Adam and Eve Reproached by the Lord*, detail of bronze doors, St. Michael's, Hildesheim, 305, 322–23, *323*
Betrayal of Jesus, The, from *Maestà Altarpiece* (Duccio), 410, *411*
Bibliothèque Ste.-Geneviève (Labrouste), *711*, *712*
Bicycle Wheel (Duchamp), 754, *755*
Biomorphic abstraction, 750
Bird in Space (Brancusi), 716, 750, *750*
Birdstone, Hopewell, 885, *885*
Birkets, Gunnar: Federal Reserve Bank Building, Minneapolis, 793, *793*
Birth of Venus (Botticelli), 8, 425, 468, 468–69
Birth of Venus, The (Bouguereau), 682, *683*
Birth of the Virgin, The (Ghirlandaio), 466, *467*
Birth of the Virgin, The (P. Lorenzetti), 421, *421*
Birthday (Kienholz), 785, *786*
Bison with Superposed Arrows (cave painting), Niaux, 30, *31*
Bison with Turned Head (Later Old Stone Age engraving), 33, 33–34
Black-figure technique (Attic pottery), 129–30
Bladen, Donald, 778–79; *X*, 779, *779*
Blam! (Lichtenstein), 717, 784, *785*
Blanket with bear design, Chilkat, 889, 889–90
Blaue Reiter, Der, 717, 724
Blenheim Palace, Oxfordshire (Vanbrugh), 579, 641, *642*
Blinding of Polyphemos and Gorgons, The (proto-Attic amphora), 127–28, *128*
Blois, Château de, Orléans wing of (F. Mansart), 622, *623*
Boar Avatar of Vishnu, cave at Udaygiri, 811, *811*
Boccioni, Umberto, 733, 749; *Unique Forms of Continuity in Space*, 749, 749–50
Bodhisattva (Early T'ang dynasty), 833–34, *834*
Bodmer, Karl, 890

Boethos: *Boy Strangling a Goose*, 176–77, *177*

Boffrand, Germain: Decorations for the Salon de la Princesse, Hôtel de Soubise, Paris, *633*, 633–34

Bologna, Giovanni da. *See* Giovanni da Bologna

Bolognese painters, 593–94, 596

Book illumination. *See* Illumination

Book of Lindisfarne, 305, 310, 311, *Plate 8-2*; St. Matthew from, 311, *311*, 313–14

Borrachos, Los (Velázquez), 600, *601*

Borromini, Francesco, 588–91; St. Ivo, Rome, 589–91, *590*; San Carlo alle Quattro Fontane, Rome, 588–89, *589*

Bosch, Hieronymus, 551–53; *The Carrying of the Cross*, 551, *551*; *The Garden of Earthly Delights*, 533, 551–53, *552*, *Plate 14-6*; *Hell*, from *The Garden of Earthly Delights*, 552, *552*

Boscoreale, Villa, Pompeii, wall painting from, 206, *207*

Botticelli, Sandro, 467–69; *The Birth of Venus*, 8, 425, *468*, 468–69; *Portrait of a Young Man*, 466–67, *Plate 12-5*

Boucher, François, 579, 637–38; *Cupid a Captive*, 638, *638*

Bouguereau, Guillaume-Adolphe: *The Birth of Venus*, 682, *683*

Bound Slave, The (Michelangelo), 495, *496*

Bouts, Dirk: *The Last Supper* (from *Altarpiece of the Holy Sacrament*), 547, *548*

Boy in a Red Vest (Cézanne), 651, 703, *703*

Boy Strangling a Goose (Boethos), 176–77, *177*

Boyle, Richard, 652–53; Chiswick House (with W. Kent), 651, 653, *653*

Bramante, Donato, 481, 483–85; St. Peter's, 484, *484*; Tempietto, Rome, 475, *483*, 483–84

Brancusi, Constantin, 750; *Bird in Space*, 716, 750, *750*

Braque, Georges, 716, 728, 731, 732; *The Table*, 732, *Plate 17-9*

Breakfast Scene (from *Marriage à la Mode*, Hogarth), 642–43, *643*

Breasted, James, 98

Breton, André, 738, 739, 754

Breuil, Abbé, 27, 28, 33

Bridge movement. *See* Brücke, Die

Bride of the Wind, The (Kokoschka), 724, *Plate 17-5*

Bridge-spouted vessel (Nasca), 877, *877*

Brihadeśvara Temple, 816

Broad Flatheads (Bury), 781, *781*

Broederlam, Melchior, 533, 536–37; *The Presentation and the Flight into Egypt*, 536–37, *537*

Bronze warrior (Greek Geometric period), 132, *133*

Bronzino: *Portrait of a Young Man*, 475, 513, *Plate 13-5*; *Venus, Cupid, Folly, and Time*, 512–13, *514*

Brücke, Die, 717, 724

Bruegel, Pieter (the Elder), 568–71; *Hunters in the Snow*, 533, 568, *570*; *The Parable of the Blind*, *570*, 571; *Peasant Dance*, 569, 571, *Plate 14-10*

Brulé art, 890–91; shirt, *891*

Brunelleschi, Filippo, 437–41; Florence Cathedral, dome of, 386, 425, 437–38, *438*; Ospedale degli Innocenti, Florence, façade of, *438*, 439; Pazzi Chapel, 440, *440*, *441*; *The Sacrifice of Isaac*, 427, *427*, *428*; Santa Maria degli Angeli, Florence, 441–42, *442*; Santo Spirito, Florence, interior of, *439*, 439–40

Bruni, Leonardo, tomb of (B. Rossellino), 459–60, *460*

Brygos Painter: *Revelers*, 132, *132*

Buddha images: Chinese, 831, 833; Indian, 807, 809–10, 818–20; Japanese, 851–52

Buddhism: in China, 831–34, 840, 841, 847; in India, 803–07, 812–13, 818, 820, 823; in Japan, 851–57

Bull's Head (Picasso), 755, *755*

Bunchō, 866

Buoninsegna, Duccio di. *See* Duccio di Buoninsegna

Burckhardt, Jacob, 394, 476

Burghers of Calais (Rodin), 709, 709–10

Burgundian school, 535

Burial at Ornans (Courbet), 690, *691*, 691–92

Burial mask (Ipiutak), 844, *885*

Burial of Atala, The (Girodet), 669, *669*

Burial of Count Orgaz (El Greco), 598–99, *Plate 15-3*

Burial of Phocion, The (Poussin), 620, *621*, 623

Burning of the Sanjo Palace, The (Kamakura period), 858, *858*

Bury, Pol, 780–81; *Broad Flatheads*, 781, *781*

Bury Bible: *Moses Expounding the Law* from, 350, *Plate 9-2*

Buson, Yosa: *Enjoyment of Summer Scenery*, detail of *The Ten Conveniences and the Ten Enjoyments of Country Life*, 862, *863*

Bust of a Little Boy (Settignano), 461, *461*

Byzantine art, 244–46, 262–86; architecture, 277–80; Byzantium, 273–77; Later, 277–86; painting, 280–86; Ravenna, 263–73

Byzantine style (*maniera bizantina*), 409–10

Byzantium, art of, 273–77. *See also* Byzantine art

C

Caere (Cerveteri), Tomb of the Reliefs at, 187, 188, *189*

Cage, John, 782

Cagliari, Paolo. *See* Veronese

Calder, Alexander, 753, *754*; *Horizontal Spines*, 717, *754*, *754*

Callicrates, 151, 160

Calligraphy, Chinese, 841–42, 844

Callixtus, catacomb of, Rome, 248, *248*

Cambio, Arnolfo di. *See* Arnolfo di Cambio

Cambodian art, 821–23

Camera degli sposi (Mantegna), 472, *473*, *Plate 12-6*

Camera obscura, 616

Campidoglio. *See* Capitoline Hill

Campin, Robert (Master of Flémalle), 533, 539; *The Mérode Altarpiece*, *539*, 539–40

Canoe-prow figure, Solomon Islands, 904, *904*

Canopic urn, Clusium, 190–91, *191*

Canova, Antonio, 660; *Pauline Borghese as Venus*, 651, 660–61, *661*

Cap Blanc, rock sculpture at, 34; *Relief Horse*, 34, *34*

Capitoline Hill, Rome (Michelangelo), 475, *502*, 502–04, *503*, *504*

Caprichos, Los: "The Dream of Reason" from (Goya), 651, 665, *665*

Caracalla (Roman bust), 235, 235–36

Caracalla, Baths of, Rome, 223–25, *225*

Caradosso: Medal of St. Peter's, 484, *484*

Caravaggio, 594–95; *Conversion of St. Paul*, 594, *Plate 15-2*

Carolingian period, 312–20

Carracci, Annibale, 593–94, 595; *Polyphemos*, 578, *593*, 593–94

Carracci, Ludovico, 595

Carrying of the Cross, The (Bosch), 551, *551*

Carson, Pirie, Scott Building, Chicago (Sullivan), 715, *715*

Caryatids, 141; of the Erechtheum, Acropolis, Athens, 144, 161–62; of the Treasury of the Siphnians, Delphi, 143–44, 162

Casa Milá, Barcelona (Gaudi), 717, 758–59, *759*

Castagno, Andrea del, 446–47; *The Last Supper*, 446, *448*; *Pippo Spano*, 446–47, *448*

Castelfranco, Giorgione da. *See* Giorgione da Castelfranco

Catacombs, 247–50, *248*, *249*

Çatal Hüyük, 40, 41, 42, 43–47

Cathedra Petri, St. Peter's, Rome (Bernini), 585–86, *Plate 15-1*

Cathedral of the Annunciation, Moscow, 279–80, *281*

Cavallini, Pietro, 412, *413*; *Seated*

Apostles, detail of *The Last Judgement*, 412, *412*

Cave art, 24–35, 817, 886

Cave temples, India, 805

Ceiling decoration: Baroque, 593–97, 635–36; of *Camera degli sposi*, 472; of catacombs, 249–50; Early Christian, 253; of Parma Cathedral dome, 509–10; Rococo, 635–36; of Sistine Chapel, 475, 495–99

Céline, Louis-Ferdinand, 771

Cellini, Benvenuto, 513–14; *Diana of Fontainebleau*, 513–14, *514*

Central-plan church, 252–55, *253*, *254*; Bramante's development of, 481, *483*, 483–84; in Renaissance, 459

Ceramics. *See* Pottery; Porcelain

Ceremonial Men's House, Abelam, 901, *901*

Cervetere (Caere), Tomb of the Reliefs at, 187, 188, *189*

Cézanne, Paul, 701–03, 727; *Boy in a Red Vest*, 651, 703, *703*; *La Montagne Sainte-Victoire*, 701, 702, *702*; *Still Life*, 701–02, *Plate 16-8*

Chagall, Marc, 716, 741–42; *Crucifixion*, 741–42, *742*

Chaitya cave, Karli, 807, 808, *809*

Chambord, Château de, 572–73, *574*, *575*

Champollion, Jean François, 75

Chandis, 820

Chang Ta-chen, 845

Chao Meng-Fu: *A Sheep and a Goat*, 843, *843*

Chapel of Henry VII, Westminster Abbey, 382, *383*

Chapel of the Santa Sindone, Turin (Guarini), 592, *592*

Chardin, Jean-Baptiste-Siméon, 638; *Grace at Table*, 638–39, *639*

Charioteer, from Sanctuary of Apollo, Delphi, 7, 147–48, *148*

Charlemagne, 2, 307, 312–16; Palatine Chapel of, 2, 315–16, *316*

Charles I Dismounted (Van Dyck), 606, *606*

Chartres Cathedral, 353, 362, *364*, 364–66, *365*, *366*, *367*, 367–69, 368, 373–74, *374*; *Good Samaritan* (window), 377, *Plate 10-2*; jamb statue from, *364*, 364–65, *365*, 431, *432*

Chartreuse de Champmol, Dijon: *Presentation and the Flight into Egypt* from (Broederlam), 536–37, *537*; *The Well of Moses* from (Sluter), 533, 535, *536*

Château de Blois, Orléans wing of (F. Mansart), 622, *623*

Château de Chambord, 572–73, *574*, *575*

Chateaubriand, François René de, 657–58

Chavín cult, art of, 875–76

Cheops. *See* Khufu

Chephren. *See* Khafre

Ch'i Pai-Shih, 845

Chiaroscuro, 11; in work of Leonardo, 478, 481

Ch'ien-lung, 846

Chilkat blanket, 889, 889–90

Chimera, Arezzo, 192, *193*

Ch'in dynasty, 828, 845–46

Chinese art, 824–47; architecture, 847; Buddhism, 831–34, 840, 841, 847; Calligraphy, 841–42, 844; Ch'in dynasty, 828, 845–46; Chou dynasty, 827–28; Five dynasties, 838–40; Han dynasty, 828–31; influence on art of Japan, 851–53, 858–60, influence on art of nineteenth-century England, 652; K'ang hsi dynasty, 846; Ming dynasty, 844–45; painting, 826, 829, 833, 834–36; People's Republic of China, 846–47; porcelain, 845–46; pottery, 838, 842; sculpture, 826–34, 846; Shang dynasty, 826–27; Southern Sung dynasty, 840–42; Sui dynasty, 833; T'ang dynasty, 833–38; Yüan dynasty, 842–43

Chinese Horse (cave painting), Lascaux, 30, *31*

Ching Hao, 838

Chirico, Giorgio de. *See* De Chirico, Giorgio

Chiswick House (Boyle and Kent), 651, 653, *653*

Chō Densu, 858

Chola temples, Tamilnadu, 816

Chou dynasty, 827–28

Christ as the Good Shepherd (mosaic), from mausoleum of Galla Placidia, 265, *Plate 7-1*

Christ Between Angels and Saints (Byzantine mosaic), 270, *Plate 7-5*

Christ Crowned with Thorns (Titian), 528, *528*

Christ Delivering the Keys of the Kingdom to St. Peter (Perugino), 425, 470, *471*

Christ in Majesty, from St. Sernin, 342, *342*

Christ in the House of Levi (Veronese), 530, *Plate 13-9*

Christian art. *See* Early Christian art

Christina of Denmark (Holbein), 533, 566, 566–67

Christina's World (Wyeth), 716, 774–75, *775*

Christus, Petrus, 547–48; *The Legend of Saints Eligius and Godeberta*, 547, 547–48

Chu Ta, 845

Chü-Jan, 839

Chün ware, 842

Church art: Baroque, 581–92, 634–37; Byzantine, 273–80; Early Christian, 250–55; Early Medieval, 315–30; Gothic, 353, 356–71, 373–91; Rococo, 634–36; Romanesque, 329–50

Cicero, 197

Cimabue, Giovanni, 413; *Madonna Enthroned with Angels and Prophets*, 403, 413, *413*

Cire perdue process, 849, 893

Citadel of Sargon II, Khorsabad, 60, 60–62, *61*

Citadel of Tiryns, 116, *117*

Cities: in ancient Near East, 43–44, *44*, 48–50, *49*, 60, *61*, 65–66, *66*; Hellenistic, 181–82; Roman, 202–05, 215–16

City, The (Léger), 733, *733*

City Square (Giacometti), 715, 716, 718, *756*, *757*

Cliff Palace, Mesa Verde, 887, *888*

Cloisonné, 308

Cloister Graveyard in the Snow (Friedrich), 685, *686*

Clouet, Jean, 533; *Francis I*, 572, *572*

Cluniac-Burgundian architecture, 330–33

Coatlicue (Aztec), 874, *875*

Codex Amiatinus: *The Scribe Ezra Rewriting the Sacred Records*, 310, 311, 313–14

Codex Aureus of St. Emmeram, 305, 314–15, 342, *Plate 8-3*

Colima dog vessel, 871, *871*

Collage: Dadaist, 736–37; of Picasso, 731; Pop Art, 783

Cologne Cathedral, 353, 386, *388*

Colonial Cubism (Davis), 775, *776*

Color, 11–13

Color theory: of Gauguin, 705; of Impressionists, 694–95; of Seurat, 700

Color-field painting, 776

Colosseum, Rome, 218–19, *219*

Column of Trajan, Rome (Apollodorus), 185, *230*, 230–31, *231*

Complementary after-image, 616n

Composition in Blue, Yellow, and Black (Mondrian), 717, 735, *Plate 17-10*

Conceptual Art, 770, 787, 788

Concordantia, principle of, 371

Concrete: in modern architecture, 762; Roman use of, 200–02

Confucius, 828

Constable, John, 684–85; *Salisbury Cathedral from the Bishop's Garden*, 684–85, *685*

Constantine the Great (Roman bust), 185, 240, 240–41

Constructivism, 752–54; Dadaism and, 736–37, 754–56, 770; in painting, 736; in sculpture, 752–54, 777–82

Contrapposto, 132

Conversion of St. Paul (Caravaggio), 594, *Plate 15-2*

Corbeled vault, 37, 871, *872*

Corbie, Pierre de, 371

Cordoba, Mosque of, 288–89, *289*, 294

Corinthian order, 140–41, 155, *170*, 170–71, 219

Cornaro Chapel, Rome (Bernini), 586–87, *587*

Coronation Gospels (*Gospel Book of Charlemagne*): *St. Matthew* from, *312*, 313

Corot, Jean Baptiste Camille, 651, 686; *The Harbor of La Rochelle*, 686, *687*

Correggio (Antonio Allegri), 475, 509–10; *The Assumption of the Virgin*, *509*, 509–10; *Jupiter and Io*, 510, *510*

Count Cagliostro (Houdon), 639, *640*

Couple (Dogon sculpture), 897, 897–98

Courbet, Gustave, 690–92; *Burial at Ornans*, 690, *691*, 691–92; *The Stone Breakers*, 651, 690, *690*, 691

Court of the Lions, Alhambra palace, 293–94, *294*

Couture, Thomas: *Romans of the Decadence*, 681–82, *682*

Coypel, Antoine, 628

Craft art: Carolingian, 314–15; Chinese, 828, 830–31; African, 892–98; Early Christian, 260–62; Germanic tribes, 307–09; Islamic, 296–98; Mycenaean, 120–21; North American Indian, 881–91; Oceanic, 898–905; Persian, 69–70

Cranach, Lucas (the Elder), 533, 558–59; *The Judgment of Paris*, 559, *559*

Creation of Adam, from the Sistine Chapel ceiling (Michelangelo), 497–98, *Plate 13-2*

Creglingen Altarpiece: The Assumption of the Virgin from (Riemenschneider), 554–55, *556*

Cretan art. *See* Minoan art

Cromlechs, 37, *38*

Cross-barrel vault, Roman, 224, *224*

Crow art, 890

Crucifixion (Chagall), 741–42, *742*

Crucifixion, from *Isenheim Altarpiece* (Grünewald), 559–60, *560*

Crucifixion (window), St. Remi, Reims, 377, *Plate 10-1*

Crucifixion, The (Byzantine mosaic), 280–82, *282*

Cryptomeria Trees (Tohaku), 861, *861*

Crystal Palace, London (Paxton), 651, 711, *713*

Cubi XVIII and Cubi XIX (Smith), 717, 777, *778*

Cubism, 717; analytic, 731; in painting, 727–35; in sculpture, 748–49; synthetic, 731

Cupbearer (fresco), palace of Knossos, 110–11, *111*

Cupid a Captive (Boucher), 638, *638*

Current (Riley), 717, 776, *777*

Cycladic art, 103–14

Cylinder seal, Ur, *54*, 55

D

Dadaism, 770; in painting, 736–37; in sculpture, 754–56

Daggers, Mycenaean, 120, *Plate 4-2*

Dali, Salvador, 740–41, 753–54, 785; *The Persistence of Memory*, 741, *741*

Damned Cast into Hell, The (Signorelli), 470, *470*

Dan art, 896

Dance relief, Angkor Wat, 821, *822*

Dancing Hunter (detail of wall painting), Çatal Hüyük, 45–46, *Plate 2-1*

Dancing Royal Couple, Gangwa, 895, *895*

Dancing Śiva Relief, Badami, 811, 811–12

Dante Alighieri, 413

Darius, Palace of, Persepolis, 66, 67, 67–69, 69, *70*

D'Artagnan (Doré), 651, 662, *663*

Daumier, Honoré, 688–89, 690–91; *Rue Transnonain*, 688, 688–89; *The Third-Class Carriage*, 651, 688, *689*; *The Uprising*, 689, *689*

David (Bernini), 586, *587*

David (Donatello), 425, *435*, 436

David (Michelangelo), 475, 493–95, *494*

David (Verrocchio), 425, 462, 462–63

David, Jacques Louis, 666–69; *The Death of Marat*, 651, 668, *668*; *Madame Récamier*, 668; *Oath of the Horatii*, *667*, 667–68

David Composing the Psalms, from *Paris Psalter*, 282–83, *284*, 285

Davis, Stuart, 775; *Colonial Cubism*, 775, *776*

De Chirico, Giorgio, 717, 738; *The Delights of a Poet*, 738, *738*

De Kooning, Willem, 773; *Woman I*, 773–74, *774*

De la Tour, Georges, 618; *The Lamentation over St. Sebastian*, 618, *618*

De la Tour, Quentin, 579, 639; *Self-Portrait*, 639, *639*

De Stijl movement, 716, 735, 751, 770

Dead Christ, The (Mantegna), 472, *473*

Death and Fire (Klee), 743, *Plate 17-11*

Death and Life (Klimt), 721, *Plate 17-1*

Death of Marat, The (David), 651, 668, *668*

Death of St. Francis, The (Giotto), 416, *417*, 418

Death of Sardanapalus, The (Delacroix), 673–74, *674*

Debarkation of Marie at Marseilles, The (Rubens), 605, *606*

Deer Hunt (wall painting), Çatal Hüyük, 45–46, *46*; *Dancing Hunter* from, *46*, *Plate 2-1*

Degas, Edgar, 651, 697–99; *Ballet Rehearsal* (*Adagio*), 697, *697*; *The Morning Bath*, 699, *699*; *Viscount Lepic and His Daughters*, 698, 698–99

Déjeuner sur l'Herbe (Manet), 692–93, *693*

Delacroix, Eugène, 18, 672–77, 681–82; *The Bark of Dante*, 677, *Plate 16-3*; *The Death of Sardanapalus*, 673–74, *674*; *Liberty Leading the People*, 651, 675–76, *676*; *Medea*, 674–75, *675*; *Paganini*, 680, *681*

Delaroche, Paul, 708

Delights of a Poet, The (De Chirico), 738, *738*

Demoiselles d'Avignon, Les (Picasso), 728, *729*, 730

Denis, Maurice, 704–05, 709, 719

Departure (Beckmann), 724–25, *725*

Derain, André: *London Bridge*, 717, 722, *Plate 17-2*

Descent from the Cross (Pontormo), 511–12, *Plate 13-4*

Deschamps, Eustache, 551

Desiderio da Settignano, 461; *Bust of a Little Boy*, 461, *461*

Diana of Fontainebleau (Cellini), 513–14, *514*

Diaphragm arch, 340

Diderot, Denis, 640

Dinkeloo, John: Oakland Museum (with Kevin Roche), 795, *795*

Diocletian, Palace of, Spalato, 237, *237*, 238

Dionysos (pediment sculpture), Parthenon, 156, *156*

Dionysos in a Sailboat (Exekias), 123, 129, *129*, 130

Dioscuri, House of the, Pompeii, wall painting from, 210, *210*

Dipteral temple, *138*, 139

Diptych of Anastasius, 261, *261*, 262

Dipylon Vase (Geometric), 123, 127, *127*

Disappointed Mistress, *Plate 18-2*

Disasters of War (Goya), 665; *Tampoco* from, 665, 665–66

Discobolos (Myron), 148–49, *149*

Disks of confusion, 616–17

District God, Harvey Islands, 899, 899–900

Djanggawul Sisters, The (Mungarawai), 905, *905*

Doge's Palace, Venice, 353, 393, *393*

Dogon art, 897–98

Dolmens, 37

Dome: Baroque, 590; Byzantine, 274–75, 279–80; of Florence Cathedral, 386, 425, 437–38, *438*; Islamic, 290; of Pantheon, Rome, 221; Romanesque, 340–41; of St. Peter's, *505*, 505–06; of stupas, 806–07

Domenichino, 578; *The Last Communion of St. Jerome*, 596, *596*

Domical vault, 359

Donatello, 429–37; *David*, 425, *435*, 436; *The Feast of Herod*, 433, *433*, 434; "*Gattamelata*," 436, *436*; *Mary Magdalene*, 437, *437*; *St. George*, 431,

431; *St. Mark*, *430*, 430–31; *St. John the Evangelist*, *15*; *"Zuccone"* (prophet figure), *432*, 432–33

Doré, Gustave: *D'Artagnan*, 651, 662, *663*

Doric order, 140, *140*, 141–43, *142*, *143*, 144–45, 151–52, 154, 155, 164, 219

Doryphoros (Polykleitos), *10*, 123, 163, *163*, 164

Dōtaku, 850

Doubting Thomas, from *Magdeburg Antependium* (Echternach Master), 323, *324*

Dream imagery in surrealist painting, 740–41

"Dream of Reason, The" from *Los Caprichos* (Goya), 651, 665, *665*

Dubuffet, Jean, 717, 771–72; *Nude, Olympia*, 771, *771*

Ducasse, Isadore, 740–41

Duccio di Buoninsegna, 403, 410–12; *The Annunciation of the Death of Mary*, from *Maestà Altarpiece*, *411*, 411–12; *The Betrayal of Jesus*, from *Maestà Altarpiece*, *410*, 411

Duchamp, Marcel, 716, 717, 737, 754; *Bicycle Wheel*, 754, *755*; *Nude Descending a Staircase #2*, 734, *734*; *To be looked at (from the other the side of glass) with one eye, close to, for almost an hour*, 716, 737, *737*

Dürer, Albrecht, 18, 533, 561–65; *Adam and Eve*, 562, *563*; *The Four Apostles*, 533, 564–65, *565*; *The Four Horsemen of the Apocalypse*, 562, *562*; *The Great Piece of Turf*, 563, *563*; *Hieronymus Holzschuher*, 563–64, *564*; *Melancolia I*, 564, *565*; *Two Lions*, 18

Durham Cathedral, England, 327, 337–38, *338*

Dutch painting, Baroque, 606–17

Dying Gaul (Hellenistic), *172*, 172–73

Dying Lioness (Assyrian relief), 18, *64*, *65*

Dying Slave, The (Michelangelo), 495, *496*

E

Eadwine Psalter: The Scribe Eadwine from, 351, *351*

Early Christian art, 244–62; architecture, 250–55; catacombs, 247–50; craft art, 260–62; illumination, 256–58; mosaic, 253, 255–56; painting, 249–50; sculpture, 258–60

Early Classical period, Greece, 123, 151–65

Early Dynastic period, Egypt, 73, 76–87

Early Empire, Rome, 185, 214–36

Early Gothic period, 356–67

Early Medieval art, 304–25; architec-

ture, 315–20, 321–22; Carolingian period, 312–20; craft art, 307–09, 314–15; illumination, 309–12, 313–14, 323–25; Migration period, 306–12; Ottonian period, 320–25; painting, 313–14, 323–25; sculpture, 322–23

Earth art, 779–80

Eastern Woodlands Indian art, 891

Echo of a Scream (Siqueiros), *743*, 743–44

Echternach Master: *Doubting Thomas*, from *Magdeburg Antependium*, 323, *324*

Ecstasy of St. Theresa, The (Bernini), 586–87, *588*

Effervescence (Hofmann), 772, *Plate 17-12*

Effigy mounds, North American Indian, 886

Egyptian art, 72–101; Amarna period, 97–101; architecture, 79–82, 90–96; Early Dynastic period, 73, 76–87; Middle Kingdom, 87–88; New Kingdom, 88–97; Old Kingdom, 73, 76–87; painting, 85–87, 88, 96–97; relief, 85–87, 91; rock-cut tombs, 87–88; sculpture, 82–85, 88, 96–97

Eighteenth-century art. *See* Baroque art

Ekkehard (Gothic statue), Naumburg Cathedral, 384–85, *386*

El Greco (Domeniko Theotokopoulos), 598–99; *Burial of Count Orgaz*, 598–99, *Plate 15-3*

Elevation of the Cross, The (Rubens), 603–04, *604*

Elgin, Lord Thomas Bruce, 156

Elgin marbles, 156

Eliot, T. S., 19, 738, 784

Embarkation for Cythera (Watteau), 636–37, *Plate 15-11*

Embryo in the Womb (Leonardo), 481, *482*

Encaustic technique, 136, 214

English art: architecture, 337–38, 380–82, 629–31, 640–41, 652–56, 658–59; Baroque, 629–31, 640–45; Gothic, 380–82; painting, 641–45, 684–85; Romanesque, 337–38, 350–51; Romantic, 652–56

Engobe, in Attic black-figure ware, 129

Engraving: German, 555–56, 562–63, 564; Italian, 464–65, 557; Later Old Stone Age, 33–34; North American Indian, 886; Polynesian, 900; Renaissance, 464–65, 555–56, 557, 562–63, 564

Enjoyment of Summer Scenery, detail of *The Ten Conveniences and the Ten Enjoyments of Country Life* (Buson), 862, *863*

Ensor, James, 707; *The Entry of Christ into Brussels*, 706, 707

Entombment, The (Pilon), 576, *577*

Entry of Christ into Brussels, The (Ensor), 706, 707

Epidaurus, theater at, *179*, 181

Equitable Building, New York, 712

Erased de Kooning by Robert Rauschenberg (Rauschenberg), 783

Erasmo da Narni, equestrian statue of (*"Gattamelata"*) (Donatello), 436, *436*

Erechtheum, Acropolis, Athens, 144, 160, *161*, 161–62

Ernst, Max, 739, 772; *Two Children are Threatened by a Nightingale*, 739, *739*

Escorial Deposition (Rogier van der Weyden), 546–47, *Plate 14-4*

Eskimo art, 884, *885*

Estes, Richard: *Nedick's*, 787, *787*

Et in Arcadia Ego (1630) (Poussin), 619, 619–20

Et in Arcadia Ego (1640) (Poussin), 620, *621*

Étienne Chevalier and St. Stephen (Fouquet), *553*, 553–54

Etruscan art, 184–94; architecture, 186–88; painting, 188–89; sculpture, 189–94

Etruscan bronze mirror, 193, *193*

Etruscan Room, Osterley Park House (Adam), 655–56, *Plate 16-1*

Euphronios: *Herakles Strangling Antaios*, 131, *131*

Euripides, 181

Euthymides: *Revelers*, 131, 132–32

Evans, Arthur, 104, 105

Evening Glow of the Ando, The (Harunobu), 651, 698, 865

Exekias: *Dionysos in a Sailboat*, 123, 129, 129, 130

Expressionism: Abstract, 769, 770, 772–74; figural, 769, 771–72; in painting, 722–27, 769–74; in sculpture, 746–47

Expulsion from Eden, The (Masaccio), 445, *445*

Expulsion from the Garden of Eden, The (Jacopo della Quercia), 428, *428*

Eyck, van. *See* Van Eyck, Hubert; Van Eyck, Jan

F

Fabriano, Gentile da. *See* Gentile da Fabriano

Fallen Warrior (pediment sculpture), Temple of Aphaia, 146, *147*

"Falling Water" (Kaufmann House) (Wright), 717, 764, *765*

Family of Charles IV, The (Goya), 663, *664*, 665

Family of Country People (Le Nain), 618–19, *619*

Fan K'uan: *Travelers Among Mountains and Streams*, 839, *839*

Fan paintings, Japanese, 855
Farnese Palace, Rome (Antonio da Sangallo), 475, 485, 486, 487; ceiling frescoes in, 593, 593–94
Faun, House of the, Pompeii, 205; mosaic from, 213, 213–14
Fauves, 717, 722–24
Feast of Herod, The (Donatello), 433, 433, 434
Feast of the Gods (Bellini), 523, *Plate 13-6*
February, from *Les Très Riches Heures du Duc de Berry* (Limbourg Brothers), 538, 538–39
Federal Reserve Bank Building, Minneapolis (Birkets), 793, 793
Feeding of Oryxes (Egyptian fresco), 88, 89
Female Head, Warka, 50, 50–51
Fetish, Luba, 883, 883
Fetish, Songye, 896, 896
Fibula, Early Medieval, 307, 307–08
Ficino, Marsilio, 426, 468, 469
Ficoroni Cist, The (Novios Plautios), 193–94, 194
Fifteenth-century art. *See* Renaissance
Fighting Téméraire, The (Turner), 684, *Plate 16-4*
Figural Expressionism, 769, 771–72
Figurines. *See* Statuettes
Finding and Proving of the True Cross, The (Piero della Francesca), 449–50, 451
Finding of the Body of St. Mark, The (Tintoretto), 475, 529–30, 530
Fiorentino, Il Rosso. *See* Il Rosso Fiorentino
Five Dynasties, China, 838–40
Flamboyant style, 378–79
Flemish art: Baroque, 603–06; illumination, 537–39; painting, 536–53, 567–71, 603–06; Renaissance, 535–53, 567–71; sculpture, 535
Florence, 404; proto-Renaissance painting in, 412–19; in Renaissance, 424–69
Florence Cathedral (Arnolfo di Cambio), 386–87, 388, 389, 389; baptistry doors of, 408, 409, 434, 434–35; campanile of (Giotto), 386–87; dome of (Brunelleschi), 386, 425, 437–38, 438
Fluting of columns, 145
Flying Horse Poised on One Leg on a Swallow (Wu-wei), 830, 830
Flying Storehouse, The, detail of *Shigisan Engi* (Fujiwara period), 856, 856
Font-de-Gaume, cave paintings at, 27, 28; *Reindeer*, 32, 33
Form, 6–7
Formalism: in Egyptian art, 77–78; in Sumerian art, 52–53. *See also* Abstract Formalism
Fortuna Primigenia, Sanctuary of, Praeneste, 200, 200–02, 201

Fortuna Virilis, Temple of, Rome, 199, 199
Forums, Roman, 219–20, 220
Fountain of the Innocents, Paris, *Nymphs* from (Goujon), 574–75, 577
Fouquet, Jean, 533, 553–54; *Étienne Chevalier and St. Stephen*, 553, 553–54
Four Apostles, The (Dürer), 533, 564–65, 565
Four Darks on Red (Rothko), 774, *Plate 17-14*
Four Horsemen of the Apocalypse, The (Dürer), 562, 562
Four Seasons: Grapevine from (Hsu Wei), 844, 845
Fourteenth-century art. *See* Proto-Renaissance
Fowling Scene (wall painting), tomb of Amenemheb, 96, *Plate 3-1*
Fragonard, Jean-Honoré, 638; *The Swing*, 579, 638, *Plate 15-12*
Francesca, Piero della. *See* Piero della Francesca
Francis I (Clouet), 572, 572
François Marius Granet (Ingres), 680, 680
François Vase, The, 128–29, 129
Frankfort, Henri, 47
Frankish ornaments, 305, 307, 307–08
Frankl, Paul, 387
French Ambassadors, The (Holbein), 566, *Plate 14-9*
French art: architecture, 329, 330–33, 336–37, 340–41, 356–62, 367–73, 378–79, 572–75, 623–28, 631–34, 656–58, 660; Baroque, 617–29, 631–34, 636–40; the Fauves, 717, 722–24; Gothic, 353–79; illumination, 349–50; painting, 553–54, 571–72, 617–23, 636–40, 666–84, 686–706, 707–09, 727–33; Renaissance, 553–54, 571–77; Romanesque, 329, 330–33, 336–37, 340–41, 342–50; Romantic, 656–58, 660, 661–62; sculpture, 342–50, 362–67, 373–76, 378, 574–77, 628–29, 639, 661–62; twentieth-century, 727–33
Fresco secco technique, 86
Frescoes: Byzantine, 282; in catacombs, 249–50; Egyptian, 86–87; Etruscan, 188–89; Italian, *see* Italian art, painting; Minoan, 109–12; in Sistine Chapel, 470, 471, 495–99, 497, 498, 499; *See also* Ceiling decorations; Murals; Wall painting
Freud, Sigmund, 721, 737, 738
Friedrich, Caspar David: *Cloister Graveyard in the Snow*, 685, 686
Fromentin, Eugène, 607n
Functionalism in modern architecture, 762
Funeral mask (Mycenaean), 120, 120
Futurism, 716, 733–34, 749–50, 770

G

Gabo, Naum, 736, 753; *Kinetic Sculpture*, 753, 754; *Linear Construction*, 716, 753, 753
Gaddi, Taddeo. *See* Taddeo Gaddi
Gainsborough, Thomas, 643–44; *The Honorable Mrs. Graham*, 644, 644; *Mrs. Richard Brinsley Sheridan*, 578, 644, *Plate 15-13*
Galatea (Raphael), 491, 491
Galen, 164
Galerie des Glaces, palace at Versailles (J. H. Mansart and le Brun), 626–27, 627
Galerie des Machines, Paris International Exhibition (1889), 712, 713
Galla Placidia, mausoleum of, Ravenna, 245, 264, 265; mosaic in, 265, *Plate 7-1*
Garden of Earthly Delights, The (Bosch), 533, 551–53, 552, *Plate 14-6*
Garden Scene (wall painting), House of Livia, Primaporta, 208, *Plate 6-4*
Garnier, Charles: Opéra, Paris, 651, 660, 660
Gasulla gorge, rock paintings at, 25, 35; *Marching Warriors*, 35, 36
"Gates of Paradise" (Ghiberti), 425, 434, 434–35
"*Gattamelata*" (Donatello), 436, 436
Gaudi, Antonio: Casa Milá, Barcelona, 717, 758–59, 759
Gauguin, Paul, 704–05; *Spirit of the Dead Watching*, 651, 705, *Plate 16-10*
Geese of Medum (Egyptian frieze), 86–87, 86–87
Gelede masquerader, 894, *Plate 22-1*
Gellée, Claude. *See* Lorraine, Claude
Gentile da Fabriano, 442–43; *The Adoration of the Magi*, 425, 442–43, *Plate 12-1*
Geometric period, Greece, 123, 126–47; bronze warrior, 132, 133
George Washington (Greenough), 661, 661
Géricault, Théodore, 671–72; *Madwoman*, 672, 673; *Mounted Officer of the Imperial Guard*, 672, 673; *Raft of the Medusa*, 671, 671–72
German art: architecture, 333–35, 336, 382, 384, 634–35; Baroque, 634–35; engraving, 555–56, 562–63, 564; Gothic, 382, 384–85; painting, 554, 555, 556–67; Renaissance, 554–67; Romanesque, 333–35, 336; sculpture, 384–85, 554–55; twentieth-century, 724–26
German Pavilion, Barcelona International Exhibition (1929) (Mies van der Rohe), 766, 766–67
Germanic tribes: craft art of, 307–09; migration of, 306–07
Gérôme, Jean-Léon: *Thumbs Down!*, 682–84, 683
Gesù, Il. *See* Il Gesù.

Ghent Altarpiece, The: Adoration of the Mystic Lamb from (H. and J. van Eyck), 540, 540–43, 541, 542; God the Father from, 542, 542

Ghiberti, Lorenzo, 426–28, 435; "Gates of Paradise" (doors of Florence Cathedral baptistry), 425, 434, 434–35; The Meeting of Solomon and the Queen of Sheba, 434, 435; The Sacrifice of Isaac, 427, 427–28

Ghirlandaio, Domenico, 466; The Birth of the Virgin, 466, 467; Giovanna Tornabuoni (?), 466, Plate 12-4

Giacometti, Alberto, 757; City Square, 715, 716, 718, 756, 757

Giacomo della Porta, 506; Il Gesú (with Giacomo da Vignola), 578, 581, 581–83

Gibbon, Edward, 235, 236, 246, 656

Giedion, Siegfried, 757

Gift (Ray), 755, 755–56

Giorgione da Castelfranco, 524; Pastoral Symphony, 524, Plate 13-7

Giotto di Bondone, 412–19; campanile, Florence Cathedral, 386–87; The Death of St. Francis, 416, 417, 418; Lamentation, 415, 416, Plate 11-1; Madonna Enthroned, 414, 414; The Meeting of Joachim and Anna, 418, 418–19

Giovanna Tornabuoni (?) (Ghirlandaio), 466, Plate 12-4

Giovanni Arnolfini and His Bride (J. van Eyck), 533, 545, 546

Giovanni da Bologna, 475, 514; Rape of the Sabine Women, 514–15, 515

Girardon, François: Apollo Attended by the Nymphs, 628–29, 629

Girodet, Anne Louis: The Burial of Atala, 669, 669

Giuliano da Sangallo, 459; Santa Maria delle Carceri, Prato, 458, 459

Giuliano de' Medici, tomb of (Michelangelo), 499–500, 500

Giulio Romano, 516; Palazzo del Tè, Mantua, 475, 516, 516–18, 517

Gizeh, Great Pyramids of, 72, 73, 79, 80, 81, 82, 83

Glaber, Raoul, 795

Gleaners, The (Millet), 686–87, 687

Glorification of St. Ignatius, The (Pozzo), 596–97, 597

Gloucester Cathedral, 382, 383

God the Father, from The Ghent Altarpiece (H. and J. van Eyck), 542, 542

Goes, Hugo van der. See Hugo van der Goes

Goethe, Johann Wolfgang von, 488, 651, 658

Gogh, Vincent van. See Van Gogh, Vincent

Golden Legend cycle: Annunciation from (Piero della Francesca), 449, 449

Gonzalez, Julio, 750–51; Woman Combing Her Hair, 751, 751

Good Government Enthroned (A. Lorenzetti), 421, 422; Peaceful City from, 422, 422; Peaceful Country from, 423, 423

Good Samaritan (window), Chartres Cathedral, 377, Plate 10-2

Good Shepherd Sarcophagus, The, 259–60, 260

Gospel Book of Archbishop of Reims: St. Matthew from, 312, 313–14

Gospel Book of Charlemagne (Coronation Gospels): St. Matthew from, 312, 313

Gospel Book of Otto III: The Annunciation to the Shepherds from, 324, 325; Otto III Enthroned Receiving the Homage of Four Parts of the Empire from, 325, 325

Gossaert, Jan, 567–68; Neptune and Amphitrite, 567, 567–68

Gothic art, 352–401; architecture, 356–62, 367–73, 378–84; Early, 356–57; English, 380–82; French, 353–79; German, 382, 384–85; High, 367–78; Italian, 386–93; Late, 378–80; sculpture, 362–67, 373–76, 378, 384–85; stained glass, 376–78

Goujon, Jean, 533, 573, 574; Nymphs (reliefs), from Fountain of the Innocents, Paris, 574–75, 577

Goya, Francisco, 662–66; Disasters of War, 665; "The Dream of Reason," from Los Caprichos, 651, 665, 665; Family of Charles IV, 663, 664, 665; The Parasol, 663, 664; Saturn Devouring His Children, 666, 666; Tampoco, from Disasters of War, 665, 665–66; Third of May, 1808, 665, Plate 16-2

Grace at Table (Chardin), 638–39, 639

Grande Odalisque (Ingres), 679, 679

Grapevine, detail of Four Seasons (Hsu Wei), 844, 845

Graphic Arts, 16; Illusion in, 16–18

Grave Stele of Hegeso, 162, 162–63

"Great Bodhisattva" (Beautiful Bodhisattva Podmapani), 817, Plate 18-1

Great Dragon, Quiriguá, (Maya), 872, 873

Great Mosque of Samarra, 245, 287, 288

Great Piece of Turf, The (Dürer), 563

Great Plains Indian art, 890–91

Great Pyramids of Gizeh, 72, 73, 79, 80, 81, 82, 83

Great Sphinx, 82

Great Stupa, The, Sanchi, 806, 806–07

Great Wave, The (Hokusai), 866, 866

Greco, El. See El Greco

Greek art, 122–83; Archaic period, 123, 126–47; architecture, 123, 138–47, 151–61, 170–71, 178–82; Early Classical period, 123, 151–65; Geometric period, 123, 126–47; Hellenistic period, 171–83; Late Classical period, 166–71; mosaics, 182–83; painting, 123, 126–32, 164–65; sculpture, 123, 132–38, 144–47, 161–64, 167–70, 171–78; Transitional period, 123, 147–50; vases, 123, 126–32

Greenberg, Clement, 776

Greenough, Horatio: George Washington, 661, 661

Greuze, Jean Baptiste, 579, 639–40; The Return of the Prodigal Son, 640, 641

Grimm, Friedrich, 654

Gris, Juan, 719, 734

Groin vault: Roman, 224; Romanesque, 332–33, 335, 357

Gropius, Walter, 765; shop block, Bauhaus, Dessau, 716, 765–66, 766

Gros, Antoine Jean, 669–70; Pest House at Jaffa, 670, 670–71

Grosz, George, 716; Punishment, 725, 726

Grünewald, Matthias, 533, 559–61; Crucifixion from Isenheim Altarpiece, 559–60, 560; Resurrection, from Isenheim Altarpiece, 560–61, Plate 14-8

Guaranty (Prudential) Building, Buffalo (Sullivan), 714–15, 715

Guarini, Guarino, 591–92; Chapel of the Santa Sindone, Turin, 592, 592; Palazzo Carignano, Turin, 578, 591, 591

Gudea Worshiping, Telloh, 56, 57, 57

Guercino, Giovanni: Aurora, 594, 595

Guernica (Picasso), 731–32, 732

Guggenheim Museum, New York (Wright), 789, 791

Guidoriccio da Fogliano (Simone Martini), 420, 420

H

Habitat, Montreal (Safdie), 794, 794–95

Hadrian (bust), 234, 234

Hagia Sophia (Anthemius and Isidorus), 7–8, 245, 273, 274, 274–77, 275, 276, 277

Hall church. See Hallenkirche

Hall of Bulls (cave painting), Lascaux, 27, 33, Plate 1-1

Hall of Mirrors. See Galerie des Glaces

Hall of the Two Sisters, Alhambra palace, 294, 295

Hallenkirche, 382, 384

Hals, Frans, 608; Archers of St. Adrian, 609–10, 610; Balthasar Coymans, 579, 608–09, Plate 15-6; Malle Babbe, 609, 609

Hamilton, Richard, 783; Just What Is It That Makes Today's Homes So Different, So Appealing?, 783, 783

Hammurabi, 52, 57–59; Stele of, 41, 57–58, 58

Han dynasty, 828–31
Han Kan: *Horse, 837, 837*
Handball (Shahn), 744, *744*
Haniwa figures, Japan, 850, *850*
Harbor of La Rochelle, The (Corot), 686, *687*
Hard-edge painting, 776
Harihara, Prasat Andet, 821, *821*
Harmony in Red (Red Room) (Matisse), 723, Plate 17-3
Harrowing of Hell, The (fresco), Mosque of the Ka'riye, 282, *284*
Harunobu, 865; *The Evening Glow of the Ando,* 651, *698,* 865
Harvester Vase, 113–14, *114*
Harvey Islands, art of, 899–900
Hasan, Sultan, Madrasah and Mausoleum of, Cairo, 294–95, *296*
Hatshepsut, Queen, Mortuary Temple of, *90, 91*
Haydon, Benjamin Robert, 156
Head Master: portals of Chartres Cathedral, 365, *365*
Head of a Roman, 185, 197, *198*
Head of Amenemhet III, 88, *90*
Head of an Akkadian Ruler, 55, *55–56*
Head of Augustus, 232, *232–33*
Head of Odysseus (Agesander, Athanadoros, and Polydoros), *175, 175–76*
Head of the God Abu, 51, 51–52
Head of the Procession (frieze, Parthenon), 157–58, *158, 160*
Heian period, Japan, 854–57
Hell, from *The Garden of Earthly Delights* (Bosch), 552, *552*
Hellenistic period, 171–83
Henry VII, Chapel of, Westminster Abbey, 382, *383*
Hepworth, Barbara, 757
Hera, Temple of, Olympia, *138, 141, 142, 143, 144*
Hera of Samos, 133, 134
Herakleitos, 158
Herakles (pediment sculpture), Temple of Aphaia, 146–47, *147*
Herakles and Antaios (Pollaiuolo), 425, 464, *464*
Herakles and Apollo Struggling for the Tripod (Andokides Painter), 130, *130*
Herakles and Telephos (Roman wall painting), 210–11, *211*
Herakles Strangling Antaios (Euphronios), 131, *131*
Hermes and Dionysos (Praxiteles), 123, *166, 167, 169*
Hermes Bringing the Infant Dionysos to Papposilenos (Phiale Painter), 165, Plate 5-2
Herodotus, 65–66, 73, 75
Herringbone perspective, 206
Hiberno-Saxon style, 309–12
Hieronymus Holzschuher (Dürer), 563–64, *564*
High Gothic period, 367–78

High Renaissance, 476–510
Hindu art, 810–20
Hinduism, 810–18, 823
Hippodameia and the Centaur (pediment sculpture), Temple of Zeus, 150, *150*
Hippodamos, 181
Hippopotamus Hunt (relief), tomb of Ti, 85–86, *86*
Hiroshige, 866
Hofmann, Hans, 772; *Effervescence,* 772, Plate 17-12
Hogarth, William, 8, 579, 641–43; *Breakfast Scene,* from *Marriage à la Mode,* 642–43, *643*
Hokke-Kyō (*Lotus Sūtra*), 855, *855*
Hokusai, 865; *The Great Wave,* 865, *865*
Holbein, Hans (the Younger), 565–67; *Christina of Denmark,* 533, *566, 566–67; The French Ambassadors,* 566, Plate 14-9
Holland, art of, 606–14. *See also* Flemish art
Holy Sepulcher, Church of the, Jerusalem, 254, *254–55*
Holy Trinity, The (Masaccio), 445–46, *446*
Homage to New York (Tinguely), 781, *782*
Homer, 103, 115, 117
Honnecourt, Villard de. *See* Villard de Honnecourt
Honorable Mrs. Graham, The (Gainsborough), 644, *644*
Honthorst, Gerard van: *The Supper Party,* 608, *608*
Hopewell art, 885–86; Birdstone, 885, *885*
Horace, 196, 212
Horizontal Spines (Calder), 717, 754, *754*
Horse (Han Kan), 837, *837*
Horsemen (frieze), Parthenon, 158, *158*
Horta, Victor: Hotel van Eetvelde, Brussels, 758, *758*
Horus, Pylon Temple of, Edfu, 92, *93*
Hosios Loukas, Greece, monastery churches at, 277–79, *278, 279*
Hotel van Eetvelde, Brussels (Horta), 758, *758*
Houdon, Jean-Antoine, 579, 639; *Count Cagliostro,* 639, *640*
House of the Dioscuri, Pompeii, wall painting from, 210, *210*
House of the Faun, Pompeii, 205; mosaic from, *213,* 213–14
House of the Vetii, Pompeii, wall painting from, 208–09, *209*
Houses: African, 895; Early Medieval, 315; Etruscan, 186–87; Hellenistic, 181–82; Japanese, 867; Roman, 204–05, 215–16; twentieth-century, 762–65

Houses of Parliament, London (Barry and Pugin), 651, 658, *659*
Howe, George: Philadelphia Savings Fund Society Building (with Lescaze), 767, *767*
Hsia Kuei, 840, 858
Hsu Wei: *Grapevine,* detail of the *Four Seasons,* 844, *845*
Huang Kung-Wang: *Landscape,* 842, *843*
Hugh of St. Victor, 376
Hugo van der Goes, 533, 548–50; *The Adoration of the Shepherds,* from *The Portinari Altarpiece,* 549, Plate 14-5; *The Portinari Altarpiece,* 549, *549–50*
Hui-tsung, 840
Huizinga, Johan, 540
Humanism: in Greece, 123–24; in Renaissance, 396–400, 407, 453–54, 468–69
Hunter, from *Lion Hunt* (Hellenistic mosaic), 123, 182, Plate 5-3
Hunters in the Snow (Bruegel), 533, 568, *570*
Hydria, *128*
Hyksos period, Egypt, 73, 88–97

I

Iatmul skull, 903, *903*
Ibex, winged, Persia, 69–70, *71*
Ibo art, 895
Iconography, 6
Icons: Byzantine, 282, 285–86; Chinese, 833; Hindu, 811, *811; See also* Buddha images
Ictinos, 151
Idol, Cycladic, 103, *105, 106*
Il Gesù (Porta and Vignola), 578, *581,* 581–83
Il Rosso Fiorentino, 512, 572; *Moses Defending the Daughters of Jethro,* 512, *512; Venus Reproving Love,* 572, *573*
Illumination: Early Christian, 256–58; Early Medieval, 309–12, 313–14, 323–25; Flemish, 537–39; French, 349–50; Islamic, 298–99; Romanesque, 349–51
Iltners, Edgards: *Strong Hands,* 744, 744–45
Impressionism, 651, 692–99
Improvisations (Kandinsky), 717, 725, 726, Plate 17-7
Inca art, 879
Incrustation wall painting, 206, *207*
India, art of, 800–23; architecture, 804–07, 810–23; Buddha image, 807, 809–10, 818–20; Buddhism, 803–07, 812–13, 818, 820, 823; Hindu resurgence, 810–18; painting, 817–18; sculpture, 804–05, 811–14, 816–23; spread of, 818–23

Indian, American, art of. *See* North American Indian art

Indifférent, L' (Watteau), 578, *632*, 632–33

Ingres, Jean-Auguste-Dominique, 18, 651, 677–81; *François Marius Granet*, 680, *680*; *Grande Odalisque*, 679, *679*; *Oedipus and the Sphinx*, 678, *678–79*; *Paganini*, 680, *681*

Insulae, 215, *215–16*

Interior of the Pantheon (Pannini), 222, *223*

Interlace pattern, in Early Medieval art, 306–07

International style, in twentieth-century architecture, 762–68

Intricate wall painting, 208–12, *209*, *210*, *211*, *212*

Ionic order, *140*, 140, 155, 160, 219

Ipiutak burial mask, 884, *885*

Iron Age house, 315, *315*

Iroquois art, 891

Ise shrine, Japan, 854, *854*

Isenheim Altarpiece (Grünewald), 533, 559–61; *Crucifixion* from, 559–60, *560*; *Resurrection* from, 560–61, *Plate 14-8*

Ishtar Gate, 66, *Plate 2-3*; *Lion from the Processional Way* from, 18, *65*, 66

Isidorus of Miletus: Hagia Sophia (with Anthemius of Tralles), 245, *273*, 274, *274–77*, *275*, *276*, *277*

Islamic art, 244, 245, 246–47, 286–99; architecture, 286–96; illumination, 298–99; influence on Romanesque sculpture, 318, *319*; object art, 296–98; textiles, 297–98

Italian art: architecture, 335–36, 338–40, 386–93, 437–42, 454–59, 481, 483–87, 498–506, 515–21, 581–92; Baroque, 581–97, 635–36; engraving, 464–65, 557; fifteenth-century, 424–73; fourteenth-century, 402–23; Gothic, 386–93; Mannerism, 510–18; painting, 409–23, 442–53, 464–73, 476–81, 487–92, 495–98, 507–10, 511–13, 521–31, 592–97, 635–36; proto-Renaissance, 402–23; Renaissance, 424–531; Romanesque, 335–36, 338–40; Romantic, 660–61; sculpture, 407–09, 426–37, 459–64, 492–95, 513–15, 586–88, 660–61; six-teenth-century, 474–531; twentieth-century, 733

J

Jacopo della Quercia, 425, 428; *The Expulsion from the Garden of Eden*, 428, *428*

Jacopo Robusti. *See* Tintoretto

Jade carvings, Chinese, 828, *828*, *830*, *830–31*, 842, 846

Jaeger, Werner, 124

Jaguar Devouring a Hare (Barye), 18, *662*, *663*

Jamb statues: Chartres Cathedral, *364*, 364–65, *365*, 431, *432*; Reims Cathedral, *375*, 375–76

Japanese art, 848–67; architecture, 849, 850, 853–54, 859–60, 866; Ashikaga period, 858–59; Buddhism, 851–57; Chinese influence on, 851–53, 858–60; Heian period, 854–57; Kamakura realism, 857–58; Momoyama period, 861–62; native traditions, 850; painting, 852, 855–57, 858–63; pottery, 850, 860; print-making, 864–67; sculpture, 849–50, 851–52, 857–58; teahouses, 859–60; Ukiyo-e, 863–64

Javanese art, 818–20

Jeanneret-Gris, Charles Édouard. *See* Le Corbusier

Jefferson, Thomas, 651; State Capitol, Richmond, 657, *658*

Jericho, 40, 41, 42–43

Jesus, Church of. *See* Il Gesù

Jesus, representations of, 255

John of Garland, 376

John of Salisbury, 366

Johns, Jasper, 783; *Painted Bronze*, 716, 784, *784*

Jones, Inigo, 629–30; Banqueting Hall, Whitehall, London, 630, *630*

Joseph Recognizes His Brothers, from the *Vienna Genesis*, 258, *258*

Josephus, 229–30

Ju Peon, 845

Judgment of Paris, The (Cranach), 559, *559*

Julii, mausoleum of the, mosaic from, 255, *256*

Jupiter and Io (Correggio), 510, *510*

Just What Is It That Makes Today's Homes So Different, So Appealing? (Hamilton), 783, *783*

Justin Martyr, 260

Justinian and Maximus (Byzantine mosaic), 269–70, *Plate 7-6*

Juvenal, 216

K

Kachina doll (North American Indian), 889, *889*

Kagle (Poro mask) (Dan), 896, *897*

Kalf, Wilhelm: *Still Life*, 13, 617, *Plate 15-9*

Kamakura realism, 857–58

Kamares pitcher (Minoan), 103, 107, *107*

Kandinsky, Vasily, 726–27; *Improvisations*, 717, 725, 726, *Plate 17-7*

K'ang hsi dynasty, 846

Kano school, Japan, 860n

Katholikon, Church of the, Hosios Loukas, Greece, 14, 277–78, *278*, *279*

Kaufmann House ("Falling Water") (Wright), 717, 764, *765*

Keats, John, 686

Kelly, Ellsworth, 783; *Red, Blue and Green*, 776, *Plate 17-15*

Kent, William, 653; Chiswick House (with Boyle), 651, 653, *653*

Kenzan, 862

Khafre, 83–84, *84*

Khafre, Pyramid of, 79, 80, 81, 82, *82*, *83*

Khnumhotep, tomb of, 87, *88*

Khufu, Pyramid of, 79, *80*, 81, *81*, 82

Kienholz, Edward, 717, 785; *Birthday*, 785, *786*

Kinetic Art, 770, 781

Kinetic Sculpture (Gabo), 753, *754*

King Riding in State Palanquin (Ashanti ceremony), 893–94, *894*

King Smenkhkare and Meritaten (Egyptian relief), 99, *100*

Kiss, The (Rodin), 710, *710–11*

Kiyomasu I, 865

Kiyonaga, 865–66

Kiyonobu I, 865

Kiyotada: *Actor*, 864, *865*

Klee, Paul, 719, 742–43; *Death and Fire*, *743*, *Plate 17-11*; *Twittering Machine*, 8, 716, 742, *742–43*

Klimt, Gustav: *Death and Life*, 721, *Plate 17-1*

Kline, Franz, 773; *Painting 1952*, 773, *773*

Knossos, palace at, 107–12, *108*, *109*, *110*, *111*, *112*; frescoes in, 110–12, *111*, *112*; Queen's Megaron in, *109*, 109–10, *111*

Koetsu, 861

Kokoschka, Oskar: *The Bride of the Wind*, 724, *Plate 17-5*

Kollwitz, Käthe, 717, 725–26; *Memorial to Karl Liebknecht*, 726, *726*

Kondo (Golden Hall), Horyu-ji, 853, *853*

Kongo art, 895–96

Kore figures, 133–36; *Kore from Chios* (?), *136*, 136; *Peplos Kore*, 134–35, *Plate 5-1*

Kōrin, 862; *White Prunus in the Spring*, 865, *Plate 20-2*

Koryūsai, 865

Kouros figures, 133–37; *Kouros from Tenea*, 133–34, *135*; *Kritios Boy*, 137, *137*; *Kroisos*, 133–34, *137*

Kraters, 117, *128*; *Argonaut Krater* (Niobid Painter), 164–65, *165*; *Dipylon Vase* (Geometric), 123, *127*, *127*; *The François Vase*, 128–29, *129*; *Herakles Strangling Antaios* (Euphronios), *131*, 131; *Hermes Bringing the Infant Dionysos to Papposilenos* (Phiale Painter), 165, *Plate 5-2*

Kritios Boy, *137*, 137

Kroisos, 133–34, *135*, 137

Ku K'ai-chih, 835–36; *Lady Feng and*

the Bear, detail of the *Admonitions of the Instructress*, 836, *836*

Kuang, (Shang dynasty), 827, *827*

Kuan-yin, (early Ch'ing dynasty), 846, *846*

Kuba art, 896–97

Kudara Kannon, 851

Kukailimoku, Hawaii, 898–99, *899*

Kuo Hsi, 839

Kwakiutl masked dancers, 882, *883*

Kylix, *128, 129*; *Dionysos in a Sailboat* (Exekias), 123, *129, 129, 130*; *Revelers* (Brygos Painter), 132, *132*

L

Labrouste, Henri: Bibliothèque Ste.-Geneviève, 711, *712*

Lachaise, Gaston, 746–47; *Standing Woman*, 717, *746, 747*

Lacquer technique, 865

Lady Chapel, Salisbury Cathedral, 381–82, *382*

Lady Feng and the Bear, detail of *Admonitions of the Instructress*, Ku K'ai-chih, 836, *836*

Lafuente, Enrique, 600

Lamentation (Giotto), 415, *416*, *Plate 11-1*

Lamentation over St. Sebastian, The (G. de la Tour), 618, *618*

Landscape (Huang Kung-Wang), 842, *843*

Landscape (Sesshū), 859, *859*

Landscape scrolls, Chinese, 835–37

Landscape with St. Jerome (Patinir), 568, *569*

Landscape with Volcanic Eruption (wall painting), Çatal Hüyük, 46, *47*

Laocoön group (Hellenistic sculpture), *174*, 174–75

Laon Cathedral, 359, *360, 361, 361, 368*, 373

Lapith and Centaur (metope), Parthenon, 157, *157*

Lascaux, cave paintings at, 24, 25, 26, *27*; *Chinese Horse*, *30, 31, 33*; *Hall of Bulls*, 27, 33, *Plate 1-1*; *Second Bull*, 27, 33, *Plate 1-2*; *Three Cows and One Horse*, *28*; *Well Scene*, 31, *32*, 35

Last Communion of St. Jerome, The (Domenichino), 596, *596*

Last Judgment, The (Michelangelo), *507*, 507–08, *508*

Last Judgment, The: Seated Apostles from (Cavallini), 412, *412*

Last Supper, The, from *Altarpiece of the Holy Sacrament* (Bouts), *547*, 548

Last Supper, The (Castagno), 446, *448*

Last Supper, The (Leonardo), 9, *9*, 475, *479*, 479–80

Late Classical period, Greece, 166–71

Late Empire, Rome, 185, 236–43

Late Gothic period, 378–80

Later Byzantine art, 277–86

"Later Canon" of Egyptian art, 78

Later Old Stone Age (Upper Paleolithic), cave art of, 24, 25, 26–35

Laurentian Library, Florence (Michelangelo), 500–02, *501*

Le Brun, Charles: east façade of the Louvre (with Perrault and le Vau), 623, *624, 625*; Galerie des Glaces, palace at Versailles (with J. H. Mansart), 626–27, *627*

Le Corbusier, 762–65, 785; Notre Dame du Haut, Ronchamp, *14*, 788–89, *790*; Unité d'Habitation, Marseilles, 788, *789*; Villa Savoye, Poissy-sur-Seine, 764, *764*

Le Nain, Louis, 618–19; *Family of Country People*, 618–19, *619*

Le Nôtre, André: park of Versailles, 627–28

Le Vau, Louis: east façade of the Louvre (with Perrault and le Brun), 623, *624, 625*; garden façade, palace at Versailles (with J. H. Mansart), 578, 626, *626*

Legend of Saints Eligius and Godeberta, The (Christus), *547*, 547–48

Léger, Fernand, 715, 732–33; *The City*, 733, *733*

Lehmbruck, Wilhelm, 746; *Seated Youth*, 7, *7*, 8; *Standing Youth*, 717, 746, *746*

Lekythos, *128*

Lely, Peter, 641

Leonardo da Vinci, 476–81; *Embryo in the Womb*, 481, *482*; *The Last Supper*, 9, *9*, 475, 479, 479–80; *Mona Lisa*, *480*, 480–81; *The Virgin and Child with St. Anne and the Infant St. John*, cartoon for, *478*, 478–79; *The Virgin of the Rocks*, *477*, 477–78

Leopards, Tomb of the, Tarquinia, *Revelers* from, 188–89, *Plate 6-1*

Lescaze, William E.: Philadelphia Savings Fund Society Building (with Howe), 767, *767*

Lescot, Pierre: Square Court of the Louvre, 533, 573–74, *576*

Lessing, Gotthold, 175

Li Lung-mien, 840

Liang K'ai, 841, 859; *The Sixth Patriarch Tearing Up a Sūtra*, 841, *841*

Liberty Leading the People (Delacroix), 651, 675–76, *676*

Lichtenstein, Roy: *Blam!*, 717, 784, *785*

Life and Miracles of St. Audomarus (Omer), The (illuminated manuscript), 350, *350*

Light: in Baroque art, 580, 610–11; additive, 11; Caravaggio's treatment of, 595; chiaroscuro, 11; in English landscape painting, 685; in Gothic churches, 358–59; in Hagia Sophia, 275; in Impressionist painting, 693–94; Masaccio's

treatment of, 444, 445; reflected, 11–12, in Roman wall painting, 207; spectrum, visible, 11–12; subtractive, 11; transmitted, 12; value, 11, *11*; *See also* Color

Limbourg Brothers: *Les Très Riches Heures du Duc de Berry*, 533, 537–39, *538*, *Plate 14-2*

Line, 8–9; axis, 8–9

Linear Construction (Gabo), 716, 753, *753*

Linear (true) perspective, 433–34, 548

Lion from the Processional Way, from the Ishtar Gate, 18, *65*, 66

Lion Gate, Boghazköy, 59, *59*

Lion Gate, Mycenae, 103, *118, 119*

Lion Hunt (Hellenistic mosaic), *Hunter* from, 123, 182, *Plate 5-3*

Lion Hunt, The (Rubens), 578, 604, *605*

Lion Portrayed from Life (Villard de Honnecourt), 18

Lipchitz, Jacques, 748–49; *Man with Mandolin*, 716, 749, *749*

Lippi, Fra Filippo, 398, 425, 452–53; *Madonna and Child with Angels*, 452–53, *453*

Livia (Roman bust), 232, *233*

Livia, House of, Primaporta, wall painting from, 208, *Plate 6-4*

Lochner, Stephan, 554; *Madonna in the Rose Garden*, 554, *554*

Lomas Rishi cave, 805, *805*

Lombardy, Romanesque architecture in, 335–36

London Bridge (Derain), 717, 722, *Plate 17-2*

Lord Heathfield (Reynolds), 645, *645*

Lorenzetti, Ambrogio, 420, 421–22; *Good Government Enthroned*, *421*, 422; *Peaceful City*, 422, *422*; *Peaceful Country*, 423, *423*

Lorenzetti, Pietro, 420–21, 422; *The Birth of the Virgin*, 421, *421*

Lorraine, Claude, 623; *The Marriage of Isaac and Rebekah (The Mill)*, 622, *623*

Lost-wax process. *See* Cire perdue process

Lot, Ferdinand, 242, 245

Louis XIV (Riguad), 578, 632, 632–33

Louvre, east façade of (Perrault, le Vau, and le Brun), 623, *624, 625*; Square Court of (Lescot), 533, 573–74, *576*; statues of courtyard façade in, 574–75, *577*

Lucifer (Pollock), 716, 772–73, *Plate 17-13*

Ludovisi Battle Sarcophagus (Early Christian), 259, *259*

Lung-men caves, 832

Luristan bronzes, 69–70; ritual cauldron, 70, 71

Luxe, Le (Matisse), 717, 722–23, *723*

Luzarches, Robert de: Amiens Cathedral, 353, 369, 369–71, *370*

Lycurgus of Sparta, 52

Lyre Player (Cycladic statuette), 106, *106*

Lysicrates, monument of, Athens, 170, *171*

Lysippos: *Apoxyomenos,* 169, *169,* 171

M

Ma Yüan, 840, 858; *Bare Willows and Distant Mountains,* 840, *840–41*

Mabuse. *See* Gossaert, Jan

Mach, Ernst, 696

Madame Récamier (David), 668

Madeleine, La, Church of, Vézelay, 346–47, *347*

Maderna, Carlo: façade from St. Peter's, 583, *583–84;* Santa Susanna, Rome, 578, *582,* 583

Madonna and Child (Robbia), 462, Plate 12-3

Madonna and Child with Angels (Lippi), 452–53, *453*

Madonna Enthroned (Giotto), 414, *414*

Madonna Enthroned with Angels and Prophets (Cimabue), 403, 413, *413*

Madonna in the Rose Garden (Lochner), 554, *554*

Madonna of the Harpies (Andrea del Sarto), 508, Plate 13-3

Madonna of the Pesaro Family (Titian), 525–26, *526*

Madonna with the Goldfinch (Madonna del Cardellino) (Raphael), 475, *488–89, 489*

Madonna with the Long Neck (Parmigianino), 512, *513*

Madrasah of Sultan Hasan, Cairo, 294–95, *296*

Madwoman (Géricault), 672, *673*

Maestà Altarpiece (Duccio), 410–12; *The Annunciation of the Death of Mary* from, *411,* 411–12; *The Betrayal of Jesus* from, *410,* 411

Magdeburg Antependium: Doubting Thomas from (Echternach Master), 323, *324*

Ma-Hsia school, 840–41

Maillol, Aristide, 745–46; *Mediterranean, 745,* 745–46

Maitreya, Yung-Kang caves, 832, *832*

Maize God, Copán, (Maya), 873, *873*

Malanggan (New Ireland mask), 900, Plate 22-1

Mâle, Émile, 374

Malevich, Kasimir, 735; *Suprematist Composition: White on White,* 735, *735*

Malle Babbe (Hals), 609, *609*

Malraux, André, 648

Man in a Red Turban (J. van Eyck), 543–44, *544,* 545

Man with Mandolin (Lipchitz), 716, 749, *749*

Man with the Glove (Titian), 527, *527–28*

Mander, Karel van, 571

Manet, Édouard, 692–95; *Bar at the Folies-Bergère,* 693–94, *694; Déjeuner sur l'Herbe,* 692–93, *693*

Maniera bizantina (Byzantine style), 409–10

Manifestatio, principle of, 371

Mannerism, 510–18; in architecture, 515–18; in painting, 511–13; in sculpture, 513–15

Mansart, François, 623; Orléans wing, Château de Blois, *622,* 623

Mansart, Jules Hardouin: Galerie des Glaces, palace at Versailles (with le Brun), 626–27, *627;* garden façade, palace at Versailles (with le Vau), 578, 626, *626;* Royal Chapel, palace at Versailles, *627,* 628

Mantegna, Andrea, 471; *Camera degli sposi, 472, 473,* Plate 12-6; *The Dead Christ, 472, 473; St. James Led to Martyrdom, 471, 471–72*

Mantiklos "Apollo," (Greek bronze), 133, *133*

Manuscripts, illuminated. *See* Illumination

Maori art, 900; door lintel, 900, *900*

Maori Chief Tupai Kupa, The, (Sylvester), *19*

Maori Chief Tupai Kupa (self portrait), *19*

Marching Warriors (rock-shelter painting, Gasulla gorge), 35, *36*

Marcus Aurelius, 214, 234–35; Column of, 231; Equestrian statue of, 185, 234–35, *235*

Marcus Aurelius Sacrificing (from an arch of Marcus Aurelius), 231, *231–32*

Mariette, Auguste, 75

Marinetti, Filippo, 733

Marquesan art, 899–900; warrior, 899, *899*

Marriage à la Mode: Breakfast Scene from (Hogarth), 642–43, *643*

Marriage of Isaac and Rebekah, The (The Mill) (Lorraine), *622,* 623

Marriage of the Virgin, The (Raphael), 488, *488*

Mars of Todi, 190, *191*

"Marseillaise, La" (Rude), 661–62, *662*

Marshall Field Warehouse, Chicago (Richardson), 651, *714,* 714

Martini, Simone. *See* Simone Martini

Martyrdom of St. Bartholomew (Ribera), 599, *599*

Martyrdom of St. Sebastian (Antonello da Messina), 473, Plate 12-7

Mary Magdalene (Donatello), 437, *437*

Masaccio, 425, 442–46; *The Expulsion from Eden,* 445, *445; The Holy Trinity,* 445–46, *446; The Tribute Money,* 443–45, *444*

Masanobu, 865

Masks: African, 883, 892, *892,* 894,

896, 897; Eskimo, 884, *885;* Melanesian, 900, *903;* 903–04; Mycenaean, 120, *120;* North American Indian, *883,* 889, *889,* 891, *891*

Maspero, G., 101

Masquerade, African art of, 894–95

Mastaba, 79, *79*

Master of Flémalle. *See* Campin, Robert

Master of the St. Francis Cycle: *St. Francis Preaching to the Birds,* 414–15, *415*

Matisse, Henri, 722–23; *Back I, 748, 748; Back IV, 748, 748; Le Luxe,* 717, 722–23, *723; Red Room (Harmony in Red), 723,* Plate 17-3

Matteo Palmieri (A. Rossellino), 425, 460–61, *461*

Mausoleum of Galla Placidia, Ravenna, 245, *264, 265; Christ as the Good Shepherd* (mosaic) from, Plate 7-1

Mausoleum of Sultan Hasan, Cairo, 294–95, *296*

Mausolus, from mausoleum at Halicarnassus, 168, *168–69*

May, from *Les Très Riches Heures du Duc de Berry* (Limbourg Brothers), 533, 538–39, Plate 14-2

Maya art, 871–73

Mbari houses (Ibo), 895

Mboom helmet mask (Kuba), 897, *897*

Medea (Delacroix), 674–75, *675*

Medea (Paolozzi), 777, *778*

Medici, 426

Medieval art. *See* Early Medieval art; Gothic art; Romanesque art

Mediterranean (Maillol), *745,* 745–46

Meeting of Joachim and Anna, The (Giotto), 418, *418–19*

Meeting of Solomon and the Queen of Sheba, The (Ghiberti), *434,* 435

Megaliths, 37–39

Mei-ping vase (Sung dynasty), 842, *842*

Melancolia I (Dürer), 564, *565*

Melanesian art, 900–05

Memling, Hans, 533, 550; *The Mystic Marriage of St. Catherine,* from *St. John Altarpiece,* 550, *550*

Memorial to Karl Liebknecht (Kollwitz), 726, *726*

Men, Boats, and Animals (Egyptian wall painting), 74, 75

Menhirs, 37

Meninas, Las (Velázquez), 579, 601–02, *602,* 603, Plate 15-4

Menkure, Pyramid of, 79, *80*

Merisi, Michelangelo da. *See* Caravaggio

Mérode Altarpiece, The (Campin), *539,* 539–40

Merz Picture 19 (Schwitters), 736, *736–37*

Meso-American art, 870–74

Mesolithic period (Middle Stone Age), rock-shelter paintings of, 24, 25, 35–36

Metamatic-Automobile-Odorante et Sonore (Tinguely), 782

Metaphysical painting. *See Pittura metafisica*

Mexican art, pre-Columbian, 870–74

Mexican school, 743

Mi Fei, 839–40

Michelangelo Buonarroti, 492–508; *The Bound Slave*, 495, *496*; Capitoline Hill (Campidoglio), 475, *502*, 502–04, *503*, *504*; *Creation of Adam*, 497–98, Plate 13-2; *David*, 475, 493–95, *494*; *The Dying Slave*, 495, *496*; *The Last Judgment*, *507*, 507–08, *508*; Laurentian Library, Florence, 500–02, *501*; *Moses*, 494, *495*; New Sacristy, San Lorenzo, Florence, 498–500, *500*; St. Peter's, 504–06, *505*, *506*; Sistine Chapel, ceiling frescoes, 475, 495–99, *497*, *498*, *499*; tomb of Giuliano de' Medici, 499–500, *500*; *Unfinished Bound Slave*, 16

Michelangelo da Merisi. *See Caravaggio*

Michelozzo di Bartolomeo, 441–43; Palazzo Medici-Riccardi, Florence, 425, 441–42, *442*, *443*

Middle Ages, art of. *See Early Medieval art; Gothic art; Romanesque art*

Middle Kingdom, Egypt, 73, 87–88

Middle Stone Age (Mesolithic), rock-shelter paintings of, 24, 25, 35–36

Mies van der Rohe, Ludwig, 760, 766–68; German Pavilion, Barcelona International Exhibition (1929), 766, 766–67; Seagram Building, New York, 716, 767–68, *768*

Migration period (Early Medieval), 306–12

Milan Cathedral, 353, 391, *391*

Miller, Sanderson: sham Gothic ruin, Hagley Park, Worcestershire, 654, *655*

Millet, Jean François, 651, 686; *The Gleaners*, 686–87, *687*

Milo of Crotona (Puget), 628, *628*

Milton, John, 580, 597

Mimbres bowl, 886–87, *887*

Ming dynasty, 844–45

Minimal Art, 770, 779–80

Minoan art, 102, 103–14; New Palace period, 103, 107–14; Old Palace period, 103, 106–07; pre-Palace period, 103, 105–06

Miracle of the Loaves and the Fishes, The (mosaic), Sant' Apollinare Nuovo, 265–66, Plate 7-2

Miracle of the Slave, The (Tintoretto), 529, *529*

Miraculous Draught of Fish, The (Witz), 554, *555*

Miró, Joan, 739–40; *Painting*, 717, 739, *740*

Miroku, Chuguji Nunnery, Horyu-ji, 851, *851*

Mission of the Apostles, The (tympanum), La Madeleine, 327, *347*, 347–48

Mrs. Richard Brinsley Sheridan (Gainsborough), 578, 644, Plate 15-13

Mitsunobu, Tosa, 860

Mnesicles, 159, 160

Mo Shih-lung, 845

Moche art, 876–77

Mochlos stoneware (Minoan), 105–06

Molière, 579, 639

Momoyama period, Japan, 861–62

Mona Lisa (Leonardo), 480, 480–81

Monastery churches: St. Gall, 10, 316, *317*, 318–19; St. Riquier, Centula, *318*, 319–20

Mondrian, Piet, 734–35; *Composition in Blue, Yellow, and Black*, 717, 735, Plate 17-10

Monet, Claude, 651, 694–95; *Rouen Cathedral*, 10, 10–11, *695*, Plate 16-5

Monogram (Rauschenberg), 783, *784*

Montagne Sainte-Victoire, La (Cézanne), 701, 702, *702*

Monument of Lysicrates, Athens, 170, *171*

Monument to the Third International (Tatlin), 752, *752*, 753

Moore, Henry, 757; *Reclining Figure*, 717, *756*, 757

Moralia in Job: St. George and the Dragon from, 327, 350, *351*

Morning Bath, The (Degas), 699, *699*

Moronobu, 865

Morris, William, 658

Mortuary temple: in Egypt, 90–92; of Queen Hatshepsut, 90, *91*; of Rameses II, *91*, 91–92, *92*

Mosaics: Byzantine, 265–72, 280–82; Early Christian, 253, 255–56; Greek, 182–83; Roman, 213–14

Moses (Michelangelo), 494, *495*

Moses Defending the Daughters of Jethro (Il Rosso Fiorentino), 512, *512*

Moses Expounding the Law (from the Bury Bible), 350, Plate 9-2

Moslem art. *See Islamic art*

Mosques, Moslem, 287–90

Motonobu, 860

Moulin de la Galette, Le (Renoir), 697, Plate 16-6

Mounted Officer of the Imperial Guard (Géricault), 672, *673*

Mshatta, unfinished palace at, *292*, 292–93, *293*

Mu Chi, 859

Muktesvar Temple, *815*, 815–16

Mummy Portrait of a Man, Faiyum, 214, Plate 6-7

Munch, Edvard, 707; *The Scream*, 707, *707*

Mungarawai: *The Djanggawul Sisters*, 905, *905*

Murals: Indian, 817–18; Mayan, 873, 874; Mexican, 743; Romanesque, 349; *See also Frescoes; Wall painting*

Musicians and Dancers (Egyptian wall painting), 98

Mycenaean art, 103, 115–21

Mykerinus. *See Menkure*

Myron: *Discobolos*, 148–49, *149*

Mysteries, Villa of the, Pompeii, frieze from, 206, Plate 6-3

Mystic Marriage of St. Catherine, from St. John Altarpiece (Memling), 550, *550*

N

Nakht, tomb of, Thebes, 97, *97*

Nanga painting, 862

Nanni di Banco, 429; *Quattro Santi Coronati*, 425, 429, *429*, 444

Naram-Sin, 55; Victory Stele of, *56*

Nasca art, 877

Nash, John: Royal Pavilion, Brighton, 651, *659*, 659

Nāṭarāja, Śiva as, from Nultanai Iśvaram Temple, 817, *817*

Native naturalism, 593

Nativity, The (G. Pisano), 407, *408*

Nature Studies (Okyo), 863, *864*

Naumburg Cathedral, statues from choir of, 384–85, *386*

Navajo art, 887–89; dry painting, Plate 22-1

Near East (ancient), 40–71; Akkad, 40, 41, 55–57; Assyria, 40, 41, 59–65; Babylonia, 40, 41, 57–64; Catal Hüyük, 30, 41, 42, 43–47; Jericho, 40, 41, 42–43; Neo-Babylonia, 65–66; Persia, 40, 41, 67–71; Sumer, 40, 41, 47–55

Nebuchadnezzar, 65, 67

Necropolis at Caere (Cerveteri), 188, *188*

Nedick's (Estes), 787, *787*

Nefertiti, Queen, 99, Plate 3-2

Neithardt, Mathis. *See Grünewald, Matthias*

Neo-Babylonian art, 65–66

Neoclassicism: in architecture, 654–57; in sculpture, 660–61

Neo-Dada. *See Pop Art*

Neolithic period (New Stone Age), 24, 25, 36–39

Neptune and Amphitrite (Gossaert), 567, 567–68

Nervi, Pier Luigi, 789–91; Palazzetto dello Sport, Rome, 647, 716, 790–91, *792*

Netherlands, art of. *See Flemish art*

Neumann, Balthasar: pilgrimage church of Vierzehnheiligen, near Bamberg, 579, 634, 634–35, *635*

New Ireland, art of, 900
New Kingdom, Egypt, 73, 88–97
New Sacristy, San Lorenzo, Florence (Michelangelo), 498–500, 500
New Stone Age (Neolithic), 24, 25, 36–39
Ni Tsan, 843
Niaux, cave paintings at, 28; *Bison with Superposed Arrows*, 30, 31
Nicolas of Cusa, 405, 544–45
Night Café (Van Gogh), 704, Plate 16-9
Nike Fastening Her Sandal, from parapet, Temple of Athena Nike, 163, 163
Nike of Samothrace, 171–72, 172
Nineteenth-century art, 650–715; architecture, 652–60, 711–15; Impressionism, 651, 692–99; painting, 662–66, 688–99; post-Impressionism, 651, 699–709; Realism, 651, 688–92, 711–15; Romanticism, 651–87; sculpture, 660–62
Niobid Painter, 164, 165; *Argonaut Krater*, 164–65, 165
Nishiki-e style, 865
Nofretari, Queen (Egyptian tomb relief), 17, 17
Nok: head, 892, 892–93
Nolde, Emil, 717; *St. Mary of Egypt Among Sinners*, 724, Plate 17-6
Nonobjective painting, 739n; of Kandinsky, 726–27; of Suprematists, 735
Norman architecture, 336–38
North American Indian art, 881–91; Eastern Woodlands, 891; Eskimo, 884; Great Plains, 890; historic era, 887–91; Northwest Coast, 889–90; prehistoric, 884–87; Southwest, 887–89
Notre Dame Cathedral, Paris, 361–62, 362, 363, 373; *The Virgin of Paris* from, 378, 378–79
Notre Dame du Haut, Ronchamp (Le Corbusier), 788–89, 790
Novios Plautios: *The Ficoroni Cist*, 193–94, 194
Nude Descending a Staircase #2 (Duchamp), 734, 734
Nude, Olympia (Dubuffet), 771, 771
Nultanai Iśvaram Temple, Punjai, 817, 817; *Śiva as Nāṭarāja* from, 817, 817
Number VII from Eight Studies for a Portrait (Bacon), 769, 771

O

Oakland Museum, Oakland (Roche and Dinkeloo), 795, 795
Oath of the Horatii (David), 667, 667–68
Oceanic art, 882–84, 898–905; Melanesia, 900–05; Polynesia, 898–900
Octopus Jar (Minoan), 112–13, 113

Odysseus' Helmsman Falling (Agesander, Athanadoros, and Polydoros), 174, 175
Odyssey Landscapes (Roman wall painting), 207–08, 208
Oedipus and the Sphinx (Ingres), 678, 678–79
Oenoche, 128
Okyo, Maruyama, 862–63; *Nature Studies*, 863, 864
Old King (Rouault), 716, 724, Plate 17-4
Old Kingdom, Egypt, 76–87
Old Market Woman (Hellenistic statue), 176, 177
Old St. Peter's, Rome, 250, 250–51, 251, 252
Oldenburg, Claes, 785; *Soft Toilet*, 785, 785
Olmec art, 870; colossal head, 870
Olympic Stadium, Munich, Model for the roofs of (Otto), 791, 792, 793
Op Art, 770, 776
Opéra, Paris (Garnier), 651, 660, 660
Orcus (Hades), Tomb of, Tarquinia, *Woman of the Velcha Family* from, 189, Plate 6-2
Orders: Corinthian, 140–41, 155, 170, 170–71; Doric, 140, 140, 141–43, 142, 143, 144–45, 151–52, 154, 155, 164, 219; Ionic, 140, 140, 155, 160, 219
Orléans wing, Château de Blois (F. Mansart), 622, 623
Ornate wall painting, 208, 209
Orvieto Cathedral, 390, 390
Oseberg ship burial, animal head from, 308, 308–09
Ospedale degli Innocenti, Florence (Brunelleschi), 438, 439
Osterley Park House, Etruscan Room in, (Adam), 655–56, Plate 16-1
Otto, Frei: Model for the roofs of the Olympic Stadium, Munich, 791, 792, 793
Otto III Enthroned Receiving the Homage of Four Parts of the Empire, from the *Gospel Book of Otto III*, 325, 325
Ottonian period, 320–25

P

Pacher, Michael, 555; *St. Wolfgang Forces the Devil to Hold His Prayerbook*, 555, 556
Paganini (Delacroix), 680, 681
Paganini (Ingres), 680, 681
Painted Bronze (Johns), 716, 784, 784
Painting: Abstract Formalism, 775–77; African, 892–93; Anatolian, 45–47; Art Nouveau, 721–22; Baroque, 592–623, 635–40, 641–45; Byzantine, 280–86; Chinese, 826, 829, 833, 834–46; Constructivism, 736; Cubism, 727–35; Dadaism, 736–37; Dutch, 606–17; Early Chris-

tian, 249–50; Early Medieval, 313–14, 323–25; Egyptian, 85–87, 88, 96–97; English, 641–45, 684–85; Etruscan, 188–89; Expressionism, 722–27, 769–74; the Fauves, 717, 722–24; Flemish, 536–53, 567–71, 603–06; French, 553–54, 571–72, 617–23, 636–40, 666–84, 686–706, 707–09, 727–33; Futurism, 733–34; German, 554, 555, 556–67; Greek, 123, 126–32, 164–65; Impressionism, 651, 692–99; in India, 817–18; Italian, 409–23, 442–53, 464–73, 476–81, 487–92, 495–98, 507–10, 511–13, 521–31, 592–97, 635–36; Japanese, 852, 855–57, 858–63; Later Old Stone Age, 24–33; Mannerism, 511–13; Melanesian, 901, 905; Middle Stone Age, 24, 25, 35–36; Minoan, 109–12; nineteenth-century, 662–66, 688–92; nonobjective, 726–27, 735, 739n; North American Indian, 887–88, 890; Pop Art, 784–87; post-Impressionism, 651, 699–709; pre-Columbian, 873; proto-Renaissance, 409–23; Realism, 607, 688–92, 743–45, 774–75; Renaissance, 442–53, 464–73, 476–81, 487–92, 495–98, 507–10, 511–13, 521–31, 553–54, 557–72; Rococo, 635–40; Roman, 205–14; Romanesque, 349; Romantic, 662–87; Spanish, 598–603; Suprematism, 735; Surrealism, 738–43; Symbolism, 720–21, 770; twentieth-century, 720–45, 768–77, 784–87; Zen, 841–42, 859
Painting (Miró), 717, 739, 740
Painting 1952 (Kline), 773, 773
Palatine Chapel of Charlemagne, 2, 315–16, 316
Palazzetto dello Sport, Rome (Nervi), 647, 716, 790–91, 792
Palazzo Carignano, Turin (Guarini), 578, 591, 591
Palazzo Medici-Riccardi, Florence (Michelozzo), 425, 441–42, 442, 443
Palazzo Pubblico, Siena, 353, 391–92, 392
Palazzo Rucellai, Florence (Alberti), 455, 455
Palazzo del Tè, Mantua (Romano), 475, 516, 516–18, 517
Palette of Narmer, 73, 76, 76–78
Palladio, Andrea, 483–84, 518–21; San Giorgio Maggiore, Venice, 520, 521, 521; Villa Rotunda, Vicenza, 475, 519, 520
Pamphilius, catacomb of, Rome, 248, 248
Panathenaic frieze, 157–58; *Head of the Procession* from, 157–58, 158, 160; *Horsemen* from, 158, 158
Panel of Hesire, 77–78, 78
Pannini, Giovanni: *Interior of the Pantheon*, 222, 223

Panofsky, Erwin, 77–78, 83–84, 371, 481

Pansa, House of, Pompeii, 204–05, *205*

Panthéon (Ste. Geneviève), Paris (Soufflot), 651, 656–57, *657*

Pantheon, Rome, 14, 220–22, *222*, *223*

Paolozzi, Eduardo, 777; *Medea*, 777, *778*

Papuan Gulf art, 902

Parable of the Blind, The (Bruegel), *570*, 571

Paradise of Amitabha (cave painting), Tun-huang, 834–35, *835*

Paradise Sects, China, 832–33

Parasol, The (Goya), 663, *664*

Parinirvana of the Buddha, Polonnaruwa, 818, *819*

Paris Opéra (Garnier), 651, 660, *660*

Paris Psalter: David Composing the Psalms from, 282–83, *284*, *285*

Parisienne, La (fresco), palace at Knossos, 112, *Plate 4-1*

Parliament, Houses of, London (Barry and Pugin), 651, 658, *659*

Parmigianino, 475; *Madonna with the Long Neck*, 512, *513*

Parthenon, Athens, 123, 151–58, *153*, *154*, 185, 214; friezes of, 157–58, *158*; pediment sculptures in, *156*, 156–57, *157*

Parting of Lot and Abraham, The (mosaic), from Santa Maria Maggiore, Rome, 255–56, *257*

Pastoral Scene (Roman wall painting), 211, *Plate 6-6*

Pastoral Symphony (Giorgione), 524, *Plate 13-7*

Pāṭaliputra, palace of Aśoka at, 804–05; capital from, *804*, 804–05

Pater, Walter, 721

Patinir, Joachim, 533, 568; *Landscape with St. Jerome*, 568, *569*

Pauline Borghese as Venus (Canova), 651, 660–61, *661*

Paulus, 274

Pausanias, 117, 141, 161

Paxton, Joseph: Crystal Palace, London, 651, 711, *713*

Pazzi Chapel, Florence (Brunelleschi), 440, *440*, *441*

Peaceful City, from *Good Government Enthroned* (A. Lorenzetti), 422, *422*

Peaceful Country, from *Good Government Enthroned* (A. Lorenzetti), 423, *423*

Peasant Dance (Bruegel), 569, 571, *Plate 14-10*

Pech-Merle, cave paintings at: *Spotted Horses* and *Negative Hand Imprints*, 29, *29*

Pendentive construction, 274–75, *279*

People's Republic of China, art of, 846–47

Peplos Kore, 134–35, *Plate 5-1*

Pericles, 123, 151, 160

Peripteral temple, *138*, 139

Peristyle court, Palace of Diocletian, 237, *238*

Perrault, Claude: east façade of the Louvre (with le Vau and le Brun), 623, *624*, 625

Persepolis, Palace of Darius, *66*, *67*, 67–69, *69*, *70*, 804

Persian art, 40, 41, 67–71

Persistence of Memory, The (Dali), 741, *741*

Perspective: aerial (atmospheric), 212, 568; of Cubists, 729–30; of Duccio, 411–12; herringbone, 206; reverse, 259; single point, 9–10; treatise on (Piero della Francesca), 448; true linear, 433–34, 548; twisted, in cave art, 33; of Uccello, 446; of J. van Eyck, 543

Perugino (Pietro Vannuci), 470; *Christ Delivering the Keys of the Kingdom to St. Peter*, 425, 470, *471*

Peruvian art, 874–79

Pest House at Jaffa (Gros), *670*, 670–71

Petrarch, 398–99, 405

Petrie, Sir W. M. Flinders, 75

Petrus Christus. *See* Christus, Petrus

Pevsner, Antoine, 736, 752, 753

Phiale Painter: *Hermes Bringing the Infant Dionysos to Papposilenos*, 165, *Plate 5-2*

Phidias, 151, 155, 156, 157, 162, 164, 165

Philadelphia Savings Fund Society Building (Howe and Lescaze), 767, *767*

Philip the Arab (Roman bust), 236, *236*

Pi (Late Chou dynasty), 828, *828*

Picasso, Pablo, 8, 708, 720, 727–28, 730–32, 755; *Accordionist*, 730, *730*; *Bathers*, 8, *8*; *Bull's Head*, 755, *755*; *Les Demoiselles d'Avignon*, 728, *729*, 730; *Guernica*, 731–32, *732*; *Portrait of Gertrude Stein*, 728, *728*; *Still-life with Chair-caning*, 13, 731, *731*; *Three Musicians*, 715, 731, *Plate 17-8*

Pico della Mirandola, Giovanni, 397–98

Piero della Francesca, 448–50; *Annunciation*, from the *Golden Legend* cycle, 449, *449*; *The Finding and Proving of the True Cross*, 449–50, *451*; *Resurrection*, 425, 450, *451*

Pilgrimage church of Vierzehnheiligen, near Bamberg (Neumann), 579, 634, 634–35, *635*

Pilon, Germain, 533, 575–76; *The Entombment*, 576, *577*

Pippo Spano (Castagno), 446–47, *448*

Piranesi, Giovanni Battista, 651; *The Temple of Saturn*, from *Views of Rome*, 656, *656*

Pisa, cathedral group of, 327, 338–39, *339*; pulpit of baptistry of (N. Pisano), *406*, 407–08

Pisano, Andrea, 409; door of baptis-

try, Florence Cathedral, 408, 409; *The Visitation*, 408, *409*

Pisano, Giovanni, 408–09, 413; *The Nativity*, 407, *408*

Pisano, Nicola, 407–09; *The Annunciation and the Nativity*, 403, *406*, 408; pulpit, Pisa Cathedral, *406*, 407–08

Pissarro, Camille, 651, 694–95; *Place du Théâtre Français*, 695–96, *696*

Pittura metafisica, school of, 738

Place du Théâtre Français (Pissarro), 695–96, *696*

Plato, 53, 139, 143, 166, 433

Plutarch, 151, 155

Pointilism, 700

Pollaiuolo, Antonio, 464–66; *Apollo and Daphne*, 465–66, *466*; *Battle of Naked Men*, 464–65, *465*; *Herakles and Antaios*, 425, 464, *464*

Pollock, Jackson, 772; *Lucifer*, 716, 772–73, *Plate 17-13*

Polonnaruwa, 818

Polydoros. *See* Agesander, Athanadoros, and Polydoros

Polygnotos, 164, 165, 214

Polykleitos, 165; canon of, 10; *Doryphoros*, 10, 123, 163, *163*, 164

Polynesian art, 898–900

Polyphemos (A. Carracci), 578, *593*, 593–94

Pompeian style, 655

Pompeii, 185, 202, *203*, 204, 204–05, *205*

Pompey the Great (Roman bust), *198*, 198–99

Pont du Gard, near Nîmes, *216*, 216–17

Pontormo, Jacopo: *Descent from the Cross*, 511–12, *Plate 13-4*

Pop Art, 770, 782–87

Pope, Alexander, 580, 637, 653

Porcelain, Chinese, 845–46

Porch of the Confessors, Chartres Cathedral, *St. Martin and St. Jerome* from, 374, *374*

Poro mask (*Kagle*) (Dan), 896, *897*

Porta, Giacomo della. *See* Giacomo della Porta

Portinari Altarpiece, The (Hugo van der Goes), 549, 549–50; *The Adoration of the Shepherds* from, 549, *Plate 14-5*

Portrait of Gertrude Stein (Picasso), 728, *728*

Portrait jar, Moche, 877, *877*

Portrait of a Lady (Roman bust), 233, *233*

Portrait of a Young Man (Botticelli), 466–67, *Plate 12-5*

Portrait of a Young Man (Bronzino), 475, 513, *Plate 13-5*

Portraits of the Emperors (Yen Li-pen), 837

Post-Impressionism, 651, 699–709

Post-Painterly Abstraction, 776

Pottery: Chinese, 838, 842; Greek, 126–32, 164–65; Japanese, 850, 860; Minoan, 107, *107*, 112–14, *113*, *114*; Mycenaean, 120–21; North American Indian, 866–67; pre-Columbian, 871, 876–77; *See also* Porcelain

Poussin, Nicolas, 579, 619–21, 623; *The Burial of Phocion*, *620*, *621*, 623; *Et in Arcadia Ego* (1630), 619, *619–20*; *Et in Arcadia Ego* (1640), 620, *621*

Pozzo, Fra Andrea, 579, 596–97; *The Glorification of St. Ignatius*, 596–97, *597*

Prabhutaratna and Śākyamuni, 833, *Plate 19-1*

Praxiteles, 167–68, *169*; *Aphrodite of Cnidus*, 167–68; *Hermes and Dionysos*, 123, *166*, 167, *169*

Pre-Columbian art, 868–79; Andes, 874–79; Aztec, 874; Chavín, 875–76; Inca, 879; Maya, 871–73; Meso-American, 870–74; Moche, 876–77; Nasca, 877; Olmec, 870; Teotihuacán, 873–74; Tiahuanaco, 877–79; West Mexico, 870–71

Presentation and the Flight into Egypt, The (Broederlam), 536–37, *537*

Priene, 122; city plan, *180*, 181; house plan, *181*, 181–82

Priests with Attendant, detail of Byzantine mural, 262–63, *263*

Prince Shōtoku and His Sons (Asuka Period), 852, *853*

Princess Tau Wan, funeral suit of, Man-ch'eng, 830, 830–31

Prints. *See* Engraving; Woodcuts

Process Art, 770, 787–88

Procession, from the Ara Pacis Augustae, 227, *227–28*

Productivist movement, 752

"Program" art, 673

Prophet Isaiah, The, from St. Pierre, Moissac, *344*, 345–46

Proportion, 10

Propylaea, Acropolis, Athens, *159*, 160

Prostyle temple, *138*, 139

Protagoras, 123

Proto-Neolithic fortifications, Jericho, *42*, 43

Proto-Renaissance, 402–23

Psalm 150, from *Utrecht Psalter*, 314, *314*

Psychedelic art, 770, 786

Pucelle, Jean, 537; *Belleville Breviary*, 533, 537, *Plate 14-1*

Pueblo Bonito (North American Indian), 887, *888*

Puget, Pierre: *Milo of Crotona*, 628, *628*

Pugin, A. W. N.: Houses of Parliament, London (with Barry), 651, 658, *659*

Punishment (Grosz), 725, *726*

Punjai, temple at, 817, *817*

Purse cover, Sutton Hoo ship burial, 308, *Plate 8-1*

Pylon Temple of Horus, Edfu, 92, *93*

Pyramids, Egyptian, 72, 73; Great Pyramids of Gizeh, 79, *80*, 81, 81–82, *82*; Stepped Pyramid of King Zoser, 79, *80*

Q

Quattro Santi Coronati (Nanni di Banco), 425, 429, *429*, 444

Queen Nefertiti, 99, *Plate 3-2*

Queen's Megaron, palace at Knossos, 109, *109–10*, *111*

Quercia, Jacopo della. *See* Jacopo della Quercia

R

Raft of the Medusa (Géricault), 671, *671–72*

Raimondi, Marcantonio, 557

Raimondi Stone, from principal pyramid, Chavín de Huantar, 875–76, *876*

Rāmāyaṇa relief, Śiva Temple, Prambanan, 820, *820*

Rameses II, court and pylon of, *95*, 95–96; mortuary temple of, *91*, 91–92, *92*

Rape of the Daughters of Leucippus (Rubens), 604, *Plate 15-5*

Rape of the Sabine Women (Giovanni da Bologna), 514–15, *515*

Raphael Sanzio, 487–92; *Baldassare Castiglione*, 492, *Plate 13-1*; *Galatea*, 491, *491*; *Madonna with the Goldfinch* (*Madonna del Cardellino*), 475, 488–89, *489*; *The Marriage of the Virgin*, 488, *488*; Sant' Eligio degli Orifici, Rome, 592, *592*; *The School of Athens*, 489–91, *490*

Rathas (Indian temples), 814–15

Raumplastik, y = ax³ − bx² + cx (Vantongerloo), *751*, 751–52

Rauschenberg, Robert, 783; *Erased de Kooning by Robert Rauschenberg*, 783; *Monogram*, 783, *784*

Ravenna, 244, 245, 315; Byzantine art in, 263–73

Ray, Man: *Gift*, *755*, 755–56

Rayonnant style, 371–73

Realism, 770; in architecture, 711–15; in Baroque Dutch painting, 607; Kamakura, 857–58; in nineteenth-century painting, 688–92; in painting, 607, 688–92, 743–45, 774–75

Reclining Figure (Moore), 717, *756*, *757*

Red, Blue and Green (Kelly), 776, *Plate 17-15*

Red Room (*Harmony in Red*) (Matisse), 723, *Plate 17-3*

Red-figure technique (Attic pottery), 130

Reims Cathedral, 374–76, *375*

Reindeer (cave painting), Font-de-Gaume, *32*, 33

Relief with dancers and musicians, Aurangabad, 813, *813*

Relief Horse (Later Old Stone Age), *34*, 34

Relief sculpture, 15; Assyrian, 62–64; Chinese, 829–30; Early Christian, 259; Egyptian, 85–87, 91; French, 576; Indian, 804–05, 806, 811–14; Javanese, 818–20; Later Old Stone Age, 33, 34; Mycenaean, 120–21; Persian, 68–70; pre-Columbian, 872, 874, 875, 877–79; Renaissance, 576; Roman, 227–32, 241–43; Romanesque, 342–49; *See also* Sculpture

Reliefs, Tomb of the, Caere (Cerveteri), 187, *188*, *189*

Rembrandt van Rijn, 579, 610–14; *The Return of the Prodigal Son*, 612, *612*; *Self-Portrait* (1652), 613, *614*; *Self-Portrait* (1660), 613, *615*; *Supper at Emmaus* (1630), 611, *611*; *Supper at Emmaus* (1648), 611, *612*; *Syndics of the Cloth Guild*, 613, *Plate 15-7*; *The Three Crosses*, 613–14, *615*

Renaissance, 394–401, 424–577; architecture, 437–42, 454–59, 481, 483–87, 498–506, 515–21, 572–75; engraving, 464–65, 555–56, 557, 562–63, 564; fifteenth-century, 535–36; Flemish art, 535–53, 567–71; French art, 553–54, 571–77; German art, 554–67; High, 476–510; in Italy, 424–531; in Northern Europe, 532–51; painting, 442–53, 464–73, 476–81, 487–92, 495–98, 507–10, 511–13, 521–31, 553–54, 557–71, 571–72; sculpture, 426–37, 459–64, 492–95, 513–15, 554–55, 574–77; sixteenth-century, 556–77; *See also* Baroque art; Proto-Renaissance

Reni, Guido: *Aurora*, 594, *594*

Renoir, Auguste, 651, 694, 696–97, 701; *Le Moulin de la Galette*, 697, *Plate 16-6*

Rent Collection Courtyard, The, Ta-yi, Szechwan, 846, *847*

Republican period, Rome, 185, 196–214

Reserve head of a prince (Egyptian bust), 84–85, *85*

Resurrection, from *Isenheim Altarpiece* (Grünewald), 560–61, *Plate 14-8*

Resurrection (Piero della Francesca), 425, 450, *451*

Return of the Prodigal Son, The (Greuze), 640, *641*

Return of the Prodigal Son, The (Rembrandt), 612, *612*

Revelers (Brygos Painter), 132, *132*

Revelers (Euthymides), *131*, 131–32

Revelers, from Tomb of the Leopards, Tarquinia, 188–89, *Plate 6-1*

Reverse perspective, 259

Reynolds, Joshua, 579, 645; *Lord Heathfield*, 645, *645*

Rib vaults: Gothic, 358, 359, 370; Romanesque, 336, 337, 338

Ribera, José de, 599; *Martyrdom of St. Bartholomew*, 599, *599*

Richardson, Henry Hobson, 712, 714; Marshall Field Warehouse, Chicago, 651, 714, *714*

Riemenschneider, Tilman, 533; *The Assumption of the Virgin*, from *Creglingen Altarpiece*, 554–55, *556*

Rietveldt, Gerrit: Schroeder House, Utrecht, 735, *763*, 763–64

Rigaud, Hyacinthe: *Louis XIV*, 578, *632*, 632–33

Riley, Bridget: *Current*, 717, *776*, *777*

Robbia, Luca della, 425, 462; *Madonna and Child*, 462, *Plate 12-3*

Robie House, Chicago (Wright), 760, *761*

Robusti, Jacopo. *See* Tintoretto

Roche, Kevin: Oakland Museum (with Dinkeloo), 795, *795*

Rock painting: African, 892–93; North American Indian, 886

Rock-cut temples, Mahabalipuram, *814*, 814–15

Rock-cut tombs, Egyptian, 87–88, *88*

Rock-shelter paintings, Middle Old Stone Age, 35–36, *36*

Rococo style, 632–40

Rodin, Auguste, 7–8, 709–11; *Balzac*, 710, *711*; *Burghers of Calais*, *709*, 709–10; *The Kiss*, 710, 710–11; *The Thinker*, 7, 7–8

Rogier van der Weyden, 533, 546–47; *Escorial Deposition*, 546–47, *Plate 14-4*

Roman art, 184–86, 194–243; architecture, 199–205, 215–25, 236–40; Early Empire, 185, 214–36; Late Empire, 185, 236–43; mosaic, 213–14; painting, 205–14; Republican period, 185, 196–214; sculpture, 197–99, 225–36, 240–43

Romanesque art, 326–51; architecture, 329–41; English, 337–38, 350–51; French, 329, 330–33, 336–37, 340–41, 342–50; German, 333–35, 336; illumination, 349–51; Italian, 335–36, 338–40; painting, 349; sculpture, 341–49

Romano, Giulio: Palazzo del Tè, Mantua, 475, *516*, 516–18, *517*

Romans of the Decadence (Couture), 681–82, *682*

Romanticism, 651–87; in architecture, 652–60; in painting, 662–87; in sculpture, 660–62

Rose, Barbara, 777–78

Rosetta Stone, 75

Rossellino, Antonio: *Matteo Palmieri*, 425, 460–61, *461*

Rossellino, Bernardo, 459–60; tomb of Leonardo Bruni, 459–60, *460*

Rossetti, Dante Gabriel, 692

Rosso Fiorentino, Il. *See* Il Rosso Fiorentino

Rothko, Mark, 774; *Four Darks on Red*, 774, *Plate 17-14*

Rouault, Georges, 723–24; *Old King*, 716, 724, *Plate 17-4*

Rouen Cathedral (Monet), *10*, 10–11, 695, *Plate 16-5*

Rousseau, Henri, 707; *The Sleeping Gypsy*, 18, 707–08, *708*

Rousseau, Jean-Jacques, 579, 640

Royal Audience Hall, stairway to, Persepolis, 66

Royal Chapel, Versailles (J. H. Mansart), 627, *628*

Royal Pavilion, Brighton (Nash), 651, *659*, 659

Rubens, Peter Paul, 603–05; *The Debarkation of Marie at Marseilles*, 605, *606*; *The Elevation of the Cross*, 603–04, *604*; *The Lion Hunt*, 578, 604, *605*; *Rape of the Daughters of Leucippus*, 604, *Plate 15-5*

Rude, François, 651; "*La Marseillaise*," 661–62, *662*

Rue Transnonain (Daumier), 688, 688–89

Ruisdael, Jacob van, 579; *View of Haarlem from the Dunes at Overveen*, 617, *Plate 15-10*

Ruskin, John, 658

S

Sacred and Profane Love (Titian), 525, *525*

Sacrifice of Isaac, The (Brunelleschi), 427, *427*, 428

Sacrifice of Isaac, The (Ghiberti), 427, 427–28

Safdie, Moshe: Habitat, Montreal, 794, 794–95

Sage Kūya Invoking the Amida Buddha, The, 857, *857*

St. Anthony Tormented by the Demons (Schongauer), 556, *557*

St. Bernard. *See* Bernard of Clairvaux

St. Denis, abbey church of, 356, 357–58, *357*, *358*, 376

St. Elizabeth, Marburg, 384, *384*, *385*

St. Étienne, Caen, 336, 336–37, *337*

St. Francis Altarpiece (Berlinghieri), *409*, 409; *St. Francis Preaching to the Birds* from, 409, 409–10

St. Francis of Assisi, 354–55

St. Francis in Meditation (Zurbarán), 579, 599–600, *600*

St. Francis Preaching to the Birds, from *St. Francis Altarpiece* (Berlinghieri), *409*, 409, 409–10

St. Francis Preaching to the Birds (Master of the St. Francis Cycle), 414–15, *415*

St. Gall, monastery church at, Switzerland, 316, *317*, 318–19

St. George (Donatello), 431, *431*

St. George and the Dragon, from *Moralia in Job*, 327, 350, *351*

St. Ivo, Rome (Borromini), 589–91, *590*

St. James Led to Martyrdom (Mantegna), 471, 471–72

St. John Altarpiece: The Mystic Marriage of St. Catherine from (Memling), 550, *550*

St. John the Evangelist (Donatello), 15

St. Lazare, Autun, 346, *346*

St. Lucy Altarpiece (Veneziano), 447–48, *Plate 12-2*

St. Maclou, Rouen, 379, *379*

St. Maria im Kapitol, Cologne, head of crucifix from, 385, *387*

St. Mark (Donatello), 430, 430–31

St. Mark's, Venice, 279, *280*, *281*

St. Martin and St. Jerome, from the Porch of the Confessors, Chartres Cathedral, 374, *374*

St. Mary of Egypt Among Sinners (Nolde), 724, *Plate 17-6*

St. Matthew, from the *Book of Lindisfarne*, 311, *311*, 313–14

St. Matthew, from *Gospel Book of Archbishop of Reims*, 312, 313–14

St. Matthew, from *Gospel Book of Charlemagne*, 312, 313

St. Michael, abbey church of, Hildesheim, Germany, 320, 321–22, *321*, *322*; bronze doors of (Bishop Bernward), 322–23, *323*

St. Michael the Archangel (Early Christian diptych), 260–61, *261*, *262*

St. Paul's Cathedral, London (Wren), 578, 630–31, *631*

St. Peter's, Rome, 7, *582*; *baldacchino* from, 585, *586*; Bramante's design for, 484, *484*; *Cathedra Petri*, 585–86, *Plate 15-1*; façade of (Maderna), *583*, 583–84; Michelangelo's work on, 504–06, *505*, *506*; piazza adjoining (Bernini), *582*, 584, *584*

St. Peter's (old), Rome, 250, 250–51, *251*, *252*

St. Pierre, Moissac, architectural sculpture of, *343*, 343–46, *344*, *345*

St. Remi, Reims, *Crucifixion* from, 377, *Plate 10-1*

St. Riquier, monastery church of, Centula, France, *318*, 319–20

St. Sernin, Toulouse, 329, *330*, 330–32, *331*; *Christ in Majesty* (ambulatory relief) from, 342, *342*

St. Theodore (jamb statue), Chartres Cathedral, 431, *432*

St. Thomas Aquinas, 405

St. Trôphime, Arles, *343*, 345, *348*, 349

St. Wolfgang Forces the Devil to Hold His Prayerbook (Pacher), 555, *556*

Ste. Geneviève (Panthéon), Paris (Soufflot), 651, 656–57, *657*

Sainte-Chapelle, Paris, *372*, 372–73

Śākyamuni Buddha, Six Dynasties, 831, *831*

Salisbury Cathedral, *380*, *381*, 381–82, *382*

Salisbury Cathedral from the Bishop's Garden (Constable), 684–85, *685*

Salon de la Princesse, Hôtel de Soubise, Paris (decorations by Boffrand), *633*, 633–34

Samarra, Great Mosque of, 245, 287, 288

Samnite House, Herculaneum: wall painting, 207

San Carlo alle Quattro Fontane, Rome (Borromini), 588–89, *589*

San Francesco, Rimini (Alberti), 456, *456*

San Giobbe Altarpiece (Bellini), *522*, 522–23

San Giorgio Maggiore, Venice (Palladio), *520*, 521, *521*

San Miniato al Monte, Florence, 339–40, *340*

San Vitale, Ravenna, 267–69, *268*, *Plate 7-4*; mosaics from, 267, 269–72, *270*, *271*, *Plates 7-5*, *7-6*, *7-7*

San Zaccaria Altarpiece (Bellini), *522*, 522–23

Sanchi, stupas at, 805–07, *806*, *807*

Sanctuary of Apollo at Delphi, *Charioteer* from, 147–48, *148*

Sanctuary of Fortuna Primigenia, Praeneste, 200, 200–02, *201*

Sangallo, Antonio da. *See* Antonio da Sangallo

Sangallo, Giuliano da. *See* Giuliano da Sangallo

Sanraku, Kano, 861

Sant' Ambrogio, Milan, *334*, 335–36, *335*

Sant' Andrea, Mantua (Alberti), 456–58, *457*

Sant' Apollinare in Classe, Ravenna, 266–67; mosaic from, 266–67, *Plate 7-3*

Sant' Apollinare Nuovo, Ravenna, 265–66, *266*

Sant' Eligio degli Orifici, Rome (Raphael), 592, *592*

Santa Costanza, Rome, *252*, 252–54, *253*

Santa Maria, Tahull, *Adoration of the Magi* from, 349, *Plate 9-1*

Santa Maria degli Angeli, Florence (Brunelleschi), 441–42, *442*

Santa Maria delle Carceri, Prato (G. da Sangallo), *458*, 459

Santa Maria della Consolazione, Todi, 485, *485*

Santa Maria Maggiore, Rome, 256;

The Parting of Lot and Abraham from, 255–56, *257*

Santa Maria Novella, Florence, façade of (Alberti), 425, *455*, 455–56

Santa Sindone, Chapel of the, Turin (Guarini), 592, *592*

Santa Sophia. *See* Hagia Sophia

Santa Susanna, Rome (Maderna), 578, *582*, 583

Santo Spirito, Florence (Brunelleschi), 439, 439–40

Sarcophagus of Archbishop Theodore, 261–62, *262*

Sarcophagus from Caere (Cerveteri), 190, *191*

Sargon II, citadel of, Khorsabad, 60, 60–62, *61*

Sarto, Andrea del. *See* Andrea del Sarto

Saturn Devouring His Children (Goya), *666*, 666

Sautuola, Marcelino de, 27

Savonarola, Girolamo, 469

Scala Regia, Vatican, Rome (Bernini), 579, 584–85, *585*

Scale, 10–11

Scenes of War, from *Standard of Ur*, *Plate 2-2*

Schliemann, Heinrich, 104, 119

Schongauer, Martin, 555–56; *St. Anthony Tormented by the Demons*, 556, *557*

School of Athens (Raphael), 489–91, *490*

Schroeder House, Utrecht (Rietveldt), *735*, *763*, 763–64

Schwitters, Kurt, 716; *Merz Picture*, *19*, *736*, 736–37

Scopas: *Warrior's Head*, 168, *168*

Scott, Sir Walter, 654

Scream, The (Munch), *707*, 707

Screen painting, Japanese, 861

Scribe Eadwine, The, from the *Eadwine Psalter*, 327, 351, *351*

Scribe Ezra Rewriting the Sacred Records, The, from the *Codex Amiatinus*, *310*, *311*, 313–14

Sculptural technique, 16; additive, 16; subtractive, 16

Sculpture: African, 892–98; Assyrian, 62–64; Baroque, 586–88, 628–29, 639; Buddha image, 807, 809–10, 818–20; Chinese, 826–34, 846; Constructivism, 752–54, 777–82; Cubism, 748–49; Dadaism, 754–56; Early Christian, 258–60; Early Medieval, 322–23; Egyptian, 82–85, 88, 96–97; Eskimo, 884; Etruscan, 189–94; Expressionism, 746–47; Flemish, 535; Formalism, 777–82; free-standing, 15; French, 342–50, 362–67, 373–76, 378, 574–77, 628–29, 639, 661–62; Futurism, 749–50; German, 384–85, 554–55; Gothic, 362–67, 373–76, 378, 384–85; Greek, 123, 132–38, 144–47, 161–64, 167–70, 171–78; in India, 804–05, 811–14;

816–23; Italian, 407–09, 426–37, 459–64, 492–95, 513–15, 586–88, 660–61; Japanese, 849–50, 851–52, 857–58; Javanese, 818–20; Later Old Stone Age, 33–35; Mannerism, 513–15; Melanesian, 900–01; Minoan, 114; Neoclassicism, 660–61; nineteenth-century, 660–62; North American Indian, 885–86, 889; Persian, 68–69; Polynesian, 898–900; Pop Art, 782–84; pre-Columbian, 870, 871, 873, 874, 875–79; proto-Renaissance, 407–09; relief, 15; Renaissance, 426–37, 459–64, 492–95, 513–15, 554–55, 574–77; Roman, 197–99, 225–36, 240–43; Romanesque, 341–49; Romantic, 660–62; Sumerian, 50–55, texture, 15–16; twentieth-century, 745–57, 768–69, 777–84

Seagram Building, New York (Mies van der Rohe), 716, 767–68, *768*

Seals, Mohenjo-Daro, 802, *803*; Ur, *54*, 55

Seated Apostles, detail of *The Last Judgment* (Cavallini), *412*, 412

Seated Boxer (Apollonius?), 123, *177*, 177–78

Seated Buddha, Gandhāra, 809, *809*, 810, *810*

Seated Goddess (statuette), Çatal Hüyük, 45, *45*

Seated Youth (Lehmbruck), 7, *7*, 8

Second Bull (cave painting), Lascaux, 27, 33, *Plate 1-2*

Self-Portrait (Q. de la Tour), 639, *639*

Self-Portrait (1652) (Rembrandt), 613, *614*

Self-Portrait (1660) (Rembrandt), 613, *615*

Seneca, 225

Senmut with Princess Nefrua (Egyptian statue), 96, *96*

Sentimentality in eighteenth-century art, 639–40

Serpent Mound (North American Indian), 886, *886*

Sesshū, 859; *Landscape*, 859, *859*

Seti I Offering (Egyptian relief), 101, *101*

Settignano, Desiderio da. *See* Desiderio da Settignano

Seurat, Georges: *Sunday Afternoon on the Island of La Grande Jatte*, 700–01, *Plate 16-7*

Seventeenth-century art. *See* Baroque art

Shahn, Ben, 717; *Handball*, 744, *744*

Shaka Triad (Tori Busshi), 851, *851*

Shang dynasty, 826–27

Sharaku, 866

Sheep and a Goat, A (Chao Meng-fu), 843, *843*

Sheikh el Beled (Egyptian statue), 85, *85*

Shen Chou, 844

She-Wolf of the Capitol (Etruscan sculpture), 185, 190–91, *192*

Shigisan Engi (Fujiwara period), 856, *856*

Shih-t'ao, 845

Shinto shrines, 853–54, *854*

Shōden, Ise Shrine, Japan, 854, *854*

Shrine of Lady Tachibana, Horyu-ji Temple, 851–52, *852*

Sibyl, Temple of the, Tivoli, *199*, 199–200

Signac, Paul, 677, 700

Signorelli, Luca, 470; *The Damned Cast into Hell*, 470, *470*

Silver Wedding, House of the, Pompeii, 206, *206*

Simone Martini, 419–20; *The Annunciation*, 419–20, *Plate 11-2*; *Guidoriccio da Fogliano*, 420, *420*

Single-point perspective, 9–10

Siqueiros, David Alfaro, 717; *Echo of a Scream*, 743, *743*-44

Sistine Chapel, Rome, frescoes (Michelangelo), 475, 495–99, *497*, *498*, *499*; frescoes (Perugino), 470, *471*

Śiva as Mahādeva, Elephanta, 812, *812*

Śiva as Nāṭarāja, Lord of the Dance, Naltunai Iśvaram, 817, *817*

Sixteenth-century art. *See* Renaissance

Sixth Patriarch Tearing Up a Sūtra, The (Liang K'ai), 841, *841*

Skull, Iatmul, 903, *903*

Skull reconstruction, Jericho, 43, *43*

Sleeping Gypsy, The (H. Rousseau), 18, 707–08, *708*

Sluter, Claus, 535; *The Well of Moses*, 533, *535*, *536*

Smith, David, 777–78; *Cubi XVIII and Cubi XIX*, 717, 777, *778*

Smithson, Robert, 779; *Spiral Jetty, Great Salt Lake*, 779, *780*

Snake Goddess (Minoan figurine), 103, 114, *115*

Snell, Bruno, 148

Social realism, 743–45

Socrates, 136–37, 166

Soft Toilet (Oldenburg), 785, *785*

Solomon Islands, art of, 904

Solomon R. Guggenheim Museum, New York (Wright), 789, *791*

Solon of Athens, 52

Songye art, 896

Sorcerer (cave painting), Trois-Frères, *32*, 32–33

Sotatsu, Tauraraya, 861–62; *Zen Priest Choka*, 862, *862*

Soufflot, Jacques Germain: Panthéon (Ste. Geneviève), Paris, 651, 656–57, *657*

Soundbox of a harp, Ur, *53*, 53–54, *54*

Space, 7–9; area, 7; volume, 7–8

Spanish painting, Baroque, 598–603

Spartianus, 234

Spectrum, visible, 11–12

Speyer Cathedral, Germany, 327, *332*, *333*, 333–34

Spiral Jetty, Great Salt Lake (Smithson), 779, *780*

Spirit of the Dead Watching (Gauguin), 651, 705, *Plate 16-10*

Spoils from the Temple in Jerusalem, from Arch of Titus, 228, *229*

Spotted Horses and Negative Hand Imprints (cave painting), Pech-Merle, *29*, 29

Square schematism in Romanesque architecture, 330, 335, 341

Stained glass: Gothic, 376–78; transmitted light and, 12

Standard of Ur, 52–53, *56*, 182, *Plate 2-2*

Standing Woman (Lachaise), 717, 746, 747

Standing Youth (Lehmbruck), 717, 746, *746*

Stanza della Segnatura, *The School of Athens* from (Raphael), 489–91, *490*

Starry Night, The (Van Gogh), 651, 704, *705*

State Capitol, Richmond (Jefferson), 657, *658*

Statuettes: Çatal Hüyük, 45, *45*; Cycladic, 106, *106*; Later Old Stone Age, *34*, 35; Sumerian, *51*, 51–52

Stein, Gertrude, 771

Stele of Hammurabi, Susa, 41, 57–58, *58*

Stepped Pyramid of King Zoser, 79, 80

Still Life (Cézanne), 701–02, *702*

Still Life (Kalf), 617, *Plate 15-9*

Still Life with Peaches and a Carafe (Roman wall painting), 209–10, *Plate 6-5*

Still-life with Chair-caning (Picasso), 13, 731, *731*

Stoas, of Athens, 125

Stone Age, art of, 24–39

Stone Breakers, The (Courbet), 651, 690, *690*, 691

Stonehenge, cromlech at, 24, 25, 37–39, *38*, 39

Strawberry Hill, Twickenham (Walpole), 651, 654, *654*

Strong Hands (Iltners), 744, 744–45

Stuart, James, 654; Doric portico, Hagley Park, Worcestershire, 654, *656*

Stupas: Indian, 805–07, 814, 818; Javanese, 818–20

Style, 2–5; artist, 5; historical period, 5; influence, 5; place of origin, 5; purpose, 4–5; school, 5

Su T'ung-p'o, 840

Subjects Bringing Gifts to the King (relief), Palace of Darius, 68–69, *70*

Suger, Abbot of St. Denis, 353, 356–59, 376

Sui dynasty, 833

Suikō style, 851

Sullivan, Louis, 651, 712, 714, 758;

Carson, Pirie, Scott Building, Chicago, 715, *715*; Guaranty (Prudential) Building, Buffalo, 714–15, *715*

Sumerian art, 40, 41, 47–55; conventionalization in, 52–53

Sunday Afternoon on the Island of La Grande Jatte (Seurat), 700–01, *Plate 16-7*

Sung dynasty, 840–42

Supper at Emmaus (1630) (Rembrandt), 611, *611*

Supper at Emmaus (1648) (Rembrandt), 611, *612*

Supper Party, The (Honthorst), 608, *608*

Suprematism, 735

Suprematist Composition: White on White (Malevich), 735, *735*

Surrealism, 717, 738–43, 770

Sutton Hoo ship burial, purse cover from, 308, *Plate 8-1*

Swing, The (Fragonard), 579, 638, *Plate 15-12*

Sylvester, John, *The Maori Chief Tupai Kupa*, 19

Symbolism, 720–21, 770

Symonds, John Addington, 425

Syndics of the Cloth Guild (Rembrandt), 613, *Plate 15-7*

Synthetic Cubism, 731

T

Table, The (Braque), 732, *Plate 17-9*

Tacitus, 246, 280

Taddeo Gaddi, 418–19; *The Meeting of Joachim and Anna*, 418–19, *419*

Taiga, Ikeno, 862

Taj Mahal, Agra, 295–96, *297*

Takayoshi: *The Tale of Genji*, 855, *Plate 20-1*

Tale of Genji, The (Takayoshi), 855, *Plate 20-1*

Tamamushi Shrine, Horyu-ji, 852, *852*

Tamerlane, 5

Tampoco, from the *Disasters of War* (Goya), 665, 665–66

T'ang dynasty, 833–38, 851

Tatlin, Vladimir, 752; *Monument to the Third International*, 752, *752*, 753

Tatooed Marquesan warrior, 899, *900*

Teahouses, Japanese, 859–60

Technology, influence of, 757, 776–77

Tectiforms, 28, *28*

Tellus Relief, from the Ara Pacis Augustae, 227, *227*

Tempietto, Rome (Bramante), 475, *483*, 483–84

Temple, Nultanai Iśvaram, Punjai, 817, *817*

Temple, William, 652

Temple B, Selinus, *138*

Temple, Khajuraho, 816, *816*

Temple of Quetzalcoatl, Teotihuacán, 874, *875*

Temple of Saturn, from the *Views of Rome* (Piranesi), 656, *656*
Temple of the Sun (now church of Santo Domingo), Inca, Cuzco, 879, *879*
Temples: Buddhist, 805–07, 818–20; Cambodian, 822–23; cave, in India, 805; Chinese, 831–32; Egyptian, 90–96; Etruscan, 187, *187*; Greek, 138–44, 151–58, 178, 180, 181; Hindu, 811–17; Meso-American, 871–74; Roman, 199–200; *See also* names of specific temples
Ten Conveniences and the Ten Enjoyments of Country Life, The, detail from (Buson), 862, *863*
Tenebrism, 595
Tennyson, Alfred, 684–85
Teotihuacán art, 873–74
Tetrarchs, The (Roman sculpture), 241, *241*
Textiles: Islamic, 297–98; pre-Columbian, 879, *879*
Thai art, 820–21
Theodora and Attendant (mosaic), San Vitale, 269–70, *271, 272*
Theotokopoulos, Domeniko. *See* El Greco
Theotokos, Church of the, Hosios Loukas, Greece, 277, *278*, 278
Thinker, The (Rodin), 7, *7–8*
Third of May, 1808 (Goya), 665, *Plate 16-2*
Third-Class Carriage, The (Daumier), 651, 688, *689*
Thirteenth-century art. *See* Proto-Renaissance
Three Cows and One Horse (cave painting), Lascaux, *28*
Three Crosses, The (Rembrandt), 613–14, *615*
Three Goddesses (pediment sculpture), Parthenon, 156–57, *157*, 163
Three Musicians (Picasso), 716, 731, *Plate 17-8*
Thucydides, 123, 125
Thumbs Down! (Gérôme), 682–84, *683*
Tiahuanaco art, 877–79; Gateway, 877–78, *878*
Tiepolo, Giambattista, 579, 636; *The Apotheosis of the Pisani Family*, 636, *636*
Timgad, North Africa, plan of, *217*, 217–18
Tinguely, Jean, 716, 781–82; *Homage to New York*, 781, *782*; *Metamatic-Automobile-Odorante et Sonore*, 782
Tintoretto (Jacopo Robusti), 528–30; *The Finding of the Body of St. Mark*, 475, 529–30, *530*; *The Miracle of the Slave*, 529, *529*
Tipi lining with pictograph of war scenes (Crow), 890, *890*
Tiryns, citadel of, *116*, 117
Titian (Tiziano Vecelli), 524–28; *Christ Crowned with Thorns*, 528,

528; *Madonna of the Pesaro Family*, 525–26, *526*; *Man with the Glove*, 527, 527–28; *Sacred and Profane Love*, 525, *525*; *Venus of Urbino*, 526–27, *Plate 13-8*
Titus, Arch of, Rome, 228, *228*
Tlingit, helmet, 882, *883*
To be looked at (from the other side of the glass) with one eye, close to, for almost an hour (Duchamp), 716, 737, *737*
Toba, Abbot (Toba Sōjō): *Animal Caricatures* (detail of scroll), 856, *857*
Tohaku, Hasegawa, 861; *Cryptomeria Trees*, 861, *861*
Tokugawa, Ieyasu, 861
Tomb of the Leopards, Tarquinia, *Revelers* from, 188–89, *Plate 6-1*
Tomb of Mausolus, 168, *168*–69
Tomb of Orcus (Hades), Tarquinia, *Woman of the Velcha Family* from, 189, *Plate 6-2*
Tomb of the Reliefs, Caere (Cerveteri), 187, 188, *189*
Tombs: Egyptian, 73, 76, 79, 87–88, 90–92, 96–97; Etruscan, 187–90, *188, 189; See also* names of specific *tombs*; Pyramids, Egyptian
Toreador Fresco, The, from palace at Knossos, 103, 111–12, *112*
Tori Busshi, 851; *Shaka Triad*, 851, *851*
Tosa school, Japan, 960n
Toulouse-Lautrec, Henri de, 651, 706; *At the Moulin Rouge*, 706, *Plate 16-11*
Tour, Georges de la. *See* De la Tour, Georges
Tour, Quentin de la. *See* De la Tour, Quentin
Town planning. *See* Cities
Toyokuni I, 866
Trabeated architecture, 237, *238*
Traini, Francesco: *The Triumph of Death*, 422–23, *423*
Trajan, Column of (Apollodorus), 185, *230*, 230–31, *231*
Transitional period, Greece, 123, 147–50
Travelers Among Mountains and Streams (Fan K'uan), 839, *839*
Treasury of the Athenians, Delphi, 138
Treasury of Atreus, Mycenae, *119*, 119–20, *120*
Treasury of the Siphnians, Delphi, 123, 143–44, 145, *145*, 160, 162
Très Riches Heures du Duc de Berry, Les (Limbourg Brothers), 533, 537–38, *538, Plate 14-2*
Tribute Money, The (Masaccio), 443–45, *444*
Triton Fountain, Rome (Bernini), 395, *395*
Triumph of Death, The (Traini), 422–23, *423*

Triumph of Titus, from Arch of Titus, 229, 229–30
Triumph of Venice, The (Veronese), 531, *531*
Trois-Frères, cave painting at: *Sorcerer*, 32, 32–33
True linear perspective, 433–34, 548
Tumulus (Etruscan tomb type), 188, *188*
Tung Ch'i-ch'ang, 845
Tung Yüan, 839
Turner, J. M. W., 651, 684; *The Fighting Téméraire*, 684, *Plate 16-4*
Tuscany, Romanesque architecture in, 338–40
Tutankhamen, painted chest from tomb of, *100*, 100
Twentieth-century art, 716–95; architecture, 757–58, 788–95; Art Nouveau, 721–22, 758–59; Conceptual Art, 770, 787, 788; Constructivism, 736, 752–54, 777–82; Cubism, 717, 727–35, 748–49, 770; Expressionism, 717, 722–27, 746–47, 769–74; the Fauves, 717, 722–24; Formalism, 770, 775–82; Futurism, 716, 733–34, 749–50, 770; International style, 762–68; Minimal Art, 770, 779–80; Op Art, 770, 776; painting, 720–45, 768–77, 784–87; Pop Art, 717, 770, 782–87; Process Art, 770, 787–88; Realism, 734–35, 770, 774–75; sculpture, 745–47, 768–69, 777–84; Suprematism, 735; Surrealism, 717, 738–43, 770; Symbolism, 720–21, 770
Twisted perspective in cave art, 33
Twittering Machine (Klee), 8, 716, 742, 742–43
Two Children Are Threatened by a Nightingale (Ernst), 739, *739*
Two Lions (Dürer), *18*
Tzu-chou ware, 842

U

Uccello, Paolo, 446; *The Battle of San Romano*, 446, *447*
Uji Bridge (Momoyama period), 860, 861
Ukhaydir, palace of, Iraq, 291, 291–92, *292*
Ukiyo-e style, 863–64
Ulysses in the Land of the Lestrygonians (Roman wall painting), 207, *208*
Unfinished Bound Slave (Michelangelo), *16*
Unique Forms of Continuity in Space (Boccioni), 749, 749–50
Unité d'Habitation, Marseilles (Le Corbusier), 788, *789*
United States, art in. *See* North American Indian art; Neoclassicism; Op Art; Pop Art
Unkei, 857

Upper Paleolithic period (Later Old Stone Age), cave art of, 24, 25, 26–35

Uprising, The (Daumier), 689, *689*

Ur: cylinder seal, *54*, 55; soundbox of a harp, 53, *53–55*, *54*; *Standard of*, 52–53, 56, 182, Plate 2-2; ziggurat at, 48, 49, 49–50

Urns, funerary (Etruscan), 189–90, *190*

Uta (Gothic statue), Naumberg Cathedral, 384–85, *386*

Utamaro, 865–66

Utrecht Psalter, 314; *Psalm 150* from, *314*, *314*

V

Van der Goes, Hugo. *See* Hugo van der Goes

Van der Weyden, Rogier. *See* Rogier van der Weyden

Van Dyck, Anthony, 578, 606; *Charles I Dismounted*, 606, *606*

Van Eyck, Hubert: *The Ghent Altarpiece (Adoration of the Mystic Lamb)* (with Jan van Eyck), 540, *540–43*, *541*, *542*

Van Eyck, Jan, 534, 540–45; *The Ghent Altarpiece (Adoration of the Mystic Lamb)* (with Hubert van Eyck), *540–43*, *541*, *542*; *Giovanni Arnolfini and His Bride*, 533, 545, *546*; *Man in a Red Turban*, 543–44, *544*, 545; *The Virgin with the Canon van der Paele*, 543, Plate 14-3

Van Gogh, Vincent, 703–04; *Night Café*, 704, Plate 16-9; *The Starry Night*, 651, 704, *705*

Van Honthorst, Gerard. *See* Honthorst, Gerard van

Van Ruisdael, Jacob. *See* Ruisdael, Jacob van

Vanbrugh, John, 641, 652; Blenheim Palace, Oxfordshire, 578, 641, *642*

Vannucci, Pietro. *See* Perugino

Vantongerloo, Georges, 717, 751–52; *Raumplastik, y = ax³ − bx² + cx*, *751*, 751–52

Vaphio Cups, The, Mycenae, 103, 120–21, *121*

Vase and cover, Peking (late Yüan or early Ming dynasty), 843, *844*

Vase painting, Greece, 123, 126–32, 164–65; *See also* Amphoras; Kraters; Kylixes

Vatican Vergil, 257, *257–58*

Vaulting: barrel, *223*, *224*, 331; cross-barrel, 224, *224*; domical, 359; Gothic, 357–58, 359, 367–68, 370; groin, 224, 332–33, 335, 357; rib, 336, 337, 338, 358, 359, 370; Roman, 223–25, *224*; Romanesque, 330, 331–38

Vecelli, Tiziano. *See* Titian

Velázquez, Diego, 600–03; *Los Borrachos*, 600, *601*; *Las Meninas*, 579, 601–02, 602, 603, Plate 15-4

Velde, Henry van de, 765

Venetian art: architecture, 518–21; painting, 521–31

Veneziano, Domenico, 447–48; *St. Lucy Altarpiece*, 447–48, Plate 12-2

Venus, Cupid, Folly, and Time (Bronzino), 512–13, *514*

Venus de Milo. See Aphrodite of Melos

Venus Reproving Love (Il Rosso Fiorentino), 572, *573*

Venus of Urbino (Titian), 526–27, Plate 13-8

Venus of Willendorf (Later Old Stone Age statuette), 34, 35, 45

Vergil, 175, 212

Vermeer, Jan, 579, 614–17; *Young Woman with a Water Jug*, 614–17, *616*, Plate 15-8

Veronese (Paolo Cagliari), 530–31; *Christ in the House of Levi*, 530, Plate 13-9; *The Triumph of Venice*, 531, *531*

Verrocchio, Andrea, 462–64; *Bartolomeo Colleoni*, *463*, 463–64; *David*, 425, 462, *462–63*

Versailles, palace at, 624, 625, 625–26; Galerie des Glaces (J. H. Mansart and le Brun), 626–27, *627*; garden façade (le Vau and J. H. Mansart), 578, 626, *626*; park of (Le Nôtre), 627–28; Royal Chapel (J. H. Mansart), *627*, 628

Vespasian (Roman bust), 233, *233*

Vetii, House of the, Pompeii, wall painting from, 208–09, *209*

Victory Stele of Naram-Sin, 56

Vienna Genesis: *Joseph Recognizes His Brothers* from, 258, *258*

Vierzehnheiligen, Bamberg (Neumann), 579, 634, 634–35, *635*

View of Haarlem from the Dunes at Overveen (Ruisdael), 617, Plate 15-10

Views of Rome: The Temple of Saturn from (Piranesi), 656, *656*

Vignola, Giacomo da: Il Gesù, Rome (with Giacomo della Porta), 578, *581*, 581–83

Villa of Agrippa Postumus, wall painting from, 211, *212*

Villa Boscoreale, Pompeii, wall painting from, 206, *207*

Villa of the Mysteries, Pompeii, frieze from, 206, Plate 6-3

Villa Rotunda, Vicenza (Palladio), 475, *519*, 520

Villa Savoye, Poissy-sur-Seine (Le Corbusier), 764, *764*

Villard de Honnecourt, 18, 371, 377, 378; *Lion Portrayed from Life*, 18; page from a notebook of, 377, *377*

Villas, Roman, 212–13

Vincent of Beauvais, 302

Vinci, Leonardo da. *See* Leonardo da Vinci

Virgin with Apostles, The (mosaic), Torcello Cathedral, 282, *283*

Virgin with the Canon van der Paele, The (J. van Eyck), 543, Plate 14-3

Virgin and Child with St. Anne and the Infant St. John, The (cartoon) (Leonardo), 478, *478–79*

Virgin of Paris, The, Notre Dame, 378, *378–79*

Virgin of the Rocks (Leonardo), *477*, 477–78

Virginia State Capitol, Richmond (Jefferson), 657, *658*

Viscount Lepic and His Daughters (Degas), 698, *698–99*

Vishnu temple, Deogarh, 813, *813*

Visitation, The (jamb statues), Reims Cathedral, *375*, 375–76

Visitation, The (A. Pisano), *408*, 409

Vitruvius, 187, 454

Vladimir Madonna, The, 4–5, 285, *285–86*

Vlaminck, Maurice de, 708

W

Wall painting: Anatolian, 45–47, *46*, *47*; Egyptian, 74, 75, 85–86; Roman, 205–13; *See also* Frescoes; Murals

Walpole, Horace, 653–54; Strawberry Hill, Twickenham, 651, 654, *654*

Wang Meng, 843

Wang Wei (fifth century), 835, 836

Wang Wei (699–759), 837

War Monument, Güstrow Cathedral (Barlach), 716, 747, *747*

Warrior Vase, The, Mycenae, 121, *121*

Warrior's Head (Scopas), 168, *168*

Watteau, Antoine, 636–37; *Embarkation for Cythera*, 636–37, Plate 15-11; *L'Indifférent*, 578, 632, *632–33*

Webster, Elon: False Face mask (Iroquois), 891, *891*

Weight-shift, principle of, 137, 430–31

Well of Moses, The (Sluter), 533, 535, *536*

Well Scene (cave painting), Lascaux, *31*, 32, 35

West Mexican art, 870–71

Westminster Abbey, Chapel of Henry VII, 382, *383*

Weyden, Rogier van der. *See* Rogier van der Weyden

White Prunus in the Spring (Kōrin), Plate 20-2

White-ground technique, 165

Whitehall, London: Banqueting Hall (Jones), 630, *630*

Whitehead, Alfred North, 401, 648

William of Ockham, 405, *406*

Winckelmann, Johann, 654–55

Winged human-headed bull, Khorsabad, 62, *62*

Winged ibex, Persia, 69–70, *71*

Wingert, Paul, 884
Witz, Conrad: *The Miraculous Draught of Fish*, 554, *555*
Wölfflin, Heinrich, 387, 480
Woman Combing Her Hair (Archipenko), 749, *749*
Woman Combing Her Hair (Gonzalez), 751, *751*
Woman I (De Kooning), 773–74, *774*
Woman of the Velcha Family, from Tomb of Orcus (Hades), Tarquinia, 189, *Plate 6-2*
Woodcuts: of Dürer, 561–62; German Expressionist, 725–26; Japanese, 864–67
Wren, Christopher, 630–31; St. Paul's Cathedral, London, 578, 630–31, *631*
Wright, Frank Lloyd, 758, 759–60, 764, 789; Kaufmann House ("Falling Water"), 717, 764, *765*; Robie House, Chicago, 760, *761*; Solomon R. Guggenheim Museum, New York, 789, *791*

Wu Chen, 843; *Bamboo*, 843, *844*
Wu Tao-tzu, 837–38
Wu Tomb, mythological scenes from, Shantung, 829, *829*
Wyeth, Andrew, 774; *Christina's World*, 716, 774–75, *775*

X

X (Bladen), 779, *779*

Y

Yamato-e style, 855–56, 858
Yayoi, 850
Yen Li-pen: *Portraits of the Emperors*, 837
Yoruba art, 894–95
Young Woman with a Water Jug (Vermeer), 614–17, *616*, *Plate 15-8*
Yu, Early Chou dynasty, 827, *827*

Yüan dynasty, 842–43
Yün-kang caves, 831–32, *832*

Z

Zaïre, art of, 895–96
Zen Buddhism, influence of, 858–60
Zen painting, 841–42, 859
Zen Priest, Choka (Sotatsu), 862, *862*
Zeus, Temple of, pediment sculpture from, *149*, 149–50, *150*
Zeus and Athena, Altar of, Pergamum, 123, *173*, 173–74
Ziggurat(s), 48–50; at Ur, *48*, 49–50, *49*
Zoser, King, Stepped Pyramid of, 79, *80*
"Zuccone" (prophet figure) (Donatello), *432*, 432–33
Zurbarán, Francisco de, 599–600; *St. Francis in Meditation*, 579, 599–600, *600*

PICTURE CREDITS

The authors and publisher are grateful to the proprietors and custodians of various works of art for photographs of these works and permission to reproduce them in this book. Sources not included in the captions are listed below.

KEY TO ABBREVIATIONS

ACL   Copyright A.C.L., Brussels
Al   Fratelli Alinari
AMNH   American Museum of Natural History, New York
An   D. Anderson
ARB   Art Reference Bureau
Bg   Giacomo Brogi
Br   F. Bruckmann K G Verlag
Bulloz   J. E. Bulloz, Paris
DAI   Deutschen Archäologisches Institut
Fototeca   Fototeca Unione, Rome
Gab   Gabinetto Fotografico Nazionale, Rome

Gir   Giraudon
Gun   L. Gundermann Photo-Verlag
Hir   Hirmer Fotoarchiv, Munich
Mansell   The Mansell Collection, London
Mar   Bildarchiv Foto Marburg
Mas   Ampliaciones Y Reproducciones MAS, Barcelona
Met   Metropolitan Museum of Art, New York
NYPL   New York Public Library
OI   Oriental Institute, University of Chicago
PRI   Photo Researchers, Inc., New York
RGP   Rapho-Guillumette Pictures
Scala   Scala Fine Art Publishers, Ind., New York

Introduction Josef Albers: FIGS. 6, 7; Al-ARB: FIGS. 9a, 10; Bibliothèque Nationale: FIG. 13; Dr. Thomas Brachert, Courtesy of *Art Bulletin*, Dec. 1971, LIII, 4: FIG. 4; Bg-ARB: FIG. 9b; Fogg Art Museum, Harvard University, Bequest of Paul J. Sachs: FIG. 3; Hir: FIG. 12; Walter Steinkopf: FIG. 14; Wilhelm-Lehmbruck-Museum: FIG. 1.

Chapter 1 Aerofilms Ltd., London: FIG. 13; AMNH: FIGS. 7, 8, 11; Caisse Nationale: FIGS. 5, 6; Colorphoto

Hinz, Basle: FIGS. 2, 4; PLATES 1, 2; Mas: FIG. 12; Edwin Smith: FIG. 14; Studio Laborie, Bergerac: FIGS. 3, 10.

Chapter 2 Al-ARB: FIG. 34; Hir: FIGS. 8, 10, 16, 17, 18, 19, 20, 23, 27; Jericho Excavation Fund: FIGS. 1, 2; Mansell: FIGS. 24, 25, Arlette Mellaart: FIGS. 5, 6, 7; James Mellaart: PLATE 1; Musées Nationaux, Paris: FIGS. 28, 31; OI: FIGS. 12, 29, 32, 33.

Chapter 3 Harvey Barad, PRI: FIG. 6; Egyptian Expedition, Met: FIGS. 16, 18, 30; Eliot Elisofon: FIGS. 22, 25; George Gerster, RGP: FIG. 7; Hir: FIGS. 2, 3, 10, 11, 12, 13, 14, 15, 21, 28, 32; from *L'Art et l'Homme*, Larousse: FIG. 1; Mar-ARB: FIGS. 23, 24, 34; Met: FIGS. 16, 18; Musées Nationaux, Paris: FIG. 35; OI: FIG. 19.

Chapter 4 Courtauld Institute Galleries, London Univ.: FIG. 22; Alison Frantz: FIG. 20; Hir: FIGS. 4, 5, 7, 8, 9, 10, 11, 12, 13, 14, 15, 16, 19, 24, 25; PLATES 1, 2; TAP Service: FIG. 23; from Christian Zervos, *L'Art de la Crète*, Editions Cahiers d'Art, Paris: FIG. 3; from Christian Zervos, *L'Art des Cyclades*, Editions Cahiers d'Art, Paris: FIGS. 1, 2.

Chapter 5 Al-ARB: FIGS. 14, 24, 53, 57, 58, 60, 64, 73; Herschel Levit: FIG. 22; Frederick Ayer III, PRI: FIG. 75; DAI, Athens: FIG. 12; Felbermeyer: FIGS. 68, 69; Alison Frantz: FIGS. 35, 36, 46, 47; Walter Hege: FIG. 40; Hir: FIGS. 2, 4, 6, 7, 8, 10, 17, 18, 21, 27, 30, 31, 32, 33, 37, 39, 42, 43, 44, 45, 48, 50, 51, 52, 55, 56, 59, 63, 70, 74, PLATES 1, 2; Mar-ARB: FIGS. 61, 62; Musées Nationaux, Paris: FIGS. 9, 54; Leonard von Matt, RGP: FIG. 67; Rev. Raymond V. Schoder, S.J.: PLATE 3; Dr. Franz Stoedtner: FIG. 26; TAP Service: FIG. 16.

Chapter 6 Al-ARB: FIGS. 4, 8, 9, 15, 23, 26, 28, 29, 30, 32, 33, 48, 51, 52, 53, 54, 55, 58, 64, 72, 73; An-ARB: FIG. 49; DAI, Rome: FIGS. 6, 12, 31, 57, 59, 71; Walter Drayer: FIGS. 2, 7, 10; Fototeca: FIGS. 5, 13, 14, 16, 17, 18, 19, 44, 47; Gab: FIGS. 3, 60; André Held: PLATE 4; Hir: FIG. 69; John Johnston: FIG. 70; G. E. Kidder Smith: FIG. 67; Foto KLM: FIG. 37; Herschel Levit: FIG. 50; Mar-ARB: FIG. 65; Leonard von Matt, RGP: FIG. 61; from Amedeo Maiuri, *Roman Painting*, Editions d'Art Albert Skira: FIGS. 24, 27; H. Roger-Viollet: FIG. 34; Charles Rotkin, PFI: FIG. 36; Scala: FIGS. 21, 40; PLATES 2, 3, 5, 6; Rev. Raymond V. Schoder, S.J.: PLATE 1.

Chapter 7 Al-ARB: FIGS. 13, 24, 29, 30, 31, 42; An-ARB: FIGS. 16, 20, 23, 45, 52; Arts et Metiers Graphiques, Paris (from G. Marçais, *L'Architecture Musulmane d'Occident*): FIG. 51; Bibliothèque Nationale: FIG. 5; Byzantine Institute, Inc.: FIG. 46; Clarendon Press: FIG. 57; from K. A. C. Creswell, *Early Muslim Architecture*, Clarendon Press: FIGS. 50, 55; Fotocielo: FIG. 40; Alison Frantz: FIGS. 37, 39; Hir: FIGS. 7, 8, 9, 17, 18, 19, 22, 25, 26, 28, 32; Iraq Mission to the United Nations: FIGS. 49, 56; G. E. Kidder Smith: FIGS. 34, 62, 63; Linares, Yale Photo Collection: FIG. 59; Mar-ARB: FIG. 48; Mas: FIGS. 53, 54, 60; Leonard von Matt, RGP: FIG. 2; OI: FIG. 21; Pontificia Commissione Centrale per l'Arte Sacra in Italia: FIG. 3; Josephine Powell: FIG. 44; Prestel Verlag, Munich: FIG. 33; Rev. Fabrica di San Pietro in Vaticano: FIG. 12; Scala: PLATES 1, 2, 3, 4, 5, 6; Staatliche Museen, Berlin: FIG. 58; Tass, Sovfoto: FIG. 43; Tiers, Monkmeyer Press Photo Service, N.Y.: FIG. 64.

Chapter 8 Dr. Harald Busch: FIG. 9; Hir: FIG. 20; PLATE 3; Mar-ARB: FIG. 18; J. Gudiol, Archives Photographiques, Paris: opening illus., Part 2; Hermann Wehmeyer: FIGS. 14, 16, 17.

Chapter 9 Al-ARB: FIGS. 8, 10, 17, 19; Bulloz: FIGS. 22, 26; Caisse Nationale: FIGS. 22, 23; Jean Dieuzaide: FIG 21; Willie Fix: FIG. 6; Fotocielo: FIG. 16; Gir: FIGS. 27, 28; J. Gudiol Archives Photographiques, Paris: FIG. 24;

Evelyn Hofer: FIG. 18; A. F. Kersting: FIG. 14; Mansell: FIG. 30; Studio Remy: FIG. 29; Yan, Reportage Photographique, Toulouse: FIG. 1; H. Roger-Viollet: FIG. 12; Jean Roubier: FIGS. 3, 11, 20; Scala: PLATE 1; Thames & Hudson Archive: FIG. 25.

Chapter 10 Aero-Photo, Paris: FIG. 15; Al-ARB: FIGS. 30, 48, 49, 50; An-ARB: FIG. 47; Belzeaux, RGP: FIG. 31; PLATE 2; P. Berger, Photo Researchers, Inc.: FIG. 8; Dr. Harald Busch: FIG. 40; Pierre Devinoy: FIGS. 1, 3; Theo Felten: FIG. 44; Gir: FIGS. 26, 28; George Holton, PRI: FIGS. 45, 51; A. F. Kersting: FIG. 36; Herschel Levit: FIG. 19; Mar-ARB: FIGS. 25, 27, 38, 42; National Monuments Record, London: FIGS. 34, 35; Revue Française de l'Electricité: PLATE 1; Rheinisches Bilderarchiv, Cologne: FIG. 43; H. Roger-Viollet: FIGS. 13, 23, 24; Jean Roubier: FIGS. 9, 12, 14; Helga Schmidt-Glassner: FIG. 41; Edwin Smith: FIG. 32; W. S. Stoddard: FIGS. 7, 10, 17; Clarence Ward: FIGS. 21, 22.

Chapter 11 Al-ARB: FIGS. 2, 4, 5, 6, 8, 9, 12, 13, 14, 15, 16, 17, 19; An-ARB: FIGS. 1, 7, 10, 20, 21, 22, 23; Bg-ARB: FIGS. 3, 18; Gab: FIG. 11; Leonard von Matt, RGP: opening illus., Part 3; Scala: PLATES 1, 2.

Chapter 12 Al-ARB: FIGS. 4, 5, 6, 8, 9, 10, 13, 14, 15, 16, 17, 20, 26, 27, 28, 32, 33, 34, 35, 36, 40, 43, 45, 46, 47, 52, 55, 56, 57, 58, 59, 60, 61; An-ARB: FIGS. 18, 22, 25, 29, 30, 31, 37, 39, 50; An-Gir: FIG. 51; Marcello Bertoni: FIGS. 1, 2; Bg-ARB: FIGS. 3, 11, 12, 24, 49; Farbenfotografie: PLATE 7; Rollie McKenna, PRI: FIGS. 38, 42; La Photothèque: PLATE 5; Scala: PLATES 1, 2, 3, 6.

Chapter 13 Al-ARB: FIGS. 1, 3, 10, 12, 13, 14, 15, 16, 17, 18, 21, 22, 24, 25, 32, 33, 37, 38, 40, 41, 49, 50, 51, 52, 53, 55, 56, 57; An-ARB: FIGS. 4, 6, 23, 28, 34, 35; Harvey Barad, PRI: FIG. 19; Fototeca: FIGS. 27, 30; Gir: FIG. 20; Rollie McKenna: FIG. 43; Phyllis Dearborn Massar: FIGS. 45, 47, 48; Met: FIG. 31; Charles Rotkin, PFI: FIG. 26; Scala PLATES 2, 3, 4, 7, 8, 9; Edwin Smith: FIG. 44.

Chapter 14 ACL: FIGS. 6, 7, 8, 13, 15, 16; Al-ARB: FIGS. 14, 37, 44; Caisse Nationale: FIGS. 1, 39; Jean Arland: FIG. 20; Br-ARB: FIG. 25; Bulloz: FIG. 43; Meyer Erwin Photo: PLATE 10; Gir: FIGS. 4, 38, 42; PLATES 2, 7, 8; Lauras-Giraudon: FIG. 2; Gun-ARB: FIG. 21; Musées Nationaux: PLATE 7; Studio Remy: FIG. 3; Rheinisches Bilderarchiv, Cologne: FIG. 19; Charles Rotkin, PFI: FIG. 40; Scala: PLATE 5; Walter Steinkopf: FIGS. 18, 30.

Chapter 15 Aero-Photo, Paris: FIG. 52a; AGRACI-ARB: FIG. 45; Al-ARB: FIGS. 9, 10, 13, 15, 22, 23, 24, 25, 33, 34, 38, 54, 56, 60, 61, 66, 68; An-ARB: FIGS. 4, 7, 12, 21, 26, 28, 29; Wayne Andrews: FIG. 62; Avery Library, Columbia Univ.: FIG. 1; Br-ARB: FIG. 30; British Crown Copyright, Reproduced with permission of the Controller of Her Britannic Majesty's Stationery Office: FIG. 58; Bulloz-ARB: FIG. 71; J. Allan Cash, RGP: FIG. 72; Editorial Photocolor Archives, Inc.: FIG. 18; Gab: FIG. 20; Gir: FIGS. 48, 57, 69; Gene Heil, PRI: FIG. 53a; Photo Henrot: FIG. 55; A. F. Kersting: FIGS. 5, 51; G. E. Kidder Smith: FIGS. 17, 19; Frank Lerner: PLATE 8; Mansell: FIGS. 46, 47; Ministry of Public Buildings and Works, London: FIG. 58; Erich Müller: FIG. 63; National Monuments Record, London: FIG. 59; NYPL: FIGS. 8, 52b; Charles Rotkin, PFI: FIG. 3; Scala: PLATES 1, 2, 11; Helga Schmidt-Glassner:

FIGS. 50, 64; Walter Steinkopf: FIGS. 35, 44; Yan, RGP: PLATE 3.

Chapter 16 ACL: FIGS. 22, 59; AGRACI-ARB: FIGS. 28, 49; Al-ARB: FIGS. 11, 14, 24, 30, 32, 33, 35, 37, 63; An-ARB: FIGS. 17, 20; Wayne Andrews: FIG. 66; British Crown Copyright, repro. with permission of the Controller of Her Britannic Majesty's Stationery Office: FIG. 1; John R. Brownlie, PRI: FIG. 8; Bulloz: FIGS. 13, 43; Bulloz-ARB: FIG. 34; J. Camponogara: FIG. 27; Chicago Architectural Photographing Co.: FIG. 65; Deutsche Fotothek, Dresden: FIG. 47; H. B. Fleming & Co.: PLATE 1; Gir: FIGS. 15, 21, 25, 26, 48; Hedrich-Blessing: FIG. 67; A. F. Kersting: FIGS. 2, 6, 9; Studio MADEC: FIG. 38; Mar-ARB: FIG. 62; Ministry of Public Buildings and Works, London: FIG. 1; NYPL: FIGS. 19, 31; Musées Nationaux: FIG. 23; PLATES 3, 6; H. Roger-Viollet: FIG. 10; Oscar Savio: opening illus., Part 4; Scala: PLATE 7; O. Vaering: FIG. 60; Virginia Chamber of Commerce: FIG. 7.

Chapter 17 Leo Castelli Gallery: FIGS. 74, 76; Chicago Architectural Photographing Co.: FIGS. 48, 49; Geoffrey Clements: FIGS. 62, 77; Colorphoto Hinz, Basle: PLATES 5, 10; David Gahr: FIG. 72; Galerie Welz: PLATE 1; Gianfranco Gorgoni: FIGS. 69, 70; The Solomon R. Guggenheim Museum: FIGS. 84, 85; Hedrich-Blessing: FIG. 9; Lucien Hervé: FIGS. 50, 52, 82, 83; Institut für Leichte Flachentragwerke: FIG. 87a; Ralph Kleinhempel: PLATE 6; Jim Knipe: FIG. 90; William Lescaze Associates: FIG. 56; Marlborough Gallery, Inc.: FIG. 67; Mas: FIG. 47; Pierre Matisse Gallery: FIG. 60; Museum of Modern Art: FIGS. 54, 57, PLATES 13, 14; Office du Film du Québec: FIG. 89a; Robert Phillips, Fortune Magazine: FIG. 88: H. Roger-Viollet: FIG. 81; *Beyond Habitat* © Moshe Safdie, MIT Press in the U.S., Tundra Books in Canada: FIG. 89b; Oscar Savio: FIG. 86; Sidney Janis Gallery, New York: PLATE 15; © foto Stedelijk Museum, Amsterdam: FIG. 51; Dr. Franz Stoedtner: FIG. 55; Ezra Stoller, copyright ESTO: FIG. 58; Walter Thiem: FIG. 87b; Tiofoto,

Chapter 18 Black Star: FIG. 28; J. LeRoy Davidson: FIGS. 13, 16, 18, 19, 22, 23, 25, PLATE 2; Eliot Elisofon, TIME/LIFE Books, Time, Inc.: FIG. 26; Government of India, Archaeological Survey of India: FIGS. 1, 2, 3, 4, 5, 6, 7, 9, 11, 12, 14, 15, 17, 20; India Tourist Office: FIG. 21; Elizabeth Lyons: FIG. 29; Josiah Martin, Auckland Institute & Museum Library: opening illus., Part 5; I. Job Thomas: PLATE 1.

Chapter 19 Chavannes: FIG. 4; Gir: PLATE 2; Robert Harding Associates, London: FIG. 21; Magnum: FIGS. 5, 6; Musées Nationaux, Paris: PLATE 1; National Commission for Protection of Cultural Properties of Japan: FIG. 16; Audrey R. Topping: FIG. 24; Charles Uht: FIG. 9; Courtesy Estate of Langdon Warner: FIG. 10.

Chapter 20 Japan Tourist Association: FIG. 23; National Commission for Protection of Cultural Properties of Japan: FIGS. 3, 4, 9, 11, 12; Sakamoto Photo Research Lab, Tokyo: FIG. 5, PLATE 1; Yoshio Watanabe: FIG. 8; Zauho Press: PLATE 2.

Chapter 21 Archaeological Institute of America, Reprinted from *Art and Archaeology*, IV, 6, copyright 1916: FIG. 5; Archive of Hispanic Culture, Library of Congress:

FIG. 13a; Chicago Natural History Museum: FIG. 13b; Susan Einstein, Museum of Cultural History, University of California, Los Angeles: FIGS. 2, 12; Field Museum of Natural History, Chicago: FIG. 3; Abraham Guillen M.: FIG. 15; Smithsonian Institution, Washington, D.C.: FIG. 1.

Chapter 22 *The American Anthropologist*, 1919: FIG. 7; H. M. Cole: FIG. 23, PLATE 4; Eliot Elisofon, TIME/LIFE Books, Time, Inc.: FIG. 3; David Gebhard, The Art Galleries, University of California, Santa Barbara: FIG. 9; from Campbell Grant, *Rock Art of the American Indian*: FIG. 8; Dr. George Kennedy, University of California, Los Angeles: FIG. 36; from J. D. Lajoux, *The Rock Paintings of Tassili*: FIG. 19; Museum of Navaho Ceremonial Art, Sante Fe: PLATE 1; National Park Service, Department of the Interior, Washington, D.C.: FIGS. 11, 12; from Karl von den Steinen, *Die Marquesaner und ihre Kunst*, I: FIG. 34; Frank Willett, Northwestern University: FIGS. 20, 21, PLATE 3.

Permission S.P.A.D.E.M. 1974 by French Reproduction Rights, Inc., for the following: FIGS. 16-52, 54, 55; 17-1, 5, 6, 7, 8, 9, 10, 13, 16, 20, 24, 29, 30, 42, 52, 62, 63, 64, 81, 82; PLATES: 16-5, 6; 17-3, 4, 5, 8, 11.

Permission A.D.A.G.P. 1975 by French Reproduction Rights, Inc., for the following: FIGS. 17-19, 35, 40, 43, 45, 60; PLATES 17-2, 7, 9.

Illustration Credits

FIG. 3-4: Adapted from the "Later Canon" of Egyptian Art, figure 1 in Erwin Panofsky, *Meaning in the Visual Arts*. Copyright © 1955 by Erwin Panofsky. Used by permission of Doubleday and Company, Inc.

FIGS. 3-17, 26; 5-25; 6-22, 38, 39, 41, 45; 7-41; 10-46; 13-11: From Sir Banister Fletcher, *A History of Architecture on the Comparative Method*, 17th ed., rev. by R. A. Cordingly, 1961. Used by permission of the Athlone Press of the University of London.

FIGS. 4-6; 7-1, 27: Hirmer Fotoarchiv, Munich.

FIG. 6-66: From Fiske Kimball, M. Arch, and G. H. Edgell, *A History of Architecture*, 1918. Used by permission of Harper & Row, Inc., publishers.

FIGS. 7-6, 10, 11: From Kenneth J. Conant, *Early Medieval Church Architecture*. Used by permission of The Johns Hopkins Press.

FIGS. 10-4, 5: From Ernst Gall, *Gotische Kathedralen*, 1925. Used by permission of Klinkhardt & Biermann, publishers.

FIG. 10-18: Used by permission of Umschau Verlag, Frankfort.

FIG. 12-41: From Nikolaus Pevsner, *An Outline of European Architecture*, 6th ed., 1960, Penguin Books, Ltd., © Nikolaus Pevsner, 1943, 1960, 1963.

FIG. 18-8: From Benjamin Rowland, *The Art and Architectural India*, 1953, Penguin Books.